Romania
& Bulgaria

Maramureş
p166

Transylvania
p76

Crişana &
Banat
p149

Moldavia & the
Bucovina
Monasteries
p183

ROMANIA   Bucharest
p34
⭐

Wallachia
p60

The Danube Delta
& Black Sea
Coast p211

The Danube & Northern Plains
p427

Sofia
p296
⭐

BULGARIA

Veliko Târnovo &
Central Mountains
p359

Black Sea Coast
p395

Plovdiv & the
Southern Mountains
p321

Mark Baker, Steve Fallon, Anita Isalska

PLAN YOUR TRIP

ON THE ROAD

WOMEN IN ROMANIAN
TRADITIONAL DRESS

Romania Contents

UNDERSTAND

SURVIVAL GUIDE

SPECIAL FEATURES

PLAN YOUR TRIP

ON THE ROAD

Bulgaria Contents

VELIKO TÂRNOVO,
BULGARIA P365

Romania & Bulgaria

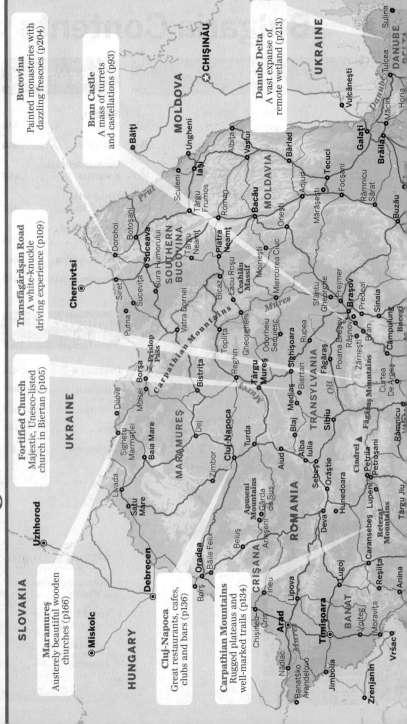

Maramureş
Austerely beautiful wooden churches (p166)

Fortified Church
Majestic, Unesco-listed church in Biertan (p105)

Transfăgărăşan Road
A white-knuckle driving experience (p109)

Bucovina
Painted monasteries with dazzling frescoes (p204)

Bran Castle
A mass of turrets and castellations (p93)

Danube Delta
A vast expanse of remote wetland (p213)

Cluj-Napoca
Great restaurants, cafes, clubs and bars (p136)

Carpathian Mountains
Rugged plateaus and well-marked trails (p134)

SLOVAKIA

HUNGARY

UKRAINE

MOLDOVA

UKRAINE

ROMANIA

TRANSYLVANIA

MOLDAVIA

SOUTHERN BUCOVINA

MARAMUREŞ

CRIŞANA

BANAT

Carpathian Mountains

Făgăraş Mountains

Retezat Mountains

Apuseni Mountains

Ceahlău Massif

✪ CHIŞINĂU

Miskolc

Debrecen

Uzhhorod

Chernivtsi

Miskolc

100 km
50 miles

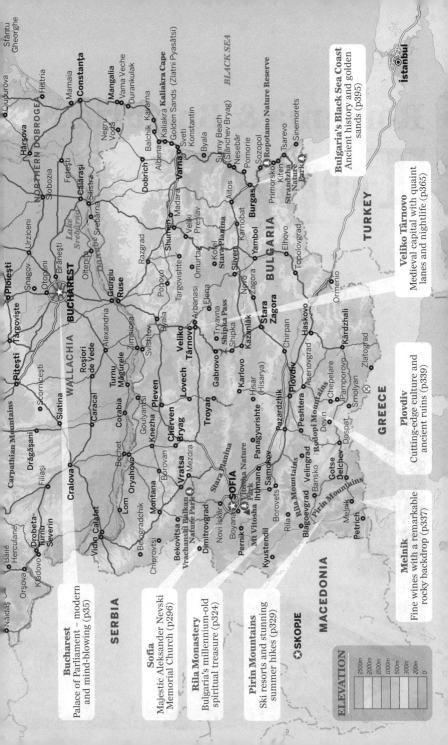

Bulgaria's Black Sea Coast
Ancient history and golden sands (p395)

Veliko Târnovo
Medieval capital with quaint lanes and nightlife (p365)

Plovdiv
Cutting-edge culture and ancient ruins (p339)

Melnik
Fine wines with a remarkable rocky backdrop (p337)

Pirin Mountains
Ski resorts and stunning summer hikes (p329)

Rila Monastery
Bulgaria's millennium-old spiritual treasure (p324)

Sofia
Majestic Aleksander Nevski Memorial Church (p296)

Bucharest
Palace of Parliament – modern and mind-blowing (p35)

ELEVATION

2500m
2000m
1500m
1000m
500m
300m
200m
0

Romania & Bulgaria's
Top 17

Palace of Parliament, Bucharest

1 Depending on your point of view, the Palace of Parliament (p35) is either a mind-blowing testament to the waste and folly of dictatorship or an awe-inspiring showcase of Romanian materials and craftsmanship, albeit applied to sinister ends. Most visitors conclude that it's a bit of both. Whatever emotions the former 'House of the People' happens to elicit, the sheer scale of Romania's entry into the 'World's Largest Buildings' competition – on par with the Taj Mahal or the Pentagon – must be seen to be believed.

Black Sea Beaches

2 Whether you're looking for all-day tanning, all-night clubbing, or something a little more relaxing, you're sure to find some patch of sand to your liking along Bulgaria's Black Sea coast (p395). Away from the big, brash package resorts, you'll come across charming seaside towns standing above smaller sandy coves, while the cities of Varna and Burgas both have lengthy, less-crowded urban beaches. If it's solitude you seek, head for the more remote beaches to the far north and south.

Below right: Albena (p424)

Rila Monastery

3 More than a thousand years of uninterrupted spiritual activity have swept through this beautiful monastery (p324), which rises from a valley in the misty Rila Mountains. Credited with safeguarding Bulgarian culture during the dark centuries under Ottoman rule, and a lightning rod for revolution in the 19th century, Rila Monastery remains Bulgaria's most storied spiritual treasure. The monastery grew from a 10th-century hermit's hut; following a fire, the breathtaking mix of elegant archways, soaring domes and apocalyptic frescoes that stands today dates mostly to the 19th century.

Bran Castle

4 Perched on a rocky bluff in Transylvania, Romania, in a mass of turrets and castellations, Bran Castle (p93) overlooks a desolate mountain pass swirling with mist and dense forest. Its spectral exterior is like a composite of every horror film you've ever seen, but don't expect to be scared. Inside, Bran is anything but spooky, with its white walls and geranium-filled courtyard. Legend has it Vlad the Impaler (the inspiration for Count Dracula) was briefly imprisoned here, and you can follow his footsteps through an Escheresque maze of courtyards and hidden passages.

Painted Monasteries of Bucovina

5 Tucked away in the eastern side of the Carpathian mountains, the Unesco-listed painted monasteries of Bucovina (p204) proudly show off Romania's unique, Latin-flavoured Orthodox tradition. The kaleidoscope of colours and intricate details in the frescoes bring to life everything from biblical stories to the 15th-century siege of Constantinople. The monasteries are largely the genius of Moldavian prince and national hero Stephen the Great (Ştefan cel Mare), who was later canonised.

Bottom right: Voroneţ Monastery (p204)

Veliko Târnovo

6 Bulgaria's long history of warring tsars and epic battles is exceptionally vivid in former capital Veliko Târnovo (p365). Topped with a medieval fortress, this town of Soviet monuments, cobblestoned lanes and handicraft shops allows for a memorable trip into Bulgaria's past. Home to the second-largest university in Bulgaria, the town also has a simmering nightlife; a creative, multicultural expat community adds to the fun. It's also a great base for local hikes, mountain biking and trips to Emen Canyon.

Below: Tsarevets Fortress (p365)

Bulgarian Wine Tasting

7 Bulgaria's winemaking tradition dates to ancient Thracian times, and its wines have been enjoyed by everyone from Roman writers to former British prime minister Winston Churchill. Melnik (p337) in southwestern Bulgaria is an especially fruitful location to sip wine, and a very scenic one: the village is lined with traditional 19th-century houses, against a backdrop of natural sandstone pyramids. Beyond Melnik, discover five distinct wine-growing regions from the Danube to the Black Sea to the Thracian Plain.

SCOTT WONG / SHUTTERSTOCK ©

Wildlife in the Danube Delta

8 After flowing 2800km across the European continent, the mighty Danube River passes through a vast expanse of remote wetland in eastern Romania – the delta – before finally emptying into the Black Sea. Under the international environmental protection of the Danube Delta Biosphere Reserve Authority, the region (p213) has developed into a sanctuary for fish and fowl of all stripe and colour. Birders, in particular, will thrill to the prospect of glimpsing species such as the roller, white-tailed eagle, great white egret and even a bee-eater or two. Above bottom: White pelican

Wooden Churches of Maramureş

9 Rising from forested hillsides like dark needles, the exquisite wooden churches of Maramureş (p166), in northern Romania, are both austere and beautiful, with roofs of shingle, and weather-beaten, Gothic-style steeples. Inside, you'll discover rich interiors painted with biblical frescoes, some of which date back to the 14th century. On Sundays, the villagers don traditional dress for church, and attending one of the services is a special treat.

Above right: Bârsana Monastery (p179)

Thracian Tombs

10 The Valley of Thracian Kings, between Shipka and Kazanlâk in Bulgaria, is dotted with tombs, and more are unearthed each year. One of the most magnificently preserved examples is the Unesco-listed Thracian Tomb of Sveshtari (p434). The tomb dates to 300 BC and harbours lovely artwork and reliefs within its three chambers, including 10 elegant female figures. A visit requires private transportation, but it's worth the effort to play Tomb Raider within its evocative confines.

Below: Tomb of Sveshtari

Cluj-Napoca

11 Romania's second-largest city (p136) has reawakened from its slumber and now offers countless bohemian cafes, great restaurants, music festivals, clubs and bars. It's also emerged as the country's contemporary arts hub. The thousands of students here lend a youthful vibe and fuel a vigorous nightlife at places like Insomnia. With increasing flight links to European cities, the city is welcoming more and more travellers, who usually shoot off to Braşov, Sibiu or Sighişoara, but who come inevitably to regret not allowing enough time for Cluj.

Trekking in the Carpathians, Romania

12 Dense primeval forests leap straight from the pages of a Brothers Grimm story, with bears, wolves, lynx and boar, rugged mountain plateaus, well-marked trails and a network of cabins en route to keep you warm. The peaks can be approached from both Transylvania and Moldavia. The Retezat Mountains (p134), with some 80 glacial lakes and peaks towering above 2000m, are a spectacular stretch of the southern Carpathians.

Above left: Hikers in the Bucegi Mountains (p82)

Stara Planina Hiking

13 Hikers have breathtaking choice across the Stara Planina (p381) mountain range, rippling for 550km across the length of Bulgaria. Strollers can walk through the meadows around Dryanovo (p376) or to peaceful monasteries such as Sokolski (p379). Meanwhile, dedicated hikers can climb the tallest peak, Mt Botev (p381), a challenging but picturesque ascent. Alternatively, seek out solitude on multiday hikes, staying at the Stara Planina's 80-odd *hizhas* (mountain huts) along the way; just prepare for changeable weather.

Top right: A *hizha*

Saxon Villages & Fortified Churches

14 Back in the 12th century, Saxon Germans were invited to settle parts of Romania's Transylvania to buffer the then-Hungarian kingdom from the threat of Tatar and Turkish attack. The architectural legacy is a row of regal fortified churches, watchtowers and impenetrable stone walls that dot the landscape between Sighişoara and Sibiu. Most visitors are drawn to the impressive Fortified Church (p105) in Biertan, though Viscri, Mălâncrav and Alma Vii are also worth exploring.

Bottom right: Biertan (p105)

NATALIYA NAZAROVA / SHUTTERSTOCK ©

Plovdiv

15 With a charming old town, revitalised artistic quarter and the most exhilarating nightlife outside Sofia, Bulgaria's second city (p339) has never looked finer. Ancient buildings nestle right in the centre of this seven-hilled town; a pleasant shopping street flows past its 2nd-century Roman stadium (which still hosts concerts) and a 15th-century mosque, in an effortless blend of old and new. Investment for Plovdiv's reign as European Capital of Culture 2019 has left the city gleaming, while the city's calendar bursts with opera, jazz, open-air art and more.

Skiing in the Pirin Mountains

16 The Pirin Mountains (p329) are truly a land of giants, with more than 100 peaks towering higher than 2000m. Their summer splendour draws hikers to Pirin National Park, but long winters and downy snowfall make Pirin Bulgaria's best skiing and snowboarding destination. Nestled at the base of Mt Vihren (2915m), Bansko is the Balkan's premium winter sports town. Its 75km of pistes, extending to a height of 2600m, have options for all levels. Just as invigorating is Bansko's après-ski culture, which culminates with the Horizon Festival (p335).

Top right: Skiers in Bansko (p332)

Driving the Transfăgărăşan Road

17 When the, high-altitude Transfăgărăşan road (p109) in southern Transylvania was built in the '70s, it was derided as a vanity project for the Ceauşescu regime. One generation later and it has been celebrated by TV's *Top Gear* as the world's most exciting length of road. Boldly charging up and down one of Romania's highest mountains provides an unforgettable, white-knuckle experience behind the wheel. The climax is glacial Lake Bâlea, which hovers like a mirror among the rocks and is sometimes totally enshrouded by clouds.

Romania

Sighişoara (p98)

Welcome to Romania

Rugged stone churches and dazzling monasteries dot a pristine landscape of rocky mountains and rolling hills. Transylvanian towns have stepped out of time, while vibrant Bucharest is all energy.

Nature & Wildlife

The Carpathian Mountains draw a wide arc through the centre of the country, leaving a swath of exposed rocky peaks surrounded by groves of pine and deciduous trees, and stretches of bright green meadow below. The harsh geography has limited human habitation, and the woods are filled with deer, elk and bear. Europe's second-longest river, the Danube, marks Romania's southern border with Bulgaria before turning suddenly northward and emptying into the Black Sea. The delta provides sanctuary for 300 species of bird and 160 species of fish. The sprawling marshes account for the largest expanse of reed beds in the world.

Castles & Medieval Towns

Transylvania, the land that gave us Dracula, has no shortage of jaw-dropping castles on rocky hilltops. There's spooky Bran Castle, of course, but don't overlook beauties such as Hunedoara's 14th-century Corvin Castle or King Carol I's sumptuous 19th-century pile, Peleş Castle. In medieval towns like Braşov, Sighişoara and Sibiu, cobbled walkways support chic streetside cafes, while the sound of cacophonous nightlife echoes off the Gothic and baroque facades in lively Cluj-Napoca. Transylvania's Saxon villages boast fortified churches that date back half a millennium.

Folk Culture

For centuries, a highly productive peasant culture thrived in much of Romania. The hilly geography and lack of passable roads necessitated the emergence of hundreds of self-sufficient villages, where crafts such as bread-making, pottery, tanning and weaving were honed to an art. Folk museums, particularly the open-air *skansens* and village museums, are a must. Many isolated hamlets, where the old folkways are still practised, are museums in themselves. This is most evident in Maramureş, where oversized hay racks, horse carts and stately wooden churches dominate, and towns and villages are straight out of the Middle Ages.

Outdoor Activities

The rocky peaks of Transylvania and Moldavia, snow-capped from mid-October in some years, call out for conquering. There are less adventurous but no less rewarding walks through woods, meadows and villages in other parts of the country. The Danube Delta is a vast and unique protected wetland and makes a perfect backdrop for fishing, boating and, especially, birdwatching in spring. In summer, Black Sea coast resorts fill up with swimmers, divers, sunbathers and partiers, who come for the all-night, open-air clubbing marathons.

Why I Love Romania

By Mark Baker, Writer

When I travel, I'm attracted to contrasts. In Romania, that means scenes of overloaded hay-and horse-carts sharing highway space with speeding Audis; or in cities, rows of regal ruins of former palaces standing side-by-side with gleaming new office buildings. There's never a dull moment. Bucharest has an unearned poor reputation, but through the cracks in the old facades, I see green shoots of creativity. It's a city of hidden gardens and quirky cafes. Further afield, the mountains and rural areas are quiet, unexplored and still highly authentic. There's a stillness and freshness in the air here that allows the mind freedom to roam.

For more about our writers, see p512

Above: Village in the Carpathian mountains

Romania

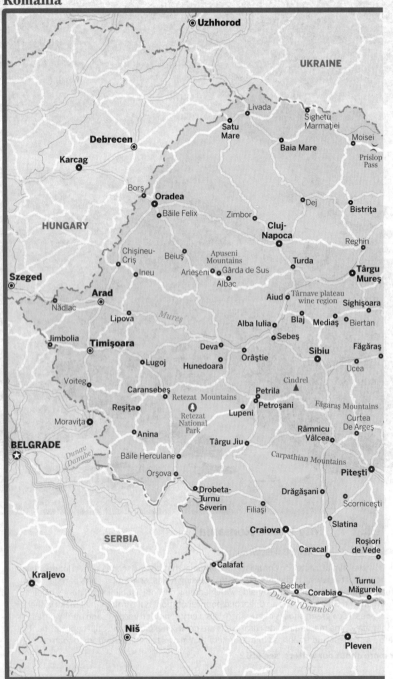

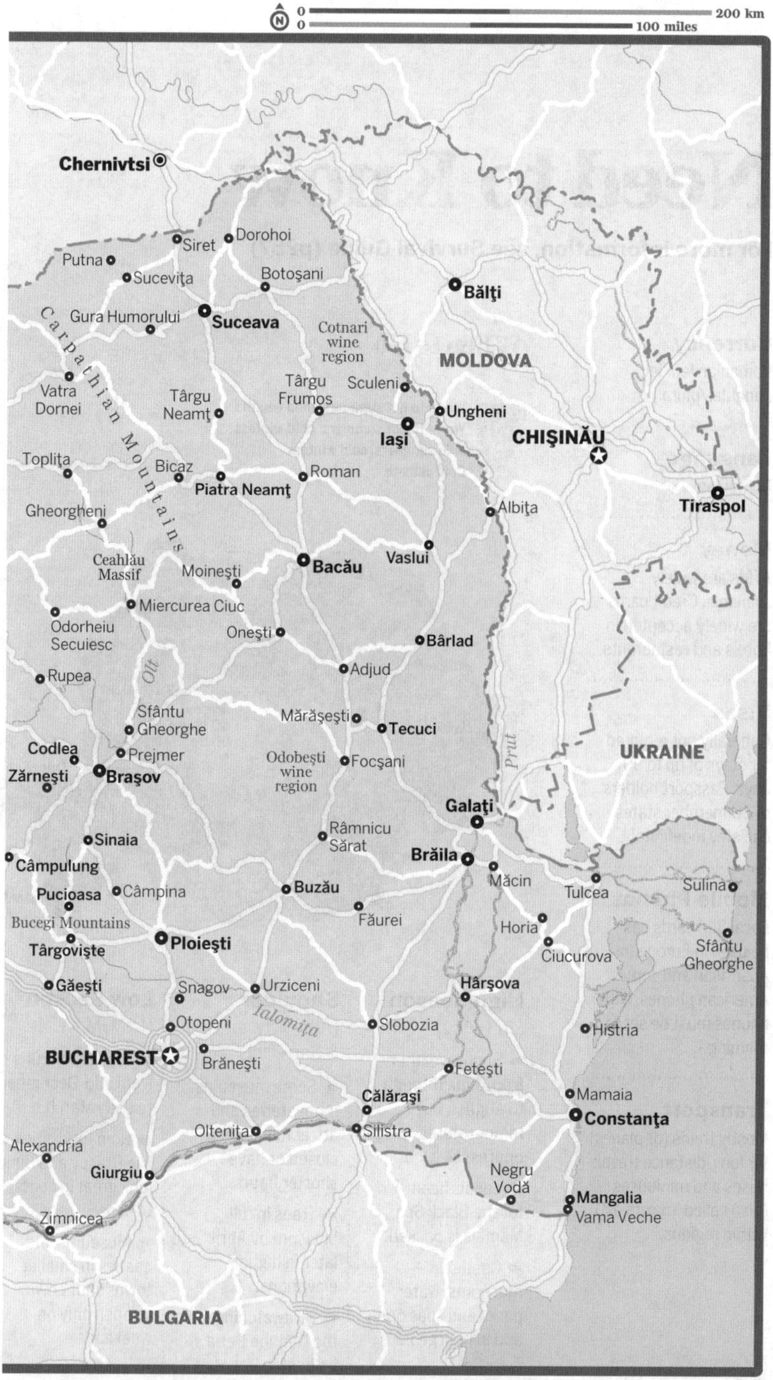

0
200 km
0
100 miles
N
Chernivtsi
Siret
Dorohoi
Putna
Suceviţa
Botoşani
Bălţi
Gura Humorului
Suceava
Cotnari wine region
Carpathian Mountains
MOLDOVA
Vatra Dornei
Târgu Neamţ
Târgu Frumos
Sculeni
Ungheni
Iaşi
CHIŞINĂU
Topliţa
Bicaz
Piatra Neamţ
Roman
Tiraspol
Gheorgheni
Albiţa
Ceahlău Massif
Moineşti
Bacău
Vaslui
Miercurea Ciuc
Odorheiu Secuiesc
Oneşti
Bârlad
Rupea
Olt
Adjud
Sfântu Gheorghe
Mărăşeşti
Tecuci
Codlea
Prejmer
Prut
UKRAINE
Zărneşti
Braşov
Odobeşti wine region
Focşani
Galaţi
Sinaia
Râmnicu Sărat
Brăila
Câmpulung
Măcin
Tulcea
Sulina
Pucioasa
Câmpina
Buzău
Făurei
Bucegi Mountains
Horia
Sfântu Gheorghe
Târgovişte
Ploieşti
Ciucurova
Găeşti
Snagov
Urziceni
Hârşova
Otopeni
Ialomiţa
Slobozia
Histria
BUCHAREST
Brăneşti
Feteşti
Călăraşi
Mamaia
Constanţa
Olteniţa
Silistra
Alexandria
Giurgiu
Negru Vodă
Mangalia
Vama Veche
Zimnicea
BULGARIA

Need to Know

For more information, see Survival Guide (p257)

Currency
Romanian leu/lei
(singular/plural)

Language
Romanian

Money
ATMs are widely
available. Credit cards
are widely accepted in
hotels and restaurants.

Visas
Generally not required
for stays of up to 90
days. Passport holders
of EU member states
can stay indefinitely.

Mobile Phones
Local SIM cards can
be used in European,
Australian and some
American phones. Other
phones must be set to
roaming.

Transport
Mostly trains (or planes)
for long-distance travel;
buses and minibuses
(also called 'maxitaxis')
within regions.

When to Go

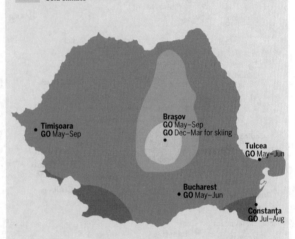

Warm to hot summers, mild winters
Warm to hot summers, cold winters
Mild summers, cold winters
Cold climate

Timişoara
GO May–Sep

Braşov
GO May–Sep
GO Dec–Mar for skiing

Tulcea
GO May–Jun

Bucharest
GO May–Jun

Constanţa
GO Jul–Aug

High Season
(Jun–Aug)

➡ Sunny weather
from June through
to August, but
temperatures can get
oppressively hot.

➡ Locals head
for the Black Sea;
Mamaia is packed.

➡ Castles,
museums, water
parks and spas open
and in high gear.

Shoulder
(Apr–May
& Sep–Oct)

➡ Some museums,
monasteries and
attractions are
closed or have
shorter hours.

➡ Trees in full
blossom by April;
later in higher
elevations.

➡ Birdwatching in
the Danube Delta at
its best in late May.

Low Season
(Nov–Mar)

➡ Ski season runs
from mid-December
to early March.

➡ Romantic cities
like Braşov and Sibiu
look great in coats
of snow.

➡ Museums and
castles in smaller
towns shut down
or open only on
weekends.

Your Daily Budget

Budget: Less than 130 lei

➡ Hostel dorm room or guesthouse: 50 lei per person

➡ Street food and self-catering: 40 lei

➡ Train/bus tickets: 30 lei

➡ Museum admission: 10 lei

Midrange: 130–360 lei

➡ Double in a midrange hotel or pension: 120 lei per person

➡ Meals in good restaurants: 60 lei

➡ Train/bus tickets: 30 lei

➡ Museum admissions: 30 lei

Top end: More than 360 lei

➡ Double in the best place in town: 200 lei per person

➡ Lunch/dinner at the best restaurants: 80 lei

➡ Taxi rides: 50 lei

➡ Museum admissions: 30 lei

Useful Websites

Bucharest Life (www.bucharest life.net) Casts a keen but critical eye on the capital.

Lonely Planet (www.lonely planet.com/romania) Destination information, hotel bookings, traveller forum and more.

Romania National Tourism Office (www.romaniatourism. com) Official tourism site.

Rural Tourism (www.rural turism.ro) Rural B&Bs across Romania.

Sapte Seri (www.sapteseri.ro) What's-on listings.

Exchange Rates

Australia	A$1	3.06 lei
Bulgaria	1 lv	2.32 lei
Canada	C$1	3.03 lei
Europe	€1	4.55 lei
Japan	¥100	3.90 lei
New Zealand	NZ$1	2.90 lei
UK	£1	5.10 lei
USA	US$1	4.00 lei

For current exchange rates see www.xe.com.

Important Numbers

Romania's country code	☏40
International access code	☏00
Ambulance & other emergency services	☏112

Opening Hours

Shopping centres and malls generally have longer hours and are open from 9am to 8pm Saturday to Sunday. Museums are usually closed on Monday, and have shorter hours outside high season.

Banks 9am to 5pm Monday to Friday; 9am to 1pm Saturday (varies)

Museums 10am to 6pm Tuesday to Friday; 10am to 4pm Saturday and Sunday

Post Offices 8am to 7pm Monday to Friday; 8am to 1pm Saturday (cities)

Restaurants 9am to 11pm Monday to Friday; 10am to 11pm Saturday and Sunday

Shops 9am to 6pm Monday to Friday; 9am to 2pm Saturday

Arriving in Romania

Henri Coandă International Airport (Bucharest) Express bus 783 runs to the centre (40 minutes, 7 lei); taxis to the centre cost 50 to 60 lei (30 to 40 minutes); trains to Gara de Nord are 10 lei (30 minutes).

Cluj Avram Iancu International Airport (Cluj-Napoca) To get to the centre take bus 5 or 8 (30 minutes, 2.50 lei), or a taxi (25 minutes, 50 lei).

Timişoara Traian Vuia International Airport (Timişoara) Express bus E4 (30 minutes, 2.50 lei) and taxis (25 minutes, 50 lei) run to the centre.

Street Scams & Annoyances

Romania is a relatively safe country, but there are some common scams to be aware of.

Watch out for jacked-up prices for tourists in Bucharest restaurants, taxis that charge extortionate fares (call for one from companies recommended by your hotel), and a lifted wallet if you're not careful in public squares or jam-packed buses – pretty much like anywhere in the world. Outside the capital, and away from touristy zones like Braşov, you'll probably end up being surprised you were ever concerned.

Stray dogs are an annoyance, but rarely pose a danger. Avoid the temptation to pat them. The best strategy is to stay out of their way and they'll stay out of yours.

For much more on getting around, see p266

If You Like...

Folk Culture

ASTRA National Museum Complex This open-air museum in Sibiu holds some 300 reconstructed peasant huts and farmhouses in a lovely park setting. (p112)

National Village Museum Romania's humbler origins are on display at this well-done skansen (open-air museum), situated incongruously in the middle of Bucharest. (p44)

Ethnographic Museum Occupying a wing of the stunningly renovated Palace of Culture, this collection of folk arts and crafts in Iaşi ranks among the most comprehensive in the country. (p187)

Huedin Microregion A bucolic paradise near the Apuseni Mountains much beloved by Hungarian folklorists as a stronghold of pastoral Transylvanian life. (p144)

Maramureş Large parts of this remote rural area to the north of Transylvania still feel untouched by modern times. (p166)

Castles & Fortresses

Fortified Church The whitewashed fortified church in Viscri, some 900 years old, is a splendidly restored feat of medieval engineering. (p106)

Royal Citadel Suceava's rugged and abandoned 14th-century fortress has received a high-tech makeover with amusing videos and touchscreen exhibits. (p200)

Bran Castle This mighty fortified castle got its start under the Teutonic knights as a watchtower over a strategic pass between Transylvania and Wallachia. (p93)

Peleş Castle If your taste runs to more aristocratic piles, this former residence of King Carol I will not disappoint. (p77)

Poienari Citadel Climb the 1480 steps up to this hilltop fortress that really was the stomping ground of feared Wallachian prince Vlad Ţepeş, aka Dracula. (p69)

Medieval Towns & Villages

Sighişoara The glorious 14th-century clock tower stands atop the town's citadel, marking out Transylvania's most picturesque Saxon town. (p98)

Curtea de Argeş This former Wallachian capital boasts the extensive ruins of a Princely Court with an intact, frescoed 700-year-old church. (p68)

Sibiel A pretty and remote Saxon village that recalls Little Red Riding Hood, with the village almost swallowed by the neighbouring forest; in recent winters packs of wolves have been spotted. (p117)

Ieud One of at least a dozen historic Maramureş villages; this one has two wooden churches and many traditional etched wooden gates. (p180)

Măgura The peaks of the Piatra Craiului mountains form a breathtaking backdrop to this tiny village near Braşov. (p98)

The Great Outdoors

Sfântu Gheorghe Relax on a pristine beach one day, scout out rare pelicans the next at the end of the Danube Delta. (p219)

Apuseni Nature Park This protected area in the northwest of the country is marked by amazing limestone formations, including arguably Romania's best caves. (p145)

Iron Gates National Park The Danube flows through a dramatic and perilously narrow gorge here along the southern border with Serbia. (p74)

Făgăraş Mountains Home to the country's tallest and most majestic mountains, with at least six peaks topping 2500m. (p106)

Interior, Palace of Parliament (p35)

Around Braşov The woods and hills around Braşov are the perfect spot for tracking wild animals, including wolves, lynx and bears, on a guided tour. (p92)

Nightlife

Bucharest's Old Town The tiny lanes that once surrounded the old Princely Court have been converted into an unbroken string of bars, pubs and clubs. (p38)

Mamaia Romania's most popular Black Sea resort is ground zero for the country's best summer beach clubs. (p225)

Timişoara You'd expect the home of the biggest university in the west to hold epic parties and you'd be right. (p151)

Cluj-Napoca Not to be outdone by Timişoara, this is another big-league college town with pubs and clubs on every corner. (p136)

Vama Veche Locals contend you haven't really partied on the Black Sea until you've pulled a beachside all-nighter here over an August weekend. (p227)

History

Palace of Parliament Former dictator Nicolae Ceauşescu's must-see alabaster albatross is an admittedly extreme example of severe, communist-era architecture. (p35)

Military Barracks The modest barracks where the Ceauşescus were executed on Christmas Day in 1989 has been reopened as a simple but chilling museum. (p65)

Former Ceauşescu Residence Grandiose or simply extreme kitsch? You be the judge as you tour the villa where the Ceauşescus lived for two decades. (p45)

Museum of the 1989 Revolution Timişoara launched the country's anticommunist revolution in 1989, and this moving exhibition tells that very brave tale. (p151)

Cucuteni Museum This gem in Piatra Neamţ highlights the ancient Cucuteni people and their provocative sculptures of feminine beauty. (p195)

National History & Archaeological Museum The amazing reach of ancient Greek and Roman cultures are displayed at Constanţa's landmark museum. (p220)

Iron Gates Museum The highlight is a scale model of the Roman bridge constructed across the Danube River in AD 103. (p74)

Month by Month

January

Expect snow and ice everywhere during, statistically speaking, the country's coldest month. Avoid slushy Bucharest and head instead for the mountains, where ski resorts are in full gear.

⭐ Winter Sports Festival

Held in Moldavia's Câmpulung Moldovenesc on the last Sunday of January. While sports are indeed the focus, they're mainly an excuse for revelry.

February

Ski resorts crowd up as school kids take their annual week-long winter break. Elsewhere, the winter freeze is going strong, and museums in the countryside are closed or have only weekend hours.

⭐ Enchanted Water Springs

Târgu Jiu's annual folk-music festival is held over the third weekend of the month.

March

March starts out festive, with the annual Mărțișor (1 March) holiday to mark the start of spring, but the rest of the month is normally cold, dark and wet.

⭐ Sighișoara Blues Festival

The highly regarded Sighișoara Blues Festival (www.blues-festival.ro) is held every year on the last weekend of March.

April

If you're partial to blossoms, this is the most beautiful month of the year. Easter is the high point of the Orthodox calendar, and Easter fairs and painted-egg festivals abound.

⭐ Bucharest International Film Festival

Annual festival brings world cinema to town over 10 days in April (www.b-iff.ro).

⭐ St George's Day Festival

Held in Sfântu Gheorghe (Transylvania; p118) in mid-April, the festival of St George's Day honours the church's patron saint with folk music, street food and nightly concerts.

May

Temperatures warm a bit in May, but expect rain. Romanians traditionally spend the Labour Day holiday (1 May) at the seashore, but it's still too cold to swim. Birdwatching starts in the Danube Delta.

⭐ Sibiu Jazz Festival

The second week in May brings headline jazz acts to Sibiu for the city's annual Jazz Festival.

June

The arrival of summer brings reliably warm, even hot, days and sunshine

throughout the country. Black Sea resorts get rolling and high-altitude zones are rich with wildflowers.

✯✯ International Theatre Festival

Sibiu's theatre festival (www. sibfest.ro) ranks as the country's most prominent performing arts event. Held over a week in mid-June.

✯✯ Transilvania International Film Festival

The Transilvania International Film Festival takes place in June at dozens of locations around Cluj-Napoca. (p136)

July

The summer sun starts to boil. Bucharest and other large cities can be unbearable if temperatures top 40°C. Locals hit the beaches on the Black Sea for relief.

☆ Electric Castle

Pop and rock festival unfolding over four days against the backdrop of Bánffy Castle (p146), near Cluj-Napoca, featuring electronica, house, metal and reggae.

✯✯ Festival of Medieval Arts & Crafts

This annual festival (www. sighisoaramedievala.ro) brings music, dance and folk crafts to Sighişoara in mid- to late July.

August

If you can take the heat, this is an ideal month to visit. Long days filled with

Top: The Romanian Athenaeum (p39), home of the George Enescu Music Festival
Bottom: Untold Festival, Cluj-Napoca (p136)

sun bring crowds to the coast and the mountains. There's a mid-month holiday (15 August), so book hotels in advance.

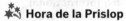

Hora de la Prislop

A folk-music festival held on the second Sunday in August at the Prislop Pass in Maramureș celebrating the sheep returning from the mountains.

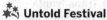

Untold Festival

Billed as 'Romania's biggest festival'; the focus is rock and indie music and it brings thousands to Cluj-Napoca (p136) in August.

September

A great month to visit. The days are warm and sunny, with plenty of daylight. The start of mushrooming season pushes city dwellers into the woods in search of the perfect fungus.

George Enescu Music Festival

This acclaimed festival (www.festivalenescu.ro) runs over the month of September at Bucharest's elegant Romanian Athenaeum (p39).

Balkanik Music Festival

High-energy Roma- and Balkan-infused world music comes to Bucharest over a long weekend in mid-September (www.balkanikfestival.ro).

Sibiu Opera Festival

The Sibiu Opera Festival (www.filarmonicasibiu.ro) brings concerts and singers to Sibiu from around the world in September.

October

The cultural calendar is in full swing in cities and towns, with concerts and theatrical performances.

International Astra Film Festival

Sibiu's International Astra Film Festival focuses on the best regional documentaries. Held in mid- to late October.

International Theatre Festival for Children

Bucharest's Ion Creangă Theatre is the host organisation for the International Theatre Festival for Children, which brings troupes from around the world.

December

The month begins with a national holiday on the 1st and then descends further into cold and darkness. By mid-month the sun is all but gone by 4.30pm each day. Christmas brings welcome relief, with parties, festivals and markets.

Winter Festival

Sighetu Marmației's undisputed annual high point comes just a couple of days after Christmas, with the Winter Festival featuring food, music, masks and a colourful oxen parade.

Itineraries

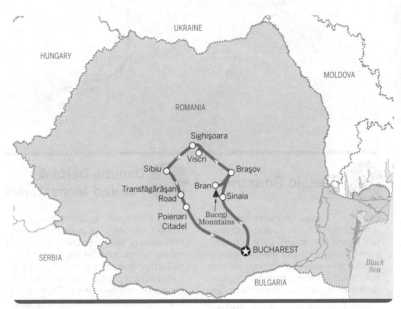

10 DAYS Transylvania Castles & Cities

Transylvania is Romania's best-known region and arguably its most beautiful. It's filled with rocky mountaintops, haunting castles and lively historic cities. This classic route is designed for travellers for whom this region is the prime focus. The tour starts in Bucharest, where most international flights arrive.

Hire a car in **Bucharest** or hop a train northward toward the mountains, stopping in **Sinaia** for a couple of nights and checking out Peleş Castle. From here, take a cable car into the **Bucegi Mountains** for a hike.

Drive or take a bus north to spend a couple of nights in **Braşov**, a lively hub with a cobbled centre. Use Braşov as a base for a day trip to the infamous **Bran Castle**.

If you have a car, spend a night in the Saxon village of **Viscri** before continuing to **Sighişoara**, where the dramatic citadel offers creature comforts and Dracula's birthplace.

Head southwest for a night or two in the cultural hub of **Sibiu**. If you have a car (and it's summer), drive south along the breathtaking **Transfăgărăşan road**. South of the pass, stop at the 'real Dracula's castle' of **Poienari Citadel**, before returning to Bucharest.

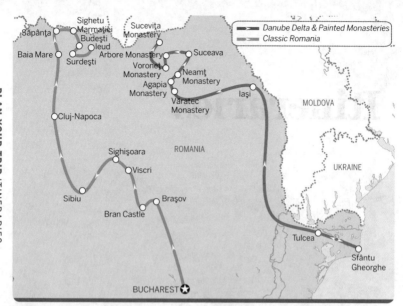

Legend:

- Danube Delta & Painted Monasteries
- Classic Romania

 Classic Romania

2 WEEKS

Romania is a deceptively large country, with physical barriers (such as high mountain passes) that make it difficult to get around easily. This tour highlights the most popular province, Transylvania, but adds neighbouring regions, including capital Bucharest, to make the most of your time.

Spend the first two nights in **Bucharest**, taking in the Palace of Parliament as well as museums and restaurants. Take the train or drive to **Braşov**, and spend at least a day or two. Use it as a base for visiting **Bran Castle** and the Saxon town of **Viscri**.

Head north to **Sighişoara** and its historic citadel. Spend the night before heading south to **Sibiu**, an eye-catching former Saxon stronghold.

From here, head north through **Cluj-Napoca**, a big university town with an abundance of awesome cafes and clubs.

Push northward to the city of **Baia Mare** or to **Sighetu Marmaţiei**, to use as a base for visiting the unspoilt region of Maramureş. Don't miss the Merry Cemetery in **Săpânţa** or the pretty wooden churches in **Budeşti**, **Surdeşti** and **Ieud**.

 Danube Delta & Painted Monasteries

1 WEEK

Eastern Romania receives the fewest number of visitors, yet possesses some of the country's most important natural and cultural attractions. For the former, look no further than the serene Danube Delta, a sprawling protected wetland that's perfect for birders. Northwest of here are the cultural wonders of the Bucovina painted monasteries.

The tour starts in **Tulcea**, the gateway to the Danube Delta. Stay overnight in Tulcea and enter the delta via boating day trips. If you've got more time, skip Tulcea and grab a passenger ferry to deeper, more scenic **Sfântu Gheorghe**.

After birdwatching and boating, return to Tulcea and take the bus or drive north to **Iaşi**, Moldavia's cultural hub and largest city. Spend a day taking in the sights. Use Iaşi as a base to explore the **Agapia**, **Văratec** and **Neamţ** monasteries.

From here, it's a short hop to the regional capital of **Suceava**, which has good hotels and a number of companies offering tours to the nearby painted monasteries. Don't miss the **Arbore**, **Voroneţ** and **Suceviţa** monasteries.

Regions at a Glance

Bucharest

Museums
Entertainment
Food

Great Galleries

Bucharest is home to the country's top museums of art, history and natural science, among many, many others. Lovers of folk art have both a quirky peasant museum and a grand, open-air collection dedicated to Romanian villages to choose from.

From Highbrow to Lowbrow

The capital has a thriving cultural calendar that runs from September through to spring, and is especially strong on classical music. In addition, nightly throughout the year, you'll have your pick of jazz, rock, indie or blues at dozens of smaller music clubs.

Romania's Dining Capital

Bucharest is the food capital of Romania. It's the place where traditional Romanian fare clashes with international organic and farm-to-table culinary trends, and the results are superb.

p34

Wallachia

History
Nature
Winemaking

Roots of Romania

Modern Romania traces its roots back to the principality of Wallachia, once ruled over by the feared Vlad Țepeș. The princely courts of Curtea de Argeș and Târgoviște tell this history.

The Danube Turns Dramatic

The Danube River defines Wallachia's southern border. In the west, below Drobeta-Turnu Severin, the river winds through a series of dramatic gorges called – appropriately enough – the 'Iron Gates'.

New Techniques & Artisanal Grapes

Wallachia is home to some of the country's finest wine regions, including the Dealu Mare area north of Târgoviște, and a promising new region in the west, at Drăgășani.

p60

Transylvania

Castles
Mountains
Scenic Villages

Counts in Black Capes

Who can blame author Bram Stoker for looking to Transylvania for inspiration on spooky castles? Bran is a national treasure, but don't neglect Corvin Castle, at Hunedoara, or Râșnov, near Brașov.

Walking Along the Peaks

Transylvania's natural borders are defined by a string of 2500m peaks that cut through the country in a sweeping arc. Many travellers are partial to the Bucegi Mountains, which are accessible by cable car from Sinaia.

Fortresses in the Middle of Nowhere

Isolated 17th-century villages, defined by fortress churches and ringed by majestic peaks, are par for the course in Transylvania. Don't miss Viscri, Biertan and Măgura.

p76

Crişana & Banat

Architecture
Hiking & Caving
Entertainment

Western Wannabes

Western Romanian cities such as Timişoara and Oradea were heavily influenced by architectural styles in Budapest and Vienna. Oradea, in particular, is drenched in glorious art nouveau detail.

Apuseni Nature Park

Often overlooked for higher peaks elsewhere, the Apuseni Mountains, southeast of Oradea, offer miles of rugged, isolated trails and dozens of caves that can be explored.

Timişoara Opera & Theatre

Timişoara takes its performing arts seriously. For something less highbrow, the city's student complex is filled with bars and dance clubs that stay open till dawn.

p149

Maramureş

Village Life
Folk Music
Wooden Churches

Back to Basics

The whole of Maramureş feels like one large exhibition of peasant life as it was lived 100 or more years ago. Traditional crafts, including the making of strong plum brandy, still thrive.

The Roots of Folk

Much Romanian folk music traces its roots to Maramureş, and traditional song and dance is on display throughout the year at festivals such as the Hora de la Prislop, held in August.

Sombre Steeples

Simple wooden churches in villages such as Budeşti, Bârsana and Ieud are a testament to both the villagers' piety and their immense woodworking skills. Try to take in a service during your visit.

p166

Moldavia & the Bucovina Monasteries

Monasteries
History
Food

Objects of Faith & Works of Art

Bucovina's painted monasteries, from the 15th and 16th centuries, are considered masterpieces for the way they harmonise colour with the surrounding countryside.

Monuments to Medieval Conquest

Fortresses in Suceava and Târgu Neamţ recall some of the greatest triumphs against the Ottoman Turks in the 15th century by Moldavian prince Ştefan cel Mare.

Hearty Regional Cooking

Moldavia is renowned for its regional traditional cooking. They lay claim to *mămăligă* (cornmeal mush), but *ciorbă Rădăuţi*, chicken soup with garlic and vinegar, is the real deal.

p183

The Danube Delta & Black Sea Coast

Wildlife
Beaches
Ancient History

Rare Pelicans & Cormorants

The Danube Delta is a protected wetland that stretches on as far as the eye can see. It's ideal for boating, hiking, fishing and birdwatching.

Sunbathing & Moondancing

Romania's coastline is dotted with beaches from the Danube Delta to the Bulgarian border. Favourites include the isolated beach at Sfântu Gheorghe and infamous party spot Vama Veche.

Stomping Ground for Greeks & Romans

The Black Sea coastline was settled by the Greeks as far back as 700 BC, and then came the Romans. Museums in Tulcea, Histria and Constanţa are particularly rich.

p211

On the Road

Maramureş
p166

Transylvania
p76

Moldavia & the
Bucovina
Monasteries
p183

Crişana &
Banat
p149

ROMANIA

Bucharest
p34
⭐

The Danube Delta
& Black Sea
Coast p211

Wallachia
p60

Bucharest

POP 1,900,000

Best Places to Eat

➜ Caru' cu Bere (p50)

➜ Lacrimi şi Sfinţi (p51)

➜ Shift Pub (p51)

➜ Gargantua in the Park (p51)

➜ Modelier (p51)

Best Places to Sleep

➜ Rembrandt Hotel (p49)

➜ Vila Arte (p49)

➜ Little Bucharest Old Town Hostel (p49)

➜ Hotel Opera (p49)

➜ Hotel Amzei (p49)

Why Go?

Romania's capital gets a bad rap, but in fact it's dynamic, energetic and fun. It's where still-unreconstructed communism meets unbridled capitalism; where the soporific forces of the EU meet the passions of the Balkans. Many travellers give the city just a night or two before heading off to Transylvania, but that's clearly not enough. Allow at least a few days to take in the good museums, stroll the parks and hang out at trendy cafes. While much of the centre is modern and garish, you'll find splendid 17th- and 18th-century Orthodox churches and graceful art nouveau villas tucked away in quiet corners. Communism changed the face of the city forever, and nowhere is this more evident than at the gargantuan Palace of Parliament, the craziest and crassest tribute to dictatorial megalomania you'll probably ever see.

When to Go
Bucharest

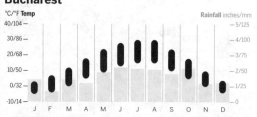

Apr & May City parks erupt into colour as trees blossom and flowers bloom.

Jul & Aug Avoid Bucharest in midsummer, when temperatures can be oppressively hot.

Sep & Oct Cooler, but still sunny, and warm enough for terrace drinking and dining.

History

Lying on the Wallachian plains between the Carpathian foothills and the Danube River, Bucharest was settled by Geto-Dacians as early as 70 BC. By 1459 a princely residence and military citadel had been established under the chancellery of infamous Wallachian Prince Vlad Țepeș. By the end of the 17th century, the city was the capital of Wallachia and ranked among southeastern Europe's wealthiest centres. It became the national capital in 1862, as it lay on a main trade route between east and west.

The early 20th century was Bucharest's golden age. Large neoclassical buildings sprang up, fashionable parks were laid out and landscaped on Parisian models and, by the end of the 1930s, the city was known throughout Europe as 'Little Paris' or 'the Paris of the East'.

Bombing by the Allies during WWII, coupled with a 1940 earthquake, destroyed much of Bucharest's prewar beauty. In 1977 a second major earthquake claimed 1391 lives and flattened countless buildings. Former dictator Nicolae Ceaușescu's massive redevelopment of the city in the 1980s, culminating in his grandiose Palace of the Parliament (sometimes still referred to as the 'House of the People'), drove a stake through the heart of Bucharest's elegant past.

The violent revolution of 1989 inflicted serious wounds, both physically and psychologically. Many buildings still bear bullet holes as testament to those chaotic days when the anticommunist uprising resembled nothing so much as a civil war. Less than a year later, in June 1990, miners poured into the centre to support a government crackdown on protesting students in a shocking wave of violence that reopened scars that had barely had time to heal.

Although it's still haunted by its recent bloody past more than a quarter century later, Bucharest is clearly recovering. The Historic Centre, particularly the area around Str Lipscani, has received a long-overdue revamp and the surrounding neighbourhoods, while still derelict in parts, seem to get nicer and nicer with each passing year.

◉ Sights

Bucharest teems with museums and attractions; all are relatively cheap and many are among the nation's best. Note, though, that many are closed on Mondays (and some on Tuesdays too), so plan your visit accordingly. The main thoroughfare, Calea Victoriei, makes a nice walk, as it connects the two main squares of the city, Piața Victoriei in the north and Piața Revoluției in the centre, before bringing you to the Historic Centre, home to countless cafes, bars and clubs.

◉ Palace of Parliament & Around

★ **Palace of Parliament** HISTORIC BUILDING
(Palatul Parlamentului, Casa Poporului; Map p40; ⤴ tour bookings 0733-558 102; http://cic.cdep.ro; B-dul Națiunile Unite; adult/student complete tours 55/28 lei, standard tours 35/18 lei, photography 30 lei; ⊙ 9am-5pm Mar-Oct, to 4pm Nov-Feb; M Izvor) The Palace of Parliament is the world's second-largest administrative building (after the Pentagon) and former dictator Nicolae Ceaușescu's most infamous creation. Started in 1984 (and still unfinished), the building has more than 3000 rooms and covers 330,000 sq metres. Entry is by guided-tour only (book in advance). Entry to the palace is from B-dul Națiunile Unite on the building's northern side (to find it, face the front of the palace from B-dul Unirii and walk around the building to the right). Bring your passport.

Several types of tours are available, including a 'standard' tour of the main rooms and hallways, and 'complete' tours that combine the standard tour with views of the terrace and basement. The standard tour takes around 45 minutes; add an extra 15 minutes to see the terrace and basement. Today the building houses the country's parliament and associated offices – though much of it stands unused.

National Museum of Contemporary Art GALLERY
(Muzeul Naționale Arta Contemporana; ⤴ 021-318 9137; www.mnac.ro; Calea 13 Sepembrie 1; adult/student 10/2.50 lei; ⊙ 10am-6pm Wed-Sun; M Izvor) The Palace of Parliament houses a superb art gallery, which displays temporary, ever-changing exhibitions of eclectic installations and video art. Check the website in advance to make sure something is on during your visit to spare yourself a long walk. The museum is located on the southwestern side of the building (at the opposite end of the Palace of Parliament to the tour entrance); look for entry E4.

Bucharest Highlights

1 Palace of Parliament (p35) Taking in the sheer enormity of former dictator Nicolae Ceauşescu's madhouse.

2 Statue of Emperor Trajan (p38) Getting that coveted Instagram snap of the city's kookiest statue – a naked Roman Emperor Trajan holding a Dacian wolf.

3 Cişmigiu Garden (p43) Kicking back in Bucharest's surprisingly peaceful central park.

4 Museum of the Romanian Peasant (p44) Learning why you might not appreciate granny's wisdom enough at this quirky but cool museum.

5 Caru' cu Bere (p50) Enjoying traditional food, along with homemade beer and an impromptu cancan performance.

6 Former Ceauşescu Residence (p45) Touring the luxe villa the Ceauşescus called home for more than two decades.

7 Grădina Verona (p52) Spending the evening drinking and talking in the open air at one of the city's pretty gardens.

8 Romanian Athenaeum (p39) Experiencing the serenity of classical music harmonising with classical architecture.

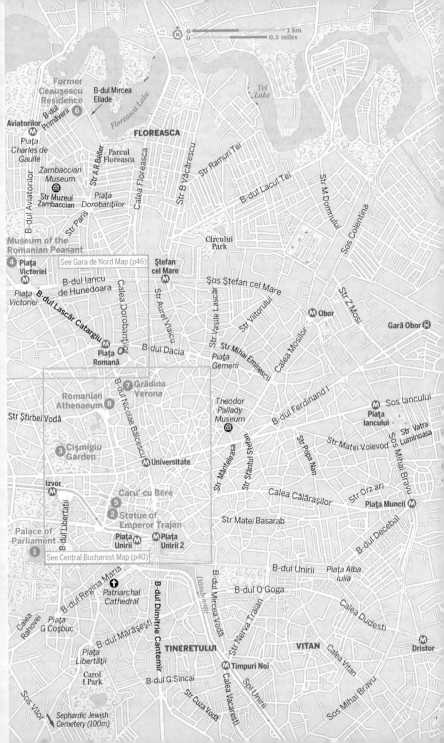

◉ Piaţa Universităţii

If Bucharest has a true centre, it would be here, midway between Piaţa Victoriei in the north and Piaţa Unirii in the south, with two major north–south arteries on each side: B-dul IC Brătianu to the east and Calea Victoriei to the west. Many university buildings are situated here (hence the name), plus government institutions and lots of restaurants and bars.

New St George's Church   CHURCH
(Biserica Sfântul Gheorghe-Nou; Map p40; cnr Str Lipscani & B-dul Brătianu; ☉ 8am-6pm; Ⓜ Universitate) FREE The New St George's Church dates from 1699 and is significant primarily as the burial place of Wallachian prince Constantin Brâncoveanu (r 1688–1714). Brâncoveanu was captured by the Turks in 1714 after refusing to take part in the Russo-Turkish War (1711). He and his four sons were taken to Istanbul and beheaded.

Museum of the History of Bucharest   MUSEUM
(Map p40; ☑ 021-315 6858; www.muzeulbucurestiului.ro; B-dul IC Brătianu 2; adult/child 10/5 lei; ☉ 10am-6pm Tue-Sun; Ⓜ Universitate) Housed in a neo-Gothic palace built in the 1830s to host fancy balls, this small museum, facing Piaţa Universităţii, is a lovely spot with an interesting collection of old artefacts, photos and costumes. Designed by two Austrian architects, the palace was built in 1832–34 for the Şuţu family, notorious for their high-society parties.

◉ Historic Centre

Bucharest's **Historic Centre** (*Centrul istoric*), sometimes referred to as the 'Old Town' or 'Lipscani', lies south of Piaţa Universităţii. It's a fascinating area that marks both the city's historic heart, formed when Bucharest was emerging as the capital of Wallachia in the 15th and 16th centuries, and the centrepiece of efforts to transform the capital into a liveable urban centre. It's home to Bucharest's **Old Princely Court** (Palatul Voievodal, Curtea Veche; Map p40; Str Francezǎ 21-23; ☉ closed to the general public; Ⓜ Piaţa Unirii), dating back to the 15th century, though the court was allowed to fall into disrepair over the centuries and is now undergoing long-term renovation.

The area around the court thrived from roughly the 16th to the 19th centuries as a merchant quarter for artisans and traders, whose occupations are still reflected in street names such as Str Covaci (street of the blacksmiths) and Str Şelari (street for saddle-makers). During much of the 20th century, in fact until as recently as a few years ago, the area had become a slum, a poor excuse for public housing for impoverished Roma.

These days, the saddle-makers are long gone to make way for the dozens and dozens of restaurants, bars and clubs. It's still very scruffy in parts, with gleaming clubs standing next to derelict buildings, but if you're in the mood for a big night out, there's no better place in town to party.

Stavropoleos Church   CHURCH
(Map p40; ☑ 021-313 4747; www.stavropoleos.ro; Str Stavropoleos 4; ☉ 7am-8pm; Ⓜ Piaţa Unirii) FREE The tiny and lovely Stavropoleos Church, which dates from 1724, perches a bit oddly a block over from some of Bucharest's craziest Old Town carousing. It's one church, though, that will make a lasting impression, with its courtyard filled with tombstones, an ornate wooden interior and carved wooden doors.

Old Princely Court Church   CHURCH
(Biserica Curtea Veche; Map p40; Str Francezǎ; ☉ 7am-8pm; Ⓜ Piaţa Unirii) FREE The Old Princely Court Church, built from 1546 to 1559 during the reign of Mircea Ciobanul (Mircea the Shepherd), is considered to be Bucharest's oldest church. The faded 16th-century frescoes next to the altar are originals. The carved stone portal was added in 1715.

National History Museum   MUSEUM
(Muzeul Naţional de Istorie a Romaniei; Map p40; ☑ 021-315 8207; www.mnir.ro; Calea Victoriei 12; adult/student 27/7 lei; ☉ 10am-6pm Wed-Sun; Ⓜ Piaţa Unirii) Houses an excellent collection of maps, statues and ancient jewels, and is particularly strong on the country's ties to ancient Rome, including a replica of the 2nd-century Trajan's Column. A local favourite, though, is not inside the museum at all, but rather on the steps outside: a controversial, and funny, **Statue of Emperor Trajan** (Map p40; Calea Victoriei 12; Ⓜ Piaţa Unirii), standing naked and holding a Dacian wolf.

◉ Piaţa Revoluţiei

To the north of Piaţa Universităţii, along Calea Victoriei, stands Piaţa Revoluţiei, a part of the city indelibly marked by the

BUCHAREST IN ...

One Day

If you've only got one day, get an early start and make your way over to the **Palace of Parliament** for a guided tour. Afterwards, stroll along Calea Victoriei and stop in at one of the big museums, such as the **National Art Museum**, and admire the **Rebirth Memorial** to the 1989 revolution. Afterwards sit with a beer at **Cişmigiu Garden** and spend the evening in the Historic Centre.

Three Days

Spend the second day in the leafy northern part of the capital, visiting **Herăstrău Park** and allowing time to see the **Former Ceauşescu Residence** and the open-air **National Village Museum**. Walk along pretty Şos Kiseleff to visit one or both of the **Museum of the Romanian Peasant** and **Grigore Antipa Natural History Museum**. For your last day, head to **Lake Snagov** to visit Dracula's, er, Vlad Ţepeş', final resting place.

events surrounding the overthrow of the Ceauşescu regime in 1989. Ceauşescu's infamous final speech was given here, from the balcony of the former Central Committee of the Communist Party building (Map p40; www.mai.gov.ro; Piaţa Revoluţiei 1; ⊘ closed to the public; Ⓜ Universitate), on 21 December 1989. Amid cries of 'Down with Ceauşescu!' he escaped (briefly) by helicopter from the roof. Meanwhile, the crowds were riddled with bullets, and many died. The building now houses the Interior Ministry.

On an island in front of the building on Calea Victoriei stands the Rebirth Memorial (Memorialul Renaşterii; Map p40; Calea Victoriei, Piaţa Revoluţiei; ⊘ 24hr; Ⓜ Universitate) – a white obelisk piercing a basketlike crown (a doughnut on a stick?). It was ridiculed when it was first erected in 2005, but the public has now grown accustomed to it.

★ Romanian Athenaeum   HISTORIC BUILDING (Ateneul Român; Map p40; ✆ box office 021-315 6875; www.fge.org.ro; Str Benjamin Franklin 1-3; tickets 20-65 lei; ⊘ box office noon-7pm Tue-Fri, 4-7pm Sat, 10-11am Sun; Ⓜ Universitate, Piaţa Romană) The exquisite Romanian Athenaeum is the majestic heart of Romania's classical music tradition. Scenes from Romanian history are featured on the interior fresco inside the Big Hall on the 1st floor; the dome is 41m high. A huge appeal dubbed 'Give a Penny for the Athenaeum' saved it from disaster after funds dried up in the late-19th century. Today it's home to the George Enescu Philharmonic Orchestra and normally only open during concerts, but you can often take a peak inside.

The peristyle is adorned with mosaics of five Romanian rulers, including Moldavian prince Vasile Lupu (r 1512–21), Wallachian Matei Basarab (r 1632–54) and King Carol I (r 1881–1914). It was built in 1888, and George Enescu made his debut here in 1898, followed five years later by the first performance of his masterpiece, *Romanian Rhapsody*.

The George Enescu Philharmonic offers a wide array of classical music concerts from September to May as well as a number of one-off musical shows and spectacles throughout the year. Buy tickets at the venue box office. Tickets go on sale Tuesday of the week a concert is taking place.

National Art Museum   MUSEUM (Muzeul Naţional de Artă; Map p40; ✆ information 021-313 3030; www.mnar.arts.ro; Calea Victoriei 49-53; 15 lei; ⊘ 11am-7pm Wed-Sun; Ⓜ Universitate) Housed in the 19th-century Royal Palace, this massive, multipart museum – all signed in English – houses two permanent galleries: one for National Art and the other for European Masters. The national gallery is particularly strong on ancient and medieval art, while the European gallery includes some 12,000 pieces and is laid out by nationality.

The Royal Palace itself is a treat. Built from 1812 to 1815 by Prince Dinicu Golescu, the palace became the official royal residence in 1834 during the reign of Prince Alexandru Ghica (r 1834–42). The facade dates from the 1930s. See the website for occasional public tours of chambers of the building that are normally off limits to visitors.

Central Bucharest

400 m
0.2 miles

See Gara de Nord Map (p46)

33

Str A Călinescu

Theodor Pallady
Museum (350m)

B-dul Carol I

Str Vasile Lascăr

Str Speranţei

Str Calmatei

Str CA Rosetti

8
21

Str Schitul Darvari

Str Thomas Masarik

Str I L Caragiale

Str Batiştei

Str Italiană

Piaţa
CA Rosetti

41

B-dul Carol I

B-dul Carol I

Piaţa
Gheorghe
Cantacuzino

Str Icoanei

Str Maria Rosetti

Str Jean Louis Calderon

36

Icoanei
Garden

Str Nicolae Filipescu

Str Tudor Arghezi

Str Nicola e Filipescu

34

58

38

49

Str Dionisie Lupu

Str Pictor Verona

Str Pitar Moş

Str CA Rosetti

Str Nicolae Filipescu

Jules Michelet

B-dul Nicolae Bălcescu

M Universitate

Str E Quinet

61
44

B-dul Gen Magheru

Str CA Rosetti

Str Ion Câmpineanu

Str Academiei

25

Str Franklin

Str D I Dobrescu

6

Str George Enescu

Str Nicolae Golescu

Piaţa
George
Enescu

Piaţa
Revoluţiei

20

Calea Victoriei

26

Str Mendeleev

46

3
**Romanian
Athenaeum**

Str Georges
Clemenceau

14

9

59

Str Matei Millo

Str George Enescu

Str Nicolae Golescu

Royal
Palace

Central
Post
Office

Piaţa
Amzei

28

Str Piaţa Amzei

Calea Victoriei

Str Ion Câmpineanu

Str Victor Eftimiu

29

56

Piaţa
Walter
Mărăcineanu

Str General Berthelot

27

Str Luterană

Str Ştirbei Vodă

43

5

Str Spiru Haret

Str Putul cu Plopi

Cişmigiu
Garden

Cişmigiu
Lake

Cişmigiu
Lake

1
**Cişmigiu
Garden**

B-dul Schitu
Măgureanu

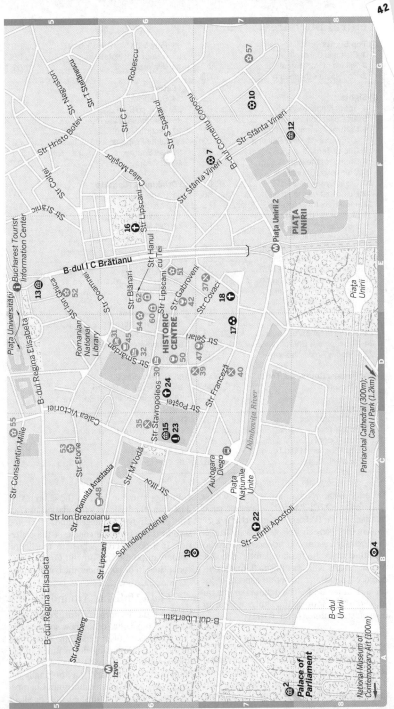

PIAȚA
UNIRII

HISTORIC
CENTRE

Piața
Unirii

Piața Unirii 2

Piața Unirii

Dâmbovița River

Piața Națiunile
Unite

Autogara
Diego

Palace of
Parliament

B-dul Unirii

B-dul Libertății

Patriarchal Cathedral (300m);
Carol I Park (1.2km)

National Museum of
Contemporary Art (100m)

Bucharest Tourist
Information Center

Piața Universității

B-dul I C Brătianu

B-dul Regina Elisabeta

B-dul Regina Elisabeta

Romanian
National
Library

Calea Victoriei

Str Lipscani

Str Gutemberg

Str Ion Brezoianu

Str Domnita Anastasia

Str Eforie

Str Constantin Mille

Str Ilfov

Str M Vodă

Str Postei

Str Stavropoleos

Str Smardan

Str Franceză

Str Selari

Str Covaci

Str Gabroveni

Str Blănari

Str Doamnei

Str Ion Ghica

Str Sf Ionic

Str Stanic

Str Lipscani

Str Hanul
cu Tei

Str Lipscani

Str Sfânta Vineri

Str Sfânta Vineri

Str Sfânta Vineri

B-dul Corneliu Coposu

Str S Spătarul

Calea Moșilor

Str C F

Str Robescu

Str Hristo Botev

Str I Neagoe

Str T Ștefănescu

Str Histori

Str Colței

Str Spl Independenței

Spl Independenței

Izvor

Str Ion Ghica

Str Lipscani

Str Sfinții Apostoli

2

11

48

53

55

35

15

23

24

30

31

45

32

54

60

50

39

40

47

42

37

51

52

13

16

7

10

57

12

18

17

62

19

22

4

Central Bucharest

Theodor Aman Museum   MUSEUM
(Map p40; ☏ 021-314 5812; www.muzeulbu
curestiului.ro; Str CA Rosetti 8; adult/child 5/2 lei;
⊙ 10am-6pm Wed-Sun; Ⓜ Piaţa Romană) This is
the lovingly restored residence and studio
of 19th-century Romanian painter Theodor
Aman. Aman's skill was in small, finely ren-
dered oil paintings depicting aspects of local and national life. The detail is so fine on
some of the paintings, the figures appear to
take on three-dimensional form.

Creţulescu Church   CHURCH
(Kretzulescu Church; Map p40; ☏ 021-410 7116;
Calea Victoriei 45-47; ⊙ 7am-8pm; Ⓜ Universitate)
FREE The modest Creţulescu Church stands
in repose near the far larger and more dramatic Royal Palace. Look for the original
paintings near the door to the church that
date from the building's foundation in 1722.
The church was damaged and renovated
several times over the course of the centuries. In front, there's a bust to the liberal
Romanian politician Corneliu Coposu, who
spent time in prison under the communists.

⊙ Piaţa Unirii & Around

South of the Historic Centre, Piaţa Unirii
stands at the centre of the new socialist city
that Ceauşescu began building in earnest
in the 1980s (knocking down much of old
Bucharest in the process). The area's broad
boulevard, B-dul Unirii, was originally intended as a kind of communist-era Champs-
Élysées. It was never finished, but the sheer

scale conveys something of the intent. The main sights, ironically, are a handful of beautiful historic churches that miraculously survived the rebuilding and demolition project.

Prince Mihai Monastery — MONASTERY
(Mânăstirea Mihai Vodă; Map p40; Str Sapienţei 4; ☺8am-7pm; Ⓜ Izvor) FREE The former symbol of Bucharest, the 16th-century Prince Mihai Monastery was built from 1589 to 1591 under the orders of Mihai Viteazul (r 1593–1601). Ceauşescu moved it 279m east in 1985 to this patch of wasteland between apartment blocks.

Antim Monastery — MONASTERY
(Mânăstirea Antim; Map p40; Str Antim 29; ☺7am-8pm; Ⓜ Piaţa Unirii) FREE This beautiful walled complex was built in 1715 by the metropolitan bishop Antim Ivireanu. Today it's hidden by communist-era housing blocks.

St Apostles' Church — CHURCH
(Biserica Sfinţii Apostoli; Map p40; Str Sfintii Apostoli 33a; ☺7am-8pm; Ⓜ Piaţa Unirii) FREE Tiny St Apostles' Church, north of B-dul Unirii (west of the Piaţa Unirii), survived Ceauşescu's 1980s demolition project – to a degree. The church, built in 1636, was not moved, but the surrounding parkland was ripped up and replaced with blocks of flats. It's overgrown, with trees and near-abandoned buildings.

Patriarchal Cathedral — CHURCH
(Catedrala Patriahală; Str Dealul Mitropoliei; ☺7am-8pm; Ⓜ Piaţa Unirii) FREE From the centre of Piaţa Unirii, look southwest to the Patriarchal Cathedral, the centre of Romanian Orthodox faith, built between 1656 and 1658. It triumphantly peeks over once-grand housing blocks on B-dul Unirii designed to 'hide' Bucharest's churches. During the 15th century, a small wooden church surrounded by vineyards occupied this site. None of the interior paintings has survived, with the exception of one icon depicting Constantin and Helen, the cathedral's patron saints.

Piaţa Victoriei & Around

Piaţa Victoriei is an important traffic hub and square that marks the northern edge of the central city. The metro station is a good access point for walks north along Şos Kiseleff or south into the centre.

George Enescu Museum — MUSEUM
(Muzeul George Enescu; Map p46; ☏021-318 1450; www.georgeenescu.ro; Calea Victoriei 141; adult/child 6/3 lei; ☺10am-5pm Tue-Sun; Ⓜ Piaţa Victoriei) A few blocks south of Piaţa Victoriei is this museum dedicated to national composer George Enescu (1881–1955). The real lure is the chance to peek inside the lovely building housing the museum: the turn-of-the-century art nouveau Cantacuzino Palace.

Art Collection Museum — MUSEUM
(Map p40; ☏021-212 1749; www.mnar.arts.ro; Calea Victoriei 111; adult/child 7/3.50 lei; ☺11am-7pm Sat-Wed; Ⓜ Piaţa Romană) A grab bag of several dozen private collections, particularly strong on folk and religious art and Romanian painting from the 19th and early 20th centuries. It's now part of the National Art Museum (p39).

Şoseaua Kiseleff

Home to some of Bucharest's finest villas and a handful of its best museums, Şos Kiseleff (metro Piaţa Victoriei) stretches north from Piaţa Victoriei to Herăstrău Park. The major landmark in this neck of the woods is the Triumphal Arch, which stands halfway up Şos Kiseleff. The 27m arch, based on Paris' namesake monument, was built in 1935 to commemorate the reunification of Romania in 1918.

Grigore Antipa Natural History Museum — MUSEUM
(Muzeul de Istorie Naturală Grigore Antipa; Map p46; ☏021-312 8826; www.antipa.ro; Şos Kiseleff 1; adult/student 20/5 lei; ☺10am-8pm Wed-Sun; Ⓜ Piaţa Victoriei) One of the few attractions in Bucharest aimed squarely at kids, this natural history museum has been thoroughly renovated and features modern bells and whistles such as video displays, games and interactive exhibits. Much of it has English signage.

DON'T MISS

CIŞMIGIU GARDEN
West of Calea Victoriei is the locally beloved Cişmigiu Garden (Map p40; ☺24h; Ⓜ Universitate) FREE, with shady walks, a lake, cafes and a ridiculous number of benches on which to sit and stare at Bucharest residents passing by. From May to September you can rent pedal and paddle boats to splash around in on the small pond.

JEWISH BUCHAREST

Once a thriving part of Bucharest, the city's Jewish community occupied many of the old streets that surrounded today's Piaţa Unirii. While much of the area was razed in the 1980s to make way for Ceauşescu's redevelopment plans, here there are scattered reminders of this once-vital group. (Note that due to security reasons, you'll usually need to show a passport or ID to enter any of the synagogues.)

The first stop would be the well-arranged Great Synagogue (Map p40; ☑ 0734-708 970; Str Adamache 11; ⊙ 9am-3pm Mon-Thu, to 1pm Fri & Sun; Ⓜ Piaţa Unirii) FREE. This important synagogue dates from the mid-19th century and was established by migrating Polish Jews. It's hard to find, but worth the effort to see the meticulously restored interior and to take in the main exhibition on Jewish life and the Holocaust in Romania. Modest displays tell the story of the around 200,000 Romanian Jews who were deported to camps in Transdniestr and Ukraine, and the well over 100,000 Jews from Transylvania who died at Auschwitz-Birkenau.

The nearby Jewish History Museum (Muzeul de Istorie al Comunitaţilor Evreieşti din România; Map p40; ☑ 021-311 0870; Str Mămulari 3; ⊙ 9am-3pm Mon-Thu, to 1pm Fri & Sun; Ⓜ Piaţa Unirii) FREE is housed in another colourful synagogue that dates from 1836 (rebuilt in 1910). Exhibits outline Jewish contributions to Romanian history. The Choral Temple (Map p40; ☑ 021-313 1782; Str Sfânta Vineri 9-11; adult/child 10/5 lei; ⊙ 9am-3pm Mon-Thu, to 1pm Fri & Sun; Ⓜ Piaţa Unirii), also not far from here, was built in 1857 and is the city's main working synagogue. It's visually stunning inside. A memorial to the victims of the Holocaust, erected in 1991, fronts the temple.

South of the Piaţa Unirii area, the old Sephardic Jewish Cemetery (Cimitirul Evreiesc de rit Sefard; Calea Şerban Vodă; ⊙ noon-dusk; Ⓜ Eroii Revoluţiei) FREE lies opposite Bellu Cemetery (metro Eroii Revoluţiei). Two rows of graves dated 21 to 23 January 1941 mark the Iron Guard's pogrom against the Jewish community, during which at least 170 Jews were murdered.

North of Piaţa Unirii is the country's formal memorial (Map p40; Str Ion Brezoianu; ⊙ 24hr; Ⓜ Izvor) FREE to Romanian Jews and Roma who died in the Holocaust. The monument was unveiled in 2009 and was widely seen as the government's first step in acknowledging Romania's part in the destruction of European Jewry.

Museum of the Romanian Peasant MUSEUM
(Muzeul Ţăranului Român; Map p46; ☑ 021-317 9661; www.muzeultaranuluiroman.ro; Şos Kiseleff 3; adult/child 8/2 lei; ⊙ 10am-6pm Tue-Sun; Ⓜ Piaţa Victoriei) The collection of peasant bric-a-brac, costumes, icons and partially restored houses makes this one of the most popular museums in the city. There's not much English signage, but insightful little cards in English posted in each room give a flavour of what's on offer. An 18th-century church stands in the back lot, as does a great gift shop and restaurant.

Don't miss the jarring communism exhibition downstairs, which focuses on the Ceauşescu-era programme of land collectivisation, which almost completely destroyed the traditional peasant way of life.

National Village Museum MUSEUM
(Muzeul Naţional al Satului; ☑ 021-317 9103; www.muzeul-satului.ro; Şos Kiseleff 28-30; adult/child 10/2.50 lei; ⊙ 9am-7pm Tue-Sun, to 5pm Mon; ♿; Ⓜ Piaţa Victoriei) On the shores of Herăstrău Lake, this museum is a terrific open-air collection of several dozen homesteads, churches, mills and windmills relocated from rural Romania. Built in 1936 by royal decree, it is one of Europe's oldest open-air museums and a good choice for kids to boot.

National Museum of Geology MUSEUM
(Muzeul National de Geologie; Map p46; ☑ 031-438 1744; www.geology.ro; Şos Kiseleff 2; adult/child 8/4 lei; ⊙ 10am-6pm Tue-Sun; Ⓜ Piaţa Victoriei) A highly worthwhile museum, this one features Romania's varied geological formations, with enough English signage on hand to give you the general idea of what's on display. The impressive building dates from the early 20th century and was originally built to house the country's Royal Geological Society.

◎ Herăstrău Park & Around

★**Former Ceauşescu Residence**   HISTORIC BUILDING

(Primăverii Palace; ☑ 021-318 0989; www.palatul primaverii.ro; B-dul Primăverii 50; guided tours in English adult/child 45/30 lei; ☺ 10am-6pm Wed-Sun; Ⓜ Aviatorilor) This restored villa is the former main residence of Nicolae and Elena Ceauşescu, who lived here for around two decades up until the end in 1989. Everything has been returned to its former lustre, including the couple's bedroom and the private apartments of the three Ceauşescu children. Highlights include a cinema in the basement, Elena's opulent private chamber and the back garden and swimming pool. Reserve a tour in advance by phone or on the website.

The overall effect is fascinating but rather depressing. The finely crafted furnishings, locally made reproductions of styles ranging from Louis XIV to art deco, feel sterile and stuffy.

Herăstrău Park   PARK

(Parcul Herăstrău; www.herastrauparc.ro; ☺ 24hr; Ⓜ Aviatorilor) FREE Sprawling over a large area north of Piaţa Victoriei, this 200-hectare park surrounding a large lake is (arguably) Bucharest's nicest park, with plenty of shaded strolls and open-air cafes, plus boats to hire. At night in summer, some of the city's best clubs decamp along the shore here and transform the park into an all-night party scene. One of the main entrances to the park is short walk from the Aviatorilor metro station.

Zambaccian Museum   MUSEUM

(Muzeul Zambaccian; ☑ 021-230 1920; www.mnar. arts.ro; Str Muzeul Zambaccian 21a; adult/student 7/3.50 lei; ☺ 10am-6pm Sat-Wed; Ⓜ Aviatorilor) Tricky to find, the little Zambaccian Museum is in a restored villa between B-dul Aviatorilor and Calea Dorobanţilor (just north of Piaţa Dorobanţilor). The small collection boasts mostly Romanian paintings from the early 20th century, plus a Matisse, a Cezanne and a couple of Renoirs – all collected by the late Armenian businessman Krikor Zambaccian.

◎ East Bucharest

The city's Historic Centre gets the glory these days, but the cobbled blocks east of Piaţa Romană and Piaţa Universităţii are some of Bucharest's most evocative. This area has undergone a facelift in the past couple of years, and hidden among the crumbling buildings are some beautifully restored villas and spruced-up parks.

Schitul Dârvari   MONASTERY

(Dârvari Monastery; Map p40; ☑ 021-212 3247; www.schituldarvari.ro; Str Schitul Darvari 3; ☺ 7.30am-7pm; Ⓜ Piaţa Romană) FREE This pretty monastery, surrounded by a lush walled garden, dates from the mid-19th century and was once the property of the private Dârvari family.

Theodor Pallady Museum   MUSEUM

(Muzeul Theodor Pallady; ☑ 021-211 4979; www. mnar.arts.ro; Str Spătarului 22; adult/student 5/2.50 lei; ☺ 10am-6pm Wed-Sun; Ⓜ Universitate) The Theodor Pallady Museum is housed inside the exquisite early-18th-century Casa Melik, a former merchant's house. It contains the private art collection of the Raut family, now part of the National Art Museum (p39).

THE CEAUŞESCUS' FINAL RESTING PLACE

Around 3km west of the Palace of Parliament (take bus 385 from outside the Parliament ticket office on B-dul Naţiunile Unite) stands the Ghencea Civil Cemetery (Cimitirul Civil Ghencea; B-dul Ghencea; ☺ 8am-8pm; ☐ 385) FREE, where you can morbidly seek out the final resting spots of Nicolae Ceauşescu and his wife, Elena, who were both executed on Christmas Day in 1989.

The two were originally buried in obscurity in separate graves shortly after the 1989 anticommunist uprising. They were quietly reburied under a common marker in 2010 after the bodies were exhumed to perform identity tests. The tests were conducted at the request of surviving family members as a way of quelling rumours that the executions had been faked and that the infamous couple had in fact survived the revolution.

The Ceauşescus remain largely shunned in death, though a fair number of nostalgic Romanians do drop by to leave flowers or light candles. The body of their son, Nicu, who died from cirrhosis of the liver in 1996, lies nearby.

Gara de Nord

See Central Bucharest Map (p40)

0 400 m
0 0.2 miles

Grigore Antipa Natural History Museum

Calea Floreasca

Şos Ştefan cel Mare

Calea Doroban ţilor

Piaţa Lahovari

B-dul Dacia

B-dul Gen Magheru

Piaţa Romană

Str C Bastiliei

B-dul Iancu de Hunedoara

Str Grigore Alexandrescu

B-dul Lascăr Catargiu

Str B Aurel

Str Nicolae Iorga

B-dul Dacia

Calea Victoriei

Str Pârs

Zambaccian Museum (1km);
Herăstrău Park, Former Ceauşescu
Residence (1.8km)

B-dul Aviatorilor

Şos Kiseleff

Piaţa Victoriei

Str Iodorescu

Str Severastu

B-dul 1 Mai

National Village Museum (2km)

Str Dr I Felix

Str Buzeşti

Str Occidentului

National Military
Museum (1km)

Şos Nicolae Titulescu

B-dul Alexandru Ioan Cuza

B-dul I G Duca

Atlassib

Str Polizu

Calea Griviţei

Bucharest National
Opera House (1km);
Cotroceni Palace (2km)

B-dul Banu Manta

Branch
Post Office

Memento
Bus

Piaţa
Gară de
Nord

B-dul D Golescu

Gară de
Nord

Hotel
Elizeu
(150m)

Str Witing

Church of the Icon CHURCH
(Biserica Icoanei; Map p40; ☑ 0766-055 565; www.bisericaicoanei.ro; Str Icoanei 12; ⊘ 8am-7pm; Ⓜ Piaţa Romană) FREE One of the city's best-known churches, the Church of the Icon takes its name from an icon of the Virgin Mary that was a gift from Constantin Brâncoveanu. The original brick church here was built by monk and former privy secretary Mihail Băbeanu between 1745 and 1750, though most of that structure was destroyed in earthquakes, and much of what you see today dates from the 19th century.

◎ West Bucharest

Cotroceni Palace MUSEUM
(☑ 021-317 3107; www.muzeulcotroceni.ro; B-dul Geniului 1; adult/student incl guided tours in English 50/25 lei; ⊘ by appt only 9.30am-5.30pm Tue-Sun; Ⓜ Eroilor) Elegant Cotroceni Palace dates from the late 19th century and is the official residence of the Romanian president. Many rooms are open to visitors, but call or email in advance to reserve a spot on the compulsory guided tour. The palace has an illustrious place in Romanian history, most notably as the home of Queen Marie, the English wife of Ferdinand I. Bring your passport.

National Military Museum MUSEUM
(Muzeul Militar Naţional; ☑ 021-319 5904; http://smg.mapn.ro/muzeumilitar/; Str Mircea Vulcănescu 125-127; adult/student 11/3 lei; ⊘ 9am-4pm Wed-Sun; Ⓜ Eroilor) The National Military Museum doubles nicely as a Romanian history museum, with its chronological rundown of how the country defended itself. In the museum entrance, note the 1988 communist mural that celebrates the Palace of Parliament (painted just a year before the revolution). In back is a hangar with early aviator Aurel Vlaicu's historic 1911 plane.

◎ Southern Bucharest

The area south of Piaţa Unirii is mostly devoid of traditional tourist sights but has some nice parks and important cemeteries.

Bellu Cemetery CEMETERY
(Cimitirul Bellu; ☑ 021-332 5744; www.bellu.ro; Şoseaua Olteniţei 3-5; ⊘ 10am-8pm; Ⓜ Eroii Revoluţiei) FREE The city's most prestigious burial ground houses the tombs of many notable Romanian writers – a map inside the gate points out locations. Many Romanians pay their respects to national poet Mihai Eminescu (1850–89) and comic playwright and humorist Ion Luca Caragiale (1852–1912), who are separated only by a bloke named Traian Savulescu; go to Figura 9 (to the right after you enter).

Martyr-Heroes of the December 1989 Revolution Cemetery CEMETERY
(Cimitirul Eroii Martiri ai Revoluţiei din Decembrie 1989; ☑ 021-336 5812; www.bisericaeroilor.ro; Calea Şerban Vodă 237; ⊘ dawn-sunset; Ⓜ Eroii Revoluţiei) Going west from the southern end of Carol I Park (⊘ 24h; Ⓜ Tineretului) FREE, near metro Eroii Revoluţiei, the road curves past this cemetery, where many of the 1000 victims of the 1989 revolution are buried.

🏃 Activities

Bucharest is highly urbanised and the main activities include walking and sightseeing. In warm weather, hire row boats or pedal boats on lakes at several parks, including Cişmigiu Garden and Herăstrău Park. Thirty-minute pleasure cruises are offered on the lake at Herăstrău Park for 10 lei. Bucharest is a dangerous city for cycling and we do not recommend it; nevertheless the bike-sharing scheme i'Velo (☑ 021-310 6397; www.ivelo.ro; Herăstrău Park; per hr/day 5/20 lei;

BUCHAREST ACTIVITIES

⊙9am-6pm May-Oct; M Aviatorilor) offers bikes for hire at Herăstrău Park.

☞ Tours

Bucharest City Tour   BUS

(☑021-307 4212; bucharestcitytour.ratb.ro; per 24hr adult/child 25/10 lei; ⊙10am-10pm) The RATB offers a daily double-decker DIY tourist bus that's a convenient way of seeing the main sights and also an efficient alternative to buses and metros for moving around town. The bus runs every 20 minutes along the major north–south axis from Piața Unirii to above the National Village Museum. Buy tickets on board at designated stops.

Cultural Travel & Tours   TOURS

(☑021-336 3163; www.cttours.ro) Offers several half- and full-day city tours, including excursions to Snagov, from 150 to 300 lei per person. It also offers longer, themed trips around the country. See the website for a full menu of tours.

Mr Tripp   TOURS

(Map p40; ☑0745-752 753; www.mrtripp.tours; Calea Victoriei 68-70; ⊙10am-8pm Mon-Sat, to 5pm Sun; M Universitate) Offers one-day guided tours of Bucharest and surrounding attractions, including day-trips to Snagov Monastery and the Danube Delta. Tours start at around 180 lei per person. Book over the telephone or directly through the company's central booking and information office.

RoCultours/CTI   TOURS

(☑0723-160 925; www.rotravel.com/cti) Reliable agent with many countrywide cultural tours and personalised itineraries listed on the website. Tour durations range from a one-day tour of Transylvania to an 11-day study tour of the country, including excursions to the painted monasteries of Bucovina and the Danube Delta. Check the website for an up-to-date list of tours. Book in advance by email or phone.

✯✯ Festivals & Events

Bucharest International Film Festival   FILM

(www.b-iff.ro; ⊙Apr) Bucharest's international film festival focuses on offbeat, art-house fare from up-and-coming directors.

Bucharest Pride   LGBT

(www.bucharestpride.ro; ⊙Jun) The city's annual gay pride festival, with events, films and dance nights around Bucharest.

Balkanik Music Festival   MUSIC

(www.balkanikfestival.ro; ⊙Sep) Outdoor festival of world music, drawing top acts and singers from across Europe over several days in early September.

George Enescu Music Festival   MUSIC

(www.festivalenescu.ro; ⊙Sep) Prestigious classical music festival, attracting some of the best orchestras and performers from around the world to perform at the Romanian Athenaeum (p39).

International Theatre Festival for Children   THEATRE

(www.teatrulioncreanga.ro; ⊙Oct) Bucharest's Ion Creangă Theatre is the host organisation for this International Children's Festival (www.fitc.ro) that brings troupes from around the world.

BUCHAREST FOR CHILDREN

Bucharest is not an extremely child-friendly destination, particularly for younger children. Distances between sights are vast and getting around involves a lot of legwork and tediously climbing up and down metro stairs.

Children of any age will appreciate the sheer vastness of the Palace of Parliament (p35) building. The most popular museums with younger visitors are likely to be the National Village Museum (p47) and the Grigore Antipa Natural History Museum (p43). The Geology Museum (p44) will appeal to older kids, especially those with a geek streak. Many kids will get a kick out of the plane hangar at the National Military Museum (p47), with parachute displays, a host of planes and all sorts of tanks outside.

The city's parks, particularly Cişmigiu Garden (p47), Herăstrău Park (p47) and Youth Park, have play areas for kids and lakes where you can rent paddle or rowing boats. Further afield, the Therme Bucharest (☑031-108 8888; www.therme.ro; DN1, Baloteşti; adult/child per day at 'Galaxy' 54/40 lei; ⊙9.30am-9.30pm Mon-Thu, 8am-midnight Fri-Sun; ➹; ☐126, 168, 68, 381, 783) water park has enough pools and slides – as well as spas and aromatherapy baths – to please both kids and their parents.

🛏 Sleeping

Hotels in Bucharest are typically aimed at business people, and prices are higher than in the rest of the country; booking in advance may help secure a discount. Room rates can drop by as much as half in midsummer (July and August), which is widely considered low season. The situation with hostels continues to improve and Bucharest now has some of the best cheap lodging in the country.

🏠 Historic Centre & Around

★ Little Bucharest
Old Town Hostel   HOSTEL $
(Map p40; ☎ 0786-329 136; www.littlebucharest. ro; Str Smârdan 15; dm 50-60 lei, r 250 lei; ❄ @ 🛜; Ⓜ Piața Unirii) Bucharest's most central hostel, in the middle of the lively Historic Centre, is super clean, white walled and well-run. Accommodation is over two floors, with dorms ranging from six to 12 beds. Private doubles are also available. The staff is travel friendly and youth oriented and can advise on sightseeing and fun. Book over the website or by email.

Pura Vida Sky Bar & Hostel   HOSTEL $
(Map p40; ☎ 0786-329 134; www.sky.puravida hostels.ro; Str Smârdan 7; dm 50-60 lei; Ⓜ Universitate) Stylish, well-run hostel, situated on the edge of the city's historic centre. Accommodation is in four-, six- or eight-bunk dorms. Beds are standard-issue pinewood, but the walls have been given a dash of colour. The main drawcard is the rooftop bar, with awesome views out over the centre. Even if you're not staying here, stop by for a drink.

★ Rembrandt Hotel   HOTEL $$
(Map p40; ☎ 021-313 9315; www.rembrandt.ro; Str Smârdan 11; s/d tourist 180/230 lei, standard 260/300 lei, business 350/380 lei; ❄ 🌸 @ 🛜; Ⓜ Universitate) It's hard to say enough good things about this place. Stylish beyond its three-star rating, this 16-room, Dutch-run hotel faces the landmark National Bank in the Historic Centre. Rooms come in three categories – tourist, standard and business – with the chief difference being size. All rooms have polished wooden floors, timber headboards and DVD players. Book well in advance.

★ Hotel Opera   HOTEL $$$
(Map p40; ☎ 021-312 4855; www.hotelopera.ro; Str Ion Brezoianu 37; s/d 400/500 lei; Ⓟ ❄ 🌸 🛜; Ⓜ Universitate) Set on a backstreet corner, this 33-room, faintly art deco hotel plays on the early-20th-century theme with historic artwork on the walls and porcelain and brass decorative objects in the rooms. Rooms come in 'standard' and slightly more-expensive 'executive' flavours, though in practice there's little difference between the two. Ask about lower weekend rates available most weeks throughout the year.

★ Hotel Amzei   HOTEL $$$
(Map p40; ☎ 021-313 9400; www.hotelamzei.ro; Piața Amzei 8; s/d 450/550 lei; ❄ 🌸 🛜; Ⓜ Piața Romană) This tastefully reconstructed villa just off Calea Victoriei has 22 rooms on four floors. The wrought-iron atrium in the lobby lends a refined feel. The rooms are in a more restrained contemporary style, but everything about the place says quality.

🏠 Outside the Historic Centre

Don't be put off by choices that aren't near the historic core of Bucharest. Many of the city's best options – including hostels – are just outside the centre.

Midland Youth Hostel   HOSTEL $
(Map p46; ☎ 021-314 5323; www.themidland hostel.com; Str Biserica Amzei 22; dm 40-60 lei; ❄ 🌸 @ 🛜; Ⓜ Piața Romană) A happening hostel, with an excellent central location not far from popular Piața Amzei. Accommodation is in four-, eight- or 12-bed dorms. There's a common kitchen too.

Doors   HOSTEL $
(☎ 021-336 2127; www.doorshostel.com; Str Olimpului 13; dm 45-60 lei, d 150 lei; ❄ @ 🛜; Ⓜ Piața Unirii) One of the better hostels in Bucharest is a 15-minute walk southwest of Piața Unirii, with a quiet, residential location and a beautiful garden set up like a Moroccan tea room. There are four-, six- and eight-bed dorms, and one private double. Friendly and welcoming staff.

★ Vila Arte   BOUTIQUE HOTEL $$$
(Map p40; ☎ 021-210 1035; www.vilaarte.ro; Str Vasile Lascăr 78; s/d 260/320 lei; ❄ 🌸 @ 🛜; Ⓜ Piața Romană, 🚃 5, 21) A renovated villa transformed into an excellent-value boutique hotel stuffed with original art that pushes the envelope on design and colour at this price point. The services are top drawer and the helpful reception makes every guest feel special. The 'Ottoman' room is done in an updated Turkish style,

SHORT-TERM APARTMENT STAYS

A short-term apartment rental makes sense if you're planning to stay longer than three days. Prices are generally cheaper than hotels, and you get a functioning kitchen and washing machine so you can regain control over your diet and dirty clothes at the same time. Note that you'll usually have to pay cash up front (sometimes in euros), so make sure you get a good look at the place before turning over your money. Most of the apartments are a little worn, but serviceable. The longer your stay, the more negotiating power you have over price. Two reputable renters include **Cert Accommodation** (☑0720-772 772; www.cert-accommodation.ro; apt 250-500 lei) and **RoCazare** (☑0721-430 000; www. rocazare.ro; apt from 225 lei).

with deep-red spreads and fabrics, and oriental carpets.

Berthelot Hotel HOTEL $$$
(Map p40; ☑031-425 5860; www.hotelberthe lot.ro; Str General Berthelot 9; s/d 360/450 lei; ☺❀@☎; ⓂPiaţa Romană) This modern boutique hotel offers bright and clean rooms, with air-conditioning and LCD TVs. The location, just off the Calea Victoriei, is in the heart of the city's fashion and boutique quarter, and is excellent for shopping. The rack rates put this property between midrange and top end, but look out for discounts that practically put it in the budget category.

🛏 Gara de Nord & Around

Though the area around the Gara de Nord is not the most appealing, there are several decent accommodation options within an easy walk of the station.

Puzzle Hostel HOSTEL $
(Map p46; ☑0733-128 887; www.puzzlehostel. ro; Calea Griviţei 32; dm 30-40 lei, d from 120 lei; ☺❀@☎; ⓂGara de Nord) Cheap, clean and within easy walking distance of the train station are three solid reasons for choosing one of the city's better hostels. Puzzle offers high-quality mattresses in multibunk (16-, eight- and six-bed) dorms as well as good-value private doubles. There are the usual hostel amenities, including a lounge where you can get a pre-party drink.

Vila 11 GUESTHOUSE $
(Map p46; ☑0722-495 900; www.vila11bucha rest.com; Str Institutul Medico Militar 11; dm 45 lei, s/d 90/120 lei; ❀@; ⓂGara de Nord) Run by a welcoming expat family, this homey *pensiune* is on a backstreet a few minutes' walk from the main train station. There are good-value six-bed dorms as well as private singles and doubles – some with en suite baths. Ask for a top-floor room, with pretty views and air-conditioning, but watch the narrow stairways.

Hotel Elizeu HOTEL $$
(☑021-319 1734; www.hotelelizeu.ro; Str Elizeu 11-13; s/d 160/240 lei; ❀@☎; ⓂGara de Nord) This 54-room hotel within easy walking distance of the main train station is comfortable and modern, with quiet rooms, minibar and decent buffet breakfast (included).

🍴 Eating

Bucharest has the country's most varied dining scene, with excellent restaurants featuring mostly Romanian cuisine supplemented by very good Italian, Middle Eastern and contemporary international places. The Historic Centre is crammed with restaurants, though the best places to eat tend to be scattered in neighbourhoods outside of the immediate centre. Dress is mainly casual, with the exception of a small number of high-priced, fine-dining establishments.

🍴 Historic Centre

★Caru' cu Bere ROMANIAN $$
(Map p40; ☑021-313 7560; www.carucubere. ro; Str Stavropoleos 3-5; mains 20-45 lei; ☺8am-midnight Sun-Thu, to 2am Fri & Sat; ☎; ⓂPiaţa Unirii) Despite a decidedly touristy-leaning atmosphere, with peasant-girl hostesses and sporadic traditional song-and-dance numbers, Bucharest's oldest beer house continues to draw in a strong local crowd. The belle-époque interior and stained-glass windows dazzle, as does the classic Romanian food. Dinner reservations are essential.

Les Bourgeois BISTRO $$
(Map p40; ☑0720-132 994; www.lesbourgeois. ro; Str Smârdan 20; mains 20-65 lei; ☺9am-2am;

☎; Ⓜ Piața Unirii) French bistro–styled place with a mouth-watering range of salads as well as chicken, fish and beef dishes. The lamb chops will not disappoint. It also serves a handy bacon-and-egg breakfast (29 lei). Eat on the terrace along a bustling corner of the Historic Centre.

St George　　　　　　　　HUNGARIAN **$$**
(Map p40; ☑ 0787-605 900; www.saint-george. ro; Str Franceză 44; mains 20-45 lei; ⊙ 10.30am-midnight; ☎; Ⓜ Piața Unirii) A festive and popular restaurant offering Hungarian and Transylvanian specialities on a lively strip in the old town. The cuisine – mainly flavourful stews and pork dishes – tends towards the heavy side, but you can wash it down with some very good wine. There's a big terrace out front.

★Lacrimi și Sfinți　　　　ROMANIAN **$$$**
(Map p40; ☑ 0725-558 286; www.lacrimisisfinti. com; Str Șepcari 16; mains 30-50 lei; ⊙ 12.30pm-2am Tue-Sun, 6pm-2am Mon; ☎; Ⓜ Piața Unirii) A true destination restaurant in the Historic Centre, Lacrimi și Sfinți takes modern trends such as farm-to-table freshness and organic sourcing and marries them to old-school Romanian recipes. The philosophy extends to the simple, peasant-inspired interior, where the woodworking and decorative elements come from old farmhouses. The result is food that feels authentic and satisfying. Book in advance.

Outside the Historic Centre

★Modelier　　　　　　　　BURGERS **$**
(☑ 0799-630 693; www.facebook.com/modelier bar; Str Duzilor 12; burgers 18-25 lei; ⊙ 1pm-2am; 🚌 70, 79) Artisanal burgers, some of the city's best French fries and homemade lemonade served in oversized carafes are a few of the main draws at this hipsterish, culture-centre-cum-restaurant located in a residential neighbourhood east of the centre. Warm summer evenings draw DJ and movie nights.

★Shift Pub　　　　　INTERNATIONAL **$$**
(Map p46; ☑ 021-211 2272; www.shiftpub.ro; Str General Eremia Grigorescu 17; mains 25-40 lei; ⊙ noon-2am; Ⓜ Piața Romană) Great choice for salads and burgers as well numerous beef and pork dishes, often sporting novel Asian, Middle Eastern or Mexican taste touches. Try to arrive slightly before meal times to grab a coveted table in the tree-covered garden.

Lente Praporgescu　　INTERNATIONAL **$$**
(Map p40; ☑ 021-310 7424; www.lente.ro; Str Gen Praporgescu 31; mains 25-40 lei; ⊙ 11.30am-1am; ☎; Ⓜ Piața Romană) The main branch of three 'Lente' restaurants scattered around the city centre. The recipe for all three is broadly the same: inventive soups and salads, an eclectic design of mismatched chairs and old books, and a relaxed, vaguely alternative vibe. A terrific choice for lunch or a casual dinner. The garden terrace offers respite on a hot day.

★Gargantua In The Park　　ITALIAN **$$$**
(Map p40; ☑ 0726-555 688; www.restaurant gargantua.ro; Str Jean-Louis Calderon 69; mains 30-55 lei; ⊙ 9am-midnight; Ⓜ Piața Romană) The peaceful setting, at the tip of Icoanei Park, is the perfect perch from which to enjoy well done Italian and international dishes, including the requisite pizza and pasta, but also delicious lamb chops, steaks and seafood. The wine list draws from some of the best local producers, and on a warm evening the terrace is a nice spot to enjoy it.

Burebista　　　　　　　ROMANIAN **$$$**
(Map p40; ☑ 0756-717 649; www.restaurant vanatoresc.ro; Str Batiștei 14; mains 40-60 lei; ⊙ noon-midnight; Ⓜ Universitate) This is a touristy, traditional grill restaurant, where the staff don 19th-century peasant-wear and everything feels kind of forced. On the other hand, the traditional food is excellent and the terrace is a relaxing spot for a beer and some grilled meats.

Drinking & Nightlife

Drinking options can be roughly broken down into cafes and bars, though there's little distinction in practice. The Historic Centre has more places to drink (and more clubs) than one could visit in a month. In summer, look for a terrace, usually in a secluded spot under a canopy of trees.

Historic Centre

Old City　　　　　　　　　　　BAR
(Map p40; ☑ 0729-377 774; www.oldcity-bucharest.ro; Str Șelari 14; ⊙ 10am-4am; ☎; Ⓜ Piața Unirii) This remains one of the favourite go-to bars in the old town; most nights, especially weekends, bring big crowds and themed dance parties. There's a large, handsome bar area and plenty of pavement seating in nice weather.

Fire Club
BAR

(Map p40; ☑ 0732-166 604; www.fire.ro; Str Gabroveni 12; ⊙ 10am-4am Sun-Thu, to 6am Fri & Sat; 🌐; Ⓜ Piaţa Unirii) A crowded student-oriented bar and rock club that's much less flash and more relaxed than some of the other venues around the Historic Centre town.

St Patrick
PUB

(Map p40; ☑ 021-313 0336; www.stpatrick.ro; Str Smârdan 23-25; ⊙ 11am-2am; 🌐; Ⓜ Piaţa Unirii) This popular pub has the authentic Irish bar look down, with dark woods and a green ceiling. Grab a table on busy Str Smârdan and settle back with a pint of Guinness or cider. They also do good renditions of standards such as steak and kidney pie (29 lei) and Irish breakfast (29 lei).

Grand Cafe Van Gogh
CAFE

(Map p40; ☑ 031-107 6371; www.vangogh. ro; Str Smârdan 9; ⊙ 8.30am-midnight Mon-Fri, 10am-midnight Sat & Sun; 🌐; Ⓜ Universitate) This well-positioned and lively cafe stands at the entrance to the old town. Very good coffee and other drinks. It also prepares light meals such as breakfasts and burgers as well as daily luncheon specials.

Outside the Historic Centre

★ **Grădina Verona**
CAFE

(Map p40; ☑ 0732-003 060; www.facebook. com/GradinaVerona; Str Pictor Verona 13-15; ⊙ 9am-midnight May-Sep; 🌐; Ⓜ Piaţa Romană) A garden oasis hidden behind the Cărtureşti bookshop, serving standard-issue but excellent espresso drinks and some of the wackiest iced-tea infusions ever concocted in Romania, such as peony flower, mango and lime (it's not bad).

M60
CAFE

(Map p40; ☑ 031-410 0010; www.facebook.com/ m60cafeamzei/; Str Mendeleev 2; ⊙ 10am-1am; 🌐; Ⓜ Piaţa Romană) M60 is a category-buster, transforming through the day from one of the city's preeminent morning coffee houses to a handy lunch spot (healthy salads and vegetarian options) and then morphing into a meet-up and drinks bar in the evening. It's been a hit since opening day, as city residents warmed to its clean, minimalist Scandinavian design and living-room feel.

Origo
CAFE

(Map p40; ☑ 0757-086 689; https://origocoffee. ro; Str Lipscani 9; ⊙ 7.30am-8pm Mon, to midnight Tue-Fri, 9am-midnight Sat & Sun; 🌐; Ⓜ Piaţa Unirii) Arguably the best coffee in town and *the* best place to hang out in the morning, grab a table and check your email. Lots of special coffee roasts and an unlimited number of ways to imbibe. There are a dozen pavement tables for relaxing on a sunny day.

Grădina Eden
BAR

(Map p40; www.facebook.com/gradinaeden107; Calea Victoriei 107, Palatul Ştirbey; ⊙ 4pm-midnight May-Sep; Ⓜ Piaţa Romană) A delightful summertime drinking garden hidden behind the derelict Ştirbey Palace. To find it, enter the gate to the palace and follow a worn footpath that runs along the palace's right side. The garden is tucked away behind some trees at the back. Line up at the bar for beer, wine or fresh lemonade, find a table and chill.

Dianei 4
CAFE

(Map p40; ☑ 0745-208 186; www.dianei4. translucid.ro; Str Dianei 4; ⊙ 10am-11pm; Ⓜ Universitate) Popular cafe and drinking garden, just off busy B-dul Carol 1. Choose from a broad menu of well-pulled espressos as well as breakfasts (around 20 lei) until noon, and salads and sandwiches throughout the day. The garden has the feel of a well-tended squat, lending a welcome alternative vibe.

Seneca Anticafe
CAFE

(☑ 0720-331 100; www.senecanticafe.ro; Str Arhitect Ion Mincu 1; per hr 8 lei; ⊙ 9am-10pm; 🌐; 🚌 24, 42, 45) A perfect spot to mix coffee with a little work. Seneca is something like a cross between a cafe and a shared co-office workspace, where you pay 8 lei per hour for unlimited coffee as well as wi-fi and a desk to work on. It's also a bookshop and cultural centre, and the staff couldn't be friendlier or more welcoming.

Piua Book Bar
BAR

(Map p40; ☑ 031-108 1011; Str Dionisie Lupu 76; ⊙ noon-midnight Mon-Fri, 3pm-midnight Sat & Sun; Ⓜ Piaţa Romană) Piua is a real gender-bender: part used bookshop, part ultracool cocktail bar, and occasionally a live music venue as well. It's situated in a renovated old mansion, and the polished floors and rickety stairs still squeak as you move from room to room. Plenty of old chairs and beanbags to lounge around on.

☆ Entertainment

Bucharest has a lively night scene of concerts, theatre, rock and jazz. Check the weekly guide *Şapte Seri* (www.sapteseri.ro) for entertainment listings. Another good source for what's on is the website www.iconcert.ro. To buy tickets online, visit the websites of the leading ticketing agencies: www.myticket.ro and www.eventim.ro.

Cinemas

Most films are shown in their original language. Check www.cinemagia.ro for film information.

Cinemateca Eforie
CINEMA
(Map p40; ☑021-313 0483; Str Eforie 2; tickets 12 lei; Ⓜ Piaţa Unirii) Plays an eclectic and often amusing mix of art-house, kitsch and Romanian films.

Cinema Pro
CINEMA
(Map p40; ☑031-824 1360; www.cinemapro.ro; Str Ion Ghica 3; tickets 10-16 lei; Ⓜ Universitate) Shows first-run features from Romania and big films from around the world.

Classical Music

The Romanian Athenaeum (p399) is the heart of Romania's classical music tradition and home to the George Enescu Philharmonic. It offers a wide array of classical music concerts from September to May as well as a number of one-off musical shows and spectacles throughout the year. Buy tickets at the venue box office.

Bucharest National Opera House
OPERA
(Opera Naţională Bucureşti; ☑box office 021-310 2661; www.operanb.ro; B-dul Mihail Kogălniceanu 70-72; tickets 10-70 lei; ☺box office 9am-1pm & 3-7pm; Ⓜ Eroilor) The city's premier venue for classical opera and ballet. Buy tickets online or at the venue box office.

Nightclubs & Live Music

Expect to pay a cover at the door of anywhere from 5 to 25 lei, which may or may not include a drink.

Control
LIVE MUSIC
(Map p40; ☑0733-927 861; www.control-club.ro; Str Constantin Mille 4; ☺noon-4am; 🛜; Ⓜ Universitate) This is a favourite among club-goers who like alternative, turbo-folk, indie and garage sounds. Hosts both live acts and DJs, depending on the night.

Club A
LIVE MUSIC
(Map p40; ☑reservations 0744-517 858; www.cluba.ro; Str Blănari 14; ☺9pm-5am Thu-Sun; Ⓜ Piaţa Unirii) Run by students, this underground club is a classic and beloved by all who go there. Most weekends bring live

ARCUB CULTURAL CENTRE

Situated in the renovated former Gabroveni Inn, ARCUB (Map p40; ☑0732-669 928; www.arcub.ro; Str Lipscani 84-90; ☺ticket office 3-8pm Tue-Fri, 6-8pm Sat & Sun; Ⓜ Piaţa Unirii) is a multidisciplinary cultural centre, with a regular line-up of art exhibitions, happenings, performances and occasional film screenings. Check the website to see if something interesting is on during your visit. Buy tickets at the venue box office.

music, with anything from rock and pop to blues and alternative.

Green Hours 22
LIVE MUSIC
(Map p40; ☑bar reservations 0751-772 275; www.greenhours.ro; Calea Victoriei 120; ☺9am-4am; Ⓜ Piaţa Romană) This old-school basement jazz club runs a lively programme of jazz and experimental theatre most nights through the week, and hosts an international jazz fest in May/June. There's also a popular bar, bistro and garden terrace. Check the website for the schedule during your trip and book in advance by email.

Spectator Sports

Bucharest is home to several local football (soccer) clubs; the two main ones are rivals Steaua Bucureşti and Dinamo Bucureşti. Both play in the country's top division, *Liga I*. The football season runs from the end of July through the following May, and catching a match during your visit is easy. With the exception of grudge matches between the two, the games rarely sell out. Steaua plays its matches at the National Arena, (Arena Naţională, Steaua FC; ☑021-410 2082, tickets 0752-120 171; www.steauafc.com; B-dul Basarabia 37-39; tickets 20-100 lei; ☺ticket office 10am-5pm Mon-Fri; 🚊40, 56) while Dinamo normally plays at Dinamo Stadium (Map p46; www.fcdinamo.ro; Şos Ştefan cel Mare 7-9; tickets 10-35 lei; ☺box office noon-7pm match day; Ⓜ Ştefan cel Mare). Buy tickets for both teams in advance at their respective stadium box offices or at the ticket window before matches. Most international matches, including those involving the Romanian national team, are played at the National Arena.

Theatre

Bucharest's theatres offer a lively mix of comedy, farce, satire and straight contemporary plays in a variety of languages, though they're normally in Romanian. Tickets usually cost no more than 40 lei. Theatres close in July and August.

National Theatre of Bucharest   THEATRE

(Teatrul Naţional Bucureşti; Map p40; ☑box office 021-314 7171, theatre 021-313 9175; www. tnb.ro; B-dul Nicolae Bălcescu 2; ◔box office 10am-4pm Mon, to 7pm Tue-Sun; Ⓜ Universitate) The National Theatre is the country's most prestigious dramatic stage. The building is a 1970s-era big box that's gotten a long-overdue facelift; the facilities inside are excellent. Most dramatic works are performed in Romanian. Check the website for the programme during your visit. Buy tickets online or at the box office.

Jewish State Theatre   THEATRE

(Teatrul Evreiesc de Stat; Map p40; ☑reservations 0721-313 736; www.teatrul-evreiesc.ro; Str Iuliu Barasch 15; tickets 12-30 lei; ◔box office 10am-noon Mon-Thu; Ⓜ Piaţa Unirii) Plays in Romanian and Yiddish.

🛍 Shopping

★Anthony Frost   BOOKS

(Map p40; ☑021-311 5136; www.anthonyfrost. ro; Calea Victoriei 45; ◔10am-8pm Mon-Fri, to 7pm Sat, to 2pm Sun; Ⓜ Universitate) Serious readers will want to make time for arguably the best small English-language bookshop in Eastern Europe. Located in a small passage next to the Creţulescu Church, this shop has a carefully chosen selection of highbrow contemporary fiction and nonfiction.

Vinexpert   WINE

(Map p46; ☑0744-481 307; www.vinexpert. ro; Calea Victoriei 155; ◔8am-midnight Mon-Fri, 11am-midnight Sat, noon-10pm Sun; Ⓜ Piaţa Victoriei) Beautiful, well-stocked wine shop with a comprehensive selection of Romanian and foreign wines, plus knowledgable salespeople to help you sort it out. In addition to selling wine by the bottle, they also dispense wine by the glass, paired with delicious cheese plates for tastings.

Cărtureşti Verona   BOOKS

(Map p40; ☑0728 828 916; www.carturesti.ro; Str Pictor Verona 13-15, cnr B-dul Nicolae Bălcescu; ◔10am-10pm; Ⓜ Piaţa Romană) This bookshop, music store, tea room and funky backyard garden is a must-visit. Amazing collection of design, art and architecture books, as well as carefully selected CDs and DVDs, including many classic Romanian films with English subtitles. Also sells Lonely Planet guidebooks.

Târgul Vitan-Bârzeşti   MARKET

(Şos Vitan-Bârzeşti, cnr Splaiul Unirii; ◔8am-4pm Sun; 🚌123) A sprawling flea market operates here, southeast of the centre, on Sundays till 4pm. Come early to get the best deals on everything from antique jewellery, books and knick-knacks to used cars. Even if you're not in the mood to buy, the energy is infectious.

Ethic Wine   WINE

(☑021-367 2283; www.ethicwine.ro; Str Banul Antonache 55; ◔1pm-9pm Mon, 10am-9pm Tue-Sat, 10am-2pm Sun; 🚌135) Impressive wine shop and tasting room, featuring some of the best Romanian wines as well as a carefully chosen list of international producers. Labels here to look out for include Bauer, Avincis and Prince Ştirbey from Drăgăşani and Chateau Vartely from neighbouring Moldova.

Cărtureşti Carusel   BOOKS

(Map p40; ☑0728-828 922; www.carturesti.ro; Str Lipscani 55; ◔10am-midnight; Ⓜ Piaţa Unirii) This impressive branch of the Cărtureşti chain of books and gifts is located in an opulent, restored early-20th-century shopping emporium in the Historic Centre. Books are on several levels and there's a decent selection of English-language titles.

Str Hanul cu Tei   GIFTS & SOUVENIRS

(Map p40; ◔10am-8pm; Ⓜ Piaţa Unirii) The little courtyard Str Hanul cu Tei is a hidden passageway in the Historic Centre with a few art galleries and art supply and antique shops. Enter from Str Blănari 5 or Str Lipscani 63.

ℹ Information

EMERGENCY

Ambulance, Fire & Police (☑112) Some operators know a smattering of English.

INTERNET ACCESS

Best Cafe (☑021-312 4816; www.best-cafe. ro; B-dul Mihail Kogălniceanu 19; per hr 5 lei; ◔24hr; 🛜; Ⓜ Izvor)

Seneca Anticafe (p52)

MEDIA

International newspapers can usually be found at newsagents in major hotels.

Bucharest In Your Pocket (www.inyourpocket. com) Bimonthly guide to Bucharest (there's a cover price, though you can usually find it free at big hotels). Opinionated and often-funny entertainment and restaurant listings.

Nine O'Clock (www.nineoclock.ro) Informative English-language news website with sections on politics, economics and culture.

Şapte Seri (www.sapteseri.ro) Weekly publication and website with entertainment listings; find it at bars and clubs around town.

MEDICAL SERVICES

You'll find pharmacies all over the centre. Sensi-Blu is a highly recommended chain with branches around town, including on **Calea Victoriei** (☑ 021-303 0267; www.sensiblu.com; Calea Victoriei 12a; ⊙ 8am-10pm Mon-Fri, 9am-9pm Sat & Sun; Ⓜ Universitate).

Emergency Clinic Hospital (☑ 021-599 2300; www.scub.ro; Calea Floreasca 8; ⊙ 24hr; Ⓜ Ştefan cel Mare) The first port of call in any serious emergency. Arguably the city's, and country's, best emergency hospital.

Medicover (☑ 021-310 1599; www.medicover. ro; Calea Plevnei 96; ⊙ 8am-8.30pm Mon-Fri, to 2pm Sat; Ⓜ Eroilor) Good, but expensive, private clinic.

Prodentcare (☑ 0724-873 551; www.prodental care.ro; Calea Rahovei 251-253; ⊙ 24hr; 🚌 23, 32) Offering dental care.

MONEY

Bank branches and ATMs are widespread in the centre. Credit cards are widely accepted, so there's no need to withdraw and carry large amounts of cash.

Most banks have a currency-exchange office and can provide cash advances against credit or debit cards. Always bring your passport, since you will likely have to show it. Most banks operate only on weekdays, though some may have limited Saturday morning hours.

Outside of normal banking hours, you can change money at private currency booths (*casa de schimb*). There is a row of these along B-dul Gen Gheorghe Magheru, running north of Piaţa Universităţii. We generally don't recommend using these, as the rates they offer tend to be the same as or lower than the banks', often with higher commission fees. If you do exchange money at a private booth, before you surrender your cash, tell the cashier exactly what you want to exchange and ask him or her to write down the amount you will receive in lei. You'll usually have to show a passport here as well.

POST

Branch Post Office (Map p46; www. posta-romana.ro; Str Gării de Nord 6-8; ⊙ 7.30am-8pm Mon-Fri; Ⓜ Gara de Nord)

Central Post Office (Map p40; ☑ 021-315 9030; www.posta-romana.ro; Str Matei Millo 10; ⊙ 7.30am-8pm Mon-Fri; Ⓜ Universitate)

TOURIST INFORMATION

Bucharest Tourist Information Center (Map p40; ☑ 021-305 5500, ext 1003; http://see bucharest.ro; Piaţa Universităţii; ⊙ 10am-5pm Mon-Fri, to 2pm Sat & Sun; Ⓜ Universitate) This small, poorly stocked tourist office is the best the city can offer visitors. While there's not much information on hand, the English-speaking staff can field basic questions, make suggestions and help locate things on a map.

Mr Tripp (p48) Private travel agency that doubles as an informal tourist information office, handing out free maps and advice, even if you're not booking one of their tours.

ⓘ Getting There & Away

Bucharest is the country's leading air gateway, and major international and European carriers fly here from around Europe and large cities in the Middle East. It's also the country's main road and rail hub.

AIR

All international and domestic flights use **Henri Coandă International Airport** (OTP, Otopeni; ☑ arrivals 021-204 1220, departures 021-204 1210; www.bucharestairports.ro; Şos Bucureşti-Ploieşti; 🚌 783), often referred to in conversation by its previous name, 'Otopeni'. Henri Coandă is 17km north of Bucharest on the main road to Braşov. Arrivals and departures use separate terminals (arrivals is to the north). The airport is a modern facility, with restaurants, newsagents, currency exchange offices and ATMs. There are 24-hour information desks at both terminals.

The airport is the hub for the national carrier **Tarom** (☑ call centre 021-204 6464, office 021-316 0220; www.tarom.ro; Spl Independenţei 17, City Centre; ⊙ 9am-5pm Mon-Fri; Ⓜ Piaţa Unirii). Tarom has a comprehensive network of internal flights to major Romanian cities as well as to capitals and big cities around Europe and the Middle East. At the time of writing, there were no direct flights from Bucharest to North America or Southeast Asia.

BUS

Domestic Destinations

Several coach companies, large and small, dominate the market for travel from Bucharest to cities around Romania. One of the cleanest and cheapest is **Memento Bus** (Map p46; ☑ 0317-105 518; www.mementobus.com; Gara de Nord; ⊙ 9am-7pm; Ⓜ Gara de Nord), a low-cost carrier that runs between major cities for as little as 5 lei per trip.

The best bet for finding a connection is to consult the websites www.autogari.ro and www.cditransport.ro. Both keep up-to-date timetables and are fairly easy to manage, though www.cditransport.ro is only in Romanian. Be sure to follow up with a phone call just to make sure a particular bus is running on a particular day. Another option is to ask your hotel to help with arrangements or book through a travel agency.

Bucharest has several bus stations and they don't seem to follow any discernible logic for which station should serve which destination. Even Bucharest residents have a hard time making sense of it. When purchasing a bus ticket, always ask where the bus leaves from.

The chief bus 'stations' – some are lots or spaces by a curb – include the following:

Autogara Diego (Map p40; ☑ 021-311 1283; www.autogaradiego.ro; Spl Independenţei 2; Ⓜ Piaţa Unirii) Near the intersection with Calea Victoriei. Destinations include Iaşi, Piatra Neamţ and Suceava, as well as several international destinations in Western Europe.

Autogara Filaret (☑ buses to Bulgaria 021-335 3290, buses to Greece 021-336 6780, domestic bus services 021-336 0692; www.acfilaret.ro; Piaţa Gării Filaret 1; ☑ 7, 47) Three kilometres south of Piaţa Universităţii; take bus 7 and 232 from Piaţa Unirii. Daily service to several Romanian cities as well as points south in Greece. Buses to and from Sofia also use this station.

Autogara Militari (☑ 0725-939 939; www.autogari.ro; Str Valea Cascadelor 1; Ⓜ Păcii) Eight kilometres west of the centre. Destinations include Curtea de Argeş, Târgu Jiu and Timişoara.

CDI (☑ 0722-418 886, reservations 0723-187 789; www.cditransport.ro; Str Ritmului 35; ☑ 69, 85) Located about 3km east of Piaţa Romană, and four blocks north of metro station Piaţa Iancului. Regular services to Braşov, Tulcea, Piteşti and Craiova, among other destinations.

International Destinations

Bucharest is a hub for long-haul coach services to Western Europe as well as parts of southeastern Europe and Turkey.

Atlassib (p268) One of the country's biggest long-haul coach companies.

Etap Grup (www.etapgroup.com) Based in Sofia, Bulgaria, this bus company runs daily between Bucharest and Sofia (about 130 lei per person one way, seven to eight hours). In Bucharest, buses depart from Autogara Filaret.

Murat Turism & Transport (p267) Runs long-haul buses daily, except Saturday, to İstanbul (160 lei per person one way, about 11 hours).

CAR & MOTORCYCLE

Driving in Bucharest is sheer lunacy and you won't want to do it for more than a few minutes

before you stow the car and use public transportation. If you're travelling around the country by car and just want to visit Bucharest for the day, it's more sensible to park at a metro station on the outskirts and take the metro into the city.

In theory, hourly parking rates apply in the centre, particularly off Piaţa Victoriei and Piaţa Universităţii – look for the wardens in yellow-and-blue uniforms – or there's paid metered parking. In many places, though, you can just pull on to the pavement like everyone else. Petrol costs around 5 lei per litre.

Bucharest offers some of the country's cheapest car-hire rates. Major rental agencies can be found at the Henri Coandă International Airport arrivals hall. Most large companies also have an in-town branch.

The cheapest rates available are from **Autonom** (☑ airport 021-232 4325, nonstop reservations 0742-215 361; www.autonom.com; Henri Coandă International Airport; per day from 150 lei), offering a Dacia Logan for around 150 lei per day (including unlimited mileage and insurance, minimum two days); rates drop if you rent for more than a week. Rates for the major international car-hire companies tend to be higher, starting at about 220 lei per day, depending on the make and length of the hire period.

Avis (☑ 0722-636 595; www.avis.ro; Henri Coandă International Airport; ⊙ 7am-11pm)

Budget (☑ 021-204 1667; www.budgetro.ro; Henri Coandă International Airport; ⊙ 7am-11pm)

Europcar (☑ 021-310 1797; www.europcar.ro; Henri Coandă International Airport; ⊙ 8am-8pm)

Hertz (☑ 021-204 1278; www.hertz.com.ro; Henri Coandă International Airport; ⊙ 8am-10pm)

TRAIN

Gara de Nord (p268) is the central station for most national and all international trains. The station is accessible by metro from the centre of the city.

Buy tickets at station ticket windows. A seat reservation is compulsory if you are travelling with an InterRail or Eurail pass.

Check the latest train schedules on either www.cfr.ro or the reliable German site www.bahn.de (when searching timetables, use German spellings for cities, ie 'Bukarest Nord' for Bucharest Gara de Nord).

Left Luggage on the main level of the Gara de Nord in the long hallway near the information stand. It's on the right side as you're walking away from the tracks.

Daily international services include two trains to Budapest's Keleti station (13 to 15 hours), and one each to Sofia (nine to 11 hours), Belgrade (12 hours), Chişinău (13 hours) and Kiev (26 hours).

INTER-CITY (IC) TRAINS FROM BUCHAREST

DESTINATION	COST (LEI)	DURATION (HR)	FREQUENCY (DAILY)
Braşov	50	2½	frequent
Cluj-Napoca	92	7½	4
Constanţa	60	2-4	3
Craiova	60	3	5
Iaşi	90	7	3
Sibiu	85	6	2
Sighişoara	70	5	3
Suceava	90	7	3
Timişoara	101	9	3

Above are sample fares and destination times from Bucharest to major Romanian cities on faster IC (Inter-City) trains.

ⓘ Getting Around

TO/FROM THE AIRPORT
Bus

To get to Henri Coandă International Airport from the centre, take express bus 783, which leaves every 15 minutes between 6am and 11pm (every half-hour at weekends) from Piaţas Unirii and Victoriei and points in between. The Piaţa Unirii stop is on the south side.

To buy a ticket, you must first buy an 'Activ' card at any RATB bus-ticket booth near a bus stop for 3.70 lei, which you then top up with credit. A single journey on the express bus costs 7 lei. Validate the card on entering the bus. Henri Coandă International Airport is 45 to 60 minutes from the centre, depending on traffic. The bus stops outside the departures hall then continues to arrivals.

To get to the centre from Henri Coandă, catch bus 783 from the ramp outside the arrivals hall; you'll need to first buy an Activ card and add credit to it from a small booth inside the terminal.

Taxi

Taking a reputable taxi from the centre to Henri Coandă International Airport should cost no more than 50 lei. To hail a taxi, go to a series of touch screens located in the airport arrivals hall, where the various taxi companies and their rates are listed. Choose any company offering rates of from 1.39 to 1.69 lei per kilometre (there's little difference in quality). The touch screen will then spit out a ticket with the taxi number clearly displayed.

PUBLIC TRANSPORT

Bucharest's public transport system of the metro, buses, trams and trolleybuses is operated by the transport authority **RATB** (Regia Autonomă de Transport Bucureşti; ☑ 021-9391; www.ratb.ro). The system runs daily from about 4.30am to approximately 11.30pm.

The ticketing situation differs for street transport (buses, trams and trolleybuses) and for the metro system. To use buses, trams or trolleybuses, you must first purchase an 'Activ' card (3.70 lei) from any RATB street kiosk, which you then load with credit that is discharged as you enter the transport vehicles. Trips cost 1.30 lei each, and the minimum amount of credit you can buy is 5 lei. Children under seven ride free. Validate your Activ card as you enter the tram or bus. Travelling without a validated Activ card risks a 50 lei on-the-spot fine. Activ cards can be topped up as needed at any RATB kiosk.

Metro stations are identified by a large letter 'M'. To use the metro, buy a magnetic-strip ticket available at ticketing machines or cashiers inside station entrances (have small bills handy). Tickets valid for two journeys cost 5 lei. A 10-trip ticket costs 20 lei. The metro is a speedy way of moving up and down the central north–south corridor from Piaţa Victoriei to Piaţa Unirii, passing through the convenient stations of Piaţa Romană and Universitate. The metro is also useful for travelling from the Gara de Nord to the centre of town and back.

TAXI

Rogue drivers are a problem, so watch for rip-offs. Always opt for a cab with a meter, and avoid the guys who line up outside the Gara de Nord as well as at Piaţa Unirii, the Inter-Continental Hotel and just outside the main arrivals hall at Henri Coandă International Airport.

Drivers are required to post their rates on both the passenger- and driver-side doors. The rate in an honest cab ranges from 1.39 lei to 1.69 lei per kilometre. Any fare significantly higher is a sign the taxi is a rip-off and should be avoided.

It's best to call one in advance – or have a restaurant or hotel call one for you. Reputable companies include **Cobalcescu** (☑ 021-9451; www.autocobalcescu.ro), **CrisTaxi** (☑ 021-9466; www.cristaxi.ro) and **Meridian** (☑ English 021-9888, general 021-9444; www.meridiantaxi.ro).

AROUND BUCHAREST

Snagov Lake

Serpentine Snagov Lake, 40km north of Bucharest and running north–south, serves as the main weekend retreat for residents of the capital looking for a place to relax. The lake has a lovely semirural setting, and there are plenty of opportunities for swimming, boating, fishing and sunbathing. Summer weekends get crowded as nature-seeking hordes from Bucharest descend. Weekdays are more peaceful. Resorts line both sides of the lake, east and west, though places on the western side, in a protected area across the lake from Snagov village, feel more exclusive and remote.

Snagov has an even bigger claim to fame: a small island at the northern end of the lake holds a fine monastery that also happens to be the reputed final resting place of none other than Vlad Țepeș (aka 'Vlad the Impaler'), the legendarily brutal Wallachian prince who served as the inspiration for Bram Stoker's *Dracula*.

◉ Sights

Snagov Monastery MONASTERY
(Mănăstirea Snagov; ☑ 0724-768 949; www.snagov.ro; Strada Mănăstirea Vlad Țepeș, Snagov Island; adult/child 15/10 lei; ☉ 7.30am-6pm) Tiny Snagov Island, at the northern end of Snagov Lake, is home to Snagov Monastery and Vlad Țepeș' alleged final resting place. The small stone church dates from the 15th century; Vlad Țepeș' purported grave is located towards the back of the church.

The island is connected to the mainland by bridge. You can also get here by boat from Snagov village or resorts along the shore. Expect to pay around 100 lei for a ride out and back.

As with many aspects of the 'Dracula' story, there is much debate as to whether the body buried here actually belongs to Țepeș. The bloodthirsty prince died in 1476 battling the Turks near Bucharest. His head was famously lopped off and carried back to Istanbul, where it was paraded on a stake. What happened to the rest of the body was never made clear. Whether or not he's actually buried here, Vlad Țepeș apparently had strong connections to Snagov. In 1456 he built fortifications around the monastery. He also built a bridge from the lake to the mainland, a bell tower, a new church, an escape tunnel

and a prison and torture chamber. The remains of the prison (behind the present-day church) can still be seen.

There's been a church here since at least the 11th century, when Mircea cel Bătrân first built a wooden structure. The monastery was added in the late 14th century during the reign of King Dan I (r 1383–86), and in 1453 the wooden church was replaced by a stone edifice that later sank into the lake. The present church came after that.

Snagov Palace HISTORIC BUILDING
(☑ 021-320 8954; www.palatulsnagov.ro; Snagov; ☉ closed to the public) On Snagov Lake's western shore you'll see an impressive-looking villa, Snagov Palace. It was built by Prince Nicolae, brother of King Carol II, in neo-Renaissance style in the 1930s. During the Ceaușescu era, the palace was used for meetings of high-level government officials. Today the building serves as a retreat for state guests and private parties.

🛏 Sleeping & Eating

Most people visit Snagov on a day trip, though there are a couple of pleasant overnight options.

Dolce Vita HOTEL $$
(☑ boat 0723-580 780; www.dolcevitasnagov.ro; Snagov Parc; r 200 lei) This hotel and restaurant complex is located on the western shore directly across the lake from Snagov village, at the edge of a protected nature reserve. There are simple rooms here for rent and pretty lakeside-terrace dining (mains 20 to 30 lei). To get here, either drive or take a maxitaxi to Snagov village and phone for someone to fetch you in a motor boat.

Complex Astoria BUNGALOW $$
(☑ 0744-372 640; Șos Snagovului; r 3-/4-star 160/190 lei; P ❋ ☵) This nine-hectare wooded resort complex east of Snagov, on the lake's northern end, has three- and four-star villas as well as space to pitch a tent. On weekends, crowds from Bucharest descend and it can get packed; on weekdays it's quieter. There's a pool (20 lei), tennis courts and boats to hire as well places to eat.

To get to here by car drive through Snagov village for a further 3km northeast to the complex (signposted 'Baza Turistică Snagov').

Hanul Vlasiei ROMANIAN $$
(☑ 0732-022 888; Str Hanul Vlasiei 1; mains 25-40 lei; ☉ 11am-10pm) On the western side of the

Around Bucharest

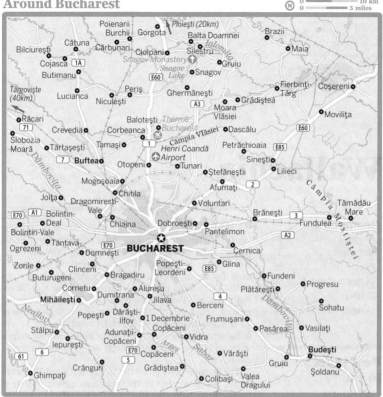

lake, across from Snagov village, this upscale terrace restaurant is one of the nicer places to eat in the Snagov area. There's an indoor restaurant, too, that borders on the stuffy and is popular with wedding parties. The menu centres on grilled meats and traditional Romanian cooking.

El Capitan BAR
(☎ 0756-385 638; Snagov Park; ☺ 2-9pm Mon-Thu, 11am-midnight Fri-Sun) Upscale terrace coffee and cocktail bar, just south of Dolce Vita on the western side of the lake across from Snagov village, attracting a glamorous boating crowd and their entourage. Relax on lakeside sofas and gaze out over lovely Snagov Lake.

❶ Information

Snagov Tur (☎ 021-323 9905; www.snagov.ro; Str Snagov 78; ☺ 9am-5pm Mon-Fri) offers information on the lake, plus guided walking and cycling tours. See the website for a current list.

❶ Getting There & Away

Though it's only 40km north of Bucharest, it's not that easy to get to Snagov without your own wheels. The best bet is to catch a maxitaxi (6 lei, 45 minutes) from stands at Piaţa Presei Libera in the north of Bucharest, which will drop you at the centre of Snagov village. The Complex Astoria, from where you can get a boat ride to Snagov Monastery, is a further 3km along the road to the northeast. To cross the lake from Snagov village, try to negotiate with a private motorboat (around 15 lei per crossing) or call Dolce Vita, and they will send a boat across the lake to get you (free ferry for customers).

To reach Snagov by car from Bucharest, follow the signs out of the city to the airport and then keep heading north along the E60 until you see the turn-off for Snagov, which lies 11km from the main road.

Wallachia

Best Places to Eat

➡ Epoca (p73)

➡ Domnesc (p70)

➡ Hanul Domnesc (p72)

➡ Taverna Dionysos (p64)

➡ La Tuciuri (p68)

Best Places to Sleep

➡ Pensiunea Ruxi (p69)

➡ Hotel Corona (p75)

➡ Pensiunea Casa Simoni (p63)

➡ La Strada (p67)

➡ Hotel Europa (p72)

Why Go?

Wallachia (Ţara Românească), the region between the Carpathians and the Danube River, admittedly lacks the must-sees of Transylvania and Moldavia. Nevertheless, it's rich in early Romanian history, particularly at the historic seats of the Wallachian princes in Curtea de Argeş and Târgovişte. This was Wallachian prince Vlad Ţepeş' old stomping ground, and north of Curtea de Argeş stands the ruins of what many consider to be the real 'Dracula's castle'. Lovers of modern sculpture will want to see Constantin Brâncuşi's work on open-air display in Târgu Jiu, close to the region of his birth.

The Danube flows along the southern edge of Wallachia and is best seen west of Drobeta-Turnu Severin, where it breaks through the Carpathians at the legendary Iron Gates. Drobeta-Turnu Severin was once a thriving Roman colony, and you can still see the remains of Emperor Trajan's mighty bridge (AD 103) that once traversed the Danube.

When to Go
Ploieşti

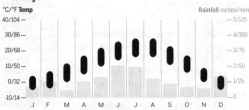

May Spring flowers cover the mountain highlands north of Curtea de Argeş.

Jun–Aug Warm afternoons are ideal for cruising the Danube near Iron Gates National Park.

Sep & Oct Regional cultural hubs like Craiova reawaken after a long summer slumber.

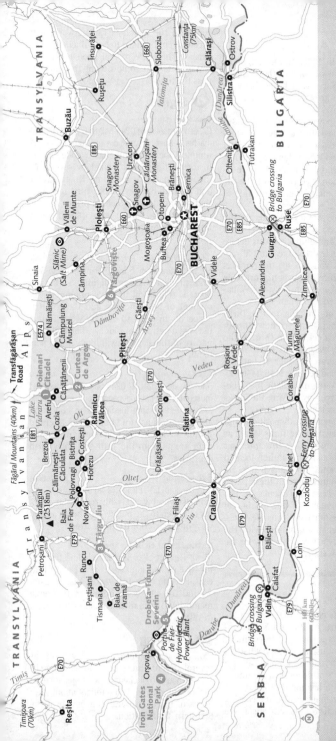

Wallachia Highlights

1 Poienari Citadel (p69)
Gasping up the 1480 steps to Vlad Țepeș' Dracula's Castle.

2 Princely Court (p69)
Gaping at 14th-century frescoes at the court's St Nicholas Church in Curtea de Argeș.

3 Endless Column (p72)
Enjoying the simple perfection of Constantin Brâncuși's sculptures, including this structure in Târgu Jiu, near the place of his birth.

4 Iron Gates National Park (p74) Admiring the dramatic beauty of the Danube as it breaks through the Carpathians west of Drobeta-Turnu Severin.

5 Iron Gates Museum (p74) Wondering at the ruins of a Roman bridge that spanned the Danube here almost 2000 years ago.

6 Târgoviște (p65)
Reliving contemporary history at the modest army base in Târgoviște, where Nicolae Ceaușescu and his wife met their bloody ends.

History

The principality of Wallachia was founded by Radu Negru in 1290. It was originally conceived as a vassal state of the Hungarian kingdom to serve as a buffer between Hungary and the growing influence of the Ottoman Turks.

As Hungarian power waned in the 13th and 14th centuries after a wave of Mongol invasions, Wallachian Prince Basarab I (r 1310–52) defeated Hungarian King Charles I in 1330 and declared Wallachia to be independent. The region is considered to be the first of the three main Romanian lands to gain independence.

The 14th century was a golden age for the Wallachian princes, who established their first capital at Câmpulung Muscel, before moving on to Curtea de Argeş and Târgovişte. To this day, you can see the remains of once-grand Princely Courts in Curtea de Argeş and Târgovişte. Eventually, the Wallachian capital moved to Bucharest.

After the fall of Bulgaria to the Turks in 1396, Wallachia faced a new threat, and in 1415 Mircea cel Bătrân (Mircea the Old; r 1386–1418) was forced to acknowledge Turkish suzerainty. Other Wallachian princes, such as Vlad Ţepeş (r 1448, 1456–62, 1476) and Mihai Viteazul (r 1593–1601), became national heroes by defying the Turks and refusing to pay tribute.

Vlad Ţepeş' legendary disposition and gruesome tactics against the Turks served as inspiration for Bram Stoker's *Dracula,* four centuries on, although the author located the 'Prince of Darkness' in Transylvania. He remains an undisputed hero in these parts. Look for the big bust of 'Dracula' in Târgovişte and the remains of one of his real castles in Poienari, north of Curtea de Argeş.

In 1859 Wallachia was united with the province of Moldavia, paving the way for the modern Romanian state.

Ploieşti

POP 209,945

Ploieşti, the main city in the Prahova region, is the centre of Romania's oil production and ranks as one of the country's most important industrial cities. It's had an oil-refining industry since 1857 and this is a source of enormous pride for its inhabitants. That said, it's not a leading destination for visitors, and your main reason for coming is likely to be practical – the city sits at the centre of the country's rail network, with excellent connections to both Bucharest and Braşov. There are several good hotels and restaurants and some decent museums to pass the time.

⊙ Sights

Clock Museum　　　　　　　　　MUSEUM

(Muzeul Ceasului; ☑ 0244-542 861; Str Nicolae Simachei 1; 8 lei; ⊙ 9am-5pm Tue-Sun) The city's unique Clock Museum has a collection of historical timepieces owned by several famous Romanians, including King Carol I, and an 18th-century rococo Austrian clock that belonged to Wallachian prince Alexandru Ioan Cuza. There's also a small collection of vintage gramophones.

Museum of Oil　　　　　　　　　MUSEUM

(Muzeul Naţional al Petrolului; ☑ 0244-597 585; Str Dr Bagdasar 8; 5 lei; ⊙ 9am-5pm Tue-Sun) This modest museum highlights the important role of oil in the economic development of both the city and the country, especially in the 19th century when Romania was a petroleum pioneer. The technical nature of the displays will likely not appeal to all.

Art Museum　　　　　　　　　MUSEUM

(Muzeul de Artă; ☑ 0244-522 264; www.artmuseum.ro; B-dul Independenţei 1; adult/child 8/2 lei; ⊙ 9am-5pm Tue-Sun) The collection at this art museum, housed in a grand Empire-style mansion, is strong on Romanian greats from the 19th and early 20th centuries.

Synagogue　　　　　　　　　SYNAGOGUE

(Str Basarab 12) Ploieşti's synagogue dates from 1901 and was lavishly restored in 2007. It's not open to the public, but there's a good view of the exterior from the street.

Cathedral of St John the Baptist　　CHURCH

(B-dul Republicii; ⊙ 8am-6pm) Ploieşti's impressive cathedral dates from the early 19th century. The 55m bell tower, visible from around the city, was finished in 1939 as a memorial to Romanian soldiers who fought in WWI.

🛏 Sleeping

Ploieşti is geared for business travel and has several decent three- and four-star hotels. There's a group of cheaper pensions north of the city, along B-dul Republicii, about 3km north of the centre and 4km north of the Southern Train Station.

Ploieşti

N 0 ——————— 400 m
0 ——————— 0.2 miles

⭐ **Pensiunea Casa Simoni** PENSION **$**
(📞0745-010 310; www.pensiunea-casa-simoni.ro;
B-dul Republicii 224; s/d 120/140 lei; 🌀❄️@)
This beautifully maintained, family-owned
pension is one of the best-value options in
town, with only one drawback: it's about
4km north of the centre. Rooms are clean
and spacious, with terraces looking out
over the front of the property. Though the
address is B-dul Republicii, the pension is
located 200m off the main road, on an unmarked road (look for the sign).

Hotel Nord HOTEL **$$**
(📞0244-516 774; www.nordhotelploiesti.com; Sos
Vestului 31; s 130-200 lei; d 160-240 lei; P🌀❄️🛜)
There's nothing fancy here at this boxy busi-
ness hotel 2km northwest of the centre, but
the rooms are clean and good value. The
Nord has two- and three-star rooms, which
aren't much different, except the latter have
air-conditioning.

Hotel Central HOTEL **$$$**
(📞0244-526 641; www.thr.ro; B-dul Republicii 1;
s 220-360 lei, d 320-420 lei; P🌀❄️@🛜) This
beautifully restored landmark hotel sits in
the dead centre of town. It offers both three-
and four-star rooms, though there is not
really much of a difference in quality. Some

Ploieşti

of the cheaper three-stars come without
air-conditioning.

Hotel Prahova Plaza HOTEL **$$$**
(📞0244-526 850; www.hotelprahova.ro; Str C-tin
Dobrogeanu Gherea 11; r 350-400 lei; P🌀
❄️@🛜) This communist-era hulk has been
given a thorough makeover into one of the
city's nicest business hotels, and prices have
been adjusted upwards accordingly. Rooms

are divided into 'economy' and 'deluxe', with the latter being larger and with updated furnishings. The location couldn't be better, just a couple of minutes' walk from the central square.

✕ Eating & Drinking

Stock up on fruit, bread and cheese for your train journey at the monster-sized **central market** (Halele Centrale; B-dul Unirii; ⊘7am-7pm Mon-Fri, to 2pm Sat).

★ **Taverna Dionysos** GREEK $$
(☑0244-338 835; Str Anul 1907 2; mains 30-40 lei; ⊘10.30am-11pm) One of the most popular restaurants in Ploiești, Dionysos offers very good, authentic Greek food, including excellent grills and fresh fish, in a lively party atmosphere. The owner is Greek and takes special pride in the food. Dine on the terrace in summer.

Bulevard ROMANIAN $$
(☑0723-617 654; Str Golești 25; mains 25-40 lei; ⊘8am-11pm Mon-Fri, 10am-2am Sat & Sun; ☎) This attractive restaurant is located within easy walking distance of the Clock Museum and other major sights. The eclectic menu is strong on Romanian cuisine, with the addition of a long list of grilled meats and fish. There's a classy dining room and an elegant summer terrace.

Sport Pub Doroftei PUB FOOD $$
(☑0244-544 112; Piața Victoriei 4; mains 20-30 lei; ⊘11am-1am; ☎) Don't be put off by the name, this 'sports' pub has great food and a fun 2nd-floor terrace that overlooks Piața Victoriei. After dinner, it does double duty as, well, a sports pub.

Dublin Pub PUB
(☑0726-352 089; B-dul Republicii 19; ⊘10am-11.30pm; ☎) A popular spot to grab a beer (although there's no Irish beer, despite the name) or occasionally see some live music or even stand-up comedy. The location is smack in the centre, an easy walk from the Hotel Central.

ⓘ Information

There's no tourist information office in Ploiești. There are banks and ATMs all around the centre, with most on the main drag of B-dul Republicii and Piața Victoriei.

Banca Transilvania (www.bancatransilvania. ro; B-dul Republicii 15; ⊘Mon-Fri 9am-5pm) Convenient full-service bank and ATM close to the centre.

Post Office (Piața Victoriei 10; ⊘7am-1pm & 1.30-8pm Mon-Fri, 8am-1pm Sat) The central post office is located on Piața Victoriei, just south of the Hotel Central following B-dul Republicii.

ⓘ Getting There & Away

BUS

Ploiești has several bus stations. The main station is the **southern bus station** (Autogara Sud; ☑0244-522 230; www.autogari.ro; Str Depoului 9-11), 200m west of the southern train station. From here, you can catch buses to Bucharest (16 lei, one hour, several daily), Câmpina (6 lei, 30 minutes, eight daily) and Târgoviște (10 lei, 90 minutes, seven daily). For other destinations, consult the website www.autogari.ro.

TRAIN

The city has two main passenger train stations, so always ask which station your train departs from. Many domestic trains, including those to

---

WORTH A TRIP

THE NICOLAE GRIGORESCU MUSEUM, CÂMPINA

If you've visited the art museums in Bucharest, Constanța or Ploiești, you've likely developed a taste for the talented and underrated (at least outside of Romania) 19th-century painter Nicolae Grigorescu (1838–1907). Best known locally for his starkly beautiful landscapes, his work ranges from portraiture to reportage (he was a war painter in the Romanian War of Independence). Grigorescu studied in Paris with Pierre Auguste Renoir and his later works were highly innovative, anticipating more modern styles, such as Impressionism, that were well in vogue by the end of his life.

The **Nicolae Grigorescu Museum** (Muzeul Nicolae Grigorescu; ☑0244-335 598; http:// grigorescu.artmuseum.ro; B-dul Carol I 166, Câmpina; adult/child 8/2 lei; ⊘9am-5pm Tue-Sun) is a modest tribute to the painter's life, with collections on two floors in a traditional wooden village house where he lived during the last seven years of his life.

From Ploiești's southern bus station there are several daily buses to Câmpina, 32km north of Ploiești. There are also daily trains from Ploiești's western station to Câmpina.

Bucovina and Moldavia, leave from the **southern train station** (Gara de Sud; ☑0244-594 799; www.cfr.ro; Strada Depoului). For trips to Transylvania and international destinations such as Budapest and Vienna, use the **western train station** (Gara de Vest; ☑0244-557 191; www.cfr.ro; Str Domnişori 95). Bucharest trains arrive at and depart from either station, so consult the timetable.

Destinations for fast Inter-City trains include Bucharest (20 lei, 45 minutes, 15 daily), Braşov (35 lei, two hours, 10 daily) and Cluj-Napoca (100 lei, eight hours, two daily).

Târgovişte

POP 79,600

The small city of Târgovişte, 50km northwest of Bucharest, has played an outsized role in Romanian history. It served as the royal capital of Wallachia from 1418 until well into the 16th century, when the capital was moved to Bucharest. The ruins of the former royal court remain the town's leading attraction. During the 15th century, Vlad Ţepeş, of impaler fame, held princely court here. In more recent times, the city made international headlines as the site where dictator Nicolae Ceauşescu and his wife, Elena, were executed on Christmas Day, 1989.

◉ Sights

★ Military Barracks   MUSEUM

(B-dul Carol I 48; adult/child 7/3.50 lei; ☺9am-5pm Tue-Sun) This small, spare museum just outside the train station contains the military barracks where former Romanian dictator Nicolae Ceauşescu and his wife Elena were tried and executed by firing squad on Christmas Day in 1989. Three rooms are open, showing where the trial took place and where the couple spent their last nights. Outside in the back, visitors can see the wall where the couple were shot. There's helpful signage in English and the modest setting adds to the powerful effect.

Before entering, take a moment to read the large bulletin board outside, which explains in detail the dramatic and terrifying days in December 1989 that lead to Ceauşescu's downfall and execution. The Târgovişte location was purely coincidental: when the couple fled Bucharest, they were captured near the city and brought here because the military barracks were well fortified.

Princely Court   MUSEUM, RUINS

(Curtea Domnească; ☑0245-613 946; www.muzee-dambovitene.ro; Calea Domnească 181; adult/child 10/5 lei; ☺9am-7pm Tue-Sun) The Princely Court was built in the 14th century for Mircea cel Bătrân (Mircea the Old) and remained a formal residence for Wallachia's princes, including Vlad Ţepeş, until the reign of Constantin Brâncoveanu (r 1688–1714). Much of the court lies in ruin, though the 27m-high Sunset Tower (Turnul Chindiei) – the symbol of the city – has a museum exhibition. Another highlight is the cathedral.

Just north of the Sunset Tower is a lovely park for strolling. Each of the Wallachian princes gets his own bust here, but the biggest prize is reserved for Vlad Ţepeş, who merits a big, suitably dramatic statue in the centre of the park – a great photo op.

Zoo   ZOO

(Grădina Zoologică; ☑0245-616 558; www.zoo targoviste.ro; Zona Calea Domnească, Parcul Chindia; adult/child 7/4 lei; ☺9am-7pm Tue-Sun May-Sep, 10am-4pm Tue-Sun Oct-Apr; 🐾) Târgovişte's small zoo, in the park just north of the Princely Court, is surprisingly comprehensive, with some large cats, a hippo, lots of chimps and a variety of other animals. The zoo shows obvious signs of wear and tear, but the animals appear adequately cared for. Kids will love how close you can come to the animals.

Târgu Church   CHURCH

(Biserica Târgului; Str Ion Rădulescu; ☺8am-6pm) Near the restaurants on Str Alexandru Ioan Cuza is the beautiful, partially frescoed Târgu Church. Dating to 1654, it was painted during the 17th and 18th centuries, but destroyed during an earthquake in 1940. Extensive renovations followed in 1941 and in the 1970s, and were still ongoing at the time of research. The church is especially pretty when lit at night.

Cathedral   CHURCH

(Catedrala Metropolitana; B-dul Mircea cel Bătrân; ☺8am-7pm) **FREE** Târgovişte's main church occupies a prominent position in the town's central Parcul Mitropoliei. The church is built of red brick in Byzantine style and dates from the early 20th century.

Museum of Printing & Old Romanian Books   MUSEUM

(Muzeul Tiparului şi al Cărţii Româneşti Vechi; ☑0245-613 946; www.muzee-dambovitene.ro;

Str Calea Domnească 181; 5 lei; ⊘9am-5pm Tue-Sun) Housed in a 17th-century palace built by Constantin Brâncoveanu for his daughter Safta, this museum is filled with original books from the beginning of Romania's printing age and manuscripts by 17th- and 18th-century Romanian writers.

🛏 Sleeping

There are a couple of acceptable hotels in town, but Târgovişte generally lacks decent places to stay.

Pensiunea Chindia
PENSION $

(📞0726-355 514; www.cazaretargoviste.ro; Calea Domenască 200; s/d/tr 70/80/120 lei; 🅿 ➗ 🗦) A good-value pension located directly across the street from the entrance to the Princely Court.

Hotel Dâmbovita
HOTEL $$

(📞0245-213 370; www.hoteldambovita.ro; B-dul Libertăţii 1; s/d 130/170 lei; 🅿 ✳ @ 🗦) If you're going to spend the night in Târgovişte, make it here, the nicest place in town. While the modern high-rise building doesn't look encouraging from the outside, the rooms are clean and quiet; some have balconies with views overlooking the central park. Breakfast (included in the room price) is served *à la carte,* a welcome relief from tired buffet spreads.

🍴 Eating

Most of the best restaurants as well as a dozen cafes and bars are clustered along Str Alexandru Ioan Cuza in the historic centre.

Bistro Alexo
PIZZA $

(📞0732-125 396; Calea Domenască 179; pizza 16-20 lei; ⊘9am-11pm; 🗦) The inviting garden terrace is a welcome spot for coffee or pizza before or after a visit to the nearby Princely Court. The salads are enormous; one is enough for the whole table. They also serve good espresso.

⭐ Queen's Corner
ROMANIAN $$

(Belvedere; Str Alexandru Ioan Cuza 22a; mains 25-40 lei; ⊘11am-midnight; 🗦) Grab an upper-level terrace table overlooking the pedestrian street and enjoy excellent Romanian and international dishes, including well-executed grilled meats and steaks. They also have very good wood-fired pizzas and a menu page of traditional Romanian dishes. The wine list is the best in town, but service can be slow.

San Marco
ITALIAN $$

(📞0723-363 635; Str Alexandru Ioan Cuza 22; mains 25-40 lei; ⊘10am-11pm; 🗦) Arguably the most attractive of several restaurants along the city's small pedestrianised strip. The focus here is pasta, risotto, pizza and salad, and there's a decent wine list on hand. There are several outside tables and a warm, inviting dining room inside.

ℹ Information

There is no tourist information office. The Hotel Dâmboviţa stocks city maps.

Arena Internet (B-dul Independenţei 2-4; per hr 2.50 lei; ⊘7am-10pm; 🗦)

Banca Comercială Română (BCR; B-dul Independenţei 6; ⊘9am-5pm Mon-Fri) Full-service bank with a row of ATMs in the centre of town on the eastern end of the large central park.

Central Post Office (Str Dr Marinoiu 2; ⊘7.30am-8pm Mon-Fri, 8am-1pm Sat)

ℹ Getting There & Away

BUS

Târgovişte has several bus stations. The main **bus station** (Autogara; www.autogari.ro; Str Gării) is located 2km south of the city centre and about 200m northwest of the train station. Buses to Bucharest (15 lei, two hours, five daily) depart from here.

Buses to Ploieşti (10 lei, one hour, several daily) leave from a small stop at Str Tudor Vladimirescu 86, about 200m south of the central Parcul Mitropoliei.

Buses to Braşov (27 lei, three hours, five daily) leave from a stop at B-dul Eroilor 38, about 1km north of the Princely Court.

For other destinations, check www.autogari.ro.

TRAIN

Târgovişte's sleepy **train station** (Gara Târgovişte; www.cfr.ro; Piaţa Gării) is 2km south of the city centre, at the end of B-dul Carol I. There are regular departures throughout the day to Bucharest Nord (10 lei, two hours, four daily). For other destinations, you're better off taking the bus.

Piteşti

POP 164,380

Piteşti is a pleasant, medium-sized city with a pretty, pedestrianised centre lined with cafes, bars and a handful of decent hotels. If you're planning an overnight stay in this neck of the woods it's a strong candidate – not so much for the sights (they are strictly second-tier), but for the energy and lively atmosphere.

◉ Sights

The city's pride and joy is an enormous stretch of green that runs west of the centre called **Trivale Park**.

Art Museum
MUSEUM

(Rudolf Schweitzer Cumpăna Art Gallery; ☑0248-212 561; www.muzeul-judetean-arges.ro; B-dul Republicii 33; adult/child 5/2 lei; ☺9am-5pm Wed-Sun) This central museum showcases the best of modern and contemporary Romanian art, including works from Nicolae Grigorescu, Nicolae Tonitza and other luminaries of the late 19th and early 20th centuries.

Princely Church
CHURCH

(Biserica Domnească; www.bisericadomneasca pitesti.ro; Str Victoriei; ☺8am-6pm) The unusual St George's Church (Biserica Sfântul Gheorghe), more commonly known as the Princely Church, was built by Prince Constantin Şerban and his wife Princess Bălasa between 1654 and 1658. The church is located on the southern end of Str Victoriei, about 200m south of the Hotel Argeş.

Piteşti Prison Memorial
MONUMENT

(Str Negru Vodă 32; ☺24hr) A modest memorial marks the spot where the city's notorious prison once stood and where insidious mind-control experiments were carried out in the late 1940s and early '50s. The main memorial is a tiled column; nearby is a map of other detention and extermination sites around Romania. It's a 15-minute walk from the centre, heading north on Str Victoriei, which becomes Str Negru Vodă.

⊨ Sleeping

Piteşti draws far more business people than leisure travellers, and accommodation is priced accordingly. Guesthouses can take the sting out of hotel rack rates.

La Storia
GUESTHOUSE $

(☑0723-889 819; http://la-storia.ro; Str Plevnei 8; r 120 lei; ☞) La Storia is a godsend for travellers on a budget in a city with few low-cost sleeping options. There are 10 clean and simply furnished rooms here, offering excellent value given the central location. There's a quiet backyard garden for coffee and light meals.

★La Strada
BOUTIQUE HOTEL $$

(☑0732-763 107; www.lastradapitesti.ro; B-dul Republicii 63; s/d 220/260 lei; P☞❀@) La Strada offers a highly tempting mix (especially if you've been travelling through the countryside) of a great location and tastefully contemporary furnishings, though at a slight premium to similar properties in the area. The hotel occupies a smartly renovated 19th-century townhouse, just a couple of minutes' walk from the centre. The terrace restaurant at the back serves good international and Romanian food.

WALLACHIA PITEŞTI

WORTH A TRIP

TASTING LOCAL GRAPES IN DRĂGĂŞANI

Few visitors would give the town of Drăgăşani, halfway between Piteşti and Craiova, a second thought if it weren't for the fact that it's home to some of the country's most innovative new wineries. Several offer tasting packages, usually paired with food.

The wine-producing merits of the region's sunny climate and low-lying hills, worn down through the years by the Olt River, have been appreciated going back centuries. The communist period, though, was not kind to Drăgăşani. Many families lost their holdings and quality suffered accordingly.

Now the area is making a comeback, with a half-dozen or so young wineries that mix modern winemaking methods with local, indigenous grapes. The best of these include **Avincis** (☑0350-522 003; www.avincis.ro; Str Valea Caselor 1a; tastings per person without food from 45 lei; ☺by arrangement), **Crama Bauer** (☑0757-098 940; www.cramabauer.com; Str Dealul Olt; tastings per person with/without food from 210/65 lei; ☺by arrangement) and **Prince Ştirbey** (☑0751-252 272; www.stirbey.com; Str Dealul Olt; tastings per person with/without food from 185/65 lei).

There are only a handful of hotels in town, though Avincis has its own rooms, and other wineries can help find accommodation. **Hotel KMZ** (☑0250-814 093; www.kmz.ro; Str Regele Carol 16; s/d 130/170 lei; P❀☞) is a funky, young-at-heart boutique hotel.

Buses leave hourly for Craiova (14 lei, one hour); at least a couple of buses run to and from Piteşti (20 lei, two hours). There are two direct trains per day between Drăgăşani and Bucharest (40 lei, 2½ hours).

★ **Hotel Argeş**   HOTEL **$$**

(📞 0248-223 399; www.hotelarges.ro; Piaţa Muntenia 3; s/d 180/220 lei; P✱@📶) On the shortlist for the best three-star hotel in the country. Ultra-clean rooms with high-thread-count linens, thick-weave carpets, sparkling baths and a warm reception add up to one of the best deals in the city. The location is dead centre, with the best cafes and restaurants at your doorstep.

✗ Eating

★ **La Tuciuri**   ROMANIAN **$$**

(📞 0348-415 343; Str Primăverii 11; mains 25-40 lei; ⊘ 8am-4am) La Tuciuri is a real find: a traditional Romanian folk restaurant, complete with peasant costumes and music some evenings, that also serves very good food in its own right. Grilled meats are the main event here, and the chef puts out very good *mititei* (grilled ground beef and pork). The party carries on to the wee hours of the morning.

Garden Pub   ROMANIAN **$$**

(📞 0733-956 280; www.gardenpub.ro; Str Victoriei 16; mains 20-40 lei; ⊘ 10am-5am; 📶) This deservedly popular restaurant and pub draws everyone from visiting business people to students on their lunch break for excellent soups, salads and grilled meats and fish. There's a streetside terrace out front, more outdoor seating on the roof, and a handsome dark-wood interior for chilly evenings. Book in advance.

🍺 Drinking & Nightlife

Guinness Pub   PUB

(📞 0726-375 619; www.guinnesspub.ro; Str Victoriei 30; mains 15-25 lei; ⊘ 8.30am-midnight Sun-Thu, to 4am Fri & Sat; 📶) Guinness Pub is a fun and rowdy drinking option most nights. If you're hungry, there's a full menu of Romanian dishes and grilled meats, too. It's located at the northern end of the pedestrianised part of Str Victoriei.

Cornel Pub & Grill   PUB

(📞 0727-362 426; Str Armand Călinescu 36; ⊘ 10am-2am Mon-Thu, to 5am Fri & Sat, 11am-2am Sun; 📶) This relaxed pub and cafe, just a short walk west of the centre, is good for a beer or light meal. There's a terrace out front and a covered bar behind. The late opening hours are a plus.

ℹ Information

There's no tourist information office, though some hotels stock the small multilingual book *Turism in Argeş* (20 lei), which has a serviceable map of the city in the front sleeve.

BRD (📞 0248-211 687; www.brd.ro; Str Victoriei 89; ⊘ 9am-5pm Mon-Fri) Full-service bank and 24-hour ATM.

Central Post Office (Str Victoriei; ⊘ 9am-7pm Mon-Fri, to noon Sat) The main post office is a little tricky to find. Walk southeast on Str Victoriei about 30m beyond the Princely Church. The post office building is on the right side. The counters are up one flight.

ℹ Getting There & Away

BUS

Piteşti has several bus stations. Many buses, including several bus and maxitaxi departures throughout the day to Bucharest (25 lei, two hours), leave from the **Southern Bus Station Targ Vale** (Autogară Sud; 📞 0248-636 302; www.autogari.ro; Str Targul din Vale 54), about 400m south of the centre. Minibuses to Curtea de Argeş (8 lei, 45 minutes) and other points to the north often leave from the **Northern Bus Station** (Autogară Nord, Girexim; 📞 0248-282 201; Str George Cosbuc 12), about 4km north of the centre. For other destinations consult the website www.autogari.ro.

TRAIN

The main train station is the **southern train station** (Piteşti Sud; 📞 0248-627 908, domestic train information 021-9521; www.cfr.ro; B-dul Republicii). Services include a handful of daily direct trains to Bucharest (30 lei, two hours) and Craiova (35 lei, two hours).

Curtea de Argeş

POP 26,133

Curtea de Argeş has a humble, likeable charm, enriched by the captivating treasures left over from the town's role as a Wallachian capital in the 14th century. St Nicholas Church in the former Princely Court is a must-see and is considered to be one of the oldest monuments preserved in its original form in the country. The town's storied cathedral, sculpted from white stone, is unique for the important royal tombs it hides and its chocolate-box architecture. In addition, the town is a gateway to the Făgăraş Mountains and just a short bus ride away from the 'real' Dracula's castle (Poienari Citadel).

THE 'REAL' DRACULA'S CASTLE

North of Curtea de Argeş the population thins out to a few scattered villages as the highway nears the Carpathians. The highlight of the region is the **Poienari Citadel** (Cetatea Poienari; Poienari; adult/child 5/2 lei; ⊙ 9am-6pm Jun-Sep, 9am-5pm May & Oct; **P**), one of the few castles in Romania that really does have a legitimate connection to the notorious Wallachian prince Vlad Țepeș (1431–76), aka 'Vlad the Impaler' or, better yet, 'Dracula'.

The Poienari Citadel was once a powerful fortress guarding entry to a strategic pass linking Wallachia with Transylvania. The castle's vantage point was recognised as early as the 13th century, when Wallachian leaders first built a tower to guard the pass. Two centuries later Vlad Țepeș enlarged the castle, using it as both a fortress and a prison. Legend has it most of the work was carried out by captured Turks.

These days there's not much of the castle left, but it's still worth the short trip from Curtea de Argeş to take in the spectacular setting and to make the invigorating climb (1480 steps) to the top. The entrance to the citadel lies just at the start of the towering **Transfăgărăşan road**, so it's an especially easy stopover if you're planning on crossing the mountains here.

If you'd like to stay the night, the **Pensiunea Dracula** (☑ 0745-473 381; www.pensiunea dracula.ro; Căpăţânenii 190; r from 140 lei; **P** 🛜) is a clean and well-run pension, whose owners get into the Dracula theme. Another good choice is **Pensiunea La Cetate** (☑ 0744-424 845; www.cabanalacetate.ro; Str Mihail Kogalniceanu 1, Poienari; r 110 lei; **P** ❄ 🛜), just 100m from the steps leading to Dracula's Castle. There's a terrace here for lunch or dinner.

The best way to come from Curtea de Argeş is by maxitaxi (5 lei, 40 minutes), signposted to Arefu.

◉ Sights

The main sights are located north of the town centre along a long stretch of B-dul Basarabilor. The Princely Court is at the southern end of B-dul Basarabilor, while the monastery complex is 2km to the north.

★**Princely Court** CHURCH, RUIN
(☑ 0248-721 446; Str Negru Vodă 2; adult/child 6/3 lei; ⊙ 9am-5pm) Curtea de Argeş was an early capital of Wallachia, and these ruins from the 13th and 14th centuries mark the spot where the court once stood. The main sight is St Nicholas Church, which dates from the time of Basarab I (1310–52). Many of the frescoes are originals and merit close inspection. In the main room to the right, just below the upper window, look for a rare painting of a pregnant Mary dating from 1370.

The church also functioned as a necropolis and holds some 21 burial tombs, including that of early ruler Vladislav I Vlaicu (d 1377). The unmarked tomb in the middle of the main room predates the church by about a century and was found in archaeological digs nearby.

Curtea de Argeş Cathedral & Monastery MONASTERY
(Mănăstirea Curtea de Argeş; ☑ 0248-721 735; B-dul Basarabilor 1; adult/child 2/1 lei; ⊙ 8am-

8pm) This cathedral and monastery complex is considered one of the country's most important ecclesiastical sights. The church was originally built by Wallachian ruler Neagoe Basarab (r 1512–21), with marble and tiles brought in from Constantinople. The current edifice dates from 1875, when French architect André Lecomte du Nouy was retained to save the complex, which was in near ruins.

The monastery is an important royal mausoleum. The white marble tombstones of King Carol I (1839–1914) and his wife Elizabeth (1853–1916) lie on the right in the church's entrance hall. On the left of the entrance are the tombstones of King Ferdinand I (1865–1927) and British-born Queen Marie (1875–1938). Neagoe Basarab and his wife are also buried here.

🛏 Sleeping

Curtea de Argeş is surprisingly popular and you never know when you might turn up on a specific saint's day, which can bring hundreds of people to town. Therefore it's a good idea to book in advance, particularly in summer.

★**Pensiunea Ruxi** PENSION $
(☑ 0727-827 675; www.pensiunea-ruxi.ro; Str Negru Vodă 104; s/d 90/100 lei; **P** ➡ @ 🛜) While

the rooms are relatively new and comfortable, the real treat here is the homely atmosphere; the family will go to heart-breaking lengths to make sure you're taken care of. The only partial drawback is the town-centre location, about 1km from the Princely Court and 2km from the monastery complex. Walk or take a local minibus.

Pensiunea Casa Domneasca PENSION $$
(☑0248-721 070; www.casa-domneasca.ro; Str Plopiş 3; s 170-220 lei, d 190-240 lei; P❀ ✴♠❄) Beautiful four-star *pensiune* with an elegant reception area and rooms that look like a spread in *Town & Country* magazine. The standard rates include breakfast; the higher rates include use of the sauna and pool. To find it, make a right at the statue of Basarab I near the Princely Court and follow the street uphill about 100m.

Hotel Posada HOTEL $$
(☑0248-721 451; www.hotelposada.ro; B-dul Basarabilor 27-29; s/d 130/180 lei; P❀✴❄) Nicely remodelled three-star hotel with a quiet location at the far northern end of B-dul Basarabilor by the monastery complex. Try to get a front room to watch the sunset over the mountains.

✕ Eating

★Domnesc ROMANIAN $$
(☑0727-364 716; www.restaurantuldomnesc. ro; B-dul Basarabilor 106; mains 20-40 lei; ❀7am-midnight; ❄) This handsome restaurant, with a large terrace, marries the best of clean, modern presentation and traditional food, featuring menu items from the surrounding Argeş region. Choose from a list of sour soups *(ciorbă)*, grilled meats, homemade sausages, and big wedges of polenta *(mămăligă)*. There's folk music and dance on Thursday evenings. Located 20m north of the Princely Court.

Curtea Veche ROMANIAN $$
(☑0745-994 345; www.curteavechekm0.ro; B-dul Basarabilor 121; mains 20-45 lei; ❀9am-11pm) Nicely restored villa with a big rambling porch and a lower-level terrace with comfy pillow seating for lounging. The menu is textbook traditional Romanian; *tochitura argeseana* is a stewy mix of pork, peppers, onions and an egg, all poured over polenta. Does pretty good pizza too. It's located 30m north of the Princely Court.

❶ Information

There is no formal tourist information office, though the private travel agency **Turism Posada** (☑0248-721 451; www.posada.ro; B-dul Basarabilor 27-29; ❀9am-5pm Mon-Fri) in the Hotel Posada may be able to answer some basic questions.

Post Office (☑0248-721 132; Str Despina Doamna 43; ❀7am-8pm Mon-Fri)

Raiffeisen Bank (B-dul Basarabilor 31; ❀8.30am-6.30pm Mon-Fri) One of several ATM options on B-dul Basarabilor. This one is next to the Hotel Posada, 100m south of the monastery complex.

❶ Getting There & Away

The main bus station is near the town centre, on a side street about 200m west of Pensiunea Ruxi. Cities served include Bucharest (30 lei, two to three hours, four daily) and Braşov (31 lei, four hours, one daily). Frequent maxitaxis to Arefu (5 lei, 40 minutes) also leave from the main bus station. Other maxitaxis go to and from Piteşti (5.50 lei, 30 minutes) from an unofficial maxitaxi stop in front of the Princely Court entrance.

Rail services have been greatly curtailed and trains are not recommended.

Craiova

POP 293,500

The university town of Craiova, founded on the site of the ancient Dacian and Roman stronghold of Pelendava, is a regional commercial centre and transport hub. All long-haul trains between Timişoara and Bucharest stop here, so it makes a convenient point to break a long journey. The modern city has greatly cleaned itself up in recent years, and the historic centre, bordered on one end by Romania's prettiest county prefecture building, is great for a relaxing stroll.

◉ Sights

Craiova has a handful of interesting museums, including an art museum with several pieces by early-modern master Constantin Brâncuşi. There are also several churches worth seeking out.

★Art Museum MUSEUM
(Muzeul de Artă; ☑0251-412 342; www.muzeul deartacraiova.ro; Calea Unirii 15; adult/student 10/8 lei; ❀10am-5pm Tue-Sun) The art museum is the only real must-see in Craiova, both for the art itself, including a small but

Craiova

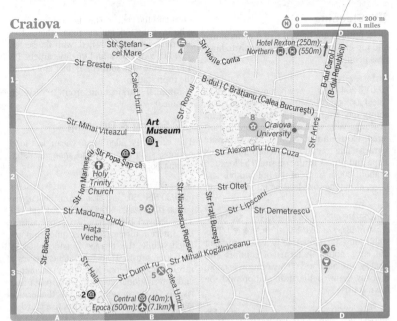

important collection of six works by internationally renowned sculptor Constantin Brâncuși, and also for the building that the works are housed in. The early-20th-century Jean Mihail Palace once belonged to Romania's richest industrial family. Over the years it has housed Romanian kings and former Yugoslav leader Josip Broz Tito, and was also home to Polish president-in-exile Ignacy Mościcki in 1939.

Ethnographic Museum   MUSEUM
(Muzeul Olteniei Secția de Etnografie; ☎ 0351-444 030; www.muzeulolteniei.ro; Str Matei Basarab 16; adult/child 5/2.50 lei; ⏱ 9am-5pm Tue-Sun) This is a highly informative, well-organised exhibition of folk traditions in the Oltenia region surrounding Craiova. The exhibition begins downstairs with bread-making and progresses through pottery, tanning, clothing, weaving and folk art. There's little English signage, but there may be someone on hand who speaks some English and can show you around. The setting is the historic Casa Băniei, dating from the 17th century. Recommended.

Natural Science Museum   MUSEUM
(☎ 0251-411 906; www.muzeulolteniei.ro; Str Popa Șapcă 8; adult/child 5/2.50 lei; ⏱ 9am-5pm Tue-

Sun) Small collection on two floors dedicated to the natural sciences. The highlights are fossils on the ground floor that include some massive mammoth tusks. On the upper level are stuffed animals representing the various fauna of the country's regions and climate zones. Very little signage in English limits the appeal.

🛏 Sleeping

Sleep options are limited to a few midrange and top-end hotels that cater mostly to business people.

Hotel Meliss
HOTEL **$$**

(☏0351-804 438; www.hotelmeliss.ro; B-dul Carol I 104; s/d 200/240 lei; ▣😊❄@🛜) This comfy modern, three-star option does a lot of things very well. The rooms are uncluttered, clean and quiet; some have private terraces. The reception is friendly and there's a spa and fitness centre on site. The location is about 200m south of the rail and bus stations, along the road leading into the centre.

Casa David
HOTEL **$$**

(☏0251-410 205; www.casadavid.ro; Str Ştefan cel Mare 18a; s/d 220/240 lei; ▣😊🛜) This small four-star *pensiune* is a step up from the city's hotels in terms of comfort and quality, and also price. The location is good, midway between the train station and the town centre.

Hotel Rexton
HOTEL **$$$**

(☏0351-462 451; www.hotelrexton.ro; B-dul Carol I 49; s/d 300/350 lei; ▣😊❄@🛜) One of the city's nicest hotels is this four-star option along the main road between the rail/bus stations and the centre. The classical motifs are a bit over the top, but the rooms themselves are more sleekly furnished, with flat-screen TVs, big comfy beds and quality carpets. It's a 10-minute walk south on B-dul Carol I from the train station.

Minimal parking out front (reserve in advance).

🍴 Eating & Drinking

The centre is filled with cheap fast-food options, such as pizza and *shoarma* (shawarma) joints.

Sofia Bistro
INTERNATIONAL **$$**

(☏0730-519 250; ww.sofiabistro.ro; Str Eugeniu Carada 17; mains 25-40 lei; ⊙9am-midnight; 🛜) This beloved bistro has two personalities: the interior dining room is quiet and refined, while the terrace outside pulsates with loud music. The same kitchen serves a mix of very well done Romanian specialities and international favourites like pasta and risotto. On warm summer nights the terrace gets crowded and service slows to a crawl.

Periniţa
ROMANIAN **$$**

(☏0251-412 412; www.restaurantperinita.ro; Calea Unirii 24; mains 20-30 lei; ⊙11am-11pm; 🛜) Very popular open-air restaurant, located in the

---

WORTH A TRIP

CONSTANTIN BRÂNCUŞI 'IN SITU' IN TÂRGU JIU

The coal-mining town of Târgu Jiu, along the Jiu River in the foothills of the Carpathians, is an unlikely setting for the breathtakingly minimalist, modern sculpture of internationally acclaimed Romanian master Constantin Brâncuşi (1876–1957). Brâncuşi was born near Târgu Jiu and spent his early years here and in nearby Craiova.

In 1935, Brâncuşi was commissioned to create a series of public works to commemorate Romanian soldiers who fought against the Germans in WWI. The works have survived to this day and constitute a unique opportunity to see the master's work in the open air.

The four main works are spread out along Calea Eroilor (Avenue of Heroes) that bisects the centre of town. Three of the works, the Gate of the Kiss, Table of Silence and Alley of Chairs, are clustered in the central park, while a fourth work, the Endless Column (Calea Eroilor; ⊙dawn-dusk) FREE, stands at the end of Calea Eroilor, about 1km to the east.

Taken together, the four sculptures constitute arguably the high point of Brâncuşi's career in the the late 1930s, showing off the artist's mastery of proportion, simplicity and symbolism. Today, works by Brâncuşi fetch as much as €30 million at auction, and the statues are under 24-hour armed guard.

For an overnight, Hotel Europa (☏0253-211 810; www.hotelrestauranteuropa.ro; Calea Eroilor 22; s/d 160/200 lei; ▣😊❄@) is a handsome historic hotel in the centre of the city and within easy walking distance of the Brâncuşi sculptures. Hanul Domnesc (☏0755-097 717; Str Victoriei 116; mains 20-30 lei; ⊙11am-11pm) is a good traditional Romanian restaurant.

Buses and maxitaxis connect the city to Timişoara (40 lei, three daily) and Drobeta-Turnu Severin (two daily). There's a regular train service to and from Bucharest (70 lei, five hours, three daily) via Craiova.

centre, specialising in traditional Romanian cooking as well as various chicken and pork grills. The grilled meatballs – *mititei* – are a house speciality and are cooked out front over an open fire. It also has pizzas and salads.

★**Epoca**   STEAK $$$
(☑0372-999 000; www.epocarestaurant.ro; Str Alexandru Macedonski 51; mains 40-115 lei; ⊘9am-midnight Mon-Fri; 🐾) This luxury steakhouse is a must for lovers of high-quality imported beef. The menu is almost exclusively grilled steaks and chops, with the speciality being cuts from Argentina and the US, served on hot plates that allow you to cook it perfectly to your liking. There's a handsome garden in the back.

Chicago   BAR
(☑0753-060 093; Str Eugeniu Carada 12; ⊘9am-midnight Sun-Wed, to 2am Thu-Sat; 🐾) The shady garden out front and the rooftop terrace are both big draws at this popular cafe and cocktail bar. Fresh lemonades, good coffees and a long list of mixed drinks lure university students in droves. There's also a small bar-food menu of mostly salads and burgers.

☆ Entertainment

A complete list of what's on can be found at www.craiova.ro/evenimente.

Oltenia Philharmonic   CLASSICAL MUSIC
(Filarmonica Oltenia; ☑0351-414 697; www.filarmonica-oltenia.ro; Calea Unirii 16; ⊘box office 10am-2pm Mon, Tue & Thu, 1-5pm Wed, 10am-2pm & 6-9pm Fri) Classical concerts are performed here by the Oltenia Philharmonic. Buy tickets at the box office.

Marin Sorescu
National Theatre   THEATRE
(☑box office 0251-413 677; www.tncms.ro; Str Alexandru Ioan Cuza 11; ⊘box office 9am-4pm Mon, 9am-4pm & 4.30-6.30pm Tue-Fri, 10am-1pm & 4.30-6.30pm Sat & Sun) For years, Craiova's main drama venue has enjoyed a national and international reputation for theatre excellence. Peformances are normally in Romanian, though the venue occasionally hosts visiting troupes from other countries. Buy tickets at the theatre box office.

❶ Information

There's no tourist information office and local travel agencies are more intent on helping Romanians than with visitors finding their way around town.

BRD (☑0251-412 282; Str Mihai Viteazul 2; ⊘Mon-Fri 9am-5pm, Sat 10am-3pm) Centrally located bank and ATM.

Central Post Office (www.posta-romana.ro; Calea Unirii 54; ⊘7am-8pm Mon-Fri, 8am-1pm Sat)

❶ Getting There & Away

BUS

The **main bus station** (Autogara; ☑0251-411 187; www.autogari.ro; B-dul Carol I 1), about 50m to the left as you exit the train station, appears at first glance like utter anarchy but is actually well organised. Regular buses and maxi-taxis leave from here to Bucharest (around 50 lei, five hours, hourly). There are also regular bus services to Timişoara (50 lei, seven hours, four daily) and Drobeta-Turnu Severin (20 lei, two hours, several daily), among other cities.

TRAIN

All fast trains between Bucharest and Timişoara stop at Craiova's **train station** (Gara Craiova; www.cfr.ro; B-dul Carol I, Piaţa Constantin Brân-cuşi; 🖳1). Services include trains to Bucharest (60 lei, three hours, 12 daily), Timişoara (70 lei, six hours, seven daily), Drobeta-Turnu Severin (35 lei, two hours) and Târgu Jiu (35 lei, two hours).

Drobeta-Turnu Severin

POP 20,500

Drobeta-Turnu Severin – usually shortened to 'Severin' in conversation – is on the bank of the Danube River bordering Serbia. Though the modern city was laid out in the 19th century, the town has a rich history stretching back nearly 2000 years, when it was an important Roman colony with a population of some 40,000. It's best known as the base of Roman emperor Trajan's colossal bridge across the Danube. You can still see ruins of the bridge as well as part of the Roman town surrounding it.

◉ Sights

The centre of town is defined by the central park, at the corner of B-dul Carol I and Str Bibicescu. There's a giant, colourful water fountain here that has nightly shows in summer starting around 9pm.

Technology geeks will want to head out of town to take a tour of the Porţile de Fier Hydroelectric Power Plant. This controversial project was a Romanian–

WORTH A TRIP

ORŞOVA & THE IRON GATES NATIONAL PARK

South and west of Drobeta-Turnu Severin, just below the town of Orşova, the Danube River begins a series of twists and turns between towering rocks that have bedevilled sailors from time immemorial.

The area is protected by the 1150-sq-km **Iron Gates National Park** (www.portile defier.ro). A similar protected area, the Djerdap National Park, sits across the river in Serbia. Highlights of the park include miles of rugged, unspoiled riverbanks and a massive stone carving of the former Dacian leader, Decebal (r AD 87–106).

There are several ways to access the park. The most popular is by private **boat** (Plimbări cu barca; ☑ 0766-522 815, 0722-502 216; Orşova Port; per passenger 50 lei; ⊗ 9am-5pm May-early Oct) along the Danube River. Several boat-rental outfits line the port in Orşova from late May to early October, depending on the weather.

Nearby Drobeta-Turnu Severin has the best selection of sleeping options, though there are a few scattered hotels in Orşova. **Pensiunea Oliver** (☑ 0726-382 246; www. pensiuneaoliver.ro; B-dul 1 Decembrie 1918 16a, Orşova; d/tr 150/180 lei; P ✳ @ ✿) is a small pension with an excellent location right on the port.

There are a couple of passable restaurants in Orşova. **Pescăruş Orşova** (☑ 0726-434 478; Str Insula Pescăruş 1, Orşova; mains 25-35 lei; ⊗ 9am-midnight Tue-Sun) is the best choice along the port. It's a seafood restaurant that offers photo-op views from its riverside terrace.

There's a regular minibus service to Orşova from Drobeta-Turnu Severin (3 lei, 30 minutes, hourly) as well as at least one train per day (5 lei, 30 minutes), though the Orşova train station is a good 2km hike to/from the centre of town.

Yugoslav joint venture, conceived in 1960 and completed 12 years later. There's a small **museum** (Muzeul Porţile de Fier I; Hwy E70; adult/child 5/2 lei; ⊗ 8am-4pm Tue-Sun) that takes you inside and provides a good idea of the scale of the plant. Guided tours (in Romanian only) go down five levels to the turbines. The museum is located on Hwy E70, 10km west of Drobeta-Turnu Severin.

Iron Gates Museum   MUSEUM
(Muzeul Porţilor de Fier; ☑ 0252-312 177; Str Independenţiei 2; adult/student 5/2 lei; ⊗ 8am-4pm Tue-Sun) While the museum houses an ethnographic and natural-sciences section, as well as an aquarium displaying Danubian species, the highlight is a scale model of the Roman bridge constructed across the Danube in AD 103 by Greek architect Apollodorus of Damascus on orders of Emperor Trajan (r AD 98–117). The bridge stood just below the site of the present museum, and the ruins (ruinele podului lui Traian) of two of its pillars can still be seen towering beside the Danube.

In its day the bridge was a tremendous feat of engineering and was more than 1100m in length and 15m wide. Nearby, you'll see scattered pieces of rock and de-bris that were once part of a Roman bath and colony along the banks of the river. The museum is located on the far eastern end of B-dul Carol I.

Water Tower   HISTORIC BUILDING
(Castelul de Apă; cnr Str Crisan & Str Dr Saidac; ⊗ 9am-9pm) FREE Severin's most striking building is this massive water tower, dating from 1910. It was one of the first buildings here to use iron in its construction. These days you can climb up the 159 steps to the top for views out over the Danube (or take the lift). It's located about six blocks north of B-dul Carol I, following Str Bibicescu.

Medieval Fortress of Severin   RUINS
(Str Portului; ⊗ dawn-dusk) FREE Just above the port and below the Hotel Continental, these restored ruins mark the spot where the mighty Fortress of Severin once stood. The fort dates from the 11th century and marked the border between the Hungarian Kingdom and the Bulgarian Empire. It was demolished in the 16th century on the orders of the then-ruling Ottoman Turks. There's not much to see now except a very tall tower and the thick walls of this legendary redoubt.

🛏 Sleeping

There are a number of roadside *pensiunes,* motels and restaurants on the main E70 highway, signposted as Str Tudor Vladimirescu, about 2km north of the town centre.

★ Hotel Corona — HOTEL $$

(✆ 0743-128 658; www.hotelcorona.ro; Str Tudor Vladimirescu 106a; s/d 150/180 lei; P ➔ ❋ @ 🛜) This clean, smart and well-run hotel occupies a nondescript strip of shops along Hwy E70, but it's set back from the highway so noise is not an issue. The rooms are bright and furnished in contemporary style. The reception is friendly and the restaurant, while lacking atmosphere, serves very good food. It's about 1km northeast of the centre of town.

Hotel Continental — HOTEL $$

(✆ 0372-528 828, reservations 0372-121 721; www.continentalhotels.ro; B-dul Carol I 2; s/d from 180/200 lei; P ➔ ❋ @ 🛜) This battered-looking high-rise from the 1970s is much nicer on the inside and the location is as good as it gets: on a ridge above the river and within walking distance of the sights. Rooms come in two categories, standard and deluxe, with the latter offering river views and updated furnishings. The reception desk has a local map.

🍴 Eating & Drinking

Along with restaurants on the E70, there's a lively **market** (Piaţa Mircea; cnr Str Horia & Str Dr Saidac; ⊙ 6am-9pm Mon-Fri, 7am-2pm Sat & Sun) just east of the town centre where you can buy fresh fruit and vegetables, breads and cheeses.

★ Trattoria Il Calcio — ITALIAN $$

(✆ 0753-118 070; www.trattoriailcalcio.ro; B-dul Tudor Vladimirescu 143; mains 20-30 lei; ⊙ 11am-midnight; 🛜) This is the local branch of a Romanian chain of Italian restaurants, but don't let that deter you. The food and service are excellent. It's in the new part of town, along the E70 highway in the direction of Craiova, about 1km north of B-dul Carol I, following Str Eminescu.

Taverna Sârbului — BALKAN $$$

(✆ 0727-353 353; www.tavernasarbului.ro; Hwy E70; mains 30-50 lei; ⊙ 9am-midnight; 🛜) Located 5km west of Drobeta-Turnu Severin along the main highway in the direction of Orşova, this Serbian-themed restaurant boasts beautiful views of the Danube and a long list of Balkan and Romanian specialities, grilled meats, stews and salads. It's 10 minutes by car from the centre of town; a taxi will run about 15 lei each way.

16,50 — BAR

(✆ 0774-431 991; www.1650.ro; Str Traian 50; ⊙ 11am-2am) About as cool as it gets in sleepy Severin. There's decent pizza and other nosh on hand, as well as a garden terrace furnished with wrought-iron sofas and chairs covered in big white pillows. Around sunset this place morphs into a fully fledged club-lounge. It's located three blocks north of B-dul Carol I, just west of the Hotel Continental.

ℹ Information

There is no central tourist information office, though there are large city maps posted at intervals around town, particulary along B-dul Carol I. The reception desk at the Hotel Continental has city maps for guests.

BRD (✆ 0252-316 074; B-dul Carol I 55, cnr Str Rahovei; ⊙ 9am-7pm Mon-Fri) One of several banks and ATMs scattered around town; located about two blocks east of the Hotel Continental near B-dul Carol I.

Post Office (Str Decebal 41; ⊙ 7am-8pm Mon-Fri, 8am-1pm Sat) The post office is situated one block north of B-dul Carol I, about 50m from the Hotel Continental.

ℹ Getting There & Away

BUS

Drobeta-Turnu Severin, as with many Romanian towns and cities, has more than one bus and minibus station. Many long-haul buses and minibuses merely service designated stops along the E70. Check details by enquiring at your hotel or consulting the website www.autogari.ro. Buses and minibuses service the entire region, with frequent departures for Orşova (3 lei, 30 minutes) and Timişoara (40 lei, four hours), among other cities.

TRAIN

The **train station** (Gara; www.cfr.ro; B-dul Dunărea) is located along the Danube River on the extreme western edge of the port, about 2km from the centre of town. On arrival at the station, hike up the steps and turn right (east) on B-dul Carol I to reach the centre or take a taxi (around 8 lei). The city has good train connections to both Bucharest (about 70 lei, five hours, five daily) and Timişoara (60 lei, four hours, four daily). Bucharest-bound trains stop in Craiova (35 lei, two to three hours). There are one or two daily trains to Orşova (5 lei, 25 minutes).

Transylvania

Best Places to Eat

➡ Szentgyörgy Pince (p119)

➡ Kulinarium (p113)

➡ Crama Veche (p148)

➡ Basa Fogadó (p122)

➡ Sergiana (p90)

➡ Roata (p141)

Best Places to Sleep

➡ Villa Hermani (p98)

➡ Youthink Hostel (p140)

➡ Casa Luxemburg (p113)

➡ Lol & Lola (p140)

➡ Select City Center (p90)

➡ Casa Georgius Krauss (p103)

Why Go?

Transylvania's forested valleys and Gothic castles are forever embedded in the popular imagination. Even before arriving, most visitors can picture this land of dark fairy-tales, where fog drapes like cobwebs over the Carpathian Mountains.

Explore these stirring landscapes on hikes through Piatra Craiului National Park, or the Bucegi (and tougher Apuseni) Mountains; or see them frozen over at winter sports centres Poiana Braşov and Predeal. Next, indulge your medieval fantasies among the watchtowers and lanes of Braşov and Sighişoara or venture to Transylvania's castles: world-famous Bran, ornate Peleş, and Hunedoara's Gothic apparition.

Deeper in the countryside, rural Transylvania's tapestry of cultures awaits: vibrant, secretive Roma communities, Székely Land hamlets where only Hungarian is spoken, and Saxon villages with crumbling citadels. And yes, Transylvania will satisfy vampire tourists – and enthral all with its jumble of edgy cities and villages that time forgot.

When to Go
Braşov

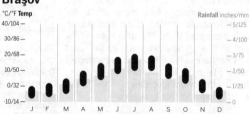

May Mild weather and meadows of wildflowers; go hiking in Piatra Craiului and Bucegi Mountains.

Jun–Sep Peak season for hiking, and medieval cities like Braşov and Sighişoara are in full swing.

Dec–Mar Check snow forecasts and head to ski slopes in Poiana Braşov.

History

Though they lived in the 5th century BC, the Dacians still elicit pride among modern Transylvanians. Fascinating traces of their history remain: metalwork, remnants of their fortifications, and even temples, such as at the Sarmizegetusa Regia archaeological site. As the Roman Empire marched across the Balkans, Dacian civilisation fizzled away. When Rome withdrew in AD 271, centuries of skirmishes followed between Huns, Slavs, Visigoths and other tribes.

For 1000 years, up until WWI, Transylvania was associated with Hungary. In the 10th century, at the behest of Stephen I of Hungary, the Székelys (a Magyar, Hungarian, tribe) settled in what they called Erdély ('beyond the forest' – the root meaning of Transylvania). In the 12th century, Saxon merchants arrived to help defend the eastern frontiers of Hungary. The seven towns they founded – Bistriţa (Bistritz), Braşov (Kronstadt), Cluj-Napoca (Klausenburg), Mediaş (Mediasch), Sebeş (Mühlbach), Sibiu (Hermannstadt) and Sighişoara (Schässburg) – gave Transylvania its German name, Siebenbürgen.

Medieval Transylvania was autonomously ruled by a prince accountable to the Hungarian crown, while the indigenous Romanians were serfs. After the 1526 Turkish defeat of Hungary the region became semi-independent, recognising Turkish suzerainty. In 1683 Turkish power was broken and Transylvania came under Habsburg rule four years later. After 1867 Transylvania was fully absorbed into Austria-Hungary. In 1918, after Austria-Hungary's defeat in World War I, Romanians gathered at Alba Iulia to demand Transylvania's union with Romania.

This unification has never been fully accepted by Hungary, and from 1940 to 1944 it set about re-annexing much of the region. After the war, Romanian communists moved to quash Hungarian nationalist sentiments. In ensuing decades, feelings of resentment subsided somewhat and Romania's relations with its western neighbour calmed.

PRAHOVA VALLEY

Wallachia funnels into Transylvania in this narrow valley at the foot of the fir-clad Bucegi Mountains. Sinaia, a king's summer retreat a century ago, is the finest town, but the real draw is up, way up, with hiking and biking trails along the flat plateau atop the mountains, and ski trails that carve down the mountainsides. If you're looking for just a taste, it's possible to do a day trip from Braşov, and take a cable-car ride up for a short hike. But it's easier if you stay a night or two.

Sinaia

POP 11,600

Nestled in a slender fir-clad valley, Sinaia teems with hikers in summer and skiers in winter. Backed by the imposing crags of the Bucegi Mountains, it's a dramatic place for a to hike for the day, or, using the network of cabanas open to walkers, several days.

The town itself is a melange of crayon-coloured wooden houses contrasted with the 'wedding-cake' style of its grander 19th-century buildings. Once home to Romania's first king, Carol I, who created a summer retreat here, Peleş Castle is a dream of hidden passages, fairy-tale turrets, vertiginous galleries and classical statues; it's so beguilingly imaginative, it could raise a swoon from the most hardened cynic.

Sinaia is administratively part of Wallachia but is most easily reached from Transylvania.

◉ Sights

★ **Peleş Castle** PALACE

(www.peles.ro; tour adult/senior/child 20/10/5 lei; ⊙9am-5pm Tue-Sun) Over 40 years, dozens of builders, artists and wood-carvers brought Peleş Castle into existence. The neo-Renaissance masterpiece was commissioned by Romania's first king, Carol I, and its first stone laid in 1875. Today this former royal summer residence is a wildly popular tourist attraction. Visits are by compulsory 40-minute guided tour; photographing inside costs a steep additional 32 lei. Inside, not a single corner is empty of silk rugs, Murano glass, carved walnut or polished marble.

In the Honorary Hallway, note the Swiss and German landscapes, fashioned from inlaid wood, to remind the king of his homeland. Beyond Iraqi carpets and alabaster Biblical scenes, you'll enter an Arms Room brimming with armour for men and

TRANSYLVANIA SINAIA

Transylvania Highlights

1 Sighişoara (p98)
Tripping along the cobbled lanes of this medieval town.

2 Fortified Saxon Villages (p104)
Marvelling at lost-in-time citadels surrounded by green meadowland, such as at charming Biertan and Viscri.

3 Libearty Bear Sanctuary (p96)
Holding your breath in a bear hide, or watching mighty mammals recuperate.

4 Apuseni Mountains (p145) Exploring the rugged Apuseni Mountains on foot or bike.

5 Bran Castle (p93) Suppressing a shiver at spooky Bran Castle, before roaming windswept ramparts at nearby Râşnov Fortress.

6 Corvin Castle (p134) Blinking in amazement at the Gothic turrets of Hunedoara's spellbinding castle, seemingly plucked from darkest fairy-tale.

7 Alba Carolina Citadel (p131) Strolling or cycling Alba Iulia's star-shaped citadel, the largest in Romania.

8 Bârgău Valley (p147) Drinking in panoramas of this scenic valley, immortalised in Bram Stoker's *Dracula*.

9 Cluj-Napoca (p136) Delving into the hidden life of an arty, festival-rich city with rough charm.

10 Sibiu (p109) Admiring baroque buildings and enjoying the cafe culture of this genteel town.

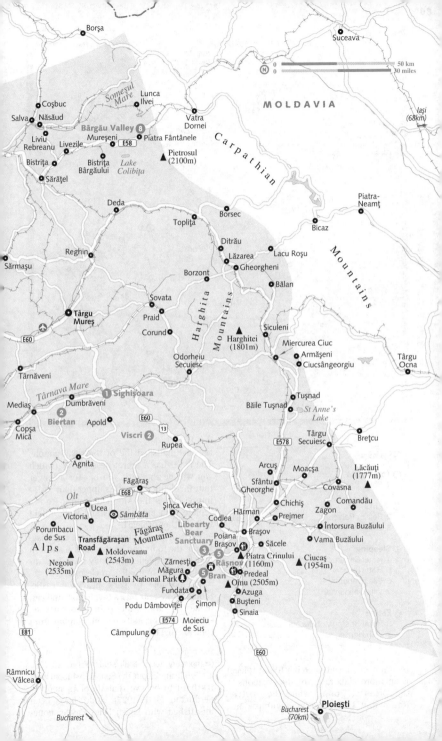

Sinaia

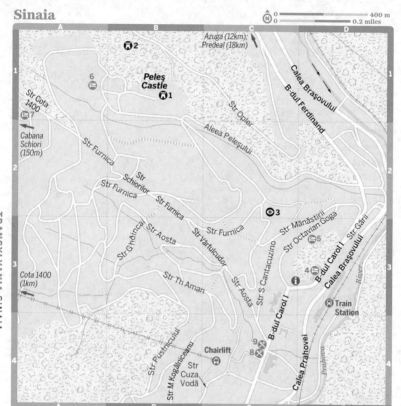

TRANSYLVANIA SINAIA

their horses (the latter weigh 100kg apiece). Even more elaborate are the weapons in the **Oriental Room**, while the **Portrait Room** and **Library** offer a glimpse into the distinguished life of the royal couple. The latter has a secret passageway (which you will be shown if you opt for a longer tour involving the castle's upper floor). Also impressive is the Moorish **Dining Room**, replete with brass lamps and walls inlaid with mother-of-pearl.

Even in peak summer season, organisation of the tours can be threadbare and you may have to queue, especially if you're waiting for a tour in English or German.

It's possible to park near the castle, though large tour buses turning around can make the parking lots painful to navigate. Otherwise it's a half-hour hike uphill from central Sinaia.

Pelişor Palace PALACE
(compulsory tours adult/student/child 20/10/5 lei; ⊙ 9.15am-4.15pm Thu-Sun, 11.15-4.15pm Wed) It's hard to believe that Carol I's nephew Ferdinand (1865–1927) could have been unsatisfied with lavish Peleş Castle; none-

theless, Pelişor Palace was built for him just next door. The smaller, art nouveau palace stands about 100m uphill from Peleş. Ferdinand's wife Queen Mary acted as Pelişor's interior designer, filling it with imported Viennese furniture. Entry is by 45-minute guided tour.

Queen Mary died in the Golden Room, the walls of which are entirely covered in gilded leaves.

Sinaia Monastery
MONASTERY

(Str Mănăstirii; 5 lei; ⊙10am-4pm Mon-Sat) The church and monks' cells on this site during the 17th century weren't ample enough to accommodate Sinaia's growing religious community, so in 1846 this serene complex was built. Its main church is a marvel of carved floral decoration, with oil paintings within. Easily as magnificent as the church itself is the backdrop of forested mountains.

🏃 Activities

Skiing and hiking are the main draws in the Bucegi with a good range of basic, intermediate and advanced runs, and similarly challenging walking routes.

Take the **Telecabina Sinaia** (www.teleferic. ro/sinaia; Str Cuza Vodă; return adult/child 25/14 lei, with bike 70 lei; ⊙8.30am-5.30pm summer, to 4.30pm winter, closed some Mon mornings) to Cota 1400, a festive scene with sleds to hire, open-air grills, a ski-hire shop and chairlift. From here you can also take the second cable car, **Telecabina Cota 1400-2000** (www.teleferic.ro/sinaia; one-way adult/child 35/17 lei, with bike 70 lei; ⊙8.30am-6pm summer, to 5pm winter, closed some Mon mornings). Between late-December and mid-March, this accesses some 20km of cross-country skiing, as well as a dozen pistes of which half suit intermediate levels (red), with a few black (advanced) and blue (beginners) runs too.

In summer the trails (at least 30 to choose from) are great for hikers.

🛏 Sleeping

Midrange to top-end hotels clamour to mimic Peleş Castle's grandeur (with varying degrees of success), so you'll find no shortage of atmospheric places to sleep in Sinaia. At the budget end of the range, the area also has plentiful pensions and hiking chalets.

Hotel Caraiman
HOTEL $$

(☑0244-312 051; www.caraimansinaia.ro; B-dul Carol I, 4; s/d/ste 165/212/270 lei; P🐕) Built in 1880, this austere yet welcoming hotel has bags of atmosphere, only slightly diminished by the number of tour groups pouring in. Some might gripe that attentive staff and a more thorough cleaning service would lift Hotel Caraiman's game, though these are small quibbles compared to its stained glass, chandeliers and sweeping stairways that once felt the footfall of Transylvania's elite.

Hotel Palace
HOTEL $$

(☑0244-312 052; www.palacesinaia.ro; Str O Goga 4; s 175 lei, d 212-270 lei; P🐕) If you're hankering for a high-end stay after exploring Peleş Castle, the 1911-built Hotel Palace assures a regal experience. Rooms have high ceilings, crimson carpets and supple beds fit for a prince. Room prices vary by size and view; opt for one with a balcony overlooking the park, if you can.

Villa Oblique
SPA HOTEL $$$

(☑0344-883 992; www.villaoblique.ro; Str Cota 1400, 3A; d from €85; P🐕) Treat yourself to an intimate getaway at this spa hotel, 700m west of Peleş Castle. There's a sauna and hot tub to linger in before you retreat to a regally furnished room with billowing drapes, high ceilings and cushioned headboards. In summer you can barbecue on the terrace, while in winter there's ski storage available.

Vila Economat
HOTEL $$$

(☑0725-310 700, 0244-311 151; Aleea Peleşului 2; d from 290 lei; P🐕) This gingerbread-roofed hotel looks to be transplanted straight from Hansel and Gretel, while inside its rooms are crisp and elegant. The location, right near Peleş Castle in the former offices of the Royal Guard, is hard to beat, and the buffet breakfasts are superb.

🍴 Eating

Hotel-Restaurant Bucegi
EASTERN EUROPEAN $$

(☑0244-312 217; www.hotelbucegisinaia.ro; B-dul Carol I, 22; mains 25-40 lei; ⊙noon-10pm) With catfish fillet, frogs' legs and pastrami of bear, this restaurant with a hint of Alpine ambiance has Sinaia's most interesting menu. If venison or tripe soup sounds heavy, you can fall back on comfort food such as Ukrainian beetroot broth or crisp Bulgarian salads.

TRANSYLVANIA SINAIA

Irish House
INTERNATIONAL $$

(www.irishhouse.ro; B-dul Carol I, 80; mains 15-25 lei; ☉8am-midnight) Eat inside or out at this busy central watering hole, popular with families and après-skiers. Service is a little slow, but coffees are suitably frothy and there's a menu spanning pancakes, pizzas and cheesy chicken schnitzels.

ℹ️ Information

Sinaia Tourism Information Centre (☑0244-315 656; www.info-sinaia.ro; B-dul Carol I, 47; ☉9am-5pm Mon-Fri) This dinky office offers free local maps, excellent hiking advice, and info on upcoming events. An essential stop before any hiking trip.

ℹ️ Getting There & Away

Sinaia and Predeal are the best connected towns in the Prahova Valley: both are on the Bucharest–Braşov train line, and have almost hourly services to each. Both towns are also served by less frequent bus services to Bucharest and Braşov. Half-hourly buses travel between Sinaia and Predeal (6 to 8 lei, 40 minutes), stopping at Buşteni.

ℹ️ Getting Around

Once arrived in the region, the best way into the Bucegi Mountains is by cable car. Hop aboard Telecabina Sinaia to reach Cota 1400 midstation, from where you can ascend even higher via Telecabina Cota 1400-2000 (hiking trails begin from both stations). From Buşteni, the cable car takes you to Cabana Babele, also an excellent starting point for treks.

Bucegi Mountains

Rising to 2505m at their tallest, the Bucegi Mountains are popular with hikers for their unspoiled scenery. This raw wilderness comes with perils: there's a sizeable population of bears and some trails are poorly marked. The Bucegi have a decent network of cabanas to shelter, eat or sleep in, but preparation is key in this high-altitude adventure playground. June to September is best for hiking (though thunderstorms are common). Winters are severe and avalanches are a particular peril during the thaw.

🛏️ Sleeping

Camping in Bucegi is only allowed in clearly signed areas and is, in fact, not altogether recommended due to the possibility of bear encounters. Cabanas provide blankets. It's sometimes hard to reserve a spot in cabanas, but they'll always make space.

Cabana Zănoaga
CABIN $

(☑0741-588 724, 0786-781 672; www.cabana zanoaga.ro; dm/d/tr 40/100/150 lei; P❄️🛜) Simple rooms for hikers, a 20-minute walk from Lake Bolboci.

Cabana Gura Diham
CABIN $

(☑0731-354 100, 0244-321 108; www.gura-diham. ro; d 110 lei; 🛜) There's been an inn on this spot since 1910, but what stands today is a thoroughly renovated modern chalet and restaurant. Rooms are simple and it serves protein-rich hiking fuel like roast lamb and soup in bread bowls, along with warming fruit brandies.

Hotel Peştera
HOTEL $$

(☑0372-733 321; www.hotelpestera.ro; d from 220 lei; P) Comfortable modern rooms with safes, mini-bars and balconies with mountain views fill this 1600m-altitude hotel, near the cave monastery.

Cabana Schiori
B&B $$

(☑0244-313 655; www.cabana-schiori.ro; Str Drumul Cotei 7; d/ste from 190/225 lei; P🛜) Some 3km from central Sinaia, this alpine lodge offers plain though homely rooms with modern fittings like flat-screens, fridges and nice bathrooms; the best rooms have balconies with mountain views. There's a chic on-site restaurant that serves schnitzels, grilled trout and (save space) *papanasi* (donuts).

Cabana Stâna Târle
CHALET $$$

(☑0731-131 953; www.stanatarle.ro; Cota 1400; d €85; 🛜) With open fires, stone walls, the scent of pine, and even a small spa (€10), this outdoorsy lodge offers a hint of luxe at 1578m altitude. Ask the welcoming owners about climbing and mountain biking.

🍴 Eating

Most cabanas have a cafe of some description but it's strongly advisable to bring food supplies on hikes.

ℹ️ Getting There & Away

The easiest way into the Bucegi from Sinaia is by cable-car. Telecabina Sinaia goes from the centre to the Cota 1400 station. From here, Telecabina Cota 1400-2000 reaches the top. In the centre, the 30-person cable-car leaves half-hourly with two station points marked by

Bucegi Mountains

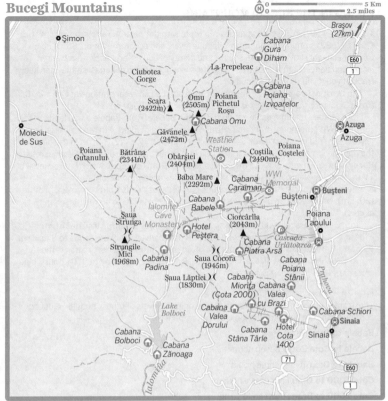

elevation. A taxi from the train station to Cota 1400 is a matter of negotiation, though expect to pay about 50 lei for the whole cab.

Roads wind up from route 71 south of the mountains all the way to Cabana Babele – although much of the road as far as Cabana Piatra Arsă is in just about passable condition, ordinary cars may struggle.

Predeal

POP 5615

Folks have been carving up mountainsides for well over a century in Predeal's ski resort. This small mountain town has a higher base elevation than neighbouring winter sports areas Poiana Braşov and Sinaia, though its runs aren't as long. Dappled with purpose-built ski lodges and three-star hotels, along with modern churches and a sci-fi-style train station, the town doesn't match the majesty of its sur-rounding mountains. But it's well equipped as an outdoor hub, with plenty of sports gear rental and ski schools. Hikers pace through Predeal in summer, and there are a few trails from town that are easy to do within a day.

🏃 Activities

There are great hiking options right from town; pick up a map from the Tourist Information Centre.

Carinthia Ski School   SKIING
(☎ 0723-931 259; www.tabere-carinthia.ro; Str Liviu Rebreanu 2; instruction per hour for group of 1/2/3 learners 80/70/60 lei; ⊕) This winter sports school offers expert instruction for skiers and boarders of all levels; book ahead. Carinithia also offers multi-day winter sports training camps for children.

Ski and snowboard rental is also available here.

HIKING IN THE BUCEGI MOUNTAINS

This is tricky terrain. Discuss your desired route with the Sinaia Tourism Information Centre (p82), confirming duration, difficulty levels and accommodation. Stock up on torch (flashlight) batteries, take snacks and plenty of liquids, and pack a lightweight jacket and fleece. Sign tourist traffic registers when you leave cabanas, so they can keep track of you if you run into difficulty.

The two most common starting points are from the cable-car stations at Cota 2000 (from Sinaia) or from Cabana Babele (in neighbouring Buşteni).

From Buşteni take the cable car up to Cabana Babele. From Babele a trail leads to the 15m-high WWI memorial cross at 2291m (one hour; it's marked with red crosses). From here a path (red crosses) leads to the top of Caraiman Peak (2384m). On the peak the path becomes wider, turning into a trail that continues towards Omu Peak across Bucegi Plateau. It gets close to the Coştila Peak (2490m) on top of which is a rocket-like TV transmitter. Nearby is a weather station that has accommodation.

Alternatively, a trail (three to four hours, blue crosses) leads from Cabana Caraiman (2025m), where you can pick up the trail to the WWI cross (30 to 45 minutes, red circles).

From Cabana Babele you can hike south following a yellow-stripe trail to Cabana Piatra Arsă (1950m). From here you can pick up a blue trail that descends to Sinaia via Cabana Poiana Stânii (three hours). An even more interesting destination is the Ialomiţei Cave Monastery (Mănăstirea Peştera Ialomiţei), accessible by trail (1½ hours, blue crosses). Hotel Peştera is nearby.

Hiking Times

These are average times. People with higher or lower levels of fitness should adjust accordingly. Browse hiking routes on www.bucegipark.ro.

Babele to Bran Nine hours

Babele to Cota 2000 Seven hours

Babele to Omu Two or three hours

Cota 2000 to Omu Four or five hours

Cota 2000 to Bran Fourteen to 16 hours

Omu to Bran Eight hours

Predeal Ski Resort SKIING
(day-pass adult/child 140/72 lei; ☉ lifts 8.30am-5pm Dec-Mar) Across an altitude difference of 480m, more than half of Predeal's 8.5km of pistes are suitable for intermediate skiers and snowboarders, with a couple of kilometres each at beginner (blue) and advanced (black) levels.

🛏 Sleeping

The road to the lift is increasingly crowded with new three- and four-star places, but simple pensions (often with attached ski hire or hiking guide outfits) are the norm. A couple of plush hotels are in the Trei Brazi district, 6km northwest.

Vila Şoimulm GUESTHOUSE $
(☎0368-104 260, 0745-150 995; www.vilasoimul. ro; Str Şoimului 4; d/tr 90/120 lei; P🖭🛜) With its faux log-cabin exterior and excellent self-catering area, this 18-room guesthouse is a winner. Rooms have fresh white walls, even fresher linen and mini-fridges, and ski storage is available. It's up a street behind the white church, the opposite side of the main road to the train station.

As in many places, rates are 10% lower during the low ski season (November to December). Minimum two-night stay at weekends.

Fulg de Nea HOTEL $
(☎0741-259 565, 0268-455 463; www.cabana fulgdenea.ro; Str Teleferic 1; d/tr/q 150/175/210 lei; P🖭🛜) This pleasant three-star has no-frills rooms and an inviting restaurant with grotto-effect walls, strung with skiing paraphernalia. It is next ext to the button lift.

ℹ Information

Salvamont (☑ 0725-826 668, 0-SALVAMONT)
Mountain rescue emergency helpline.

Tourist Information Centre (☑ 0268-455 330;
www.predeal.ro; Str Intrarea Gării 1; ⊘10am-
6pm) Helpful information kiosk facing the
train station, offering maps, hiking advice and
updates on winter sports conditions.

ℹ Getting There & Away

The **train station** (B-dul Mihail Săulescu) and
bus/maxitaxi stop are right on the main street,
B-dul Mihail Săulescu, which goes north to
Braşov and south to Sinaia and Bucharest. The
lifts are a 10-minute walk southeast.

Predeal is on the main Cluj-Napoca–Braşov–
Bucharest line and you'll never wait long for a
train heading to Braşov (13 lei, 40 minutes, 20
daily) or Bucharest (18 to 40 lei, two to three
hours, 19 daily). Outside, buses or maxitaxis
show up almost half-hourly in the train-station
parking lot heading for Braşov (6 to 8 lei, 30 to
50 minutes) or Sinaia (6 to 8 lei, 40 minutes).
Less frequent buses reach Bucharest (38 lei,
three hours, four daily).

BRAŞOV

POP 275,000

Gothic spires, medieval gateways, Soviet
blocks and a huge Hollywood-style sign:
Braşov's skyline is instantly compelling.
A number of medieval watchtowers still
glower over the town. Between them sparkle baroque buildings and churches, while
easy-going cafes line main square Piaţa Sfatului. Visible from here is forested Mt Tâmpa,
sporting 'Braşov' in huge white letters.

According to local legend, the Pied Piper
of Hamelin reemerged in Braşov. Indeed,
this playful town has many tales as colourful as its pastel-hued streets. Locals will ea-
gerly spin a yarn about Vlad the Impaler's
romantic dalliances, a noblewoman revived
from her grave, and the time a bear wad-
dled into the main square (at least the last
one's true).

Braşov is a good base for skiing in nearby
Poiana Braşov, or trekking in Piatra Craiului
National Park, 30km west. Most travellers
use it as a gateway to castles in Bran and
Râşnov.

History

Though sporadically settled since 100 BC,
the town was established on an ancient Dacian site in AD 1211 by Teutonic knights. Its
old Roman name, Corona, is still reflected
in the crown on the town's coat of arms.
Braşov grew into a German mercantile
colony named Kronstadt (Brassó in Hungarian). The Saxons built ornate churches
and townhouses, protected by a massive
wall that still remains. The Romanians
lived at Schei, just outside the walls, to the
southwest.

One of the first public oppositions to the
Ceauşescu government flared up here in
1987. Thousands of disgruntled workers took
to the streets demanding basic foodstuffs.
Ceauşescu called in the troops and quashed
the uprising, though it paved the way for
protests across Romania that would topple
the regime two years later.

◉ Sights

◉ Central Braşov

Black Church CHURCH
(Biserica Neagră; ☑ 0268-511 824; www.honterus
gemeinde.ro; Curtea Johannes Honterus 2; adult/
student/child 9/6/3 lei; ⊘10am-7pm Tue-Sat
& noon-7pm Sun Apr-Oct, 10am-3pm Tue-Sat &
noon-3pm Sun Nov-Mar) Romania's largest
Gothic church rises triumphantly over
Braşov's old town. Built between 1385 and
1477, this German Lutheran church was
named for its charred appearance after the
town's Great Fire in 1689. Restoration of
the church took a century. Today it towers
65m high at its bell tower's tallest point.
Organ recitals are held in the church three
times a week during July and August,
usually at 6pm Tuesday, Thursday and
Saturday.

Draped across the church's spare interior
are 16th- to 19th-century Anatolian rugs;
these were once placed on pews reserved
for church donors. Look closely at the columns, a couple of which bear scars from
projectiles fired into the church during the
events of 1989. Find also a collection of ornate funerary stones and a 4000-pipe organ
(1839).

The exterior of the church bears scrape
marks, thought to be from soldiers sharpen-
ing their swords – after all, who better than
God to prime a weapon for battle?

Piaţa Sfatului SQUARE
This wide square, lined with cafes, was once
the heart of medieval Braşov. In the centre
stands the 1420 Council House (Casa Sfatului), topped by the Trumpeter's Tower, in

TRANSYLVANIA BRAŞOV

Braşov

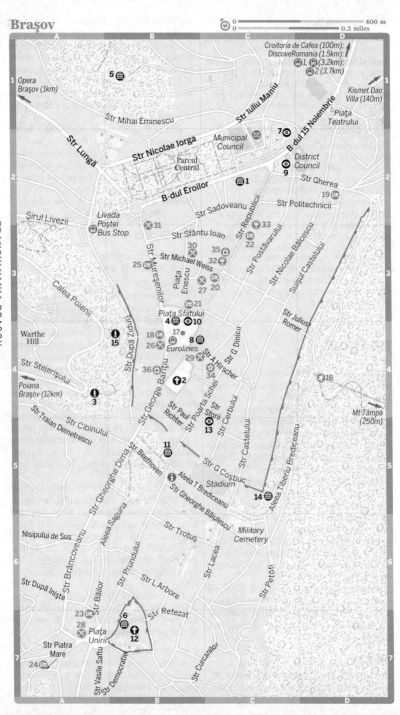

0 400 m
0 0.2 miles

Croitoria de Cafea (100m);
DiscoveRomania (1.5km);
I. (3.2km);
2 (3.7km)

Kismet Dao
Villa (140m)

Opera
Braşov (1km)

Str Mihai Eminescu

Str Nicolae Iorga

Str Iuliu Maniu

Piaţa
Teatrului

Str Lungă

Municipal
Council

B-dul 15 Noiembrie

Parcul
Central

7

District
Council

9

Str Gherea

B-dul Eroilor

1

Str Sadoveanu

Str Politechnicii

19

Şirul Livezii

Livada
Poştei
Bus Stop

31

Str Sfântu Ioan

Str Republicii

33

22

Calea Poienii

Str Mureşenilor

25

Str Michael Weiss

30

35

32

Str Nicolae Bălcescu

Suişul Castelului

27

20

Piaţa
Enescu

Warthe
Hill

21

Str Dima

Impiz Dima

Piaţa Sfatului

4

10

Str Julius
Romer

15

18

17

26

8

Eurolines

Str Stejerişului

29

Str A Hirscher

Str G Dimiu

34

Poiana
Braşov (12km)

3

36

2

16

Str George Bariţiu

Str Paul
Richter

Str Poarta Schei

Str
Sforii

Str Cerbului

Mt Tâmpa
(250m)

Str Cibinului

13

Str Castelului

Str Traian Demetrescu

Str Gheorghe Dima

Str Beethoven

11

Str G Coşbuc

Stadium

14

Aleea T Brediceanu

Str Gheorghe Băiulescu

Aleea Tiberiu Brediceanu

Nisipului de Sus

Aleea Saguna

Str Trotuş

Military
Cemetery

Str Lacea

Str Petofi

Str Brâncoveanu

Str Prundului

Str L Arbore

Str Curcanilor

Str Băilor

23

6

Str Retezat

28

Piaţa
Unirii

12

Str Piatra
Mare

24

Str Vasile Saftu

Str Democraţiei

5

Braşov

TRANSYLVANIA BRAŞOV

which town councillors would meet. These days at midday, traditionally costumed musicians appear at the top of the tower like figures in a Swiss clock.

Braşov Historical Museum MUSEUM
(www.brasovistorie.ro; Piaţa Sfatului; adult/student 7/1.50 lei; ☉10am-6pm Tue-Sun) The old City Hall houses the two-floor, by-the-numbers Braşov Historical Museum, in which the region's history from Roman times via medieval military history to the Saxon guilds is recounted (sometimes in English).

Hirscher House HISTORIC BUILDING
(Str Apollonia Hirscher) The Renaissance Hirscher House, completed in 1545, was once the largest building in Braşov. It was commissioned by Apollonia Hirscher, the widow of Braşov mayor Lucas Hirscher, so that merchants could do business without getting rained on.

Strada Sforii HISTORIC SITE
(www.stradasforii.ro) Formerly an access route for firefighters, Strada Sforii is one of the narrowest streets in Europe at 1.2m wide. Lurid tales have sprung up about Vlad Ţepeş snatching a kiss from his future wife in this very lane, but it's mostly modern-day lovers who squeeze through.

East of the Centre

Mt Tâmpa MOUNTAIN
(Muntele Tâmpa) Rising 940m high and visible around Braşov, Mt Tâmpa is adorned with its very own Hollywood-style sign. Hard as it is to imagine, it was the site of a mass-impaling of 40 noblemen by Vlad Ţepeş. Banish such ghoulish images from your head as you take the cable car (Telecabina; ☎0268-478 657; Aleea Tiberiu Brediceanu; adult one way/return 10/16 lei, child one way/return 6/9 lei; ☉9.30am-5pm Tue-Sun, noon-6pm Mon), or hike (about an hour), to reach a small viewing platform offering stunning views over the city. There's a slightly drab cafe at the top.

North of the Centre

Running north of Piaţa Sfatului, the pedestrianised Str Republicii provides respite from the traffic that detracts from the charm of the rest of the Old Town. At the promenade's northern end is the wooden-cross Memorial to Victims of the 1989 Revolution (cnr Str Republicii & B-dul 15 Noiembrie). Across B-dul 15 de Noiembrie is the Heroes' Cemetery (B-dul 15 de Noiembrie), a memorial slab listing 69 local victims.

A block west of the memorial, the Art Museum (Muzeul de Artă; ☑ 0268-477 286; www.muzeulartabv.ro; B-dul Eroilor 21; adult/student 5/1 lei; ☺ 10am-6pm Tue-Sun) and the Ethnographic Museum (☑ 0268-476 243; www.etnobrasov.ro; B-dul Eroilor 21A; adult/student 5/2 lei; ☺ 10am-6pm Tue-Sun summer, 9am-5pm Tue-Sun winter) adjoin each other. The former has a mishmash of Romanian paintings and decorative arts. The latter has laminated handouts in several languages explaining how hemp and goat hair were transformed into Transylvania's traditional scarlet and white village-wear.

Citadel HISTORIC BUILDING
(Cetatea; Dealul Cetatii; ☺ 11am-midnight) `FREE`
In 1524 a new wooden citadel was built in Braşov, on top of Citadel Hill just north, though the stone wall ruins you now see are from the 16th and 17th centuries. It's a steep trek from the old town, but these old walls are a pleasant spot to watch the sun set over Braşov.

◉ Around the Walls

Old Braşov was once enclosed by mighty fortified walls, 12m high and more than 3km-long. Built in stages between 1400 and 1650, these walls and defence towers were built in anticipation of attacks by the Turks. The most popular viewing area is along the western section, which runs along a stream and pedestrianised Str După Ziduri, north towards B-dul Eroilor. A good access point is 200m south of the Black Church.

Seven bastions were raised around the city at the most exposed points, each one defended by a guild whose members, pending danger, tolled their bastion bell. Above on the hillside are two towers – the Black Tower (Turnul Negru) and White Tower (Turnul Alb) – offering nice views, particularly when the setting sun casts a golden hue on Braşov.

On the wall's southeast corner, past the Schei Gate (Str Poarta Schei), is the 16th-century Weavers' Bastion. Visit the Weavers' Bastion Museum (Muzeul Bastionul Ţesătorilor; Str George Coşbuc 9; adult/child 7/4 lei; ☺ 10am-6pm Tue-Sun), housed in Braşov's only 15th-century building. The simple exhibits – in German and Romanian only – include an impressive cityscape model of Braşov in the 17th century, made in 1896 by a German teacher.

◉ Schei District

In Saxon Braşov, Romanians were not allowed to enter the walled city but were banished to the Schei quarter in the southwest. Entry to this quarter from the walled city was marked by the Schei Gate.

St Nicholas' Cathedral CHURCH
(Biserica Sfântul Nicolae; Piaţa Unirii 1; ☺ 7am-7pm) With forested hills rising behind its prickly Gothic spires, St Nicholas' Cathedral is one of Braşov's most spectacular views. First built in wood in 1392, it was replaced by a Gothic stone church in 1495 and later embellished in Byzantine style. It was once enclosed by military walls; today the site has a small cemetery. Inside are murals of Romania's last king and queen, covered by plaster to protect them from communist leaders and uncovered in 2004.

First Romanian School Museum MUSEUM
(Prima Şcoala Românească; www.primascoalaromaneasca.ro; Piaţa Unirii 2-3; adult/student/child 10/5/5 lei; ☺ 10am-5pm Tue-Sun) This venerable museum near St Nicholas' Cathedral time-travels into the history of Romanian education. Students have been educated on this site since the late 16th century. The museum houses recreated schoolrooms, a library of 4000 antique books, and one of the country's oldest Bibles.

🏃 Activities

Hikes are everywhere – from atop Mt Tâmpa in town, Poiana Braşov or Zărneşti, or into the Bucegi Mountains. Pick up maps from Himalaya (www.himalaya.ro; Str Rebublicii 23; ☺ 10am-7.30pm Mon-Fri, to 4pm Sat, 11am-2pm Sun) or talk with a travel agent specialising in hikes. You can also ski on day trips to Poiana Braşov, Predeal and Sinaia.

★ **Transylvanian Wolf** TOURS
(☑ 0744-319 708; www.transylvanian.ro; ☺ year-round) This family-run nature-tour company, with award-winning Romanian guide Dan Marin at its helm, leads walks on the trail of animals such as wolves, bears and lynx (€40 per person, minimum two people). Adventurous rambles in pure nature are guaranteed, though sightings aren't. Alternatively, sightings are very likely on excursions to a bear hide (€55 per person for two-hours; price includes transfers).

FROM BRAȘOV WITH LOVE

Between 1950 and 1960, when Romania still considered itself Moscow's buddy, Brașov was named 'Orașul Stalin'. Some claim that the Russian dictator's name was emblazoned into the side of Mt Tâmpa, though this has since been discredited by many historians. Stalin's rule tampered with much more than the town name: ruthless forced industrialisation yanked thousands of rural workers from the countryside and plunked them down on the city in an attempt to crank the totalitarian motor of industry.

Transylvanian Wolf can also arrange cosy accommodation and traditional, organic food in the family's guesthouse in Zărnești.

Roving România TOURS

(☏ 0724-348 272, 0744-212 065; www.roving -romania.co.uk; ⊘ Apr-early Dec) Tailormade trips with Roving România allow small groups to access Transylvania's natural splendour, and enjoy authentic village life. A founder member of the Association of Ecotourism in Romania, tour guide Colin leads environmentally friendly excursions to track wildlife and spot birds, plus immersive experiences at shepherd camps (May to September) and in Roma communities. Prices start at €130 per group per day, plus expenses.

DiscoveRomania TOURS

(☏ 0722-746 262; www.discoveromania.ro; Str Mihai Viteazul 17; ⊘ 10am-3pm Mon-Fri) Tailormade small-group trips with this environmentally sensitive operator can lead you hiking between monasteries, encountering Roma communities, or following Princes Charles' footsteps through Transylvania. The emphasis is local culture and the outdoors, with wolf-tracking and nature-spotting along the way. DiscoveRomania can also arrange bird-watching excursions in the Danube Delta.

Walkabout Tour WALKING

(www.brasov.walkaboutfreetours.com; ⊘ 3pm daily) **FREE** These informative two-hour strolls around Brașov, led by a bubbly young guide, weave local history in with Dracula myths and urban legends. Essential landmarks such as the Black Church and Schei Quarter are covered, with a good dose of wit. Ideal if you're short on time. Meet by the fountains in Piața Sfatului.

🛏 Sleeping

Brașov has a superb range of friendly hostels, well-equipped apartments and cheerful, family-run guesthouses. Larger hotels tend to be hit-and-miss, offering a less personal and less atmospheric experience than Brașov's many daintier boutique offerings.

Rolling Stone Hostel HOSTEL $

(☏ 0268-513 965; www.rollingstone.ro; Str Piatra Mare 2A; dm/r €10/30; P @ ☏) Powered by enthusiastic staff, Rolling Stone has clean dorm rooms that sleep between six and 10. Most rooms have high ceilings and convenient touches like lockers and reading lamps for each bed. Private doubles are comfy, or you can sleep in the wood-beamed attic for a stowaway vibe. Maps and excellent local advice are supplied the moment you step through the door.

Centrum House Hostel HOSTEL $

(☏ 0727-793 169; www.hostelbrasov.eu; Str Republicii 58; dm/r from €11/33; ☏) This huge hostel has plenty of natural light and cosy common areas, including a shared kitchen, alongside hostel must-haves like lockers. Buzzing and social, there's always a new way to make friends here, from baking nights to movies and pub crawls. Beyond the eight to 14-bed dorms, places to snooze continue in the attic, a love-it-or-hate-it space decorated with trilby hats and silver insulation.

Women-only four-bed dorms cost €12. There's a free beer on arrival.

Kismet Dao Villa HOSTEL $

(☏ 0268-514 296; www.kismetdao.ro; Str Neagoe Basarab 8; dm/d with shared bathroom €10/27; P @ ☏) The vine-draped walls of Kismet Dao Villa add more than charm: they're the source of this friendly hostel's mulled wine each winter. Communal living at a relaxed pace rules this characterful place with six-bed dorms, three private rooms and a bean-bag-strewn games room. You even get a free drink for each night of your stay.

★ **Select City Center** APARTMENT $$

(☎0742-224 028; www.select-apartments-brasov.
ro; Str Mureşenilor 17; studio €30, apt €40-50; 🐾) Less than five minutes' walk from Piaţa Sfatului, these individually decorated apartments allow you to live like the most glamorous of Braşov locals. Polished bathrooms, modern kitchens and spacious lounge rooms are fitted around the elegant bones of this high-ceilinged building. The apartments cultivate different atmospheres: one has a fireplace and leather love seats, another is framed by arches and flooded with natural light.

Breakfast not included. The helpful manager can help arrange paid parking (from €3 per day).

★ **Bella Muzica** HOTEL $$

(☎0268-477 956; www.bellamuzica.ro; Piaţa Sfatului 19; s/d/apt from 220/270/540 lei; ❀🐾) A regal feel permeates Bella Muzica, housed within a 400-year-old building, thanks to its tastefully restored wooden beams, exposed brick, high ceilings and occasional antiques. The main square location of this refined hotel is hard to top.

Casa Reims B&B $$

(☎0368-467 325; www.casareims.ro; Str Castelului 85; s/d from €48/56; Ⓟ❀🐾) Pastels and acid tones mingle beautifully with bare brick and wooden beams at this boutique B&B. Personalised service from the friendly owners adds to the VIP feel, and most rooms have views of Mt Tâmpa.

Casa Wagner HOTEL $$

(☎0268-411 253; www.casa-wagner.com; Piaţa Sfatului 5; d from 245 lei; 🐾) This former 15th-century German bank has been converted into a luxury boutique hotel, with 24 well-appointed rooms. Right in the heart of the city, exposed-brick walls, tasteful furnishings, modern en suites and pleasant management make this an excellent choice.

Pensiunea Curtea Braşoveană HOTEL $$

(☎0268-472 336; www.curteabrasoveana.ro; Str Băilor 16; s/d €50/60; ❀@🐾) This courtyard hotel in a 100-year-old house has nine comfy double rooms and four suites, some with low-hanging wood beams, and all with trim modern bathrooms. Sauna and friendly management top it off nicely.

Casa Rozelor BOUTIQUE HOTEL $$$

(☎0268-475 212; www.casarozelor.ro; Str Michael Weiss 20; s/d €62/74, ste €68-84; 🐾) This hidden courtyard oasis has five beautiful apartments, some with split-level floors adjoined by spiral staircases. Each is defiantly individual but all fuse contemporary chic with European antiques. Some rooms have air-conditioning. Street parking is available.

✖ Eating

Piaţa Sfatului is great for cafes and breakfast, while Str Republicii is more suited to coffees and ice cream. Braşov does high-end cuisine very well, with several romantic and refined restaurants standing out among a slew of satisfyingly rustic Romanian diners.

★ **Bistro de l'Arte** BISTRO $$

(☎0720-535 566; www.bistrodelarte.ro; Piaţa Enescu 11; mains 15-35 lei; ⊙9am-midnight Mon-Sat, noon-midnight Sun; 🐾✍) Tucked down a charming side-street, this bohemian joint can be spotted by the bike racks shaped like penny-farthings. There's an almost Parisian feel in Bistro de l'Arte's arty decor and champagne breakfasts (59 lei), though its menu picks the best from France, Italy and beyond: bruschetta, fondue, German-style cream cake, and a suitably hip cocktail list.

★ **Sergiana** ROMANIAN $$

(☎0268-419 775; www.sergianagrup.ro; Str Mureşenilor 28; mains 25-40 lei; ⊙11am-11pm) Steaming soups in hollowed-out loaves of bread, paprika-laced meat stews, and the most generous ratio of cheese and sour cream we've ever seen in a polenta side-dish – do not wear your tight jeans for a feast at Sergiana. The subterranean dining hall, lined with brick and wood, is lively and casual – fuelled by ample German beer and loud conversation.

Bella Muzica ROMANIAN, MEXICAN $$

(☎0268-477 946; www.bellamuzica.ro; Str George Bariţiu 2; mains 20-30 lei; ⊙noon-11pm) In a vaulted cellar that flickers with candlelight, this intimate dining spot offers paprika stew, goulash and other country favourites alongside a well-executed range of Mexican meals such as fajitas.

Casa Românească ROMANIAN $$

(Piaţa Unirii; mains 15-30 lei) Unapologetically gut-busting Romanian peasant cuisine is served with aplomb at this brooding tavern crowned with a stag's skull. Feast on salted chicken, smoked mutton or *sarmale* (stuffed cabbage) with polenta and sour cream.

Keller Steak House
STEAK $$$

(📞 0268-472 278; www.kellersteakhouse.ro; Str Apollonia Hirscher 2; mains 60-90 lei; ⊙ 11am-11pm; 🍴) Bloody steaks and smooth red wine, served decadently in Keller's cavernous interior... there's more than a hint of a vampire's lair about this upmarket steakhouse. The meat is premium quality, with equally classy wines, brandies and desserts. If a whopping sirloin with Roquefort is more than you can handle, you can choose from Mediterranean-inspired fish dishes, a few vegetarian options and pasta.

Prato
ITALIAN $$$

(📞 0720-444 422; www.prato.ro; Str Michael Weiss 11; pizzas 30 lei, mains 40-60 lei) The extensive menu of this elegant (and very popular) place spans pizzas, seafood and rocket risotto, cheese-stuffed ravioli and beautifully seared steaks. Pasta is made in-house from Italian flour. There is an Italian-inspired cocktail list too.

🍸 Drinking & Nightlife

There's a bohemian bent to Braşov's nightlife, with arty cafe-bars to linger in and a busy calendar of live music, but no shortage of rough and ready pub-and-club action too. Browse entertainment listings on Zile şi Nopţi (Days and Nights; www.zilesinopti.ro/brasov).

Croitoria de Cafea
COFFEE

(📞 0770-263 333; Str Iuliu Maniu 17; ⊙ 8am-7pm Mon-Fri, 9.30am-6pm Sat, to 4pm Sun) The best coffee in town can be sipped at this hole-in-the-wall cafe, which has a few wooden stools for you to perch amid bulging bags of beans.

Deane's Irish Pub
PUB

(Str Republicii 19; ⊙ 10am-3am) As if transplanted from Donegal, this subterranean Irish pub with its early-20th-century cloudy mirrored bar, shadowy booths and old-world soundtracks, is a haven for the Guinness-thirsty. Live music some nights.

Festival 39
BAR

(📞 0743-339 909; www.festival39.com; Str Republicii 62; ⊙ 7am-midnight) Jazz flows from this vintage-feel watering hole and restaurant, an art-deco dream of stained-glass, high ceilings, wrought-iron finery, candelabra and leather banquettes. As good for clanking together beer glasses as for cradling a hot chocolate over your travel journal.

☆ Entertainment

Filarmonica Braşov
CLASSICAL MUSIC

(www.filarmonicabrasov.ro; Str Apollonia Hirscher 10; concert tickets adult/child from 20/10 lei) Lavish your ears with the sound of Braşov's venerable Philharmonic Orchestra, established in 1878, which hosts concerts throughout the year. Tickets for performances can be bought at the booth on B-dul 15 Noiembrie 50 (noon to 3pm Monday and Wednesday, 4pm to 6pm Tuesday and Thursday).

Puppet Theatre
THEATRE

(Teatrul Arlechino; 📞 0268-475 243, tickets 0735-870 773; www.teatrularlechino.ro; Str Apollonia Hirscher 10) Teatrul Arlechino hosts whimsical puppet shows aimed at children. Reserve tickets by phone or buy from the ticket office (1.30pm to 4pm Tuesday and Wednesday, to 6pm Thursday, 9.30am to 1.30pm Saturday and Sunday).

Opera Braşov
OPERA

(📞 0268-415 990; www.opera-brasov.ro; Str Bisericii Române 51; tickets adult/student from 20/10 lei) Opera classics, plus a few productions geared towards children, take to the stage of this 1953-founded venue.

🔒 Shopping

Transylvania Folk Art
GIFTS & SOUVENIRS

(Str George Bariţiu; ⊙ 9.30am-8pm) Beckoning across the road from the Black Church, this handicrafts shop sells sparkly decorative eggs, woven linen shirts, and other gifts with a taste of traditional Transylvania.

ℹ Information

You'll find ATMs and banks along Str Republicii and B-dul Eroilor.

Raiffeisen Bank (Piaţa Sfatului 18; ⊙ 9am-5.30pm Mon-Fri) Main square bank and ATM.

Tourist Information Centre (www.brasov tourism.eu; Str Prundului 1; ⊙ 9am-5pm Mon-Fri) Cordial staff offer maps and local advice.

Check www.brasovtravelguide.ro for general info.

ℹ Getting There & Away

BUS

Maxitaxis and microbuses are the best way to reach places near Braşov, including Bran, Râşnov, Sinaia and Sfântu Gheorghe. The most accessible station is **Bus Station 1** (Autogara 1;

TRANSYLVANIA BRAŞOV

☎ 0268-427 267; www.autogari.ro; B-dul Gării 1), next to the train station.

From 6am to 7.30pm maxitaxis leave every half-hour for Bucharest (from 35 lei, 2½ to 3½ hours), stopping in Buşteni and Sinaia. About 12 daily buses or maxitaxis leave for Sibiu (30 lei, 2½ hours), stopping in Făgăraş town. Three go daily to Sighişoara (30 lei) and press on to Târgu Mureş (35 lei, 3½ to four hours). Less frequent buses reach Cluj-Napoca (65 lei, five to 5½ hours, three daily), Constanţa (70 lei, 5½ hours, two daily) and Iaşi (70 lei, six to eight hours, three daily).

Half-hourly daily buses to Sfântu Gheorghe (8 lei, 45 minutes) leave from a parking lot on the opposite side of the train station from Bus Station 1. Regular buses go to Prejmer (4 lei, 30 minutes), some from Bus Station 1, others from the corner of Str Andreescu and Str Lunga; check www.autogari.ro for details.

Bus Station 2 (Autogara 2; ☎ 0268-426 332; www.autogari.ro; Str Avram Iancu 114), 1km northwest of the train station, sends half-hourly buses marked 'Moieciu-Bran' to Râşnov (4 lei, 25 minutes) and Bran (7 lei, 40 minutes) from roughly 6.30am to 9pm. Take bus 12 to/from the centre (it stops at the roundabout just north of the station). A dozen daily buses go to Zărneşti (5 to 10 lei, 40 minutes to one hour).

The main bus stop in town is **Livada Poştei** (B-dul Eroilor 31) at the western end of B-dul Eroilor. From here bus 20 goes half-hourly to Poiana Braşov (5 lei, 20 minutes). Buy your ticket from a kiosk before boarding.

European routes are handled by **Eurolines** (☎ 0268-474 008; www.eurolines.ro; Piaţa Sfatului 18; ⊙ 9am-8pm Mon-Fri, 10am-2pm Sat), which sells tickets for buses to Germany, Italy, Hungary and other European destinations.

TRAIN

The **train station** (Gara Braşov; ☎ 0268-410 233; www.cfrcalatori.ro; B-dul Gării 5) is 2km northeast of the town centre. Left luggage service is available at the station.

International train service prices vary widely according to the time of the train and whether you opt for a seat or couchette. There are three daily trains to Budapest (13 to 16 hours), one to Vienna (17 hours) and one to Prague (21 hours).

ⓘ Getting Around

Minibus 51 runs from the train station and Bus Station 1 through the centre, stopping at Piaţa Unirii south of the centre. From Bus Station 2, take bus 12 from the 'Stadionul Tineretului' stop on nearby Str Stadionului (just north of the bus station). At time of research a single bus ticket cost 1.50 lei, a day pass 5 lei. Stamp tickets aboard the bus.

Most of the centre is walkable though it's fun to hire a bike from centrally located **I'Velo** (www.ivelo.ro; Piaţa Sfatului; per hour/day 4/15 lei; ⊙ 11am-10pm Mon-Fri, 10am-10pm Sat & Sun Jul & Aug, 11am-8pm Mon-Fri, 10am-8pm Sat & Sun Mar & Apr, 11am-9pm Wed-Fri, 10am-9pm Sat & Sun May, Sep, Oct).

Autonom (☎ 0268-415 250; www.autonom.com; Str Nicolae Bălcescu 20) usually has the best car-hire prices (from 155 lei per day, with discounts for long-term rentals) and will deliver a car to locations inside Braşov for no extra charge. **Sixt** (☎ 021-9400; www.sixt.ro; Str Apollonia Hirscher 14) has an office in town too.

Taxis line up outside the train station. A couple of reputable companies include **Martax** (☎ 0268-313 040) and **Tod** (☎ 0268-321 111).

AROUND BRAŞOV

Beyond historic Braşov, many more diversions await in the surrounding hills. Most popular is Bran Castle, thanks to vampiric associations that most visitors are content to leave un-factchecked. Also in easy daytrip distance of Braşov are soaring Râşnov Fortress and Libearty Bear Sanctuary (near Zărneşti). Once you've had your fill of fortresses, this is superb terrain to stretch your legs in Piatra Craiului National Park or Poiana Braşov's ski resort.

TRAINS FROM BRAŞOV

DESTINATION	COST (LEI)	DURATION (HR)	FREQUENCY (DAILY)
Bucharest	49	2½	10
Cluj-Napoca	73-80	7	5
Iaşi	92	8½	1
Sfântu Gheorghe	5-15	30min	15
Sibiu	20-45	2¾-4	6
Sighişoara	18-40	2½-3½	7

Bran

POP 5345

Illuminated by the light of a pale moon, the vampire's lair glares down from its rocky bluff... but regrettably, Bran Castle's blood-drinking credentials don't withstand scrutiny. Claims that Vlad Ţepeş – either 'the Impaler' or 'protector of Wallachia', depending on who you ask – passed through here are unproven. Nor did the castle inspire Bram Stoker, much as souvenir-sellers attempt to link Bran to the iconic Gothic novel *Dracula*.

These seem minor quibbles when you gaze up at the turreted fortress, guarded from the east by the Bucegi Mountains and from the west by the Piatra Craiului massif. Meanwhile, the castle's museum pays greater homage to Romanian royals than immortal counts. Ignoring this, a gauntlet of souvenir sellers hawk fang-adorned mugs and Vlad-the-Impaler compact mirrors (really).

The bulk of visitors see Bran as a half-day trip, with a stop at Râşnov Castle. Daring hiking trails down from the Bucegi wind up here too.

◎ Sights

Bran Castle   CASTLE
(☑ 0268-237 700; www.bran-castle.com; Str General Traian Moşoiu 24; adult/student/child 35/20/7 lei; ⊘ 9am-6pm Tue-Sun, noon-6pm Mon Apr-Sep, same hours to 4pm Oct-Mar) Rising above the town on a rocky promontory, Bran Castle holds visitors in thrall. An entire industry has sprouted around describing it as 'Dracula's Castle'. The liberties taken with Bran's reputation are quickly forgotten on a visit: you'll climb up its conical towers, admiring views over thick forest, and stroll through creaky-floored rooms furnished with bearskin rugs and 19th-century antiques.

Noting Bran Pass' strategic location, Teutonic knights built a citadel here in the 13th century. The structure was destroyed in battle, but fears of Turkish invasion led to a new citadel being built in the same place in 1382, as part of a 14th-century boom in castle-building. Bran Castle languished as an administrative building during the 18th century. The town of Bran was offered to Queen Maria of Romania in 1920, as a thank you for her efforts in uniting the country.

Indeed, you'll learn rather more about Queen Maria than Dracula. One room exhibits a half-hearted account of Romanian vampire lore, and rather infuriatingly shoehorns together some displays on Vlad Ţepeş – popularly, 'the Impaler' – and author Bram Stoker.

Several displays are devoted to Maria, the castle's former royal resident, and her belongings are lovingly displayed alongside video footage. One of the finest rooms is her husband King Ferdinand's former bedroom, with decorated furniture and ceramic fireplaces.

Bran Castle hosts atmospheric events around Halloween; check the castle's website for details. It also hosts a late-summer Jazz Festival (www.bran-castle.com; ⊘ late Aug).

Bran Village Museum   MUSEUM
(Muzeul Satului Brănean; adult/student 8/2 lei; ⊘ 9am-6pm Tue-Sun & noon-6pm Mon summer, 9am-4pm Tue-Sun winter) Just east of Bran Castle, this museum displays original items found in the castle, with open-air displays of traditional architectural styles of the region.

🛏 Sleeping & Eating

Bran's coven of villas and *pensiunes* grows every year, though most visitors day trip from Braşov. Browse agrotourism and homestay listings on www.ruraltourism.ro.

Vampire Camping   CAMPGROUND $
(☑ 0268-238 430; www.vampirecamping.com; Str Cavaler Ioan de Puscariu 68; per adult/child/tent €4.50/2/3; ⊘ Apr-Oct; ℗) This standard, rather than spooky, campground is 1.5km north of Bran Castle. There's a pizzeria in high summer, bike hire, laundry facilities (€4 per load) and wi-fi around the reception area.

The GuestHouse   PENSION $$
(☑ 0744-306 062; www.guesthouse.ro; Str General Traian Moşoiu 7; d 135-165 lei, tr 170 lei; ℗ 🛜) Six trim rooms, where modern fittings mingle with rustic touches like wooden beams, offer terrific views of Bran Castle. It's clean, friendly, and has perks for families including a kids playground and communal lounge and dining room.

Hanul Bran   HOTEL $$
(☑ 0268-236 556; www.hanulbran.ro; Str General Traian Moşoiu 4; s/d/apt €35/40/65; ℗ 🛜) Rooms are a little old-fashioned at Hanul Bran, but it's a comfortable option and only

TRANSYLVANIA BRAN

10 minutes on foot from Bran Castle. The attached Transylvanian restaurant, with tables beneath elegant archways, has an agreeable lost-in-time feeling.

Popasul Reginei PENSION **$$**
(☎0268-236 834; www.popasulreginei.ro; Str Aurel Stoian 398; d/tr/ste 156/178/312 lei; P✿❄) Just across the park and down the street from Bran Castle, this seven-room place has homely rooms removed from the touristic bedlam of the castle. There's also a decent restaurant serving traditional Romanian fare.

The small pool is summer only.

ℹ️ Getting There & Away

Bran is an easy DIY day trip from Braşov. Buses marked 'Bran-Moieciu' (7 lei, 45 minutes, half-hourly) depart Braşov's Bus Station 2 (Autogara 2), stopping in Râşnov.

From Zărneşti (5 lei, 40 minutes), travel via Moieciu de Jos. One daily bus reaches Piteşti (30 lei, 3½ hours).

Poiana Braşov

POP 400

With a dusting of snow, the little mountain resort of Poiana Braşov makes a sparkling day trip from Braşov (12km down the road). Carving up its 20km of pistes, many of them wide and tree-lined, is time well spent. But dedicated skiers and snowboarders won't find enough to keep them for longer than a couple of days.

Locals make much of Jude Law and Nicole Kidman's glamorous visit to Poiana Braşov during the filming of *Cold Mountain* (2003), but in reality this is a small, though lively and family-friendly, winter sports area. Aside from a few hikers, Poiana Braşov goes quiet outside the December to March ski season.

◉ Sights

Sf Ioan Botezătorul Church CHURCH
(Str Poiana Soarelui; ⊙hours variable) This ornate church shaped like a witch's hat, built in Maramureş style entirely out of wood, has a stunning mountain backdrop.

🏃 Activities

Hiking

The Postăvaru Massif nestles between the Cheii Valley, Timişului Valley and Poiana Braşov, and has dozens of trails of varying levels of difficulty to choose from. Leave details of your intended route with your guesthouse, wear layers and bring water.

A two-hour circuit, beginning and ending in Poiana Braşov, begins at Poiana Ursului following blue circles via Poiana Drester before descending to Pârtia Bradul.

From Poiana Braşov you can hike to Cabana Postăvaru (two to 2½ hours, marked with red crosses) for stunning mountain views. From Cabana Postăvaru, you can follow a trail marked with yellow bars to Pietrele lui Solomon (three hours). Or you can hike down to Timişu de Jos from Cabana Postăvaru in four hours: the trail is marked from the cabana with blue stripes, then blue crosses. Instead of following the blue-cross trail where the path diverges, you can continue following the blue-stripe trail, which eventually takes you over the top of Mt Tâmpa to Braşov. This trail (1½ to two hours) follows the old Braşov road. All are medium difficulty.

From Poiana Braşov you can also hike to Râşnov (three hours, yellow crosses, then left on the road to the trail marked with blue stripes) or tackle the more strenuous hike to Predeal (five to seven hours, yellow stripes).

Skiing

The ski season runs from December to March, sometimes later. It's a small, family-friendly winter sports area best suited to beginner and intermediate skiers and boarders.

Among its 20km of pistes, across a 775m elevation difference, are a few gentle nursery slopes and three red (intermediate) runs, plus a couple of blacks (difficult). They are accessed by two cable-car lifts, plus two chairlifts and five drag lifts. Lift passes start at 140/80 lei per adult/child. The main cable car, a 15-minute walk up the road southwest from the bus stop (past Sf Ioan Botezătorul Church), operates all year. Another is next to AnaHotel Sport.

Several hotels can arrange lessons and gear hire. Club Rossignol (☎0722-794 162; www.clubrossignol.ro), across from the main lift, also hires skis or snowboards from 45 lei per day.

🛏️ Sleeping & Eating

Choose from a good range of Alpine-style lodges and midrange to luxe ski hotels, or stay down the road in Braşov town. Room rates vary wildly according to demand:

prices rise during high season (December to mid-March) and drop by 25% or more at other times.

Hotel Crisalpin
HOTEL $$

(☑ 0757-050 833; www.hotelcrisalpin.ro; Str Poiana Ursului; d/ste from 220/265 lei; P 🛜) Less than 500m from the ski lifts, welcoming three-star Crisalpin offers rooms with comfortable beds, fridges and underfloor heating. Ask for a balconied room with mountain views. There's a sauna and ski storage.

Vila Zorile
CHALET $$

(☑ 0268-262 286; www.vila-zorile.ro; Str Poiana Ruia 6; d/ste from 220/270 lei; P 🛜) Jude Law and Nicole Kidman stayed at this cosy chalet while filming *Cold Mountain*. Some doubles aren't huge, but everything is furnished with an eye for rustic mountain chic, with polished wood, decorative rugs and a soothing powder-blue-and-white colour scheme.

Poiana Ursului
CHALET $$

(☑ 0268-262 216; www.poianaursului.ro; Str Poiana Ursului 1; s/d/apt from €40/45/70; P 🛜) Forty-two rooms and suites, in bright primary colours and crisp monochrome, fill this amicable guesthouse. It's a 10-minute walk from the ski lift.

★ AnaHotel Sport
HOTEL $$$

(☑ 0268-407 330; www.anahotels.ro/sporthotel; Str Valea Dragă; d from 420 lei; P 🛜🏊) This swish, four-star complex with spacious modern rooms and flower-filled balconies acts as a luxurious one-stop shop for stays in Poiana Braşov. Multilingual staff can arrange ski passes, gear rental and even massages. There are fabulous indoor and outdoor (summer only) pools, a gym, and ski storage.

ℹ️ Information

The www.poiana-brasov.ro and www.poiana brasovinfoturist.ro websites are useful sources of info on Poiana Braşov. The former has accommodation finders and booking tools; the latter has ski, bike and walking trails.

ℹ️ Getting There & Away

From Braşov, bus 20 (5 lei, 20 minutes, every 30 minutes) runs from the Livada Poştei bus stop, at the western end of B-dul Eroilor, to Poiana Braşov. A 10-trip bus card costs 20 lei.

Zărneşti

POP 21,680

Though it's perched on the eastern edge of craggy Piatra Craiului National Park, Zărneşti shares none of its drama. This low-key little town is a useful base for day-hikes into the park, or to circle your wagons before a longer trek; otherwise there's no reason to hang around. Some 7km east is Libearty Bear Sanctuary, though this is just as easy to visit on an excursion from Braşov or Bran (plus transfers and guided

---

WORTH A TRIP

RÂŞNOV FORTRESS

Commonly paired with Bran Castle on day-trips from Braşov, **Râşnov Fortress** (Cetatea Râşnov; adult/child 12/6 lei; ⊘ 9am-6pm) might just be the more enchanting of the two. The medieval citadel, built by Teutonic knights to guard against Tatar and Turkish invasion, roosts on a hilltop 19km southwest of Braşov by road. Visitors are free to stroll between sturdy watchtowers, browse medieval-themed souvenir and craft stalls, and admire views of rolling hills from the fortress' highest point. Walk from the village or take the **lift** (cnr Str Ion Luca Caragiale & Str Cetăţii; adult/child 12/6 lei; ⊘ 8.30am-4.30pm Mon-Fri, 9am-4pm Sat & Sun).

A Dacian settlement perched on this hilltop around the 1st century BC, but was abandoned after Roman conquest. The stocky-walled fortification today was built and rebuilt between the 14th and 17th centuries, passing between Hungarian and Saxon ownership, eventually losing its military significance in the 18th century. Today it's emblazoned with a Hollywood-style 'Râşnov' sign.

Audioguides are available (10 lei) for a more detailed romp through Râşnov's history. Tourist information booths operate just outside the citadel, following its opening hours.

From Braşov, frequent Bran-bound buses stop in Râşnov (4 lei, 25 minutes).

tours are easier to find from there than Zărneşti).

◉ Sights

Libearty Bear Sanctuary   NATURE RESERVE (www.ampbears.ro/en/bear-sanctuary; Zărneşti; adult/child 40/10 lei; ◷ tours 9am, 10am & 11am Tue-Sun Apr-Oct, 10am, 11am & 12pm Tue-Sun Nov-Mar) Not enough time to join a bear hide excursion to see these impressive carnivores lumbering through their natural habitat? Libearty Sanctuary is the next best thing. This 69-hectare enclosure is the leafy retirement home of former captive bears, most of whom endured horrific confinement (and sometimes torture) at the hands of circuses, zoos and private owners. Visits are by guided tour, at times when bears approach the fences for some of the tasty entrails thrown their way by staff. It's 7km east of Zărneşti.

Romania outlawed the keeping of wild bears in 2005. Most of the bears at the sanctuary are Romanian, but some have been rescued from as far afield as Albania and Texas. The giant of the sanctuary, at 400 kilos, hails from Armenia. It's impressive to see these enormous mammals but undeniably sad to see scars of what they endured: some pace in circles, despite the abundant space. You may also spot tiny deer or the nine wolves who also make their home here.

Many local hostels and guesthouses offer tours, sometimes combined with Bran Castle; otherwise it's a 45-minute drive from

PIATRA CRAIULUI NATIONAL PARK

With a spectacular 25km limestone ridge, giving way to spruce forests and glacial lakes, drama is everywhere in Piatra Craiului National Park. Wolves, bears, deer, eagle owls and 17 species of bat are at home in these woodlands and crags, first declared a nature reserve in 1938.

Some 42 marked trails weave through the park, including plenty of day-hikes from Zărneşti, 2km from the park's northeasterly edge. Entry tickets for the park (week/season ticket 10/20 lei) are available from booths in Zărneşti and at the **park office**.

Before setting out on any hikes, be sure to check weather conditions, and ask the info centre for trails suitable for the season. In May/June and September, Piatra Craiului receives heavy rainfall. Summer storms are possible too. In winter much of the mountain cannot be accessed and avalanches are common.

Day-hike loops from Zărneşti are a popular way to experience the park. Suitable for all levels is the three-hour return hike along **Zărneşti Gorge**; park your car at Culmea Prăpăstiilor. Alternatively, walk from Zărneşti, adding an extra two hours each way (total return journey seven hours).

A tougher day-hike begins south from Zărneşti past **Cabana Gura Râului** (red cross markings). The trail then veers northwest (yellow vertical-stripe markers) to **Cabana Curmătura** (☑ 0745-454 184; www.cabana-curmatura.ro; dm 30 lei), before circling back along the same trail to Zărneşti. It takes about six hours in total. An alternative, heavy-going return route splinters east on the blue-dot trail up **Piatra Mică** (a challenging 1816m peak, assisted by chains); seek local advice on weather and trail conditions before attempting this route.

Several trails meet up behind Cabana Curmătura, from where you can follow a blue-stripe trail in a looping direction west and north to **Colţul Chiliilor Monastery** peak (1125m, two hours return). The blue-stripe trail back to the northwestern edge of Zărneşti from here is relatively flat (about two hours).

Hikers with a high level of fitness, and climbing experience, can eye tougher routes on the western side of the range. Even so, it's strongly advisable to hire a guide who knows the area (ask at the park office). From northwestern Zărneşti, a road marked with red-stripe signs goes 11km to 849m **Cabana Plaiu Foii** (☑ 0726-380 323; www.cabanaplaiulfoii.ro; d 140 lei). From the cabana, start early for a very difficult trail (red stripes, four hours one-way) up ghostly pale limestone cliffs to **La Lanturi** (or 'to the chains', as you'll need to use the permanent cables to navigate some of the narrow canyon walls). Nearby is the vigorous climb up to the highest peak in the park, **La Om** (2237m). Trails along the ridge usually take two days and are for hiking experts only.

Braşov (the last few minutes along an exceedingly bumpy gravel road). Call ahead outside high season as the sanctuary requires 10 visitors to guarantee a tour.

🛏 Sleeping

A couple of plain pensions in central Zărneşti offer adequate rooms for the night, if you want to pause before a long hike, but consider sleeping in Măgura, which has options within the park itself.

Cabana Gura Raului　　　　　　HOSTEL **$**
(📞0744-307 978; http://cabanaguraraului.ro; Str Raului 86; r 65-80 lei) With comfortable accommodation in two- and four-bed dorm rooms, and well positioned at the foot of Piatra Craiului National Park, this simple hiker's lodge is perfectly placed if you want to start trekking early in the morning. Breakfast not included.

ℹ Information

Piatra Craiului National Park Office (📞0268-223 165; www.pcrai.ro; Str Topliţei 150; ⊘8am-4.30pm Mon-Thu, to 2pm Fri) In a building shaped like a mountain range, about 2km west of Zărneşti towards the park, this excellent information centre sells maps (20 lei) and can arrange mountain guides with a week's notice (225 lei per day).

Tourist Information Centre (Str Tiberiu Spârchez; ⊘10am-4pm Tue-Thu & Sat, to 2pm Fri & Sun) Helpful tourist office on the roundabout, open year-round.

ℹ Getting There & Away

Buses stop at a roundabout near the post office, about 100m past the city hall and centre along Str Metropolit Ion Meţianu. The train station is about 1km east of (before) the city hall.

Trains connect Zărneşti with Braşov (5 lei, 40 minutes, nine daily); there are also several daily buses between Braşov's Bus Station 2 (Autogara 2) and Zărneşti, but the journey takes longer (one hour). About five or six daily buses head to Bran (5 lei, 40 minutes). If you're headed to stay in Măgura village, you'll need to organise a lift from up there, take a **taxi** (📞0742-223 111, 0726-223 111) for roughly 50 lei, or hike.

Hărman & Prejmer

Step into Transylvania's Saxon past at the fortified churches of Hărman and Prejmer. Twelve kilometres north of Braşov is Hărman (or Honigberg, as it was known to

Transylvania's medieval Saxons), home to a stocky 16th-century citadel. Just 7km further north stands Prejmer (once Tartlau), whose 15th-century citadel – enclosing a splendid Gothic church – boasts the thickest defensive walls of all Transylvania's Saxon churches. These two Unesco-listed sights are easily combined into a single day trip from Braşov.

◉ Sights

Hărman Fortified Church
　　　　　　　　　　　　　　　CHURCH, CASTLE
(www.harmaninfo.com; Hărman; adult/child 10/5 lei; ⊘9am-noon & 1-5pm Mon-Sat, from 10am Sun) From the outside, Hărman's fortified church resembles a bright white layer cake. Enclosed by its mighty walls is a triple-naved basilica, the **Church of St Nikolaus**, which has retained its Romanesque style (dating to 1240) despite reconstruction. The centrepiece is a circa-1300 bell tower, rising 56m above the complex. Watch your step as you climb the narrow spiral staircase up the tower (and guard your eardrums if you reach the top when the hourly chimes ring out).

The main church harbours a fine baroque altar and women's benches that date to 1753; the lack of backrests is a deliberate design feature, as ladies' stiff attire didn't allow them to lean back (or nod off).

A small museum in the outbuildings displays traditional furniture and embroidery. Don't miss climbing the stairs to the smaller chapel building, which has magnificent 15th-century murals of Heaven and Hell.

Prejmer Fortified Church
　　　　　　　　　　　　　　　CHURCH, CASTLE
(Prejmer; 10 lei; ⊘9am-6pm Mon-Fri, to 5pm Sat, 11am-5pm Sun May-Oct, 9am-4pm Mon-Sat, 11am-4pm Sun Nov-Apr) If we had a choice of fortresses in which to wait out a siege, we'd opt for Prejmer. This superbly preserved complex has the most powerful fortified walls in Transylvania at 4.5m thick. Prejmer's fortress was originally constructed in the early 1200s by Teutonic knights. A 15th-century reconstruction shaped it into the battering-ram-proof fortification that stands today, encircling a Gothic church. The 270 store rooms were once packed with produce to allow inhabitants to stay fed while under attack.

🛏 Sleeping & Eating

Hărman and Prejmer each have a few sleepy, budget guesthouses, but you're far better off staying in Brașov (12km south of Hărman).

Dining options are also limited. In Prejmer, find a couple of cafes and restaurants on Strada Mare (the end that runs south from the church). Hărman has a couple of restaurants along Strada Ștefan cel Mare, including a good pizzeria.

Althaus PIZZA $$
(☑0268-367 850; Str Ștefan cel Mare 295, Hărman; mains 20 lei; ☺noon-11pm) One of few options in Hărman, this bustling little spot serves good thin-crust pizza within steps of the fortified church, and there's a shady garden to relax in.

❶ Getting There & Away

By bus, it's fairly easy to visit both Prejmer and Hărman on a day trip from Brașov. Head to Prejmer first, from a stop near Brașov's Bus Station 1 (Autogara 1; 4 lei, 20 minutes, regular). Then take a Brașov-bound bus and exit at the Hărman stop on the way back (3.50 lei, 20 minutes, four daily); it's a 20-minute walk from the highway to Hărman's church.

If you're visiting only Hărman, connections to and from Brașov are frequent (2.50 lei, 15 minutes).

SAXON LAND

North of the Carpathian Mountains roll the immortal villages of Saxon Land. For many travellers, this area of golden cornfields and fortified churches is the 'real Transylvania'. Rattling along the dirt roads of a Saxon village, past blue-and-white houses and the odd horse and cart, is a guaranteed highlight – particularly if journey's end is a haunting castle or fortified church.

Most popular is vampire tourist spot Sighișoara, though the poised city of Sibiu increasingly pulls crowds for its festivals and gastronomy. The most memorable journeys revolve around fortified Saxon villages, like Viscri and Alma Vii, for thriving handicrafts, homespun Transylvanian food, and guesthouses tucked inside authentic Saxon homes.

Sighișoara

POP 28,100

So resplendent are Sighișoara's pastel-coloured buildings, stony lanes and medieval towers, you'll rub your eyes in disbelief. Fortified walls encircle Sighișoara's lustrous merchant houses, now harbouring cafes, hotels and craft shops. Lurking behind the roofs and turrets of the Unesco-protected

---

WORTH A TRIP

THE KALIBASH VILLAGES

Snoozing on the northeastern edge of Piatra Craiului National Park (p96) are **Măgura** and **Peștera**, known as the Kalibash Villages. This alpine idyll of fields flecked with cottages, backed by Mt Craiului, is interrupted only by crowing cocks (and sheepdogs chasing your car). Although tiny, Măgura and Peștera are superb bases to launch into the national park or join a bear-tracking tour.

The villages' first inhabitants lived in mud huts dug into the ground, known as *coliba*, which gave the area its name. Meadows continue to be cut by scythe. While Peștera is just outside the national park boundary, Măgura is reachable only by rattling along a steep gravelled road, giving the area a wild, lost-in-time feel.

Măgura-based **Carpathian Nature Tours** (☑0745-512 096; www.cntours.eu; Villa Hermani) can help you spot bears, boar, birds of prey and more. The tour operator specialises in immersive wildlife experiences, plus trekking and cultural trips. Most popular are bear-hide trips, which take you by minibus from Măgura (an hour's drive) into a protected nature reserve.

For hiking, May to September is prime season, or June to August if you're heading to high alpine locations. There may already be snowfall in some areas from October.

Măgura's excellent **Villa Hermani** (☑0740-022 384; www.cntours.eu; Măgura; half-board per person s/d €58/43; 🅿❄🖥) makes a good base in the national park; book well in advance. Meanwhile Peștera, just south of the park boundary, has a bigger choice of B&Bs and hotels.

Măgura and Peștera are a 17km drive from Bran and 7km drive from Zărnești. Roads are winding and buses don't come here, so you'll need private transport.

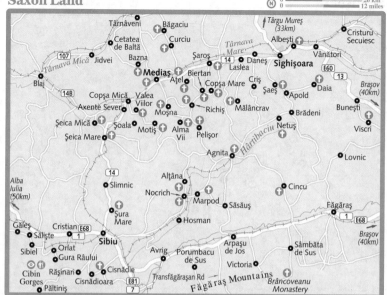

old town is the history of Vlad Ţepeş, Transylvania's most notorious ruler; he was born in a house that is visitable to this day. Revered by many Romanians for protecting Transylvania from Turkish attacks, Ţepeş is better remembered as Vlad the Impaler, or Dracula, fuelling a local industry of vampire-themed souvenirs.

Allow time to lose yourself along Sighişoara's alleys, hike to its hilltop church, and sip coffee at cafes half a millennium old. If Sighişoara doesn't sate your thirst for medieval splendour, it also makes a great jumping-off point to explore Saxon villages like Viscri and Biertan.

◎ Sights

Citadel   FORTRESS

Sighişoara's delightful medieval buildings are enclosed within its citadel, a Unesco-listed complex of protective walls and watchtowers. Walking in the citadel is today a tranquil, fairytale-like experience, but these towers were once packed with weapons and emergency supplies, guarding Sighişoara from Turkish attacks (note the upper windows, from which arrows could be fired).

From the 14th to 16th centuries each of the 14 towers and five artillery bastions was

managed by a different town guild, and the walls extended 903m. Surviving today are nine towers and two bastions.

Dating from the 16th century, the **Bootmakers' Tower** (Turnul Cizmarilor; Str Zidul Cetăţii; ⊘ closed to the public) was a key point of defence from the northern end. Just south, the **Tailors' Tower** (Turnul Croitorilor; Str Zidul Cetăţii; ⊘ closed to the public) was built to guard over the back entrance to the citadel. As with many of the buildings here, the tower was engulfed in a massive fire in 1676 and rebuilt afterward. On the eastern edge of the citadel is the **Blacksmiths' Tower** (Turnul Fierarilor; Piaţa Muzeului; ⊘ closed to the public), a pointy-roofed watchtower dating to 1631. Finally, the southerly (and top-heavy) **Tinsmiths' Tower** (Turnul Cositorarilor; Piaţa Răţuştelor; ⊘ closed to the public) is one of the most easily recognisable in the citadel, both for its height (25m) and its octagonal upper level. A siege in 1704 left scars in the building that are visible to this day.

Clock Tower   MUSEUM
(Turnul cu Ceas; Piaţa Muzeului 1; adult/child 14/3.50 lei; ⊘ 9am-6.30pm Tue-Fri, 10am-5.30pm Sat & Sun) The multicoloured tiled roof of Sighişoara's Clock Tower glitters like the scales of a dragon. The tower was built in

Sighişoara

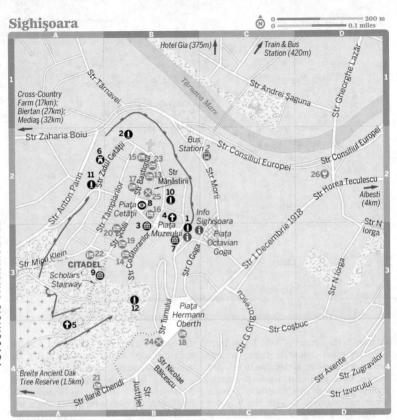

the 14th century and expanded 200 years later. It remains the prettiest sight in town, offering a magnificent panorama from the top. The views are as good a reason to visit as the museum inside, a patchy collection of Roman vessels, scythes and tombstones, and a scale model of the fortified town (English-language explanation is variable).

Casa Vlad Dracul　　　　HISTORIC BUILDING
(www.casavladdracul.ro; Str Cositorarilor 5; 5 lei; ☺10am-10pm) Vlad Ţepeş (aka Dracula) was reputedly born in this house in 1431 and lived here until the age of four. It's now a decent restaurant, but for a small admission, the staff will show you Vlad's old room (and give you a little scare). Bubble-burster: the building is indeed centuries old, but has been completely rebuilt since Vlad's days.

Church of the Dominican Monastery　　　　CHURCH
(Biserica Mănăstirii; Piaţa Muzeului; 5 lei; ☺10am-5pm) This late-Gothic church has a spooky air, and guards a trove of baroque finery inside. First mentioned in 1298, the church was rebuilt between 1482 and 1515 after Mongol and Tatar invasions, and again after Sighişoara's great fire in 1676. The bronze baptismal font dates to 1440, though most of its treasures are baroque, including the altar. There's an impressive collection of Anatolian carpets from the 16th and 17th centuries.

Mass for the Saxon community is held here to this day.

Piaţa Cetăţii　　　　SQUARE
Gem-sized Piaţa Cetăţii is the heart of old Sighişoara. It was here that markets, craft fairs, public executions, impalings and witch trials were held.

Scholars' Stairway　　　　HISTORIC BUILDING
(Scara Şcolarilor; Str Şcolii) From Piaţa Cetăţii, turn south up Str Şcolii to reach the 176-step covered stairway, which has tunnelled its way up the hill since 1642. With light dappling through the roof and buskers at the top, it's a charming ramble.

Church on the Hill　　　　CHURCH
(Biserica din Deal; 5 lei; ☺10am-5pm) Don't miss hiking up the covered stairway to 'School Hill' (418m) to admire this evocative late-Gothic, triple-naved church. Originally a 13th-century Romanesque basilica, it was restored in Gothic style across the 14th and 15th centuries. Inside, find traces of 15th-century frescoes, Renaissance furnishings, and an impressive Gothic altarpiece (1520).

Breite Ancient Oak Tree Reserve　　FOREST
(☎0265-506 024; www.rezervatia-breite.ro) `FREE`
Escape the crowds and visit the enchanting Breite Ancient Oak Tree Reserve, 2km west of town. Its 133 hectares boast 800-year-old oaks, with circumferences of 400cm to 600cm.

Statue of Vlad Ţepeş　　　　MONUMENT
Behind the Church of the Dominican Monastery is a Statue of Vlad Ţepeş (sometimes known as 'The Impaler'), showing the legend with a bewildered look and his trademark circa-1981 porno moustache.

🏃 Activities

Rent bikes in summer at Pensiune Cristina & Pavel (p102).

Some 17km outside town, **Cross-Country Farm** (☎0369-086 012; www.cross-country.ro; horse riding per hour 80 lei) offers horseback riding past traditional villages and wagon rides for beginners (from 100 lei).

☞ Tours

Eye Tours　　　　CULTURAL, HIKING
(☎0747-375 715; www.facebook.com/Eyetours -Transylvania-140617032968093; 3-day trips from €70) Run by a Dutchman who fell in love with Romania and never looked back, Eye Tours specialises in tailormade multiday trips into Saxon Land, from hiking to visiting shepherds, charcoal burners and other local trades. Friendly owner Marco Nawjin can also help arrange accommodation. Get in touch via Facebook a few days in advance of your trip.

Wanderlust Tour　　　　CULTURAL, CYCLING
(☎0765-156 653, 0728-216 212; www.wanderlust -tour.ro) Wanderlust offers day trips to Saxon villages and cycling tours. You can also experience rustic life by meeting traditional charcoal burners and cheese makers. Tours are available in Romanian, English or German. Wanderlust can also help with bike hire and transfers.

🎭 Festivals & Events

International Vampire Film & Arts Festival　　　　ART, FILM
(www.ivfaf.com; ☺late-May) Don your best black cloak for this four-day celebration of the dark arts. A varied program of horror

TRANSYLVANIA SIGHIŞOARA

movie screenings, Gothic literature readings and provocative art shows are sure to thrill children of the night.

Festival of Medieval Arts & Crafts CULTURAL
(www.sighisoaramedievala.ro; ⊙ Jul) Over three days, Sighişoara embraces its medieval history through costumed reenactments, parades, live concerts and plenty of beer spilling, street-food-nibbling fun around the citadel.

🛏 Sleeping

From hostels in medieval buildings to boutique hotels in the attics of merchant mansions, Sighişoara has evocative accommodation to suit most budgets. Staying in a creaky, centuries-old building is one of the pleasures of visiting Sighişoara. Book well ahead for summer. Prices often rise at weekends.

Pensiune Cristina & Pavel PENSION $
(🖉 0744-159 667, 0744-119 211; www.pensiune afaur.ro; Str Cojocarilor 1; dm/d/tr 50/140/180 lei; 🅿 🕏) This cosy, family-run place is a calm haven outside the citadel, with a friendly welcome. Dorm rooms are well maintained and have lockers, private rooms are homely, and there's a shared kitchen including free tea and coffee. Breakfast costs 20 lei.

Casa Saseasca GUESTHOUSE $
(🖉 0265-772 400; www.casasaseasca.com; Piaţa Cetăţii 12; s/d from 140/154 lei; 🕏) Casa Saseasca houses nine rooms with traditionally painted Saxon furniture and widescreen views of the nearby square. There's an inviting courtyard out back and a terraced restaurant at the front. Excellent value. Breakfast not included.

Burg Hostel HOSTEL $
(🖉 0265-778 489; www.burghostel.ro; Str Bastionului 4-6; dm 45 lei, s/d 90/110 lei, without bathroom 85/100 lei; 🕏 ▣) A great budget choice without compromising on charm, Burg Hostel has spacious dorms (with handy touches like plug sockets close to beds). Common areas have chandeliers made from old cartwheels, ceramic lamps, vaulted ceilings and other rustic touches. Staff are friendly and there's a relaxing courtyard cafe. Breakfast not included, but you can buy meals from the cafe.

Hotel Gia HOTEL $
(🖉 0722-490 003; www.hotelgia.ro; Str Libertăţii 41; s/d/tr 90/110/140 lei; 🅿 @ 🕏) Spacious and chic rooms are frilled with satin and floral decorations, each with comfortable beds and mini-fridges. Barely 100m from the train station, Gia is an excellent choice for late arrivals or early starts.

Hotel Sighişoara HOTEL $$
(🖉 0265-771 000; www.sighisoarahotels.ro; Str Şcolii 4-6; d/ste from 205/340 lei; 🅿 🕏) Sighişoara lost many of its venerable buildings to a 17th-century fire, but this 1502 mansion survived. Though its 32 rooms (all with en suites) are modern and the hotel boasts a trim spa with sauna and jacuzzi and a decent **restaurant** (mains 25 lei), this cavernous place has retained a heritage feel thanks to stained-glass windows and old frescoes.

Pensiunea Legenda GUESTHOUSE $$
(🖉 0748-694 368; www.legenda.ro; Str Bastionului 8; r €26-39; 🕏) The owners of this historic guesthouse whisper that Vlad Ţepeş once wooed a beautiful young woman within these walls, a myth that will either charm or chill you. All five rooms at this well-run guesthouse have snug beds and occasional vampiric twists like black chandeliers and dungeon-like doors. Breakfast not included.

Casa Wagner HOTEL $$
(🖉 0744-388 321, 0265-506 014; www.casa-wagner.com; Piaţa Cetăţii 7; r 178-288 lei; 🕏) This appealing 16th-century hotel has 32 rooms spread across three buildings. Think pastel-coloured walls, antique furniture and tasteful rugs. The rooms in the eaves are smaller though still cosy.

★ Casa Barocă GUESTHOUSE $$$
(🖉 0742-512 711, 0365-424 929; http://casa-baroca.ro; Str Cositorarilor 9; r €120-160; 🕏) You'll feel some trepidation as you tread down stone passageways and up a creaking wooden staircase to tiny Casa Baroca. Despite this ominous beginning – or perhaps because of it – all three rooms feel thrillingly antique, retaining original wooden beams and decorated with Gothic touches like blood-red velvet armchairs and silver candlestick holders. Bathrooms, on the other hand, are polished and modern.

★ **Fronius Residence**　　GUESTHOUSE **$$$**
(☑0265-779 173; www.fronius-residence.ro; Str
Şcolii 13; d €70-120; P ❀ 🐾) Stride past walls
lined with medieval weaponry towards el-
egant rooms, some with rib-vault ceilings,
within this 400-year-old building. In the
citadel's heart, Fronius has a noble, nostal-
gic atmosphere, enhanced by vintage-style
chairs, ornate candelabra and faded pictures
of Sighişoara. Rooms are priced by their var-
ying sizes and facilities.

Ask ahead about the limited parking (five
spaces).

★ **Casa Georgius
Krauss**　　BOUTIQUE HOTEL **$$$**
(☑0365-730 840; www.casakrauss.com; Str Bas-
tionului 11; r 243-450 lei; P ❀ 🐾) This dazzling
boutique hotel is hived out of an old burgher's house at the northern end of the citadel. The restoration left period details like
wood-beamed ceilings, while adding tasteful
modern bathrooms and plush-linened beds.
The Krauss Room, number 2, has original
paintings including a medieval coat of arms,
plus a four-poster bed.

Other rooms are a little smaller, though
all have quality hardwood furnishings and
unique touches, like a fireplace in number
1 and a sunken bed in the attic room, number 9.

Staff are friendly and accommodating
and there's a quality restaurant with a fabulous wine list. Rooms are priced by size and
some have air-conditioning.

Central Park　　HOTEL **$$$**
(☑0365-730　006; www.hotelcentralpark.ro;
Piaţa Hermann Oberth 25; s/d/ste €77/90/110;
P ❀ @ 🐾) Prepare to crane your neck as
you enter this opulent hotel, where artwork
hangs high on the walls, European antiques
decorate the hallways, and chandeliers spar-
kle above a grand stairway. Rooms continue
the aristocratic feel with writing desks,
high-thread-count sheets and velvet trim-
mings, plus mod cons like TVs and safes. It's
a five-minute walk to the citadel.

Hotel-Restaurant Claudiu　　HOTEL **$$$**
(☑0744-823　101, 0265-779　882; www.hotel
-claudiu.com; Str Ilarie Chendi 28; r 315-360 lei;
P 🐾) Duck through an archway on main
drag Str Chendi to reach this intimate
guesthouse, run with loving care within a
1638 building. Hotel Claudiu's peachy colour scheme gives it a warm, soothing feel.
Meanwhile the clean rooms are decorated

in a smart modern style, and they're very
quiet.

✗ Eating & Drinking

Well-touristed Sighişoara has a mixed bag
of authentic Saxon and Romanian eateries,
often in historic buildings, and overpriced
cafes designed to squeeze a few lei out of
foreign visitors. Either way, expect a wait if
you're dining here in busy midsummer.

Café International　　CAFE **$**
(House on the Rock; Piaţa Cetăţii 8; mains 13
lei; ☺8.30am-7.30pm Mon-Sat Jun-Sep, 9am-
6pm Mon-Sat Oct-May; 🐾 🍴) This delightful
family-run cafe dishes up pies, cookies,
quiches and sandwiches. Inside is rustic
chic, while outside chairs and tables spill
onto the cobbles. Homebaked goodies range
from carrot cake to cheesecake and fruit
pies, precisely the fuel you need to make it
up to the Church on the Hill.

Central Park　　INTERNATIONAL **$$**
(☑0365-730 006; www.hotelcentralpark.ro; Cen-
tral Park Hotel, Piaţa Hermann Oberth 25; mains
25-40 lei; ☺11am-11pm; P 🐾) Even if you're
not staying at the Central Park hotel, try to
plan a meal here. Sighişoara is short on good
restaurants and this is one of the best. The
food is a mix of Romanian and international
dishes, and the carefully selected wine list
offers the best domestic labels. Dress up
for the lavish dining room or relax on the
terrace.

Altepost　　ROMANIAN **$$**
(☑0365-430 270; www.gasthaus-altepost.ro; Piaţa
Hermann Oberth 38; mains 25 lei; ☺10am-midnight)
Within a venerable 1851 building, this
guesthouse-restaurant prepares satisfying
portions of Saxon and Romanian cuisine, including spicy soups, *spätzle* (German pasta),
chicken paprika and stuffed cabbage leaves.
Pick a table either within the brick-lined
vault or on the outdoor terrace.

Casa Vlad Dracul　　ROMANIAN **$$**
(☑0265-771　596; www.casavladdracul.ro; Str
Cositorarilor 5; mains 24-35 lei; ☺11am-11pm;
🐾) The link between Dracula and tomato
soups, or medallions with potato and
chicken roulade, we'll never quite under-
stand. But the house where Vlad was born
could have been dealt a worse blow than
this atmospheric, wood-panelled restau-
rant. The menu of Romanian, Saxon and
grilled specials is dotted with Dracula

references. With a little embellishing from you, your kids will love it.

It's 5 lei to ascend to the upper room where Vlad was born (brace yourself).

Aristocrat CLUB
(www.club-aristocrat.ro; Str 1 Decembrie 1918, 57; ⊙10pm-late) Sip cocktails or boozy coffees in this converted theatre space, or twirl for live music, themed club nights and DJ sets at this catch-all cafe and nightclub.

🛍 Shopping

★ Arts & Crafts ARTS & CRAFTS
(www.thespoonman.ro; Str Cositorarilor 5; ⊙10am-6pm) Inside Casa Vlad Dracul, this wondrous handicraft shop is the brainchild of self-styled 'Spoonman' Mark Tudose, who employs traditional woodcarving methods to fashion Transylvanian spoons (each with a local legend behind it), as well as painted-glass icons, clay statues, painted eggs and much more. It's a beautiful place to browse, and your best bet for finding a culturally meaningful souvenir.

Ask about wood-carving classes inside.

ℹ Information

BRD (Str 1 Decembrie 1918, 20; ⊙9am-5pm Mon-Fri) One of several banks with 24-hour ATMs along Str 1 Decembrie 1918.

Farmacia Genţiana (Piaţa Hermann Oberth 45; ⊙7.30am-8pm Mon-Fri, from 8am Sat & Sun) Pharmacy at the bottom of the citadel.

Info Sighişoara (☏0744-372 073; www.infosighisoara.ro; Str O Goga 8; ⊙10am-6pm Tue-Sat) Private accommodation service; can help find rooms.

Tourist Information Centre (☏0788-115 511; Piaţa Muzeului 6; ⊙9am-5pm) Cordial, multilingual information service adjoining the Clock Tower, with maps and transport information.

ℹ Getting There & Away

Direct trains connect Sighişoara's **train station** (☏0265-771 130; www.cfrcalatori.ro; Str Libertăţii 51) with Braşov (18 to 40 lei, 2½ to 3½ hours, six daily), Bucharest (67 lei, five to 5½ hours, three daily; more via Braşov), Cluj-Napoca (30 to 60 lei, 4½ to six hours, four daily; more via Teius) and Sibiu (13 lei, 2½ to three hours, two daily; more via Mediaş).

For Oradea, change trains in Cluj-Napoca. For Alba-Iulia, head to Teius and switch trains there.

The station provides a **left luggage** (per day 7 lei; ⊙24hr) service.

Next to the train station, the **main bus station** (Autogara Sighişoara; ☏0265-771 260; www.autogari.ro; Str Libertăţii 53) sends buses of various sizes and colours to Braşov (18 to 25 lei, 2½ hours, three daily), Făgăraş (19 lei, 2½ hours, one daily) and Sibiu (20 lei, 2½ hours, four daily). Maxitaxis pass by hourly for Târgu Mureş (18 lei, 1½ hours). There is a handful of daily services to Daneş (4 lei, 20 minutes). Additionally, some international bus services leave from **Bus Station 2** (Autogara 2; Str Morii 21).

ℹ Getting Around

Find paid parking along Str 1 Decembrie 1918. Buy tickets from the roadside machines (per hour/day 1.50/5 lei).

Taxis wait at the bottom of the main entrance to the citadel, with rates per kilometre around 2.40 lei. Hotels and guesthouses can negotiate with honest taxi drivers for a return trip to Biertan for around 120 lei.

Rent-a-Car Sighişoara (☏0744-759 433, 0748-220 940; www.rent-a-car-sighisoara.com.ro; cnr Str 1 Decembrie 1918 & Piaţa O Goga; from 90 lei per day; ⊙9am-5pm Mon-Fri) Reputable car hire operator who can bring a vehicle to your chosen address.

Fortified Saxon Villages

Remote, romantic villages along the Târnave plateau have the power to plunge you deep into Transylvania's past. Dotted between Sighişoara and Sibiu, churches flanked by watchtowers and stocky walls rise from tumbledown villages. These imposing constructions hark back to medieval Transylvania, when the threat of attacks from the Turks prompted a frenzy of defence-building.

Though Saxon residents largely drifted away from these villages from WWII onwards, Saxon flavour can be strongly sensed through well-preserved churches and in rarer cases, German-speaking locals. Today the villages are slow-paced places, where horses and carts rattle along gravel roads and flocks of sheep force you to snap off your car engine and wait.

Most visitors are drawn to Biertan and Viscri, though tiny Mălâncrav and Alma Vii have charms worth exploring.

History

In 1123 Hungarian King Géza II invited Saxons – mainly from the Franken region in western Germany – to settle here. In the 15th and 16th centuries, following the increased threat of Turkish attacks on their towns, the settlements were strengthened with bulky city walls and fortified churches. Defensive towers in the churches served as observation posts. Town entrances were guarded with a portcullis that could be quickly lowered.

Transylvania's Saxons began to leave for Germany and Austria after WWII. Many more departed after the 1990 revolution, leaving pretty villages ghostly and untended. Many were swiftly inhabited by Roma people.

Subsequent inhabitants felt little connection to the region's Saxon heritage. The Mihai Eminescu Trust (www.mihaieminescu trust.org) is attempting to bridge the gap and instil a sense of pride in regional history, with restoration projects and tourism initiatives that involve local people.

Biertan

POP 2500

Rising sharply above a huddle of Saxon-style buildings, Biertan's fortified church is a poetic sight. Medieval-themed inns and pastel-coloured houses surround the church, charming countless visitors to make a day-trip here from Sighişoara (30km) and Sibiu (80km).

◉ Sights

Fortified Church CHURCH
(adult/child 8/4 lei; ⊙9am-5pm Mon-Sat Apr-Oct) Biertan's late-Gothic church, ringed by concentric walls and flanked by towers, is among the largest and most impressive in Transylvania. The triple-naved church was built between 1493 and 1522, housing superbly preserved Renaissance artwork, an intricately carved pulpit and mosaicked door. The church and its majestic fortifications won a Unesco listing, along with the medieval core of Biertan village.

Near the altar in the church is the sacristy that once held treasure behind its formidable door with an even more formidable lock: it has 19 locks activated by a single key, a marvel of engineering that made waves at the Paris World Expo in 1900.

Inside the grounds are many buildings of interest, including a small bastion, which is famous in local lore: couples wanting a divorce were supposedly locked in here for two weeks as a last attempt to resolve differences. There was only one bed, one table and one set of cutlery. The method has been so successful that stories claim that only one

couple decided to go through with divorce in more than 300 years.

✪ Festivals & Events

It's impossible to imagine a more perfect location for the **Lună Plină Film Festival** (www.lunaplinafestival.ro; ⊙late Aug) of horror and fantasy film than the Gothic fortress of Biertan. International and Romanian films are screened at various locations. Book accommodation well ahead.

🛏 Sleeping & Eating

There are a dozen guesthouses around town, most of them family-run affairs. It's best to call ahead.

Pensiunea Thomas APARTMENT $$
(⌨0742-024 065; Str 1 Decembrie; apt €90) Both of these 100-sq-m apartments within a renovated Saxon building enjoy fortress views, and have refined decor and crisp linens. At a pinch, the apartments can sleep up to six people, making use of two bedrooms and a pull-out sofa.

It's a sister property to Unglerus Medieval Resort.

Unglerus Medieval Resort GUESTHOUSE $$
(⌨0742-024 065; www.biertan.ro; Str 1 Decembrie, 1; d/apt €40/65; 🛜) Brassy bedframes, wood beams and the occasional antique make this guesthouse a refined and atmospheric spot to bed down in Biertan. Book ahead.

Unglerus Medieval Restaurant ROMANIAN $$$
(⌨0742-024 065; www.biertan.ro/restaurant/ unglerus-restaurant.htm; Str 1 Decembrie, 1; mains 30-65 lei; ⊙10am-10pm) Steps away from the guesthouse of the same name, Unglerus Restaurant instantly evokes time-worn grandeur with its high-backed chairs, wood-beamed ceilings, ornately carved banisters and oil paintings of knights and maidens. Satisfying goulash with polenta, spaghetti, tarragon and pork soup, and fried trout are on offer, though the wine cellar is the standout reason to stop by.

❶ Getting There & Away

Visiting Biertan is easiest by car, but four to six daily buses connect Biertan with Mediaş (10 to 12 lei, 45 minutes), which is reachable by train from Sighişoara. It's possible to hire a taxi from Sighişoara to Biertan for around 60 lei each way.

Viscri

POP 400

With a medieval fortification at its heart and bucolic meadows in its surrounds, Viscri epitomises the romance of rural Transylvania. Flowing from Viscri's medieval fortified church are cobbled lanes flanked by rows of cornflower-blue houses. The only sounds are the rattle of horse-drawn carts and the clank of a blacksmith's workshop.

The Saxon population may have thinned to around a dozen, but this remains one of the best-preserved Saxon villages in Romania. Transformative investment from the Mihai Eminescu Foundation has turned traditional buildings into guesthouses and established sustainable, informative ways to experience local crafts such as hand-stitched felt.

⊙ Sights & Activities

Gerhild Gross (📞0742-077 506) can help arrange 90-minute horse-and-cart trips (60 lei) with the opportunity to see shepherds and blacksmiths perform their traditional crafts. Through Gerhild, you can also visit local women who make felt hats and slippers; you're encouraged to buy, though there's no hard-sell and delicately hand-stitched goods do the talking.

Fortified Church   MUSEUM
(adult 8 lei, student 4 lei, child free; ⊙10am-1pm & 2-7pm mid-Jun–mid-Sep, 10am-1pm & 2-6pm Apr–mid-Jun & mid-Sep–mid-Oct) The whitewashed and tile-roofed fortified church in Viscri is a splendidly restored feat of medieval engineering. Its outbuildings display decorated furniture and agricultural tools, alongside village ceramics, and there's a tower to climb for views across Viscri's farmland. The centrepiece of the complex is a 1724 church displaying original wood carvings, paintings

and a baroque chandelier. Watch out for those floorboards.

Established by Székely builders in the early 12th century, Viscri's fortification was seized by Saxon colonists in 1185. Walls were strengthened and towers added from the 14th to 16th centuries.

🛏 Sleeping

Viscri 125   GUESTHOUSE $$$
(📞0723-579 489; www.viscri125.ro; s/d/chalet incl breakfast from €70/90/100; 🅿🛜) Wood-beamed rooms in an elegantly spare style, with Saxon touches such as rugs and floral paintwork, occupy this beautifully renovated house and barn on Viscri's main street. Hearty lunches and dinners (€15/18 per person) are available. Reserve in advance. Prices are 10% higher at weekends.

ℹ Information

Mihai Eminescu Trust (MET; 📞0265-506 024; www.mihaieminescutrust.org) Background information on restoration projects in Viscri and local guesthouses, and accommodation booking.

ℹ Getting There & Away

Reaching Viscri requires private transport. By road, it's 45km southeast of Sighișoara along route 13 and the E60, or 80km north of Brașov along the E60. When we passed through, the gravelly road through Viscri was in dire condition beyond the E60 turn-off, so prepare to dodge potholes.

Făgăraș Mountains

Slicing through the forbidding Făgăraș Mountains, the Transfăgărășan Rd offers some of Transylvania's most memorable views. You're sure to have an iron grip on the steering wheel as you navigate its sharp bends. Road access is seasonal, usually be-

---

PRINCE CHARLES: TRANSYLVANIA'S ROYAL FAN

Transylvania has found an unexpected ally in Prince Charles. The prince once quipped that with his genealogical links to Vlad the Impaler, he naturally has a *stake* in the country. Since his first visit in 1998, Prince Charles has campaigned to preserve Transylvania's countryside and Saxon architecture. And though they won't admit it, the royal stamp of approval inspires plenty of curious Brits to follow the prince's footsteps. The royal purchased a house in Viscri in 2006, and a second one in the village of Zalanpatak in 2010. Both can be rented out when Prince Charles isn't stopping by (though at the time of writing, the former was serving as a local handicrafts training centre). Learn more on http://zalan.transylvaniancastle.com.

Făgăraş Mountains

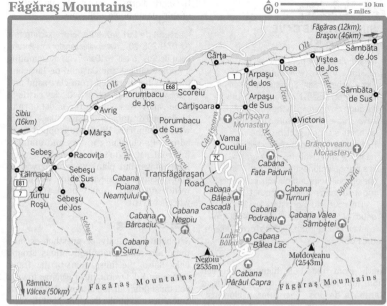

tween June and early October, but check weather conditions locally.

Access points from the north – Făgăraş and Victoria – are situated outside the mountains and lack any sort of mountain-air quaintness. Still, the monumental citadel in Făgăraş town and Şinca Veche's mysterious cave shrine warrant driving beyond the Transfăgărăşan Rd.

Făgăraş

Făgăraş (fuh-guh-*rash*) town is 25km east of the start of the Transfăgărăşan Road, but has more services than any access point north of the mountain range. Dead-centre Piaţa Republicii is handy for banks, shops and services.

◉ Sights

★ **Făgăraş Citadel** CASTLE
(Cetatea Făgăraşului; Str Mihai Viteazul 1, Făgăraş town; adult 15 lei, student 7 lei, child under 7yr free; ⊙ 8am-7pm Tue-Fri, 10am-6pm Sat & Sun Jun-Sep, 8am-5pm Tue-Fri, 9am-5pm Sat & Sun Oct-Mar) Encircled by a moat fringed with willow trees, Făgăraş Citadel is an impressively intact fortification from medieval Transylvania. The oldest part of this mighty fortress is the 14th-century Red

Tower (actually a warm beige), with impenetrable 3m-thick walls. Included in the ticket price is entry to the **Valer Literat Museum** (⏍ 0268-211 862; www.muzeufagaras. ro; Făgăraş Citadel, Str Mihai Viteazul 1), whose visual highlights include delicately painted Saxon furnishings and a room exhibiting splendid glassware from Porumbacu de Sus village.

Built over a 12th-century wooden fortress razed to the ground by Tatars, the citadel began to take shape in 1310. It soon gained a reputation as Transylvania's strongest fortress; in parts of the complex, two walls run parallel creating a barrier 8m thick. Exploring the site, you'll also see a bastion used to store artillery, and a rather too accessible scaffold (complete with hangman's noose).

Don't miss seeing the **Black Tower** (again beige), which first belonged to Wallachia's 14th-century rulers, Mircea cel Bătrân and stake-loving Vlad Ţepeş, before being completed by Prince Stefan Báthory in the 16th century.

Sâmbăta

Mountain-backed meadows and an impressive monastery have turned placid Sâmbăta into a surprise tourist hit. The region rolls

ȘINCA VECHE CAVE MONASTERY

Mystery and awe hang thick in the air in Șinca Veche (www.sincaveche.ro; Șinca Veche; ⊙ 8am-8pm summer, 9am-6pm winter) FREE. Natural light pours through an opening in the ceiling of a cave-shrine; the faithful arrive to stand within this simple grotto, bathe in its healing light, and pray for fertility or health. A short walk from the grotto is a tranquil monastery. You can visit the outbuildings and church, but dress modestly and respect the quiet.

The cave and monastery are 1km south of Șinca Veche village, itself 30km east and south from Făgăraș town (take the E68).

south from the E68 highway between Sibiu and Făgăraș town; the turn-off is at **Sâmbăta de Jos**. Thereafter, a gloriously scenic drive bypasses acres of cornfields, with the Făgăraș Mountains beckoning behind them. First you'll reach **Sâmbăta de Sus** village (6km); another 7km south is the touristic complex, where stately Brâncoveanu Monastery (one of Romania's wealthiest) stands peacefully amid *pensiunes* and cafes.

◉ Sights

Brâncoveanu Monastery　　　MONASTERY
(📞 0730-556 342; www.manastireabrancoveanu.ro; Sâmbăta de Sus; ⊙ 8am-6pm) FREE Wondrously decorated with carved columns, apocalyptic frescoes and gardens with barely a petal out of place, Brâncoveanu Monastery is as pristine as its mountain backdrop. Named after its original founder, Wallachian prince Constantin Brâncoveanu (1688–1714), a few dozen monks still live here, meditating in the glittering Orthodox church and fashioning the glass icons for which Sâmbăta is famous. Ask for entry to the onsite Glass Icon Museum to see examples.

Founded in 1696, Brâncoveanu Monastery has been a lightning rod for spirituality in the Făgăraș Mountains ever since. Restorations between 1929 and 1936 polished up the belfry and added stone colonnades. Today it's popular with Romanian visitors. Bring a bottle to fill with holy water from the marked urns, if you want to take a splash of spirituality home with you.

Castelul de Lut Valea Zanelor　ARCHITECTURE
(📞 0721-298 207; www.valeazanelor.ro; Porumbacu de Sus; 5 lei; ⊙ 10am-7pm) Resembling a gnome village, the Castelul de Lut complex has been created from clay, sand and pure whimsy. The self-styled 'clay castle of pixie valley' was built in the midst of tumbledown Porumbacu de Sus village, 26km west of Sâmbăta. When we stopped by to admire its charming towers and undulating roofs, it hadn't yet opened for overnight stays. But plans were underway to allow visitors to sleep in this weird and wonderful place. You'll need your own wheels to visit.

🛏 Sleeping

Sâmbăta has plenty of guesthouses, and there are some charming options around Lake Bâlea, the finish point of the Transfăgărășan Rd. Overnight in Făgăraș town if you must (after all, it has most of the region's amenities and public transport) but its humdrum *pensiunes* aren't likely to prolong your stay.

Făgăraș town has the biggest choice of cafes and fast food, followed by Sâmbăta. In general, dining choices are unreliable (especially outside summer) so stock up, especially for road trips or hikes.

Casa Marta　　　　　　　　PENSION $$
(📞 0760-454 533, 0764-141 414; sscumpika88@ yahoo.com; Sâmbăta de Sus; r 225 lei; 🅿) Around 250m from the Brâncoveanu Monastery, this agreeable pension feels a little 1970s, but in the most comforting way. Satellite TVs, decent bathrooms and a peaceful garden are among Casa Marta's simple perks.

Cabana Bâlea Cascadă　　　　HOTEL $$
(📞 0724-244 463; www.balea-turism.ro; s/d/tr 130/160/195 lei; 🅿 🛜) Right near the cable car up to Lake Bâlea, this lodge offers roomy but simply furnished rooms with dreamy views of the mountains.

Cabana Bâlea Lac　　　　ROMANIAN $$
(📞 0745-072 602; www.balealac.ro; mains 15-35 lei; 🖉) Bordering Lake Bâlea, this cabin and restaurant has seasonal cuisine from soups and cheese plates to mushroom stews. It's the perfect finish after a thrilling drive along the Transfăgărășan Rd.

ⓘ Getting There & Away

Drivers rule the Făgăraş Mountains. Main draws are the Transfăgărăşan Rd and poorly connected Sâmbăta, so private transport is ideal. You can hire a car in Sibiu or Braşov (www.autonom.ro).

The main public transport hub is Făgăraş town, 13km east of the turn-off to Sâmbăta and 25km east of the start of the Transfăgărăşan Rd. Buses and maxitaxis pass Făgăraş from Braşov (15 lei, 1½ hours, 12 daily) on their way to Sibiu.

Făgăraş' train station sends direct trains to Braşov (9 to 22 lei, 1½ hours, 11 daily), Sibiu (12 to 28 lei, two hours, eight daily) and Bucharest (60 lei, 4½ hours, two daily).

Sibiu

POP 154,890

Sibiu is awash in aristocratic elegance. Noble Saxon history emanates from every art nouveau facade and gold-embossed church. Renowned composers Strauss, Brahms and Liszt all played here during the 19th century, and Sibiu has stayed at the forefront

---

THE TRANSFĂGĂRĂŞAN ROAD

The Transfăgărăşan Rd (the 7C) is Romania's highest asphalted road. Driving its hairpin bends is a white-knuckle adventure: along some stretches, you're hemmed in by sharp cliffs and forest. After a few twists and turns, these abruptly give way to breathtaking mountain views. The two-lane 'road to the clouds' sometimes has the narrowest of shoulders separating it from the edge of a cliff. Voted by TV's *Top Gear* as the world's best road, it provides an unforgettable experience behind the wheel.

Ceauşescu's most celebrated project was built in the 1970s over the course of 4½ short years – 6 million kg of dynamite was used to blast out 3.8 million cu metres of rock, and at least 38 overworked soldiers died in accidents during its hasty construction. Though other routes east and west of here cut an easier north–south route, Ceauşescu thought it wise to secure the Carpathian crossing at the traditional border between Wallachia and Transylvania, in case of invasion.

How to tackle it: The Transfăgărăşan Rd is most commonly accessed from the northern end, where a 35km drive will take you south from Hwy 1 to the haunting glacial Lake Bâlea (2034m). No public transport follows this route, parts of which are closed from October to May (roughly). Driving here isn't permitted at night.

Starting from Hwy 1 in the north, the drive gets interesting at Km12, when the road begins a series of jagged turns through forest. As you keep climbing, the trees start to thin, their veil replaced by unfolding views of sheer rock face. By Km20, your ears are popping. At Km22, you arrive at the *cascadă* (waterfalls). The 360-degree views here are stunning: walls of mountains surround the area, and the distant waterfalls' slash of white appears like a lightning bolt in a grey sky. There are souvenir stands, a restaurant and the Cabana Bâlea Cascadă (p108) as well as the Telecabina Bâlea (one-way adult/child 30/15 lei; ⊙9am-5pm), a cable car that whisks you up to Lake Bâlea. Alternatively, follow the scenic blue-flecked trail (2½ to three hours). The remaining 13km up to Lake Bâlea is a maze of razor-sharp zigzags hanging over precipices framing breathtaking views.

The crowning glory: Lake Bâlea hovers like a mirror among the rocks, sometimes totally enshrouded by clouds that come billowing over the peak above it. Cabana Bâlea Lac (p108) is here, a chalet and restaurant with seasonal cuisine from soups and cheese plates to mushroom stews. To get here during snow, you'll have to park at Cabana Bâlea Cascada and take the cable car the rest of the way. And remember, temperatures here can be very cold even if it's boiling at the foot of the mountain, so wrap up.

Dedicated road trippers can continue an additional 118km south to Piteşti, via Curtea de Argeş. After an 887m-long tunnel through rock under the Palţinu ridge, the road descends the less impressive south side along the Argeş Valley. After re-entering forest, just when you think the fun is over, the road suddenly hugs the shores of the picturesque Lake Vidraru and crosses a 165m-high arched dam (1968). Beyond the lake, just off the road, is the Poienari Citadel (p69), the real Dracula's castle (where Vlad Ţepeş ruled).

of Romania's cultural scene through its festivals of opera, theatre and film, as well as rock, jazz and more. The country's first hospital, school, library and pharmacy were all established here, and locals are justly proud of the spirit of enterprise that endures to this day.

Beyond its grand architecture, Sibiu has a good dose of bohemian flair. Houses with distinctive eyelid-shaped windows (imagine a benign 'Amityville Horror' House) watch a cast of artists and buskers bustling below them. Cafes and bars inhabit brick-walled cellars and luminously decorated attics. Sibiu's soul lies somewhere in between genteel coffee culture and unbridled creativity; go find it.

History

Founded on the site of the former Roman village of Cibinium, during the peak of Saxon influence, Sibiu had some 19 guilds (each representing a different craft) within the sturdy city walls protected by 39 towers and four bastions. Under the Habsburgs from 1692 to 1791 and again from 1849 to 1867, Sibiu (Hermannstadt in German) served as the seat of the Austrian governors of Transylvania. A great deal of Sibiu's architecture has roots in this colourful history. In 2000 Johannis Klaus of the German Democratic Forum was elected mayor, remaining hugely popular until the end of his tenure in 2014, when he moved on to become Romania's president.

◎ Sights

★ **St Mary's Evangelical Church**   CHURCH
(Catedrala Evanghelică Sfânta Maria; Piaţa Huet; adult/child 5/2 lei, with tower 8/3 lei; ⊙ 9am-8pm Mon-Sat, 11.30am-8pm Sun) Sibiu's Gothic centrepiece rises more than 73m over the old town. Inside, marvel at ghoulish stone skeletons, 17th-century tombs and the largest organ in Romania, all framed by a magnificent

Sibiu

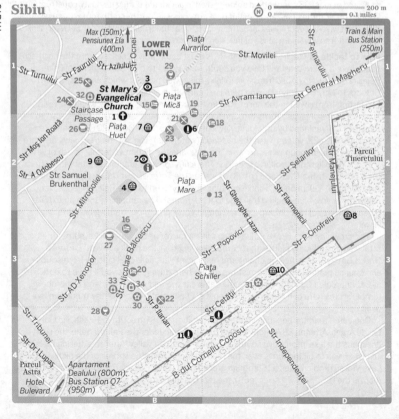

arched ceiling. Built in stages from the mid-1300s to 1520, the church was planted atop the site of an older 12th-century sanctuary. The four turrets on its tower once signified the right of the town to sentence criminals to death.

The tomb of Mihnea Vodă cel Rău (Prince Mihnea the Evildoer), son of Vlad Ţepeş, is behind the organ. The prince was murdered in front of the church in 1510.

Brukenthal Palace   GALLERY
(European Art Gallery; ☏0269-217 691; www.brukenthalmuseum.ro/europeana; Piaţa Mare 5; adult/student 20/5 lei; ☉10am-6pm Tue-Sun summer, closed Tue winter) Brukenthal Palace is worth visiting as much for its resplendent period furnishings as the European art within. Duck beneath the Music Room's chandeliers to admire colourful friezes and 18th-century musical instruments, before sidling among chambers exhibiting 17th-century portraits amid satin chaise longues and cases packed with antique jewellery. Sumptuously curated.

History Museum   MUSEUM
(Casa Altemberger; www.brukenthalmuseum.ro/istorie; Str Mitropoliei 2; adult/child 20/5 lei; ☉10am-6pm Tue-Sun Apr-Oct, 10am-6pm Wed-Sun Nov-Mar) This impressive museum begins with reenactments of cave dwellers squatting in the gloom and dioramas of Dacian life. Out of these shadowy corridors, the museum opens out to illuminating exhibitions about Saxon guilds and local handicrafts (most impressive is the 19th-century glassware from Porumbacu de Sus). There's plenty of homage to Saxon efficiency: you could expect a fine for improperly crafting a copper cake tin.

Pharmaceutical Museum   MUSEUM
(www.brukenthalmuseum.ro; Piaţa Mică 26; adult/student 10/2.50 lei; ☉10am-6pm Tue-Sun Apr-Oct, 10am-6pm Wed-Sun Nov-Mar) On the site of Sibiu's first documented apothecary, this museum delves into the herb-scented history of medicine. More than 6600 items such as microscopes, mortars and pestles, pills, powders and shudder-inducing suppository moulding kits and surgical kits are presented around the three rooms of this 1568 building.

Bridge of Lies   BRIDGE
(Podul Minciunilor) The 1859-built iron bridge is nicknamed the Bridge of Lies. Depending on who you ask, it stems either from tricky merchants who met here, or young lovers swearing their undying affection (or virginity). If you tell a lie upon it, it's supposed to creak.

Roman Catholic Cathedral CHURCH

(Piaţa Mare; ☉9am-6pm) The inside of this baroque church, built between 1726 and 1738, gleams with gold decoration and bright frescoes.

Franz Binder Museum
of World Ethnology MUSEUM

(www.franzbinder.sibiu.ro; Piaţa Mică 11; adult/child 20/10 lei; ☉10am-6pm Tue-Sun Jun-Sep, 9am-5pm Tue-Sun Oct-May) Named for a 19th-century collector from Sibiu, the Franz Binder Museum of World Ethnology was undergoing a revamp when we passed through. A scattering of musical instruments and a mummy were on display, but a reopening of its vast, global collection of objets d'art was imminent.

Banca Agricolă LANDMARK

(Piaţa Mare 2) Banca Agricolă is one of Piaţa Mare's most impressive sights; the art nouveau building, dating to the early 20th century, now houses the town hall and tourist information centre.

ASTRA National Museum Complex MUSEUM

(Muzeul Civilizaţiei Populare Tradiţionale ASTRA; ☑0269-202 447; www.muzeulastra.ro; Str Pădurea Dumbrava 16-20; adult/child 17/3.50 lei; ☉8am-8pm May-Sep, 9am-5pm Oct-Apr) Five kilometres from central Sibiu, this is Europe's largest open-air ethnographic museum, where churches, mills and traditional homes number among 400 folk architecture monuments on site. In summer, ASTRA hosts numerous fairs, dance workshops and musical performances, so it's worthwhile checking the website for events. There's also a nice gift shop and restaurant with creekside bench

seats. Get there via bus 13 from Sibiu's train station.

🏃 Activities

Carpathian Travel Centre TOURS

(☑0740-843 678; www.carpathian-travel-center. com; Piaţa Mare 12; ☉9am-6pm Mon-Fri, to 1pm Sat May-Oct) Offers city tours as well as hiking and cycling trips in the surrounding countryside.

✨ Festivals & Events

Sibiu Jazz Festival MUSIC

(www.sibiujazz.ro; ☉May) Many consider Sibiu to be Romania's jazz capital. During this spring festival, the town is awash in smouldering sounds: open-air jazz parades, jam sessions and performances in intimate venues.

International Theatre Festival THEATRE

(www.sibfest.ro; ☉Jun) This 10-day festival is the most prominent annual performing arts event in Romania, with 70 countries involved.

International Opera
Music Festival PERFORMING ARTS

(www.filarmonicasibiu.ro; ☉mid-Sep) Welcoming a host of international acts, this popular festival is staged in September.

International Astra Film Festival FILM

(☑0269-202 430; www.astrafilm.ro; ☉mid-Oct) Since 1993 this film festival has given a spotlight to Eastern European and Romanian documentary filmmakers.

🛏 Sleeping

Sibiu has a sophisticated range of digs: boutique guesthouses in medieval buildings, palatial hotels, and even hostels with

---

CITY WALLS

South of Piaţa Mare, Str Cetăţii lines a section of the old city walls, constructed during the 16th century. As in Braşov, different guilds protected each of the 39 towers. Walk north up Str Cetăţii past a couple – the **Potters' Tower** (Turnul Olarilor; Str Cetăţii) and **Carpenters' Tower** (Turnul Dulgherilor; Str Cetăţii) – to reach the **Natural History Museum** (☑0269-436 545; www.brukenthalmuseum.ro/naturale_en; Str Cetăţii 1; adult/child 13/3.25 lei; ☉10am-6pm Tue-Sun summer, closed Tue winter), which has an average collection of stuffed animals that dates from 1849, and frequent temporary exhibitions. Further north, the street curls around the **Haller Bastion** (Str Onofreiu). When Sibiu was hit by the plague, holes were drilled through the walls to enable corpses to be evacuated more quickly from the city.

Meanwhile in the centre of the old town, guarding over Piaţa Mică, is the **Council Tower** (Turnul Sfatului; Piaţa Mică; 2 lei; ☉10am-8pm). It was first built in the 13th century and refortified in the 16th.

a touch of elegance. Beyond the central squares, homely pensions are dotted along Sibiu's residential streets. Book well ahead for summer weekends and when festivals are on.

PanGeea
HOSTEL $

(📞 0369-801 232; www.sibiuhostel.ro; Str Avram Iancu 4; 6-/8-bed dm 50/48 lei, d 120 lei; 🛜) Psychedelic decorations muddle alongside baroque-style furnishings at this unique, welcoming hostel. Six- and eight-bed dorms are comfortable, while essentials such as the shared kitchen, laundry (free) and wi-fi function nicely.

Don't miss the fabulously colourful bar, Geea Caffe (p114).

Welt Kultur
HOSTEL $

(📞 0269-700 704; www.weltkultur.ro; Str Nicolea Bălcescu 13; dm 45-53 lei, d from 137 lei; 🛜 @ 🛜) Almost too chic to be dubbed a hostel, Welt has elegant wrought-iron bunks in its spotless four-, six- and eight-bed dorms (one is women-only). Meanwhile doubles are plain but easily as comfortable as Sibiu's pricier midranges. The best rooms face the street: they have more light and better views. There are lockers and a friendly chill-out room.

Old Town Hostel
HOSTEL $

(📞 0269-216 445; www.hostelsibiu.ro; Piaţa Mică 26; dm/d 50/150 lei; 🛜) Though housed in a 450-year-old building, the dorms and private rooms at Old Town Hostel are crisp and modern, with views of the square that deserve a far steeper price tag. Benefits include a welcome drink, lockers, free tea and coffee and laundry facilities; plus the cheery staff can help arrange car and bike hire. Breakfast is an extra 5 lei.

Pensiunea Ela
PENSION $

(📞 0269-215 197; www.ela-hotels.ro; Str Nouă 43; s/d/tr 110/130/180 lei; 🛜) Down a quiet street in a 17th-century building, this homely pension has eight basic rooms with a retro feel. The flower-filled courtyard, complete with wagon wheels, completes the rustic air, and owner Ela is a genial host. There are larger rooms designed for families, and a small children's playground.

The Council
BOUTIQUE HOTEL $$

(📞 0369-452 524; www.thecouncil.ro; Piaţa Mică 31; s/d/apt from €50/55/109; 🛜 🛜) Tapping into Sibiu's medieval lifeblood, this opulent hotel occupies a 14th-century hall

in the heart of the old town. Individually designed rooms are equipped with desks, security safes and plenty of contemporary polish, but there are aristocratic touches like crimson throws, bare wooden rafters and Turkish-style rugs.

Am Ring
HOTEL $$

(📞 0269-206 499; www.amringhotel.ro; Piaţa Mare 14; s/d/ste 250/290/390 lei; 🛜 🛜) Centrally located and decorated in a smorgasbord of styles, this is Sibiu's most lavish place to sleep. From the vaulted brick dining room to bedrooms styled with original wooden beams, throne-like chairs and baroque touches like gold candelabra, Am Ring exudes old-world elegance.

Apartament Dealului
APARTMENT $$

(📞 0741-179 800; Str Dealului 21; 1-/2-bed apt from 160/180 lei; 🅿 🛜 🛜) These modern, if occasionally bare, apartments have gleaming kitchens and bathrooms, 700m southwest of Sibiu's old town. The excellent breakfast spread, with eggs, cold meats, bread and jam brought right to your apartment, is a huge bonus.

★ Casa Luxemburg
HOTEL $$$

(📞 0269-216 854; www.casaluxemburg.ro; Piaţa Mică 16; s/d/tr from 290/320/370 lei; 🛜) Rooms with a clean, classic design are ornamented with Saxon-style paintwork and pine furniture at this eager-to-please hotel in the centre. Staff can help arrange bike and car rental, and they can advise on where to park your car.

Hotel Împăratul Romanilor
HOTEL $$$

(📞 0269-216 500; www.imparatulromanilor.ro; Str Nicolae Bălcescu 2-4; s/d/ste from 240/315/365 lei; 🅿 🛜 🏊) If a baroque bedroom seems a fitting place to sleep in grand Sibiu, this hotel is sure to please. One hundred plush rooms fill the 1895 building (though some feel a little worn), and there's a sauna, gym and indoor pool.

✖ Eating

Foodies will find many, many excuses to linger in Sibiu, from authentic Italian diners to rustic Romanian cuisine. Restaurants around the main square get busy, and some of the best places are only a staircase or alley away from the centre.

★ Kulinarium
ROMANIAN, EUROPEAN $$

(📞 0721-506 070; www.kulinarium.ro; Piaţa Mică 12; mains 25-35 lei; ⊗ noon-midnight) Fresh,

TRANSYLVANIA SIBIU

well-presented Italy- and France-leaning cuisine, using seasonal ingredients, graces plates at Kulinarium. The restaurant has an intimate, casual feel, with roughly painted stone walls and dangling modern lampshades. Choose from smoky Austrian sausages, spinach soup with quail eggs, rare-beef salad, trout with polenta or well-executed pasta dishes.

★ Crama Sibiul Vechi ROMANIAN $$

(☑0269-210 461; www.sibiulvechi.ro; Str Papiu-Ilarian 3; mains 25-30 lei; ☉11am-10pm) Hidden in an old wine cellar, this is the most evocative restaurant in Sibiu. Explore Romanian fare such as cheese croquettes, minced meatballs and peasant's stew with polenta. Show up early, or reserve ahead; it's very popular.

Max ITALIAN $$

(☑0269-233 003; www.max-restaurant.ro; Str Ocnei 22; mains 20-35 lei; ☉noon-midnight) Locals' favourite Italian food is served within a restored, wood-shuttered 14th-century house, on a quiet street north of the old town. The Italian owner has perfected a menu spanning porcini-stuffed chicken, authentic *tagliatelle al ragù*, and gorgonzola gnocchi.

Crama Sibiană ROMANIAN $$

(☑0729-614 260; Piața Mică 31; mains 26-30 lei; ☉noon-midnight) Juicy seasoned ribs, meatstuffed *sarmale* (cabbage rolls) topped with duck and sour cream, and outdoor tables looking right onto Piața Mică: this is a satisfying and popular spot, with food to compensate for the sluggish service.

Weinkeller ROMANIAN $$

(☑0269-210 319; www.weinkeller.ro; Str Turnului 2; mains 20-30 lei; ☉noon-midnight) Mixing Romanian mains such as stuffed cabbage leaves with Austro-Hungarian-influenced fare like *Tafelspitz* (boiled beef) and goulash, this romantic wine cellar and restaurant is the best date spot in Sibiu.

Pasaj BISTRO $$

(☑0369-437 687; Str Turnului 3A; mains 20-25 lei; ☉11am-11pm Mon-Fri, from noon Sat & Sun; 🖘🍽) At the foot of Pasajul Scărilor, the stairs between Sibiu's upper and lower town, this intimate Italian diner serves perfect pizzas alongside Romanian soups and salads. Service is attentive, and the low-lit interior and wrought-iron tables outside are equally atmospheric.

🍷 Drinking & Nightlife

Piața Mică and Str Nicolae Bălcescu are excellent places to start on a night out, though even at weekends the outdoor drinking scene quietens down shortly after midnight. Seek out cellar bars and cafes secreted away on upper floors to keep the party going later.

Music Pub BAR

(☑0369-448 326; www.musicpubsibiu.ro; Piața Mică 23; ☉8am-3am Mon-Fri, from 10am Sat & Sun) Skip down the graffitied corridor and rub your eyes in astonishment as a cellar bar and airy verandah opens up. One of the merriest spots in town, Music Pub sparkles with straw lamps and little candles, while '90s dance and rock plays on. There's table service, it's friendly, and there's occasional live music: a surefire winning night out.

Espressee COFFEE

(Str Alexandru Dimitrie Xenopol 1; ☉8am-midnight Mon-Fri, from 10am Sat & Sun) One of a new slew of upmarket coffee places, Espressee prepares its brews with loving care, and it shows. Decadent iced coffees are a meal in themselves; try the Snickers, sprinkled with peanuts, caramel syrup and whipped cream.

Geea Caffe BAR

(Str Avram Iancu 4; ☉5pm-midnight Wed-Mon) Adjoining the whimsical PanGeea hostel (p113), this bar was decorated with animal skulls, vintage furniture and mind-bending paintings by the owner's artist husband. It's an eclectic setting for a cocktail, and frequented by plenty of travellers.

Cafe Wien CAFE

(☑0269-223 223; www.cafewien.ro; Piața Huet 4; ☉10am-2am Mon, 9am-2am Tue-Sun; 🖘) There's no more genteel Viennese tradition than *Kaffee und Kuchen* (coffee and cake), and Cafe Wien has just the right blend of refinement and relaxation to accompany your strudel or Sachertorte (chocolate cake).

Imperium Club BAR

(Str Nicolae Bălcescu 24; ☉9am-3am) Cosy barfly joint with vampish vaulted ceilings, dimly lit booths for canoodling, great cocktails (15 to 18 lei) and occasional live acts and screenings of sports events.

☆ Entertainment

Agenția de Teatrală BOOKING SERVICE

(Str Nicolae Bălcescu 17; ☉11am-6pm Mon-Fri, to 3pm Sat) Sells tickets for concerts and events.

State Philharmonic CLASSICAL MUSIC (www.filarmonicasibiu.ro; Str Cetăţii 3-5; tickets 16-30 lei; ☺ box office noon-4pm Mon-Fri) Founded in 1949, this has played a key role in maintaining Sibiu's prestige as a main cultural centre of Transylvania. It's the key venue for performances at the annual opera festival (p112).

🛍 Shopping

Gossip Tree CLOTHING (☑ 0742-985 489; www.facebook.com/GossipTreeBoutique; Str Turnului 2; ☺ 10am-8pm Mon-Fri, 11am-7pm Sat) Hand-stitched kitten ears, painted shoes and bags made from repurposed floppy discs... The imaginations of over 40 Romanian designers have run riot, filling this little boutique with inventive accessories and clothing you won't find anywhere else.

Librăria Humanitas BOOKS (Str Nicolae Bălcescu 16; ☺ 10am-8pm Mon-Sat, 11am-5pm Sun) Buy road maps for Romania and other European countries, pick up some hiking maps, or grab a drink in the cavernous cafe attached.

Souvenir Market ARTS & CRAFTS (cnr Str Papiu-Ilarian & Str Nicolae Bălcescu; ☺ hours variable) On weekends and in high summer, this small pop-up souvenir market peddles jewellery, fridge magnets and other trinkets.

ℹ Information

ATMs are located all over the centre as well as in most hotels. **Banca Comercială Română** (Str Nicolae Bălcescu 1; ☺ 9am-5.30pm Mon-Fri) is one of several banks with ATMs along Str Nicolae Bălcescu.

Farmasib (☑ 0269-217 897; Str Nicolae Bălcescu 53; ☺ 7am-10pm Mon-Fri, from 8am Sat & Sun) Sells toiletries and over-the-counter medicine.

Tourist Information Centre (☑ 0269-208 913; www.turism.sibiu.ro; Piaţa Mare 2; ☺ 9am-8pm Mon-Fri, to 6pm Sat & Sun May-Sep, 9am-5pm Mon-Fri, to 1pm Sat & Sun Oct-Apr) Based at the town hall; staff can offer free maps and plenty of local transport advice.

ℹ Getting There & Away

AIR

Sibiu International Airport (SBZ; ☑ 0269-253 135; www.sibiuairport.ro; Şoseaua Alba Iulia 73) is 5km west of the city centre.

Austrian Airlines (☑ 0256-490 397; www.austrian.com) Connects Vienna and Sibiu through daily flights.

Blue Air (☑ UK +44 (0)151 230 1590; www.blueair-web.com) Offers direct flights to Stuttgart (three weekly).

Tarom (☑ call centre 021-204 6464; www.tarom.ro; ☺ call centre 8am-8pm Mon-Fri, 9am-2pm Sat) Has direct flights to Munich and Vienna.

WizzAir (☑ premium rate 0903-760 105; www.wizzair.com) Budget airline connecting Sibiu with European destinations including London Luton (four weekly), Madrid (two weekly) and Dortmund (two weekly).

BUS

The main **bus station** (Autogara Sibiu; ☑ 0269-217 757; www.autogari.ro; Piaţa 1 Decembrie 1918) is opposite the train station; the other station, **bus station Q7** (Autogara Q7; ☑ 0269-232 826; Str Şcoala de Înot), is southwest of central Sibiu. Bus and maxitaxi services reach the following destinations. Ask locally, or look on www.autogari.ro, to see which station your service leaves from (hit the 'vezi detalii' button after making your search).

Services run to Alba Iulia (20 lei, one to 1½ hours, almost hourly), Braşov (28 lei, 2½ to three hours, 12 daily), Bucharest (50 to 55 lei, 4½ hours, 10 daily), Cluj-Napoca (35 lei, 3½ to 4½ hours, 17 daily), Deva (30 lei, two to 2½ hours, eight daily), Timişoara (60 to 65 lei, 4½ to six hours, seven daily) and Târgu Mureş (20 to 28 lei, 2½ to 3½ hours, six daily).

Maxitaxis to Cisnădie (7 lei, 25 minutes) leave half-hourly from the main bus station. Another microbus heads west five times daily, stopping in Sălişte (9 lei, one hour), 4km from Sibiel, and on to Jina (14 lei, 2½ hours).

Eurolines (www.eurolines.ro) sells tickets to many European destinations, including Vienna and Budapest.

TRAIN

Sibiu's **train station** (Gara Sibiu; ☑ 0269-211 139; www.cfrcalatori.ro; Piaţa 1 Decembrie 1918, 6) has direct trains to Braşov (40 lei, three hours, nine daily), Bucharest (61 lei, six hours, four daily; more via Braşov) and Timişoara (61 lei, 6½ hours, two daily; more via Arad).

Mostly indirect services reach Cluj-Napoca (56 lei, five hours, 12 daily) and Sighişoara (9 to 17 lei, three hours, six daily). Change at Copşa Mică or Vinţu de Jos for the former, and Copşa Mică or Mediaş for the latter. For Alba Iulia (11 to 26 lei, 2½ hours), there are two direct; otherwise change at Vinţu de Jos.

The station has self-service luggage storage (6 lei per day) available round the clock.

ℹ️ Getting Around

Trolleybus 1 connects the train station with the centre, but it's only a 500m walk along Str General Magheru to get there by foot. Bus 11 runs between central Sibiu and the airport.

Autonom (☑ 0749-151 037; www.autonom. com; Str Nicolae Bălcescu 1-3) car rental typically has the best rates, from €39 per day (or from €28 for long rentals). Also has an office at Sibiu Airport.

There's a taxi stand at the west end of Str Nicolae Bălcescu. To order a taxi, dial ☑ 0269-953 from a local phone or ☑ 0724-333 953.

Around Sibiu

Hypnotised by Sibiu's old town, smart dining scene and heady nightlife, many visitors neglect to explore its surroundings. Only a few kilometres south of Sibiu, city hubbub melts into the Transylvania of centuries past. Villages in the so-called Mărginimea Sibiului ('borders of Sibiu') have preserved traditional farming methods – look out for horses and carts – and crafts such as woodwork and icon-painting continue to thrive.

Sibiel's glass icons are an especially lovely example of the region's handicrafts; meanwhile local ethnographic museums lovingly present fine embroidery and wood-carvings. Hikers will also find joy in the numerous trails extending from Păltiniş.

Cisnădie & Răşinari

Cisnădie is worth a stop for its fortified 15th-century **Fortified Church** (Biserica Evanghelică Fortificată; www.ekh.ro; adult/student 7/4 lei; ☉ 10am-1pm & 2-6pm Mon-Sat, from 11am Sun). A museum of communism, with English translations, is found on the 1st floor of the citadel walls. Take route 106C south from Sibiu for 11km to reach the church.

Almost in the skirts of the Cindrel Mountains and 12km south of Sibiu, Răşinari is peppered with faded facades and has a little **Ethnographic Museum** (Str Octavian Goga 152, Răşinari; 4 lei; ☉ 9am-4pm Tue-Sat, to 2pm Sun) (west of the centre, follow the brown sign, then take the first left).

From Cisnădie, drive west and then north along route 106D for 8km until you see a turn-off to Răşinari, which lies another 5km southwest.

🛏️ Sleeping & Eating

Don't expect luxury in Sibiu's tranquil surrounds: the guesthouses in Cisnădie, Răşinari and along roads in between are simple, home-run affairs, and all the more charming for it. There are plenty of options listed on www.ruraltourism.ro. More glamorous digs, and efficient hostels, await in Sibiu itself.

Pensiunea Sub Cetate PENSION $
(☑ 0740-220 035; www.sub-cetate.ro; No 252, Cisnădioara; s/d/tr 100/120/160 lei; Ⓟ🛜) Saxon-style furnishings, painted with pretty floral designs, infuse this otherwise simple and homely guesthouse with traditional flavour. The restaurant (closed Mon) serves Transylvanian comfort food such as stuffed cabbage rolls and pork stew. It's between Cisnădie and Răşinari. Breakfast is an extra 22 lei.

Trattoria dei Fiori PIZZA $
(www.trattoriadeifiori.ro; Str Măgurii 57, Cisnădie; pizza 10-16 lei; ☉ 10am-10pm Mon-Fri, from noon Sat & Sun) This poky pizzeria is excellent value, serving puffy pies with a smile. Consider choosing the pizza named for your nationality: the English has ham and boiled eggs while the German is topped with sausage and pickles.

Păltiniş

Modest mountain resort Păltiniş, 35km southwest of Sibiu, is a scenic place for a short skiing or hiking trip. The resort was established in 1895, making it Romania's oldest. The ski area might be small and the mountains long enjoyed by skiers, but Păltiniş' sport facilities are modern and is served by an array of well-equipped spa hotels. In summer, hikers can enjoy spectacular trails into the Cindrel Mountains.

🏃 Activities

Arena Platoş Pătiniş (www.arenaplatos.ro; day-pass adult/child 58/38 lei; ☉ Dec-Apr) has six runs, plus a fun park and tiny 50m beginners' slope, 3km north of Păltiniş. The main chair lift **Statie Telescaun** (Chair Lift; www. telescaunpaltinis.ro; return ticket 10 lei; ☉ 9am-6pm) is open year-round and accesses skiing and hiking terrain with stunning views of the Cindrel Mountains.

🛏 Sleeping & Eating

Accommodation in Păltiniş is mostly geared towards midrange (and above) travellers looking to hike and ski, though you'll also find a scattering of budget pensions, usually no-frills affairs run by families. Book ahead for the winter sports season between December and March.

Hotel Cindrel HOTEL $$
(☑0269-574 056; www.hotelcindrel.ro; Str Cindrel; d from 216 lei; [P][🅟][🛜][🏊]) From the pool and spa centre to billiards, Cindrel has plenty of ways to while away bad-weather days in the mountains. It's 500m from the ski lifts. Standard rooms feel a little small, while superiors (from 279 lei) are huge. Ski storage is available.

Curmătura Ştezii GUESTHOUSE $$
(☑0269-557 310; www.curmaturastezii.ro; DJ 106A, KM16; s/d/tr 140/160/210 lei; [P]) Modern guesthouse with a chalet feel, on the road from Păltiniş to Răşinari (about 3km west of the latter). Rooms are well-maintained and wood-furnished, and there's a pleasant stone-walled restaurant. Owners can arrange bike hire, or horse riding with a little notice.

Cabana Păltiniş B&B $$
(☑0745-279 789; www.cabana-paltinis.ro; r from 150 lei; [P]) Hip guesthouse with an attached wine bar.

Hohe Rinne SPA HOTEL $$$
(☑0269-215 000; www.hoherinne.ro; Str Principala 1; s/d from €67/70, superior rooms from €96; [P][🛜][🏊]) Eighty-eight modern rooms with writing desks, safes, minibars and mountain chalet accents fill this satisfying hotel, named for Păltiniş' old German name. It's on the main road within easy access of hiking trails. The highlight is the spa area, with a small pool, salt chamber, jacuzzi and three (count 'em) kinds of sauna (day-pass weekday/weekend 69/88 lei).

ℹ Information

The **tourist information centre** (☑0269-223 860; centre Păltiniş; ☺8am-5pm) has information on resorts, hiking trails and maps.

ℹ Getting There & Away

Păltiniş is 35km south and west of Sibiu, along route 106A. Bus 22 links Păltiniş with Sibiu (9 lei, one hour, three to four daily).

Sibiel & Around

Surrounded by forest, there's a hint of fairytale menace in Sibiel's stark setting. A rainbow of well-tended houses is strung along Sibiel's main street, while a milk-white 18th-century church rises in front of its main draw, the Glass Icons Museum. This highly memorable collection of religious paintings is a popular detour between Sibiu and Alba Iulia.

From Sibiel, head 6km north to **Sălişte**, a quaint village with a strong shepherd tradition. Some 2km west of Sălişte are the Saxon houses of hill-backed **Galeş**, a scenic place to drive through. Exploring Sibiel and surrounding villages is an evocative day trip from Sibiu.

◎ Sights

★Zosim Oancea Glass Icons Museum MUSEUM
(☑0269-552 536; Str Bisericii 329; adult/student 5/3 lei; ☺8am-1.30pm & 2-8pm May-Sep, 7am-1.30pm & 2-7pm Oct-Apr) This museum of painted icons, named after the priest who collected them, is a true hidden gem. Unlike the sombre wooden icons you'll see elsewhere in Romania, these religious images were painted using a 300-year-old method: on the back of glass, with gold leaf decoration stuck down using egg white and garlic. Proud St Georges, tearful Virgin Marys and allegorical Bible scenes are among the 700 icons displayed across two floors, most of them in a luminous naive style.

The museum is behind the late-18th-century **Sfânta Treime** (☺8am-1.30pm & 2-8pm May-Sep, 7am-1.30pm & 2-7pm Oct-Apr) church, which has a finely frescoed interior and time-worn graveyard.

🛏 Sleeping & Eating

Sibiel has several budget *pensiunes,* most of them folksy and family-run. Other guesthouses are dotted along the main road to Sălişte and Galeş.

Restaurants serving home-cooked Romanian food tend to be tied to local guesthouses. Pickings are slim outside summer.

Pensiunea Mioriţică GUESTHOUSE $
(☑0269-552 640, 0740-175 287; coldeasv@ yahoo.com; Str Râului 197A; r/ste 80/140 lei; [P][🛜]) Mioriţică sits in a bee-humming garden with a stream passing at its feet. Amid the vivid flowers are intimate nooks for

reading and a small communist museum set up by the owner. The chalet-style buildings are enticing, housing a cosy breakfast room and rooms wrapped in verandahs to take in the forest views. Follow the stream for around 700m west from the village centre.

ℹ️ Getting There & Away

Sibiel train station, 2km east of town, has connections to Sibiu (4 lei, 30 minutes, five daily). The area is best visited by car from Sibiu.

SZÉKELY LAND

Székely Land's meadows, spa towns and occasional urban sprawl have one thing in common: their distinctly Hungarian spirit. In many places, conversation is almost entirely in the local Hungarian dialect, while signs list place names bilingually across much of Székely Land (that is, Ţara Secuilor in Romanian, Székelyföld in Hungarian). The shift from Saxon flavour in nearby Braşov and Sighişoara feels instant.

Charismatic cultural centre Târgu Mureş (Marosvásárhely in Hungarian), with a population evenly split between Romanian and Hungarian-speakers, should be your first stop. Further east, ethnic Hungarians comprise the majority in Odorheiu Secuiesc (Székelyudvarhely) and Miercurea Ciuc (Csíkszereda). Quintessential experiences are soaking in mineral-rich waters, perhaps Sovata's 'Red Sea' or a glossy spa in Băile Tuşnad, and dipping into Székely culture at the fine museums in Sfântu Gheorghe and Odorheiu.

History

The origins of Székely people are disputed. Debates rage as to whether they are descendants of the Huns, who arrived in Transylvania in the 5th century and adopted the Hungarian language, or whether they are Magyars who accompanied Attila the Hun on his campaigns in the Carpathian basin and later settled there. Three 'nations' were recognised in medieval Transylvania: the Székelys, the Saxons and the Romanian nobles.

During the 18th century, thousands of young Székely men were conscripted into the Austrian army. Local resistance in Székely Land led to the massacre of Madé-falva in 1764, after which thousands of Székelys fled into Romanian Moldavia. Following the union of Transylvania with Romania in 1918, some 200,000 Hungarians – a quarter of whom were Székelys – fled to Hungary.

A level of tension still exists between Romanians and Hungarians, who battled each other during WWI and WWII. Mention of Székely Land (in particular ethnic Hungarians not learning the Romanian language in some parts of Romania) can bring out verbal editorials, as can Romania's treatment of Hungarians in the 20th century.

Today, many Hungarian tourists flock to the area to experience pastoral customs that are fading in their motherland. Meanwhile, protests for Székely autonomy (rather than full independence from Romania) have gathered pace. In 2013, an estimated 100,000 demonstrators formed a human chain across Transylvania, with a protest of thousands in Budapest declaring solidarity. Demonstrations are often timed for 10 March, dubbed Székely Freedom Day.

Sfântu Gheorghe

POP 56,000

Sfântu Gheorghe – or Sepsiszentgyörgy, as the town is known to its Hungarian majority population – doesn't brim with sights, but it's an attractive place to delve into Székely culture. Some 32km north of Braşov, this town in Covasna county has an excellent museum on the history and traditions of Székely people, and a park fringed with Habsburg buildings and pleasant cafes. An agreeable detour.

◎ Sights

The most interesting area of town surrounds the park, **Parcul Elisabeta**. Just north is **Piaţa Libertăţii**, featuring an impressive equestrian statue of Mihai Viteazul (Michael the Brave). On the park's western flank, Stra Gábor Áron, you'll see a **plaque** showing the building where Gábor Áron and other local revolutionaries planned their armed resistance against Austrian rule (1848–9).

Strolling east from the park along Str Gróf Mikó Imre, after about 500m you can admire the outside of the **Fortificată Reformată Church**. Its cemetery contains striking examples of traditional Székely wooden crosses and graveposts.

Muzeul Naţional Secuiesc
MUSEUM

(Székely Nemzeti Múzeum; ☑ 0267-312 442; www.sznm.ro; Str Kós Károly 10; adult/child 10/5 lei; ☉ 9am-5pm Tue-Sun Jun-Aug, to 4pm Tue-Fri, to 2pm Sat & Sun Sep-May) About 200m south of Parcul Elisabeta, this wide-ranging museum has exhibitions on natural history, local history, Székely crafts and costumes, plus displays of archaeological discoveries from around the region. There's also a library with the oldest surviving Hungarian-language version of the Bible. The building holding these varied exhibitions is itself a masterpiece, in the style of a fortified church with colourfully tiled spiked roofs; it was designed by leading Hungarian architect Kós Károly between 1911 and 1912.

The museum's earliest incarnation dates even earlier, to 1875.

🛏 Sleeping

Attractive *pensiunes*, and a couple of three-star business hotels, are easy to find within walking distance of the park.

Pensiunea Lucia
PENSION $$

(☑ 0741-200 165; Str Kossuth Lajos 17; s/d 150/170 lei; P 🛜) With a grandmotherly furniture style and cheerful welcome, Pensiunea Lucia has a soothing, homely atmosphere. Rooms are large and clean, and breakfast is a spread of homemade jams and omelettes sizzled up before your very eyes.

Ferdinand B&B
PENSION $$

(☑ 0740-180 502; www.restatferdinand.ro; Str Decembrie 1918, 10; s/d/q 160/170/230 lei; P 🛜) This guesthouse, named for the owner's grandfather, is a family affair with modern rooms and a lavish breakfast spread of local products. It's just off the street in a courtyard.

🍴 Eating

Sfântu Gheorghe's dining scene comprises good-value Hungarian cuisine and a scattering of casual Italian and mixed European joints. Piaţa Libertăţii, and the stretch of Str 1 Decembrie 1918 closest to the park, have a good concentration of options.

Central
DINER $

(☑ 0744-757 515; www.centralrestaurant.ro; Str 1 Decembrie 1918, 8; mains 15 lei; ☉ 8am-midnight Mon-Fri, from 10am Sat & Sun) Breakfasts, all-you-can-eat lunch specials (22.50 lei), do-it-yourself salad buffets, pancakes... This pleasant diner with an outdoor terrace has a filling and fuss-free range of food.

★ Szentgyörgy Pince
HUNGARIAN $$

(☑ 0267-352 666; www.szentgyorgypince.ro; St Gábor Áron 14; mains 14-25 lei; ☉ 10am-midnight; 🚗) Vaulted ceilings and brick walls adorned with crests of bygone nobles establish the tone of this restaurant within an old wine cellar. Plates are heavy with Hungarian fare such as deer goulash, Transylvanian pork soup and beef stroganoff. Vegetarians will also need to wear their stretchy pants for rich dishes like paprika mushrooms with cheese-laden polenta.

COVASNA'S SPA HOTELS

Known as 'the resort of 1000 springs', there is something in the water in Covasna. The largely Hungarian spa town lies 30km east of Sfântu Gheorghe, and 45km southeast of fellow spa haven Băile Tuşnad. While the centre has few attractions, secreted away at the eastern end of Covasna is something of a spa hotel neighbourhood. Visitors flock to immerse themselves in Covasna's mineral-rich waters (along with salt chamber therapy, massage and more). **Hotel Clermont** (☑ 0267-342 123; www.clermonthotel.ro; Str Mihai Eminescu 225A, Covasna; d €68-79, ste from €101; P ❄ 🛟) has double rooms awash in yellow and gold, surgically clean bathrooms, plus a pool with sauna and whirlpool. Spa treatments include manicures and massages (from 28 lei). Nearby, despite its air of a doll's house, **Hotel Mercur** (☑ 0367-800 594; www.hotelmercurcovasna.ro; Str Mihai Eminescu 225, Covasna; s/d/ste from 290/330/500 lei; P ❄ 🛜 🛟) is one of Covasna's slickest spa hotels. Bedrooms are in soothing beige with marbled bathrooms, while deluxe apartments have a country manor feel. Pick from electrotherapy, heat therapy, or a tried-and-trusted pool and sauna combo at the wellness centre.

ⓘ Information

Tourist Information Bureau (☑ 0267-316 474; www.sepsiszentgyorgy.ro; Str 1 Decembrie 1918, 2; ⊙ 7.30am-3.30pm Mon-Wed, to 5pm Thu, to 2pm Fri Jul & Aug) Summer-only information office providing free city maps and guesthouse listings.

ⓘ Getting There & Away

The **bus station** (Str Gării) is 50m north of the train station. Direct services reach Braşov (8 lei, one hour, half-hourly), Miercurea Ciuc (12 to 15 lei, one to 1½ hours, five daily), Piatra Neamţ (40 lei, five to six hours, two daily) and Târgu Neamţ (50 lei, six hours, one daily).

From Sfântu Gheorghe **station** (☑ 0267-325 850; Str Gării), daily trains go to Covasna (4.50 lei, one hour, four daily) and Braşov (5.50 lei, 30 to 45 minutes, 12 daily), with most stopping in Hărman (4.50 lei, 30 minutes). Buy advance train tickets at the **Agenţia de Voiaj CFR** (☑ 0267-311 680; Str Gróf Mikó Imre 13; ⊙ 8am-8pm Mon-Sat).

Miercurea Ciuc

POP 42,100

Hockey, Hungarian cafe culture and a local beer are Miercurea Ciuc's three main passions. Despite this appealing trio, it's a rather benign town. Not that you'd dream of saying so to its face: for Miercurea Ciuc (Csíkszereda in Hungarian) is an earnest, family-friendly place, eager to please but too sleepy to detain you beyond a day. Dally long enough to dip into its Hungarian cafes and the castle, but then press on to Târgu Mureş or Braşov.

◉ Sights

The art nouveau **Palace of Justice** (Str G Doja 6) and **City Hall** (Piaţa Cetăţii 1) (1884–98), both built in an eclectic style, and a **Soviet Army Monument**, face Piaţa Cetăţii. Miercurea Ciuc is a hockey town: there's a heroic **hockey statue** (Str Nicolae Bălcescu) in front of the town's rink, just 200m northwest of Piaţa Cetăţii.

Csiki Sör Brewery Tour   BREWERY
(☑ 0755-030 895; www.csikisor.com/gyarlatogatas; Sânsimion; tour with 2-beer tasting/unlimited beers 25 lei/55 lei) Learn the secrets of Miercurea Ciuc's beloved brew at this factory tour, 12km south of Miercurea Ciuc, through tastings and traditional Hungarian beer snacks. After a few sips, you too will be singing the praises of the Harghita Mountains' spring water and quality hops. Tours are according to demand, so book a few days ahead by phone or the website.

Mikó Castle   CASTLE
(Csíki Székely Múzeum; www.csszm.ro; Piaţa Cetăţii; adult 10 lei, student 7 lei, child under 7yr free; ⊙ 9am-6pm Tue-Sun May-Oct, to 5pm Sep-Apr) Miercurea Ciuc's centrepiece, and the proud source of the Ciuc beer logo, is Mikó Castle. Today it houses the impressive Csíki Székely Múzeum, which hosts rotating displays of mostly Hungarian art within its venerable walls.

Built from 1623 to 1630, the castle was burnt down by Tatars in 1661 and then rebuilt in 1716. It later played a role as defence

---

WORTH A TRIP

SIMMERING IN SALTY WATER AT BĂILE TUŞNAD

Known as 'Transylvania's pearl', dainty Băile Tuşnad is hidden among the volcano-made Harghita Mountains, 32km south of Miercurea Ciuc. Its heart is tiny **Lacul Ciucaş**, fringed by tall evergreens with invigorating spas close to its shore.

Legends say that in 1842 a shepherd boy's festering ulcers were cured with a splash of Băile Tuşnad's water. An industry took off only a few years later, bottling these salty, thermally warmed waters and using them to target ailments as wide-ranging as paleness, nerves, and rheumatic trouble.

Wellness Tuşnad (☑ 0756-118 479; www.wellness-tusnad.ro; 3hr session adult/child 30/15 lei, per 30min thereafter 5/3 lei; ⊙ 10am-9pm Tue-Sun, 2-9pm Mon), bordering the lake, looks a little like a Saxon citadel and has swimming pools, salt chambers, a sauna and a steam room.

Beyond simmering in salty water, Băile Tuşnad has walking trails in the bracing, pine-scented air, and it's a good base to visit St Anne's Lake, 24km southeast by road. The **InfoTur Stand** (☑ 0744-693 814; Str Oltului; ⊙ 8am-4pm Mon-Fri), opposite the impossible-to-miss Hotel Tuşnad, offers maps and posts a list of local pensions on the outside.

Miercurea Ciuc

sions tend to be well-worn; apartments are often more modern.

Hilcon Family Apartments APARTMENT $
(www.apartments.hilcon.ro; Str Salciei; ste from 65 lei; P 🛜) The stripey apartment blocks in Miercurea Ciuc's residential areas seem endless, but judging by Hilcon Family Apartments, they're exceedingly pleasant inside. Simple and serviceable 'studios' include access to a kitchen (shared with one other room). Furnishings are bare but washing machine, zippy fast wi-fi and can-do hosts make up for it. Bookings through website only.

Hotel Korona HOTEL $
(📋0266-310 993; www.korona.panzio.ro; Str Márton Áron 40; r from 140 lei; P 🛜) This graceful Habsburg-era building is ornamented in stucco casts and carriage lamps and has 16 functional rooms with en suites.

✖️ Eating

Pedestrianised Str Petöfi Sándor is comprised almost entirely of cafes and pizza joints.

La Jupânu ROMANIAN $
(www.lajupanu.ro; Str Zöld Péter 1; mains 12-20 lei; ⊘8am-midnight Mon-Fri, from 10am Sat, from noon Sun) Popular with a lively crowd of eaters and drinkers, this traditional restaurant has bench seats and locally recommended food (pork schnitzels, chicken breast and more).

Novák CAFE
(Str Petőfi Sándor; ⊘7am-10pm Mon-Fri, from 8am Sat, from 9am Sun) Creamy Black Forest gateau, Sachertorte (Viennese dark chocolate cake), macarons and coffee are all the more enjoyable when served to diverting views of locals ambling down Miercurea Ciuc's pedestrian drag.

for the Habsburg empire, housing the first Székely infantry in 1849.

Franciscan Monastery CHURCH
(Str Szék 148) Some 2km northeast of the centre in the Şumuleu district (Csíksomlyó in Hungarian) is a fine Franciscan monastery, built in 1442 by Iancu de Hunedoara (János Hunyadi), governor of Hungary from 1446 to 1452, to commemorate his great victory against the Turks at Marosszentimre.

The monastery today is the site of the city's main tourist draw, the **Pentecostal Pilgrimage**. About 300,000 Székelys flock here on Whitsunday (late May/early June) to celebrate their brotherhood.

🛏️ Sleeping

There is a handful of budget and midrange options for stays in Miercurea Ciuc. Pen-

ℹ️ Information

Banca Comercială Română (Str Kossuth Lajos 17; ⊙ 9.30am-5pm Mon-Fri) One of several banks with ATMs along Str Kossuth Lajos.

Tourist Information Centre (📋 0266-317 007; www.szereda.ro; 1st fl, City Hall, Piaţa Cetăţii 1; ⊙ 8am-4pm Mon-Fri summer) A well-hidden seasonal information office on the 1st floor of city hall.

ℹ️ Getting There & Away

From Miercurea Ciuc **train station** (📋 0266-315 102; Str Braşovului 1), services reach Braşov (30 lei, two to 2½ hours, 10 daily, some at night), several via Sfântu Gheorghe (22 lei, 1½ hours); three continue to Bucharest (67 lei, 5½ hours). There are also 11 daily trains to Gheorgheni (18 lei, 1½ hours), and one to Iaşi (80 lei, seven hours).

The **bus station** (Str Braşovului) is 50m north of the train station. Buses go to Braşov (20 lei, two hours, three daily), six to Gheorgheni (12 lei, 1½ to two hours), plus five to Sfântu Gheorghe (15 lei, 1½ hours), nine to Odorheiu Secuiesc (12 lei, one hour), and one to Budapest (130 lei, 11½ hours).

Gheorgheni

POP 20,020

Gheorgheni's Hungarian heritage and flashes of Armenian history are diverting enough, but this languid town is best used as a springboard to the countryside. Gheorgheni is in the midst of superlative road-trip country: roads meander between towering forests (especially along the 13B to Sovata), the best restaurants are snuggled within small villages, and 25km east lies forest-fringed **Lacu Roşu** (Red Lake).

⊙ Sights

Look out for the runic Old Hungarian alphabet, which can be seen on street signs around Gheorgheni. This writing form is so ancient that linguists can't agree on it precise origin. Locals proud of their Székely heritage think it's due for a comeback. Another unexpected influence is Armenian culture: Gheorgheni had a sizeable Armenian minority in the 18th century and is home to an **Armenian Church** (on, appropriately named, Str Biserica Armeană).

Lăzarea Castle   CASTLE
(Lázár Kastély; Lăzarea) Just 6km northwest of Gheorgheni on the road to Topliţa is the tiny village of Lăzarea (Gyergyószárhegy in

Hungarian). The predominantly Hungarian village is dominated by its 16th-century castle, whose walls are crowned with unique sculpted designs. Gábor Bethlen, later to become prince of Transylvania (r 1613–29), was raised within this Renaissance-style citadel. When we passed through, the castle doors were closed indefinitely and renovations were hotly expected.

🛏️ Sleeping & Eating

Gheorgheni has serviceable budget guesthouses, though few have charisma. For a slice of Székely country living, visitors with private transport can explore surrounding villages Borsec, Lăzarea and Borzont, each of which has *pensiunes*.

Astoria   HOTEL **$**
(📋 0266-365 600; www.astoria-hotel.ro; Str Două Poduri 2; s/d 100/150 lei; 🅿️ 🛜) Gheorgheni's most mellow place to stay is the Astoria Hotel, in a turreted building down a quiet street off Str Márton Áron. Yellow-tinged bedrooms are contemporary and well-tended, if a little bare. Friendly staff can arrange horse-riding excursions into the countryside.

Lázár Panzió   PENSION **$**
(📋 0266-362 042; www.lazarpanzio.ro; Str Băii 3; s/d/tr 78/98/128 lei; 🅿️ 🛜) Family-run since the 1930s, this guesthouse-restaurant 30m west of Piaţa Libertăţii offers no-frills rooms with home comforts like fresh sheets, reading lights and small TVs. Breakfast is an extra 10 lei.

⭐ **Basa Fogadó**   HUNGARIAN **$$**
(📋 0745-399 286; www.basafogado.com; Str Principala 131, Borzont; mains 20 lei; ⊙ 8am-11pm; 🍴) Driving the Gheorgheni–Sovata road, it's impossible to miss this folksy inn, marked with a giant roadside knife and fork. Fifteen kilometres west of Gheorgheni, this country dining room with knee-slapping hospitality is worth travelling for. The inn was established in 1897, and it has been whipping up chicken stew, bacon-wrapped garlic pork, and green pea soup ever since.

Erdélyi Gondűző   HUNGARIAN **$$**
(📋 0752-048 874; www.erdelyi-gonduzo.ro; 12C Km6.5; mains 20 lei; ⊙ 10am-9.30pm) En route to Lacu Roşu, tuck into juicy roasted sausage, grilled trout, fried cheese – or heck, maybe all three – at this inviting restaurant and pension. It's 7km east of Gheorgheni.

ℹ Information

Tourist Information Centre (☎0730-710 965; www.visitgheorgheni.ro; Piața Libertății 22; ⊙8am-4pm Mon-Fri) Superbly helpful staff offer maps, outdoor advice and good humour at Gheorgheni's tourist office.

ℹ Getting There & Away

The **bus station** (☎0266-363 999; Str Gării) and **train station** (Str Gării) are 2km west of the centre.

There are direct buses to Brașov (30 lei, 2½ hours, three daily) and Odorheiu Secuiesc (30 lei, 2½ to three hours, two daily). Routes also extend to Târgu Mureș (25 to 30 lei, two to four hours, seven daily), continuing to Cluj-Napoca (35 lei, 4½ to 6½ hours). Bus services also reach Lacu Roșu (5 lei, 30 minutes, five to seven daily).

Trains go to Brașov (45 lei, three to 3½ hours, seven daily) and Baia Mare (73 lei, seven hours, one daily) and Bucharest North (73 lei, six hours, three daily).

Odorheiu Secuiesc

POP 36,530

With baroque buildings, galleries and genteel cafe culture, Odorheiu Secuiesc is a pleasant spot to enjoy some Hungarian flavour. Around 96% of the town's residents identify as Hungarian, which is reflected in the language and cuisine: you'll spot signs in both Romanian and Hungarian, and enjoy poppyseed cake and *gulyás* (goulash) galore.

Most locals refer to the town as Székelyudvarhely, unfortunately no easier for foreigners to pronounce than its Romanian name. It's an agreeable detour between Sighișoara and the east.

History

Settlements have been scattered around the southeastern stretch of the Transylvanian basin since the late Stone Age, though the first mention of the town – then 'Uduorhel' – was in 1333. Uduorhel grew as a market town and was granted privileges by Queen Isabella (then regent of Transylvania) in 1557, allowing it to thrive. Transylvanian prince Gábor Bethlen affirmed its status and rights in 1615. Several buildings in town are restorations of structures that date to its prosperous 16th to 18th centuries.

◉ Sights

If you're short on time, a stroll along Piața Primeriei allows a glimpse of the prettiest architecture, including the City Hall (1895–96) and 18th-century baroque Hungarian Reformed Church (Református Templom).

Haáz Rezső Museum   MUSEUM
(www.hrmuzeum.ro; Str Bethlen Gábor 2; adult/child 5/2.50 lei; ⊙9am-6pm Tue-Fri, from 10am Sat & Sun Apr-Sep, 9am-5pm Tue-Fri, 10am-2pm Sat & Sun Oct, 9am-4pm Tue-Fri Nov-Mar) This lacy-looking building, 1900-built Haberstumpf cottage, seems slightly lost, standing next to the roaring main road through town. But the gallery within is excellent. It features mostly 20th-century art, much of it modern interpretations of the Hungarian and Romanian countryside, with plenty of striking sculptures and surreality around its several exhibition rooms.

Chapel of Jesus   CHURCH
(Jézus Kápolna; Str Bethlen Gábor; adult 2.50 lei, child free; ⊙9am-4pm Tue-Fri, 10am-2pm Sat & Sun) Some 2km south of town, a striking wooden gateway carved in filigree leads to the small, conical Jesus Chapel, encircled by a stone wall. Estimated to date to the 16th century, it's the only standing medieval remainder from Odorheiu's long history.

There is a telephone number posted outside the chapel; call for access between the visiting hours.

Citadel   RUINS
The crumbling walls of Odorheiu Secuiesc's medieval citadel can be spied from Str Eötvös József.

⊨ Sleeping

There is a handful of budget and midrange guesthouses in the centre of town, mostly aimed at business travellers and overnighting tourists (few stay longer than one night). There's also an enormous range of budget pensions north of the centre, along route 13A.

Petőfi Panzió   GUESTHOUSE $
(☎0756-093 926; www.petofipanzio.ro; Str Petőfi Sándor 2; s/d 90/140 lei; P 🛜) This popular guesthouse has little rooms with hardwood furnishings, in a soothing location away from the square and main roads. The sauna,

jacuzzi and traditional Hungarian restaurant are enjoyable perks.

Korona Panzió
HOTEL $

(☑ 0266-216 946; www.koronapanzio.ro; Piața Primăriei 12; s/d/tr €18/26/39; @ 🛜) Just off the prettiest part of the main square, Korona has the best location in town. Duck beneath the archway to access this courtyard hotel with pine-accented rooms. Lodgings are plain, but the flowery beer garden and restaurant compensate (and, unexpectedly, a free solarium). Breakfast is an additional €4.

✖ Eating & Drinking

Hungarian coffee-and-cake culture brightens Odorheiu's food scene. Find places to eat and drink in Piața Primăriei and its surrounding roads. There are fast-food joints and supermarkets along Str Bethlen Gábor.

Gondüző
ROMANIAN $$

(☑ 0266-218 372; www.gonduzo.ro; Str Sântimbru 18; mains 20-40 lei; ☺ 10am-midnight) This upscale hotel-restaurant serves refined Romanian dishes such as trout stuffed with chanterelles, duck with potatoes and cabbage, pork trotters with sour cream... and a few soups and salads if you need a time-out from filling peasant fare.

GPont
CAFE

(www.gpont.ro; Str Sântimbru 8; ☺ 8am-late Mon-Sat, 9am-midnight Sun; 🛜) Bookish and brick-lined, this boho cafe and community space serves up live jazz, literary meet-ups and great coffee. Sink into a faded leather armchair and let your eye wander across antique photos and candlebra, while lounge music and intellectual chatter forms the soundtrack.

ℹ Information

There are ATMs and banks along Str Kossuth Lajos and around Piața Primăriei.

Tourinfo (☑ 0266-217 427; www.tourinfo.ro; Str Bethlen Gábor 43; ☺ 8am-8pm Mon-Fri summer) Seasonal tourist information point with maps and brochures.

ℹ Getting There & Away

From the **bus station** (☑ 0266-212 034; Str Târgului), a 400m walk southwest of the **train station** (Str Bethlen Gábor), there are buses to Sovata (12 lei, 1¼ hours, six daily), Miercurea Ciuc (12 lei, one hour, three to five daily) and

Târgu Mureş (22 lei, two to 3½ hours, 10 daily). For Sibiu or Cluj-Napoca, travel via Târgu Mureş.

Hungary-bound buses are run by **Csavargó** (☑ 0266-217 377; www.csavargo.ro) and **Scorpion Trans** (☑ 0266-218 495; www.scorpion trans.eu); both have ticket windows at the bus station. Services reach Budapest (120 to 130 lei, 11 hours, one daily) and Pécs (160 lei, 15½ hours, one daily).

Trains clank out towards Sighişoara (7 lei, 1½ hours, three daily).

Odorheiu Secuiesc to Târgu Mureş

Praid

Eight kilometres north of Corund on the road to Sovata, Praid is home to a salt mine (Salina Praid; ☑ 0266-240 200; www.salinapraid. ro; Str Minei 44, Praid; adult/child 25/15 lei; ☺ entry 8am-2.50pm Mon-Sat, 10am-1pm Sun), a bizarre underground world with a church, sculpture, swing sets, slides, and a cafe selling soda and beer. Locals come for extended underground treatments for bronchitis and other respiratory illnesses at the base, 120m below the surface. A bus leads down dark tunnels – it's almost apocalyptic. There's a saltwater outdoor pool a couple of hundred metres west of the entrance to the salt mine. Seven daily buses connect Praid with Sovata (4 lei, 20 minutes).

Sovata

POP 10,385

Since the 19th century, bathers have eased their achey bodies into Sovata's Bear Lake. The warm, salty waters at this forest-hugged beauty spot, 35km north of Odorheiu Secuiesc, have long been famed for their healing powers. A couple of high-rise hotels, cashing in on Sovata's continued popularity, risk encroaching on the views. But overall, this spa town retains a nostalgic feel, with faded villas lining the road and bathers idling on lakeshore wooden decking each summer.

🛏 Sleeping

Vila Sara
PENSION $

(☑ 0265-570 159; www.vilasara.ro; Str Trandafirilor 86; r from 126 lei; ℙ 🛜) Opposite a coal-black orthodox chapel, and rather mimicking its spiky wooden style, is this richly decorated wooden chalet. It has 10 simple rooms with marble floors and pine furniture (some with balconies) plus a lounge with fireplace to relax in. Breakfast not included.

Danubius Health Spa Sovata   RESORT **$$$**
(☑ 0265-570 151; www.danubiushotels.com; Str Trandafirilor 82; d from €86; P ❄ 🛜 🏊) If you want to do Sovata's salt lake in style, stay at the shiny four-star Danubius and make full use of the pool, sauna, steam bath and bewildering array of wellness treatments from mud packs to massages. Rooms have all the polish you'd expect from this prestigious hotel chain, with wonderfully comfortable beds and views of forest or the lake.

ℹ️ Information

Salt Lake Travel Tourist Office (☑ 0265-577 421; www.sovatatravel.ro; Str Bradului 2A; ⊗ 10am-8pm Mon-Sat, to 4pm Sun Jul & Aug, 9am-5pm Mon-Fri Sep-Jun, plus to 4pm Sat Jun) Book wellness treatments and transport, and get local information from this small travel agency.

ℹ️ Getting There & Away

Daily buses connect Sovata with Odorheiu Secuiesc (12 lei, one to 1½ hours, five daily), Târgu Mureș (14 lei, two hours, hourly) and Gheorgheni (15 lei, 1½ hours, one daily).

Târgu Mureș

POP 142,000

Târgu Mureș is Transylvania's most underrated town. This spirited place is an ideal starting point to explore Székely Land; its own population is almost an even Romanian-Hungarian split. Târgu Mureș' showpiece is Piața Trandafirilor, which preens with statues, two cathedrals, and the unique Culture Palace, the region's most riotously decorated building. Given its location at the heart of Transylvania, there are plenty of ways to whittle a Târgu Mureș detour into your travels – you'll be very glad you did.

History

Târgu Mureș (Marosvásárhely in Hungarian, Neumarkt in German) was first documented as a market town, 'Novum Forum Sicolorum', in 1322. It developed as a leading garrison town and later as an important cultural and academic centre. In 1658 it was attacked by Turks, who captured 3000 inhabitants and transported them back to Istanbul as slave labour.

During the Ceaușescu regime, Târgu Mureș was a 'closed city', with ethnic groups other than Romanians forbidden to settle here, in an effort to dilute the Hungarian community.

In 1990 Târgu Mureș was the scene of bloody clashes (now known as 'Black March') between Hungarian students, demonstrating for a Hungarian-language faculty, and Romanians who raided the local Hungarian political party offices. Both sides had casualties. The Romanian mob attempted to gouge out the eyes of playwright András Sütő, who remained blind in one eye until his death in 2006. According to Human Rights Watch World Report for 1990, the violence was stirred by rumours that Romanian peasants were being bussed in from outlying villages to fortify Romanian protesters.

Wounds haven't healed, though demonstrations in the 2000s have largely been orderly. Demonstrations in Târgu Mureș calling for Székely autonomy are usually timed for 10 March, so-called 'Székely Freedom Day'. In 2014, an estimated 10,000 demonstrators gathered in Târgu Mureș.

◉ Sights

◉ Piața Trandafirilor & Around

The effervescent central Piața Trandafirilor is filled with statues, open-air cafes, restaurants, a cinema and theatre, as well as Târgu Mureș' two unmissable sights: the Culture Palace and Ethnographic Museum. At its northeastern end are two contrasting churches.

★ Culture Palace   MUSEUM
(Palatul Culturii; ☑ 0265-267 629; www.palatul culturiimures.ro; Str Enescu 2; 12 lei; ⊗ 9am-6pm Tue-Sun summer, to 4pm winter) This ornate secessionist-style building, ostentatiously tiled on the outside and colourfully furnished within, is unlike anything else in Transylvania. Built 1911–13, the Culture Palace harbours busts and glass portraits of composers, glinting chandeliers, Carrara marble stairways, mirrors imported from Venice, a regally decorated concert hall, and display rooms on local history and art (all included in the entry price). The undisputed highlight is the Hall of Mirrors (Sala Oglinzi), where Székely village life and

Târgu Mureş

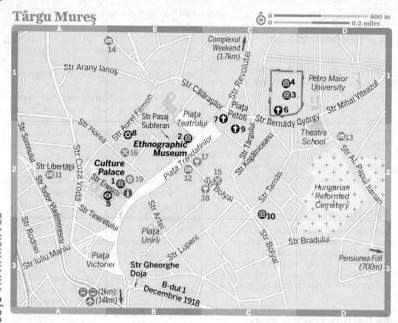

Târgu Mureş

dark fairy-tales are immortalised in stained glass.

The windows in the 45m-long Hall of Mirrors feature cautionary tales, odes to maternal love, and women being ravaged by the Devil, all captured in colourful stained glass. Elsewhere, a small museum of regional history is within the Dandea Hall, while the Secession Hall exhibits medals, costumes and large late-19th-century and early-20th-century paintings. Peep inside the Concert Hall to see ox-blood vel-

vet seats and a ceiling dripping with gold decoration.

★ **Ethnographic Museum**   MUSEUM
(Muzeul de Etnografie; ☑ 0265-250 169; Piaţa Trandafirilor 11; 6 lei; ☺ 9am-4pm Tue-Fri, to 2pm Sat, to 1pm Sun) Ethnographic exhibitions can be humdrum, so Târgu Mureş' hay-strewn and vividly soundtracked museum is a welcome surprise. A voiceover (in Romanian), supplemented by a multilingual booklet, guides you through a racy story of moral

dilemmas from a century ago, set in rural Transylvania. The museum is furnished with great attention to period detail. Vintage coats on hooks and discarded antique tea-cups allow you to imagine the characters in the story have only just left the room.

County Council Building NOTABLE BUILDING
(Prefectura; Piaţa Victoriei 1) Next door to the Culture Palace is the County Council Building (1905–7), also secessionist in style. Its decorative orange and green tiled roof and ornate 60m watchtower have made it one of Târgu Mureş' most photographed buildings. You can glimpse inside to see hand-painted ceilings and stained glass facing a grand staircase, but tourists can enjoy a more in-depth fix of architectural splendour at the Culture Palace.

Orthodox Cathedral CHURCH
(Piaţa Trandafirilor; ☺8am-6pm) The dominating Orthodox Cathedral (1925–34) was designed to impress, with Byzantine-style paintings and gold-haloed icons of saints – plus a politically charged mural of a 'Romanian peasant' Jesus being whipped by nobles in Hungarian costumes.

Teleki-Bolyai Library MUSEUM
(www.telekiteka.ro; Str Bolyai 17; donations welcome; ☺10am-6pm Tue-Fri, to 1pm Sat & Sun) FREE Opened in 1802, this is one of the oldest libraries in Transylvania, named for its founder Count Sámuel Teleki de Szék. Technically still used as a public library, it's now a 240,000-strong collection with treasures including 15th- to 19th-century encyclopedias and an engraved copy of the USA's Declaration of Independence (1819). Visitors may need to knock to gain entry. No, you can't touch the books.

Roman Catholic Church CHURCH
(Biserica Sfântul Jonos; Piaţa Trandafirilor; ☺8am-6pm) Built by Jesuit monks between 1728 and 1764, this baroque-style church was given a neo-Renaissance makeover in the 1930s. It's across the street from the Orthodox Cathedral.

Orthodox Synagogue SYNAGOGUE
(www.izraelsarokms.ro; Str Aurel Filmon 23; by donation; ☺9am-12.30pm Mon-Fri) A block west of the Ethnographic Museum is an ornate and well-preserved synagogue from 1899–1900. Before WWII more than 6000 Jews lived in Târgu Mureş; in the early 2000s, surveys found about 200 still reside here.

◉ The Citadel & Around

A block northeast of Piaţa Trandafirilor, the huge citadel dates from 1492. It houses the Fortress Church, the oldest church in town, and City Museum, and its green gardens are a soothing space for an afternoon stroll.

Citadel HISTORIC BUILDING
(Cetatea Medievală; www.cetatespum.ro; B-dul Cetăţii; ☺8am-9pm Tue-Sun) FREE Visitors can wander freely within the walls of Târgu Mureş' citadel, whose foundations date to 1492. It houses the Fortress Church and **City Museum** (Citadel, B-dul Cetăţii; adult/student 4/1 lei; ☺9am-4pm Tue-Fri, 10am-2pm Sat & Sun), and its gardens are a soothing space to stroll.

Fortress Church CHURCH
(Citadel, B-dul Cetăţii; ☺hours variable) Enclosed by the walls of the citadel, this oft-closed late-Gothic church is the oldest one in Târgu Mureş. Construction began in the mid-14th century, though it wasn't completed for a century.

Complexul Weekend SWIMMING POOL
(cnr Str Luntraşilor & Str Plutelor; adult/child 6/3 lei; ☺8am-7pm Tue-Sun May-Aug) In high summer when the mercury tops 40°C, this swimming complex, 2.5km north of the centre, is a welcome oasis. There's a couple of giant pools, a few kids pools, waterslides, plus a beach volleyball area.

🛏 Sleeping

Hotels rise and fall in Târgu Mureş' ever-changing accommodation scene. Still, several excellent stalwarts endure, while more and more enterprising locals are renting flats privately on booking and accommodation websites. Boutique and high-end hotels are easy to find around Piaţa Trandafirilor, although the best value can be found at guesthouses in residential streets one or two kilometres from the centre.

Pension Ana Maria PENSION **$**
(☏0265-264 401; Str Papiu Ilarian 17; d/tr from €30/35; P🛜) This family-run hotel of 20 years boasts traditional Austro-Hungarian furnishings, and some rooms even have decorative awnings over the blue beds. Breakfasts are very generous.

★ Atlantic Hotel
HOTEL $$

(☎ 0265-268 381; www.atlantichotel.ro; Str Libertății 15; r/apt from €43/58, with jacuzzi €85; P ❄ 🛜) Instantly seizing attention with its deer-antler furniture and marbled entrance, the Atlantic is an oasis despite its central location. Flamboyant antiques and wooden furnishings fill its spacious rooms, green plants breathe life into common areas, and staff are just the right blend of cheerful and cordial. A sophisticated choice.

Pensiunea Full
PENSION $$

(☎ 0265-311 030; www.pensiuneafull.ro; Str Cornești 61; s/d 130/160 lei; P ❄ 🛌) This well-run guesthouse, 1.5km east of Piața Trandafirilor, is ideal for those seeking respite from the din of central Târgu Mureș. The decor might feel a touch 1970s, but rooms come with fridges and safes, bathrooms are in great nick, and there's a relaxing pool area with sun loungers and trimmed lawns.

Pensiunea Tempo
PENSION $$

(☎ 0265-213 552; www.tempo.ro; Str Morii 27; s 160-205 lei, d 175-220 lei; P ❄) Festooned in baskets of flowers, this motel-style courtyard accommodation is one of Târgu Mureș' top picks. Standard rooms are clean and cosy, while the more expensive superior rooms are large with an upmarket chalet feel, plus occasional Saxon-style furnishings. As a bonus, you're in prime position to grab a coveted table at Laci Csárda next door.

Hotel Concordia
BOUTIQUE HOTEL $$

(☎ 0265-260 602; www.hotelconcordia.ro/hotel. html; Piața Trandafirilor 45; s/d/ste €56/64/75; P 🛜 🛌) With retro-nodding furniture and bohemian touches, Hotel Concordia seems to take inspiration from London's Soho in the 1980s. Rooms have zebra-patterned chairs and claret-red carpets, there's a small spa and pool area (included in the price) and the hotel poses right on the main square.

✖ Eating

Pick any street leading from Piața Trandafirilor – itself overflowing with cafes and restaurants – and you'll find somewhere pleasant to eat. Befitting Târgu Mureș' ethnic mix, you'll find a medley of Hungarian and Romanian kitchens, along with ever-present pizzerias and bistros.

★ Laci Csárda
ROMANIAN $$

(☎ 0265-213 552; www.tempo.ro/restaurant-laci -csarda; Str Morii 27; mains 20-30 lei; ⊘ 10am-mid-night) Shaped like a wooden church, this striking restaurant with an outdoor terrace prepares heaving platefuls of nourishing peasant fare such as *koloszvari*-style stuffed cabbage (with pork and rice), paprika mushrooms, and stewed beef with polenta.

Emma
ROMANIAN $$

(Str Horea 6; mains 11-25 lei; ⊘ 8am-11pm Mon-Fri, from 10am Sat, from 11am Sun) Hearty schnitzels, paprika chicken and veggie chilli is on the menu at this local lunch favourite. The embroidered tablecloths and cosy interior matches the homestyle cooking perfectly. Lunch specials are available at a reasonable 13 lei.

Donuterie
DESSERTS

(www.donuterie.ro; Str Bolyai 3; donut 2.50 lei; ⊘ 9.30am-6.30pm Mon-Fri) Want to quell the munchies as you museum-hop around Târgu Mureș? Try grabbing one of Donuterie's rainbow-coloured, chocolate-covered or Oreo-sprinkled creations.

🍷 Drinking & Nightlife

Piaf
COCKTAIL BAR

(www.piafcafe.ro; Str Bolyai 10; ⊘ 8am-3am Thu-Sat, to 1am Mon-Wed) The illuminated wall of red and white bottles is clue enough: Piaf is mixology central. Cocktail creation extends beyond the excellent mojitos. There is an ample selection of mocktails, infused with exotic flavours from coconut to buckthorn. Modern art and jazzy seats, along with sultry portraits and exposed brick, conspire to make it one of Târgu Mureș' most enticing spots for a drink.

Old City Pub
BAR

(Piața Trandafirilor 43; ⊘ 9am-1am Sun-Wed, till late Thu-Sat) Just off the square through an archway, this cafe and pub is a favourite with locals thanks to its cosy but chic atmosphere, and occasional program of karaoke, quizzes and more. Cocktails are good, and there is a pleasing range of food on offer, from salads and spaghetti to French-style desserts.

☆ Entertainment

The lovely Culture Palace (p125) houses the Agenție de Bilete (⊘ noon-5.30pm Mon-Fri), which sells tickets for a wide variety of shows, including opera and the State Philharmonic (Filarmonica de Stat; ☎ tickets 0265-261 420; www.filarmonicams.ro; Str George Enescu 2; tickets from 20 lei) concerts.

ℹ Information

ATMs are easy to find in the centre, including at **Banca Carpaţi** (Str Poştei 1; ⊙ 8.30am-5pm Mon-Fri).

Tourism Information Centre (☐ 0365-404 934; www.cjmures.ro/turism; cnr Piaţa Trandafirilor & Str Enescu; ⊙ 8am-4pm Mon-Thu, to 3pm Fri) Occupying the enviable corner spot at the Culture Palace, this superbly run centre offers free maps and information on the region, as well as advice on accommodation and transport.

ℹ Getting There & Away

AIR

Târgu Mureş Airport (☐ 0265-328 259; www.aeroportultransilvania.ro; Str Ludus Km14.5) is 14km southwest of town (on the road to Cluj-Napoca). Catch a bus from outside the theatre (buses are usually timed for major flights).

At the time of writing, Wizz Air (www.wizzair.com) ran flights to/from Budapest (twice weekly), London Luton (four weekly), Madrid (twice weekly), Paris Beauvais (twice weekly) and more.

BUS

The **bus station** (☐ 0265-237 774; Str Gheorghe Doja 143) sends daily bus and maxitaxi services.

TRAIN

From the **train station** (☐ 0265-236 284; Piaţa Gării) there is one daily direct train each to Bucharest (90 lei, 8½ hours) Cluj-Napoca (26 to 60 lei, five hours), Sibiu (30 lei, six hours) and Timişoara (66 lei, 7½ hours). There are more services if you change trains.

ℹ Getting Around

Central Târgu Mureş is small enough to cover by foot. Bus 18 goes from the stop at Piaţa Teatrul and Piaţa Trandafirilor to the bus station; bus 5 goes to the train station (ticket 2 lei). A taxi to or

from the airport is about 40 lei. Taxis are easy to find around town; rates are 2 to 2.50 lei per kilometre.

SOUTHWEST TRANSYLVANIA

Southwest Transylvania's history was built on ancient gold and medieval might. Stretching between the Retezat and Apuseni Mountain ranges, west of the Cluj-Napoca–Sibiu highway, the region is littered with citadels. Corvin Castle has doomy towers and drawbridges to inspire envy in even the most dastardly of Counts. Câlnic's fortification and crumbled Deva fortress whisper of the medieval past. Alba Iulia's citadel encloses monuments, churches and the hall where the union between Romania and Transylvania was signed in 1918.

But on southwest Transylvania's timeline, these castles are youngsters. The gold-rich hills have been mined for nearly 2000 years (you can admire glistening remnants at the gold museum in Brad), and ancient Dacian civilisation has left traces at mysterious Sarmizegetusa Regia. Contemplate this vast history among southwest Transylvania's most enduring features, the Retezat Mountains, where hiking trails climb to lofty glacial lakes.

Alba Iulia

POP 63,530

Alba Iulia's star-shaped citadel is one of Transylvania's most overlooked sights. The walls of this magnificently preserved citadel – the largest in Romania – enclose grand monuments and museums, glittering churches, and archaeological treasures.

BUSES FROM TÂRGU MUREŞ

DESTINATION	COST (LEI)	DURATION (HR)	FREQUENCY (DAILY)
Bistriţa	22	2½-4	3
Braşov	35	3-4	3
Bucharest	60	7	2
Budapest	100	9	3
Cluj-Napoca	25	2-2½	13
Sibiu	20-30	2½-3½	6
Sighişoara	13	1½	almost hourly
Sovata	14	1½-2	at least hourly

Alba Iulia

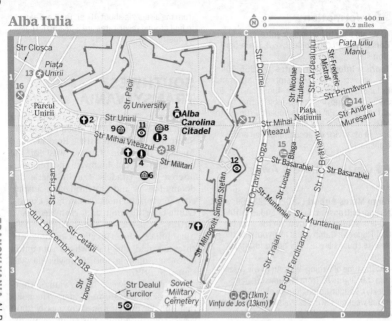

Over recent years, these attractions have been thoroughly rejuvenated and sprinkled with plenty of multilingual information. As the place where the agreement was signed to unify Transylvania with Romania, Alba Iulia is the natural focus of 2018's centenary of the union. So it's no wonder the town has a spring in its step.

Outside the citadel, Alba Iulia is a busy, sprawling place with no shortage of Soviet-era concrete. It's a worthy stop if you're travelling from Sibiu towards the castles of Deva and Hunedoara, or up to Cluj-Napoca and the Apuseni Mountains.

History

The nation announced the union of Transylvania with Romania here in 1599 and 1918, which were both hugely important occasions to Romanians. Alba Iulia was known by the Dacians as Apulum, serving both as the capital of Upper Dacia and, later, during Roman times, as the largest centre in the Dacian province of the Roman empire. From 1542 to 1690 Alba Iulia was the capital of the principality of Transylvania. Romania's national day (1 December) is always a time of major celebrations in Alba Iulia.

◉ Sights

It's worth timing a stroll inside the citadel for the daily changing of the guard (Str Mihai Viteazul; ☺noon) ceremony, in which uniformed guards trot on horseback between the old gates, while solemn drumrolls and brass boom out.

★ **Alba Carolina Citadel** CASTLE
FREE Alba Carolina Citadel is the crowning attraction of Alba Iulia. Within this star-shaped citadel are museums, churches and the Unification Hall that sealed the union of Transylvania with Romania in 1918. Originally constructed in the 13th century, the present fortification dates mostly to the 18th century. If you're short on time, focus on the dazzling Coronation Cathedral and National Union Museum. Ideally, spend a full day strolling museums, posing at grand gateways, and idling in cafes. The citadel is free, but the museums carry entry charges.

Str Mihai Viteazul runs up from the lower town to the first gate of the fortress, adorned with sculptures inspired by Greek mythology. From here, a stone road leads to the third gate of the fortress, dominated by a horseback statue of Carol VI of Austria. Above the gate is Horea's death cell (Celula lui Horea), a reproduction of where Horea, the leader of the 1784–85 peasant riots, awaited his unpleasant end. He and fellow revolutionary Cloşca were crushed to death on wheels on Forks Hill (Dealul Furcilor) in 1785; Crişan killed himself in prison to avoid this fate. A nearby 22.5m-high granite column, the Uprising Memorial (Str Mihai Viteazul), was erected in 1937 to commemorate these events. It also offers a superb panorama over the surrounding hills.

Just before you enter the third gate, a footpath leads 500m south to out-of-sight Michael the Brave Church (Biserica Memorială Sfânta Treime; www.biserica-mihai-viteazul. ro; Str Mitropolit Simion Stefan 5; ☺8am-7pm). The wooden church, brought to Alba Iulia in 1992 from Maramureş, stands on the site of a former Metropolitan cathedral built by Mihai Viteazul in 1597 and destroyed by the Habsburgs in 1714.

Inside the gates, about 200m west, is the Custozza Monument. This obelisk was raised in 1906 to commemorate soldiers and officers of the 50th infantry regiment of Alba Iulia, who were killed while fighting in the Habsburg army against Italy in the Battle of Custozza in 1866. Close by is the Muzeul Principia (☑0258-813 300; www. castrul-apulum.ro; Str Unirii; adult/child 10/6.50 lei; ☺10am-9pm Tue-Sun); archaeologists unearthed the largest fort in Roman Dacia at this site, and you can admire the old walls and old hypocaust (heating system) within.

Just west is the Union Hall (Sala Unirii; Str Muzeului) **FREE**. Within this 1900-built hall, the union between Romania and Transylvania was signed and sealed on 1 December 1918. Facing the hall from the south is a large equestrian statue of Mihai Viteazul (Michael the Brave), ruler of Wallachia, then Transylvania and Moldavia, in the late 16th century; this union crumbled after his execution in 1601. Behind the statue is the Former Princely Palace (☺not open to public), once residence of John Sigismund of Transylvania, built in several stages from the 16th century onwards. Mihai Viteazul stayed here briefly too.

Immediately west is St Michael's Cathedral (☺9am-6pm), Romania's most venerable Roman Catholic cathedral, as well as the country's longest at slightly over 89m. Royal tombs, including Queen Isabella and her son (the first prince of Transylvania) are inside, plus a 2209-pipe organ framed by baroque and Gothic decorations.

On the other side of the road is the impressive National Union Museum (Muzeul Unirii; ☑0258-813 300; Str Mihai Viteazul 12; adult/child 8/4 lei; ☺10am-7pm Tue-Sun summer, to 5pm Tue-Sun winter), which celebrates the 1918 signing of the union between Transylvania and Romania. Close by, near the western entrance of the citadel, rises the highly impressive Coronation Cathedral (Str Mihai Viteazul 16; ☺hours variable), built in 1921–22 and designed in the shape of a Greek circumscribed cross. A 58m-tall bell tower marks the main entrance.

🏃 Activities

A 5km cycling trail and pedestrian path wends through woodlands between the Miceşti and Pâclişa neighbourhoods, via lofty hilltop views. It's best accessed via a rental bike from I'Velo (Parcul Unirii; per hour/day 4/15 lei; ☺Apr-Oct).

🛌 Sleeping

Alba Iulia's accommodation choices range from sumptuous guesthouses and themed hotels to barebones pensions. Finding lodgings within walking distance of the citadel is easy on all budgets.

Villa Preciosa
BOUTIQUE HOTEL **$$**

(☑0258-814 033; www.preciosa.ro; Str Lucian Blaga 10; s/d from 150/220 lei; P🖤) This refined and romantic guesthouse, on a quiet residential lane just a 10-minute walk from the citadel, is Alba Iulia's most stylish place to stay. The columned exterior sets the tone, with chandelier dangling within, while rooms are plump of pillow and very clean.

The attached restaurant serves a medley of European cuisine with a standout wine menu.

Hotel Parc
HOTEL **$$**

(☑0258-816 642; www.hotelparc.ro; Str Primăverii 4; s/d/apt 240/260/360 lei; P❄🖤💺) Looking like a '70s cruise ship on the outside, this businessy hotel has art deco aspirations with a spangly lobby and bright crimson dining room. Rooms are decorated either in trim monochrome or a fetching shade of mustard, and there's a heated pool and two saunas to toast in.

★ Hotel Medieval
HOTEL **$$$**

(☑0374-079 990; www.hotel-medieval.ro; Str Militari 13; d/apt from €110/170; P🖤) Housed in former 18th-century barracks within the citadel, this five-star belle beguiles guests with carved hardwood furnishings, occasional antiques and gleaming modern bathrooms with clawfoot tubs.

✕ Eating & Drinking

The dining scene in Alba Iulia has been lifting its game in recent years, with choices that span country fare in medieval-style surroundings, French brasseries and Italian *trattorie*. Options within the citadel are touristy but good, and there's a sprinkling of restaurants across town (though opening hours can be erratic outside summer).

★ Pub 13
ROMANIAN **$$**

(☑0728-444 415; www.pub13.ro; Aleea Capistrano, 3rd gate, Citadel; mains 20 lei; ⊙noon-midnight) If you want to face down a suit of armour while gnawing on steak, or swirl a fork through cheesy polenta beneath coats of arms slung across brick-lined walls, this medieval restaurant will delight. This is no cheap theme restaurant: Pub 13 is built into the wall of the citadel and bedecked with historic regalia, ambiently lit by chandeliers.

Gavroche
EUROPEAN **$$**

(☑0358-401 203; www.restaurantgavroche.ro; B-dul 1 Decembrie 1918; mains 16-25 lei; ⊙8am-midnight Mon-Thu, 9am-1am Fri-Sun) Though it takes inspiration from French brasserie chic, Gavroche's satisfying menu spans burgers, curry and deep-fried cheese, alongside well-executed pasta dishes. Gourmet options include duck in sour-cherry sauce and mustard-glazed pork (30 to 35 lei).

ℹ Getting There & Away

Direct bus and maxitaxi services from Alba Iulia's **bus station** (☑0258-812 967; Str Iaşilor 94) reach Bucharest (60 lei, six hours, six to eight daily), Cluj-Napoca (20 lei, two hours, hourly), Deva (18 to 20 lei, 1½ hours, 10 daily), Sibiu (15 lei, 1½ hours, hourly), Târgu Mureş (32 to 35 lei, 2½ hours, three daily) and Timişoara (44 lei, 4½ to six hours, four daily).

From Alba Iulia's **train station** (Str Maramureşului), there are daily runs to Cluj-Napoca (35 lei, 2½ hours, five daily), Deva (9 to 22 lei, two hours, four daily), Timişoara (67 lei, five hours, three daily) and Sibiu (12 lei, 2½ hours, two daily). One daily train reaches Bucharest (94 lei, 11 hours), with more via Deva and Simeria.

ℹ Getting Around

Local buses 103 and 104 run between the train station and citadel (single fare 2.50 lei; buy from ticket machines and validate on the bus). Otherwise Alba Iulia is easy to explore on foot.

Deva
POP 61,125

Deva is crowned by its 13th-century citadel and Hollywood-style sign. Apart from grabbing a pizza or popping into a handful of museums, Deva does little to warrant an extended stay. That said, if you're on a castle hunt headed to Corvin Castle, stopping in Deva is definitely preferable to staying in Hunedoara's industrial sprawl.

◉ Sights

Deva Citadel
FORTRESS

(Cetatea Deva) **FREE** Deva's crumbling citadel looms from a rocky hilltop 300m above town. A steep climb leads up behind Parcul Cetăţii at the west end of B-dul 1 Decembrie 1918. Alternatively, take the funicular (☑0254-220 288; adult return/one-way 10/6 lei; child return/one-way 5/3 lei; ⊙9am-9pm May-Sep, 8am-8pm Oct-Apr) – hang on tight. At the top there are plenty of stone walls to ponder and 360-degree views of the surrounding

Deva

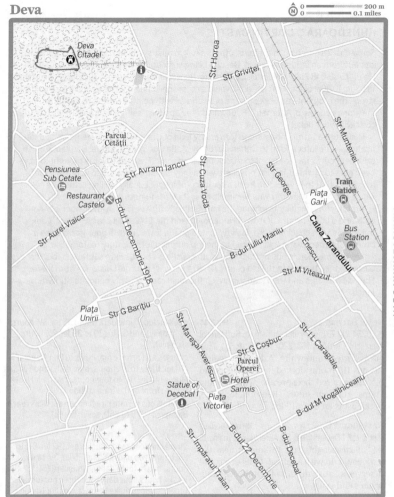

hills. There are no opening hours to access the ruin.

Work started on the stone fortress in the mid-13th century. In 1453 Iancu de Hunedoara expanded the fort, just in time to imprison Unitarian activist Dávid Ferenc (1510–79), who died here. In 1784, during the peasant uprising led by Horea, Crişan and Cloşca, the fortress served as a refuge for terrified nobles fearful of being killed by militant peasants. In 1849 Hungarian nationalists attacked Austrian generals held up in the fort. The four-week siege ended with the mighty explosion of the castle's gunpowder deposits, which left the castle in ruins.

🛏 Sleeping & Eating

Budget and midrange hotels are dotted around Deva, though few will lure you to stay longer than a night.

Pensiunea Sub Cetate   PENSION $
(📞 0254-212 535; http://devacazare.ro; B-dul 1 Decembrie 1918, 37B; s/d 100/120 lei; 🅿 ❄ 📶) On a leafy residential lane, this exceptionally friendly guesthouse has clean, homely rooms, some with balconies.

HUNEDOARA'S CORVIN CASTLE

Some castles perch on mountains, others skulk in mist-shrouded hills, but Hunedoara's juts out from an industrial jungle. Despite being surrounded by steel mills, **Corvin Castle** (✆0786-048 718; www.castelulcorvinilor.ro; Hunedoara; adult/student 30/5 lei; ⊙9am-7pm Tue-Sun, 10.30am-7pm Mon) is Transylvania's most spellbinding fortress. You'll be thunderstruck the moment you walk over the drawbridge, with pointed turrets rising above, into the stone courtyard. Alternatively, download the app for a self-guided walk (8 lei; buy the code with your ticket).

Built atop a 14th-century stone fortress by Ioan of Hunedoara, new elements and fortifications were later added to Corvin Castle by Matia Corvin and Gabriel Bethlen. Turkish prisoners performed much of this back-breaking work. The castle well is thought to have been cursed by three Turkish prisoners when they were condemned to death in spite of a promise that they would be freed after its completion. Equally chilling is the **Bear Pit**, where prisoners were thrown to animals after their usefulness expired.

Architectural highlights include the late-Gothic **Knights Hall**, with armour, cannonballs and a bulky bronze of Ioan of Hunedoara, and the 1440-built **Mace Tower**. Look out for the faint checkerboard design painted on the tower, and lift your gaze to see a bronze of a medieval knight, placed at the top during a 19th-century restoration.

From Hunedoara's bus or train station, the castle is about 1.5km southwest, but it's easier to take the bus to the old centre (2 lei) then walk the short distance from there. Hunedoara's bus and train stations are off the main road, roughly opposite Str Avram Iancu.

Hotel Sarmis
HOTEL **$$**

(✆0254-214 731; www.unita-turism.ro; Str Mareşal Averescu 7; s/d/apt 163/220/356 lei; P🛜) This queasy green-and-white Aztec-style colossus has 118-rooms decked in dark wood and biscuit-coloured bedspreads, with reading lamps and en suites. Reasonable value. Breakfast is an extra 16 lei.

Restaurant Castelo
INTERNATIONAL **$**

(cnr B-dul 1 Decembrie & Str Aurel Vlaicu; mains 15 lei; ⊙9am-midnight) This restaurant near the park could do with a refresh to its decor, but it serves a satisfying set of schnitzels, sandwiches and grills.

ℹ Information

Raiffeisen Bank (B-dul Iuliu Maniu; ⊙9am-1pm & 1.30-5.30pm Mon-Fri) Near the train station.

Tourist Information Centre (Str Stadion; ⊙9am-9pm summer) Right next to the funicular up to the castle, this info kiosk has maps and English-speaking staff.

ℹ Getting There & Away

BUS

The **bus station** (Calea Zarandului) spills across the parking lot in front of the train station. Frequent buses and microbuses go to Hunedoara (7 to 10 lei, 40 minutes). Other services include Timişoara (28 to 35 lei, 3½ hours, eight daily) and Sibiu (20 to 30 lei, 2½ hours, six daily).

Buses and private maxitaxis to Cluj-Napoca (40 lei, three to 3½ hours, nine daily) and Târgu Mureş (40 lei, 3½ to four hours, two daily) leave from in front of the train station.

Numerous private direct coach services reach Budapest (€25 to €50, seven hours).

TRAIN

Direct services reach Bucharest (92 lei, 8½ to 9½ hours, two daily), Sibiu (35 lei, 3½ to 4½ hours, two to three daily), Timişoara (50 to 60 lei, 3¼ hours, four daily) and three nocturnally timed services make their way to Cluj-Napoca (25 to 53 lei, 4½ to five hours).

Retezat Mountains

Bejewelled by 80 glacial lakes and with peaks towering above 2000m, the Retezat Mountains are a spectacular stretch of the southern Carpathians. **Retezat National Park** (www.retezat.ro), the oldest reserve in Romania, is the primary draw as much for its wildlife as its dizzying walking trails. The town of Haţeg, north of the park, is a good place for hikers to circle their wagons before embarking on trails. Haţeg is an equally good base for road trippers to explore intriguing sights such as a small bison reserve, some minor monasteries and fortresses, and Sarmizegetusa Regia, ancient Dacian remains that bring to mind a Romanian Stonehenge.

⊙ Sights

★ **Sarmizegetusa Regia**   ARCHAEOLOGICAL SITE
(adult/child 5/3 lei;   ⊙9am-8pm May-Sep, to 6pm Mar-Apr & Oct-Nov, closed Dec-Feb) The Sarmizegetusa Regia archaeological site is Romania's Stonehenge. Only stones remain, enclosed by pretty woodlands, but they reveal compelling clues about the region's pre-Roman Dacian civilisation. The site grew into a commercial centre around 1st century BC, thanks to rich iron ore, and the outlines of houses, granaries and workshops can be seen here. Most intriguing are the remains of limestone temples, oriented according to the solstice. Its destruction by the Romans in AD 106 was a symbolic end to Dacian spirituality.

🏃 Activities

Walkers are spoilt for choice with 516km of marked trails, most of them substantial five-plus hour treks. Excellent hikes begin from Râuşor, northwest of the park, to Cabana Pietrele and deeper into the park. Cabana Gura Zlata is another key entry point. Retezat

Park Administration Centre (☏0254-779 969; www.retezat.ro; Nucşoara 284; ⊙8am-4pm Mon-Thu, to 2pm Fri) is a superb first port of call for hikers.

Worthy trails include the following. Approximate durations are one-way, and vary according to fitness levels.

Râuşor to Lake Ştevia (three to four hours) This medium-difficulty trail follows red markings past spruce forests to a glacial lake.

Cabana Codrin to Poiana Pelegii (5½ hours) Start at Cârnic north of the park towards Cabana Pietrele along the blue trail, peaking at Lake Bucura (total elevation difference is more than 1200m) before a descent to Poiana Pelegii.

Cabana Pietrele to Lake Bucura (6½ hours) The challenging yellow trail leads hikers to 2041m-altitude Bucura, the largest glacial lake in the Retezat Mountains. The lake is also reachable by seven-hour hike from Cabana Gura Zlata.

🛏 Sleeping

Choose between no-frills hiking huts within the park, and simple pensions on its outskirts. Sleeping options in the Retezat Mountains aren't usually luxurious, or indeed charming, but the scenery amply

Retezat Mountains

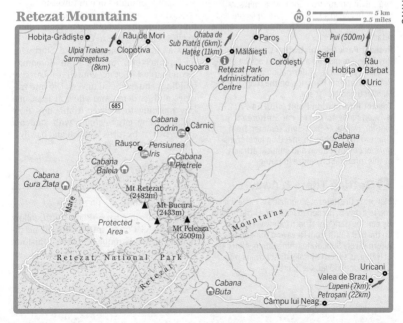

compensates. Haţeg is a good base if you have a car and want access to restaurants, supermarkets and other amenities.

Vila Silva GUESTHOUSE $
(📞 0760-938 844; www.silva.cazareinhateg.ro; Str Carpaţi 3, Haţeg; s/d 100/125 lei; 🅿🛜❄) This pointy-eaved guesthouse on the outskirts of Haţeg has white-walled rooms with colourful accents. Though simply furnished, it's a convenient base if you prefer digs in town to sleeping out in the Retezat wilds. Breakfast costs an extra 15 lei.

Cabana Codrin CABIN $
(📞 0742-793 620; www.codrin.ro; Cârnic; d with shared bathroom 80 lei, camping per person 5 lei, half-board per person 45 lei; 🅿) These simple cottages and guestrooms are located on the road between Nucşoara and the edge of Retezat National Park.

Pensiunea Iris PENSION $
(📞 0744-605 262; http://geraico.ro/pensiunea-iris -bradatel; Valea Riului Mare; d/tr from 90/120 lei; ☺May-Sep; 🅿) If you're arriving by car and want to dip in and out of Retezat National Park without resorting to barebones hiking huts, rooms at Pensiunea Iris have a dash more comfort.

ℹ Information

You can buy maps from the park administration centre. Bel Alpin's 1:50,000 *Retezat Mountains* map ships internationally from numerous online retailers.

Retezat Park Administration Centre (p135) Buy hiking maps and ask for trail advice at the official (and helpful) information centre for Retezat National Park. It's on the road between Mălăieşti and Nucşoara.

Tourist Information Point (📞 0254-770 273; www.en.hateg-turism.ro; cnr Str Horea & Str Florilor, Haţeg; ☺9am-5pm summer, from 10am winter) Get up to speed on local transport, accommodation and cultural attractions at this information centre in Haţeg.

ℹ Getting There & Away

Exploring the Retezat Mountains is easiest if you're a driver, hardened hiker, or a little of both. By car, the park's northern gateway Haţeg is on the E79 south from Deva and Hunedoara. Alternatively Subcetate train station, 4km east of Haţeg, is served by daily direct trains from Cluj-Napoca (60 lei, 4½ hours).

NORTHERN TRANSYLVANIA

Raw mountainscapes and a bite of Bram Stoker are the main reasons to linger in northern Transylvania, though city chic isn't far behind. Just south of Maramureş, the region's heart is Cluj-Napoca: Romania's second city is criminally underrated, and chock full of bars and galleries. The challenging hiking terrain of the Apuseni Mountains ripples westward.

Northeast of Cluj, passing the proud remains of Bánffy Castle, extends the perilous terrain of Bram Stoker's imagination: Bistriţa and the Bârgău Valley, key locations in *Dracula,* each now boast a themed hotel. But the more rewarding travels here are timed for Untold or Electric Castle, two of the music festivals transforming this region into a musical hub.

Cluj-Napoca

POP 324,500

Bohemian cafes, music festivals and vigorous nightlife are the soul of Cluj-Napoca, Romania's second-largest city. With increasing flight links to European cities, Cluj is welcoming more and more travellers, who usually shoot off to the Apuseni Mountains, Maramureş or more popular towns in southern Transylvania. But once arrived, first-time visitors inevitably lament their failure to allow enough time in Cluj.

Don't make the same mistake. Start with the architecture, ranging from Romania's second-largest Gothic church to baroque buildings and medieval towers. Dip into galleries and gardens. And allow at least one lazy morning to recover from Cluj's fiery nightlife. The city, teeming with students and artists, is by turns bookish and bawdy – intrigue is guaranteed.

◉ Sights

◉ Old Town

From the north edge of Piaţa Unirii, follow Strada Matei Corvin into a cobbled neighbourhood of baroque churches, historic houses and quaint restaurants. The monuments and museum of Piaţa Muzeului are just north of here.

St Michael's Church CHURCH

(Biserica Sfantul Mihail; ☑0264-592 089; Piaţa Unirii; ⊘8am-6pm) The showpiece of Piaţa Unirii is 14th- and 15th-century St Michael's, the second biggest Gothic church in Romania (after Braşov's Black Church). Its neo-Gothic clocktower (1859) towers 80m high, while original Gothic features – such as the 1444 front portal – can still be admired. Inside, soaring rib vaults lift the gaze towards fading frescoes.

Statue of Matthias Corvinus STATUE

(Piaţa Unirii) Hogging the limelight in front of St Michael's Church is a bulky 1902 statue of horseback Matthias Corvinus, the famous 15th-century Hungarian king.

Pharmacy History Collection MUSEUM

(Piaţa Unirii 28; adult/child 6/3 lei; ⊘10am-4pm Mon-Wed & Fri, noon-6pm Thu) Cluj-Napoca's oldest pharmacy building holds an intriguing collection of medical miscellany. 'Crab eyes', skulls, and powdered mummy are just a few of the cures on display in these antique-filled rooms. The prettiest is the Officina, a polished room with dark filigree swirling around its walls. You'll also learn that the 18th-century recipe for a love potion sounds suspiciously like mulled wine...

It's just past the northeast corner of the square, towards Str Regele Ferdinand I.

Hungarian Reformed Church CHURCH

(Str Mihail Kogălniceanu; ⊘9am-5pm) Commissioned by the king of Hungary, Matthias Corvinus, in 1486, this church took more than 20 years to complete. Its interior seems spare at first glance, but the carved wooden seats display grand Hungarian heraldry, and there's a rococo church organ (1765).

Matthias Corvinus House NOTABLE BUILDING

(cnr Str Matei Corvin & Str Puşcariu) A block south of the National History Museum is the birthplace of Matthias Corvinus, a 15th-century Hungarian king. This Gothic building is now the library of Cluj university's Faculty of Arts.

National Art Museum GALLERY

(Muzeul de Arta; ☑0264-596 952; www.macluj.ro; Piaţa Unirii 30; adult/student 8/2 lei; ⊘10am-5pm Wed-Sun) The permanent collection of this sizeable gallery has creaky rooms featuring 18th- and 19th-century art, mostly portraits of nobles and their bewigged wives, plus landscapes and religious icons. It's a pleasant collection, though not unmissa-

ble. The reason to visit is the stately setting within baroque Bánffy Palace, which hosted Habsburg Emperor Franz Joseph I.

National History Museum of Transylvania MUSEUM

(Str Constantin Daicoviciu 1; adult/child 6/3 lei; ⊘noon-6pm Wed, 10am-4pm Tue & Thu-Sun) Within this museum of regional history you'll discover Dacian artefacts, mostly from Sarmizegetusa's archaeological sites, including glass blow pipes, blacksmithing tools, reconstructed urns and silver bracelets. English information is scant, but there are a few virtual reality games aimed at children, to immerse you in historic Romanian dwellings (if you can get them to work). The museum is on the 2nd floor.

Ethnographic Museum of Transylvania MUSEUM

(Muzeul Etnografic al Transilvaniei; www.muzeul-etnografic.ro; Str Memorandumului 21; adult 6 lei, student 3 lei, child free; ⊘10am-6pm Wed-Sun) On the upper floor of a renovated neo-Gothic building, dating to the 16th century, find well-tended exhibitions on Romanian peasant life throughout the centuries. You'll see beeswax presses and whey-boiling vats, admire colourful ceramics, and be able to delight friends and family with trivia about Romanian embroidery long after.

◉ Student Quarter

A bookish, cafe-lined neighbourhood beloved of students spreads southwest of the centre, along Strada Universităţii and along the lanes flowing west of here. There are literary haunts, superb coffee shops and bohemian open-air bars. It's quieter in summer.

Alexandru Borza Botanic Gardens GARDENS

(Str Republicii 42; adult/child 10/5 lei; ⊘8am-8pm summer, 9am-6pm winter, museum 8am-3pm Mon-Fri) These wonderfully relaxing gardens comprise rockeries, neoclassical statues peeping from tangles of rose, and a Japanese-style garden with a crimson bridge spanning a turtle pond. At the heart of the gardens, find the Botanical Museum (Muzeul Botanic), exhibiting vegetal curios from bottled fruits to fern fossils.

Hungarian Cemetery CEMETERY

(Házsongárdi Temető; Str Matei Basarab; ⊘dawn-dusk) Founded in the 16th century, this stately cemetery is a memorable place to

Central Cluj-Napoca

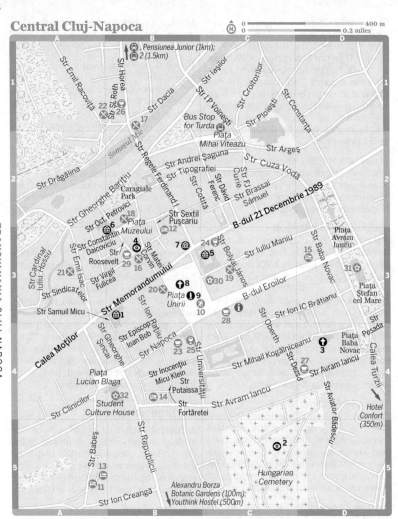

stroll among the elegant tombs and mausoleums of Transylvanian poets and composers, while crows call from the surrounding trees. Enter the cemetery downhill from Str Avram Iancu, south of the main square.

Outside the Centre

Parcul Etnografic
Romulus Vuia   MUSEUM, PARK
(www.muzeul-etnografic.ro; Aleea Muzeului Etnografic; adult/child 6/3 lei; ⏰10am to 6pm summer, 9am to 4pm winter) Traditional architecture from around Romania has been

faithfully reassembled at this open-air museum, located 5km northwest of central Cluj. Most impressive is the Cizer Church; get the attention of a caretaker to allow you inside to view frescoes covering its wooden interior.

Fabrica de Pensule   ARTS CENTRE
(Paintbrush Factory; ☎0727-169 569; www.fabricadepensule.ro; Str Henri Barbusse 59-61; ⏰tours 4-8pm Mon-Fri) FREE More of a living, breathing creative space than a gallery, Fabrica de Pensule teems with just-made artwork by local and foreign creators who

Central Cluj-Napoca

use this former paintbrush factory as a studio. Visits are by free guided tour, and depending on when you visit you'll spy anything from haunting urban photography to surreal Icelandic ceramics. Depending on how you like your art, you'll either adore visiting this artistic community in a post-industrial setting, or be bemused by the work-in-progress art within boxy gallery spaces.

🏃 Activities

Cluj-Napoca is a popular centre for caving and mountain-biking enthusiasts, with the Apuseni Mountains to the southwest offering a wealth of caves and trails. Alongside regular operators, Retro Hostel (p140) also has a travel agency that can organise short and long tours to Turda salt mine, Sibiu, the Apuseni Mountains, and much more.

Green Mountain Holidays   HIKING
(☑0744-637 227; www.greenmountainholidays. ro) ✎ This terrific ecotourism organisation is recommended for an environmentally friendly, activity-filled week. Check its website for caving, hiking and biking tours in the Apuseni Mountains with guides, transport, meals and accommodation, as well as self-guided trips.

Cluj Guided Tours   WALKING
(www.facebook.com/clujguidedtours; Piaţa Unirii; ⊘6pm daily May-Oct) [FREE] Informative English-language walking tours of Cluj begin at the Matthias Corvinus statue on Piaţa Unirii. The walks are led by volunteers, though tips are welcome at the end. They're roughly two hours long and cover the major old town sights.

🎆 Festivals & Events

**Transilvania International
Film Festival**   FILM
(www.tiff.ro; ⊘early–mid-Jun) International and local movie screenings take place in dozens of locations around Cluj-Napoca, from major cinemas to enchanting gardens, for this celebration of the silver screen. Browse schedules on the website well ahead of time, or buy a TIFF Card (300 lei) and you can settle in for as many as 35 movies.

★Untold Festival   MUSIC
(www.untold.com; ⊘early Aug) Romania's largest music festival has been scooping up awards since it began in 2015. An explosive mix of dubstep, house and EDM takes to the stage over four euphoric days. Book tickets, and accommodation in Cluj, well ahead of time – this is a local favourite rapidly gathering international praise.

TRANSYLVANIA CLUJ-NAPOCA

🛏 Sleeping

A slew of excellent hostels has boosted Cluj-Napoca's budget accommodation scene in recent years. There are comfy guesthouses and a couple of standout boutique hotels, and only a few drab, business-focused hotels to avoid. Strada Republicii, extending along the botanic gardens, has plenty of family-run pensions.

★ Youthink Hostel — HOSTEL $

(☑ 0745-202 911; www.youthinkhostel.com; Str Republicii 74; dm/d €15/35; P 🐾) 🧭 A labour-of-love restoration project has transformed a 1920 building, abandoned for a decade, into something between a hostel and an ecotourism retreat. Original wood beams, fireplace and hardwood floors retain the building's early-20th-century splendour, while the seven- and eight-bed dorms are clean and modern. Aptly for such a cheery and eco-conscious hostel, you'll be greeted by friendly dogs and a cat.

Zen Hostel — HOSTEL $

(www.zenboutiquehostel.ro; B-dul Eroilor 47; dm/d from 60/160 lei; @🐾) Sparkling stained-glass and swaying hammocks set the pace of this hostel haven at the eastern end of B-dul Eroilor. All the essentials are here – lockers, maps, laundry facilities (15 lei), kitchen – plus there's a mini-library and plenty of colourful nooks and crannies to chill in. Breakfast not included.

Retro Hostel — HOSTEL $

(☑ 0264-450 452; www.retro.ro; Str Potaissa 13; incl breakfast dm/s/d without bathroom 55/100/150 lei, s/d 120/170 lei; @🐾) The modern-nostalgic blend at Retro Hostel works like a charm. Minimalist murals of head-scarf-clad women dance across its corridors, while elsewhere you can spy original medieval stone walls. Dorms and private rooms are nicely maintained, decorated in cooling shades of blue, but certain dorms are not for tall travellers. The homecooked breakfasts, included in the price, are a highlight.

★ Lol & Lola — BOUTIQUE HOTEL $$

(☑ 0264-450 498; www.loletlolahotel.ro; Str Neagră 9; s/d €67/79; P ❄🐾) This enjoyably zany hotel has a rainbow of individually styled rooms to choose from, with themes ranging from Hollywood, ballet, and a rock 'n' roll room with vinyl and guitars. It's ultra-modern with friendly service.

Pensiunea Junior — PENSION $$

(☑ 0264-432 028; www.pensiune-junior.ro; Str Câii Ferate 12; d 160 lei; P 🐾) Far superior to the average train-station-skirting hotel, Junior has immaculately clean bathrooms adjoining its modern double rooms with floral trimmings. Worth a longer stay than just an overnight before an early train journey (the terminal is 300m away).

Hotel Confort — HOTEL $$

(☑ 0264-598 410; www.hotelconfort.ro; Calea Turzii 48; s/d/ste 200/220/255 lei; P ❄🐾) Huge rooms with wooden floors and fuzzy rugs are accented with flower arrangements and arty prints at this chic hotel. Four rooms have balconies, and most have big windows and billowy drapes. It's a car-friendly location, a 15-minute walk outside central Cluj. Parking is free but limited; ask ahead. Breakfast is an extra 12 lei.

Fullton Hotel — HOTEL $$

(☑ 0729-999 444; www.fullton.ro; Str Sextil Pușcariu 10; s 195-235 lei, d 215-250 lei; ❄🐾) This grey-green hotel has a superb location in the old town, and its furnishings continue the old-timey feel. 'Attic' and 'canopy' rooms are worth the higher price tag for their wood beams and billowing four-poster beds.

Capitolina City Chic — BOUTIQUE HOTEL $$$

(☑ 0264-450 490; www.hotel-capitolina.ro; Str Victor Babeș 35; d €86-97; P ❄🐾) Breezy design touches such as chandeliers, flowing drapes and literary quotes lend an upbeat feel to this boutique hotel, 400m west of the botanical gardens. The individually decorated rooms are light-filled, colourful and modern, with spotless marble bathrooms; the larger ones have cosy couches to slump in.

🍴 Eating

Cluj's varied restaurant scene can satisfy every taste, from hole-in-the-wall coffee spots, hearty Hungarian restaurants, polished bistros and all-vegetarian cafes. Piața Unirii and the old town have plenty of choice.

One warming local dish is *varză a la Cluj,* layers of cabbage, minced pork and soured cream.

Bistro Viena — DESSERTS, AUSTRIAN $

(☑ 0757-082 590; www.bistroviena.ro; Str Matei Corvin 3; dessert 10 lei; ⊙ 9am-midnight Mon-Thu, to 1am Fri & Sat, 10am-1pm Sun) Channelling Austria's sweet tooth and coffee culture, this cafe with outdoor seating has tempting desserts including Sachertorte, strudels and poppyseed dumplings, with a range of refreshing cocktails (13 lei) if caffeine simply won't do. It's next door to Restaurant Matei Corvin.

★ Roata
ROMANIAN $$

(☑0264-592 022; www.restaurant-roata.ro; Str Alexandru Ciurea 6; mains 20-28 lei; ☺noon-11pm; ☑) Transylvanian cuisine just like granny made it, in an untouristed part of Cluj. Settle in beneath the vine-covered trellis in the outdoor area, and agonise between roasted pork ribs and pike with capers. Or go all out with a 'Transylvanian platter' for two (52 lei), with homemade sausages, meatballs, sheep's cheese, aubergine stew and spare elastic for when your pants snap (we wish).

Nuka Bistro
BURGERS $$

(☑0742-687 769; Piaţa Unirii 16; mains 21-28 lei; ☺8am-late) Choose from Vlad, Monroe or JFK burgers at this smart bistro (the count has chilli, while Marilyn is slathered with sweet caramelised onion). There's also a fine pan-European menu with good breakfasts, seafood and cakes. One of several elegant spots on the western side of Piaţa Unirii.

Samsara
VEGETARIAN $$

(☑0736-073 073; www.samsara.ro; Str Ştefan Ludwig Roth 5; mains 21-26 lei; ☺11am-11pm; ☑) Cluj's hippie haven is this health-conscious veggie place with a convivial outdoor garden seating. Nibble brown-rice sushi and raw cakes with a few gulps of green smoothie as the ultimate antidote to heavy Romanian cuisine. There are vegan options too.

Camino
INTERNATIONAL $$

(☑0749-200 117; Piaţa Muzeului 4; mains 20-30 lei; ☺9am-midnight; ☎) This boho restaurant has a raffish charm, its peeling interior decked in candelabra and threadbare rugs, and outdoor seating spilling into monumental Piaţa Muzeului. Italian, Spanish and Indian dishes grace the menu. Ideal for solo book-reading over a pressed lemonade or alfresco tapas for two.

Restaurant Matei Corvin
ROMANIAN $$

(☑0264-597 496; Str Matei Corvin 3; mains 16-42 lei; ☺noon-11pm Mon-Sat) Sit down at one of the tables tumbling onto the stony pedestrian lane, and tuck in to Transylvanian cuisine such as paprika chicken with mămăligă (cornmeal) and big crunchy salads on the side.

Bricks – (M)eating Point Restaurant
STEAK $$$

(☑0364-730 615; www.bricksrestaurant.ro; Str Horea 2; mains 33-58 lei; ☺11am-11pm; ✷☎) Jazz flows right along with the cocktails at this chic steakhouse overhanging the river. Italian pasta dishes, burgers and barbecued meats dominate the menu, alongside a couple of vegetarian options and plump desserts like cottage-cheese pancakes. Lunch specials (15 lei) offer the best value.

Mátyás Étterem
HUNGARIAN $$$

(☑0264-406 523; www.hotelagape.ro; Str Iuliu Maniu 6; mains 25-50 lei; ☺noon-11pm) Based at the Hotel Agape, rustically painted wooden walls and finely carved furniture complement a menu of Hungarian dishes with a twist, such as Marmite goulash and meat stew with rosehip jam. Polish it off with cheesecakes, pancakes and a lavish list of local wines.

🍷 Drinking & Nightlife

The clubs don't rival Bucharest, but Cluj-Napoca uses its smaller scene to great advantage: bars and venues are geared towards culture, music and good conversation, and nightclubs tend to be fun-loving and unpretentious, without onerous dress codes. Cafe-bars within cavernous cellars and repurposed historic buildings ooze charm. Many of the best bars are in the student quarter, and along B-dul Eroilor and Piaţa Unirii.

Insomnia
BAR, BEER GARDEN

(www.insomniacafe.ro; Str Universităţii 2; ☺9am-1am Mon-Fri, 11am-1am Sat & Sun) Squeezed into a narrow courtyard, a jaunty beer garden adjoins this zanily decorated bohemian cafe. Insomnia is one of a slew of bars catering to Cluj's arty crowd (which seems to be half the city) within the student quarter.

Roots
CAFE

(B-dul Eroilor 4; ☺7.30am-11.30pm Mon-Fri, 9am-11.30pm Sat, to 5pm Sun) Competition for Cluj's best brew is stiff, but Roots' silky coffee is the front runner. Staff are as friendly as the flat whites are smooth.

Joben Bistro
CAFE

(www.jobenbistro.ro; Str Avram Iancu 29; ☺8am-2am Mon-Thu, noon-2am Fri-Sun; ☎) This steampunk cafe will lubricate the gears of any traveller with a penchant for Victoriana. Aside from the fantasy decor, with skull designs, taxidermied deer heads and copper pipes on bare brick walls, it's a laid-back place to nurse a lavender-infused lemonade or perhaps the potent 'Drunky Hot Chocolate'.

Irish & Music Pub
BAR
(☑ 0729-947 133; www.irishmusicpub.ro; Str Horea 5; ⊘ 10am-4am Mon-Sat, 6pm-4am Sun) Before you flee from the hackneyed 'Irish pub abroad' theme, know that this subterranean place has plenty of atmosphere resounding from its cavernous brick walls, plus a menu of steak sandwiches and veggie-friendly bar snacks to line your stomach.

Delirio Gay Club
GAY & LESBIAN
(www.delirio.ro; B-dul 21 Decembrie 1989, 8; ⊘ 6-11pm Sun-Wed, to 5am Thu, 11pm-5am Fri & Sat) Cluj's only LGBT club is a laid-back bar on weeknights, and a vodka-fuelled, scantily-clad late-night party at weekends. Boys are banned between 11pm and 5am on Thursday for the weekly ladies' night.

Caffe Meron
CAFE
(www.caffemeron.com; Str Napoca 3; ⊘ 8am-10pm) While this cafe is almost a little too trendy, with its polished tables and trance soundtrack, the coffee is to die for.

Tabiet Cafe
CAFE, BAR
(Str Virgil Fulicea 2; ⊘ 7am-10pm Mon-Fri, 9am-10pm Sat, 10am-10pm Sun) Sip good coffee and great cocktails in Tabiet's snug, stone-walled bar or on the terrace, which spills into the cobbled old town. It also serves *piadina* (stuffed flatbread) and other Italian-inspired fare.

☆ Entertainment

Zile și Nopți (www.zilesinopti.ro/cluj-napoca) and *24-Fun* are biweekly entertainment listings (in Romanian).

Flying Circus
CONCERT VENUE, CLUB
(www.flyingcircus.ro; Str Iuliu Maniu 2; entry before/after 1am 7/10 lei; ⊘ 5pm-dawn) Arrive around midnight to see this student-oriented club

begin to swing. Punters come for the music rather than to pose, so check the theme before you rock up: events vary from doom metal to euphoric drum and bass. There's usually a free shot with the entry fee.

National Theatre
THEATRE
(Teatrul Național Lucian Blaga; www.teatrulnational cluj.ro; Piața Ștefan cel Mare 2-4; tickets from 20 lei) From Molière and Shakespeare through to modern drama, the Romanian language performances at the National Theatre are the slickest productions in town. Buy tickets in advance at the nearby box office (☑ tickets 0264-595 363; Piața Ștefan cel Mare 14; ⊘ 11am-2pm & 3-5pm Tue-Sun & 1 hour before performances).

The National Theatre was designed in the 19th century by the famed Habsburg architects Fellner and Helmer.

State Philharmonic
CLASSICAL MUSIC
(Filarmonica de Stat; ☑ box office 0264-430 060; www.filarmonicatransilvania.ro; Piața Lucian Blaga 1-3; concerts adult/student from 25/13 lei) Hear choirs, quartets and rousing orchestras at Transylvania's State Philharmonic Theatre.

ⓘ Information

The city is full of ATMs and banks that exchange currency. **Banca Comercială Română** (Str Gheorghe Barițiu 10-12; ⊘ 9am-5.30pm Mon-Fri) is one of several banks and ATMs along busy Str Gheorghe Barițiu.

Tourist Information Office (☑ 0264-452 244; www.visitcluj.ro; B-dul Eroilor 6; ⊘ 8.30am-8pm Mon-Fri, 10am-6pm Sat & Sun) Super-friendly office with free maps, thoughtful trekking advice, and tons of info on transport links, accommodation, events and more.

ⓘ Getting There & Away

AIR
Cluj International Airport (CLJ; ☑ 0264-416 702, 0264-307 500; www.airportcluj.ro; Str Traian Vuia 149) is 7km east of the old town.

DOMESTIC BUS SERVICES FROM CLUJ-NAPOCA

DESTINATION	COST (LEI)	DURATION (HR)	FREQUENCY (DAILY)
Baia Mare	35-53	3	12
Bistrița	20	2¼	8
Brașov	35-65	4¾–5½	4
Bucharest	70-90	9	6
Sibiu	30-35	3¼-4	almost hourly

TRAINS FROM CLUJ-NAPOCA

DESTINATION	COST (LEI)	DURATION (HR)	FREQUENCY (DAILY)
Bistriţa	16	3	2 (more via Sărăţel)
Braşov	62-75	6-8	6
Bucharest	78-87	10-11	5
Budapest	140	5	2
Huedin	6-15	¾-1¼	20
Iaşi	78	9½	4
Oradea	38	2¼-4	14
Sibiu	46	4	1 (more via Vinţu De Jos)
Sighişoara	52	4½	4 (more via Teiuş)
Suceava	63	7	4
Târgu Mureş	12-23	2¼	1 (via Aiud or Războieni)
Timişoara	63	5½–7½	4 (more via Teiuş)
Zalău	33-38	4	1 (more via Jibou)

Buses 5 and 8 connect the airport with central Cluj (Piaţa Mihai Viteazul). Services are every 10 to 20 minutes between 5am and 10pm. The journey takes 30 minutes. The airport is served by numerous airlines.

Austrian Airlines (www.austrian.com) Services between Cluj and Vienna.

Lufthansa (www.lufthansa.com) Sends daily flights to Munich.

Tarom (www.tarom.ro) Domestic flights between Cluj and Bucharest.

Turkish Airlines (www.turkishairlines.com) Links Cluj with İstanbul.

Wizz Air (www.wizzair.com) Budget carrier flies to London Luton, Paris Beauvais, Valencia, Tel Aviv, Barcelona, Cologne, Eindhoven and more.

BUS

Domestic and international bus services depart mostly from **Bus Station 2** (Autogara 2, Autogara Beta; ☑ 0264-455 249; www.autogara-beta-cluj.ro; Str Giordano Bruno 1-3).The bus station is 350m northwest of the train station (take the overpass).

Buses to Turda run both from a **stop** at Piaţa Mihai Viteazu and Bus Station 2 (7 lei, 45 minutes, half-hourly).

TRAIN

Trains from Cluj-Napoca's **train station** (www.cfrcalatori.ro; Str Căii Ferate) reach the following destinations; routes are direct unless stated. The **Agenţia de Voiaj CFR** (☑ 0264-432 001; Piaţa Mihai Viteazu 20; ⊘ 8.30am-8pm Mon-Fri) sells domestic and international train tickets in advance. Left luggage service is available at the station.

Turda

POP 55,800

A breathtaking but bizarre salt mine reels visitors in to Turda, while the epic hiking terrain of Turda Gorge detains them a while longer. The town itself, featuring a pedestrianised square lined with Hapsburg facades, is a pleasant enough detour, though most people pop in on a day-trip from Cluj, 30km north.

Back in the days when salt was currency, Turda's salt-mining industry (dating back to the 13th century) made it a powerhouse. The main mine shut down in 1932, though it's a much-visited curiosity in its current form. Whether you're seeking amenities, hotels or food, life revolves around Turda's central street, Str Republicii.

☉ Sights

Salt Mine   MINE

(Salina Turda; ☑ 0364-260 940; www.salinaturda.eu; Str Aleea Durgaului 7; adult/child 20/10 lei, parking per car 5 lei; ⊘ 9am-5pm, last entry at 4pm; ℗) The meadowlands and chalky hills surrounding Turda have a secret underworld: a salt mine so impressive, it could be a supervillain's lair. Walking along 900m of cave corridors, zebra-striped with salt and dirt, you'll discover a chapel with a salt-encrusted Jesus and Mary; salt miners used to pray here before their shift. When you see the hefty 1881 extraction apparatus, you'll understand why. Then descend into the most spectacular chamber, befitting a Bond nemesis. It's a chilly 10°C to 12°C, so wear layers.

WORTH A TRIP

TURDA GORGE

Precipitous **Turda Gorge** (Cheile Turzii; www.turism-cheile-turzii.ro; May-Sep adult/child 4/2 lei) lies 8km west of town (as the crow flies), and it makes a stunning, if leg-stiffening, half-day hike. The canyon is nearly 3km long, with 300m-high walls sculpted in weathered limestone. Walking the gorge's length takes roughly 1½ hours each way.

To get there, take a bus from Turda to the centre of Cheia (4 lei, 30 minutes). From there it's a straightforward roadside 5km hike to the gorge (follow the 'cheile turzii' signs). It's possible to drive down this road, but ask locally about road conditions and don't attempt it in poor weather.

Dress for temperatures several degrees lower than in the surrounding uplands, and wear grippy footwear. Pay the entry fee after the first bridge (high season only).

🛏 Sleeping & Eating

Turda offers a modest array of midrange hotels, some with a spa theme in line with the healing powers of the salt mine. But most visitors day-trip here from Cluj-Napoca, 30km north.

★ **Hunter Prince Castle & Dracula Hotel**   HOTEL $$
(Castelul Printul Vanator; ☑0264-316 850; www.huntercastle.ro; Str Şuluţiu 4-6; s/d/ste from 204/247/294 lei; 🅿✳🛜) The fanged face of Vlad Ţepeş, beaming down from a stone wall, might not be the warm welcome you'd hope from a hotel. But it's hard to resist staying at this turreted homage to Vlad, crowned with iron flagpoles, with hunting regalia decorating it within. Comfy twin rooms have suitably spiky wrought-iron bed frames; meanwhile the suites are stupendous, with carved armoires and mosaic-style stonework.

Alegria Centrale   PIZZA $
(☑0364-888 444; www.pizzaalegria.ro; Piaţa Republicii; mains 15 lei; ⊗8am-midnight) A good stop for a coffee, pizza or salad; eat inside its Europop-blasted interior or, better still, outside on the Piaţa-facing terrace.

✈ Getting There & Away

Maxitaxis leave frequently from the centre for Cluj-Napoca's Piaţa Mihai Viteazul (7 lei, 40 minutes). The bus station in Piaţa Romană, a 10-minute walk south of Piaţa Republicii, has buses heading for Alba Iulia (15 lei, 1½ to two hours, hourly), Sibiu (28 lei, three hours, almost hourly) and Bucharest (70 to 80 lei, six or seven daily, eight hours).

If arriving by car, note that parking around Turda's main streets starts from 1 lei per half-hour; there are machines and signs showing a number to pay by SMS (if you have a Romanian SIM card).

Huedin Microregion

Centuries-old traditions endure in this peaceful region of chalky hills and farmland, just off the Cluj–Oradea highway. Scattered around chief town Huedin, just north of the Apuseni Mountains, the 42 villages comprising the Huedin Microregion (or Kalotaszeg) are rewarding terrain for road trippers and hikers.

The Kalotaszeg is much beloved by Hungarian folklorists as a stronghold of pastoral Transylvanian Magyar culture. Experience it through immersion: stay the night in a never-changing village like Sâncraiu, indulge in Hungarian pastries, and learn woodwork and embroidery from local artisans.

The area's namesake, Huedin (Bánffyhunyad in Hungarian), 52km west of Cluj-Napoca, is an unengaging highway town. Nonetheless, it has the bulk of local amenities, so it's worth pausing here to stock up on food, fuel or mobile-phone credit.

◉ Sights

Exploring the area surrounding Huedin brings fascinating insights into Transylvanian Magyar culture.

Driving west from Cluj-Napoca towards Huedin, you can't fail to notice the famous 'souvenir village' of **Izvoru Crişului** (Körösfő to Hungarians). Shops are stacked along the main road running through town, peddling traditional ceramics, linen womenswear and menswear, beaded jewellery (from 15 lei), baskets, embroidered tablecloths (800 lei and beyond), and plenty of cheap souvenirs and toys too.

Continue west for 7km to Huedin, then take the southbound route 1R for 5km to **Sâncraiu**. **Davincze Tours** (☑0745-637 352,

0264-257 580; www.kalotaszeg-davincze.ro; No 291, Sâncraiu) can arrange hiking guides (€55 per day) and horse-drawn carriage rides (€20 per hour) into the sweeping hills here. But most compelling are the authentic cultural and gastronomic experiences on offer.

Twelve kilometres southwest of Sâncraiu lies Mănăstireni (Magyargyerömonostor in Hungarian), a quaint village noted for its 13th-century church. During the 1848 revolution, 200 Hungarians died at the battle of Mănăstireni; you can see bullet holes from Turk guns in the church. Twenty-three kilometres south of here is a dam-flooded village submerged beneath Lake Beliş-Fântânele – at very low water levels, you can see the church tower come up for air.

🛏 Sleeping & Eating

Main town Huedin might seem like an obvious base for exploring the region, but accommodation here is uninspiring and thin on the ground. *Pensiunes* in Sâncraiu or Răchiţele are much more comfortable.

★ **Püspök Panzió**   PENSION $
(📞 0745-637 352; www.kalotaszeg-davincze.ro; Sâncraiu; s/d €15/20; 🅿 🛜) Brimming with charm and colour, this former barn has been transformed into a welcoming guesthouse with unique hand-painted decoration, firm beds and spotless white linens. Chairs and bedframes are a riot of blue-and-red patterns, expertly finished by a local furniture painter. Breakfast is an extra €3. Traditional Kalotaszeg dinners (€7) are available on request. It's expertly run by the Davincze Tours (p144) team.

ℹ Getting There & Away

Huedin is accessible from Cluj-Napoca by train (17 lei, one to 1½ hours, 12 daily), and bus or maxitaxi (8 to 10 lei, one to two hours, 12 daily). From here, taxis can drop you to villages (about 20 to 25 lei for Sâncraiu). You'll see plenty of hitchhikers, though we don't recommend it. A rental car from Cluj is best.

Apuseni Mountains

Southwest of Cluj-Napoca, the Apuseni Mountains are sheer drama. Beneath silhouettes of mountains lie thatches of conifer forest, while sinkholes and grottoes are secreted away in the karst plateaus. Some 760 sq km here are protected as the Apuseni Nature Park, best accessed from Oradea. Meanwhile the Padiş Plateau is the park's central point, and a popular outdoor excursion from Cluj.

🏃 Activities

The Apuseni Mountains have challenging hiking terrain, so it's worth considering going with a guide; **Pan Travel** (📞 0264-420 516; www.pantravel.ro; Str Grozăvescu 13; ⊙ 9am-5pm Mon-Fri) and Green Mountain Holidays (p139) in Cluj can help, as well as organise other adventure activities such as caving and biking.

Hiking

Cabana Padiş, signposted just off Str Principală running through Padiş, is a starting point for several good hikes. One popular circuit leads southwest via Glăvoi to the fantastic **Cetăţile Ponorului** or 'fortress cave'

WORTH A TRIP

RĂCHIŢELE

Travelling south from Huedin towards the Apuseni, the last base with guesthouses before the mountains is Răchiţele, surrounded by rolling pastureland, farmsteads and thick forest. Six kilometres west of the village, reached by a patchy dirt road, is 30m-high **Cascada Vălul Miresei** (Bride's Veil Waterfall). The cascade takes its name from a folk tale in which a bride fell over the cliff, leaving her veil draped on the rocks.

It's also on this road you'll find some welcoming *pensiunes*, including **Pensiunea Susman** (📞 0744-653 294, 0744-475 758; www.pensiuneasusman.home.ro; Răchiţele; d/tr/q from 70/80/100 lei; 🅿). Less than two kilometres from Bride's Veil waterfall, this pretty wood cabin offers warm welcomes and simple rooms with forest views. Two of its eight rooms have shared bathrooms. Speak to the hospitable owners about hiking and rock climbing in summer, and ice climbing and sleigh rides in winter.

From Cluj, a scenic approach to the Apuseni is by driving west to main highway town Gilău (16km west of Cluj) and on to Lake Beliş-Fântânele (60km total). There's accommodation around Beliş and neighbouring Mărişel.

WORTH A TRIP

BÁNFFY CASTLE

Thirty kilometres northeast of Cluj and 3km east of the highway, the village of Bonţida holds the manicured gardens and orchards of the 17th-century Bánffy Castle (Castelul Bánffy de la Bonţida; www.heritagetraining-banffycastle.org; Bonţida; 3 lei; ⊙ 10am-8pm Tue-Sun), once referred to as 'Transylvania's Versailles'. The aristocratic Bánffy family resided between these thick walls; but where once stood ornate windows and stucco, today you see only exposed brick and cracked stone awaiting restoration. In summer, it hosts the Electric Castle (www.electriccastle.ro; Bonţida; ⊙ mid-Jul) music festival of house and electronica.

WWII was cruel to the castle: the long-resident Bánffy family had fled, and the castle's renowned library and archive was lost when the retreating German army set fire to its main buildings. Slow, painstaking restoration works have been in motion since 1999.

There are buses from Cluj-Napoca to Bonţida (6 lei, one hour, three daily), while trains reach the station 3km north of the castle (4.50 lei, 45 minutes, five daily).

(2½ hours one way, blue circles), so called because of its 76m entrance, like the portal to a magical underworld. While much of this walk is on road, the last part is down an uneven path winding through forest. As the path veers sharply downhill you'll have to pick your way across boulders and sprawling tree roots and, for the final 200m descent, you'll need the aid of a ladder and cables to get you to the great mouth of the cave (those prone to vertigo should stop before this point).

The cave itself, with a main gallery 2km long, and one of the country's largest underground rivers – fraught with whirlpools and sinkholes – is only advisable with a guide and equipment including good boots, a helmet and a torch.

Another trail, a long full-day trek, is marked first by red stripes then by red circles, leading from Cabana Padiş north for three or four hours to a meadow at Poiana Vărăşoaia. From here, red circles continue two hours to the Rădesei Citadel (Cetăţile Rădesei), another underground chamber with impressive rock formations (and tent sites). The route then circles Someşul Cald, a river in a deep gorge, after which you can head back south to the cabana.

🛏 Sleeping & Eating

Padiş has simple chalet accommodation, there are pensions aimed at hikers elsewhere in the park, and camping is possible at Glăvoi, 2km southwest of Padiş. Check ahead, as some accommodation is seasonal.

Pack a picnic or eat at your guesthouse; the Apuseni Mountains are wild, and guesthouse-restaurants open erratically.

La 5 Casute CHALET $
(☎ 0732-833 783; Padiş; d 130 lei; P 🛜) On the main road through Padiş, this tourist complex's five pinewood cabins are simple but romantic, with comfy beds, TVs and mountain views. Wi-fi doesn't extend to all the cabins. Payment is in cash only.

Cabana Cetaţile Ponorului CHALET $
(☎ 0740-007 814; www.padis.ro; r with/without bathroom per person €15.50/13.50; P 🛜) The double and quad rooms at this friendly chalet are a good place to rest your head after adventures to the caves of Apuseni Nature Park. Staff can prepare picnics to take on hikes. It's 1.7km downhill from Glăvoi, past the turn-off for the fortress cave.

ℹ Information

Apuseni Nature Park Visitors Centre (☎ 0372-702 242, 0748-126 924; www.parcapuseni.ro; Sudrigiu 136; ⊙ 8am-4.30pm Mon-Thu, 8am-2pm Fri) An immensely useful stop if you are visiting the Apuseni Mountains independently, rather than on guided tours or hikes. The park's administration office sell maps (15 lei) and offers advice on activities and accommodation.

ℹ Getting There & Away

From Cluj-Napoca, it's possible to reach Padiş by car along the 108C from Huedin via Rachiţele, though the road wasn't in good condition when we rattled in. Ask locally for the latest road advice, and don't even think about it in bad weather. You may wish to take the long way around, entering the park from the western side. Much nicer is route 1R south from Huedin, though it doesn't plough as deep into the park; still, there are numerous roadside guesthouses along the way.

Public transport from Cluj-Napoca isn't straightforward: board a bus from Cluj to Huedin (7 to 10 lei, one hour, 12 daily). Infrequent local minibuses run from Huedin to Rachiţele, from where you can hike into the park (some travellers hitchhike).

Bistriţa

POP 113,260

Travellers following the Transylvanian vampire trail may be quietly disappointed by amiable Bistriţa. Spangled with pastel-coloured Renaissance buildings and whitewashed churches, the town bears little resemblance to the Bistritz (its German name) described in Bram Stoker's *Dracula*. In the novel, Jonathan Harker stays in Bistriţa before heading to the Count's lair in Borgo (Bârgău) Pass, despite locals' anguished warnings of the horrors ahead.

Modern Bistriţa has barely a garlic-clutching villager in sight. Cobbled streets lined with cafes radiate from its Gothic centrepiece, the 14th-century Evangelical Church. Several well-preserved Renaissance buildings attest to its history of Saxon merchants and renowned silversmiths. It's a relaxing place to stay before pressing on to Lake Colibiţa or the forbidding Bârgău Valley.

⊙ Sights

Walk from Piaţa Unirii south along Str Teodoroiu through narrow alleys to **Parcul Municipal**. The park has long boulevards for cycling and walking, and a lily pond with giant goldfish. Amble southwest along its leaf-lined promenade, past the buttercream-coloured **Centrul Cultural** building. You'll soon see the **Turnul Dogarilor**

(Cooper's Tower; Str Dogarilor), part of Bistriţa's 13th-century fortifications.

County Museum   MUSEUM
(Muzeul Judetean; B-dul General Grigore Bălan 19; adult/child 4/2 lei; ☉ 10am-6pm Tue-Sun Apr-Sep, 9am-5pm Tue-Sun Oct-Mar) Did you know that Bistriţa is the only place in Transylvania where men's traditional headwear involves a crown of peacock feathers? Inside a former garrison, Bistriţa's County Museum offers interesting tidbits of local history around its three exhibition spaces: ancient history, with Thracian bronze tools; the rural past, with handicrafts and farming tools; and a collection of modern art.

Evangelical Church   CHURCH
(Biserica Evanghelică; Piaţa Centrală; tower adult/child 10/5 lei; ☉ 9am-5pm Mon-Fri, 10am-6pm Sat, noon-6pm Sun) Bistriţa's number one landmark is the Evangelical Church, whose 76m Gothic tower dominates its main square. Construction began in the 14th century, and Italian architect Petrus Italus de Lugano gave it a Renaissance-style makeover in 1563, adding its portals. It's worth climbing the tower for views over the town.

Silversmith's House   MUSEUM, GALLERY
(Casa Argentului; Str Dornei 5; ☉ 10am-6pm Tue-Sun) **FREE** Formerly the home of Bistriţa's most renowned jeweller, this restored Gothic and Renaissance building is worth a peep for its rotating exhibitions of art and local history.

⊨ Sleeping

Bistriţa has a small choice of mostly budget and midrange hotels, with a couple that stand out for charm and good service.

WORTH A TRIP

DRACULA'S BÂRGĂU VALLEY

Writing his timeless Gothic novel *Dracula*, Bram Stoker gave his count a lair overlooking the forbidding forests of Bârgău Valley, 45km east of Bistriţa. Today, a themed hotel has sprung up at this very spot, near Piatra Fântânele village. While Hotel Castel Dracula is camp compared to the fictional den of Dracula and his bloodthirsty sirens, it's an awe-inspiring location, especially when night falls and wind whips across the valley.

The hotel draws as many day-trippers as overnight guests. Snap a selfie with the bust of Stoker outside, peep inside to shiver at taxidermied hawks and wolves and – if you don't have a heart condition – visit 'Dracula's tomb'.

Bârgău Valley is difficult to explore without private transport. On request, buses between Bistriţa and Vatra Dornei (20 lei, two to 2½ hours, two to four daily) stop in Piatra Fântânele for Hotel Castel Dracula.

BUSES FROM BISTRIȚA

DESTINATION	COST (LEI)	DURATION (HR)	FREQUENCY (DAILY)
Alba Iulia	44	4	3
Cluj-Napoca	20	2½	9
Oradea	50	6	2
Suceava	45	6	3
Târgu Mureş	25	2½-4	3
Vatra Dornei	20	2-3	6

★ Coroana de Aur   HOTEL $$
(☑ 0263-232 470; www.hotelcoroanadeaur.ro;
Piaţa Petru Rareş 4; s/d/apt 185/210/330 lei;
P ❋ �🛜) It's named for the guesthouse
where Jonathan Harker stayed in Bram
Stoker's *Dracula,* but this is a faultless busi-
ness hotel rather than a forbidding old inn.
Its prettily lit cream decor, plush beds and
bright modern bathrooms are very pleasant
indeed. There's an occasional nod to the
vampire theme, though 'Jonathan Harker
Conference Room' doesn't spook us. Peas-
ants brandishing crucifixes not included.

Hotel Bistriţa   HOTEL $$
(☑ 0263-231 154; www.hotel-bistrita.ro; Piaţa Petru
Rareş 2; s/d/apt from 130/175/350 lei; P ❋ �🛜)
Guarded by a phalanx of conifers, this
imposing hotel has a plush '80s feel and
friendly staff. Rooms are down-lit and come
with a perky coral colour scheme, clean en
suites, safe deposit boxes and, in some cases,
balconies.

✖ Eating

There is a fine selection of cafes and restaurants in Bistriţa, from fast-food spots to
refined Romanian fare. Hotels and guesthouses have the most upmarket cuisine.
Pietonalul Liviu Rebreanu, extending east
from Piaţa Centrală, is lined with cafes and
casual eats.

★ Crama Veche   ROMANIAN $$
(☑ 0730-011 812; www.crama-veche.ro; cnr
Str Albert Berger & Str Dogarilor; mains 22 lei;
⊙ noon-midnight; �🛜) Feast like a medieval no-
ble in this stone-floored restaurant, where
walls are slung with guild regalia and lights
twinkle beneath low-slung beams. Bring a
healthy appetite for paprika chicken, veal
stew, meatballs and sausage (by the metre).
With 24 hours notice, they'll roast you a
piglet. We'd advise leaving room for jam-
crammed pancakes or fruit dumplings, but
it's almost impossible.

Coroana de Aur Restaurant   ROMANIAN $$
(☑ 0263-232 470; www.hotelcoroanadeaur.ro/
restaurant-bistrita; Piaţa Petru Rareş 4; mains 20-
45 lei; ⊙ 10am-11pm) Setting aside the decid-
edly retro feel to the Coroana de Aur hotel's
restaurant, it's considered the finest place to
eat in town. Indulgent game dishes include
wild boar leg with venison sauce, while
Romanian classics such as grilled trout are
faultlessly prepared. Otherwise there's a
daredevil dining choice: pork brains with
egg and onion.

ℹ Information

Tourist Information Office (☑ 0263-235 377;
www.primariabistrita.ro; Piaţa Centrala 13)
Information office equipped with brochures,
maps and more, but whimsical opening hours.

ℹ Getting There & Away

BUS

Bistriţa has a busy **bus station** (☑ 0256-
493 471) serving numerous Transylvanian
destinations.

TRAIN

The **train station** (☑ 0256-491 696) sends daily
trains to Sibiu (from 26 lei, 6½ hours, one daily),
Cluj (16 lei, 2½ to 3½ hours, five daily), Vatra
Dornei (21 lei, five hours, one daily) and Braşov
(70 lei, six hours, one daily direct, many more
via Saratel).

Crişana & Banat

Best Places to Eat

➡ Caruso (p156)

➡ Casa Bunicii (p155)

➡ Graf (p160)

➡ Don Restaurant (p164)

➡ Nora (p155)

➡ Picasso Restaurant (p165)

Best Places to Sleep

➡ Picasso Boutique Hotel (p163)

➡ Hotel Elite (p159)

➡ Vila La Residenza (p155)

➡ Hostel Costel (p155)

➡ Hotel Arad (p163)

➡ Casa Noastră (p163)

Why Go?

Western Romania, with its geographic and cultural ties to neighbouring Hungary and Serbia and its historical links to the Austro-Hungarian Empire, enjoys an ethnic diversity that much of the rest of the country lacks. Timişoara, the regional hub, has a nationwide reputation as a beautiful and lively metropolis, and for a series of 'firsts'. It was the world's first city to adopt electric street lights (in 1884) and, more importantly, the first city to rise up against dictator Nicolae Ceauşescu in 1989.

The three major centres of Timişoara, Oradea and Arad all boast some wonderful examples of art nouveau (or Secession) architecture and many buildings are now getting a long-awaited facelift. Outside these metropolitan areas, there are spas at Băile Felix, while the remote and pristine western ranges of the Apuseni Mountains are criss-crossed with kilometres of isolated hiking trails and dozens of amazing caves that cry out for exploration.

When to Go
Timişoara

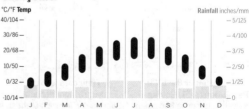

Apr–May Budding tree blossoms make a striking backdrop to a city break in Timişoara, Arad or Oradea.

Jun–Aug Summer brings warm, sunny days perfect for hiking in the western Apuseni Mountains.

Sep–Oct Timişoara's cultural scene awakens from its summer slumber.

Crişana & Banat Highlights

1 **Museum of the 1989 Revolution** (p151) Getting a riveting lesson in Romanian history in Timişoara.

2 **Oradea** (p157) Exploring the city's stunning and increasingly renovated art nouveau monuments.

3 **Timişoara** (p151) Enjoying a night of opera, dinner at a fine restaurant and a nightcap on Piaţa Victoriei or Piaţa Unirii.

4 **Bears Cave** (p161) Looking at the ancient stalactites and stalagmites in this magnificent limestone underworld.

5 **Apuseni Mountains** (p161) Hiking around or simply gazing at the Apuseni's western ranges.

6 **Băile Felix** (p161) Taking to the thermal waters at this spa resort.

History

The western Romanian regions of Crişana and Banat have always been the stepping stone between east and west. The area was first settled in the 6th century BC, and by AD 106 had become part of the Roman province of Dacia. The two regions both fell under Hungarian rule around the end of the 9th century and remained part of the Hungarian kingdom right up until the Ottoman conquest of Crişana and Banat in 1552.

The Turks ruled these parts for around 150 years, losing control of Crişana and Banat to the Austrian Habsburgs in 1716 after the Turks were defeated in battle by Habsburg prince Eugene of Savoy. Two years later, the regions formally became part of the Habsburg Empire, ruled from Vienna.

Austria lost no time in shoring up the regions against any possible return of the Turks, building state-of-the-art military fortresses in Arad, Oradea and Timişoara, which remain standing to this day. As a way of furthering their claims to Banat, the Austrians opened the area to settlement, and today you'll still come across small scattered communities of ethnic Czechs, Croats, Slovaks and others, living much as they did 100 years ago. Most Schwab Germans, who settled here after the expulsion of the Turks, have since emigrated to Germany.

The anti-Habsburg bourgeois uprisings of 1848 were felt keenly in these parts. Independence-seeking Hungarians fought to make these part of a newly formed Hungary, against armed resistance from the Austrians and, in some cases, bands of Romanian brigands. The Austrians eventually prevailed, but ultimately ceded the territories to Hungary when Austria and Hungary agreed to form a 'dual monarchy' in 1867.

Crişana and Banat largely thrived in this dual monarchy up to WWI. The amazing art nouveau and Secession architecture found in the major cities, especially Oradea, is evidence of this prosperity. Under the terms of the Treaty of Trianon after WWI, Hungary lost two-thirds of its territory, including Crişana and Banat, which were awarded to a newly independent Romania.

BANAT

Timişoara

POP 319,280

Romania's third-largest city (after Bucharest and Cluj-Napoca) is also one of the country's most attractive urban areas, built around a series of beautifully restored public squares and lavish parks and gardens. It's known as Primul Oraş Liber (The First Free City), for it was here that anti-Ceauşescu protests first exceeded the Securitate's capacity for violent suppression in 1989, eventually sending Ceauşescu and his wife to their deaths. With western Romania's nicest hotels and finest restaurants, it makes a perfect base for exploring the Banat region.

Timişoara has been named European Capital of Culture 2021.

◎ Sights

◎ Piaţa Unirii & Around

Piaţa Unirii is Timişoara's most picturesque square, featuring the imposing Catholic and Serbian churches facing each other to the east and west.

★**Museum of the 1989 Revolution** MUSEUM
(☑0256-294 936; www.memorialulrevolutiei.ro; Strada Popa Şapcă 3-5; entry by donation; ⊙8am-4pm Mon-Fri, 10am-2pm Sat) This is an ideal venue to brush up on the December 1989 anticommunist revolution that began here in Timişoara. Displays include documentation, posters and photography from those fateful days, capped by a graphic 20-minute video (not suitable for young children) with English subtitles. Enter from Str Oituz 2.

Synagogue in the Fortress SYNAGOGUE
(Sinagoga din Cetate; Str Mărăşeşti 6) Built in 1865 by Viennese architect Ignatz Schuhmann, the synagogue acts as an important keynote in Jewish history – Jews in the Austro-Hungarian Empire were emancipated in 1864, when permission was given to build the synagogue. It was closed at the time of research for a massive renovation, but the fine exterior is worth taking in.

Timişoara Art Museum MUSEUM
(Muzeul de Artă Timişoara; ☑0256-491 592; www.muzeuldeartatm.ro; Piaţa Unirii 1; adult 10 lei, child free; ⊙10am-6pm Tue-Sun) This museum displays a representative sample of paintings

Central Timişoara

EANAT

```
0                    200 m
0                    0.1 miles
```

CRIŞANA & BANAT TIMIŞOARA

Parcul Botanic

Piaţa Mărăşti

1 — Museum of the 1989 Revolution

Str Oituz

Str Gheorghe Dima

East Eurolines (1.3km)

Str Gheorgle Lazăr

19
Str N Grigorescu

18

7

5

B-dul Tache Ionescu

Piaţa IC Brătianu

Str Mărăşeşti

Str Ungureanu

Piaţa Unirii

Str P Chinezu

Str V Alecsandri

10

11

Str 1 Mai

Str Omul Tinta

Str 9 Mai

9

3

Str F Mercy

Str Pacha

Str Eugeniu de Savoya

Str Palanca

Str Popa Şapcă

Str Hector

Hostel Costel (850m)

8
Piaţa Libertăţii

Str Proclamaţia de la Timişoara

B-dul Revoluţiei 1989

Str Col Enescu

Str V V Delamarina

16

15

Str Lucian Blaga

Parcul Civic

Str Traian Grozăvescu

26

22
i

24

Str Alba Iulia

Piaţa Huniades

B-dul Republicii

Piaţa Victoriei

2

B-dul I C Brătianu

Str Rene Brassey

Str Nicolae Paulescu

Str N Lenau

Str Patriah Miron Cristea

Str Camil Petrescu

Str Piatra Craiului

17

6

21

B-dul 20 Decembrie 1989

B-dul Mihai Eminescu

B-dul Michelangelo

B-dul Regele Ferdinand I

20

Parcul Central

Parcul Catedralei

4

B-dul C D Loga

Str Acad Alexandru Borza

Parcul Rozelor

Reformed Church (500m)

25

Parcul Justiţiei

Parcul de Cultură

Bega Canal

Spl Tudor Vladimirescu

12

B-dul Regele Ferdinand I

23

B-dul Pârvan Vasile

Student Complex (550m)

Spl Tudor Vladimirescu

14

University of West Timişoara

B-dul Mihai Viteazu

Str Remus

13

Str Sfânta Rozalia

Communist Consumers Museum, Casa Bunicii, Scârţ loc lejer (250m); Vila La Residenza (550m)

Central Timişoara

and visual arts over the centuries as well as regular, high-quality temporary exhibitions. It's housed in the baroque **Old Prefecture Palace** (built 1754), which is worth a look inside for the graceful interiors alone.

Roman Catholic Cathedral CATHEDRAL
(Catedrală Episcopală Romano-Catolică; ☑ 0256-430 671; Piaţa Unirii 12; ⊙ 8am-6pm) The city's fine baroque cathedral on the east side of Piaţa Unirii was built in the mid- to late 18th century, after the Austro-Hungarian Empire had finally secured the area from Turkish influence. The main altar painting (1754) of St George slaying the dragon was carried out by Michael Angelo Unterberger, who was the director of the Fine Arts Academy in Vienna at the time of the cathedral's construction.

Timişoara Fortress FORTRESS
(Cetatea Timişoara; Str Hector; ⊙ 24hr) **FREE**
A couple of blocks to the east of Piaţa Unirii, following Str Palanca, is a classic 18th-century Austrian fortress with three fortification rings and nine bastions. It's been partially remodelled into a complex of shops and cafes.

Serbian Orthodox Church CHURCH
(Biserica Ortodoxă Sârbă; Str Ungureanu 12) Fronting the west side of Piaţa Unirii, the Serbian Orthodox Church was built at approximately the same time as its Catholic coun-

terpart across the square. Local Banat artist Constantin Daniel painted the interior.

⊙ Piaţa Libertăţii & Around

Sandwiched between Piaţa Unirii and Piaţa Victoriei, Piaţa Libertăţii is a shady square that lies at the heart of the city. There are few traditional sights here, but there are several interesting old buildings, including the **Old Town Hall**, and monuments.

St John of Nepomuk
& Virgin Mary Statue MONUMENT
The statue of St John of Nepomuk and the Virgin Mary, located in the centre of Piaţa Libertăţii, was made in 1756 in Vienna and brought to Romania in memory of the victims of the 1738–9 plague. Etched around the monument's base is the story of hapless St John of Nepomuk, who was reputedly flung off Charles Bridge in Prague to his death on the orders of the king for failing to reveal the queen's confessions.

⊙ Piaţa Victoriei & Around

Piaţa Victoriei is a leafy pedestrian mall dotted with central fountains and lined with shops and cafes. The square's northern end is marked by the 18th-century National Theatre and Opera House (p156). It was here that thousands of demonstrators gathered on 16 December 1989. A memorial on the front of the opera house reads: 'So you, who pass by this building, will dedicate a thought for free Romania'. Towards the centre, is the **Romulus and Remus Column**, a copy of the statue in Rome presented to Timișoara by that city in 1906 to mark Romania's Latin origins.

Orthodox Metropolitan Cathedral CATHEDRAL

(Catedrala Ortodoxă Mitropolitană; www.mitropolia-banatului.ro; B-dul Regele Ferdinand I; ⊙6am-8pm) The Orthodox cathedral was built between 1936 and 1946. It's unique for its Byzantine-influenced architecture, which recalls the style of the Bucovina monasteries; the floor tiles recall traditional Banat carpets. At 83m, the dome is the highest in Romania.

Banat History Museum MUSEUM

(Muzeul Banatului; ☑0256-225 588; Piața Huniades 1) This museum is housed in the historic Huniades Palace, whose origins date to the 14th century and to Hungarian king Charles Robert, Prince of Anjou. The museum was closed at the time of research for protracted renovations. The exterior of the palace, though, is still worth a look.

◎ South of the Centre

The **Bega Canal** snakes around the city south of Piața Victoriei. While parts of the banks remain scruffy in spots, the parks that line the canal on both sides are pleasant places to stroll.

Reformed Church CHURCH

(Biserica Reformată; Str Timotei Cipariu 1) The 1989 revolution began at the Reformed Church, where Father László Tőkés spoke out against Ceaușescu. You can sometimes peek in at the church, and it is usually open during times of worship.

Communist Consumers Museum MUSEUM

(Muzeul Consumatorului Comunist; ☑0751-892340; www.facebook.com/muzeuconsumatorcomunist; Str Laszlo Szekely 1; donation accepted; ⊙9am-11pm Mon-Fri, 11am-11pm Sat, 2-11pm Sun) This museum houses an odd collection of pre-1989 consumer goods manufactured in Romania. It fills to the point of overflowing three rooms and a hallway below a popular cafe south of the centre. Most of the toys, appliances and periodicals will mean nothing to foreigners but it's worth a visit just to watch older Romanians take a nostalgic stroll down memory lane.

Reach it on tram 6 or 8.

◎ North of the Centre

Banat Village Museum MUSEUM

(Muzeul Satului Banațean; ☑0256-491 339; www.muzeulsatuluibanatean.ro; Str Avram Imbroane 1; 4.50 lei; ⊙10am-5pm Tue-Sun) This open-air 'village' was created in 1917 and exhibits more than 30 traditional peasant houses dating from the 19th century. Take tram 1 (black number) from the Northern Train Station.

🏃 Activities

Rent **pedal boats** (☑0771-675 881; per hr 15 lei; ⊙9am-4pm Mon-Thu, 10am-5pm Sat & Sun May-Sep) to splash around the Bega Canal.

⌲ Tours

Several companies and individuals offer guided tours of the city and the Banat region. Recommended guides include **Tymes Tours** (☑0722-525 734; www.tymestours.ro), **Alexandra Irimia** (☑0742-112 174; www.timisoaratourguide.com), **Ludovic Satmari** (☑0762-519 797; www.timisoaracitytours.com) and **Claudiu Preda** (☑0745-519 934; www.claudiupreda.eu).

🎊 Festivals & Events

The city has an active cultural calendar, with high points coming in spring and autumn. The website of the **Timișoara Tourist Information Centre** (p157) has a complete list under 'Events'.

European Festival of Performing Arts PERFORMING ARTS

(FEST-FDR; www.tntimisoara.com; ⊙May) Nine-day annual festival that highlights the best of Romanian drama and theatre.

Hearts Folk Festival CULTURAL

(Festivalul Inimilor; www.facebook.com/FestivalulInimilor; ⊙Jul) One of the most important folklore festivals in Europe, held in Roses Park over four days in July.

International Jazz Festival MUSIC

(www.jazztm.ro; ⊙Jul) Held over three days in early July, this is one of the most important jazz festivals in Eastern Europe.

PLAI Festival MUSIC

(www.plai.ro; ⊙Sep) This very popular annual festival of ethnic and world music takes places on the grounds of the Banat Village Museum (p154) in mid-September.

🛏 Sleeping

Timişoara offers a range of choices, from a converted villa moonlighting as a hotel, boutique hotels and uber-comfortable guesthouses to a canal-side hostel.

★Hostel Costel   HOSTEL $

(☑0356-262 487; www.hostel-costel.ro; Str Petru Sfetca 1; dm 50-60 lei, d 135 lei; @🛜) This charming 1920s art nouveau villa is the city's best-run hostel. The vibe is relaxed and congenial. There are three dorm rooms with six to 10 beds and one private double, plus ample chill rooms, a kitchen and a big garden with hammocks for relaxing.

The hostel is 1km east of the centre, across the Bega Canal near the Decebal Bridge; take tram 1.

★Pensiunea Casa Leone   PENSION $$

(☑0256-292 621, 0723-329 612; www.casaleone. ro; B-dul Eroilor de la Tisa 67; s/d/tr 140/160/225 lei; P⊖🕸🛜) This lovely, very welcoming 10-room *pensiune* offers exceptional service and individually decorated rooms. The surrounding garden is a cool and leafy oasis in summer. To find it, take tram 8 from the train station, alight at Deliblata Station and walk one block northeast to B-dul Eroilor. Or phone ahead to arrange transport.

Boutique Pensiunea Park   PENSION $$

(☑0356-264 039, 0733-274 035; www.pensiunea park.ro; Str Remus 17; s/d/ste 200/250/295 lei; P🕸🛜) This is a small, family-owned 'boutique *pensiune*' in an old villa on a leafy side street, about 10 minutes' walk from Piaţa Victoriei. Lots of period touches, including beautiful chandeliers and fixtures in the public areas, though the 10 rooms themselves are modestly furnished with metal-frame beds.

There's a small terrace in the back for morning coffee and bikes to ride for free during your stay.

★Vila La Residenza   HOTEL $$$

(☑0256-401 080; www.laresidenza.ro; Str Independenţei 14; s/d/ste €80/92/108; P🕸@🛜♒) This charming converted villa recalls an English manor, with a cosy reading room and library off the lobby and an enormous, well-tended garden in the back with swimming pool. Its 15 rooms are comfort-driven in a similar understated way. A first choice for visiting celebrities and *the* place to stay if price is no object.

La Residenza is about 2km south of the centre. Take tram 6.

Hotel Savoy   HOTEL $$$

(☑0256-249 900; www.hotelsavoytimisoara.ro; Splaiul Tudor Vladimirescu 2; s/d/ste 295/385/510 lei; P🕸🛜) This stylish refurbished villa from the 1930s has some lovely art deco details in the older wing's 21 rooms (eg corner room 208 and the large 303). The 33 rooms in the newer area are swankier, with soft tones and white carpets. It's a short walk to the centre or to the banks of the Bega Canal.

🍴 Eating

There are plenty of lovely terrace cafes surrounding Piaţa Unirii and Piaţa Victoriei that serve a mix of drinks and food. *The* spot for cheap eats, kebabs and pizza joints is the student complex (Complexul Studentesc; Str Socrate; ⏱hours vary), south of the centre across the Bega Canal.

Massimo Timişoara   ICE CREAM $

(☑0256-200 606; www.facebook.com/massimo timisoara; Piaţa Victoriei 8; 1/2/3 scoops 3/4/5 lei; ⏱10am-11pm) OK, it is a popular Italian eatery on leafy Piaţa Victoriei, but we come here for the attached gelateria, which serves the best Italian ices and ice creams in Timişoara.

★Casa Bunicii   ROMANIAN $$

(☑0356-100 870; www.casa-bunicii.ro; Str Virgil Onitiu 3; mains 20-50 lei; ⏱noon-midnight; 🍴) The names translate to 'Granny's House' and indeed this casual, family-friendly restaurant specialises in home cooking and regional specialities from the Banat, with an emphasis on dishes based on *spätzle* (egg noodles). The duck soup with dumplings (10 lei) and grilled chicken breast served in sour cherry sauce (20 lei) both come recommended. Folksy surrounds.

★Nora   ROMANIAN $$

(☑0256-218 204; www.restaurantnora.ro; B-dul Dâmboviţa 40; mains 15-29 lei; ⏱11am-11pm) Reservations are a must to nab a spot on the terrace at this popular, casual Romanian restaurant with a reputation for grilled meats. Nora is about 2km out of the centre to the southwest but worth the taxi fare (10 lei).

Casa cu Flori   ROMANIAN $$

(☑0721-180 011, 0256-435 080; www.casacuflori. ro; Str Alba Iulia 1; mains 23-55 lei; ⏱8am-midnight; 🕸) One of the best-known restaurants in the city and for good reason, the 'House of Flowers' serves excellent high-end

Romanian cooking with refined service at moderate prices in a delightful 1st-floor dining room. In warmer weather, climb three flights to the flower-bedecked rooftop terrace. Always a warm welcome here.

★ **Caruso** INTERNATIONAL **$$$**
(📋 0256-224 771; www.restaurantcaruso.ro; Str Enrico Caruso 2; mains 56-115 lei; ⊙ noon-midnight) Probably Timişoara's finest restaurant, Caruso serves superb international and New Romanian cuisine that puts a 21st-century spin on old favourites. Foie gras with cocoa? Breast of pigeon with pear mouse? Or try veal sweetbreads with bacon mash and morel sauce. Seating on two levels and minimalist decor with lots of photos of the celebrated Italian tenor.

It has an excellent wine selection but not much by the glass. There's a blowout 10-course gourmet menu with wine pairings for 1100 lei.

 Drinking & Nightlife

In summer, Piaţa Unirii and Piaţa Victoriei are lined with cafes. For a decent listing of hot spots, pick up a free copy of *Zile şi Nopti* (Days & Nights) at the Tourist Information Centre.

Aethernativ CAFE
(📋 0724-012 364; www.facebook.com/Aethernativ; Str Mărăşeşti 14; ⊙ 10am-1am Mon-Fri, noon-1am Sat, 5pm-1am Sun) This trendy cafe, cafe and bar occupies a courtyard of an old building two blocks west of Piaţa Unirii and has eclectic furnishings and an alternative, student vibe. There are no signs to let you know you're here; simply find the address and push open the door. Always a fun crowd on hand.

Scârţ loc lejer CAFE
(📋 0751-892 340; www.facebook.com/scartloclejer; Str Laszlo Szekely 1; ⊙ 9am-11pm Mon-Fri, 11am-11pm Sat, 2-11pm Sun; 🖥) An old villa that's been retro-fitted into a funky coffeehouse called something like the 'Creaky Door', with old prints on the walls and chill tunes on the turntable. There are several cosy rooms in which to read and relax, but our favourite is the garden out back, with shady nooks and even hammocks to stretch out.

It's about 1km south of the city centre. Take tram 6 or 8.

Bierhaus BEER HALL
(📋 0721-279 039; www.bierhaus.ro; Str Emanoil Ungureanu 15; ⊙ 11.30am-1am) This German-style bar with a red British phone box and black-and-white photos of old Temeschburg (Timişoara in German) on the walls may have something of an identity problem, but it's a great place to down a pint or two (five beers on tap) amid good company.

Club 30 CLUB
(📋 0760-027 785, 0256-201 115; www.facebook.com/club30.timisoara; Piaţa Victoriei 7; ⊙ 6pm-3am Thu & Sun, 10pm-5am Fri & Sat) This club has been a staple on the dance scene for years and shows no signs of slowing down, particularly on retro '80s and '90s dance nights. There's live music on some evenings, with jazz usually on Thursday and Sunday.

Opera CAFE
(📋 0720-149 813; www.facebook.com/pages/Opera-Cafe/115891888493329; Piaţa Victoriei 6; ⊙ 8am-midnight Mon-Fri, 9am-midnight Sat & Sun; 🖥) One of over a dozen similar cafes on large Piaţa Victoriei serving a mix of hot and cold beverages and usually some variation of salads and sandwiches (10 to 19 lei). We can say this one has the best cakes on the square.

☆ **Entertainment**

La Căpiţe LIVE MUSIC
(📋 0720-400 333; www.lacapite.ro; B-dul Pârvan Vasile; ⊙ 10am-1am Mon-Sat, 10am-noon Sun; 🖥) Shaggy riverside beer garden and alternative hang-out strategically located across the street from the university, ensuring lively crowds on warm summer evenings. Most nights have live music or DJs. The name translates as 'haystack', and bales of hay strewn everywhere make for comfy places to sit and chill.

National Theatre & Opera House THEATRE, OPERA
(Teatrul Naţional şi Opera Română; 📋 opera 0256-201 286, theatre 0256-499 908; www.tntimisoara.com; Str Mărăşeşti 2) The National Theatre and Opera House features both dramatic works and classical opera, and is highly regarded. Buy tickets (from around 40 lei) at the **box office** (📋 0256-201 117; www.ort.ro; Str Mărăşeşti 2; ⊙ 11am-7pm Tue-Sun) or via email, but note that most of the dramatic works will be in Romanian.

State Philharmonic Theatre CLASSICAL MUSIC
(Filharmonica Banatul Timişoara; 📋 0256-492 521; www.filarmonicabanatul.ro; B-dul C D Loga 2; tickets 10-30 lei; ⊙ box office 10am-2pm Mon, Wed & Fri, 2-7pm Tue & Thu) Classical music concerts are held here most evenings. Tickets can be

bought at the box office inside the theatre one hour before performances.

German State Theatre   THEATRE
(TeatrulGermandeStat; ☑ 0256-201291; www.teatrul german.ro; Str Mărăşeşti 2) The German State Theatre, located near the National Theatre, has regular performances in German. Buy tickets from its box office (☑ 0256-435 743; www.teatrulgerman.ro; Str Alba Iulia 2; ⊗10am-3pm & 5-7pm Tue-Fri, 10am-3pm Sat).

🛍 Shopping

Calina Contemporary Art Space   ART
(www.calina.ro; Str Mărăşeşti 1-3; ⊗10am-6pm Mon-Fri, 11am-3pm Sat) This very high-end contemporary art gallery showcases the work of artists from Romania and abroad.

ℹ Information

Central Post Office (☑ 0256-491 999; B-dul Revoluţiei 1989 2; ⊗8am-7pm Mon-Fri, to noon Sat)

Timişoara County Emergency Hospital (Spitalul Clinic Judeţean de Urgenţă Timişoara; ☑ 0356-433 111; www.hosptm.ro; B-dul Iosif Bulbuca 10) Modern hospital, located 2km south of the centre, with 24-hour emergency service.

Timişoara Tourist Information Centre (Info Centru Turistic; ☑ 0256-437 973; www. timisoara-info.ro; Str Alba Iulia 2; ⊗9am-7pm Mon-Fri, 10am-4pm Sat May-Sep, 9am-6pm Mon-Fri, 10am-3pm Sat Oct-Apr) This great tourist office can assist with accommodation and trains, and provide maps and Banat regional info.

UniCredit Bank (www.unicredit.ro; Piaţa Victoriei 2; ⊗9am-4pm Mon-Fri)

ℹ Getting There & Away

AIR

The **Timişoara Traian Vuia International Airport** (TSR; ☑ 0256-386 089; http://aerotim.ro/en; Str Aeroport 2, Ghiroda) is 12km northeast of the centre. Timişoara has excellent air connections to nearly every big city in the country and destinations around Europe thanks to budget carriers **WizzAir** (☑ calls per min €0.62 0903-760 105; www.wizzair.com) and **Ryanair** (☑ UK, calls per min £0.13 +44 871 246 0002; www.ryanair.com/ro/en).

Express bus E4 connects the airport and the city centre (2.5 lei, 20 minutes).

BUS

Timişoara lacks a centralised bus station for its extensive domestic services. Buses and minibuses are privately operated and depart from several points around the city, depending on the company. Consult the website www.autogari.ro for departure points. Sample fares include Arad (15 lei), Cluj-Napoca (75 lei) and Sibiu (65 lei).

International buses leave from the **East Bus Station** (Gara de Est; www.autogari.ro). The main international operators include **Atlassib** (☑ 0256-226 486, local office 0757-112 370; www.atlassib.ro; Calea Stan Vidrighin 12) and **Eurolines** (☑ 0372-766 478, 0256-288 132; www.eurolines.ro; Str M Kogălniceanu 20). Belgrade-based **Gea Tours** (☑ 0316-300 257; www. geatours.rs) offers a daily minibus service between Timişoara and Belgrade (one way/return €15/30); book over the website.

TRAIN

Trains depart from the **Northern Train Station** (Gara Timişoara-Nord; ☑ 0256-200 457; www. cfrcalatori.ro; Str Gării 2), though it's actually west of the centre. Daily express trains include services to Bucharest (112 lei, nine hours, two daily), Cluj-Napoca (80 lei, six hours, two daily), Arad (18 lei, one hour, four daily) and Oradea (49 lei, three hours, three daily).

Agenţia de Voiaj CFR (☑ 0256-491 889; www.cfr.ro; B-dul Republicii 10; ⊗10am-6pm Mon-Fri) sells domestic and international train tickets and seat reservations.

CRIŞANA

Oradea

POP 196,370

Fans of art nouveau and Viennese and Hungarian Secession architecture dating from the late 19th and early 20th centuries will want to make a special stop in Oradea. While many of the once-elegant buildings here have been allowed to fall into disrepair, a lot more are getting long-awaited facelifts. Visitors with a sharp eye will see Secession's signature lyric design elements and inlaid enamelwork on buildings up and down the main pedestrian walkway, Calea Republicii, and across the Crişul Repede river in Piaţa Unirii.

◎ Sights

The best way to see the city is to stroll along pedestrian-only Calea Republicii, lined on both sides with architectural gems, and cross over the river to dramatic Piaţa Unirii.

Darvas-La Roche House   MUSEUM
(Casa Darvas-La Roche; www.oradea.travel; Str Josif Vulcan 11; adult/child 5/3 lei; ⊗noon-7pm Tue-Sun Apr-Oct, shorter hours in winter) This delightful Secession-style burgher house (1912) designed by brothers József and László Vágó, who also

Oradea

built Oradea's stunning **Moskovits Palace** (Palatul Moskovits; Calea Republicii 13), has now opened as a museum of interiors, furnishings and applied arts. Don't miss the stunning stained glass and dining room. A 10-lei entry fee includes admission to the Zion Neolog Synagogue and Town Hall Tower.

Town Hall Tower TOWER
(Turnulk Primăriei; www.oradea.travel; Str Tudor Vladimirescu 2; adult/child 5/3 lei; ☉ noon-7pm Tue-Sun Apr-Oct, shorter hours in winter) The 50m-high tower, which is now open to the public, counts four main levels, three of which have viewing platforms. A 10-lei entry fee includes admission to the Zion Neolog Synagogue and Darvas-La Roche House.

Orthodox Synagogue SYNAGOGUE
(Sinagoga Ortodoxă; www.oradeajc.com; Str Mihai Viteazul 4; ☉ closed to the public) Oradea's Orthodox synagogue dates from 1890 and was the main house of worship for around

a third of the city's Jewish residents before WWII. It survived the war intact, but was badly neglected afterwards and at the time of research was undergoing a thorough renovation, which was close to completion.

Just behind and to the left of the synagogue is a small **Holocaust Memorial** remembering some 30,000 Oradea Jews who perished. Most of the victims were executed at the German Nazi extermination camp at Auschwitz-Birkenau in Poland in May and June 1944, after being forced to live in a cramped, sealed ghetto here. The ghetto was located in the area surrounding the synagogue and remains a depressed area to this day.

Zion Neolog Synagogue SYNAGOGUE
(Neolog Synagogue; www.oradeajc.com; Str Independenței 22; adult/child 5/3 lei; ☉ noon-7pm Tue-Sun Apr-Oct, shorter hours in winter) Of the reformist Conservative (as opposed to Orthodox) branch of Judaism and dating from 1878,

Oradea

this synagogue, with its graceful dome, is one of the most striking elements of the Oradea skyline. It's open to the public and a 10-lei entry fee includes admission to the Town Hall Tower and Darvas-La Roche House.

Oradea Fortress FORTRESS
(Cetatea Oradea; Piaţa Independenţei; ⊙9am-5pm) FREE Oradea's fortress dates from the 15th and 16th centuries and played a key role in conflicts between the Turks, Austrians and Hungarians over the years. The fortress is shaped like a pentagon, with five towers and thick defensive walls, and has frescoed interior walls. It is largely still under reconstruction but you can stroll around the grounds.

Canon's Corridor ARCHITECTURE
(Sirul Canonicilor; Str Sirul Canonicilor) Just east of the Roman Catholic cathedral, Canon's Corridor forms a series of 57 arches built between 1750 and 1875, part of the original baroque design as laid out by the Austrian master architect Franz Anton Hillebrandt.

Roman Catholic Cathedral CHURCH
(Catedrală Romano-Catolică; Sirul Canonicilor; ⊙9am-6pm) This cathedral, 2km north of the centre, was built between 1752 and 1780 and is the largest baroque church in Romania. Organ concerts are occasionally held here.

🚌 Tours

Apuseni Experience ADVENTURE
(☑0747-962 482, 0745-602 301; www.apuseni experience.ro) This Oradea-based outdoor-travel outfit arranges multiday hiking and biking trips in the Apuseni Mountains, plus ski touring and snowshoeing in winter.

🛏 Sleeping

★**Hotel Elite** HOTEL **$$**
(☑0359-332 211, 0259-414 924; www.hotelelite. ro; Str IC Bratianu 26; s/d from €55/65; 🅿 🛜 ☷) This beautiful hotel has 38 spotless and well-maintained rooms, but the major drawcard is its gorgeous heated (and child-friendly) outdoor pool straight out of a Hollywood mansion. Swim into the night and dine on the terrace. There's a small spa too.

Nonresidents can use the pool for 30/40 lei on weekdays/weekends. Add 10 lei for the spa.

Hotel Stokker HOTEL **$$**
(☑0359-444 994; www.facebook.com/Stokker Hotel; Parcul Petőfi 16; s/d/apt 170/210/290 lei; 🅿 ❄ 🛜) Renovated, rebranded and renamed, the Stokker is a good choice if you're coming to Oradea by train as it's only a 10-minute walk from the station. The 17 rooms are smallish but spotless and have decent artwork; a few have balconies over the garden and fountain. The outdoor restaurant is a festive place for a summer-evening meal.

Hotel Qiu HOTEL **$$**
(☑0733-666 555; www.qiu.ro; Calea Republicii 15; r without breakfast from €40; ❄ 🛜) This modern hotel boasts an excellent location, right on Calea Republicii in the centre of town. There's no reception; instead, book via the hotel website or by phone. The building is an art nouveau palace in need of renovation, but the five rooms themselves have been given a stylish update and are clean, quiet and comfortable. They also have kitchenettes.

🍴 Eating

★**Butoiul de Aur** BISTRO **$**
(☑0359-427 162; www.butoiuldeauroradea.ro; Str Iosif Vulcan 1; mains 13-30 lei; ⊙9am-11pm Mon-Fri, 9am-midnight Sat & Sun) The impossibly ornate 'Golden Barrel', with its stained-glass cupola and painted stucco work, dates to 1892. Though there are more complex dishes on the menu, most punters seem to come for

the pasta and pizza (14 to 23 lei), the live music at weekends and the stunning surrounds.

Lactobar
CAFE $

(☑0723-234 187, 0259-455 154; www.facebook.com/Lactobar-Retro-Bistro-152884041477820; Calea Republicii 11; mains 12-23 lei; ⊙9am-midnight Mon-Fri, 10am-midnight Sat & Sun; 🕾🗖) Worth even just a look, this charming, very kid-friendly 'retro bistro' with a big cow statue on the main street is decked out in colourful period-piece found objects, including an orange, ultra-cool Dacia automobile. The menu is less amazing, mostly burgers – what's lacto got to do with it? – and sandwiches.

Rosecas
ROMANIAN $$

(☑0756-260 185; www.rosecas.ro; Str Traian Moșoiu 17; mains 25-55 lei; ⊙11am-11pm Mon-Thu, 11am-midnight Fri & Sat, 11am-10.30pm Sun; 🕾) This upbeat, now rather posh place serves excellent home-cooked Romanian and Hungarian fare, such as chicken paprika and duck, as well as delicious salads and home-made chicken soup. In summer, sit on the cosy terrace squeezed in between two buildings. The weekday set lunch is a snip at 18 lei.

Cyrano Cafe Restaurant
ROMANIAN $$

(☑0728-284 722; www.facebook.com/pages/Cyrano/101250046625819; Calea Republicii 7; mains 15-30 lei; ⊙10am-11pm Mon-Sat, 11.30am-11pm Sun; 🕾) Popular hang-out ideal for people-watching from the coveted terrace tables. Though the menu teems with Romanian favourites, the incredible beef stew with tarragon in a hollowed bread loaf (*ciorbă de vițe cu tarhon in chiflă;* 13 lei) is all the nourishment you'll need.

★ Graf
INTERNATIONAL $$$

(☑0259-421 421; www.restaurantgraf.ro; Str Barbu Stefanescu Delavrancea 3; mains 35-70 lei; ⊙5-11pm Mon-Sat, noon-3pm Sun; 🕾) Graf is arguably Oradea's nicest restaurant and a perfect splurge option. The menu features wood-grilled steaks, fish and pork; the caramelised duck leg served on our visit was one of our best meals in Romania. Desserts feature cheesecake and home-made ice cream, and the wine list is top notch. It's undergone a recent renovation.

☆ Entertainment

The weekly *Zi de Zi* (Day by Day) events brochure covers what's on.

Oradea State Theatre
PUPPET THEATRE

(Teatrul de Stat Oradea; ☑0259-440 742; http://teatrulreginamaria.ro/trupa-arcadia; Piața Ferdinand I 4-6; ⊙10am-7pm Mon-Fri, 10am-1pm Sat & Sun; 🗖) The State Theatre, also known as the Queen Mary Theatre (Teatrul Regina Maria; completed in 1900), is one of the most important heritage buildings in Oradea. Kids will enjoy the puppet shows put on by the Arcadia Troupe (Trupa Arcadia).

State Philharmonic
CLASSICAL MUSIC

(Filarmonica de Stat; ☑0259-430.853; www.oradeaphilharmony.com; Str Moscovei 5; tickets 10-25 lei; ⊙box office 11am-5pm Mon-Fri) Tickets for performances at the State Philharmonic, with its traditional program of classical music, can be purchased in advance from the theatre box office or one hour before show time. The exterior was undergoing a massive renovation at time of research.

🛍 Shopping

Humanitas
BOOKS

(☑0259-472 955; www.humanitas.ro; Calea Republicii 11; ⊙9am-8pm Mon-Fri, 10am-7pm Sat, 10am-3pm Sun) Humanitas is a small but helpful bookshop, with a tiny collection of titles in English.

ℹ Information

Banca Transilvania (☑0259-410 932; Calea Republicii 5; ⊙9am-5pm Mon-Fri)

Oradea Tourist Information Centre (☑0259-437 000; http://oradea.travel; Piața Unirii; ⊙9am-5pm Mon-Fri) In the Town Hall.

Post Office (☑0259-435 040; Str Roman Ciorogariu 12; ⊙8am-7pm Mon-Fri, 8am-1pm Sat)

ℹ Getting There & Away

BUS

A small **bus station** (autogara; ☑0259-418 998; www.autogari.ro/Oradea; Str Râzboieni 81) is situated 2km south of the centre. From here you can catch frequent maxitaxis and regular buses to Băile Felix (3 to 5 lei, 10 minutes), Ştei (for access to Bears Cave; 14 lei, 90 minutes) and Arieşeni (26 lei, 2½ hours).

There's a small **maxitaxi stand** north of the train station for services to cities north of Oradea, such as Baia Mare (40 lei, 3¾ hours).

TRAIN

Oradea's **train station** (☑0259-414 970; www.cfr.ro; Calea Republicii 114) is 2km north of the centre. Daily fast trains from Oradea include

CAVING IN THE APUSENI NATURE PARK

The Apuseni Mountains lie for the most part in Transylvania, but their western ranges are easily accessed from Oradea along Hwy 76. The area is known for its spectacular cave systems – both 'show caves' open to the public and 'technical caves' restricted to guided groups.

The best source of information is the **Apuseni Nature Park Visitors Centre** (☑0372-702 242, 0748-126 924; www.parcapuseni.ro; Sudrigiu 136; ☺8am-4.30pm Mon-Thu, 8am-2pm Fri), with headquarters at Sudrigiu on the approach to Bears Cave near the village of Chişcău.

Travelling from Oradea along Hwy E79 (local Hwy 76), the first major cave is **Meziad Cave** (Peştera Meziad; ☑0742-115 303; Meziad; adult/child 15/10 lei; ☺10am-6pm Jun-Sep, 10am-5pm Mar-May), 24km northeast of the town of Beiuş. The cave features an enormous opening and is split into three levels. Wear sturdy shoes and bring a torch (flashlight).

Meziad Cave is not easy to reach with public transport. From Beiuş, take a local minibus (four a day on weekdays only) to the village of Meziad and hike the final 4km. By car from Beiuş, follow signs to the cave for 12km via the villages of Remetea and Meziad.

Bears Cave (Peştera Urşilor; ☑0744-638 244, 0359-411 083; www.pesteraursilor.ro; Chişcău; adult/child 20/10 lei; ☺10am-5pm Tue-Sun), 82km from Oradea, is one of Romania's finest and worth a special trip. The cave was discovered by quarry workers 40 years ago. It's named after skeletons of the extinct cave bear (Ursus spelaeus) found inside. The magnificent galleries extend over 1km on two levels. Guided tours allow you to spend an hour inside.

From Sudrigiu, home of the park visitor centre, take the 763 road east for about 15km; the cave is signposted and there's a car park nearby. Without private transport, the region around the cave is tricky to navigate. Infrequent buses run between Beiuş, Chişcău and Ştei. For a nearby overnight option, **Pensiunea Laura** (☑0768-539 401; Chişcău 81a; d/tr/ste 70/80/150 lei; P☎) is a wooden chalet with eight rooms and a charming restaurant.

The most famous cave in the Apuseni Nature Park, the **Ice Cave** (Peştera Ghețarul; ☑0753-470 285; Scărişoara; adult/child 10/7 lei; ☺9am-6pm Mon-Fri, 10am-5pm Sat & Sun) houses one of the largest underground glaciers in Europe – one of just 10 – and is filled with 7500 cu metres of ice dating back to the Ice Age. Tours of 10 to 50 people depart between six and seven times a day. The tour lasts 20 minutes and involves a steep descent to the opening, a peek inside and then back up again.

The cave can be reached on foot from Gârda de Sus (9km, two hours). You can drive to the cave via a paved but narrow 8km-long road.

services to Budapest (89 lei, five hours, one daily), a slow overnight to Bucharest (112 lei, 12 hours), Cluj-Napoca (45 lei, three hours, six daily), Braşov (102 lei, nine hours, two daily) and Timişoara (49 lei, three hours, three daily).
Agenţia de Voiaj CFR (☑0259-416 565; Str Roman Ciorogariu 4; ☺8am-8pm Mon-Fri) sells domestic and international train tickets and seat reservations.

Băile Felix

Băile Felix, 9km southeast of Oradea, is a summer oasis, with huge, open-air, kid-friendly swimming pools filled with warm thermal water. It's close enough to Oradea for an easy day trip, and the pools provide welcome relief if you get caught in a midsummer heatwave. Mind you, like every resort it can be raucous and cheesy too. Be warned.

◉ Sights & Activities

Strand Felix　　　　　　　　THERMAL BATHS
(www.bailefelix.net; adult/child 30/15 lei; ☺8am-7pm Mon, 8am-8pm Tue-Fri, 7am-8pm Sat & Sun May-Sep; ⛤) Of the two main pool complexes in Băile Felix, this is the larger and more popular one. It's located just south of Strand Apollo, near the Stația Băile Felix bus stop. The Felix has water slides and attracts families and kids.

Strand Apollo　　　　　　　　THERMAL BATHS
(www.bailefelix.net; adult/child 30/15 lei; ☺8am-7pm Mon, 8am-8pm Tue-Fri, 7am-8pm Sat & Sun) There are two main pool complexes in Băile Felix – this one, at the north end of Băile Felix, is the smaller and quieter of the two. The entrance is just opposite the Stația Băile Felix bus stop. Strand Apollo also has a wave pool.

CRIŞANA & BANAT BĂILE FELIX

🛏 Sleeping & Eating

There are plenty of private rooms on offer, so if the hotels are booked, simply look for signs saying *camere* (rooms), *cazare* (accommodation) or *pensiunea* (pension).

Casa Veronica   PENSION $

(☑ 0723-008 367, 0259-318 481; www.casaveronica. ro; Str Primăverii 9a; d/tr/apt 100/120/160 lei; 🅿 ❀ 🛜) This well-maintained canary-yellow chalet with eight rooms is in tip-top shape. Located opposite the entrances to the pools, it's convenient for families.

Termal Hotel   HOTEL $$$

(☑ 0359-089 930, 0259-318 214; www.hotel -termal.ro; Str Victoria 24; half-board s/d 260/385 lei; 🅿 ❀ ❀ 🛜 🏊) This institutional-looking modern building houses a comfortable spa resort. The 184 rooms reek of cleanliness, with firm beds and balconies (request a forest view).

Restaurant Union   ROMANIAN $

(☑ 0259-317 005; www.pensiuneaunion.ro; Str Primăverii 106a; mains 13-20 lei; ⊙ 8am-midnight) Feast on a full menu of Romanian food, including a delicious bean soup with smoked ham. The set lunch is just 14 lei.

❶ Getting There & Away

Maxitaxis run either every 15 minutes or when full between Oradea bus station and Băile Felix (3 to 5 lei). Many maxitaxis and buses heading south for Ştei and the Apuseni Mountains stop at Băile Felix en route.

Arad

POP 160,000

The border town of Arad, some 50km from the crossing into Hungary, lies astride the main road and has good transport connections in and out of Romania. There are not many traditional sights here, but the city is a convenient stopover on your first or last night in the country. Fans of late-19th- and early-20th-century architectural styles such as neoclassical and Secession will enjoy a stroll up the city's long tree-lined central boulevard, B-dul Revoluţiei, running north–south.

⊙ Sights

Arad Town Hall   HISTORIC BUILDING

(Primăria Arad; www.primariaarad.ro; B-dul Revoluţiei 75) The U-shaped, neoclassical town hall is Arad's most impressive building,

with neoclassical and neo-Renaissance influences. The clock atop the 54m-high tower was brought from Switzerland in 1878.

Archaeology & History Museum   MUSEUM

(Muzeul de Arheologie şi Istorie; ☑ 0257-281 847; www.museumarad.ro; Piaţa George Enescu 1; 1 lei; ⊙ 9am-5pm Tue-Sun) Arad's modest history museum housed in the Palace of Culture is a good primer for anyone interested in the city's complex origins, including 150 years of Ottoman occupation until 1699. After that the city served as a military bastion of the Habsburgs and, briefly, in 1849, as a centre of the Hungarian uprising – the museum has good coverage of that period and of the 1989 revolution.

Neolog Synagogue   SYNAGOGUE

(Sinagoga Neologă; Str Truibunal Dobra 10 (entrance Str Cozia 12)) Arad's Neolog (Conservative) synagogue, built between 1827 and 1834, lies southwest of Piaţa Avram Iancu. It was closed to visitors at the time of research, but the Moorish-style exterior is worth a look. About 10,000 Jews lived in Arad before WWII.

Arad Fortress   FORTRESS

(Cetatea Arad) Arad's star-shaped fortress was built on the orders of the Habsburg empress Maria Theresa between 1763 and 1783. It stands on the site of an old fortress built in 1551 by the Turks. It housed a military base until recently and there are plans to open it up to the public as a museum complex.

Reconciliation Park   MONUMENT

(Parcul Reconcilieri) This monument park, three blocks west of Piaţa Avram Iancu, contains two notable statues. In the centre, the Liberty Monument was erected in 1890 to honour 13 Hungarian generals executed after the 1849 Hungarian uprising. Nearby, an even more impressive Triumphal Arch was built in 2004 to remember the Romanian fighters killed in the same insurrection.

☀ Activities

Neptun Water Park (Strandul Neptun; ☑ 0757-038 901; http://reconsarad.ro/strand.html; adult/child 13/7 lei; ⊙ 1-10pm Mon, 8am-10pm Tue-Sun May-Sep; 🛝) is a sprawling swimming complex and a godsend on a hot summer day.

🛏 Sleeping

There are no youth hostels and very few budget options in Arad. Book a room in a

ENJOYING THE AIR IN ARIEŞENI & GÂRDA DE SUS

Arieşeni and Gârda de Sus are wonderfully picturesque alpine villages that straddle both the Arieş River and scenic national Hwy 75 along a narrow valley in the Apuseni Mountains. They're 7km apart and both are filled with guesthouses.

Most visitors come here to relax and take in the mountain air or to hike or cave in the adjacent nature park, a remote expanse of mountains in the 1600–1800m range that fans out to the north. Hiking trails leave from the villages of Vârtop, Arieşeni and Gârda de Sus. Ask the **Apuseni Nature Park Visitors Centre** (Arieşeni Branch; ☎ 0358-402 537; www.parcapuseni.ro; Hwy 75, btwn Arieşeni & Gârda de Sus; ⊗ 8am-4.30pm Mon-Thu, 8am-2.30pm Fri) for a trail map or buy the 1:150,000 Apuseni Mountains map (15 lei). The website www.padis.ro is an excellent source of information in English.

For longer hikes, **Cabana Cetatile Ponorului** (☎ 0740-007 814; www.padis.ro/ro/cabana-cetăţile-ponorului; dm 50-60 lei; ☺) is a well-equipped mountain hut, northwest of Arieşeni, that offers 65 beds in dorm rooms of two, four and six beds. The hut is about three to four hours on foot from the Vârtop Pass (1140m) along a red-marked trail.

If you're travelling by car, Hwy 75 is chock-a-block with hotels, pensions and private rooms (*camere*). **Casa Noastră** (☎ 0724-350 451, 0744-322 215; www.pensiunea-casa-noastra.ro; Arieşeni; s/d 120/150 lei; ☺ ❀ ☎), a family-owned guesthouse, is arguably the area's most handsome *pensiune*, with a dozen snug timber-lined rooms, an attractive garden along a babbling brook, and a lovely terrace. It's 1km west of the centre of Arieşeni in the village of Izlaz on Hwy 75.

Mama Uţa (☎ 0735-164 098; www.mamauta.ro; Gârda de Sus 97; campsite 15 lei, cabin 80-120 lei; ☎) is a popular summer spot, situated just on the western side of Gârda de Sus. It has 14 attractive cabins. The restaurant is one of the best around, so come for a meal even if you're not staying here.

From Arieşeni and Gârda de Sus there are decent bus and maxitaxi connections to Ştei, Beiuş, Oradea and Arad. The main bus station is located in the centre of Arieşeni village.

private home (from 80 lei) through the **Arad Tourist Information Centre**.

★ Hotel Arad
HOTEL **$$**

(☎ 0257-280 894; www.hotel-arad.com; B-dul Decebal 9; s/d/ste 135/155/177 lei; P ❀ ☎) In a building that dates to 1876, this wonderful old hotel has 28 huge rooms with high ceilings that feature art deco details throughout. It's in an excellent central location too, just two minutes' walk from B-dul Revoluţiei.

Pensiunea Belanco
BOUTIQUE HOTEL **$$**

(☎ 0747-880 965; www.belanco.ro; Str Cocorilor 36; s 155 lei, d 190-220 lei; P ❀ ☎) This family-run hotel offers 16 well-proportioned rooms with air-conditioning and balconies. There's a lovely garden terrace for breakfast at the back of the house; room 8 is a good choice. Be aware that it is in a noisy workaday neighbourhood 3km northwest of the centre, with absolutely nothing of interest nearby. Take a taxi (10 to 15 lei) from the train station.

★ Picasso Boutique Hotel
BOUTIQUE HOTEL **$$$**

(☎ 0357-424 484; www.facebook.com/Picasso-Ristorante-Boutique-Hotel-977020529007884/info; B-dul Decebal 2; r €50-100; P ❀ ☎) One of the finest small hotels in western Romania, the Italian-owned six-room Picasso is housed in a delightful 19th-century townhouse. Rooms are designed in creams and chocolates with hard-wood floors and tubs in the bathrooms. The Cubist prints on the wall won't let you forget where you are staying. There's a fantastic in-house restaurant.

Hotel Continental Forum
HOTEL **$$$**

(☎ reservations 0372-121 721, 0372-578 800; www.continentalhotels.ro; B-dul Revoluţiei 79-81; s/d €65/80; P ❀ @ ☎) Arad's upmarket choice has international standards of accommodation and service and an impressive lobby with a large circular staircase. Most of the 160 rooms have balconies. The buffet breakfast is the best in town. Discounted room rates during slow periods.

Arad

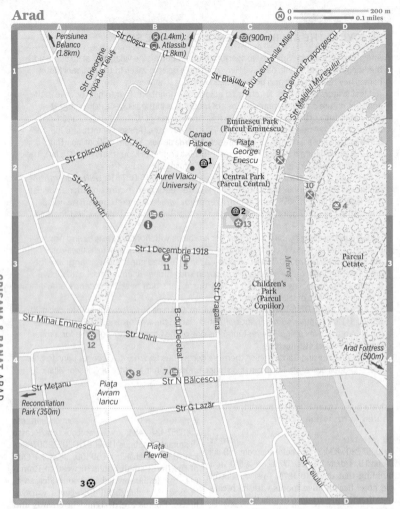

✗ Eating & Drinking

Perla Mureşului ROMANIAN **$**

(📞 0745-876 744; Str Malulul Mureşului; mains 15-30 lei; ⊙ 9am-11pm) The popular riverside 'Pearl of the Mureş' is an excellent (if somewhat frayed) choice on a warm summer's evening, with a cool breeze and fleeting glimpses of the Mureş River opposite. The traditional Romanian food is short of gourmet, though that doesn't diminish the festive feel.

★ Don Restaurant ITALIAN **$$**

(📞 0357-431 788; www.restaurant-don.ro; Str Nicolae Bălcescu 1; mains 29-55 lei; ⊙ 11am-11.30pm; 📶)

This very stylish neighbourhood eatery done up in brick and wood serves some excellent (and quite authentic) dishes, including an excellent *zuppa di pesce* (fish soup). There's also a fairly good choice of vegetarian pasta (20 to 28 lei) and pizza (17 to 25 lei).

Restaurant Ratio ROMANIAN **$$**

(📞 0731-317 420, 0257-285 477; www.restaurant ratio.ro; mains 22-40 lei; ⊙ 10am-midnight) Location, location, location... This flower-bedecked, chalet-like eatery perched atop a hill on the left bank of the Mureş just over the footbridge has decent Romanian dishes and

Arad

grills. But it's all about the views and watching the lazy river roll by.

★ **Picasso Restaurant**   ITALIAN $$$
(☎0722-222 199; www.facebook.com/Picasso
-Ristorante-Boutique-Hotel-977020529007884/
info; B-dul Decebal 2; mains 22-85 lei; ☺10am-
11pm Mon-Sat) Overseen by a Roman and subtitled the 'Italian Food Academy', this hotel restaurant in a charming circular corner room with hard-wood floors and cheery yellow walls just has to be the real McCoy. Try the spaghetti *vongole* (pasta with clams) to start and a veal dish as a main course.

Euphoria Biergarten   BEER HALL
(☎0745-393 333; http://biergarten-arad.euphoria.
ro; Str 1 Decembrie 1918 6; ☺8am-2am) This place is a fully fledged restaurant with sandwiches and mains such as fish 'n' chips, *pljeskavica* (spicy grilled meat patties) and pizza (18 to 26 lei) served in the pub, the dining room and in the lovely back beer garden. But we come to this massive, colourful place for liquid libation, with its six beers on tap and double that available by the bottle.

☆ **Entertainment**

For a decent listing of hot spots, pick up a free copy of *Zile şi Nopti* (Days & Nights) at the Tourist Information Centre.

Ioan Slavici Theatre   THEATRE
(Teatrul Ioan Slavici; ☎0257-280 016, box office 0257-281 554; www.teatrulclasic.ro; B-dul Revoluţiei 103; tickets 10-30 lei; ☺box office 10am-2pm & 5-7pm Tue-Fri, 10am-noon & 5-7pm Sat & Sun) Arad's Ioan Slavici Theatre is nationally celebrated, though note that performances are in Romanian. The theatre also hosts concerts and musical performances.

Philharmonic Orchestra   CLASSICAL MUSIC
(Filarmonica de Stat Arad; ☎box office 0257-281 554; www.filarmonicaarad.ro; Piaţa George Enescu 1; tickets from 10 lei) The Philharmonic Orchestra is based in the Palace of Culture and holds classical-music concerts. Tickets are sold at the venue box office two hours before performances begin.

ℹ **Information**

Arad Tourist Information Centre (☎0728-116 412; http://romaniatourism.com/arad.html; B-dul Revoluţiei 81; ☺9am-5pm) Helpful staff provide brochures and free maps and give accommodation recommendations.

Banca Transilvania (☎0257-213 320; B-dul Revoluţiei 76; ☺9am-5pm Mon-Fri, 9.30am-12.30pm Sat)

Eurocomputer (B-dul Decebal 20; per hr 4 lei; ☺8am-11pm Mon-Fri, 10am-11pm Sun; ☎) Basement internet cafe.

Post Office (Str Caius Iacob 4; ☺7am-7pm Mon-Fri)

ℹ **Getting There & Away**

The border crossing into Hungary is 50km west of Arad at Nădlac.

BUS

Arad's **bus station** (Calea 6 Vânători 2-4) is west of the train station, separated by the enormous Galleria Mall. It's the hub for **Atlassib** (☎0747-045 337, 0257-338 000; www.atlassib.ro; Calea 6 Vânători 2-4; ☺7.30am-4pm Mon-Sat), the main international coach operator. Daily domestic destinations include Timişoara (about 17 lei, 1½ hours, hourly) and Oradea (24 lei, three hours, four daily).

TRAIN

Arad's **train station** (☎0257-230 633; Piaţa Gării 8-9) is a major railway junction. Daily fast services include five to Budapest (115 lei, four hours), with onward connections to Western Europe, and Bucharest (168 lei, 10½ hours, five daily), Timişoara (18 lei, one hour, four daily) and Cluj-Napoca (70 lei, four hours, two daily).

CRIŞANA & BANAT ARAD

Maramureş

Best Places to Eat

➡ Michael Pascale (p170)

➡ Village Hotel (p177)

➡ Butoiaşu' cu Bere (p170)

➡ Restaurant Casa Iurca de Călineşti (p174)

Best Places to Sleep

➡ Village Hotel (p177)

➡ Floare de Colţi (p170)

➡ Casa Iurca de Călineşti (p173)

➡ Casa Muntean (p179)

➡ Cobwobs Hostel (p173)

Why Go?

Widely regarded as Romania's most traditional region, dotted with steepled wooden churches and farmhouses fronted by ornately carved gates, Maramureş feels as if you are climbing into a horse-drawn time machine and heading back a couple of centuries. Indeed, Maramureş' tapestry of pastureland, peopled by colourfully garbed peasants, jumps straight out of a Brothers Grimm fairy tale. Welcome to the heart of folkloric, medieval Romania, where the last peasant culture in Europe continues to thrive. Medieval Maramureş exists in the Mara and Iza Valleys, and eight of their churches are on Unesco's list of World Heritage sites. Among the best are Deseşti in Mara Valley and Poienile Izei in Iza Valley, not just for their architecture but for their well-preserved interior wall paintings.

When to Go
Baia Mare

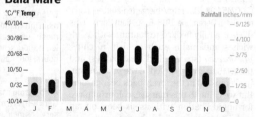

May & Sep Warm temperatures, meadows strewn with wildflowers and cooler temperatures for touring.

Dec–Mar The best time for skiers to head for Maramureş' snowy slopes.

Jun–Aug The hot summer months are the perfect time for hiking and cycling in the Carpathians.

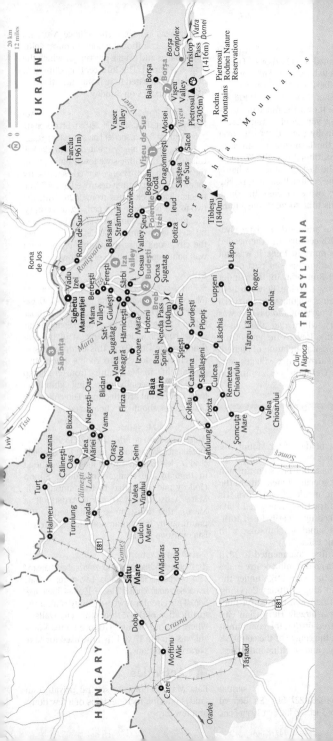

Maramureş Highlights

1 Vişeu de Sus (p181) Chugging through the beautiful Vaser Valley on Europe's last steam-powered forest train.

2 Budeşti (p176) Knocking on the door of this village's wooden church – one of the most beautiful (and largest) in Maramureş.

3 Merry Cemetery (p178) Wandering through Săpânţa's colourful and humorous forest of painted wooden grave markers.

4 Iza Valley (p178) Travelling back in time with a rustic homestay in this isolated valley.

5 Poienile Izei (p180) Witnessing the fiery visions of hell at this village's scary church.

6 Breb (p177) Observing traditional ways of life in Maramureş's most folkloric village.

7 Borşa (p182) Hiking in the hills above Maramureş' best ski resort.

History

Maramureş (of which Baia Mare is the capital) was first documented in 1199 though Dacian tribes are thought to have settled here around 1000 BC. When the Roman emperor Trajan conquered the rest of Romania in AD 106, his forces never made it over the range of mountains protecting the villages of Maramureş.

Hungary gradually exerted its rule over the region from the 13th century onwards. Tatar invasions continued into the 17th and 18th centuries; the last documented battle took place on the Prislop Pass in 1717. Numerous churches were erected in Maramureş around this time to mark the Tatars' final withdrawal.

Maramureş was annexed by Transylvania in the mid-16th century and then ceded to the Austrian empire in 1699. It was not until 1918 that Maramureş – or part of it – formally rejoined Romania; the remainder went to what is now Ukraine. Between 1940 and 1944 Maramureş – along with northern Transylvania and parts of Moldavia – was ruled by Hungary, which had allied itself with Nazi Germany. Toward the end of the war the entire Jewish population of Sighetu Marmaţiei and surrounding villages was shipped to Nazi Germany's extermination camps in Poland.

Baia Mare

POP 136,480

Lying at the foot of the Gutâi Mountains, Baia Mare does not offer a particularly attractive first glimpse, but press on through the bleak husk of socialist tenements to the inner pearl of the medieval Old Town. Its centerpiece, the attractively renovated Piaţa Libertăţii, is flanked by cheerily hued 16th- and 17th-century buildings bursting with lively bars and chic cafes.

The town was first documented in 1329 and developed as a gold-mining centre in the 14th and 15th centuries. In 1469, under the rule of Hungarian king Matthias Corvinus, the town was fortified, and thrived for hundreds of years as a largely Hungarian city. Baia Mare prospered during the communist period, becoming the centre of the country's non-ferrous mining and smelting industries.

◎ Sights

Village Museum
MUSEUM

(Muzeul Satului; ☎ 0262-227 517; Str Bernard Shaw; adult/child 5/3 lei; ☉ Tue-Sun 10am-6pm, shorter hours in winter) The Village Museum displays 15 traditional wooden houses (plus gates, barns and even a pigsty), for which the region is famed. The 16th-century Church of St George relocated here from Budeşti is still used for services on Sunday.

Stephen's Tower
TOWER

(Turnul Ştefan; Piaţa Cetăţii; ☉ 8am-6pm Mon-Fri, noon-4pm Sat & Sun, shorter hours in winter) FREE Looming above newly created Piaţa Cetăţii, this 40m-high Gothic-style tower dating from the mid-15th century once served as the belfry for an adjoining church destroyed in 1847. The mechanical clock dates from 1628, with the two-tonne bell from the early 20th century. The tower can be climbed via 136 mostly spiral steps for stunning 360-degree views over the city. Don't miss the Gothic chapel with wall paintings at the base of the tower.

Ethnographic & Folk Art Museum
MUSEUM

(Muzeul de Etnografie şi Artă Populară; ☎ 0262-276 895; www.etnografie-maramures.ro; Str Dealul Florilor 1; adult/child 5/3 lei; ☉ 10am-6pm Tue-Sun, shorter hours in winter) Northwest of the stadium in the City Park, this comprehensive collection in four large rooms traces traditional life in Maramureş from cradle to grave, with especially interesting exhibits on local trades and architecture. The collection of carriages should not be missed.

County Art Museum
MUSEUM

(Muzeul Judeţean de Artă; ☎ 0262-213 964; www.muzeumm.baiamare.rdsnet.ro; Str 1 Mai 8; adult/child 7/3 lei; ☉ 10am-4.30pm Tue-Sun) Founded in 1896 by the Hungarian painter Simon Hollósy and dedicated to the famous Baia Mare Artist Colony (Centrul Artistic Baia Mare), this museum exhibits some 400 paintings by Romanian and Hungarian artists over two levels.

Butchers' Bastion
TOWER

(Bastionul Măcelarilor; http://muzeubaiamare.ro/category/bastionul-macelarilor-baia-mare; Piaţa Izvoarelor; adult/child 3/1 lei; ☉ 10am-4.30pm Tue-Sun) This circular tower, the only remaining fortification of the 15th-century city walls, is where famous brigand Grigore Pintea Viteazul was shot in 1703. It is now used for temporary exhibitions.

☆ Activities

Baia Mare is home to several private tour guides offering regional trips of a few hours or a few days.

Baia Mare

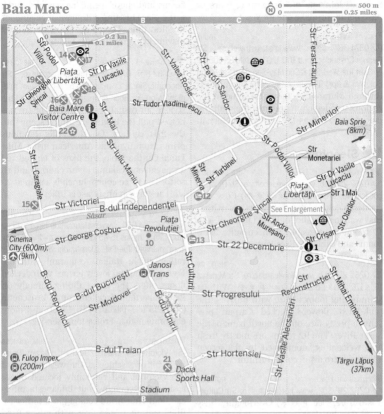

Baia Mare

⊙ Sights

Rada Pavel   TOURS

(☎ 0753-780 800; www.maramurestourism.com)
A long-term employee at the Tourist Information Centre Maramureș in Baia Mare,
where she impressed even hard-to-please

Lonely Planet writers, experienced guide
Rada knows Maramureș like the back of her
hand and can unlock both proverbial doors
and some of those impressively carved gates

for you. Join one of her existing tours or have her tailor-make one for you.

Travel Kristakis TOURS
(📞0374-367 139; www.kristakistravel.ro; Str George Coşbuc 5; adult 100-120 lei, child 85-105 lei; ⊙8am Tue, Wed, Sat & Sun May-Sep, 8am Sat & Sun Oct, Mar & Apr) This agency runs two circuits through Maramureş, taking in some of the region's wooden churches and other cultural landmarks, such as the Merry Cemetery in Săpânţa.

🛏 Sleeping

★Floare de Colţi GUESTHOUSE $
(📞0262-250 216; www.floaredecolti.ro; Str Dr Vasile Lucaciu 48; s/d 105/140 lei; 🅿❄🛜) Cosy and spotlessly clean, the 'Edelweiss' is within easy walking distance of Piaţa Libertăţii. The 13 rooms are sizeable, with en suite bathrooms and cable TV. Excellent value.

Hotel Carpaţi HOTEL $$
(📞0262-214 812; www.hotelcarpati.ro; Str Minerva 16; s 170-240 lei, d 280-300 lei; 🅿❄🛜) With its shimmering lobby ablaze with mirrors, the pink-hued, flower-bedecked Carpaţi presents a pretty face on the north bank of the Săsar River. The 92 rooms are mostly fresh and welcoming, dominated by flat-screen TVs and retro art-deco-ish furniture.

Rivulus Hotel HOTEL $$
(📞0262-216 302; www.hotelrivulus.ro; Str Culturii 3; s/d 179/219 lei; 🅿❄🛜) Overlooking busy Piaţa Revoluţiei, the 60-room Rivulus has a workaday lobby and rooms to match, with comfortable, standard-issue furniture. Cable TV, choice oils on the walls and the warm welcome are incentives to stay.

🍴 Eating

Hanu Igniş ROMANIAN $
(📞0362-405.503; Piaţa Libertăţii 16; mains 14-24 lei; ⊙10am-midnight) As authentic a Romanian *han* (inn) as you'll find, with colourful plates on the wall, embroidered covers on the tables and folk music in the air, this place serves rib-sticking specialities such as polenta with, well, ribs (20 lei) and the very porky, very cheesy 'Shepherd's Purse' (22 lei). You won't eat again for a week.

★Butoiaşu' cu Bere ROMANIAN $$
(Beer Keg; 📞0751-409 057; Str Gheorghe Şincai 15; mains 10-39 lei; ⊙8am-midnight) One of the most fun places to eat in town, this rustic eatery with its stone walls, exposed wooden beams and encyclopedic 'newspaper' menu is the place to sample Romanian cuisine for the first time. There's an energetic quartet playing gypsy music most nights.

★Michael Pascale FRENCH $$
(📞0362-807 078; www.michaelpascale.ro; Str Gheorghe Şincai 2; mains 26-62 lei; ⊙9am-midnight Mon-Fri, noon-midnight Sat & Sun) This stylish but casual French-owned bistro has helped pull the Baia Mare dining scene into the 21st century. On the walls, fabulous prints from dynamic American artist Mike Lana. On the table, the likes of chilled red gazpacho and calamari with chorizo and risotto. The three-course lunch is a snip at 29 lei. The English breakfast is 18 lei.

Lumiere ITALIAN $$
(📞0262-214 020; www.restaurantlumiere.ro; Piaţa Libertăţii 3; mains 16-45 lei; ⊙noon-midnight Mon, 8am-midnight Tue-Sat, 10am-midnight Sun) This rather chichi Italian restaurant with the French name and lovely terrace with decked floors offers the finest dining directly on Piaţa Libertăţii. Excellent soups, bruschetta (10 to 15 lei), pasta (16 to 45 lei) and more elaborate mains. Professional service.

Budapesta HUNGARIAN $$
(Str Victoriei 94; mains 20-50 lei; ⊙8am-10pm) It's a bit of a schlep at the western end of Str Victoriei and randomly located above a shopping complex, but Budapesta offers excellent Hungarian cooking in a rather refined setting. Goose liver with crispy fried onion and lamb cutlet with rosemary jus are just two of the dishes on offer.

ℹ Information

Baia Mare Visitor Centre (📞0262-211 003; www.baiamare.ro; Piaţa Libertăţii, Stephen's Tower; ⊙8am-6pm Mon-Fri, noon-4pm Sat) At the foot of Stephen's Tower, this centre deals primarily with Baia Mare and its surrounds.

Tourist Information Centre Maramureş (📞0262-206 113; www.visitmaramures.ro; Str Gheorghe Şincai 46; ⊙9am-4pm Mon-Thu, to 2pm Fri) This jewel of a tourist resource is hidden in a communist-era building with a verdigris roof. Helpful staff can recommend homestays, suggest itineraries and trekking guides, and sort out transport options.

ℹ Getting There & Away

BUS
Infrequent services run from the **bus station** (📞0262-221 777; Str Gării 2) to outlying villages. There are daily buses to Satu Mare (15 lei,

1¼ hours), Cluj-Napoca (30 lei, three hours), and Sighetu Marmaţiei via the Gutâi Pass or Cavnic (15 lei, 1½ to two hours).

Maxitaxis, also departing from the bus station, run daily (except Sunday) to Satu Mare (15 lei) and Bistriţa (25 lei).

Fulop Impex (📞 0745-600 796; http:// efitravel.ro) operates both daily and overnight bus services to Budapest, with departures from Baia Mare's bus station. Satu Mare–based **Janosi Trans** (📞 0261-758 620, 0749-268 676; www.janositrans.ro/en; B-dul Unirii) also operates bus services to Budapest, departing from the McDonald's parking lot (80 to 95 lei, about seven hours).

TRAIN

Advance train tickets are sold at **Agenţia de Voiaj CFR** (📞 0262-219 113; Str Victoriei 5-7). From Baia Mare's **train station** (📞 0262-220 950; Str Gării 4) there are around four daily trains to Satu Mare (8 lei, two hours), two to Bucharest via Braşov (from 141 lei, 13 hours), one to Cluj-Napoca (27 lei, four hours) and one to Timişoara (80 lei, 6½ hours). At the time of research there were no direct trains to Budapest, but you can catch an early train (departing just after 4am, arriving 8.50am) to the Hungarian city of Debrecen, from where there are frequent departures to Budapest (60 lei, 5½ hours).

Around Baia Mare

From Baia Mare, there are easy excursions southeast and southwest to a number of villages with some of the finest wooden churches in the county. Most of the churches now have wooden info kiosks and regular opening times, though some still post a telephone number for you to locate the church's key-holder. A trip northeast passes remote villages en route to some natural springs.

Surdeşti & Around

Approaching Surdeşti via Hwy 184 from Baia Sprie, after 5km you'll pass through **Şişeşti** village, home to the **Vasile Lucaciu Memorial Museum** (📞 0262-298 024; Şişeşti; donation requested; ⊙ 10am-noon & 2-4pm Mon-Fri). Vasile Lucaciu (1835–1919), a reformer and activist who was appointed parish priest in 1885, built a church for the village in 1890 that was supposedly modelled on St Peter's in Rome. Now Greco-Catholic, the church is signposted about 2km from the main road.

The **church** (Surdeşti; 5 lei; ⊙ 10am-6pm, shorter hours in winter) at **Surdeşti**, with its 54m-high steeple, is one of the most magnificent in the Maramureş region and is listed as a Unesco monument. It's well worth a visit for its splendid wall and ceiling paintings of Christ's Passion and the Apocalypse (note the seven-headed dragon). The church, signposted 'Biserică de Lemn' (wooden church) from the road, was built in 1721 as a centre of worship for the Greco-Catholic faithful. Two kilometres south in **Plopiş** is another Unesco-protected **church** (📞 0757-333 731; Plopiş; 10 lei; ⊙ 10am-4pm Tue-Sun) dating from the late 18th century, with a towering steeple and paintings of Christ's Passion, Adam and Eve and the Archangels Michael and Gabriel. A further 7km southeast is the town of **Lăschia**. Its **church** (Lăschia; 2 lei; ⊙ 10am-6pm Tue-Sun, shorter hours in winter) dates from 1861 and has an unusually bulbous steeple.

Baia Mare to Izvoare

North of Baia Mare a small road designated Rte 183 twists and turns through the remote villages of Firiza, Blidari and Valea Neagră, culminating some 38km from the centre of town at Izvoare, where there are natural springs.

Viewing churches is not on the agenda here; come to enjoy the mountainous countryside dotted with the odd wooden cottage and ramshackle farm. The most popular hiking destination in the area is **Igniş Peak** (1307m), which is used by paragliders.

This route is not served by public transport and, if driving, you must return the way you came as there is no exit onto Hwy 18 from Rte 183. A **hiking trail** (five to six hours, waymarked with red triangles) leads from Baia Mare to Izvoare; it starts about 3km north of the city along the Baia Mare–Izvoare road.

Ţara Chioarului

The Ţara Chioarului region in the southwestern part of Maramureş takes in the area immediately south of Baia Mare. The numerous villages, most of which contain traditional wooden churches, form a convenient loop that is ideal for a two-hour drive, though hard to do by public transport.

⊙ Sights & Activities

From Baia Mare follow the main road (Hwy 1C) south towards Cluj-Napoca for 17km to Satulung. Three kilometres south of Satulung, take the unmarked turn-off on the left (east) to Fînteuşu Mare and continue for 5km until you reach the village of Posta. A small wooden church (1675) opposite a more modern one sits at the top of the hill.

Nine kilometres south of Şomcuţa Mare lies Valea Chioarului, the southernmost village in Ţara Chioarului. Its delightful tall church (Valea Chioarului; ⊙hours vary), with decent interior wall paintings, stands next to the bus stop in the centre of the village. Seek the key in the shop opposite.

From Şomcuţa Mare, 5km south of the Posta turnoff, a largely unmade road wends its way to Remetea Chioarului, 8km to the northeast. Its tiny church (☑0757-617 349; Remetea Chioarului; ⊙10am-4pm Mon-Fri, 2-8pm Sat & Sun), dating from 1800, is the highlight of Ţara Chioarului, with its interior paintings and vaulted ceiling.

Săcălăşeni, 7km further north, has a small church, built in 1442, making it the oldest wooden church in Maramureş. To reach it, turn east at the modern church dominating the village.

Sighetu Marmaţiei

POP 37,640

The sleepy town known as 'Sighet' has a few sights for a morning's browsing, a pretty square edged by churches, and the Ukrainian border crossing just a few minutes away. The real reason for visiting Maramureş is its rural charm, so you needn't linger long. For centuries Sighet formed a cultural and geographic border between Slav-dominated territories to the north and Hungary and Romania to the south. Its name is derived from the Thracian and Dacian word 'seget' (fortress).

Sighetu Marmaţiei, first documented in 1334, was also an important Jewish settlement until the spring of 1944, when most of the Jews were transported to Auschwitz-Birkenau. After WWII the communist government established one of the country's most notorious prisons here, for dissidents, intellectuals and anyone else who could challenge the regime. It is now a memorial museum and one of the city's most important tourist sights.

⊙ Sights

Piaţa Libertăţii and surrounds are awash in churches of all denominations, including the 1804 Ukrainian Orthodox church, the Hungarian Reformed church, parts

of which date to the 12th century, and the 18th-century Roman Catholic church.

Village Museum MUSEUM

(Muzeul Satului; ☑0262-314 229; www.muzeul maramuresului.ro; Str Dobăieş 40; adult/child 4/2 lei; ⊙10am-6pm May-Sep, 8am-4pm Oct-Apr; ⓘ) Allow two to three hours to wander through the incredible constructions at the open-air Village Museum, about 2.5km southeast of Sighetu Marmaţiei's centre. Children in particular will love the wooden dwellings, cobbled pathways and 'mini villages'.

Elie Wiesel Memorial House HISTORIC BUILDING

(Casa Memorială Elie Wiesel; www.muzeulmara muresului.ro; Str Tudor Vladimirescu 1; adult/child 4/2 lei; ⊙10am-6pm May-Sep, 8am-4pm Oct-Apr) The late Jewish writer and 1986 Nobel Peace Prize winner Elie Wiesel (1928–2016) was born in and later deported from this house on the corner of Str Dragoş Vodă and Str Tudor Vladimirescu. The museum traces Wiesel's life and work and examines the history of the Jews and Jewish culture in Maramureş. There's a monument (Monumentul Holocaustului; Str Gheorghe Doja) to the victims of the Holocaust along Str Gheorghe Doja.

Jewish Cemetery CEMETERY

(Cimitirul evreiesc; Str Szilagyi Istvan) Organise visits to the cemetery through the Jewish Community Centre (☑0743-853 975, 0262-311 652; Str Bessarabia 8; ⊙10am-4pm Tue-Sun). To reach the cemetery from Str Gheorghe Şincai in the centre follow Str Izei for a couple of blocks south and then turn right into Str Szilagyi Istvan.

Maramureş Ethnographic Museum MUSEUM

(www.muzeulmaramuresului.ro; Piaţa Libertăţii 15; adult/student 4/2 lei; ⊙10am-6pm May-Sep, 8am-4pm Oct-Apr) One of three branches of the Maramureş Museum – the others are the Elie Wiesel Memorial House and the Village Museum – this ethnographic museum displays colourful folk costumes, rugs and carnival masks.

Sephardic Synagogue SYNAGOGUE

(☑0262-311 652, 0743-553 975; Str Bessarabia 10; ⊙9am-4pm Mon-Fri, or call ahead) Sighet's only remaining synagogue is north of Piaţa Libertăţii. It was built in the Moorish-Renaissance style in 1904. You can look around for free, but it's customary to leave a donation (10 lei). Before WWII the Jewish community here numbered just over 10,000 people – about 40% of Sighet's population at the time. Sadly, today the local Jewish community numbers around 200.

Most of the Jews perished at Auschwitz-Birkenau after being shipped there in 1944, when Hungary (which ruled over the area at the time) agreed to surrender its Jews to Nazi Germany. Some 38,000 eventually perished and the majority of the survivors chose to emigrate.

🏃 Activities

Teofil Ivanciuc TOURS
(📞 0745-944 555; www.maramurestour.com; one-day tours €60-100) Teofil Ivanciuc is a local writer who works as a fixer with outfits such as National Geographic, and can take you to the mountains to explore remote villages by car or horse cart. Homestays can also be arranged in his traditional wooden **Amizadil House** (📞 0745-944 555; www.amizadil. com; Str Mocăniței 51a, Valea Cufundoasă; s/d from €30/40).

🛌 Sleeping

★ Cobwobs Hostel GUESTHOUSE **$**
(📞 0740-635 673; www.facebook.com/cobwobs hostel; Str 22 Decembrie 1989 42; dm/d with shared bathroom 40/100 lei; @ 🛜) Friendly Cobwobs sits down a leafy lane in a pleasant house whose garden is so crowded with fruit trees, flowers, chickens and goats that you may forget you're in a town. All-wooden doubles and family rooms are homely and large, all with shared bathrooms. There are also three dorms with between four and six beds.

Outside are tables to read at and bikes for rent (30 lei per day). Owner Lia is charm itself and a great source of local info, especially on transport.

Motel Buți HOTEL **$**
(📞 0262-311 035; www.hotelbuti.ro; Str Simion Bărniuțiu 6; s/d/tr/ste 120/140/180/220 lei; ✳ @ 🛜) The 23 rooms may be a bit on the small side, but considering the Buți's standard and location, and the rooms' flatscreens, decent furniture and crisp linen, this is very good value. There's a bar and pizzeria downstairs.

★ Casa Iurca de Călinești HOTEL **$$**
(📞 0262-318 882; www.casaiurca.ro; Str Dragoș Vodă 14; s/d 110/175 lei; 🅿 ✳ 🛜) The 22 rooms and suites here are elegant and cool but only a handful are in the fine, old-wood-accented villa, with most in a newer annexe. Expect tasteful furniture, flat-screen TVs, tiled floors, leather chairs and spotless linen for your money. There are also fridges, fans and cable TV. Hands down the most atmospheric digs in town.

Hotel Grădină Morii HOTEL **$$**
(📞 0372-721 210; www.hotelmarmatia.ro; Str Mihai Eminescu 97; s 170-195 lei, d 250-300 lei; 🅿 ✳ 🛜) A top-to-tail revamp has turned the old Hotel Marmația into a comfortable destination hotel called the 'Mill Garden'. It's in an appealing, partially wood-clad building, hard by the Iza River at the foot of a nearby mountain and surrounded by parkland. Its 49 international-style rooms are comfortable, and there's a posh lobby and an excellent restaurant.

SIGHET PRISON: A SUFFERING NATION

In May 1947, the communist regime slaughtered, imprisoned and tortured thousands of Romanians who could or might oppose the new leadership. While many leading prewar figures were sent to hard-labour camps, the regime's most feared intellectual opponents were held in Sighet's maximum-security prison.

Between 1948 and 1952 about 180 members of Romania's academic and government elite were imprisoned here and some 51 died. The prison, housed in the old courthouse, was closed in 1974. In the early '90s it reopened as the **Memorial Museum to the Victims of Communism & to the Resistance** (📞 0262-319 424; www.memorialsighet. ro; Str Corneliu Coposu 4; adult/child 6/3 lei; ⏱ 9.30am-6.30pm daily, to 4pm Tue-Sun in winter).

Photographs and objects with short descriptions are displayed in the torture chambers and cells on two levels. There's also a small bookstore and gift shop. The heart-rending bronze statues in the courtyard, shielding themselves and covering their mouths in horror, are dedicated to those who died. Many of these victims are buried in the **Paupers' Cemetery** (Cimitirul Săracilor; Str Avram Iancu) some 2.5km west of the centre.

Sighetu Marmaţiei

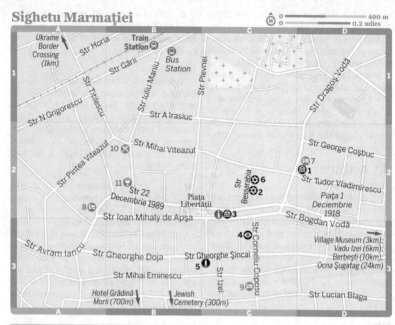

Sighetu Marmaţiei

⊙ Sights

1 Elie Wiesel Memorial House...............D2
2 Jewish Community Centre.................C2
3 Maramureş Ethnographic Museum...C2
4 Memorial Museum to the Victims
   of Communism & to the
   Resistance...C3
5 Monument to Holocaust Victims........C3
6 Sephardic Synagogue.........................C2

⊜ Sleeping

7 Casa Iurca de Călineşti D2
8 Cobwobs Hostel....................................A2
9 Motel Buţi...C3

⊗ Eating

10 Casa Veche...B2
   Restaurant Casa Iurca de
   Călineşti .... (see 7)

⊕ Drinking & Nightlife

11 Old Pub...B2

✕ Eating & Drinking

★ **Restaurant Casa Iurca de
Călineşti**   ROMANIAN $$
(☎0371-056 449; www.casaiurca.ro; Str Dragoş
Vodă 14; mains 18-38 lei; ⊙9am-11pm; 🛜) With
seating both at rustic wooden tables and in a
leafy courtyard, this is the top spot in Sighet

for a proper sit-down meal. Dishes include
seared pork, skewered lamb and Maramureş
stew with polenta (28 lei). There's a bargain
three-course set lunch for just 25 lei.

Casa Veche   ROMANIAN $$
(☎0744-110 299; Str Iuliu Maniu 27; mains 15-36
lei; ⊙7am-11pm) Probably the busiest joint in
town, Casa Veche has a bubbly terrace in the
evening, and an elegant, high-ceilinged interior dining room. Most punters come for the
big pizzas but there are also succulent steaks,
salads and all manner of Romanian specialities, including Transylvanian soup with pork
(4 lei) and 'Outlaw's Stew' (22 lei) with beef.

Old Pub   IRISH PUB
(☎0262-314 231; www.facebook.com/oldpub
sighet; Str Iuliu Maniu 5; ⊙8am-10pm Mon-Fri,
9.30am-10pm Sat & Sun) This less-than-raucous
Irish-style boozer is not a place to party but
rather to enjoy a pint in the courtyard.

ⓘ Information

**Tourist Information Centre Sighetu Mar-
maţiei** (☎0371-347 133; www.turismsighet.ro;
Piaţa Libertăţii 26; ⊙9am-5pm) Central and
very helpful tourist office down some steps on
Piaţa Libertăţii; will assist with general enquiries as well as accommodation, transport and
guided tours.

[side margin] MARAMUREŞ SIGHETU MARMAŢIEI

❶ Getting There & Away

BUS

The **bus station** (Str Gării) is opposite the train station north of the centre.There are up to five local buses departing daily to Baia Mare (12 lei, 65km) as well as services to Satu Mare (25 lei, 106km), Oradea (45 lei, 240km) and Timişoara (70 lei, 408km). From here you can also reach Borşa (15 lei), Budeşti (7 lei), Călineşti (7 lei), Vişeu de Sus (12 lei) and Săpânţa (5 lei), as well as Bârsana, Botiza, Ieud and Mara (all about 7 lei).

Atlassib (✆ 0751-519 365; Str Bogdan Vodă 5; ⊙ 9am-1.30pm & 2.30-5pm Mon-Fri) Books bus trips to major destinations in Romania.

Eurolines (✆ 0729-618 009; Str Bogdan Vodă; ⊙ 9am-6.30pm Mon-Fri, 10am-2pm Sat) Just off Piaţa Libertăţii. Offers Europe-wide long-distance coach services.

TRAIN

There are daily fast trains to Timişoara (100 lei, 12 hours), Bucharest (103 lei, 12 hours), Cluj-Napoca (43 lei, six hours) and Braşov (79 lei, eight hours).

Mara Valley

The Mara Valley (Valea Marei), with its beautiful rolling hills, is really the heart of Maramureş. Villages here are famed for their spectacular churches and carved gateways.

Giuleşti & Around

Heading south from Sighetu Marmaţiei on Hwy 18, you first reach the tiny village of Berbeşti, famed for its large, 300-year-old *troiţă*, a wayside shrine of a roofed carved crucifix with solar symbols. It stands by the roads at the northern end of the village. Traditionally, travellers prayed – or at least blessed themselves – by the cross to ensure a safe journey.

Continuing south you'll find Giuleşti, the main village in the Mara Valley, notable for its crumbling wooden cottages with 'pot trees' in their front yards, upon which a colourful array of pots and pans signify the eligibility of a daughter. It was here in 1918 that the revolutionary Ilie Lazăr summoned delegates from all over Maramureş prior to their signing of Transylvania's union agreement with Romania. Ilie Lazăr's simple three-room farmhouse built in 1826 is preserved and open to tourists as a memorial museum (Casa Museum Ilie Lazăr; Giuleşti; adult/child 4/2 lei; ⊙ by appointment). During the communist crackdown in the early 1950s,

❶ CROSSING OVER TO UKRAINE

There's a vehicular and foot bridge over the Tisa River to Ukraine just north of the centre of Sighet, making an excursion into Ukraine a snap. EU and US citizens need only fill out some forms and show a passport; nationals from other countries may need to secure a visa beforehand. Formalities on the Romanian side are fast and hassle-free. To reach the 24-hour crossing point from the centre follow Str Nicolae Titulescu northward for about 2km.

Ilie Lazăr was arrested and imprisoned at Sighet prison.

The village of Deseşti is a few kilometres southwest of Giuleşti on the road to Baia Mare. Its Orthodox church, built in 1770, was struck by lightning in 1925, destroying much of the outer walls and the steeple. Fortunately, its interior paintings, to the right as you enter the porch, have survived. The work of Radu Munteanu, they date from 1780 and feature a harrowing glimpse of Sodom and Gomorrah.

Close to the church is a 400-year-old oak tree measuring almost 5m in diameter. It has been preserved as a monument to the extensive oak forest that once covered the area before people felled the trees to build their homes.

Mara, just a couple of kilometres south of Deseşti, is known for its elaborately carved wooden gates (*porţi de lemn*). These are a unique architectural feature of the Maramureş region. In more recent times, their spiritual importance has been overridden by the social status attached to them.

Sat-Şugatag & Around

Four kilometres south of Giuleşti is Sat-Şugatag, home to a wooden church dating from 1642. The church is famed for its fine, ornately carved wooden gate and 18th-century interior paintings (though they are not very well conserved). Sat-Şugatag was first documented in 1360 as the property of Dragoş of Giuleşti, a *voivode* and probably Moldavia's first ruler.

Mănăstirea is 1km east of Sat-Şugatag. Its tiny church, about 150m up the hill from a gravel road and a very rickety bridge, was built by monks in 1633. It was dissolved in

1787 during the reign of Austro-Hungarian Emperor Joseph II. The original monks' cells are on the northern side of the church, which can be seen through the window if the church is closed.

Three kilometres south of Sat-Şugatag is **Hărniceşti**, home to a marvellous **Orthodox church** dating from 1770. A footpath from the main road leads through a graveyard to the hillside church.

Four kilometres southwest of the village and resort of **Ocna Şugatag**, famed for saltwater thermal pools, is **Hoteni**, known for its folk festival, **Tânjaua de pe Mara**, held in early May to celebrate the first ploughing.

Budeşti & Around

Heading south on the main road from Sighetu Marmaţiei, bear left onto Hwy 186B at Fereşti, which leads to some of Maramureş' more remote villages. If starting out from Baia Mare, you can approach this area on Hwy 184 through Cavnic and the Neteda Pass (1058m).

Corneşti, the first village along this stretch, has a small 18th-century **church** with interior paintings by Hodor Toador. It is about 250m west of the main road and over a very shaky bridge. **Călineşti**, 4km

further south, has two churches; to distinguish them they are called the Susani ('upper-dweller') church and the Josani church ('lower-dweller') church. The **Susani church** (1683; ☏ 0765-126 734, 0724-188 163) is on the right side of the road at the end of the village if coming from the north. The **Josani church**, built 20 years earlier, is 1km to the east on the road to Bârsana.

From Călineşti a road leads 8km to **Sârbi**, inhabited since 1402. Its two churches are built from oak. The **Josani church** (Sârbi Lower-Dweller Church), the first on the right and dating from 1665, has two icons by Radu Munteanu. The **Susani church** (1667; Sârbi Upper-Dweller Church) is at the other end of the village and 100m off the main road. Below this church there's a collection of buildings associated with traditional industry that used the waters of the Cosău River for power: a flour mill, a distillery and a fulling mill. The last of these is something like a natural 'laundrette' and used to clean and prepare wool for processing into clothing and blankets.

Budeşti, 5km to the south, is a larger village of intricately carved wooden gates and cosy cottages stacked with firewood. There are a couple of shops scattered about

---

WOODEN MARAMUREŞ CHURCHES & GATEWAYS

Dating back to the 14th century when Orthodox Christian Romanians were forbidden by their Roman Catholic Hungarian rulers to build their churches in stone, the master builders of Maramureş used wood in an architecturally unique way to express the faithful's spirituality. There are eight Unesco-listed churches you can visit today: Bârsana (p179), Budeşti (p176), Deseşti (p175), Ieud (p180), Plopiş (p171), Poienile Izei (p180), Rogoz and Surdeşti (p171). All were built in the 18th and 19th centuries after the Tatar invasions ended in 1717. These churches' weather-beaten exteriors have taken on an eerie, blackened hue, their Gothic-style spires rising austerely to almost needle-like shape. However, inside you'll find them vibrant and cosy, with packed congregations of fervently religious villagers, and walls painted in naive biblical frescoes and representations of traditional rural life. TTraditionally, homes of the Mara, Cosău and Iza Valleys used oak, while in Bârsana they were built from pine, and this is still largely the case. Roofs are tall and steep, many finished in shingle tiles that look like fish scales, while the oldest ones are covered in thatch.

Immense, intricately carved wooden gates (*porţi de lemn*) fronting homes are common. Often used to emphasise the social status and wealth of the inhabitants, originally they were built only by royal landowners to guard against the forces of evil. The gates were the symbolic barrier between the safe interior and the unknown outside world, and people placed money, incense and holy water under them for further protection against evil. Gate carvings include the 'tree of life', a snake (guardian against evil), birds (symbols of the human soul) and a face (to protect from spirits). Other common motifs are the sun and a coiled rope (symbols of life and continuity).

Some of the most beautiful wooden gates are found in the villages of Giuleşti, Deseşti, Sârbi, Vadu Izei and, in particular, Bârsana.

and a pension. The village also has one of the most beautiful (and largest) wooden churches in Maramureş. **Budeşti Josani church** (Budeşti Lower-Dweller Church; 🖉0764-206 302; ☉9am-1pm & 2-5pm), built in 1643 and measuring 18m by 8m, features four small turrets surrounding the bell tower. Among the church's wooden and glass icons is a prized 18th-century painting of the Last Judgment.

🛏 Sleeping & Eating

Private rooms and homestays are fairly plentiful here; just look for signs offering *camere* (rooms) or *cazare* (accommodation). For pensions check out www.la pensiuni.ro.

Pensiunea Mara   PENSION $
(🖉0749-459 331; www.pensiuneamaradesesti.ro; Deseşti 322; s/d from 100/140 lei; 🅿☏) In the heart of Deseşti village, hard by the Mara River and less than a kilometre from the village's wooden church, this modern *pensiune* has five rooms with balconies, private bathrooms and satellite TV, as well as an on-site restaurant. The surrounding garden is a delight.

Păstrăvăria Alex Happy Fish   SEAFOOD $
(Alex Happy Fish Trout Restaurant; 🖉0262-372 686, 0741-662 269; off Hwy 18, Mara; mains from 10 lei; ☉24hr) This local institution just off Hwy 18 in the picturesque village of Mara serves fresher-than-fresh trout pulled straight out of the lake. It's spread over a large, leafy and hilly tract of land, with ponds, waterfalls and various cabanas for dining almost alfresco. Worth a stop to or from Baia Mare, 40km to the southwest.

❶ Getting There & Away

Infrequent buses link Baia Mare with some of the outlying villages, including Mara, Călineşti and Budeşti up to five times a day between 6am and 7pm.

Breb

Just off the road linking Budeşti and Hwy 18 between Baia Mare and Sighetu Marmaţiei, rustic Breb is an isolated village replete with ancient wooden houses and a 16th-century church. The village and surrounds are home to a panoply of traditional craftspeople, including the famous woodcarver Patru Pop, who welcome visitors to watch them while they work.

🛏 Sleeping & Eating

Breb features a charming traditional guesthouse with separate cottages, a comfortable *pensiune* and even a camping ground.

Pensiunea Lucia   PENSION $
(🖉0262-374 584, 0752-527 485; www.pensiunealucia.com; Breb 285; per person B&B/half-board 55/90 lei; 🅿☏) This lovely *pensiune* has two rooms in an old traditional house with embroidered pillows, handwoven rugs and coffered wooden ceiling, and two more rooms in a newer neighbouring building; each pair share a bathroom. Meals served here – considered the best in Breb – are prepared with all-organic produce from the family farm.

Owner Ion is a guide and eco-enthusiast who will take you hiking and trekking.

Babou Maramureş Campsite & Hostel   HOSTEL, CAMPGROUND $
(🖉0747-687 747; www.baboumaramures.com; Breb 149; camping adult/child 25/10 lei; dm 50 lei; ☉Apr-Oct; 🅿☏) 🅿 Babou's sits in glorious hammock-strung meadowland with views of Ukraine. There's a pine-accented hostel with a six-bed dorm, an up-to-date kitchen and communal area, and a huge garden to pitch in (tent to rent: 75 lei). Extremely clean and efficiently run by affable Dutch couple Matthijs and Eveline.

★**Village Hotel**   GUESTHOUSE $$
(🖉0725-141 545; www.villagehotelmaramures.com; Breb; d/tw/q €35/40/45, cottage €50-75; 🅿☏) 🅿 Run by a charming English couple, Duncan and Penelope, this idyllic property has three rooms in the main farmhouse and three traditionally styled cottages with daub-and-wattle walls, wood-beamed rooms, log burners, immaculately clean kitchens and bedrooms carpeted with sheepskin rugs.

Breakfast is self-serve, with milk delivered daily along with cheese and freshly baked bread, while dinner (30 lei) is cooked around the open outdoor barbecue or at nearby farmhouses; mixing with locals is not just encouraged but mandatory in these parts. Rustic chic gets no better.

A font of local information and lore, Duncan can organise treks in the mountains, visits to traditional workshops, and excursions farther afield in Maramureş and Transylvania. As a professional photographer, his speciality is photography tours (see www.photographytoursromania.com).

MARAMUREŞ MARA VALLEY

❶ Getting There & Away

A half-dozen buses link Breb with Baia Mare daily (with the last one leaving Baia Mare at 5pm) and there are a couple of regular minibuses to/from Sighetu Marmației. The Village Hotel in Breb can organise transport to/from Sighetu Marmației (€15) and Baia Mare (€30).

Săpânța

Săpânța, 18km northwest of Sighetu Marmației, exudes pastoral charm with vividly hued rugs hanging over walls, fields dotted with hayricks, and horses and carts trundling at a snail's pace. The main draw of the village, however, is its unique Merry Cemetery (p178): the church graveyard famous for the colourfully painted wooden crosses that adorn its tombstones. The crosses attract busloads of visitors who marvel at the gentle humour that created them and, curiously, villagers seem unfazed by the daily circus. Outside the church, a gauntlet of souvenir stalls hawk embroidered tablecloths, carved gewgaws and woven rugs.

Five hundred metres down a paved road to the right, just before you reach the centre of the village, is the Săpânța-Peri Monastery (Mănăstirea Săpânța-Peri), whose adjoining wooden church claims to be the tallest wooden structure in Europe (75m).

🛏 Sleeping & Eating

Pensiunea Ileana PENSION $
(🌐0745-491 756, 0262-372 137; www.sapanta maramures.ro/pensiuni/pensiuneaileana; s/d 100/130 lei; 🅿🛜) With its five large and bright traditional rooms nestled round a courtyard and its garden stacked with freshly sheared

wool, this place is old-school Maramureș. Ileana, the eponymous hostess, has her own weaving workshop where you can watch her at work. The *pensiune* is just opposite the Merry Cemetery's main entrance.

Casa Ana &
Săpânța Camping PENSION, CAMPGROUND $
(🌐0740-593 380; www.sapantamaramures.ro/pensiuni/camping-poieni-casa-ana; tent/campervan/d 30/40/100 lei; 🛜) Located 3km south of Săpânța village, this pension and campsite is idyllically positioned by a stream, and has a restaurant in the main house. Guests can use the clay oven too. The *pensiune* has four rooms. Shared showers and WC.

❶ Getting There & Away

From Sighetu Marmației two or three buses a day go to Săpânța (one in the morning and one or two in the afternoon, weekdays only, 5 lei), but with no fixed-time return bus.

Iza Valley

The Iza Valley (Valea Izei) follows the Iza River southeastward from Sighetu Marmației to Moisei. A tight-knit procession of quintessentially Maramureș peasant villages nestles in the valley, almost all featuring the region's famed elaborately carved wooden gates and tall wooden churches.

Vadu Izei

Vadu Izei lies at the confluence of the Iza and Mara Rivers, 7km southeast of Sighetu Marmației. An old wooden house dating to 1750 next to the church in the centre forms part of the Village Museum (p172) in Sighetu Marmației.

MERRY CEMETERY

Săpânța's Merry Cemetery (Cimitirul Vesel; 5 lei; ⊙8am-6pm) was the creation of Ioan Stan Pătraș, a simple wood sculptor who, in 1935, started carving crosses to mark graves in the old church cemetery. He painted each cross in blue – the traditional colour of hope and freedom – and on top of each he inscribed a witty epitaph to the deceased.

Every cross tells a different story, and the painted pictures and inscriptions illustrate a wealth of traditional occupations: shepherds tend their sheep, mothers cook for their families, barbers cut hair and weavers bend over looms.

Pătraș carved and painted his own cross, complete with a portrait of himself. His grave is directly opposite the main entrance to the old church. Since Pătraș' death his former house and studio have been converted into a fascinating museum (Casa Memorială Ioan Stan Pătraș; Săpânța 380; adult/child 4/2 lei; ⊙7am-8pm). It's a short detour 400m to the right of the cemetery entrance.

🛏 Sleeping & Eating

⭐**Casa Muntean** PENSION $
(☑ 0766-755 267; www.casamuntean.ro; Vadu Izei 505; s/d without bathroom 40/80 lei; ☻@☎) Five colourful rooms (only one with private bathroom) are enlivened by richly coloured rugs, wooden ceilings and wall hangings, as well as cable TV. Breakfast/dinner is an additional 15/25 lei. Owner Florin can take you on a guided tour (from 135 lei per person) to local wooden churches and the Merry Cemetery (p178).

Casa Muntean also hires bikes (25 lei per day) and can organise four-hour horse-and-cart trips (100 lei per person). The owners will pick you up at Sighet station.

Pensiunea Teodora Teleptean PENSION $
(☑ 0742-492 240; www.pensiuneateleptean.ro; Vadi Izei 506; s/d 100/120 lei; ℗☎) Some 10 rooms with private bathrooms in a pretty all-wooden building. Rooms are spacious and decorated with antique armoires, wood-raftered ceilings and TVs. Take breakfast (15 lei) or dinner (30 lei) in the large dining room.

ⓘ Information

Guide and glass-painter **Ioan Borlean** (☑ 0742-749 608, 0728-316 425) functions as a quasi-official source of tourist information. Give him a call if you need help.

Bârsana

From Vadu Izei you can continue for 13km through Onceşti to the village of Bârsana, dating back to the 14th century.

⊙ Sights

Bârsana Monastery MONASTERY
(Mănăstirea Bârsana; ☑ 0262-331 101; www.manastireabarsana.ro) This enormous all-wooden Orthodox monastic complex counts some 10 massive buildings atop a steep hill, including a beautiful church built in 1993, and is a popular Maramureş pilgrimage site. Check out the small museum with icons dating back to the 16th century.

The 10.45am Sunday service is a magical experience among the rolling hills and wildflowers, and on 30 June the monastery celebrates the feast of the 12 Apostles. Some nine nuns and a priest reside here.

BârsanArt ARTS CENTRE
(☑ 0740-490 152, 0262-331 015; http://barsanart.ro; Bârsana 524; ☺9am-8pm) Not a gallery

as such but a garden workshop, this place is operated by master artisan Ioan Bârsan, who whittles wood and produces everything from life-size bears to the ubiquitous carved wooden entrance gates. Definitely worth a stop.

Bârsana Church CHURCH
(☑ 0760-863 342, 0262-331 316; ☺9am-4pm Mon-Sat, 1-6pm Sun) Bârsana's Unesco-listed wooden church, which contains interior paintings by local masters Hodor Toador and Ion Plohod, dates to 1720. It is signposted 700m up the hill to the north from the centre of the village.

🛏 Sleeping

Bârsana has a couple of comfortable pensions and even a large campsite.

Camping Bradova CAMPGROUND $
(☑ 0746-993 061, 0262-331 200; http://camping-bradova.ro; Bradova 803; tent/campervan 30/40 lei, cottage from 50 lei) This large campsite with an impressive carved wooden entrance gate is a couple of kilometres up the hill from Bârsana's church and offers dramatic views over the rolling countryside. Stilted wooden cottages for two are also available here, and there's a restaurant on-site.

Pensiunea Fratii Pasca PENSION $
(☑ 0762-609 352; www.fratiipasca.ro; Str Principala 1338a; r without/with bath from 60/70 lei; ℗☎) Situated 2km outside of Bârsana on the road to Călineşti is this two-part pension offering 13 cosy rooms with driftwood furniture, TV, clean linen, en suite and bright, fresh walls. Breakfast (15 lei) and dinner (30 lei) available.

Botiza

From Şieu you can take the turn-off to the right (Hwy 171A) for the sleepy village of Botiza, one of the prettiest in all of Maramureş and site of the some of the region's best homestays. Botiza's Unesco-listed old wooden church (☏ 0262-211 947; ⊘ 10am-4pm Tue-Sun), built in Vişeu de Jos in 1690 and moved here more than two centuries later, is overshadowed by the giant new church, constructed in 1974 to serve the Orthodox faithful.

The 9am Sunday service is the major event of the week in Botiza. The *entire* village flocks to the church to partake in the religious activities, which continue well into the afternoon.

🛏 Sleeping

Casa Berbecaru PENSION $
(☏ 0723-775 848; http://ruralturism.ro/maram/pensmar/botiza/berbecaru%20victoria/html/berbecaruen.html; Botiza 743; r from 80 lei) Four spick-and-span rooms are available at this pension, run by the warm, French-speaking Victoria. Better still are the two rooms in the 19th-century wooden house just opposite, where you can stay in simple, cosy cells that feel like being in a ship's cabin. There's a shop here selling Victoria's beautifully designed, hand-woven rugs.

George Iurca PENSION $
(☏ 0722-942 140; iurcageorge@yahoo.com; Botiza 742; r per person from €15; @⊚) George is a guide licensed to conduct tours throughout Romania. He rents out a couple of clean, comfortable rooms as well as mountain bikes (25 lei per day) and vehicles with a driver-guide (€80 to €100 per day for a group). You'll find his house two doors to the right of Botiza's new church.

Poienile Izei

From Botiza an unmade road leads northwest to Poienile Izei, home of a church (☏ 0744-811 899; adult/child 4/2 lei; ⊘ 9am-1pm & 2-6pm Mon-Sat, noon-4pm Sun) with some of the most dramatic frescoes of hell you're likely to see. The early-17th-century church's frescoes eerily depict infernal visions of torments inflicted by the devil on sinners.

Three kilometres further north along a gravel road is the village of Glod, the birthplace of the popular Maramureş folk-singing duo Fratii Petreuş (Petreuş Brothers).

🛏 Sleeping & Eating

La Domniţa PENSION $
(☏ 0724-175 757; domnita-ilies@yahoo.com; Poienile Izie 138; d from 50 lei) This delightful *pensiune* run by French-speaking Ilies has eight rooms (four with en suite bathroom) and a seven-bed dorm in the main building, and five chalets in the back of an enormous garden. Some of the best food in the area is served here in La Domniţa's restaurant, with produce coming directly from the back garden.

Breakfast/lunch/dinner costs 15/20/25 lei.

Ieud

Packed with traditional houses and pensioners in traditional garb, this fervently Orthodox village (8km off the road south from Şieu) has as its main draw its 17th-century wooden Orthodox church (adult/child 4/2 lei; ⊘ 10am-4pm Tue-Sun). Under its rooftop was found the Ieud Codex, a document dating from 1391–92 considered to be the oldest example of written Romanian. Today it is kept in the archives of the Romanian Academy in Bucharest.

Ieud's other wooden church (adult/child 2/1 lei; ⊘ 10am-4pm Tue-Sun), now Graeco-Catholic in denomination, was built in 1717. The church, at the southern end of the village, is unique to the region as it has no porch. It houses one of the largest collections of icons on glass found in Maramureş. Cross the nearby bridge to the modest Ethnographic Museum (Muzeul Etnografic; adult/child 5/2 lei; ⊘ 8am-noon & 1-8pm) contained in two traditional Maramureş cottages.

🛏 Sleeping & Eating

Meals are available at Pensiunea Chindris and Pensiunea Ilea.

Pensiunea Ilea PENSION $
(☏ 0747-940 260; www.cazarelapensiune.ro/ieud/cazare-ieud/pensiunea-ilea-804; Ieud 333; r per person incl breakfast/half-board €15/20; P⊚) This wooden *pensiune* (found at the base of a hill at the end of a lane) is signed 1km out of town, and has four simple rooms, two with en suite bathroom. The friendly owner can arrange to pick you up in Sighetu Marmaţiei (55 lei) or Baia Mare (175 lei).

Pensiunea Chindris PENSION $
(☏ 0743-811 077, 0262-336 197; www.ruraltourism.ro/maram/pensmar/ieud/ChindrisVasile/html/chindrisro.html; Ieud 201; r per person incl breakfast/half-board €17/28; P) The three rooms

STEAMED UP!

Operated by **CFF Vişeu de Sus** (p182) and known as the 'Vaser Valley Forest Railway' or 'Carpathian Forest Steam Train' in English, this former logging train travels a network of some 60km of narrow 12-gauge track (though travellers only get to ride on 22km of it), and is probably the last forestry railway still powered by steam working in Europe today. Started in 1932 as an alternative to transporting logs by river, the track wends through soaring forested crags that a traveller might otherwise have trouble reaching. And it's an excellent ride as you smell the wood-smoke and hear the train whistle blaring.

The journey proper starts at 9am, but you'll need to secure a ticket by arriving at the **railway station** (📞0262-353 381; Str Cerbului 5) at 8.30am (the train only seats 210). In summer call ahead or book online. Due to the damage sustained to the track by flooding in 2008, the journey ends at Paltin, where you'll alight by the river for a 1½-hour lunch break. There are benches in a meadow, and grilled sausages and cold drinks are sold nearby. From Paltin the intrepid can trek higher into the mountains, or it's possible to camp near the warden's lodge (at Paltin) if you seek his permission (arrange with the CFF Vişeu de Sus office to catch a return train the following day).

The magic ends somewhere between 2.30pm and 3.30pm (depending on the season) as you return to the station. The railway runs daily from mid-June to late September, with an extra train or two sometimes added at 9.30am and 10am in July and August. It runs from Thursday to Sunday only from April to mid-June and late September to October.

with shared bathroom are clean and homely in these central digs. The husband-and-wife team can drive you around. Meals cost 28 lei.

🛈 Getting There & Away

The region is best explored by car, heading south out of Sighetu Marmaţiei along the main road (Hwy 18) to Baia Mare and then bearing left in Vadu Izei, 7km southeast of Sighetu Marmaţiei along a quieter road (Hwy 186) in the direction of Bârsana. Three minibuses run along this road daily, serving Vadu Izei, Bârsana, Poienile Izei, Botiza and Ieud.

Vişeu & Vaser Valleys

Wooded mountains rise to dizzying heights around the beautiful Vişeu Valley (Valea Vişeu), which tracks the Vişeu River on its journey southeast from Sighet. The equally picturesque Vaser Valley (Valea Vaser) is carved out by the river of the same name, which meets the Vişeu River at Vişeu de Sus.

Vişeu de Sus

POP 15,050

Essentially a one-street affair dotted with a few banks, cafes and restaurants, the town's narrow lanes radiate towards the Vaser Valley railway station where you can board the celebrated steam train. If you're headed into the rural wilds of Maramureş this is a good stop to fuel up on gasoline and lei, and there are a couple of solid hotels.

🏃 Activities

Most travellers come to Vişeu de Sus for the chance to ride a steam-powered locomotive high into the hills along a narrow-gauge track originally built for transporting logs. It's a grand day out and combines the thrill of a good ride with a chance to start a hike into the upper reaches of the Vaser Valley.

🛏 Sleeping

Hotel Gabriela   HOTEL $
(📞0757-114 972, 0262-354 380; www.hotel-gabriela.ro; Str Rândunelelor 1; s/d 120/140 lei; P🐾❄️🛜) Located 2km east of Vişeu de Sus, reliable Hotel Gabriela offers 29 clean, modern rooms with verandahs, cable TV, en suites and hearty breakfasts. The hotel restaurant serves decent pizza.

Pensiunea Stancuta   PENSION $
(📞0745-096 481; www.pensiuneastancuta.ro; Str Alexandru Ioan Cuza 56; r 120 lei) Handy for catching the early-morning train, Stancuta is 1km past the train station from the centre of town and on the other side of the tracks. The five rooms are clean and welcoming, with fine views of the nearby mountains. There's a large garden – almost a farm – and a wooden terrace to sun or read on.

🍴 Eating & Drinking

Pizzeria Andra   PIZZA $
(📞0741-226 055; www.facebook.com/pizzeriarestaurantandra; Str 22 Decembrie 1989 25;

WORTH A TRIP

HIKING THE PRISLOP PASS

From the Borşa Complex, a tight, winding road climbs for 10km to the remote 1413m-high Prislop Pass. Hikers can trek north into the Maramureş Mountains or head south into the Rodna Mountains and onward to Moldavia. Red triangles then blue stripes lead to the peak of the Gărgălău Saddle (1925m, two hours). You can then either continue east (red stripes) to the Rotunda Pass, then southeast to Vatra Dornei, or west to the highest part of the massif and on to La Cruce (four to five hours). From here the weather station on the summit of Mt Pietrosul (2305m, blue stripes) is only 90 minutes away, which, among the mind-bending views here, allows for a good long gaze into Ukraine without the hassle of border checks. At this point, it's a direct hustle back down to Borşa (two to three hours).

Do not attempt to stray too far from these trails without a good map and compass.

pizza 12-20 lei; ⊙7am-midnight) With chartreuse-coloured seats and wooden-tile panelling, Andra is a local favourite, with a huge menu of pizza, pasta (11 to 17 lei), schnitzel and bruschetta to choose from. There's a back terrace too.

Café Maya CAFE
(www.facebook.com/MayaCaffeBar; Str 22 Decembrie 1989 12; ⊙7am-10pm) With its vaguely Parisian interior, this is a good stop for cappuccinos and, come evening, mojitos and daiquiris.

ⓘ Information

CFF Vişeu de Sus (☑0744-686 716, 0262-353 381; www.cffviseu.com; Str Cerbului 5; adult 48-57 lei, child 33-39 lei; ⊙8am-6pm) All your information needs are taken care of by the tirelessly helpful staff at CFF Vişeu de Sus, the agency that operates the narrow-gauge railway from the train station. They can assist you with walking maps and eating and accommodation advice. They can also help organise guides.

ⓘ Getting There & Away

Regular buses and maxitaxis link the Vişeu Valley with the cities of Sighet and Baia Mare, making it more accessible for travellers without private transport. There are between five and six departures for Vişeu de Sus and Borşa from both cities on weekdays. Service is limited to two or three buses on Saturday.

Borşa

POP 27,600

Grubby little Borşa has an ace up its sleeve: the Borşa Complex some 10km east, a ski resort set amid insanely pretty countryside

with dark green forests, sun-dappled streams and midsize mountains. As well as having some decent intermediate and beginner slopes (1km-long Ştiol, 2km-long Poiana), it's the main entry point for hikers keen to experience the beauty of the Rodna Mountains, part of which forms the Pietrosul Rodnei Nature Reservation (5900 hectares).

🏃 Activities

Hiking information is scarce, but there are clearly marked trails with red stripes leading from the top of the Borşa Complex Ski Lift (Str Brădet 10; one way/return 15/30 lei; ⊙9am-5pm). Trails include a two-hour hike (in good weather) to the Prislop Pass (1413m) and a pleasant, 90-minute walk to Cascada Cailor (Horseshoe Waterfall), which is 90m high. If you want to stretch your legs before starting on the trails, there's a path leading up underneath the ski lift.

🛏 Sleeping & Eating

Motel Rodna GUESTHOUSE $
(☑0744-699 052, 0262-344 122; Str Libertaţii 37; d from 80 lei; 🅿🛜) It might not sound like much but this 18-room guesthouse is just about the best place to stay in Borşa. It's about 300m west of the centre and has an in-house restaurant.

Pensiunea Vila Focus CHALET $
(☑0721-290 239, 0262-344 038; Str Brădet 12; r 120 lei; 🅿🛜) At the Borşa Complex and by the chairlift, the Vila Focus is a timber and stone affair with a tempting restaurant and 11 immaculate rooms. Try for digs facing the mountain.

Moldavia & the Bucovina Monasteries

Best Places to Eat

➡ Cuib (p190)
➡ Restaurant Centru Vechi (p203)
➡ Q'usine (p210)
➡ Noir (p197)
➡ Antique (p208)

Best Places to Sleep

➡ Hotel Select (p189)
➡ Hotel Lacu Roşu (p197)
➡ Irene's Hostel (p202)
➡ Eden (p194)
➡ Casa Bunicilor (p208)
➡ Gerald's Hotel (p208)

Why Go?

Less visited than other parts of Romania, Moldavia rewards those intrepid enough to seek it out: from glorious medieval monasteries to rugged mountains ideal for hiking, this singular region combines natural beauty with plenty of action. Moldavia's bucolic villages and oddly endearing towns feature some of Romania's friendliest locals. Beyond the hinterland, Moldavian modernity is fully displayed in Iaşi, one of Romania's largest cities and a vibrant student town famous for its nightlife. Bucovina, to the northwest, is home to Romania's pride and joy: a half dozen Unesco-protected painted monasteries from the 15th and 16th centuries that attest to the region's artistic skills and enduring faith. Everywhere you'll find signs of Moldavian prince (and Romanian national hero) Ştefan cel Mare and his epic battles with the Ottoman Empire, above all at the mighty fortresses at Suceava and Târgu Neamţ.

When to Go
Iaşi

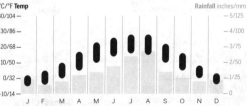

Apr & May Enjoy Iaşi when it's rejuvenated by spring flowers, boisterous students and live music.

Jul & Aug Escape the summer heat by hiking the Ceahlău and Rarău Mountains.

Sep & Oct Visit the Bucovina painted monasteries minus the crowds, as the autumn leaves change colour.

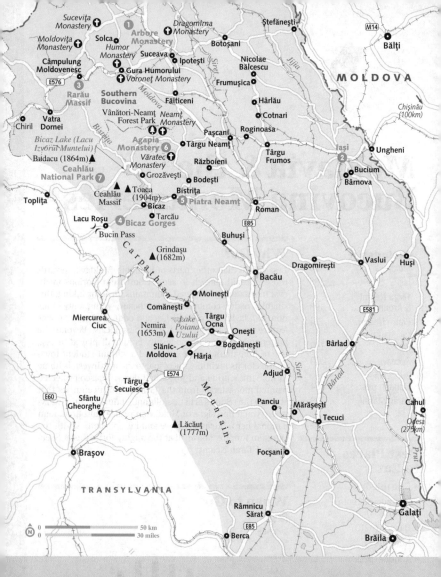

Moldavia & the Bucovina Monasteries Highlights

1 Arbore Monastery
(p204) Admiring the artistry of this church and surrounding painted monasteries.

2 Palace of Culture
(p186) Gawking at the size and gleam of Iaşi's now fully renovated grand royal palace.

3 Lady's Stones
(p209) Gazing at this string of soaring limestone rock formation, part of the Rarău Massif.

4 Bicaz Gorges (p197) Bearing down for some white-knuckle driving through these stupendously steep gorges.

5 Cucuteni Museum
(p195) Blushing at the more-than-*zaftig* female figurines created by the neolithic Cucuteni people, at this museum in Piatra Neamţ.

6 Agapia Monastery
(p193) Enjoying the tranquil beauty of the often-overlooked Neamţ monasteries.

7 Ceahlău National Park
(p198) Looking out over Lake Bicaz from Moldavia's highest mountain, the Ceahlău Massif.

History

In prehistoric times, the territory of Moldavia was the centre of a remarkable neolithic culture known as Cucuteni-Trypillian. Thriving from 6000 to 3500 BC, the Cucuteni were known for their beautiful, modern-looking pottery and highly sexualised female figurines. Many pieces have survived and are on display at Piatra Neamţ's Cucuteni Museum.

Later, Moldavia was occupied by Thracian and Dacian tribes in the millennium up to the Common Era, and was then under partial Roman occupation for some centuries. It also experienced waves of peoples, including Goths, Huns, Slavs and Bulgars, moving across the land from the 4th to 10th centuries.

Moldavia achieved its own identity between the 13th and 16th centuries, when it and its sister Romanian principality, Wallachia, emerged as buffers to protect the Hungarian kingdom from the growing might of the Ottoman Empire. This opposition to the Ottoman Turks gave rise to a string of Moldavian heroes, chief among them Prince Ştefan cel Mare (Stephen the Great; r 1457–1504).

Ştefan cel Mare and subsequent rulers, including his illegitimate son Petru Rareş (r 1527–38), established impregnable fortresses and monasteries, among them the Bucovina painted monasteries, which formed the crux of the region's identity. Ştefan cel Mare's Moldavian principality stretched to the east into the territory of the present-day Republic of Moldova, leaving us with the confusing nomenclature of Moldavia/Moldova, which continues to this day.

Both Wallachia and Moldavia eventually fell to the Turks, but were briefly united, along with Transylvania in the west, at Alba Iulia under the leadership of Mihai Viteazul (Michael the Brave; r 1593–1601).

In 1775 part of Moldavia's territory, Bucovina, was annexed by Austria-Hungary. This was followed in 1812 by the loss of its eastern territory – Bessarabia (modern-day Republic of Moldova) – to Russia. After the Russo-Turkish War of 1828–29, Wallachia and Moldavia became Russian protectorates while remaining within the Ottoman Empire.

As the Ottoman Empire weakened throughout the 19th century, leaders in both Moldavia and Wallachia saw the opportunity to fuse together as a united Romania. This eventually took place in 1961 under the leadership of Moldavian Prince Alexandru Ioan Cuza. Later, the defeat of Austria-Hungary in WWI paved the way for the return of Bucovina.

From this point onward, Moldavia's fortunes rise and fall with the rest of the country, with a low point during WWII. The alliance of Romania with Nazi Germany in June 1941 eventually led to the destruction of Moldavia's sizeable Jewish community. The horrific pogrom of that month in Iaşi, where some 13,000 people were killed, and the mass deportations to Bessarabia in the east reduced the number of Jews living in Moldavia to just a few thousand.

MOLDAVIA

Apart from the painted monasteries in Bucovina, the eastern half of Romania gets relatively few tourists. That's their loss, as vibrant cities like Iaşi, filled with students, exude both cultural energy and impressive historic and sacral architecture.

This was the stamping ground of early national heroes such as Prince Ştefan cel Mare, and many churches and fortresses, especially the impregnable rock at Târgu Neamţ, bear his stamp. The region's numerous monasteries lack the dazzling colours of Bucovina but arguably compensate with a more genuine sense of living spirituality. The Bicaz Gorges and Ceahlău Massif in the west are stark natural wonders.

Iaşi

POP 290,422

Exuberant, cultured Iaşi (pronounced 'yash') clearly enjoys being the biggest city in Moldavia. Once dubbed the 'city of the hundred churches', Iaşi is indeed bursting with centuries of architectural creations. Yet besides the monasteries, theatres and other historic buildings, this eclectic place has botanical parks, big squares and (for better or for worse) both communist-era concrete structures and gleaming modern shopping malls.

As with its shopping scene, Iaşi's innumerable eateries, drinking holes and lively clubs depend on the robust university population. You'll find students from all over the world here – making this little corner of Romania unexpectedly cosmopolitan.

○ Sights

The city's elaborate system of boulevards and squares centres on Piaţa Unirii, from

Iaşi

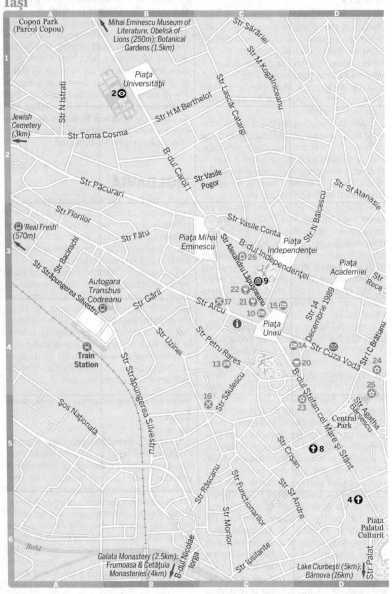

Copou Park
(Parcol Copou)

Mihai Eminescu Museum of
Literature, Obelisk of
Lions (250m); Botanical
Gardens (1.5km)

Str Sărăriei

Str M Kogălniceanu

Piaţa
Universităţii

2

Str N Istrati

Str H M Berthelot

Str Lascăr Catargi

Jewish
Cemetery
(3km)

Str Toma Cosma

B-dul Carol I

Str Vasile
Pogor

Str Sf Atanasie

Str Păcurari

'Real Fresh'
(570m)

Str Florilor

Str Fătu

Str Vasile Conta

Piaţa
Independenţei

Str N Bălcescu

Str Bacinschi

Piaţa Mihai
Eminescu

Str Alexandru Lăpuşneanu

B-dul Independenţei

Piaţa
Academiei

Str
Rece

Str Străpungerea Silvestru

Autogara
Transbus
Codreanu

Str Gării

26

9

22

21

17

15

Str Arcu

10

Str 14 Decembrie 1989

Piaţa
Unirii

Str C Brătianu

Train
Station

Str Uzinei

Str Petru Rareş

14

Str Cuza Vodă

24

25

Şos Naţională

Str Străpungerea Silvestru

13

20

B-dul Ştefan cel Mare şi Sfânt

Str Agatha Bârsescu

16

Str Săulescu

23

Central
Park

8

Str Crişan

Str Sf Andra

Bahl

Str Răscanu

Str Funcţionarilor

Str Morilor

Str Ipsilante

B-dul Nicolae Iorga

4

Piaţa
Palatul
Culturii

Str Palat

Galata Monastery (2.5km);
Frumoasa & Cetăţuia
Monasteries (4km)

Lake Ciurbeşti (5km);
Bârnova (16km)

which B-dul Ştefan cel Mare şi Sfânt extends south to Piaţa Moldova. Between the
two squares are some of the town's most
famed historic buildings, including the
Moldavian Metropolitan Cathedral and the
Palace of Culture.

★ **Palace of Culture**   MUSEUM
(Palatul Culturii; 0232-275 979; www.palatul
culturii.ro; Piaţa Ştefan cel Mare şi Sfânt 1; adult/
child combined entry 40/10 lei, tower only 16/4 lei;
10am-5pm Tue-Sun) Iaşi's premier attraction and symbol of the city is the grandiose

stands over Prince Alexandru cel Bun's ruined 15th-century princely court. Visitors can tour the palace, climb the tower and explore four major museums.

The project to restore the palace ranks among the largest public-works projects undertaken in Romania since 1989. The building's floor plan covers some 34,000 sq metres and there's said to be 365 rooms (one for each day of the year), though the actual count is around 300. The structure's dominant feature is the central clock tower, with immense clock faces on three sides decorated in stained glass. As you enter, the grand central hall shows off the architect's infatuation – in keeping with the neo-Gothic style – with medieval beasts: dragons, lions and griffons to name a few.

The four main museums are the **Ethnographic Museum** (adult/child 12/3 lei), **Art Museum** (adult/student 16/4 lei), **History Museum** (adult/child 16/4 lei), **Science & Technical Museum** (adult/student 12/3 lei). It's possible to buy separate entrances to each museum or a discounted combined-entry ticket to the museums and palace.

Golia Monastery   MONASTERY
(☑ 0232-216 693; Str Cuza Vodă 51) **FREE** This beautiful late Renaissance–style monastery is guarded by thick walls and the 30m-high Golia tower, which you can climb (120 steps) for views out over the city. The 17th-century church is notable for its vibrant Byzantine frescoes and intricately carved doorways, and features bastions from 1667. The complex also contains a small museum dedicated to writer and one-time resident Ion Creangă (1837–89), renowned for his Moldavian folklore–inspired short stories.

After repeated fires and closure from 1900 to 1947, the monastery was rejuvenated in 1992 and renovations continue.

Botanical Gardens   GARDENS
(Grădină Botanică; ☑ 0232-201 373; www.botanica. uaic.ro; Dumbrava Rosie 7-9, Parcul Expoziţiei; 5 lei; ⊙ 9am-7pm) Iaşi's Botanical Gardens are Romania's first (1856) and largest (100 hectares). They sprawl across Parcul Expoziţiei's western side and offer 21km of shady lanes, 800 rose varieties and orchid gardens, plus greenhouses with tropical flowers and carnivorous plants. Kids will enjoy the lawns and small lake. The gardens are about 3km northwest of the centre, so take a taxi (8 lei) or walk (20 minutes) up on B-dul Carol I.

Gothic-revival Palace of Culture that dominates the horizon at the southern end of B-dul Ştefan cel Mare şi Sfânt. Though it looks as if it stepped out of a medieval fairy tale, the building is only around 100 years old (built from 1906 to 1925). The palace

Iaşi

Moldavian Metropolitan Cathedral　CHURCH
(Mitropolia Moldovei; ☑ 0232-215 300; www.mmb.
ro; B-dul Ştefan cel Mare şi Sfânt 16; ☺8am-6pm)
FREE This cavernous cathedral, built between 1833 and 1839, was designed by architect Alexandru Orascu and decorated by painter Gheorghe Tattarescu. Since 1889, when the cathedral claimed the relics of Moldavia's patron saint, St Paraschiva, from the Church of the Three Hierarchs, the faithful have flocked here each October to see them displayed.

Great Synagogue　SYNAGOGUE
(☑0232-313 711; Str Sinagogilor 7) The Great Synagogue, built in 1671, is wedged between concrete apartment blocks. At the time of research, the synagogue was closed for renovation. Victims of the June 1941 pogroms are commemorated on a statue here.

Bărboi Monastery　MONASTERY
(Biserica Bărboi; Str Bărboi 12; ☺8am-6pm) **FREE**
Built in 1841 over a 1615 church foundation, the Bărboi has an eccentric combination of a Byzantine stone-and-brick interior and a neoclassical portico supported by Doric columns – apparently a homage to similar churches at Greece's monastic community of Mt Athos.

Alexandru Ioan Cuza University　UNIVERSITY
(☑0232-201 000; www.uaic.ro; B-dul Carol I 11; ☺9am-5pm Mon-Fri) **FREE** This is the impressive headquarters of Romania's first university, founded in 1860. The building dates from around the turn of the 20th century and the inauguration was overseen by King Carol I himself. One of the highlights of the interior is the Gheorghe Asachi Technical Library, a beautifully restored historic reading salon dating from the building's origins. Find it in the northern wing of the building.

Jewish Cemetery　CEMETERY
(Cimitiru Evreiesc; ☑0232-234 570; Aleea Cimitirul Evreiesc; ☺dawn-dusk; ☐43) Jewish victims of the fascist Iron Guard's pogroms are buried in four concrete bunkers at this cemetery on Mountain Hill (Dealul Munteni), 5km west of centre off Str Păcurari. Here stands a monument to the victims, as well as a (very small) synagogue. A taxi ride from the centre costs about 10 lei.

Union Museum　MUSEUM
(Muzeul Unirii; ☑0232-314 614; Str Alexandru Lăpuşneanu 14; adult/student 12/3 lei; ☺10am-5pm Tue-Sun) This impressive neoclassical palace was Alexandru Cuza's home for three years (1859–62) and later housed King Ferdinand during his WWI retreat from Bucha-

rest. It displays the Cuza family's opulent furniture, pictures and personal effects.

Church of the Three Hierarchs
CHURCH

(Biserica Sfinților Trei Ierarhi; B-dul Ştefan cel Mare şi Sfânt; ⊙ 9.30am-noon & 1-5.30pm) **FREE** Built by Prince Vasile Lupu between 1637 and 1639, and restored between 1882 and 1904, this is one of Iaşi's most beautiful churches. Its exterior stone pattern work is exquisite and reveals Turkish, Georgian and Armenian influences. It also contains the marble tombs of Prince Lupu and his family (to the left), plus those of Prince Alexandru Ioan Cuza (to the right) and Moldavian prince Dimitrie Cantemir.

In 1994 the church reopened as a monastery. The three saints are celebrated here on 30 January with an all-monk choir performance.

Mihai Eminescu Museum of Literature
MUSEUM

(☑ 0232-144 759; Copou Park; adult/child 10/3 lei; ⊙ 10am-5pm Tue-Sun) This museum documents the writings, life and loves of Eminescu (1850–89), Romania's favourite writer and poet. The great love of the married poet, Veronica Micle, was married also. They each outlived their spouses but never married due to Eminescu's deteriorating health. The busts of Micle and Eminescu face each other by his favourite linden tree on Junimea Alea.

Jewish Museum
MUSEUM

(Comunitatea Evreiasca din Iasi; ☑ 0742-515 290; Str Elena Doamna 15; 5 lei; ⊙ 10am-1pm Mon-Fri) Run by the city's ever-dwindling Jewish community, this tiny, hard-to-find museum is currently the only source of background information on Jewish history in Iaşi. The museum's custodian apparently doesn't feel bound by the opening hours, so it may very well be closed when you turn up. To find the museum, turn down tiny Str Benjamin Fondane. It's the first house on the right.

Copou Park
PARK

(Parcol Copou; B-dul Carol I; ⊙ dawn-dusk) Designed between 1834 and 1848 under Prince Mihail Sturza, this 10-hectare park is allegedly where poet Mihai Eminescu wrote beneath a linden tree. The tree still stands behind the 13m-high Obelisk of Lions (supposedly modern Romania's oldest monument), which is opposite the main entrance. A bronze bust of Eminescu sits in front.

🛏 Sleeping

Iaşi's accommodation is business-oriented and relatively expensive. Dedicated bargain hunters can find deals, however.

Iaşi Apartment
APARTMENT $

(☑ 0746-067 979; www.iasi-apartment.com; apt from 120 lei; ▣ @ 🛜) Run by a congenial local, these downtown apartments have kitchens, air-con, internet and cable TV. Compare apartments, if possible, as quality and location varies, but price differences are minimal.

★ Hotel Select
HOTEL $$

(☑ 0232-210 715; www.selectgrup.ro; Str 14 Decembrie 1989 2; s/d/ste 250/300/400 lei; ▣ ▣ 🛜) The Select hits all the sweet spots: excellent central location, clean, stylish room decor, gleaming baths and friendly staff. The setting is a renovated 19th-century mansion, and many period details – such as the grand stairway – have been retained. There's an elegant outdoor cafe and patisserie open to nonguests as well.

Hotel Eden
HOTEL $$

(☑ 0332-144 486; www.hotels-eden.ro; Str Sf Sava 1; s/d 160/170 lei; ▣ 🛜) An excellent three-star option, the Eden is central and has a good restaurant. The fresh-smelling rooms are spacious and some have balconies. Breakfast (20 lei) is not included in the room rate.

Grand Hotel Traian
HOTEL $$

(☑ 0232-266 666; www.grandhoteltraian.ro; Piaţa Unirii 1; s 220-240 lei; d 260-280 lei; ▣ ▣ ▣ 🛜) Right in the centre, the elegant Traian was designed by Gustave Eiffel himself. The rooms are appropriately outfitted with billowing curtains, high ceilings and big baths, and a general old-world ambience prevails. Rooms are divided into 'standard' and only slightly more expensive 'deluxe' classes. The latter are larger and come with balconies.

Hotel Majestic
HOTEL $$

(☑ 0232-255 557; www.hotel-majestic.ro; Str Petru Rareş 7; s/d from 175/220 lei; ▣ ▣ 🛜 ▣) This formerly humble central pension has been renovated and expanded, its sharp rooms decorated with ornate furniture, elegant curtains and wallpaper. The facilities include, rare for Iaşi, an indoor pool. Room rates are cut over the weekend and guests receive discounts at the in-house restaurant.

Hotel Unirea
HOTEL $$$

(☑ 232-205 000; www.hotelunirea.ro; Piaţa Unirii 5; s/d/ste 225/295/395 lei; P ❋ 🛜 ⊠) Although several contenders around the main square vie for the title of Iaşi's best hotel, an indoor pool, a spa centre and a 13th-floor panoramic restaurant (with expansive views) sets the high-rise Unirea apart. Rooms are bright and business style, with comfortable beds and all amenities.

Hampton by Hilton
BUSINESS HOTEL $$$

(☑ 0232-242 000; www.hamptoninn3.hilton.com; Str Anastasie Panu 26; s/d/ste 300/400/500 lei; P ⊖ ❋ 🛜) The international Hilton chain has completely revamped the former Hotel Europa and transformed it into one of the city's premier business hotels. The setting is a 15-storey high-rise, full of amenities the chain's mainly corporate customers demand. The location is the eastern end of Str Anastasie Panu (south of the centre, but an easy walk from the Palace of Culture).

Little Texas
HOTEL $$$

(☑ 0232-272 545; www.littletexas.ro; Str Moara de Vant 31; s/d from 250/275 lei; P ❋ 🛜) On the airport road (a 10-minute drive from the centre), this four-star Texan-run hotel is outfitted in Americana decor and has business-class amenities, plus a Tex-Mex restaurant. Free airport pickups are offered.

✖ Eating

As on many other matters, Iaşi takes its dining cues from its student population. The city excels in fast food and burgers and has an increasing number of good vegan and vegetarian options.

★ Cuib
VEGETARIAN $

(☑ 0747-485 053; Str Gavriil Musicescu 14; mains 15-25 lei; ⊙ 10am-11pm; 🛜 ✏) Slow food, raw food, vegan items; there is something for everyone at this student-run restaurant not far from the university quarter. Favourites include creamy vegetable soup or baked peppers stuffed with tofu. Dine in the leafy front garden in nice weather or browse through handmade notebooks and bags at the small gift shop inside.

Vivo Fusion
BURGERS $

(☑ 0332-417 727; www.vivofoodbar.com; Str Zimbrului 5; burgers 15-25 lei; ⊙ noon-11pm) Great burgers, fries and salads are dished up at this upscale burger bar just south of the Palace of Culture. The exposed-brick interior, the old bikes mounted on the wall, and the

generally laid-back attitude of the staff are all subtle clues you've entered a hipsterish enclave, but the price-for-value ratio works and for a light lunch, it's a perfect choice.

La Castel
INTERNATIONAL $$

(☑ 0749-225 220; www.lacastel.com; Aleea M Sadoveanu 54, Copou; mains 20-35 lei; ⊙ noon-11pm; ⏹) With spacious, breezy lawns, La Castel incorporates French and Bavarian flourishes, a long wine list and sinful desserts. Restless youngsters will be appeased by the playground, and there's live music most nights.

It's a 15-minute drive from town, or you can catch bus 6 (a 20-minute trip) from Piaţa Unirii or in front of Alexandru Ioan Cuza University in the Copou area.

Buena Vista
SOUTH AMERICAN $$

(☑ 0232-242 244; http://buena-vista.ro; Str Petru Movila 43; mains 20-40 lei; ⊙ noon-midnight) Buena Vista calls itself a Latin American restaurant, but there are enough Romanian staples, such as polenta, on the menu to attract a mainly local following. The specialities here are large cast-iron plates of grilled meats, mixed with potatoes, rice or cornmeal. There's outdoor seating on the upper terrace.

Trattoria Lavric
ITALIAN $$

(☑ 0232-229 960; Str Sf Atanasie 21; mains 20-40 lei; ⊙ 11am-11.30pm) For years Lavric was known as one of the most elegant Romanian restaurants in town. They've now switched to a Italian menu. The quality is still high and the setting of brick walls, tiled floors and white linens is both dressy and romantic. The location, in a renovated residence northeast of the centre, can be hard to find.

🍷 Drinking & Nightlife

Having failed as a commercial centre, the concrete expanse known as the 'Cub' (or Cube) at B-dul Ştefan cel Mare şi Sfânt 8 hosts several subterranean student bars. Look for the giant cube tipped on its side out front by the street, find the stairs and walk down to the lower level.

★ Cafeneaua Acaju
BAR

(☑ 0727-255 514; www.facebook.com/Acaju-Cafenea; Str Sf Sava 15; ⊙ 10am-1am) Easy to miss and hard to forget, this hip, unpretentious bar is barely signposted near the corner of Str Armeană. Its regulars include local artists, musicians and others of all ages. A small bar-top box reading 'nice things for nice people' purveys inexpensive handmade jewellery. Come for coffee by day.

Jassyro
CAFE

(☑ 0747-771 771; www.jassyro.ro; B-dul Ştefan cel Mare şi Sfânt 1c; ☻ 7.30am-2pm & 4pm-7.30pm Mon-Fri, 9am-5pm Sat & Sun) Why settle for your hotel's undrinkable breakfast coffee when this high-quality, next-gen roaster is waiting with vacuum presses, French presses, special filter blends and plain old espresso. There's a couple of tiny seats on the steps outside; otherwise take it to go and find a cosy bench nearby.

Terasa Corso
PUB

(☑ 0728-920 092; www.corsoterasa.ro; Str Alexandru Lăpuşneanu 11; ☻ 9am-2am; 🐾) Hedges and gardens adorn the centre of this expansive, amphitheatre-shaped pub with overlapping rows of long tables. It's good for coffee by day and drinks by night, and serves tasty pastas, pizzas and other fare (mains 15 to 30 lei).

Radio Ga Ga English Pub
PUB

(☑ 0232-274 037; www.facebook.com/radiogaga englishpub; Str Alexandru Lăpuşneanu 7; ☻ noon-midnight) Popular student watering hole, serving Guinness on tap as well as a wide range of decent cocktails, coffee and wine. Sit on the pavement terrace and watch the crowds saunter down pedestrianised Str Lăpuşneanu.

La Bază
CLUB

(☑ 0332-408 146; B-dul Ştefan cel Mare şi Sfânt 8, Cub; ☻ 4pm-2am) This festive indie fave down in the Cub complex has outlandish green walls and surrealist versions of Romanian monastic murals. The beer is cheap and the crowd is young; there's sometimes live music and film screenings.

☆ Entertainment

Filarmonica
CLASSICAL MUSIC

(☑ tickets 0332-882 025; www.filarmonicais.ro; Str Cuza Vodă 29; tickets 20 lei; ☻ box office 10am-1pm & 5-7pm Mon-Fri) The Iaşi State Philharmonic Orchestra's home hall is excellent for classical music; there's a 50% student discount.

Underground The Pub
CLUB

(☑ 0735-004 001; B-dul Ştefan cel Mare şi Sfânt 8, Cub; DJ nights 15 lei; ☻ 9pm-6am) Slightly posher than its neighbouring bars in the Cub complex, Underground specialises in mainly DJ dance parties. To find it, walk downstairs from the Agenţia de Opera ticket office.

Vasile Alecsandri National Theatre
THEATRE

(☑ 0232-267 763; www.teatrulnationaliasi.ro; Str Agatha Bârsescu 18) The National Theatre performs an impressive mix of high-brow and experimental plays, mainly in Romanian language. The theatre is located in the same impressive neobaroque building as the Romanian National Opera. Tickets start at around 30 lei, with 50% student discounts.

The building dates from the 1890s and is the work of the renowned, at the time, Viennese architects Fellner and Helmer.

Romanian National Opera
OPERA

(Opera Naţională Română Iaşi; ☑ tickets 0332-888 448; www.operaiasi.ro; Str Agatha Bârsescu 18; ☻ box office 10am-5pm Mon-Fri, to 1pm Sat) The Romanian National Opera of Iaşi occupies the same impressive neobaroque building as

MOLDAVIA & THE BUCOVINA MONASTERIES | IAŞI

WORTH A TRIP

TASTING THE WHITES OF COTNARI

The vineyards at Cotnari (☑ 0740-234 040, tours 0741-117 751; www.cotnari.ro; tours per person without/with food €10/55), 54km northwest of Iaşi, are among the most fabled in Romania, and the sweet whites made here are exported worldwide.

The town got its start in 1491, when Ştefan cel Mare built a small church, followed by a Latin college in 1562. But it was incoming French monks who transformed Cotnari into a wine power. By the late 19th century, Cotnari wine was prominent at international exhibitions. King Michael I's half complete royal palace from 1947 (restored in 1966) today houses the winery offices.

Popular varietals include white table wines such as *frâncuşa* (dry) and *cătălina* (semi-sweet), and the sweet, golden *grasă* and *tămâioasă* dessert wines.

The winery offers a menu of tours and tastings, some paired with food. Tours without food normally start at 10am on Monday, Wednesday and Friday and don't require prebooking. Tours with food require a 10-person minimum and prior appointment.

Cotnari makes for a fairly easy day trip from Iaşi. Hârlău-bound buses make the trip in a little more than an hour.

the Vasile Alecsandri National Theatre. The annual repertoire includes all of the Viennese, German, French and Italian classics. The website has an up-to-date schedule in English; buy tickets at the theatre box office or at the Agenţia de Opera (☑0232-255 999; B-dul Ştefan cel Mare şi Sfânt 8; ⊙10am-5pm Mon-Sat). Performances normally start at 6.30pm.

Gate   LIVE MUSIC
(www.facebook.com/thegatebar.iasi; B-dul Ştefan cel Mare şi Sfânt 8, Cub; ⊙noon-1am) Metalheads unite! This dingy, compact bar specialises in speed metal, death metal and all varieties of morose head-pounding music, including regular live concerts. It's located below ground in the Cub complex. To find it, walk downstairs from the Agenţia de Opera ticket office.

Shopping

Palas Mall   SHOPPING CENTRE
(☑0232-209 920; www.palasiasi.ro; Str Palas 7a; ⊙8am-9pm) If Moldavia is truly impoverished, you'd never know it from this sleek hybrid of airport duty-free shops and American-style megamall.

Anticariat Grumazescu   ANTIQUES
(☑0232-225 566; www.facebook.com/Anticariat Grumazescu; Str Alexandru Lăpuşneanu 24; ⊙10am-5.30pm Mon-Fri) This long-standing local antiques shop sells everything from folk heirlooms and jewellery to rare, expensive icons. It can provide authorised sale certificates for anything that might excite border-point customs agents.

ℹ Information

Forte Cafe (B-dul Independenţei 27; per hr 3 lei; ⊙24hr) Down a passage off the footpath.

Post Office (Str Cuza Vodă 10; ⊙9am-6pm Mon-Fri, to 1pm Sat)

Sfântu Spiridon University Hospital (☑0232-240 822, ext 193; www.spitalspiridon.ro; B-dul Independenţei 1) Iaşi's largest hospital.

Tourist Information Centre (☑0232-261 990; www.turism-iasi.ro; Piaţa Unirii 12; ⊙8am-4pm Mon-Fri) Helpful staff provide city maps and activity brochures.

ℹ Getting There & Away

Iaşi, the biggest city in the east of the country, is a major transport hub, with good air, rail and bus connections to the rest of the country.

AIR

Iaşi Airport (Aeroportul Internaţional Iaşi, IAS; ☑0232-271 590; www.aeroport.ro; Str Moara de Vant 34) is 5km east of the centre. Both Tarom and Blue Air (www.blueairweb.com) fly to Bucharest as well as to Cluj-Napoca and Timişoara. There are also flights to various European destinations, including London (Luton).

BUS

The **Autogara Transbus Codreanu** (Autogara Vama Veche; ☑0232-250 985; www.transbus codreanu.ro; Str Gării 22), across the street from the main train station, is Iaşi's most useful and convenient bus and minibus station. Buses and minibuses regularly depart from here for towns and cities around the country, as well as for Chişinău in neighbouring Moldova. There's a timetable posted at the station entrance. Buy tickets from the driver.

A second smaller station, **Bus Station 'Real Fresh'** (Autogara Real Fresh; ☑0232-240 000; www.autogari.ro; Str Moara de Foc 15a), is located about 1km north of the main train station. It serves mainly smaller regional destinations, though it's also used by a handful of long-haul coaches to Western Europe.

TRAIN

Nearly all domestic and international trains use the **Central Train Station** (Gara Centrală; ☑reservations 0232-202 777; www.cfrcalatori. ro; Piaţa Gării 2; 🚇2). The central **Agenţia de Voiaj CFR** (www.cfrcalatori.ro; Piaţa Unirii 10; ⊙7.30am-8.30pm Mon-Fri) sells advance tickets. A 24-hour left-luggage office is by the car park.

BUSES FROM IAŞI

DESTINATION	COST (LEI)	DURATION (HR)	FREQUENCY (DAILY)
Bucharest	80	7	6
Chişinău	25	5	9
Cluj-Napoca	90	9	4
Piatra Neamţ	30	3	13
Suceava	30	2	12
Târgu Neamţ	20	2	8

TRAINS FROM IAŞI

DESTINATION	COST (LEI)	DURATION (HR)	FREQUENCY (DAILY)
Braşov	92	8½	1
Bucharest	92	7	3-4 direct
Chişinău	40	2	1
Cluj-Napoca	92	9	1
Suceava	22-40	2½	several daily
Târgu Neamţ, change at Paşcani	26	2½	several daily
Timişoara, via Oradea	121	16	2

Târgu Neamţ & Around

POP 18,695

Târgu Neamţ (literally 'German Market') is a quiet market town which wouldn't figure on most travellers' itineraries if it wasn't for its proximity to the Neamţ county monasteries. The half-dozen or so major monasteries in the surrounding area lack the colour of Bucovina's painted monasteries, but they certainly have historic cred and, more importantly, they're still very much working monasteries. This lends a feeling of living spirituality that sometimes gets drowned out by the tour buses pulling into the painted monasteries to the north. Târgu Neamţ's own claim to fame is the Neamţ Citadel, a 14th-century stronghold that repelled invaders for nearly 300 years.

◎ Sights

Neamţ Citadel is the only major sight within the town limits of Târgu Neamţ. The monasteries are located in a cluster 10km to 15km southwest of town.

Neamţ Citadel
FORTRESS

(Cetatea Neamţului; ☑ 0744-702 415; Târgu Neamţ; adult/child 5/2 lei, photography 10 lei; ☉ 10am-6pm Tue-Sun) Medieval Neamţ Citadel had already long been considered Moldavia's finest fortress before recent renovations improved it again. It was built in 1359 by Prince Petru I Muşat, who picked an impregnable location. The castle successfully resisted attacks by Hungarians in 1395 and by Turks in 1476, and was only conquered by Polish forces in 1691. The citadel is 2km west of the centre, following the main road B-dul Ştefan cel Mare. It's a 15-minute scramble to the top.

Agapia Monastery
MONASTERY

(Mănăstirea Agapia; ☑ 0233-244 736; Agapia; museum adult/child 5/3 lei; ☉ 9am-7pm May-Sep, to 4pm Oct-Apr) Agapia Monastery is an active nunnery, housing 300 to 400 nuns in two locations. The main monastery, Agapia din Vale, stands at the western end of Agapia village. It was built in 1644 by Gavril Coci (Vasile Lupu's brother). It has relaxing gardens and an impressive facade, but most come to see the interior frescoes painted from 1858-61 by Romanian master Nicolae Grigorescu. A second, smaller monastery, Agapia din Deal (sometimes called Agapia Veche), is 1.6km up a steep road.

The main monastery also has a small museum, which exhibits 16th- and 17th-century icons, and a shop where you can buy icons and other religious articles. To find the monastery from Târgu Neamţ, head south along the main road to Piatra Neamţ, bearing right at the sign to Agapia village. The monastery is 7km further at the end of the road.

Sihla Monastery
MONASTERY

(Schitu Sihla; ☉ 9am-7pm May-Sep, to 4pm Oct-Apr) FREE Placid Sihla Monastery, inhabited by 30 monks, occupies a solitary wooded plateau about 8km southwest of Agapia Monastery along a marked, partly paved forest road. The remote location keeps the number of visitors to a trickle. Here you may observe *pustnici* (hermit monks), who regularly kneel in prayer, sometimes remaining so for hours. Nearby the venerated Cave of Pious St Teodora was where the eponymous nun lived for 60 years, sleeping on a rock slab. The hermitage is candlelit.

Sihla is accessible by car from Agapia Monastery along the forest road. Alternatively, the 8km hike following the road takes around an hour and is largely uphill.

Văratec Monastery
MONASTERY

(Mănăstirea Văratec; Văratec; ☉ 9am-7pm May-Sep, to 4pm Oct-Apr) FREE Văratec Monastery is the country's biggest nunnery, inhabited by some 400 to 500 nuns. Founded in 1785, the complex houses an icon museum and small embroidery school. The main church, whitewashed in 1841, incorporates neoclassical elements and grounds featuring a small botanic garden. The lavishly decorated interior has numerous frescoes. The monastery is 7km south of Agapia along a main road.

Neamț Monastery   MONASTERY
(Vânători-Neamț; ☉ 9am-7pm May-Sep, to 4pm Oct-Apr) FREE The 14th-century Neamț Monastery is Romania's oldest and largest male monastery. Founded by Petru I Mușat, it doubled as a protective citadel. Ștefan cel Mare built today's large church in the 15th century, though some of the paintings date from Mușat's time. The fortified compound houses a medieval art museum and a house museum dedicated to novelist Mihail Sadoveanu (1880–1961). The library, with 18,000 rare books, is the largest of any Romanian monastery.

🛏 Sleeping & Eating

Târgu Neamț has a handful of hotels and *pensiunes*. The village of Agapia, near the monastery of the same name, is loaded with decent *pensiunes*.

Aristocratis   PENSION $$
(☎ 0233-791 986; www.aristocratis.ro; B-dul Ștefan cel Mare 245, Târgu Neamț; s/d 220/250 lei; P ❖ ✳ @ ⊛ ✿) This snazzy four-star *pensiune* (priced to match) offers spotless rooms, an excellent Italian restaurant (open to nonguests), a beautiful rural setting and an open-air swimming pool. There's also a playground for kids.

It's 4km east of the centre of Târgu Neamț, following B-dul Ștefan cel Mare.

Doina   HOTEL $$
(☎ 0233-790 270; www.hotel-doina.ro; Str Mihail Kogălniceanu 6-8, Târgu Neamț; s/d 130/170 lei; P ⊖ ✳ ⊛) The Doina is a tastefully renovated modern hotel in the centre of Târgu Neamț that represents excellent value for money, given the clean rooms and location. There's a decent in-house restaurant.

★ Eden   PENSION $$$
(☎ 0728-821 013; www.edentur.ro; Hwy DN15C, Agapia; s/d 200/240 lei; P ⊖ @ ⊛) Family-owned Eden, in an updated farmhouse setting, boasts the nicest rooms in the general area of the Neamț monasteries. There's an excellent restaurant here (open to nonguests) and plenty of pretty gardens to stroll or to let the kids play in.

The pension is situated outside Agapia village, 5km south of Târgu Neamț on the main highway to Piatra Neamț.

Venezia   ITALIAN $$
(☎ 0757-512 259; Str Serafim Lungu, Târgu Neamț; mains 20-30 lei; ☉ 9am-11pm; P ⊛) This pizzeria and grill house is the best of a meagre range of options in Târgu Neamț. That said, the pizzas are excellent and the grilled pork and chicken offerings are spiced up with homemade tomato sauce. There's a covered terrace in nice weather. Find it down the side street that leads south from the Tourist Information Centre.

❶ Information

Tourist Information Centre (☎ 0233-790 154; B-dul Ștefan cel Mare 60, Târgu Neamț; ☉ 8am-4pm Mon-Fri) Every town should be so lucky to have such a helpful and efficient tourist information office. Cheerful English-speaking staff are happy to advise on monastery visits and figuring out travel logistics. The free town map includes coverage of the Neamț county monasteries. The office is located along the main boulevard, near the centre of town.

❶ Getting There & Away

At least four daily buses go to Suceava (20 lei, two hours) and several maxitaxis run to Iași (13 lei, two hours). Hourly buses run to Piatra Neamț (10 lei, one hour). Check the website www.autogari.ro for an up-to-date timetable.

❶ Getting Around

Getting around to all of the monasteries from Târgu Neamț on public transport is possible, though schedules don't allow for seeing them all in one day – it's much easier and more efficient to drive or take an organised tour.

Several buses make the 15km journey from the centre of Târgu Neamț to Neamț Monastery and from Târgu Neamț to Agapia Monastery. You can hike to Văratec from Agapia (two hours) and on to Sihăstria Monastery along clearly marked trails. There are maxitaxis to Văratec from Târgu Neamț (10 daily).

Piatra Neamț

POP 104,605

Up-and-coming, easy-going Piatra Neamț (literally 'German Rock') sprawls in three directions across a valley, gripped by forested mountains. Moldavia's third-biggest town was home to Ștefan cel Mare's 15th-century Princely Court and has a smattering of de-

Piatra Neamţ

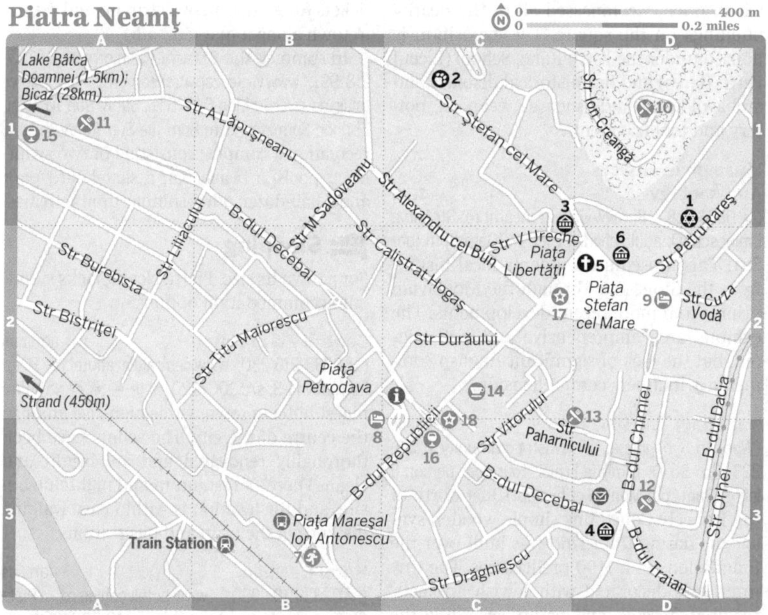

Map markers:
- 2 Cozla Zoological Park
- 10 Cercul Gospodinelor
- Str Ştefan cel Mare
- 3 Cucuteni Museum
- 6 Princely Court Exposition
- 1 Bal Shem Tov Synagogue
- 5 Nativity of St John the Baptist Church
- Piaţa Ştefan cel Mare
- 9 Hotel Ceahlău
- 17 Tineretului Theatre
- 14 Casablanca
- Piaţa Petrodava
- 8 Central Plaza Hotel
- 18 Tonique Club
- 16 Temple Pub
- 13 Times
- 12 Noir
- 4 Museum of History and Archaeology
- 7 Telegondola
- Train Station
- Piaţa Mareşal Ion Antonescu

Piatra Neamţ

cent museums and cultural offerings, including a couple of the region's best restaurants. It's also a decent base for forays into the nearby Bicaz Gorges and Ceahlău Massif. ATMs, groceries and pharmacies line Piaţa Ştefan cel Mare and central B-dul Decebal.

◉ Sights

Cucuteni Museum   MUSEUM
(Muzeul Cucuteni; ☎0233-226 471; www.viziteazaneamt.ro; Str Ştefan cel Mare 3; adult/child 4/2 lei; ⊙10am-6pm Tue-Sun) This is by far the city's best museum, with three floors of well-done displays on the Cucutenians, a neolithic culture with advanced pottery skills that lived in the area from around 6000 BC to 3000 BC. The ground floor is given over to the stunning symmetry of Cucutenian vases and vessels, while the upper floors feature the frank sexuality of Cucutenian sculpture.

Princely Court Exposition   HISTORIC BUILDING
(Expozitia Curtea Domnească; ☎0233-217 496; www.viziteazaneamt.ro; Str Ştefan cel Mare 4; adult/child 4/2 lei; ⊙10am-6pm Tue-Sun) This exposition features the dank ruins of Ştefan cel Mare's 1497 Princely Court complex,

which once encompassed all of the nearby buildings on the square. The exposition is housed under the Petru Rareș School (Liceul Petru Rareș) and has historical displays and archaeological finds such as weapons, pottery and tool fragments.

Museum of History and Archaeology MUSEUM

(☑ 0233-218 108; www.viziteazaneamt.ro; Str Mihai Eminescu 10; adult/child 4/2 lei; ☉ 10am-6pm Tue-Sun) This museum documents local history from the Stone Age through the Moldavian princes and more recent developments. The exhibits are comprehensive and well laid-out, but the lack of significant English commentary hampers comprehension.

Bal Shem Tov Synagogue SYNAGOGUE

(Wooden Synagogue; ☑ Jewish community 0233-223 815; Str Dr Dimitrie Ernici; tours per person 5 lei; ☉ 8am-1pm Mon-Fri or by appt) Just north of the Princely Court, this simple wooden synagogue dating from 1766 was built over the foundations of a 1490 predecessor. The tiny interior is decorated with Jewish artefacts, restored frescoes and paintings. While the synagogue keeps nominal opening hours, it's often closed. The best bet is to call ahead to make sure it's open.

Nativity of St John the Baptist Church CHURCH

(Biserica Domneasca; Piața Libertății 2; tower adult/child 5/2 lei, church free; ☉ church 8am-7pm, tower 10am-6pm Tue-Sun) St John Church dates from 1498 and was originally part of Ștefan cel Mare's Princely Court complex. It has a lovely but sombre interior. Standing in front of the church is a free-standing, 19m-high tower that served both as a bell tower and watchtower. You can climb up for views out over the town.

Cozla Zoological Park ZOO

(Parcul Zoologic Cozla; www.viziteazaneamt.ro; Piața Ștefan cel Mare; adult/child 4/2 lei; ☉ 8am-8pm) Northwest of the centre along Str Ștefan cel Mare, this petting zoo is situated on successive terraces running up Mt Cozla.

🏃 Activities

A year-round telegondola (Cabin lift; ☑ 0724-538 928; www.cozlaparc.ro; adult/child return 20/12 lei; ☉ 10am-8pm Mon-Thu, to 8.30pm Fri-Sun) runs regularly throughout the day from a base near the main train station high up to the foot of Mt Cozla (639m). The eight-passenger gondolas make the nearly 2km run in about 10 minutes. Buy round-trip

tickets (or go for one-way trip up and return to town along a marked path).

In summer, the Strand (☑ information 0233-218 991; www.viziteazapiatraneamt.ro; Alee Tineretului; adult/child Mon-Fri 7/5 lei, Sat & Sun 10/5 lei; ☉ noon-8pm Mon, 8am-8pm Tue-Sun Jun-Aug) is a recreational complex consisting of two swimming pools, a beach bar, a skateboard park and a half-dozen other summertime activities.

🛏 Sleeping

For a town its size, Piatra Neamț lacks standout accommodation options.

Central Plaza Hotel HOTEL $$

(☑ 0233-216 230; www.centralplazahotel.ro; Piața Petrodava 1-3; s/d 200/220 lei; P ❄ ✳ @ 🛜) The nicest hotel in town is this high-rise affair in the centre of the city. The rooms have been thoroughly renovated and are bright and clean. There's a restaurant and nightclub on-site, and the location is within easy walking distance of the train and bus stations.

Hotel Ceahlău HOTEL $$

(☑ 0233-219 990; www.hotelceahlau.ro; Piața Ștefan cel Mare 3; s/d/ste 140/190/260 lei; ❄ ✳ @ 🛜) This big, old three-star hotel has rooms that are slightly old-fashioned but perfectly fine, and some have balconies with excellent views. The restaurant chefs are kind to breakfast slackers and the menu is reasonably priced.

🍴 Eating

Times ROMANIAN $$

(☑ 0333-401 489; www.facebook.com/TheTimes Restaurant; Str Paharnicului 3; mains 20-35 lei; ☉ 10am-11pm; 🛜) The setting couldn't be prettier: a restored 19th-century mansion in a green area a block north of the main artery B-dul Decebal. The menu runs the gamut from meats and seafood to cheaper (but excellent) pastas, and the desserts and pastries are some of the best in town. There's a big garden and terrace for dining out in nice weather.

Cercul Gospodinelor ROMANIAN $$

(☑ 0233-223 845; Str Ion Creangă; mains 15-30 lei; ☉ 10am-midnight) Located at the top of the road to Cozla Park, this is a good pick for traditional Romanian cuisine, with gorgeous views and nightly live music in summer. Watch for wedding and private parties, though, which can bring service to a crawl.

Laguna PIZZA $$

(☑ 0233-232 121; www.restaurantlaguna.ro; B-dul Decebal 80; mains 15-30 lei; ☉ 10am-11pm; 🛜)

This long-time favourite is known for very good pizza, but the cooks here also turn out good grilled meats, soups and salads. After 9pm or so it devolves into a drinking den, and there are a couple of billiard tables on hand to help you work off the beer.

★ **Noir**   INTERNATIONAL **$$$**
(📞 0233-211 886; www.restaurantnoir.ro; Piaţa Mihail Kogalniceanu; mains 25-50 lei; ⊗ noon-11pm; 🎧) Intelligent and well-thought-out menu combinations, such as grilled pork tenderloin served with baked apple or glazed pork ribs paired with diced potato and coleslaw, feature at Noir. The interior is done out in modern minimalism; the wine list is long and very good. The only drawback might be inattentive service, but with food this good, it's worth the wait.

🍸 **Drinking & Nightlife**

The centre is filled with some old-school coffee bars, where the main attractions are ice cream and homemade cakes. While there's no major university in town, city residents do their best to maintain a lively drinking and clubbing vibe.

Casablanca   CAFE
(📞 0233-213 214; www.cafecasablanca.ro; B-dul Republicii 7; ⊗ 8am-midnight; 🎧) An elegant continental-style cafe, Casablanca has subdued decor with striped wallpaper and matching ornate chairs. Young lawyers, visiting television personalities and other socialites come for the good coffee, wine and beer.

Chaplin's Pub   PUB
(📞 0749-061 414; www.facebook.com/chaplinspub piatraneamt; Str Luceafarugui 22; ⊗ 9am-late; 🎧) This popular pub consists of lots of weathered wood, historic photos, and small enclosed bars and tables with candles adding a touch of intimacy. It's very popular on Saturdays, when live bands perform.

Temple Pub   PUB
(📞 0233-215 215; B-dul Republicii 15; ⊗ 7am-late; 🎧) This big eclectic bar at the B-dul Decebal intersection combines Greek fast food and decent grills with Irish (and other) beer.

MOLDAVIA & THE BUCOVINA MONASTERIES PIATRA NEAMŢ

WORTH A TRIP

WINDING YOUR WAY THROUGH BICAZ GORGES

National highway 12C weaves precariously through the dramatic **Bicaz Gorges** (Cheile Bicazului), 20km west of Bicaz. It's a spectacular ride as the road cuts through sheer 300m-high limestone cliffs along which pine trees improbably cling.

Along the roadside, artisans hawk their crafts (some original, some mass-produced) from stalls beneath the rocks, at the points where it's wide enough for parking. The Bicaz Gorges belong to the **Hăşmaş-Bicaz Gorges National Park** (Parcul Naţional Hăşmaş-Cheile Bicazului).

A few kilometres west begins Transylvania's Harghita County and **Lacu Roşu** (Red Lake), a pretty lake where you can get a bite and rent a **boat** (Barcă; Hwy 12C, Lacu Roşu; boat rental per 30 min from 20 lei; ⊗ 10am-6.30pm May-Oct) or hike around. The road continues on for another 20km to Gheorgheni via the similarly scenic Bucin pass. Note the season runs from May to October and things pretty much shut down in winter.

Lacu Roşu, in fairness, is more a large pond than a real lake. The murky waters here have no healing powers, but do conceal dead tree stumps that jut from the surface at odd angles. One cheerful legend attests that a picknicking group crushed by a fallen mountainside oozed their blood into the site where the lake amassed. (An 1838 landslide did in fact occur, eventually flooding the valley and damming the Bicaz River).

Though it feels (and is) remote, there are a couple of decent overnight options. **Hotel Lacu Roşu** (📞 0374-473 728; www.hotellacurosu.ro; Hwy 12C, Str Principala 32; s/d 100/150 lei; 🅿🌐❄🎧) offers big bouncy beds with mirrored headboards. The best attraction is the excellent restaurant. **Hotel Turist** (📞 0266-380 042; www.lacurosu.hostvision.ro; Hwy 12C, Str Lacu Roşu 1; s/d 100/150 lei; 🅿🌐❄🎧🏊) has comfortable rooms with spacious bathrooms.

Numerous buses and minibuses ply the stretch from Bicaz to Gheorgheni (13 lei, 1½ hours) through the day, passing through the gorges and stopping (on request) at Lacu Roşu. If you're trying to catch a bus out of Lacu Roşu, hail down passing buses on the main road, near the lakefront. Buy your ticket from the driver.

There are plenty of outdoor tables and it's a popular weekend nightspot.

☆ Entertainment

Tineretului Theatre THEATRE
(☑ tickets 233-211 036; www.teatrultineretuluint.ro; Piaţa Ştefan cel Mare 1; tickets 20 lei; ⊙ box office 11am-noon Tue-Fri, 4-7pm Tue-Sun) Though the name means 'Youth Theatre', this is an active and well-respected dramatic theatre, with performances appealing to audiences of all ages. Productions are normally staged in Romanian. Consult the website for an up-to-date schedule.

Tonique Club CLUB
(☑ 0233-213 388; www.facebook.com/toniqueclub; B-dul Republicii 18; ⊙ 24hr) There's something obscure, bordering on the mysterious, about this dark underground bar that works 24 hours a day. It has a few gambling video machines in the corner, and is frequented by muscular men singing traditional Romanian drinking songs, though weekend 'club nights' are more lively.

ℹ Information

Post Office (B-dul Decebal 2; ⊙ 8am-7pm Mon-Fri, 9am-1pm Sat)
Tourist Information Centre (☑ 0233-271 591; www.cniptpiatraneamt.ro; Piaţa Petrodava 1; ⊙ 10am-5pm Mon-Fri) Very helpful tourist information office situated in a kiosk in front of the Central Plaza Hotel. They hand out free city maps and can advise on sightseeing in the city and further afield in the area around Bicaz and the Ceahlău Massif.

ℹ Getting There & Away

BUS

The **bus station** (☑ 0233-211 210; www.autogari.ro; Str Bistriţei 1), near the train station, has 11 buses and maxitaxis to Târgu Neamţ (10 lei, one hour) for connecting services to Agapia. Buses also run to Gura Humorului (25 lei, three daily). Other popular bus routes include Suceava (35 lei, two hours, four daily), Iaşi (32 lei, 2½ hours, six daily), Braşov (45 lei, six hours, one or two daily) and Bicaz (6 lei, 30 minutes, several daily).

TRAIN

The **Agenţia de Voiaj CFR** (☑ 0233-211 034; Piaţa Ştefan cel Mare 10; ⊙ 9.30am-5pm Mon-Fri) sells train tickets. Trains to Bucharest (73 lei, seven to eight hours, several daily), Suceava (47 lei, four hours, several daily) and Iaşi (47 lei, four hours, several daily) all usually require a change in Bacău. Around five daily trains serve Bicaz (5 lei, 45 minutes).

Ceahlău National Park

The Ceahlău National Park, including the 1907m high Ceahlău Massif, Moldavia's most impressive peak, spreads out for some 77 sq km and offers great hiking and stunning mountain views. The range is part of the Eastern Carpathians and climbs dramatically to the west of the sprawling artificial Lake Bicaz (Lacu Izvorul Muntelui). An early-morning photo from the peaks out over the misting lake in the distance is the stuff of Instagram legend. Access the park via hiking trails that fan out from bases in Izvorul Muntelui, near Bicaz on the southeastern side, or from Durău in the north.

🏃 Activities

Seven signposted walks of varying difficulty fan out toward the peaks from various access points around the park. The Bicaz Tourist Information Centre website has descriptions of each in English. Note that trails covering the highest elevations are generally closed from October to April and there's a nominal fee (adult 5 lei, child 2 lei) to enter the park. Contact Salvamont (☑ 0734-889 133, 0-SALVAMONT, 0244-311 922) mountain rescue if you run into problems on the trails.

The quickest route to the top begins near the village of Izvorul Muntelui. A blue-striped path brings you to near the top, near Cabana Dochia, in about four hours (change in elevation: 950m). Alternatively, a red-striped path covers the same elevation change in about seven hours. The two trails allow for unique hikes during ascent and descent.

From Durău (elevation 850m), on the mountain's northwestern side, a steep track (red stripe, one hour) leads to Cabana Fântânele at 1220m. From there, the red stripe trail carries on to Cabana Dochia near the peak, or use a connecting path to reach a second trail, marked by a red cross. The cumulative difference in elevation from Durău is nearly 1000m.

🎪 Festivals & Events

Ceahlău Mountain Festival MUSIC
(www.ceahlaupark.ro; ⊙ Aug) The annual mountain festival of folk music and dance takes place over a long weekend in early August at Durău.

Ceahlău Massif

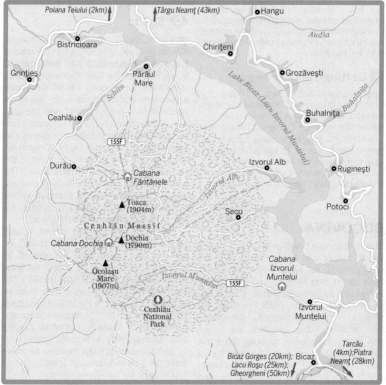

🛏 Sleeping & Eating

Cabana Izvorul Muntelui   LODGE **$**
(☎0233-234 269, 0728-325 559; www.bicaz-turism. ro; Izvorul Muntelui; r from 70 lei) This mountain chalet (797m) is situated at the foot of the eastern side of Ceahlău. Offers accommodation in private doubles as well as four-person bungalows (from 110 lei). Reserve in advance.

Cabana Fântânele   LODGE **$**
(☎0744-186 360; Durău; dm from 30 lei, s 60 lei) Handy mountain chalet on the northern side of the Ceahlău Massif at an altitude of 1220m. It's reachable by trail from Durău and offers 80 beds, including multibunk dorms and private singles. Book in advance by phone.

Pensiune Igor   GUESTHOUSE **$**
(☎0233-256 503; Str Principala 268, Durău; r 85-110 lei) This *pensiune* has five double rooms with shared bathroom. Breakfast is not provided, but there's a self-catering kitchen.

Pensiuna Paulo   GUESTHOUSE **$**
(☎0722-769 400; www.pensiunea-paulo.ro; Str Principala 266, Durău; d with/without bathroom 100/75 lei) Simple, clean rooms, some en-suite, are available at this old Durău standby.

Cabana Dochia   LODGE **$**
(☎reservations 0730-603 801; www.cabana-dochia. ro; dm 40-60 lei) At 1750m, Cabana Dochia is a godsend for hikers hoping to break up the climb to the top of the Ceahlău Massif. The cabana, near the peak, offers dorm accommodation in four- to 19-bunk rooms and cold showers. There's also a passable restaurant on-site. Book in advance by phone.

ℹ Information

Bicaz Tourist Information Centre (☎0233-254 028; www.bicaz-turism.ro; Str Barajului 4, Bicaz; ☉9am-5pm Mon-Fri) Good source of information on Bicaz and the Ceahlău Massif. Provides free maps and can help work out hikes and accommodation options.

Ceahlău National Park Visitor Centre
(☑ 0233-256 600; www.ceahlaupark.ro; Hwy 155F, Izvorul Muntelui; ☺ 9am-5pm Tue-Sun) Information on hikes and accommodation options in the Ceahlău National Park. The office is located on Hwy 155F, just outside of the village of Izvorul Muntelui.

❶ Getting There & Away

Three daily trains connect Bicaz and Piatra Neamţ (5 lei, 30 minutes). In addition, numerous buses and maxitaxis (6 lei, 30 minutes) run between the two towns throughout the day.

From Bicaz heading north, public transport options start to thin out, though you might find a bus for the onward journey to Izvorul Muntelui (otherwise it's a 4km hike). Reach Durău by car following hilly Hwy 155F from Izvorul Muntelui.

BUCOVINA

Bucolic Bucovina is dotted with slant-roofed village houses and lovely groves of beech trees (indeed, the name 'Bucovina' derives from the ancient German and Slavic roots for beech). As in neighbouring Maramureş, across the mountains, you'll encounter old women in colourful traditional dress, fearless children riding bareback on horses, and enterprising locals scouring the forest for some truly massive mushrooms. It's an ornery place, and both public transport and foreign languages can be lacking, but Bucovina is nevertheless highly worthwhile for hill walks, cycling, rural idylls and, of course, taking in those unforgettably colourful monasteries.

Suceava

POP 92,121

Judging by its small centre, Suceava would hardly seem Moldavia's second-biggest town; however, it has sufficient urban sprawl to ensure runner-up status. While Suceava can't compete with Iaşi in things cultural or learned, it does make an incredibly useful and affordable base for visiting fortresses and the Bucovina monasteries, with myriad worthwhile tours offered. Suceava also has good eats and rudimentary nightlife.

As Moldavia's capital from 1388 to 1565, Suceava thrived commercially on the Lviv–Istanbul trading route. It boasted approximately 40 churches when Ştefan cel Mare's reign concluded in 1504. However, stagna-

tion followed a 1675 Turkish invasion. A century later, Austria-Hungary took over.

◉ Sights

★ **Royal Citadel** FORTRESS
(Cetatea de Scaun; ☑ 0230-216 439; www.muzeul bucovinei.ro; adult/child 10/3 lei, photography 10 lei; ☺ 10am-7pm Tue-Sun) Suceava's rugged, abandoned 14th-century citadel has gotten a high-tech makeover, allowing visitors to scramble over the rocks and into the various chambers and learn the structure's history through clever video presentations and hands-on touchscreen exhibits. It's great for kids, the only downside being most of the text and video is only in Romanian. The unconquerable fortress withstood multiple attacks, including one by Ottoman Sultan Mehmed II in 1475, just 22 years after his conquest of Constantinople (Istanbul).

The original fortress was dubbed 'Muşat's Fortress' (after founder Petru II Muşat). Its eight square towers were surrounded by trenches. Ştefan cel Mare added 4m-thick, 33m-high walls, foiling archers outside. The exasperated Ottomans finally blew it up in 1675; a century later, home builders were still pillaging the ruins. The fortress is located 3km east of the centre by road (about 12 lei by taxi). Alternatively, hike from the centre (1km) by finding a marked footpath across the street from the Union Apartment (p202), next to McDonald's. It's 250 steps to the top.

Bucovinian Village Museum MUSEUM
(Muzeul Satului Bucovinean; ☑ 0230-216 439; www.muzeulbucovinei.ro; Royal Citadel; adult/child 6/2 lei; ☺ 10am-6pm Tue-Sun) Located next to the Royal Citadel, this small museum displays relocated Bucovinian traditional homes, with their original furnishings, accessories and appliances.

Mirăuţi Church CHURCH
(☑ 0744-304 470; Str Mirăuţilor 17; ☺ 8am-7pm) Suceava's oldest surviving church, Mirăuţi is 500m northwest of the main square. Founded by Petru II Muşat in 1375, it was Moldavia's original coronation church (Ştefan cel Mare was crowned here), and the initial Moldavian bishops' seat. The church was largely restored between 1898 and 1901, preserving the original design.

Monastery of St John the New MONASTERY
(Mănăstirea Sfântu Ioan cel Nou; Str Ioan Voda Viteazul 2) This monastery off Str Mitropoliei, built between 1514 and 1554, remains an impor-

Suceava

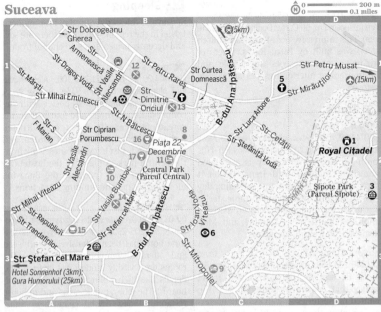

Suceava

tant pilgrimage destination: in a decorated silver casket it houses the relics of St John the New, which ruler Alexandru cel Bun had brought to Moldavia in 1415. The church and grounds come alive on 24 June (p202), when faithful from around the country come here and camp on the grounds.

Bucovina History Museum MUSEUM
(Muzeul Naţional al Bucovinei; ☑ 0230-516 439; www.muzeulbucovinei.ro; Str Ştefan cel Mare 33; adult/child 10/3 lei; ☉ 10am-6pm Tue-Sun) Displays here range from the Bronze Age to the present, and highlight Moldavia's famous rulers, particularly Ştefan cel Mare. While

the numismatics, medieval armour and tools are interesting, Ştefan's 'Hall of Thrones' court re-creation seems rather contrived. The exhibits on WWI, WWII and the communist period are particularly interesting.

Gah Synagogue SYNAGOGUE
(Str Dimitrie Onciul 7) By the post office, this 1870 structure is Suceava's only surviving synagogue out of an original 18. The well-preserved and elaborately decorated temple is still used by the tiny Jewish community, though it's normally closed to the public. Contact Suceava's Jewish community (☑ 0230-213 084) to arrange a visit.

St Dumitru's Church
CHURCH

(Biserica Sf Dumitru; ☑ 0745-672 429; www.sfantul dumitrusuceava.ro; Str Curtea Domnească; ☺ 9am-6pm) This impressive post-Byzantine church (1535) was built by Petru Rareș. Traces of original exterior frescoes are visible and the impressive interior frescoes are largely restored.

🕼 Tours

Hello Bucovina
TOURS

(☑ 0744-292 588; www.hellobucovina.com; Aleea Nucului 1, bldg 1, apt 3; ☺ 9am-5pm Mon-Fri) This youth-oriented travel agency is associated (and shares an office) with Irene's Hostel. It offers a wide variety of tours, including day trips to the Bucovina painted monasteries and other regional sights, as well as more ambitious journeys to Ukraine and Moldova. See the website for details.

Explore Bucovina
TOURS

(☑ 0746 933 659; www.explorebucovina.com; Str Nicolae Bălcescu 2) Highly regarded travel agency that organises group tours of the painted monasteries as well as of monasteries and attractions in neighbouring Neamț county. These include the Neamț Citadel, Agapia Monastery, Văratec Monastery and Neamț Monastery.

AXA Travel
TOURS

(☑ 0741-477 047; www.axatravel.ro) AXA is run by experienced local tour guide Sebastian 'Gigi' Traciu. One-day and multiday tours visit the Bucovina monasteries, Târgu Neamț, the Bicaz Gorges, Lacu Roșu and Maramureș. Tour prices depend on participant numbers, and can be as cheap as 160 lei per person. Other day trips include horseback riding and river rafting.

🎎 Festivals & Events

Suceava Days
RELIGIOUS

(☺ 24 Jun) Patron St John is celebrated each 24 June, with most of the action taking place at the Monastery of St John the New. To welcome the pilgrims who come from around the country, the city pulls out all the stops, offering beer, street food and music.

Festival of Medieval Arts
CULTURAL

(Festival de Artă Medievală Ştefan cel Mare; ☺ Aug) The annual Festival of Medieval Arts highlights the costumes and customs of Suceava's glory days in the 14th and 15th centuries. It's held in mid-August at the Royal Citadel.

🛏 Sleeping

Suceava is blessed with the best modern hostel in the region. Otherwise there are several decently priced hotels to choose from.

★ Irene's Hostel
HOSTEL $

(☑ 0744-29 25 88, 0721-280 100; Aleea Nucului 1, bldg 1, apt 3; dm from 50 lei; P ☯ @ 🖗) A cheerful, well-maintained hostel with accommodation in three- and four-bed dorms spread out over half a dozen rooms. There's a shared kitchen and peaceful garden, and the location is just a few minutes' walk from the central park. A big plus: the hostel can help arrange tours (p202) to the Bucovina monasteries and surrounding attractions.

★ Hotel Balada
HISTORIC HOTEL $$

(☑ 0330-100 026; www.hotel-balada.ro; Str Mitropoliei 5; s/d 205/250 lei; P ☯ ❋ @ 🖗) This historic hotel has been extensively refurbished and offers uncommonly good value. The rooms are stylishly modern yet sport period details like high ceilings and padded headboards. The lobby, public areas and in-house restaurant boast crystal chandeliers, shiny wood panelling and elegant tiles. The location is within easy walking distance of the centre.

Union Apartment
APARTMENT $$

(☑ 0741-477 047; www.union-apartments.ro; B-dul Ana Ipătescu 7; apt from 180-300 lei; ❋ 🖗) Accommodation offered in a central, three-room private apartment. There are two bedrooms and a pull-out sofa in the living room, providing decent value for self-caterers. The price varies depending on the number of people. The owner can provide airport pickup and arrange day trips to the painted monasteries through AXA Travel.

Hotel Sonnenhof
HOTEL $$$

(☑ 0230-220 033; www.hotelsonnenhof.ro; B-dul Sofia Vicoveanca 68; s/d from 260/320 lei; ❋ 🖗) This fancy four-star place is good for drivers and those not so budget-conscious. It's 3km from town on the Târgu Neamț road (12 lei by taxi), and has excellent rooms loaded with amenities and decorated in soothing tones. The hotel's Restaurant Mozaik (☑ 0230-220 099; www.hotelsonnenhof.ro; B-dul Sofia Vicoveanca 68; mains 30-65 lei; ☺ 10am-11pm) is well regarded.

🍴 Eating

★ Natanael
ICE CREAM $

(☑ 0230-533 033; www.natanael.ro; Str Ştefan cel Mare 3; cones 5-10 lei; ☺ 8.30am-6pm Mon-Fri,

9am-2pm Sat) Arguably (okay, definitely) the region's best ice cream is sold here at the outlet of a Christian aid group based in Suceava. The ice cream and dairy products are sourced from the group's own cows and the recipes tend toward the buttery, creamy end of the ice-cream spectrum.

★ **Restaurant**

Centru Vechi INTERNATIONAL $$
(☑ 0749-222 202; www.centruvechisv.ro; Str Vasile Bumbac 3; mains 20-35 lei; ⊙ 8am-midnight) This big local favourite serves hearty grills and salads, and has a local wine and beer selection. Start with a creamy chicken soup *(ciorbă rădăuţeană),* and move on to exquisitely prepared lamb chops or roast pork. Dine on the spacious terrace in warm weather.

Latino ITALIAN $$
(☑ 0730-920 920; www.restaurant-latino.ro; Str Curtea Domnească 9; mains 20-45 lei; pizza 20-30 lei; ⊙ 8am-11pm) In the eyes of locals, this is Suceava's best Italian restaurant, with subdued class and attentive (if not always prompt) service. There are numerous pizza options, and the varied pasta and grilled meat dishes are all excellent.

▼ Drinking & Nightlife

From Thursday through Saturday nights, most bars become 'clubs' with DJ music, flashing lights – the works.

Apropos CAFE
(☑ 0330-111 725; www.apropocafe.ro; Str Republicii 10; ⊙ 8am-11pm Mon-Fri, 9.30am-midnight Sat, 10.30am-11pm Sun) A local favourite for good coffee and homemade lemonade, stylish modern decor and a convenient central location. It also serves cakes, light bites and breakfast (12 to 15 lei), including an excellent and otherwise hard-to-find eggs Benedict.

Oscar Wilde PUB
(☑ 0751-350 575, 0330-803 102; www.oscarwilde.ro; Str Ştefan cel Mare 26; ⊙ 8am-1am) Suceava's nearest thing to an Irish pub (look for the giant black Guinness canopies), Oscar Wilde is a big, wood-floored bar with outdoor seating. It serves food, including a decent breakfast, and on weekends becomes a slightly chaotic 'club.'

Lounge CLUB
(☑ 0755-181 968; www.loungesuceava.ro; Str Ştefan cel Mare 20a; ⊙ 7am-midnight Mon-Fri, noon-4am Sat, noon-midnight Sun) One of several similar clubs around town, Eclipse does double duty

as a coffee bar by day and a cocktail bar/club by night. The central location is a big plus. There are DJ parties, karaoke nights and the like most weekends.

ℹ Information

ATMs and exchange offices line Piaţa 22 Decembrie and Str Ştefan cel Mare.

Infoturism (☑ 0230-551 241; www.turism-suceava.ro; cnr B-dul Ana Ipătescu & Str Mitropoliei 4; ⊙ 8am-4pm Mon-Fri) Provides maps and information on local sites.

Post Office (☑ 0230-531 872; Str Dimitrie Onciul 6; ⊙ 8am-7pm Mon-Fri)

ℹ Getting There & Away

AIR

Ştefan cel Mare International Airport (SCV; ☑ 0230-340 400; www.aeroportsuceava.ro; Salcea) is 15km northeast of Suceava, but has limited flights. **Tarom** (☑ 0230-214 686; www.tarom.ro; Str Nicolae Bălcescu 2; ⊙ 10am-7pm Mon-Fri, 9am-1pm Sat) has daily flights to Bucharest.

BUS

The central **bus station** (Autogara; ☑ 0230-524 340; Str Vasile Alecsandri, cnr Str Armenească) is near the southern end of Str Armenească. Bus and maxitaxi services departing from here include the following:

Bucharest (90 lei, eight hours, four daily)

Gura Humorului (8 lei, one hour, 13 daily)

Iaşi (30 lei, three hours, 12 daily) Maxitaxis depart from a car park behind the bus station, dubbed 'Autogara Intertrans'.

Piatra Neamţ (25 lei, three hours, three daily)

Rădăuţi (8 lei, 45 minutes, 13 daily)

Târgu Neamţ (15 lei, two hours, three daily)

See the website www.autogari.ro for timely information.

TRAIN

Suceava's two train stations, Gara Suceava (aka Gara Burdujeni, Gara Sud and Gara Principala) and Gara Nord (aka Gara Iţcani), are both roughly 5km north of the centre, and easily reached by bus or maxitaxi (7 lei). The **Agenţia de Voiaj CFR** (www.cfrcalatori.ro; Str Nicolae Bălcescu 8; ⊙ 7.30am-8.30pm Mon-Fri) sells advance tickets. Most trains originate or terminate at the Gara Suceava.

Train services include the following:

Bucharest (91 lei, seven hours, six daily)

Cluj-Napoca (73 lei, seven hours, four daily)

Gura Humorului (7 lei, 70 minutes, five daily) Disembark at the Gura Humorului Oraş stop.

Iaşi (40 lei, two hours, nine daily)

Timişoara (121 lei, 14 hours, two daily)

Bucovina Monasteries

Bucovina's painted monasteries are among the most distinctive in all Christendom. They're cherished not only for their beauty and quality of artisanship, but also for their endurance over the centuries and their over-all cultural significance. The half-dozen or so monasteries, scattered over a large swathe of Bucovina, date mainly from the 15th and 16th centuries, a time when Orthodox Moldavia was battling for its life with forces of the expanding Ottoman Empire.

The monasteries are hailed mainly for their colourful external frescoes, many of which have survived the region's cruel winters relatively intact. The frescoes served as both expressions of faith and as an effective method of conveying important biblical stories to a mostly illiterate parish. But don't pass up the rich interiors, where every corner is filled with religious and cultural symbolism.

⊙ Sights

The main attractions here are the churches and monasteries themselves, though most of the monasteries also have smaller, separate museums tucked somewhere within the grounds. Normally, a single admission fee (adult/child 5/2 lei) gives access to the churches, gardens and museums. A photography tax (normally 10 lei) allows for taking photos of the church exteriors, but interior photography is always off limits.

There are a handful of common-sense rules for visiting the monasteries, the main one being visitors should act and dress 'respectfully'. In practice, this means no short pants for men and covered shoulders and longer skirts or pants for women. If you turn up in shorts, cover yourself with one of the capes or cloaks hanging on pegs near the entry.

★ **Arbore Monastery**　　　　　　　CHURCH
(Manastirea Arbore; ☑ 0740-154 213; www.manastire aarbore.ro; Hwy DN2K 732, Arbore; adult/student

> ### ℹ CONSIDER A GUIDED TOUR
>
> A guided tour is the most time-efficient and informative way to visit. Several travel companies offer guided tours, including transport and meals, from their base in Suceava. Câmpulung Mold-ovenesc is also a practical starting point for exploring the monasteries.

5/2 lei, photography 10 lei; ⊙ 8am-7pm May-Sep, to 4pm Oct-Apr) This Unesco-protected church in the village of Arbore receives a fraction of the visitors of the other painted monasteries and hence feels more private and special. The small scale allows you to study the paintings up close, to appreciate the skills and techniques. The monastery dates from 1503 and was the brainchild of local nobleman Luca Arbore.

The tiny interior consists of three chambers. That nearest the altar has a particularly well-preserved votive painting (on the facing wall) of Arbore offering the church to God. The tombs of Arbore and his family sit in another chamber. The interior is in the process of long-term restoration and preservation. The exterior paintings on the western wall are in relatively good shape, while the paintings that covered the rest of the outside have been lost to the ravages of time.

Voroneț Monastery　　　　　　　MONASTERY
(Mănăstirea Voroneț; ☑ 0230-235 323; Str Voroneț 166, Voroneț; adult/child 5/2 lei, photography 10 lei; ⊙ 8am-7pm May-Sep, to 4pm Oct-Apr) Built in just three months and three weeks by Ştefan cel Mare following a key 1488 victory over the Turks, Voroneț Monastery is the only painted monastery that has had an internationally recognised colour associated with it. 'Voroneț Blue', a vibrant cerulean hue created from lapis lazuli and other ingredients, is prominent in its frescoes. A 2011 restoration of frescoes in the entryway revealed the incredible quality of these paintings even more clearly.

The wondrous size, scope and detail of the *Last Judgement* fresco, which fills the entire exterior western wall of the Voroneț Monastery, has earned near-universal accolades as being the most marvellous Bucovina fresco. Angels at the top roll up the zodiac signs, indicating the end of time, while humanity is brought to judgement in the middle. On the left, St Paul escorts the believers, while a stern Moses takes the nonbelievers on the right. Heaven and the Garden of Eden is on the bottom left, the Resurrection is on the bottom right.

On the northern wall is *Genesis*, from Adam and Eve to Cain and Abel. The southern wall features the Tree of Jesse (King David's father) with the biblical genealogy. The first three rows portray St Nicholas' life and miracles. The next two rows recount the martyrdom of Suceava's St John the New. The bottom row, from left to right, features the monastery's patron saint, St George,

KNOW YOUR MONASTERIES

You don't have to be an art snob to wow your friends with monastery fresco facts. While each monastery is different, they share many common motifs. Inside the churches, for example, check out the facing wall in the main altar room to see an image of the church's patron or builder (and his family) offering the church to god. The exteriors almost always depict some version of a ladder to heaven.

While the monasteries usually depict similar stories and images, the differing preservation qualities mean that some monasteries are more strongly associated with a particular colour or image. The following need-to-know details help to keep things straight.

Arbore Monastery
Representative colour: green
Famous fresco: Scenes from the book of Genesis that adorn the western exterior wall

Humor Monastery
Representative colours: red and brown
Famous frescoes: *The Annunciation, The Life of St Nicholas*

Voroneţ Monastery
Representative colour: blue
Famous fresco: *The Last Judgement*

Moldoviţa Monastery
Representative colour: yellow
Famous frescoes: *The Siege of Constantinople, The Story of Jesus' Life*

Suceviţa Monastery
Representative colour: green
Famous frescoes: *The Genealogy of Jesus, The Ladder of Virtues, The Story of Moses' Life*

---

fighting the dragon, St Daniel the Hermit (Daniil Sihastrul) with Metropolitan Grigorie, a Deisis icon, and the 1402 procession of St John the New's relics into Suceava.

In the antechamber lies the tomb of Daniel the Hermit, the ascetic who encouraged Ştefan cel Mare to fight the Turks, and then became the monastery's first abbot. Daniel's cave (p206) is located near Putna Monastery.

The monastery is located about 6km from the town of Gura Humorului.

Suceviţa Monastery MONASTERY
(☑ 0230-417 110; www.manastireasucevita.ro; Suceviţa; adult/student 5/2 lei, photography 10 lei; ⊙ 8am-7pm May-Sep, to 4pm Oct-Apr) Suceviţa Monastery (built 1582–1601) is the largest Bucovina monastery, and some regard it as the finest. It's perhaps best known for its exterior *Ladder of Virtues* fresco, with its 32 steps to heaven, near the main entry. It exhorts priests to righteous behaviour and to avoid the unfortunate fate of the clerics depicted tumbling from the ladder due to sins like greed or vanity. The church's tomb room contains the coffins of monastery founders Simion and Ieremia Movilă.

The continuity of the Old and New Testaments is emphasised on the southern exterior wall, where a tree grows from the reclining figure of Jesse, flanked by ancient Greek philosophers. The Virgin, depicted as a Byzantine princess, stands nearby, with angels holding a red veil over her head. More good cheer appears on the porch's south-side archway, where frescoes depict the Apocalypse and the dark visions of St John in Revelations. The western wall is bare. Legend says the fatal plunge of the artist from the scaffolding there dissuaded other painters.

Suceviţa was the last painted monastery built. Ieremia Movilă (d 1606) is depicted with his seven children on the western wall.

Moldoviţa Monastery MONASTERY
(Mânăstirea Moldoviţa; Vatra Moldoviţei; adult/student 5/2 lei, photography 10 lei; ⊙ 8am-7pm May-Sep, to 4pm Oct-Apr) Built in 1532, Moldoviţa Monastery occupies a fortified enclosure with tower, gates and well-tended lawns. The central painted church has been partly restored and features frescoes from 1537. The southern exterior wall depicts the siege of Constantinople in AD 626, under a combined Persian-Avar attack. Interestingly, the besiegers are depicted in Turkish dress – keeping parishioners concentrated on the contemporary enemy.

Inside the sanctuary, on a wall facing the carved iconostasis, a pious Prince Petru Rareş offers the church to Christ. The monastery's small museum displays Rareş' original throne.

Humor Monastery
MONASTERY

(Mănăstirea Humorului; Gura Humorului; adult/student 5/2 lei, photography 10 lei; ⊙ 8am-7pm May-Sep, to 4pm Oct-Apr) Founded by Chancellor Theodor Bubuiog under Moldavian Prince Petru Rareş, Humor Monastery, built in 1530, is surrounded by ramparts, with a three-level brick-and-wood lookout tower. The narrow walls enclosing the last stretch of stairway were designed so that defending soldiers could kill off attacking Turks one by one. Humor's predominantly red-and-brown exterior frescoes (1535) are divided topically. On the southern wall's left-hand side, patron saint the Virgin Mary is commemorated; on the right, St Nicholas' life and miracles are captured.

Other features include a faded depiction of the 1453 siege of Constantinople, with a parable depicting the prodigal son's return, on the right of the southern wall. St George appears on the northern wall. The porch contains a painting of the Last Judgement: the long bench on which the 12 Apostles sit, the patterned towel on the chair of judgement, and the long, hornlike *bucium* (pipe) announcing Christ's coming are all typical Moldavian elements. The three square images in red, white and black (on the bottom right) are unique to Humor: they represent the fire, the coldness and the darkness (or boiling tar) of hell.

Humor shelters five chambers. The middle one (the tomb room) hides a treasure room *(taİniţa)*, which safeguarded monastic riches. On the right-hand wall, a votive painting depicts Bubuiog offering (with the Virgin Mary's help) a miniature monastery replica to Christ, a common motif in the Byzantine artistic tradition. Bubuiog's tomb (1539) is on the room's right side, that of his wife on the left side; above the latter is a painting of his wife praying to the Virgin Mary.

Putna Monastery
MONASTERY

(☏ 0230-414 055; www.putna.ro; Putna; adult/student 5/2 lei, photography 10 lei; ⊙ 8am-7pm May-Sep, to 4pm Oct-Apr) Some 28km northwest of Rădăuţi, along a forested road dotted by traditional villages, Putna Monastery (1466–81) was built by Ştefan cel Mare, following his victory over the Turks at Chilia. About 60 monks live here. While Putna lacks spectacular frescoes, its royal inhabitants

(Ştefan cel Mare is buried in the tomb room) keep it close to the Romanian heart.

Putna Museum, behind the monastery, houses one of Eastern Europe's largest Byzantine collections. Treasures include medieval manuscripts and the Holy Book that Ştefan cel Mare carried into battle. The largest of three bells inscribed in Old Church Slavonic outside dates from 1484, and was rung for royal deaths. The price of admission is included in the general monastery entry fee.

Dragomirna Monastery
MONASTERY

(Mănăstirea Dragomirna; www.manastireadrago mirna.ro; Mitocul Dragomirnei; adult/student 5/2 lei, photography 10 lei; ⊙ 8am-7pm May-Sep, to 4pm Oct-Apr) About 10km north of Suceava in Mitocul Dragomirnei, the 60-nun-strong Dragomirna Monastery was founded between 1602 and 1609 by scholar, calligrapher, artist and bishop Anastasie Crimca. The intricate rope lacing around the midsection of the main church's exterior (and repeated throughout the interior) represents the Holy Trinity, and the short-lived unification of the Moldavian, Wallachian and Transylvanian principalities in 1600.

Dragomirna's **Museum of Medieval Art** contains carved cedar crosses mounted in silver-gilt filigree and religious texts. There's also a small shop here where the nuns sell wood and glass icons as well as cheese products. Drive or take a taxi from Suceava (30 lei).

Egg Museum
MUSEUM

(☏ 0723-541 643; www.muzeuloualorluciacondrea. ro; Str Stadionului 87, Vatra Moldoviţei; adult/child 5/3 lei; ⊙ 9am-8pm) This small, private museum shows off the painted egg creations of local artist Lucia Condrea. Condrea's eggs mix traditional Romanian Easter and holiday motifs with strong Slavic, Ukrainian and folk influences. The 2nd floor has several cases filled with painted eggs from around the world, so you can compare and contrast the various styles and colours.

Daniel the Hermit's Cave
CAVE

(Chilia lui Daniil Sihastrul; ☏ 0753-020 678; Putna; ⊙ 10am-7pm May-Sep) FREE About 2km from Putna, this cave contains a wooden table and memorial plaque to the 15th-century hermit and seer Daniel Dimitru. A monk by age 16, Daniel later dug and inhabited this rock cave; his fame was such that Ştefan cel Mare consulted him before doing battle. From Putna Monastery, you can walk to the cave in about 30 minutes. By car, leave Putna village and follow the signs to 'Chilia lui Daniil Sihastrul'.

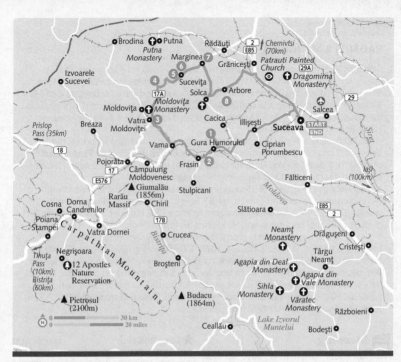

🏃 Driving Tour
Bucovina Monasteries

START/FINISH SUCEAVA
LENGTH 231KM; 8 HOURS

Bucovina's painted monasteries are Moldavia's top cultural draw. Dazzling frescoes run from top-to-bottom in churches where monks and nuns follow traditional Orthodox vigils and services. On either a round-trip circuit or organised tour from Suceava, visiting the five most spectacular monasteries is achievable in a day. For a more leisurely tour, and to visit monasteries like Putna and Dragomirna, overnight at a rural guesthouse.

Leaving Suceava, take the southwest road for 50km (one hour) towards Gura Humorului village and **1 Humor Monastery** (p206). Along with elaborate frescoes, this fortified monastery's tower offers nice views.

Continue on the south side of the Gura Humorului road for 10km (20 minutes) to **2 Voroneţ Monastery** (p204), a spectacular structure known for its unique blue paint and detailed fresco of *The Last Judgement*.

From here, head west and then northwest, passing through Vatra Moldoviţei for

3 Moldoviţa Monastery (p205), a pretty place known for its frescoes *The Story of Jesus' Life* and *The Siege of Constantinople*.

Backtrack to Vatra Moldoviţei and continue northeast on a winding mountain road, peaking at 1100m at **4 Ciumârna Pass**, dubbed 'Palma' (a giant human-palm statue stands here). You'll find great views, refreshing breezes and local vendors selling crafts.

Continue northeast for 10km to **5 Popas Turistic Bucovina** (p209), an excellent lunch stop. Local forest mushrooms are used here in traditional sauces for chicken and pork dishes, and in hearty soups.

Another 4km north is **6 Suceviţa Monastery** (p205), with paintings including the *Ladder of Virtues* and *The Genealogy of Jesus*.

Travel 6km on the road to Suceava to pass through Marginea, known for its unique black pottery, available in **7 AF Magopat Gheorghe** (p208), where potters work on traditional wheels. On the return to Suceava, don't forget tiny **8 Arbore Monastery** (p204), whose smaller scale allows for a closer inspection of the beautifully preserved frescoes.

WORTH A TRIP

RĂDĂUŢI & MARGINEA

Side trips from the Bucovina monastery trail include Rădăuţi and Marginea. Rădăuţi is a small market town with Moldavia's oldest church, the mid-14th-century **Bogdana Monastery** (Manastirea Bogdana; ☎0230-563 005; www.bogdana.ro; Str Bogdana Vodă 4-6, Rădăuţi; ⊙8am-7pm May-Sep, to 4pm Oct-Apr) FREE, built by Prince Bogdan I, which is also the mausoleum for eight early Moldavian rulers and their families, including Bogdan I, Latcu, Roman Muşat and Ştefan I.

Rădăuţi's square, Piaţa Unirii, features a multidomed **cathedral**. Opposite, the **Museum of Bucovina Folk Techniques** (☎0230-562 565; Piaţa Unirii 63, Rădăuţi; adult/child 5/2 lei; ⊙8am-5pm Mon-Fri, to 4pm Sat & Sun) is Moldavia's oldest ethnographic museum and displays over 1000 items, including regional pottery.

Tiny Marginea, 9km west of Rădăuţi, produces a unique black pottery, made with a technique dating to neolithic times. Here **AF Magopat Gheorghe** (Black Pottery Workshop; ☎0745-922 949; www.ceramicamarginea.ro; House 1265, Marginea; ⊙8am-6pm Mon-Sat) displays and sells these items, and showcases the last traditional potters in action.

This area also has remarkably good guesthouses, many signposted, catering to all budgets. In Rădăuţi, **Gerald's Hotel** (☎0330-100 650; www.geraldshotel.com; Str Piaţa Unirii 3, Rădăuţi; s/d 380/420 lei; P ❄ @ ☎) is among Moldavia's nicest hotels. It's loaded with business-class amenities, like a fitness centre and elegant bathrooms adorned with dark-wood furniture, plus a restaurant and bar. Rădăuţi is also blessed with **Antique** (☎0230-560 011; www.restaurant-antique.ro; Al Primaverii 12, Rădăuţi; mains 20-50 lei; ⊙9am-10pm; ☎), one of Bucovina's best restaurants.

Sleeping

Pensiunes and guesthouses have sprung up in all of the towns and villages where the monasteries are located. Good places to hunt include Gura Humorului, near the Humor and Voroneţ Monasteries, Putna and Suceviţa. Along with the guesthouses, homes with *cazare* (accommodation) signs abound.

Pensiunea Emilia GUESTHOUSE $
(☎0743-117 827; Str Bercheza 173, Suceaviţa; r per person 80 lei) The most appealing local *pensiune* in Suceviţa, Emilia has charming rooms and is 500m up the road from the village, opposite the monastery.

Pensiunea Aga GUESTHOUSE $
(☎0740-613 901; House 165, Putna; r with shared bathroom 70-90 lei) Right outside Putna Monastery, Pensiunea Aga has 10 rooms, with those in the main house the best. No English spoken; breakfast 15 lei.

Ieremia Movilă GUESTHOUSE $
(☎0230-417 501; www.ieremiamovila.ro; Str Suceviţa 459, Suceviţa; s/d/tr 100/120/180 lei; P ❄ ☎) This modern place has nice rooms with great bathrooms, balconies and wi-fi. Some rooms have monastery views. The on-site restaurant is decent.

★ **Casa Bunicilor** GUESTHOUSE $$
(☎0747-512 291; www.casabunicilor.com; Str Chilia 22, Mănăstirea Humorului; s/d 120/180 lei; P ⊖ ❄ ☎) A piece of paradise in an isolated spot north of Humor Monastery. Guests sleep in restored traditional Bucovina houses. There's an excellent restaurant and plenty of horses and goats for the kids to play with. To find it, drive north from the monastery along the main highway for 3km, and watch for a signposted turn-off to the left.

Pensiunea Muşatinii GUESTHOUSE $$
(☎0744-503 536; www.pensiuneamusatinii.ro; Str Mănăstirii 513a, Putna; s/d/apt 120/160/220 lei; ⊖ ❄ ☎) This large, modern place in the centre of Putna has the village's best rooms. There's a sauna and on-site restaurant.

La Roata GUESTHOUSE $$
(☎0230-230 400; www.la-roata.ro; Str Wurzburg 21f, Gura Humorului; s/d/apt from 160/200/290 lei; P ❄ ☎) This collection of detached guesthouses is 500m west of the Gura Humorului town centre. It offers spacious rooms, a restaurant and kid-friendly attractions like a playground and table tennis.

Hilde's Residence GUESTHOUSE $$
(☎0230-233 484; www.lucy.ro; Str Şipotului 2, Gura Humorului; s/d/ste from 200/240/300 lei; P ❄ ☎) Among Gura Humorului's more atmospheric

and pricier guesthouses, long-established Hilde's has nine uniquely designed rooms; it's just off the village's main road. The on-site Romanian restaurant is good too.

Casa Doamnei   GUESTHOUSE **$$**
(📞0752-111 859; www.casa-doamnei.ro; Str Voroneț 255, Gura Humorului; s/d from 120/160 lei) On the Voroneț road (500m after the train tracks, 3.5km before Voroneț Monastery), this guesthouse has stylish wooden furniture, balconies and nice bathrooms.

Pensiunea Crizantema   PENSION **$$**
(📞0230-336 116; www.vilacrizantema.ro; Str Mănăstirii 284a, Vatra Moldoviței; s/d half-board 150/190 lei; 🅿 😒 🛜) Near the Moldovița Monastery, this rustic eight-room place has cute, smallish rooms (bathrooms are simple), some with monastery views.

🍴 Eating

Restaurants are few and far between on the roads that connect the monasteries, though sizeable towns like Rădăuţi and Gura Humorului have a decent selection. Hotels and pensions normally cook for nonguests as well.

Popas Turistic Bucovina   ROMANIAN **$$**
(📞0230-417 000; www.popas.ro; Str Movileştilor 305, Suceviţa; mains 18-35 lei; ⏱7.30am-10pm) The perfect spot to grab a well-prepared lunch of traditional Bucovinian cooking near the Suceviţa Monastery. Specialities include cabbage rolls with polenta and trout wrapped in pine, among others. Dine outside in a camplike setting in nice weather. It also offers overnight accommodation in four villas, and it's possible to camp as well.

ℹ Getting There & Away

From Suceava, trains run to Gura Humorului (7 lei, 70 minutes, five daily), near the Humor and Voroneţ Monasteries. Bus and maxitaxi services include Gura Humorului (10 lei, one hour, 19 daily) and Rădăuţi (8 lei, 45 minutes, 13 daily). To access Putna, five daily buses make the trip from Rădăuţi (7 lei, 45 minutes).

From Câmpulung Moldovenesc, regular maxitaxis pass through Gura Humorului (7 lei) on their way to Suceava (14 lei).

ℹ Getting Around

Public transport is sporadic in these parts, requiring hopping around and backtracking. Infrequent buses and maxitaxis service towns and villages. See the website www.autogari.ro.

Rarău Massif

Rarău Massif refers to a modest (the highest point is 1651m) but dramatic outcropping of the Eastern Carpathian Mountains that rises to the south of Câmpulung Moldovenesc. The massif is accessible by road or hiking trail from May to October, with the most popular trails leading south from Câmpulung or from the neighbouring village of Pojorâta, 5km to the west. Highlights of a hike or drive here include unusual limestone rock formations, most notably the beloved Lady's Stones (Pietrele Doamnei), and dramatic vistas over steep, deep-green valleys.

🏃 Activities

Hiking is far and away the major activity here. There's also a modest ski run that operates from December through March most years. If you have your own wheels, it's possible to drive near the top of the massif.

Hiking

Hiking is the main activity in these parts and marked trails to the peak at Cabana Rarău (p210) and further on to the Lady's Stones fan out from Câmpulung and Pojorâta. Cabana Rarău is also accessible on foot from the southern side, starting in Chiril village. From Câmpulung, count on about four to five

Rarău Massif

CÂMPULUNG MOLDOVENESC

Situated at 621m, placid Câmpulung Moldovenesc dates from the 15th century. Known for logging, fairs and outdoor sports, it's an excellent base for exploring the painted monasteries and for hiking the Rarău Massif, 15km south. In winter the town transforms into a modest ski resort – there's a short 800m ski slope with a chairlift.

There are dozens of *pensiunes* along the main highway and around the town. Try to book in advance over summer weekends, when the town fills up with hikers.

Dor de Bucovina (☑0723-523 083; www.puravidahostels.ro; Str Simion Florea Marian 8; s/d 80/100 lei; 🔊) is a simple, well-maintained guesthouse off a quiet side street 1km east of the centre. **Eden Hotel** (☑0230-314 733; www.hotel-eden.ro; Calea Bucovinei 148; s/d/ste 150/200/340 lei; 🅿🌐🔊🏊) is an oasislike complex with hotel-, chalet- and bungalow-style rooms. It's well furnished, with large bathrooms with hydromassage tubs.

There are a couple of decent restaurants near the town centre. **Q'usine** (☑0752-502 948; www.facebook.com/qusine2016; Str Dimitrie Cantemir 14; mains 25-40 lei; ⏱11.30am-11.30pm; 🔊) is an unexpected touch of sophistication. The industrial decor is softened by exposed wood beams and cushioned Eames chairs. The menu offers a nice selection of steaks, lamb and duck. It's two blocks north of Str 22 Decembrie (the town centre).

Regular maxitaxis run throughout the day to Suceava (14 lei) via Gura Humorului (7 lei), departing from a small station along the main road, Calea Bucovinei, about 100m east of the central square at Str 22 Decembrie. The tiny train station is situated 1km west of the centre. Daily services include several trains to Suceava (12 lei, two hours), two to Iaşi (60 lei, four hours) and one to Bucharest (90 lei, 90 minutes).

hours to the top at a moderate pace, following one of two main paths (one marked by a red circle and the other by a yellow triangle).

From Cabana Rarău, a signposted trail (30 minutes) leads to the foot of the **Lady's Stones**. Several crosses crown the highest stone, a memorial for those who have died climbing here. Views from the top are superb. A trail marked by red stripes and red triangles (five hours) leads from the cabana to the **Slătioara Forest Reservation**. From here another trail (red triangles) leads to the **Todirescu Flower Reservation**.

Driving

By car, the drive to the top at Cabana Rarău (15km) takes about 30 minutes along the superb **Transrarău highway** (marked as Hwy DJ175B). The Transrarău begins in Pojorâta, 5km west of Câmpulung (look for signs to 'Rarău'). From Cabana Rarău, it's possible to continue by road another 10km south to Chiril village, from where you can return to Pojorâta, or proceed onward to Vatra Dornei, 24km to the west. Winter conditions can close the road from late October to April.

🛏 Sleeping & Eating

There are a few scattered mountain lodges near the peaks that allow for a more leisurely assault on the top. The best facilities are offered at the base station shelter Cabana Rarău. Be sure to arrange sleeping in advance to make sure there's room. There are plenty of guesthouses and private rooms in both Câmpulung Moldovenesc and Pojorâta.

Cabana Rarău　　　　LODGE **$**
(☑0720-538 197; www.rarau-turism.ro/cazare_cabana.html; d 100 lei)　Up at 1520m, this simple mountain lodge has a somewhat ramshackle exterior that belies its cosy, rustic-decor common area. Rooms are simple but well-maintained.

Pastravaria Izvor　　　ROMANIAN **$$**
(Transrarău/Hwy DJ175B, Pojorâta; mains 25-40 lei; ⏱11am-9pm)　This traditional restaurant serves excellent river fish dishes as well as Moldavian and Romanian specialities. It's located along the Transrarău highway heading south toward the Cabana Rarău, about 4km outside the village of Pojorâta.

❶ Getting There & Away

Câmpulung Moldovenesc is the natural entry point into the Rarău Massif. The town lies on the main highway across the mountains and is well-served by buses and maxitaxis from Suceava (14 lei) via Gura Humorului (7 lei). Câmpulung Moldovenesc is also reachable by train from Suceava (12 lei, two hours), Iaşi (60 lei, four hours) and Bucharest (90 lei, nine hours).

The Danube Delta & Black Sea Coast

Best Places to Eat

➜ Ivan Pescar (p216)

➜ Sandalanda (p228)

➜ Irish Pub (p224)

➜ Chevalet (p226)

➜ Pizzico (p224)

Best Places to Sleep

➜ Hotel Cherica (p223)

➜ Pura Vida (p227)

➜ Vila Petru & Marcela Stefanov (p219)

➜ Vila Caviar (p217)

➜ Hotel Europa (p227)

Why Go?

Romania's 194km Black Sea coastline is remarkably diverse, from both an environmental and a cultural standpoint. In the north, the mighty Danube River (Râul Dunărea) empties into the sea after completing its 2800km-long journey across the continent. The river's mouth, the Danube Delta, is a largely unspoilt wetland that draws bird lovers and seekers of solitude alike. It's a fantastic, tangled network of ever-eroding canals, riverbeds and marshlands with remote fishing villages and stretches of deserted coast.

Further south, around Constanţa, a string of lively beach resorts draws a different kind of wildlife altogether. Everywhere you go you'll find evidence of Romania's long historical connections to ancient Greece and Rome, as well as surviving pockets of more recent Turkish, Tatar and Lippovani/Old Believer cultures.

When to Go
Tulcea

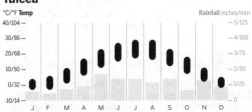

May & Jun Cool, fresh mornings are ideal for boating the Danube Delta wetlands.

Jul & Aug Black Sea resorts Mamaia and Vama Veche in peak season; book hotels far in advance.

Sep & Oct Beach towns seasonally close; culture and clubbing action shifts to Constanţa.

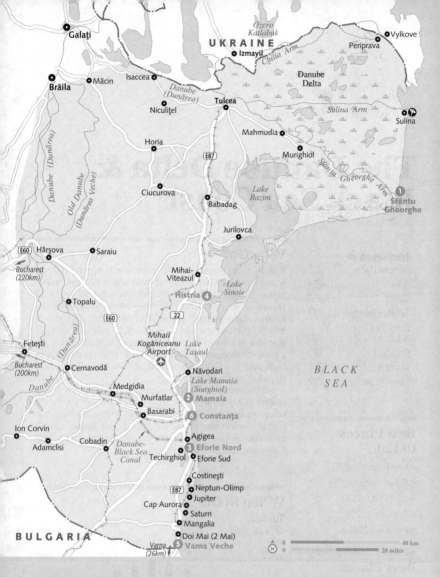

The Danube Delta & Black Sea Coast Highlights

1 **Sfântu Gheorghe Beach** (p219) Enjoying one of Romania's most beautiful, unspoiled beaches with fine white sand, clear water and few visitors.

2 **Crush Beach** (p225) Testing the limits of sun and of your modesty at one of Mamaia's trendy beaches.

3 **Mud Baths** (p227) Disregarding prudence and wallowing in the stinky, black (healthful?) mud at Eforie Nord.

4 **Histria Archaeological Complex & Museum** (p224) Reliving a piece of ancient Greece where you'd least expect it.

5 **Plaja de Carta** (p227) Soaking up some counter-culture and a glass of wine on the beach at Vama Veche.

6 **Statue of Ovid** (p220) Paying your respects to an unhappy Ovid as you stroll Constanța's rejuvenating old port area.

History

Archaeologists have discovered evidence of human civilisation dating back several thousand years all along the Black Sea coast. The ancient Greeks arrived around the 7th century BC. Histria, founded in 657 BC, was the oldest Greek settlement in Romania.

The Romans arrived around the 1st century BC and conquered the coastal region. They considered the Black Sea to be on the very fringe of the empire. Indeed, it was to ancient Tomis – today's Constanţa – where Emperor Augustus chose to banish the poet Ovid (43 BC–AD 17) in AD 8 for transgressions that remain unclear to this day. Ovid was by all accounts not a happy camper being so far from Rome.

In 1418 the coastal area was conquered by the Ottoman Turks, who stayed for more than four centuries. The cultural impact of the Ottoman Empire was profound, as the presence of grand mosques to this day in both Tulcea and Constanţa testify.

In 1878 the territory became part of Romania when a combined Russo-Romanian army defeated the decaying Ottoman Empire. Once Romanian flags flew over the area, much was done to integrate it in to the rest of the country as quickly as possible.

DANUBE DELTA

After passing through several countries and absorbing countless lesser waterways, the Danube empties into the Black Sea south of the Ukrainian border. The Danube Delta (Delta Dunării), included on Unesco's World Heritage list, is one of Romania's leading attractions. At Tulcea, the river splits into three separate channels: the Chilia, Sulina and Sfântu Gheorghe arms, creating a constantly evolving 4187-sq-km wetland of marshes, floating reed islets and sandbars. The region provides sanctuary for 300 species of bird and 160 species of fish. Reed marshes cover 1563 sq km, constituting one of the largest single expanses of reed beds in the world. The delta is a haven for wildlife lovers, birdwatchers, fishers and anyone wanting to get away from it all for a few days. There are beautiful, secluded beaches at both Sulina and Sfântu Gheorghe, and the fish and seafood, particularly the fish soup, are the best in Romania.

National Parks

Much of the delta is under the protection of the Danube Delta Biosphere Reserve Authority, headquartered in Tulcea, with branch offices in the delta, including in

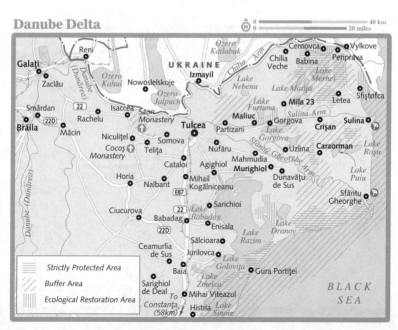

Danube Delta

N 0 ——————— 40 km
   0 ——————— 20 miles

Strictly Protected Area

Buffer Area

Ecological Restoration Area

Sfântu Gheorghe. There are around 20 strictly protected areas covering about 500 sq km that are off-limits to tourists, including the 500-year-old Leţea Forest and Europe's largest pelican colony. Visitation is limited in other areas. Note that visitors to the reserve are required to purchase an entry permit. Camping in the reserve is only allowed in official camping grounds.

❶ Getting Around

There is no rail service in the delta and few paved roads, meaning the primary mode of transport is ferry boat. Regularly scheduled ferries, both traditional 'slow' ferries and faster (and more expensive) hydrofoils, leave from Tulcea's main port on select days throughout the week and access major points in the delta. The helpful staff at the Tourism Information Centre in Tulcea can help piece together a journey depending on your time and budget.

Note that the delta covers a large area, and depending on where you want to go it will usually not be possible to depart and return on the same day. Give yourself at least a few days for more leisurely exploration. Ferries can get crowded in summer, so try to arrive at least an hour prior to departure to secure yourself a seat. Note that, though the ferries run year-round, service is far less reliable in winter.

Tulcea

POP 93,050

The Danube port of Tulcea (pronounced tool-*cha*) is the largest city in the delta and the main entry point for accessing the region. It's got good bus and minibus connections to the rest of the country, and is home to the main passenger ferries. If you've only got a short amount of time (one to three days), you'll want to base yourself here and explore the delta via boating day trips. If you've got more time, you'll likely only transit through Tulcea on your way to deeper destinations like Sulina and Sfântu Gheorghe. There are plenty of good hotels and restaurants, and several interesting museums if you're caught up in bad weather.

◉ Sights

Tulcea has several worthwhile museums, most of which are grouped around the eastern end of the port. The area just to the east and behind the museums is a traditional Turkish quarter. Following Str Independenţei brings you to the minaret of 1863-built **Moscheia Azizie** (Azizie Mosque; Str Independenţei; ⊗ closed to the public).

Tulcea

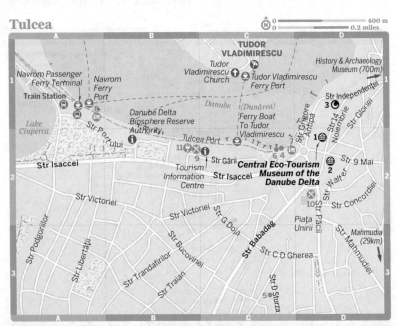

★ **Central Eco-Tourism Museum of the Danube Delta**   MUSEUM, AQUARIUM

(Centrul Muzeal Ecoturistic Delta Dunării; ☑ 0240-515 866; www.icemtl.ro; Str 14 Noiembrie 1; adult/child 20/5 lei; ☺ 10am-6pm Tue-Sun) This combined museum and aquarium is a good primer on the delta's varied flora and fauna. There are stuffed animals on the main floor and a small but fascinating aquarium on the lower level, with ample signage in English. Highly recommended if you're traveling with kids and want to get the most out of your visit.

History & Archaeology Museum   MUSEUM

(Muzeul de Istorie şi Arheologie; ☑ 0240-513 626; www.icemtl.ro; Parcul Monumentul Independenţei, Str Gloriei; adult/child 6/3 lei; ☺ 10am-6pm Tue-Sun) This well-worth-visiting museum is presented on two levels, with the upper level given over to extensive Roman findings and the lower level displaying even more fascinating artefacts of pre-Roman civilisations going back some 6000 years. The museum is situated on the site of the ancient fortress of Aegyssus, around 1km east of the centre.

Folk Art & Ethnographic Museum   MUSEUM

(Muzeul de Etnografie şi Artă Populară; ☑ 0240-516 204; www.icemtl.ro; Str 9 Mai 4; adult/child 6/3 lei; ☺ 10am-6pm Tue-Sun) This modest museum displays the ethnic and cultural diversity of the delta region over the centuries, and the interaction of Romanians with Turks,

---

ℹ DANUBE DELTA PERMITS

All visitors to the protected areas of the delta, including those on private hiking or boating excursions from Tulcea, Sulina or Sfântu Gheorghe (but not on the large public ferries), are required to purchase an entry permit. Permits are available for one day (5 lei), one week (15 lei) or one year (30 lei) from Danube Delta Biosphere Reserve Authority offices in Tulcea (DDBRA; ☑ 0240-518 924; www.ddbra.ro; Str Portului 34A; ☺ 9am-4pm Mon-Fri) or Sfântu Gheorghe (p220). Boats are subject to spot inspections and if you're caught without a permit you could be fined. Note you need separate permits to fish or hunt.

Russians, Ukrainians and Bulgarians. There is some signage in English, though you can get the general idea without linguistic help.

🏃 **Activities**

Tulcea's main activities are boating, fishing and birdwatching. The port is lined with private boat operators offering a variety of excursions on slow boats, speedboats and pontoon boats; these can be tailored to accommodate special pursuits. Prices vary according to the operator, length of time, type of boat and number of passengers. Hotels and the Tourism Information Centre can help plan trips and choose operators.

Escape   BOATING

(☑ 0743-609 626; www.deltaescapetravel.ro; Tulcea Port; tours per person from 130 lei; ☺ tours 9am) This private operator comes highly recommended. Offers a standard mix of five-, seven- and nine-hour boat trips, on both slow and speed boats. Most tours leave at 9am daily from June to September. It will also tailor trips to accommodate special interests, such as fishing or birdwatching.

Ibis Tours   TOURS

(☑ 0722-381 398, 0240-512 787; www.ibis-tours. ro; Str Dimitrie Sturza 6; ☺ 9am-6pm Mon-Sat) Arranges wildlife and birdwatching tours in the delta and Dobrogea led by professional ornithologists.

Safca Delta Tours   BOATING

(☑ 0721-725 176, 0744-143 336; www.egretamica. ro; Tulcea Port; tours per person from 150 lei) This small father-and-son company offers a variety of boat excursions for individuals or groups of up to around eight people. It has both faster boats and a pontoon boat. Among its tours is a popular seven-hour 'slow' tour that includes a fish lunch and an all-day 'hyper' trip to Sulina that includes a visit to the beach.

🛏 Sleeping

⭐ **Hotel Select** HOTEL $$
(📞 0240-506 180; www.calypsosrl.ro; Str Păcii 6; s/d 140/170 lei; P🅿❄@🛜) A likeable version of a boxy high-rise, with the biggest selling points being the friendly staff and very good inhouse restaurant. The rooms are plain but very good value, with big and comfortable beds and light-blocking blinds on the windows.

Hotel Delta HOTEL $$
(📞 0240-514 720; www.deltahotelro.com; Str Isaccei 2; s/d 3-star 220/280 lei, 4-star 280/360 lei; ❄❄🛜❄) This landmark hotel situated toward the eastern end of the port offers both three- and four-star accommodation in adjoining buildings. The three-star rooms, with air-con and balcony views, are better value. The four-star side represents

arguably Tulcea's most luxurious property. There's an indoor pool and the location is superb.

Hotel Esplanada HOTEL $$$
(📞 0240-516 607; www.hotelesplanada.ro; Str Portului 1; s/d 280/360 lei; P❄❄🛜) This luxury property has smart rooms with contemporary furnishings and excellent views out over the Danube. There's a good in-house restaurant. It's conveniently located next to the bus station.

🍴 Eating & Drinking

⭐ **Ivan Pescar** SEAFOOD $$
(📞 0240-515 861; www.facebook.com/Ivan-Pescar-1456721501301741; Str Gării 28, Faleza Tulcea; mains 25-40 lei; ⊘noon-11pm) An awesome fish restaurant such as this is long overdue on Tulcea's Danube port. Expect very good traditional fish soup, as well as grilled fish and various stews and concoctions, pairing river species with various spices and polenta. There's an excellent wine list and very good homemade lemonade. A gift shop in the back sells wines and locally made honey and trinkets.

TRAVELLING BY PASSENGER FERRY

State-run **Navrom** (📞 0240-511 553; www.navromdelta.ro; Str Portului 26; ⊘ticket office 11.30am-1.30pm) operates both slower, traditional ferries (referred to as 'classic ships' on timetables) as well as faster hydrofoils to the main destinations in the delta. Ferries from Tulcea to Sulina (64km) tend to leave nearly every day in season (May to September), while ferries along less-travelled arms in the delta, including to Sfântu Gheorghe (109km), may only leave every other day. Be sure to check the schedule carefully to make sure a boat is departing on the day you need to leave.

Ferry tickets can only be purchased on the day of departure. In Tulcea, buy ferry tickets at ticket counters at the Navrom passenger ferry terminal along the Tulcea riverfront. In places outside of Tulcea, buy tickets at the local ferry terminal just ahead of the departure time. Try to arrive a bit early to make sure you get a ticket.

Ferry schedules vary from season to season. At the time of writing, Navrom boats were sailing according to the following summer timetable:

Tulcea to Sulina (via Crişan): Slow ferries ('classic ships') leave Tulcea at 1.30pm (46 lei, four to five hours) on Monday, Wednesday, Friday and Saturday, and return at 7am on Tuesday, Thursday, Saturday and Sunday. Fast ferries leave Tulcea at 1.30pm (56 lei, two to three hours) on Tuesday, Thursday and Sunday, returning at 7am on Monday, Wednesday and Friday.

Tulcea to Sfântu Gheorghe (via Mahmudia): Slow ferries leave Tulcea at 1.30pm (48 lei, five to six hours) on Wednesday, Thursday, Friday, and Sunday, returning at 7am on Monday, Thursday, Friday and Saturday. Fast ferries depart from Tulcea at 1.30pm (60 lei, three hours) on Monday and Saturday, returning at 7am on Tuesday and Sunday.

In addition to the scheduled passenger ferries, private companies offer water-taxi service to and from Tulcea to popular destinations in the delta. For the 90-minute journey to Sulina, for example, expect to pay around 60 lei per person.

Restaurant Select ROMANIAN **$$**

(📖 0240-506 180; www.calypsosrl.ro; Str Păcii 6; mains 20-35 lei; ⊙9am-11pm; P🔊) Though it's a couple of blocks away from the port and lacks any buzz to speak of, this hotel restaurant is still one of the best places in town. The varied menu offers fresh fish, pizza and the local speciality, *tochitura dobrogeana* (pan-fried meat with spicy sauce).

Cheers Pub PUB

(📖 0340-401 637; www.facebook.com/cheers. tulcea; Str Gării 30; ⊙9am-midnight) The liveliest pub on the Tulcea waterfront draws an eclectic mix of local fishers and tourists trudging to the nearby ferries. Serves mainly beers and coffee, but they also pop popcorn in the evenings in case you get hungry.

ⓘ Information

The helpful **Tourism Information Centre** (📖 0240-519 130; www.cnipttulcea.ro; Str Gării 26; ⊙8am-4pm Mon-Fri) can sort through the confusing ferry schedules as well as advise on various travel agencies, hotels and restaurants.

ⓘ Getting There & Away

Train service has been greatly scaled back and is not recommended.

BUS

The **bus station** (📖 0240-513 304; Str Portului 1) adjoins the main ferry terminal. As many as 10 buses and maxitaxis head daily to Bucharest (45 lei, five hours); there are two daily buses to Iași (85 lei, five hours). Maxitaxis to Constanța (35 lei, two hours) leave every half-hour from 5.30am to 8pm.

Sulina

POP 3500

The sleepy fishing port of Sulina is Romania's easternmost point (64km east of Tulcea) and the highlight of any journey along the Danube's central arm. There's a beautiful, tranquil (during the day) beach here as well as a charming canalside promenade. It's also an excellent base for forays deeper into the delta or on to the Black Sea. While Sulina has a year-round population, most hotels, restaurants and activities run only from May to September.

🎣 Activities

Sulina is a quiet place. The main activities include strolling the main promenade (Str I), soaking up the sun at the beach, 4km east of the centre, or hiring a tour boat to take you around the delta.

A bike can be handy for moving from the centre to the beach and back. There's a seasonal **Rent a Bike** (📖 0748-369 173; Str I, cnr Str Mihail Kogălniceanu; per 2hr/day 10/20 lei; ⊙9am-8pm Jun-Aug) outfit on the riverfront promenade.

Danube Delta Excursions BOATING

(Excursii în Delta Dunării; 📖 0744-821 365; Str I, cnr Str Mihail Kogălniceanu; per person 40-60 lei) One of a number of private operators along the promenade that offer boat trips into the delta and to the Gulf of Musura on the Black Sea that last from two to four hours. Make reservations and buy tickets at a display table located in front of the commercial complex near the intersection with Str Mihail Kogălniceanu.

Sulina Beach BEACH

(Plaja Sulina; ⊙May-Sep) Sulina's clean, sandy beach is ideal for kids because of the shallow water that goes out only waist-high to a distance of 100m. There are no showers, but two small restaurants have toilets. Wild camping is permitted. It's located 4km east of the passenger ferry port. Walk or take a taxi (8 lei) or minibus (2 lei).

🛏 Sleeping

There are several *cazares* and *pensiunes* here: you can accept an offer from those who greet the passenger ferries, or ask around. Expect to pay around 100 lei per room, excluding board. Wild camping is possible on the beach.

Pensiunea Ana PENSION **$**

(📖 0724-421 976; pensiuneana@yahoo.com; Str IV 144; r 120 lei; ❄❂🔊) This charming family-run affair has four rooms and a beautifully shaded garden. The view from the street is not promising but once inside the blue gate things start to look up. To find it, walk 200m west from the ferry port along the main promenade, bear left on Str Mihail Kogălniceanu, and walk four blocks inland.

★**Vila Caviar** PENSION **$$**

(📖 0744-559 213; www.pensiuneacaviarsulina.ro; Str IV 142; r 180 lei; ❄❂🔊) Clean and comfortable family-owned *pensiune*. The rooms are spacious, with hardwood floors, armoires and writing desks. There's a small garden to relax in with coffee. Meals available on request. The location is four blocks inland

SULINA'S HISTORY: MORE THAN MEETS THE EYE

Sulina has a richer history than most small towns in these parts. It was selected in the mid-19th century to serve as the headquarters of the European Commission of the Danube – an early multinational effort to transform the canals of the delta into a navigable waterway.

As the seat of an international organisation, Sulina rapidly became home to a diverse group of residents, including Romanians, Russians, Greeks, Turks and Jews, as well as a smattering of citizens from countries across Europe, including Britain, France and Germany. A taste of this diversity in action, and the comic and dramatic overtones of having so many nationalities crammed into such a small space, was captured in the popular 1933 novel *Europolis*, by the Romanian author Eugeniu Botez (writing under the pen name Jean Bart). From the book at least, little Sulina was apparently quite a bawdy place at one point.

Sadly, little of this vitality survived WWII, but you can still visit Sulina's **Lighthouse** (Farul Sulina; www.icemtl.ro/sulina-en; Str II-a 43; adult/student 5/2.50 lei; ⊘10am-6pm Tue-Sun), the actual headquarters of the commission. Indeed, the founding plaque of the commission can still be seen on the side of the building. The best place to get a feel for the seaport in its heyday is, ironically, **Sulina Cemetery** (Cimitir; DC5; ⊘sunrise-sunset) **FREE**, where the various faiths and mix of nationalities still rub shoulders, so to speak, in a tiny, harmonious setting. Don't miss the row of fallen British sailors from the 19th century, arrayed just in front of the cemetery's small chapel.

from the riverfront, just near Str Mihail Kogălniceanu.

Hotel Casa Coral   HOTEL $$
(☏0742-974 016; www.casacoralsulina.ro; Str I 195; r 150 lei; ❄☎) This modern three-star property lacks character but is arguably the nicest hotel in Sulina centre. You'll have to book in advance in summer as it tends to fill up fast. You'll find it on the main promenade 100m west of the passenger ferry port.

✖ Eating & Drinking

Perla   ROMANIAN $$
(☏0754-200 300; www.perla-sulina.ro; Str I 155; mains 20-35 lei; ⊘10am-11pm May-Sep; ☎) Reliably good restaurant, slightly west of the centre, meaning fewer crowds. Enjoy Romanian sour soups, and traditional specialities, as well as very good fish soup and grilled and fried variations of delta fish. There are a few tables outside with a nice view out onto the river canal.

Restaurant Marea Neagră   ROMANIAN $$
(☏0240-543 130; Str I 178; mains 20-30 lei; ☎) This large, popular open-air terrace offers more than a dozen fish specialities, including sturgeon. It's on the riverfront promenade, just next to Sulina's small city hall.

Irish Stoker Pub   PUB
(☏0744-696 842; Str I 181; ⊘3pm-midnight; ☎) Popular watering hole on the river promenade with decent coffee and relatively rare nonfiltered Ciuc beer on tap for 6 lei per glass. It's about 300m west of the passenger ferry port, just next to the Sulina town hall (Primăria).

ℹ Information

Farmacie (Str I, cnr Str Mihail Kogălniceanu; ⊘10am-6pm Mon-Fri, 9am-1pm Sat & Sun) Convenient pharmacy in the commercial complex, next to the supermarket and post office.

Sulina Visitor Centre (Centrul de Informare Turistica Sulina; Str I; ⊘8am-3pm Mon-Fri, to 11am Sat & Sun May-Oct) Sulina's sparsely furnished information centre has basic information on the delta, including a helpful exhibition of delta flora and fauna on the upper floor. The office is located on the seafront promenade on the extreme western edge of the pedestrianised portion, 700m west of the Navrom passenger ferry port.

ℹ Getting There & Away

There's regular Navrom passenger ferry and hydrofoil service between Tulcea and Sulina. The **ferry port** (☏information 0240-519 008; www. navromdelta.ro; Str I) is on the eastern end of the riverfront promenade, about 200m east of the centre.

In addition to the big Navrom ferries, several smaller, private companies operate a water-taxi service from Sulina to Tulcea, with most also stopping at Crişana (about midway). Be sure to reserve in advance and expect to pay around 60 lei per person for the 90-minute journey. Two reliable water-taxi companies operating between May and September are **Eco Delta** (☑ 0742-529 011; www.delta-trip.ro; Str 1; per person 60 lei; ☺ May-Sep), with daily boats departing at 10am and 3pm, and **Travel Delta Star** (☑ 0752-917 592; www.excursii-delta-dunarii.ro; Str 1; ☺ May-Sep), with boats leaving at 7am, 8am, noon and 4pm daily.

At the time of research, the only access to Sfântu Gheorghe (30km south) was by private boat. Negotiate rates on the waterfront. Expect to pay upwards of 400 lei for the one- to three-hour journey (depending on the type and speed of the boat).

Sfântu Gheorghe

POP 1000

First recorded in the mid-14th century by Visconti, a traveller from Genoa, the remote seaside village of Sfântu Gheorghe, on the eastern end of the Sfântu Gheorghe channel (109km from Tulcea), retains an ever-so-slight alternative vibe, fed by the town's lovely, lonely beach and its sleepy, noncommercial core. It's also one of the best places in the delta to sample traditional cooking (including some fabulous fish soup). Each August the village hosts what just might be the world's most remote film festival, the Anonimul fest.

🏃 Activities

There's not much to do here and that's precisely the point. Take your pick between lazing on the beautiful sandy beach and exploring the waterways on a boat trip. Several private boat owners offer excursions into the delta or to the Black Sea. Negotiate your itinerary and prices in advance. The Delta Marina hotel organises boat trips too. See the reception desk for details.

Delta Boat Trips BOATING
(☑ 0744-586 360; Portul; boat trip per person 50-60 lei) This private boat operator just west of the ferry terminal is one of several along the waterfront offering two- to six-hour trips around the delta. Rates vary but start at around 50 lei per person for a standard two-hour tour. Popular tours include visiting pelican colonies and the mouth of the Danube, where it enters the Black Sea.

Sfântu Gheorghe Beach BEACH
(Plaja Sfântu Gheorghe; ☺ 9am-8pm Jun-Aug) Sfântu Gheorghe's wild beach is one of Romania's most beautiful. Fine, white sand, clean water and rarely more than a handful of sunbathers make this a beach worth seeking out. There are few facilities, so bring food and whatever else you might need. It's 4km east of the centre. Walk about 30 minutes or take the Transport Plaja (Trocarici; ☑ 0740-572 269; Str Principala (Str 1); per person 3 lei).

🛏 Sleeping

There are several *cazares* and *pensiunes* here: you can accept an offer from those who greet the incoming passenger ferries, or ask around. Wild camping is possible on the beach, but it gets windy and it's a long 4km hike in the dark.

★**Vila Petru & Marcela Stefanov** PENSION $
(☑ 0240-546 811, 0763-088 859; near Str Principala (Str I); s/d incl half board 120/150 lei) This family-run *pensiune* offers clean and comfortable accommodation just a few metres' walk from the town centre. Rates include half-board, which means delicious homemade fish soup followed by more grilled fish. The street and property are unmarked, but the *pensiune* is three houses north (on the left-hand side) of the *complex comercial* and supermarket, just beyond Str Principala (Str I).

Delta Marina HOTEL $$
(☑ 0240-546 946; www.deltamarina.ro; Str Principala (Str I); r 150 lei; ❋ ☎) This small, modern hotel is situated on the water about 200m west of the ferry port. The 15 rooms here are modestly sized but outfitted with comfortable beds, up-to-date baths and minibars. The popular terrace restaurant is one of the few places in town to grab a sit-down meal (mains 20 to 25 lei).

Green Village RESORT $$$
(☑ 0731-818 511, 0241-487 090; www.greenvillage.ro; Str Principala (Str 1); s/d 400/500 lei; ☺❋☎⊠) This four-star resort has the best facilities in Sfântu Gheorghe. Accommodation is in bungalows with thatched roofs designed to harmonise with the delta setting. The restaurant is open to the public. There's a pool, spa and bike rental (per hour 10 lei). It's located 1.5km east of the centre (a 15-minute walk east of the ferry port).

🍴 Eating & Drinking

There are few restaurants around, so you're best off booking full- or half-board deals with your hotel or pension. The Delta Marina hotel has a decent terrace restaurant that also opens at 7am for breakfast if necessary.

Bar Terasa CAFE

(Str Principala (Str I); ⊙8am-2am May-Sep; 🛜) When it comes to evening drinking, this centrally located open-air terrace is the only game in town. Serves beer and coffee throughout the day to a pulsating pop soundtrack that changes over to live music some evenings around 9pm.

ℹ Information

Danube Delta Biosphere Reserve Authority (🗷 0240-518 926; www.ddbra.ro; Str Ia 39; permits day/week 5/15 lei; ⊙7am-noon & 4-7pm Tue-Fri, 9am-1pm Sat & Sun May-Oct) Decent source for what to see and do on the delta. Sells visitors permits. Located on the harbour, 50m from the entrance to the passenger ferry port.

ℹ Getting There & Away

There's a regular Navrom ferry and hydrofoil service between Tulcea and Sfântu Gheorghe. The **ferry port** (🗷 information 0240-519 008; www.navromdelta.ro) is 100m southeast of the village centre. The only access to Sulina (30km to the north) is by water taxi. Negotiate rates on the waterfront. Expect to pay upwards of 400 lei for the one- to three-hour journey (depending on the type and speed of the boat).

BLACK SEA COAST & LITTORAL

Romania's Black Sea coast is not well known outside the country. And, indeed, the beach resorts in neighbouring Bulgaria generally offer superior facilities and better prices. That said, Romania's coast has a charm of its own, especially if you like your beaches loud and summer nights long. The two main resorts, Mamaia and Vama Veche, tend to draw different crowds. Mamaia is the larger and brasher of the two, and beaches here co-exist alongside big package-tour hotels and swish nightclubs (especially in the northern end of the resort). 'Vama' attracts a counter-culture crowd and feels much more down to earth, though the facilities here are more primitive.

Constanţa

POP 283,000

Constanţa is Romania's largest and most important port city on the Black Sea; in summer it's also the gateway to the country's seaside resorts. Accommodation here is cheaper than in Mamaia and maxi taxis cover the journey in about 15 minutes, so it may be worthwhile to consider basing yourself here even if you're only coming for Mamaia's beaches and clubs. The city is working hard to scrub up the long-neglected area around the port, and there are some very good museums and a pretty portside walk. The restaurants are the best in this part of the country.

◉ Sights

◉ City Centre & Ovid Square

The city centre and the area around Ovid Square (Piaţa Ovidiu) have the city's most important museums. Ovid Sq is easy to find. Just look for the landmark Statue of Ovid (Piaţa Ovidiu) standing at the centre. The famed Roman poet (43 BC–AD 17) was banished here by Emperor Augustus in AD 8 for reasons that remain unclear to this day. By all accounts, he hated being so far away from his beloved Rome. The statue dates from 1887 and is the work of Ettore Ferrari.

National History & Archaeological Museum MUSEUM

(Muzeul de Istorie Nationala si Arheologie Constanta; 🗷 0241-618 763; www.minac.ro; Piaţa Ovidiu 12; adult/child 13/5 lei; ⊙9am-8pm Jun-Sep, to 5pm Tue-Sun Oct-May) This is the city's most important museum, though on balance it's a minor disappointment. The stunning ground-floor exhibits of vases, jewellery and statuary from the Greek and Roman periods, lasting until about AD 500, justify the admission price, but the upper floors on more recent times and Romanian national history are poorly lit and lack signage in English. Skip the top floor altogether.

Roman Mosaic RUINS

(Edificiul Roman cu Mozaic; Piaţa Ovidiu 12; adult/child 10/5 lei; ⊙9am-8pm Tue-Sun Jun-Sep, 10am-6pm Oct-May) Located just behind and south of the National History & Archaeological Museum, a modern building protects what's left of a Roman floor mosaic dating from the 4th century that was discovered in the 1960s. The site is near where the forum of ancient Tomis is thought to have existed. On the grounds surrounding the mosaic are old Roman tombstones, complete with highly moving and surprisingly modern epitaphs that have been translated into English.

Great Mahmudiye Mosque
MOSQUE

(Carol I Mosque; Str Arhiepiscopiei 5; adult/child 5/3 lei; ⊙9am-5pm) This impressive mosque is the seat of the mufti and was built in 1910 by King Carol I. It's the spiritual home of the 50,000 Muslims in the coastal region. The highlight is the enormous Persian rug, said to be the largest carpet in the country. You can climb the 140 steps of the minaret.

Folk Art Museum
MUSEUM

(Muzeul de Artă Populară; ☑ 0241-616 133; B-dul Tomis 32; adult/child 5/2.50 lei; ⊙9am-7.30pm) This large and impressive collection features folk costumes, implements, household items and interiors of traditional homes from around Romania.

Naval History Museum
MUSEUM

(Muzeul Marinei Române; ☑ 0241-619 035; Str Traian 53; adult/child 10/5 lei; ⊙10am-6pm Wed-Sun) This museum offers a fascinating if slightly confusing stroll through 2000 years of maritime history on the Black Sea. The exhibit begins in the Greco-Roman period, with some intricate models of old Roman boats, but quickly moves to the 19th and 20th centuries. The garden is strewn with relics of real propellers, landmines and torpedoes that seem to be rusting into the ground.

◎ Seaside Promenade & Around

One of the city's finest assets is a peaceful promenade that meanders along the waterfront, offering sweeping views of the Black Sea. The crown jewel of the promenade is the gloriously derelict casino.

Casino
HISTORIC BUILDING

(Faleza Casino Constanţa; B-dul Elisabeta 1; ⊙closed to the public) Constanţa's stunning but sadly derelict art nouveau casino, dating from 1910, was awaiting a long overdue renovation at the time of research and closed to the public. The building was commissioned by King Carol I and once drew monied holidaymakers from across Europe. It fell on hard times after the fall of communism and has struggled to find a suitor ever since.

Aquarium
AQUARIUM

(Acvariu; ☑ 0241-481 461; www.delfinariu.ro; Faleza Casino Constanţa, B-dul Elisabeta 1; adult/child 20/10 lei; ⊙9.30am-8.30pm Jun–mid-Sep, 10am-6pm Tue-Sun mid-Sep–May) This waterfront aquarium focuses on fish native to the Black Sea, including a large selection of endangered sturgeon, as well as local freshwater species.

Black Sea Coast

THE DANUBE DELTA & BLACK SEA COAST CONSTANŢA

Central Constanţa

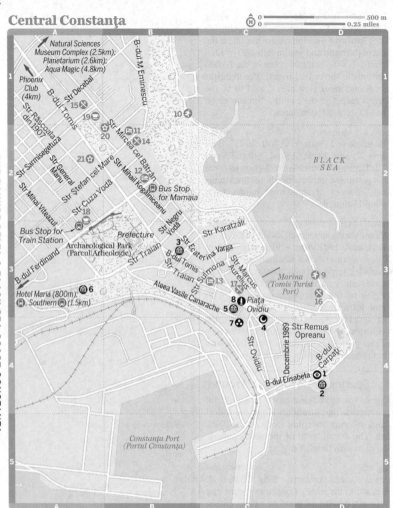

THE DANUBE DELTA & BLACK SEA COAST CONSTANŢA

⊙ Outside the Centre

Natural Sciences
Museum Complex   MUSEUM
(Dolphinarium/Delfinariu; ☑ 0241-481 230; www.
delfinariu.ro; B-dul Mamaia 255; adult/child 25/12
lei; ⊙ 9am-8pm) The museum complex is
more of a zoo than traditional museum,
with exhibits on flora and fauna, including
live birds and other animals, common to
the Black Sea region. The complex features
a dolphinarium, with daily performances
of trained dolphins. Bear in mind that
sea-animal encounters and similar shows

have received criticism from animal-welfare
groups who claim the captivity of marine
life is debilitating and stressful for the animals, and that this is exacerbated by human
interaction.

Planetarium   PLANETARIUM
(www.delfinariu.ro; B-dul Mamaia 255; adult/
child 10/5 lei; ⊙ shows at 10am, 11.30am, 1.30pm,
3.30pm, 4.30pm) Constanţa's planetarium,
located just next to the Natural Sciences
Museum Complex, is a fun rainy-day treat
for kids. The 3D projection shows throughout the day are narrated in Romanian, but

Central Constanţa

the visual effects are stunning and will wow small kids.

🏃 Activities

Swim in the Black Sea at **Modern Beach** (Plaja Modern; Str Ştefan cel Mare), situated at the eastern end of Str Ştefan cel Mare (walk down the steps). It's a pleasant enough place to get your feet wet, but the facilities at nearby Mamaia are superior.

Condor Cruise Boat (Plimbari pe mare; ☑0729-199 538, 0742-817 916; www.facebook. com/CondorsiTomis; Marina, Portul Tomis; per person per hour 25 lei, min 6 persons; ◷9am-10pm May-Sep) offers tailored sightseeing tours suitable for six to 12 people. You'll find the boat anchored at the city's tourist port (Tomis Turist Port), in front of the On Plonge restaurant.

🛏 Sleeping

During the summer season, don't be surprised if you're approached at the train station with offers of private rooms. The prices are attractive (rooms for 60 to 100 lei) compared to hotels, but the rooms are likely to be nothing special, with shared bathrooms and scant privacy. The nearest camping ground is north of Mamaia.

★**Hotel Cherica** BOUTIQUE HOTEL **$$**
(☑0756-617 174; www.cherica.ro; Str Ştefan cel Mare 4; s/d 240/280 lei; P❂❉@❉) Beautifully refurbished townhouse with spacious, suite-like rooms on three floors. The rooms have retained period details like large windows and panelled walls, but given a

modern makeover with thick carpets and gleaming baths. The location is just next to Constanţa's beach and within easy walking distance of the old port area.

Hotel Maria HOTEL **$$**
(☑0241-611 711; www.hotelmaria-ct.ro; B-dul 1 Decembrie 1918, 2d; s/d 160/200 lei; ❉❉) This simple, modern hotel sits across the park from the train station and close to the bus station and makes sense if you're arriving late or departing early. The rooms feature big windows, modern baths and writing desks.

Hotel Ferdinand HOTEL **$$**
(☑0241-617 974; www.hotelferdinand.ro; B-dul Ferdinand 12; s/d/ste 220/260/380 lei; P❂❉❉) Arguably the best three-star hotel in town. Nothing fancy, just a well-run property in a smart, nicely restored 1930s townhouse. Rooms have fridges and big, comfy beds. The hotel is within easy walking distance of virtually everything, including the city beach. Mamaia-bound maxitaxis leave from across the street.

Villa Anticus HOTEL **$$$**
(☑0722-611 114; www.vilaanticus.ro; B-dul Tomis 23; s 260 lei, d 290-360 lei; ❂❉@❉) This stylishly renovated boutique hotel on the pedestrianised section of lower B-dul Tomis is close to the city's beach, port and most sights. All rooms feature top-quality mattresses as well as high-end towels and toiletries; pricier rooms are more spacious. The neighbourhood is slowly gentrifying but still spotty in sections.

✖ Eating

Constanța has some of the best restaurants in this part of Romania. Enjoy fresh fish by the port and a range of other restaurants scattered around the centre.

★ **Irish Pub**   INTERNATIONAL **$$**
(📞 0241-550 400; www.irishpub.ro; Str Ştefan cel Mare 1; mains 20-40 lei; ⊙ 8am-midnight; 📶)
Several years after it opened to an enthusiastic reception, this is still *the* place to see and be seen, and one of the best restaurants in town. There are a couple of pub staples like burgers, and fish and chips, but the menu has higher aspirations, with steaks and grilled fish. It's equally good for beer or coffee. Reservations at meal times are essential.

★ **Pizzico**   INTERNATIONAL **$$**
(📞 0746-013 004; www.pizzico.ro; Piaţa Ovidiu 7; mains 15-40 lei; ⊙ 8am-2.30am; 📶) Pizzico has greatly expanded its range in the past couple of years, moving beyond very good wood-fired pizza to excellent grilled meats, seafood and chops. The location, on Piaţa Ovidiu, makes it easy to pair lunch here with a visit to a nearby museum.

On Plonge   SEAFOOD **$$**
(📞 0241-601 905; www.onplonge.ro; Tomis Turist Port; mains 15-40 lei; ⊙ 10am-11.30pm) This brawny portside eatery with an informal, everyman vibe specialises in fresh fish hauled in off the boat. Gets packed on summer nights and service suffers accordingly. The views out over the port and the old town are stunning.

Marco Polo   ITALIAN **$$$**
(📞 0241-617 357; Str Sarmizegetuza 2, cnr Str Mircea cel Bătrân; mains 30-50 lei; ⊙ noon-10.30pm; 📶) A swanky Italian restaurant where servers swarm to keep patrons happy. Portions are generous and the pizza, pasta, meat, fish and veg dishes are all delicious. You might consider dressing up for this one.

🍷 Drinking & Nightlife

Cafes usually do double duty as drinking establishments after sunset. In summer much of the drinking and clubbing action shifts to Mamaia, and Constanța can feel like a ghost town.

★ **Barissimo**   CAFE, COCKTAIL BAR
(📞 0736-366 101; www.barissimo.ro; B-dul Ferdinand 32; ⊙ 8am-1am; 📶) Worth a trip to admire the stunning steampunk-inspired interior of tiles and colours and big bar built from stacks of pulped paperback books. Great coffee, superb cocktails and a smart, hipsterish vibe make this a great stop for a coffee break or a longer evening session over drinks. There's a small lunch menu as well, with salads, sandwiches and burgers.

Crazy   CAFE, BAR
(📞 0726-779 292; www.crazycafe.ro; Str Mircea cel Bătrân 97a; cocktails 20 lei; ⊙ 9am-2am; 📶) This is a stylish and secluded spot for coffee or drinks, and works equally well for relaxing in the afternoon or partying in the evening. The main draws are the generous open-air terrace, decent cocktails and a bar built wholly from tree branches laid horizontally. They also do breakfasts (15 to 21 lei) and light bites throughout the day.

WORTH A TRIP

THE ANCIENT GREEK POLIS OF HISTRIA

About 65km north of Constanța, Histria, or Istros, settled in 657 BC by Greek traders, is Romania's oldest town. Its founding by Greek colonists, through the Hellenic decline, the rise and fall of the Roman Empire and then the rise of Byzantium, forms a fascinating microcosm of early settlement in this part of the world.

Over the centuries, Histria became a key commercial port, superseding even that at Constanța. But subsequent Goth attacks coupled with the gradual sand-locking of the harbour led to its equally rapid decline. By the 7th century AD the town was abandoned.

Its ruins were discovered and excavated in the late 19th and early 20th centuries. Relics uncovered at the site are displayed in the **Histria Archaeological Complex & Museum** (📞 0241-618 763; www.histria-cheiledobrogei.ro; Istria; adult/child 20/5 lei; ⊙ 9am-8pm). From the entrance to the site, paths lead visitors through the ancient city's remains, and pass by the big tower into the western sector, where most of the public buildings, the thermal baths and the civil basilica stood. Close by is the Christian basilica, built with stones from the old theatre in the 6th century AD.

⭐ Entertainment

Phoenix Club LIVE MUSIC
(📞0730-617 787; www.club-phoenix.ro; Str Capitan Dobrilă Eugeniu 1; ⏰7pm-3am) Legendary rock club with a rep that goes back to the '90s for bringing to Constanța Romania's biggest rock and metal acts. Check the walls for a list of groups that have played here over the years. It's still going strong, with live music most weekends. Check the website for details.

Oleg Danovski
National Theatre OPERA, BALLET
(Teatrul Național de Operă și Balet 'Oleg Danovski'; 🎫tickets 0241-481 460; www.tnobconstanta.ro; Str Mircea cel Bătrân 97; tickets 15-30 lei; ⏰box office 10am-5pm Mon-Fri) The city's premier venue for opera and dance. Buy tickets at the theatre box office or the central **ticket office** (📞0241-488 247; www.opera-balet-constanta.ro; B-dul Tomis 97; ⏰10am-7pm Wed-Fri, 4-8pm Sat & Sun).

ℹ Information

There are abundant banks and ATMs in the centre.

Constanța Country Emergency Hospital
(Spitalul Clinic Județean de Urgență Constanța; 📞0241-662 222; www.spitalulconstanta.ro; B-dul Tomis 145)

Forte-Games (📞0241-551 251; www.forte-games.ro; B-dul Tomis 235; per hour 6 lei; ⏰24hr)

ℹ Getting There & Away

BUS

Constanța, like many large Romanian cities, has several bus stations, depending on which bus line is operating the route. Buses to Bucharest (60 lei, three to four hours) and to the southern resorts, including Vama Veche (13.50 lei, one hour, several daily), often depart from outside the train station. Most other buses use the large **southern bus station** (Autogara Sud; 📞0241-665 289; B-dul Ferdinand), about 200m north of the train station. Buses to Tulcea (35 lei, two to three hours) and points north often leave from other parts of town. Your best best is to check the website www.autogari.ro to see times and departure points.

Several buses and minibuses make the 30-minute run out to Mamaia throughout the day. A convenient bus stop for Mamaia is located on B-dul Ferdinand, across the street from the Hotel Ferdinand.

TRAIN

Constanța's **train station** (📞0241-614 960; www.cfrcalatori.ro; B-dul Ferdinand 45) is near the southern bus station, 2km southwest of the centre; buses run from a central stop on B-dul Ferdinand to the station. There are several fast Inter-City trains a day to Bucharest (60 lei, two to three hours). There are also daily services to Suceava (100 lei, eight hours), Iași (90 lei, eight hours), Timișoara (120 lei, 14 hours), via Arad, and other destinations. In summer, several trains a day head from Constanța south to Mangalia (8 lei, 1½ hours), with stops at resorts in between.

Mamaia
POP 200
Mamaia, a thin strip of sand extending north from Constanța, is Romania's most popular and expensive package-holiday resort. In season, from early June to early September, the 8km-long beachfront is lined end to end with sunbathers from all around Romania, who compete for that precious patch of seaside real estate. By night, Mamaia morphs into what feels like one long nightclub, with dozens of high-adrenaline dance places and impromptu beach parties.

🏃 Activities

Mamaia's main activities are sunbathing and swimming. The beach stretches for 8km, with the southern end, towards Constanța, being the most crowded and least appealing. The further north you go the more exclusive the resorts become, with correspondingly nicer sand and cleaner water. The beachfront is sectioned off into smaller private beaches, usually belonging to a hotel or sponsored by companies; entry is free but you'll be expected to rent a lounge chair (15 lei per day) or daybed (single/double 35/50 lei per day).

Crush Beach BEACH
(📞0767-488 944; www.facebook.com/ClubCrush.ro; Telegondola Station (northern end); free admission, s/d daybed 35/50 lei; ⏰8am-11pm Jun-Sep) Popular beach located beside the northern terminus of Mamaia's telegondola line.

Aqua Magic WATER PARK
(📞0241-831 176; www.aqua-magic.ro; adult/child Jun & Sep 40/20 lei, Jul & Aug 70/30 lei; ⏰10am-6pm Jun & Sep, 9am-7pm Jul & Aug) This amazing water park (at the southern end of the telegondola station) has pools, slides and inner-tube rides galore. It can get very crowded on summer weekends, so try to arrive early to snag a decent chair, or go during the week.

THE DANUBE DELTA & BLACK SEA COAST MAMAIA

Boats to Ovidiu Island BOATING

(Insula Ovidiu; ☑ 0241-550 550; B-dul Mamaia; per person one-way 20 lei, child under 7 yr free; ⊗ boats 10am-11.30pm) In summer boats ferry tourists across Lake Siutghiol to Insula Ovidiu (Ovidiu Island), where there's a good restaurant and Ovid's tomb is said to be located. They depart every 30 minutes from a small unmarked wharf on the lake (*not* the beach) toward the northern end of the Mamaia resort.

🛏 Sleeping

Mamaia is flush with resort complexes that are better attuned to handling package tours than walk-ins. If you know your dates in advance and plan to stay at least three days, you're better off arranging a package through a travel agency like Mistral Tours. You'll save plenty on the rack rate and spare yourself the hassle of going from hotel to hotel trying to find a free room. See www.turist info.ro for a complete list of Mamaia hotels.

Hotel Ovidiu HOTEL $$

(☑ 0241-831 590; www.hotelovidiu.ro; Aleea Falezei; d/tr 250/350 lei; ⊜ ❊ 🛜) This simple two-star hotel offers basic, clean rooms at a good price and not much else. Request an upper-floor room to get a better sea view. It's located about the middle of the resort, just south of the northern telegondola station.

Hotel Splendid HOTEL $$$

(☑ 0341-412 541; www.splendidhotel.ro; B-dul Mamaia, Mamaia Nord; s/d 480/560 lei; P ⊜ ❊ @ 🛜) This five-storey modern hotel, built in 2007, is a quiet option since it's on the western side of the main road (away from the beachfront, along Lake Siutghiol). The 31 rooms get high marks for cleanliness and the adjoining restaurant is a decent choice for a meal. You'll find it on the northern end of the resort.

🍴 Eating

Almost every hotel has its own adjoining restaurant and there are numerous fast-food stands and self-serve restaurants lining the boardwalk.

La Mama ROMANIAN $$

(☑ 0730-526 262; www.lamama.ro; Faleza Casino Mamaia; mains 20-35 lei; ⊗ 9am-2am May-Sep; 🛜) This branch of a reliable local chain serves up huge portions of traditional Romanian specialities at affordable, family-friendly prices. You'll find it on the main promenade

about 200m south of the northern telegondola station.

★ Chevalet INTERNATIONAL $$$

(☑ 0721-421 501; www.restaurantchevalet.com; Complex Enigma; mains 50-80 lei; ⊗ 11am-11pm; 🛜) Head chef Nelu Păucă trained around the world before opening this romantic beachfront restaurant on the far northern end of Mamaia. Specialities include steak tartare, frog legs and a mouthwatering array of beef, pork and seafood. Book in advance to secure a table on the sea.

🍷 Drinking & Nightlife

Mamaia is known around the country for its vibrant party scene. In season, the clubs decamp from Constanţa and reopen en masse on the coast, filling the air with the beat of dance music nightly, starting at around 10pm and continuing until the wee hours.

Crazy Beach CLUB

(☑ 0726-676 666; www.crazybeach.ro; B-dul Mamaia Nord; ⊗ 8am-1am) One of the hottest clubs in Mamaia is this open-air lounge and cocktail bar, situated in the extreme north of Mamaia, about 4km beyond the northern telegondola station. Take a taxi (about 10 lei from central Mamaia). By day, this is a chilled out beach, with clean sand and lounge chairs.

ℹ Information

Mistral Tours (☑ 0728-281 676; www.mistral tours.ro; ⊗ 9am-5pm Mon-Fri, to 1pm Sat) This helpful travel agency, located at the southern end of Mamaia's telegondola line, should be your first port of call. Staff can help find accommodation, plan day trips and excursions, including to the Danube Delta and Bulgarian Black Sea coast, and sell the Constanţa City Pass discount card.

ℹ Getting There & Away

Frequent maxitaxis (2 lei, 15 minutes) ply the route between central Constanţa and Mamaia from June to September. Maxitaxis 301 and 303 depart regularly from Constanţa's train station. You can wave them down conveniently on B-dul Ferdinand, across the street from both the Hotel Class and the Hotel Ferdinand.

ℹ Getting Around

Once in Mamaia, stroll the boardwalk or take the *telegondola* (cable car) that runs from the **station** (one way 20 lei; ⊗ 9am-10pm Jun-Oct) at the southern end of the resort to the **northern station** (one way 20 lei; ⊗ 9am-10pm Jun-Oct) at approximately the midway point.

BATHING IN THE MUD AT EFORIE NORD

Eforie Nord, 14km south of Constanţa, is a honky-tonk seaside resort, free of pretension, where families come to soak up the sun by day and gorge on junk food by night. That said, there's another reason for making a detour here: the amazing mud. Lake Techirghiol, within walking distance of the centre, is famous for its dark sapropel mud. This black sediment is dense with organic matter and when slathered over your body is said to be restorative for skin and bones.

Most of the big hotels in town offer some kind of mud-bath package, but the easiest – and cheapest – way to take the mud is to head to the public **mud baths** (Bai Reci; adult/student 13/5 lei; ⊙7am-7pm) on the southern end of town. At the baths, single-sex changing rooms lead to separate beaches, where convalescence seekers stand around nude, apply the glop and bask in the sun until the mud cracks.

Eforie Nord gets incredibly crowded in July and August, so advance hotel bookings are essential. There are tonnes of accommodation options in town. For budget travellers, **Hotel Clas** (✆0725-528 296; www.hotel-clas.ro; Str Armand Călinescu 8; r 120-230 lei; P❋⊛) is clean and well run. A decent midrange choice, close to the beach, is the **Hotel Regal** (✆0241-741 069; www.hotelregaleforie.ro; B-dul Ovidiu 20; d 235-270 lei; P❋⊛). For top end, go for the **Hotel Europa** (✆0725-702 818; www.anahotels.ro; Str Panselelor 23; s/d 240/450 lei; P⊖❋@⊛⊠), which offers a full range of mud treatments.

Vama Veche

POP 280

The southernmost point on the Romanian Black Sea coast just happens to be party central. Vama Veche is *the* place where ageing hippies and bearded hipsters mingle, let their hair down and bond over beers and beach. 'Vama' has stubbornly resisted attempts by developers to drag it upmarket and still retains a whiff of counterculture rebellion – a rep it developed in the '80s when it was a haven for artists, hedonists and free thinkers. That said, don't come looking for peace and quiet. Vama can get impossibly crowded in July and August. Instead, this is the place to dance all night and sleep it off on the beach the next day.

🏃 Activities

The main activities are swimming, sunbathing, drinking and partying, and not necessarily in that order. There's a 5km bike path to an adjoining seaside village to the north called Doi Mai (2 Mai), that starts from the northern end of Vama Veche.

Plaja de Carta　　　　BEACH
(day beds 20 lei; ⊙9am-8pm Jun-Aug) This relaxed beach is situated on the far northern end of the resort and tends to be less crowded. The draw is a lending library, where you can borrow books (some in English) to read on the beach. It's a 'mixed' beach, meaning nudist on the northern side, though no one cares whether you're wearing a suit or not.

Amphora Beach　　　　BEACH
(✆0755-141 420; Str Falezei; day beds 20 lei; ⊙9am-midnight Jun-Sep) Arguably Vama's prettiest beach, occupying a long strand of fine sand on the southern end of the resort, with comfortable day beds, lounge chairs and umbrellas for rent. Come back for sunset and evenings, when Amphora morphs into a cocktail bar and (on weekends) dance club.

🛌 Sleeping

Alas, Vama's growing popularity means it's no longer possible to show up in July or August and expect to find a room. This is doubly true on weekends. Book as far ahead as possible. There's wild camping at both the far southern and northern ends of the beach. Hotels normally operate from June to September.

★ Pura Vida　　　　HOSTEL **$**
(✆0786-055 288; www.puravidahostels.ro; Str Falezei; dm from 50 lei, d from 140 lei; P⊖⊛) Clean, well-run hostel with a perfect perch, on the northern end of Vama beach. There are a handful of private doubles as well as a couple of multibed dorm rooms on two floors. The hostel has a beautiful terrace with beach views and a popular, chilled-out coffee bar. No credit cards.

Elga's Punk Rock Hotel
HOTEL $

(☑ 0241-858 070; www.punkrockhotel.com; Str Mihail Kogălniceanu; r 80-100 lei; P ⊖ ✳ 🌐) This welcoming family-run hotel offers small but ultra-clean rooms with either double or twin beds in two price categories. 'A' level rooms are slightly larger and have air-conditioning, while category 'B' rooms are smaller and have fans. There's a shared kitchen on the premises.

Club d'Or
HOTEL $$

(☑ 0743-335 114; www.clubdor.ro; Str Ion Creangă; r 180 lei; P ⊖ 🌐 ≋) Clean, quiet and close enough to the beach to drift in and out when you want. The rooms resemble a motel and fan out around a gigantic, clean swimming pool. It's located 100m west of Str Mihail Kogălniceanu (Hwy E87) at approximately the centre of the village.

BazArt
HOSTEL $$

(☑ 0722-889 087; www.bazarthostel.ro; Str Ion Creangă, cnr Str Tudor Vladimirescu; d 100-180 lei, q 280 lei; ✳ 🌐) This popular student choice on Vama Veche's main drag offers a variety of rooms, including comfortable private doubles with en suite baths and air-conditioning, as well as budget twins and quads with shared facilities and no air-con. The location is convenient to the bars and clubs. Rents bikes (2hr/day 10/25 lei; ⊙ 9am-sundown Jun-Sep).

✕ Eating

The main street that connects the highway to the beach, Str Ion Creangă, has plenty of fast-food stalls and mini-markets. Most restaurants are uniformly mediocre, though there are a couple of decent places worth seeking out. Restaurants run from late May to mid-September.

★ Sandalandala
INTERNATIONAL $$

(☑ 0749-551 476; www.sandalandala.ro; mains 25-40 lei; ⊙ 8am-11pm Jun-Sep) This spacious summertime terrace bar and restaurant, connected to a campground on the northern end of the resort, feels like a relaxing antidote to the general chaos of Vama. Grilled meats, cooked over an enormous outdoor smoker, are the specialities. There's a terrific wine list and it also does good breakfasts, starting from 8am.

Casa Double M
ROMANIAN $$

(☑ 0749-057 557; www.casadoublem.ro; Str Mihail Kogălniceanu 3A; mains 20-40 lei; 🌐) This family-run inn on the main highway that passes through town takes home-cooking to a new level. Traditional Romanian dishes, as well as ample fish and seafood, are paired imaginatively with local sides such as polenta. Double M has a good wine list and offers both indoor and outdoor seating. This place gets very popular in season, so reserve in advance.

Cherhana
SEAFOOD $$

(Str Falezei; mains 20-30 lei; ⊙ 10am-11pm Jun-Sep) This informal grill-and-picnic-tables beachfront place draws big crowds, particularly campers from the nearby wild campsites. The fresh fish is grilled on the spot. To find it, follow the main street, Str Ion Creangă, to the beach and turn left. It's situated on the northern edge of Vama Veche.

♇ Drinking & Nightlife

Vama has a legendary rep in Romania as a summertime party spot. Most of the serious partying takes places over weekends in July and August, but there's usually plenty of drinking and dancing options available any night of the week. The scene typically ends the last weekend in August.

Expirat
CLUB

(☑ 0733-974 782; Str Falezei 32; ⊙ 24hr) Expirat is widely considered Vama's premier dance club and weekend parties in July and August routinely last well into the next morning. On off nights, Expirat is a relatively tame cocktail bar with a nice view out over the beach.

Stuf
BEACH BAR

(www.stufvamaveche.ro; Plaja Vama Veche; ⊙ 9am-2am Jun-Sep) This is the oldest and most likeable of several beachside drinking shacks with their signature thatched roofs and picnic tables. To find it, walk down the main drag, Str Ion Creangă, to the beach and turn left.

ⓘ Information

There's no tourist information office, but it's small enough to negotiate on your own. The main street, Str Ion Creangă, which runs east from Hwy E87 to the beach, has everything you're likely to need, including a handy ATM and a pharmacy.

ⓘ Getting There & Away

There are no trains to Vama Veche; instead take a maxitaxi from Constanța (about 12 lei) or take a train to Mangalia and a maxitaxi from there (8km, 5 lei).

Understand Romania

Romania Today

Romania finds itself in a clean-up phase, both physically and metaphorically. Towns and cities around the land are sprucing themselves up, renovating and modernising in step with the country's expanding reputation as a tourist destination. The new emphasis on tidiness extends to the upper reaches of government. Officials have launched a long-awaited crackdown on corruption in the hope of winning the favour of Brussels and finally gaining all of the benefits of EU membership.

Best on Film

4 Months, 3 Weeks & 2 Days (2007) Breakthrough drama on illegal abortion that kicked off the 'Romanian New Wave'.

Tuesday, After Christmas (2010) Slow dissolution of a marriage, with the pressure of the holidays in the backdrop.

Child's Pose (2013) Gripping story about bending the system to get a man absolved of a crime.

Best in Print

Between the Woods and the Water (Patrick Leigh Fermor; 1986) Reminiscences of an Englishman who undertakes a remarkable journey through Transylvania in the '30s.

The Historian (Elizabeth Kostova; 2005) Brilliantly reanimates the Dracula myth focusing on Vlad Țepeș.

Nostalgia (Mircea Cărtărescu; 2005) Short stories on modern Romanian life weaving together dream and reality.

Best in Music

Band of Gypsies (Taraf de Haïdouks; 2001) Roma-inspired folk music.

OM (Negură Bunget; 2006) Metal band blending folk and noise.

Romanian Rhapsodies (George Enescu; 1901) The best-known compositions of Romania's greatest classical composer.

Not Quite a 'Full' EU Member

While Romania has been a formal member of the EU since 2007, visitors to the country will notice that not all perks of membership appear to apply.

The first major difference is that entry into the country from the EU requires you to show a passport. Romania is still not a member of the EU's common border and customs 'Schengen Zone'. Membership in Schengen was part of the original package when Romania and Bulgaria were negotiating EU membership in the run-up to 2007, but Brussels delayed the decision for both. More recently it has again deferred the question of Schengen entry, and at the time of research it wasn't clear when or if Romania would receive this coveted perk.

The other big difference is that Romania still does not use the euro. It is among a handful of EU states where old national currencies still circulate. The reasons are complex. At first, Romania didn't meet stringent EU budget and inflation standards for joining the common currency. Later, in the aftermath of the 2008 economic crisis, particularly with problems in EU-member Greece, neither Bucharest nor Brussels appeared eager to force the euro on Romania. Central banks still make occasional noises about joining the euro, but the date keeps getting pushed off further and further into the future.

Growing 'Colectiv' Conscience

The evolution of Romanian society since the fall of communism in 1989 has been an amazing process. In the first decade after the revolution, it looked (from the outside at least) as if little had changed. After all, the new election cycles seemed only to return the same old and familiar faces to power. More often than not, these leaders had ties to the old regime.

In more recent years, though, it appears this former acquiescence to the status quo – the belief that nothing will change – is itself starting to change. Many point to the Roşia Montană environmental dispute of 2013 and 2014 as the first glimmer of a population willing to fight back. The dispute involved a deal between a Canadian mining company and the Romanian government to exploit a gold seam in a protected part of Transylvania. Fearing the project would destroy the area, thousands of demonstrators took to the streets around the country and eventually forced the government to halt the deal.

Less than two years later, a tragic nightclub fire at the 'Colectiv' club in Bucharest killed more than 60 people, and protestors came back out in force. This time the enemy was widespread corruption – the argument being that bribes and protection rackets had allowed the owners of the nightclub and similar places to skirt fire and safety rules.

The result was a breath-taking crackdown on corruption at all levels that had Romanians joking there were more public officials behind bars than hardened criminals. Corruption remains a hot-button issue. A governmental decree to relax parts of the crackdown sparked another round of massive protests in Bucharest and other cities in early 2017 as many suspected the government's motive was merely a partisan effort to free corrupt politicians.

The Place Never Looked Better

Romania is sprucing itself up and credit for that probably goes to Sibiu. The Saxon city served as the EU's Cultural Capital in 2007 and used the opportunity to polish the cobbles and transform itself from a shabby Transylvanian town to a top-shelf destination.

Other cities around the country took notice. Cluj-Napoca took the bait in 2015, when it served as the EU's Capital of Youth. The city converted that honorific into a chance to renovate, innovate and reinvent itself as a lively student hub.

Indeed, everywhere you go, cities and towns sport a new shine. In 2016 Iaşi pulled the scaffolding down from the long-idle Palace of Culture. After eight years in the planning and nearly €30 million in investment, the former seat of Moldavian power now looks like a glimmering Taj Mahal.

Fix-up fever has even reached scruffy Bucharest, with central Calea Victoriei getting a long-awaited spruce-up by way of new bike lanes and trendy boutiques. Timişoara will serve as the EU's Cultural Capital in 2021, and is also cleaning itself up at a feverish pace.

POPULATION: **19.9 MILLION**

AREA: **238,391 SQ KM**

GDP GROWTH (2016): **5%**

INFLATION RATE (2015): **-0.6%**

AVERAGE MONTHLY SALARY (2016): **2108 LEI (€467)**

if Romania were 100 people

89 would be Romanian
7 would be Hungarian
3 would be Roma
1 would be Other

belief systems
(% of population)

81 Orthodox Christian

 6 Protestant

5 Roman Catholic

 8 Other

population per sq km

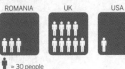

ROMANIA   UK   USA

 ≈ 30 people

History

Sometimes referred to as 'Europe's great survivor', this melting pot of Romanians, Hungarians, Germans and Roma has been constantly invaded and occupied throughout its existence. The name 'Romania' didn't refer to Wallachia or Moldavia until 1859 and, in fact, Transylvania remained part of the Austro-Hungarian empire until 1918 – so what exactly is 'Romania'? Understanding its ancient past and the surrounding empires and countries who influenced it is probably the best way to get a grip on this fascinating country.

Roman Dacia

For thousands of years, the territory of what was to become modern Romania was inhabited by various Neolithic and Bronze Age tribes. These include the fascinating Cucuteni people, who thrived from 6000 to 3500 BC and left behind a legacy of beautiful, modern-looking pottery.

From around the 7th century BC the Greeks established trading colonies along the Black Sea at Callatis (Mangalia), Tomis (Constanța) and Histria. In the 1st century BC, a strong state was formed by indigenous Dacian tribes, led by King Burebista, to counter the growing might in the area of the Roman Empire. The last Dacian king, Decebal (r AD 87–106), consolidated this state but was unable to stave off attacks led by the Roman emperor Trajan between AD 101 and 102, and Dacia became a Roman province.

The name 'Romania' supposedly comes from Romanus (Latin for 'Roman') but others say it could also be from *rumân* (dependent peasant).

The slave-owning Romans mixed with the conquered tribes to form a Daco-Roman people who spoke Latin. The reflected glory of Rome was short lived when, after increasing Goth attacks in AD 271, Emperor Aurelian (r 270–75) decided to withdraw the Roman legions to south of the Danube River, meaning Rome governed here for fewer than 175 years. Romanised peasants remained in Dacia and mixed with the locals; hence the Roman heritage of contemporary Romanians.

Medieval Principalities

Waves of migrating peoples, including the Goths, Huns, Avars, Slavs, Bulgars and Magyars, swept across the territory from the 4th to the 10th centuries, each one leaving its mark on the local culture, language and

TIMELINE	650 BC	AD 106	896
	Dacians are first recorded in the area of present-day Transylvania from their trade with Greeks, who established colonies at Callatis, Tomis (now Constanța) and Histria.	Dacia becomes a Roman province for 175 years, until Goth attacks (AD 271) force Emperor Aurelian to withdraw Roman legions south of the Danube.	Magyars settle in the Carpathian Basin, integrating Transylvania into Hungary.

ŞTEFAN CEL MARE

It's a rare day when you don't hear the name 'Ştefan cel Mare' (Stephen the Great; r 1457–1504) somewhere: Moldavia's greatest prince adorns squares, boulevards, streets, statues and landmarks nationwide. During his reign, Ştefan beat back Polish, Hungarian and Ottoman forces, his resistance to the Ottomans winning him widespread admirers, including Pope Sixtus IV, who declared Ştefan an *Athleta Christi* (Champion of Christ). Despite allegedly fathering over 20 illegitimate children, Ştefan's heroic deeds and church building won him canonisation by the Romanian Orthodox Church, as 'The Right-Believing Voivod Stephen the Great and the Saint'.

Although Ştefan is often overshadowed by his infamous cousin, Wallachian prince Vlad Ţepeş (Vlad the Impaler), his battle record (34–2) speaks for itself, and he did erect 44 churches and monasteries – several now Unesco World Heritage sites. Both in battle and in church building, the prince kept up Romanian spirits and traditions, preventing the Ottomans from disrupting traditional cultures as they did almost everywhere else in the Balkans. Without Ştefan, Europe might well have turned out differently.

gene pool. By the 10th century a fragmented feudal system ruled by a military class appeared. Around this point, the Magyars (Hungarians) expanded into Transylvania, and by the 13th century the area had become an autonomous principality under the Hungarian crown. Following devastating Tatar raids on Transylvania in 1241 and 1242, King Bela IV of Hungary persuaded German Saxons to settle in Transylvania with free land and tax incentives. He also granted the Székelys – a Hungarian ethnic group who had earlier migrated to the region with the Magyars – autonomy in return for their military support.

In the 14th century, Prince Basarab I (r 1310–52) united various political groups in the region south of the Carpathians to create the first Romanian principality – Wallachia, dubbed Ţara Românească (Romanian Land). Its indigenous peasantry became known as Vlachs. Around this time, a similar process of state formation was underway along the eastern and northern sides of the Carpathians that would eventually form a second Romanian principality: Moldavia. In the early days, these two principalities served mainly to buffer the Hungarian Kingdom from the growing Ottoman Empire, but the two would eventually form the nucleus of a future Romanian state. They were ruled by a prince who was also the military leader. Most noblemen at this time were Hungarian; the peasants were Romanians.

Lucian Boia's *Romania* (2004) is a rare account of the country written by a local; the philosophical, even playful, overview covers various viewpoints about the sometimes debated truths behind the origin of Romania.

Ottoman Expansion

Throughout the 14th and 15th centuries Wallachia and Moldavia offered strong resistance against the Ottoman's northward expansion.

1000	1241	14th century	1431
Byzantine, Slavic, Hungarian and Oriental records first mention the existence of Romanians under the name of Vlachs.	After the Tatars invade Transylvania, King Bela IV of Hungary offers free land to entice German Saxons to Transylvania, fortifying the defence.	Prince Basarab I creates the first Romanian principality: Wallachia. The region is known as Ţara Românească (Romanian Land).	Vlad Ţepeş (Vlad the Impaler) is born. He grows a handlebar moustache then spends much of his cumulative eight years in power terrorising and slaughtering invading Turks.

Mircea cel Bătrân (Mircea the Old; r 1386–1418), Vlad Țepeș ('The Impaler'; r 1448, 1456–62, 1476) and Ștefan cel Mare (Stephen the Great; r 1457–1504) were legendary figures in this struggle. When the Turks conquered Hungary in the 16th century, Transylvania became a vassal of the Ottoman Empire, retaining its autonomy by paying tribute to the sultan, as did Wallachia and Moldavia. In 1600 these three principalities were briefly united at Alba Iulia under the leadership of Mihai Viteazul (Michael the Brave; r 1593–1601), who shortly after was defeated by a joint Habsburg-Transylvanian noble army and beheaded.

Following the defeat of the Turks in the 1687 Battle of Mohács in Hungary, the area of Transylvania came under Habsburg rule. Large pieces of Wallachia and Moldavia, however, remained under Ottoman control, though both areas retained some autonomy.

The 18th century marked the start of the Transylvanian Romanians' fight for political emancipation. Romanian peasants constituted around 60% of the population, yet continued to be mostly excluded from political life. In 1784, three serfs named Horea, Cloșca and Crișan led a major uprising against Hungarian rule. The uprising was quashed and two of the instigators were executed; nevertheless the revolt was not without some success. In 1785, Habsburg Emperor Joseph II abolished serfdom in the then-Hungarian province of Transylvania.

The 17th century in Wallachia, under the reign of Constantin Brâncoveanu (r 1688–1714), brought a period of prosperity characterised by a cultural and artistic renaissance. In 1775 part of Moldavia's northern territory – Bucovina – was annexed by Austria-Hungary. This was followed in 1812 by the loss of its eastern territory – Bessarabia (most of which is in present-day Moldova) – to Russia. After the Russo-Turkish War of 1828–29, Wallachia and Moldavia became Russian protectorates while remaining nominally in the Ottoman Empire.

One State

In the 19th century, the Austrian-led Habsburg Empire came under threat from within by the growing might of individual nations within the empire – above all from nationalist Hungarians agitating for their own state. To quell the rebellion, the Habsburgs struck a deal with Transylvania's Romanians, promising them national recognition in return for joining forces with them against the Hungarian revolutionaries. Thus Transylvanian Romanians fought against and enacted revenge upon the Hungarians in the province for what was seen as centuries of mistreatment. Russian intervention finally settled the issue in favour of the Habsburgs and ended a revolution that had shocked all sides in its viciousness.

In the aftermath, the region fell under the direct rule of Austria-Hungary from Budapest. Ruthless 'Magyarisation' followed: Hungarian was estab-

Romanians are proud the Turks never completely conquered their land, but in quiet tones some admit that Bucharest wasn't even on the way between Constantinople and the Ottomans' main goal, Vienna.

In 1462 Vlad the Impaler lived up to his name, skewering 20,000 Turkish soldiers outside the city walls of Târgoviște.

1453	1467	1475	16th century
The fall of Constantinople. The Ottomans block trade on the Black Sea, deepening Romania's isolation.	Ștefan cel Mare (Stephen the Great) defeats the Hungarian army (Hungary's last attempt to conquer Moldova), then defeats Tatar forces at Lipnic and finally invades Wallachia to repel the Ottomans.	Moldavian Prince Ștefan cel Mare wins a decisive battle against a numerically superior Ottoman army at Vaslui.	The Turks conquer Hungary, and Transylvania becomes a vassal of the Ottoman Empire.

WALLACHIA UNDER VLAD'S RULE

If you were a Boyar (nobleman), Saxon merchant, unchaste woman or Turk during the time of Vlad Țepeș (r 1448, 1456–62, 1476), your life hung in the balance. Throughout his reign, Vlad finessed his torture methods – which included flaying, strangulation, burning, blinding and amputation – to a frightening degree. Legend has it that as a test of respect to him, a gold cup could be placed in any town square, and while anyone could drink freely of its contents, the cup had to remain. Not surprisingly, it never strayed.

In 1462 the famous 'Forest of the Impaled' incident occurred, which immortalised Vlad's infamy in history books. In a daring bid to drive out Turkish invaders from the Danube River valley, Vlad burnt the crops and poisoned the wells, while his soldiers, disguised as Turks, snuck into the Turkish camp to surprise them. To add gore to injury, when the Turkish sultan marched on Țepeș' city, Târgoviște, he discovered 20,000 of his men impaled outside the city walls in a forest of flesh. The wooden stakes were driven through the victims' anuses, emerging from the body just below the shoulder, in such a way as not to pierce any vital organs. This ensured at least 48 hours of unimaginable suffering before death.

Tellingly, it transpires that many of Vlad's youthful years were spent in a Turkish prison, where he was allegedly raped by members of the Turkish court. Revenge? For an individual soaked in others' blood, it seems fitting he himself was beheaded in 1476, his head preserved in honey and taken to the sultan in Constantinople.

lished as the official language and any Romanian who dared oppose the regime was severely punished. Austria-Hungary would rule the region uncontested until WWI.

By contrast, Wallachia and Moldavia prospered. In 1859, with French support, Alexandru Ioan Cuza was elected to the thrones of Moldavia and Wallachia, which created a national state known as the United Romanian Principalities on 11 December 1861. This was renamed Romania in 1862. The reform-minded Cuza was forced to abdicate in 1866 by mutinous army officers, and his place was taken by the Prussian prince Carol I. With Russian assistance, Romania declared independence from the Ottoman Empire in 1877. In 1881 it was declared a kingdom and on 22 May 1881 Carol I was crowned the first king of Romania.

WWI & Greater Romania

Through shrewd political manoeuvring, Romania greatly benefited from WWI. Despite having formed a secret alliance with Austria-Hungary in 1883, it began WWI as a neutral state. In 1916 the government, under pressure from the Western allies, declared war on Austria-Hungary, with the ultimate prize being to annex Transylvania.

1600	1606	1683	1784
Wallachia, Transylvania and Moldavia are united for 15 months under Mihai Viteazul.	The Treaty of Vienna gives religious and constitutional rights to Hungarian-speaking Transylvanians but none to Romanian-speaking people.	The Ottomans' siege of Vienna ends in the defeat of the Turks; the Habsburg Empire moves in to take control of Transylvania.	A peasant uprising results in Habsburg Emperor Joseph II abolishing serfdom in Transylvania the following year.

The defeat of Austria-Hungary in 1918 paved the way for the formation of modern Romania. Through settlements and treaties after the war, the country gained Bessarabia, the area east of the Prut River that had been part of Moldavia until 1812, part of Bucovina that had been in Austro-Hungarian hands since 1775, part of the Banat, and eventually Transylvania. By the end of WWI, Romania had more than *doubled* its territory (from 120,000 to 295,000 sq km) and population (from 7.5 to 16 million). The acquisition of the new lands was ratified in 1920 under the Treaty of Trianon – a settlement that has never rested easily with Hungary.

Fifty years after his death in 1953, Carol II's remains were transferred back to Romania from Portugal, where he had died. He was interred in Curtea de Argeş.

Carol II & the Iron Guard

In the years leading up to WWII, Romania sought an alliance with France and Britain, and joined Yugoslavia and Czechoslovakia in the Little Entente. Romania also signed a Balkan Pact with Yugoslavia, Turkey and Greece, and later established diplomatic relations with the USSR. These efforts were weakened by the Western powers' appeasement of Hitler and by Romania's own King Carol II, who succeeded his father Ferdinand I to the throne. Extreme right-wing parties opposed to a democratic regime emerged, notably the anti-Semitic League of the National Christian Defence, which consequently gave birth to the Legion of the Archangel Michael in 1927. This notorious breakaway faction, better known as the fascist Iron Guard, was led by Corneliu Codreanu, and by 1935 it dominated the political scene.

Finding himself unable to manipulate the political parties, Carol II declared a royal dictatorship in February 1938. All political parties were dissolved and laws were passed to halve the size of the electorate. Between 1939 and 1940 alone, Romania had no fewer than nine different governments. In 1939 Carol II clamped down on the Iron Guard, which he had supported until 1937. Codreanu and 13 other legionaries were arrested, sentenced to 10 years' imprisonment and then assassinated. In revenge for their leader's death, Iron Guard members murdered Carol II's prime minister, Armand Călinescu, leading to the butchering of 252 Iron Guard members by Carol II's forces. In accordance with the king's wishes, the corpses were strung up in public squares. Only with the collapse of the Axis powers at the end of WWII did the Iron Guard disintegrate.

The US Holocaust Memorial Museum paints a harrowing portrait of anti-Semitic horror in Romania during WWII, chronicling how the state used various brutal methods – aside from organised murder – to rid itself of Roma and Jews.

Romania, formally allied to the West, was isolated after the fall of France in May 1940, and in June 1940 Greater Romania collapsed in accordance with the Nazi-Soviet Nonaggression Pact of 1939. The Soviet Union re-occupied Bessarabia. On 30 August 1940, Romania was forced to cede northern Transylvania to Nazi-ally Hungary by order of Germany and fascist Italy. In September 1940 Southern Dobrogea was given to Bulgaria. Not surprisingly, the loss of territories sparked widespread popular demonstrations. Even Carol II realised he could not quash the

1812	1819–34	1864	1881
Treaty of Bucharest, signed at the conclusion of the Russo-Turkish War, grants Russia control of eastern Moldavia. The Ottoman Empire gains control of western Moldavia.	Wallachia and Moldavia are occupied by Russia.	In retaliation, after Romanian Jews refuse to provide financial support, Alexandru Ioan Cuza inserts a clause to deny suffrage to all non-Christians in his draft of a constitution. Jews are forbidden to practise law.	Prince since 1866, Carol I is crowned the first king of Romania.

increasing mass hysteria and on the advice of one of his councillors, the king called in General Marshall Ion Antonescu. To defend the interests of the ruling classes, Antonescu forced King Carol II to abdicate in favour of the king's 19-year-old son Michael. Antonescu then imposed a fascist dictatorship, with himself as *conducător* (supreme leader).

Romanian–Nazi Alliance

German troops were allowed to enter Romania in October 1940, and in June 1941 Antonescu joined Hitler's anti-Soviet war. The results of this Romanian–Nazi alliance were gruesome, with over 200,000 Romanian Jews – mainly from newly regained Bessarabia – and 40,000 Roma deported to transit camps in Transdniestr and later murdered. After the war, Antonescu was turned over to the Soviet authorities who condemned him to death in a show trial.

As the war went badly and the Soviet army approached Romania's borders, on 23 August 1944 an opportunistic Romania suddenly changed sides again, joining the Soviet and Western alliance, by capturing the 53,159 German soldiers stationed in Romania and declaring war on Nazi Germany. By this dramatic act, Romania salvaged its independence and shortened the war. By 25 October the combined Romanian and Soviet armies had driven the Hungarian and German forces out of Transylvania, replacing the valued territory back under Romanian control. And the cost? About 500,000 Romanian soldiers died fighting for the Axis powers, and another 170,000 died after Romania joined the Allies.

Romanian People's Republic

Of all the countries that burst forward into the mass-industrialised, communist experiment in the 20th century, Romania and Russia were the least prepared, both being overwhelmingly rural, agricultural countries. Prior to 1945 Romania's Communist Party had no more than 1000 members. Its postwar ascendancy, which saw membership soar to 710,000 by 1947, was a consequence of backing from Moscow. The Soviet-engineered return of Transylvania greatly enhanced the prestige of the left-wing parties, which won the parliamentary elections in November 1946. A year later Prime Minister Petru Groza forced King Michael to abdicate (allegedly by holding the queen mother at gunpoint), the monarchy was abolished and a Romanian People's Republic was proclaimed. The year 1948 saw a shift to collectivisation – the process by which industry was redesigned as a state farm, and villagers were ripped from their ancestral land and forced to live in dehumanising city high-rises.

A period of terror ensued in which all the prewar leaders, prominent intellectuals and dissidents were imprisoned or interned in hard-labour camps. The most notorious prisons were in Piteşti, Gherla, Sighetu Mar-

Best Places to Catch the Ghost of Vlad Ţepeş

Ţepeş' birthplace in Sighişoara

Bran Castle, where he was allegedly interned

Poienari Citadel, his high-altitude stronghold

Târgovişte, where he had 20,000 Turks impaled

Snagov Monastery, his reputed burial site

Bucharest's Athénée Palace is a spectacular hotel, but this beautiful building was a warren of spies and informers during WWII. To get a first-person look, read the excellent *Athene Palace* by RG Waldeck, an American journalist who was there.

1897	1916	Feb 1938	1940
Bram Stoker's *Dracula* is published.	Romania relinquishes its WWI neutrality and declares war on Austria-Hungary in order to annex Transylvania.	King Carol II declares a royal dictatorship. All political parties are dissolved.	Romania is forced to cede northern Transylvania to Hungary by order of Nazi Germany.

matiei and Aiud. Businesses were nationalised, and in 1953 a new Slavi-cised orthography was introduced to obliterate all Latin roots of the Romanian language, while street and town names were changed to honour Soviet figures. Braşov was renamed Oraşul Stalin. Romania's loyalty to Moscow continued until Soviet troops withdrew in 1958, and after 1960 the country adopted an independent foreign policy under two 'national' communist leaders, Gheorghe Gheorghiu-Dej (leader from 1952 to 1965) and his protégé Nicolae Ceauşescu (leader from 1965 to 1989). By 1962 the communist state controlled 77% of Romania's land.

Ceauşescu famously refused to assist the Soviets in their 1968 armed 'intervention' in Czechoslovakia, his public condemnation earning him 'maverick' status in the West and more than US$1 billion in US-backed credits in the decade that followed. And when Romania condemned the Soviet invasion of Afghanistan and participated in the 1984 Los Angeles Olympic Games despite a Soviet-bloc boycott, Ceauşescu was officially decorated by Great Britain's Queen Elizabeth II.

On Clowns (1993) is a cutting rant on Romanian dictatorship by Jewish author Norman Manea (b 1936), who was deported to the Transdniestr concentration camp as a child in 1941.

Ceauşescu & the Grand Delusion

It's all but impossible to fully appreciate how hard life became under the megalomaniacal 25-year dictatorship of Nicolae Ceauşescu and his wife Elena. Political freedom was *verboten,* as was freedom of the media (ownership of a typewriter could be punishable by death). TV and radio programs entirely revolved around the personality cult of their venerable leader; the brainwashing of the population even stretched its tentacles into schools. In the 1980s, in his attempts to eliminate a $10 billion foreign debt and impress the world, Ceauşescu exported Romania's food while his own people were forced to ration even staple goods. Unless you were a high-ranking member of the Communist Party you had to queue for two hours for basics such as milk and potatoes, returning to a house where electricity was turned off to save energy.

Along with bugged phones and recorded conversations there were strict curfews. Few of the dictator's sinister schemes were more frightening than the pro-birth campaign, designed to increase the working population from 23 to 30 million. In 1966 it was decreed: 'The fetus is the property of the entire society...' A celibacy tax was charged on offenders with up to 10% of their monthly wages docked until they had children. Romania's birth rate predictably swelled, with the country's infant-mortality rate soaring to 83 deaths in every 1000 births. Women under the age of 45 were rounded up at their workplaces and examined for signs of pregnancy (in the presence of government agents – dubbed the 'menstrual police'). Many fled to Hungary, leaving a legacy of millions of hungry orphans – many with serious developmental problems – to the outrage of the international community when the story broke in 1990.

June 1941	1944	1947	1968
The citizens of Iaşi, whipped into a far-right frenzy, commit an atrocious pogrom against Jews, eventually killing 13,000 people.	Following secret talks between Stalin, Churchill and Roosevelt, the Soviet Union gains a 90% share of 'influence' in Romania.	The monarchy is abolished and a Romanian People's Republic is proclaimed.	Nicolae Ceauşescu's public condemnation of the Soviet-led invasion of Czechoslovakia is lauded by the West, which rewards him with economic aid.

The Securitate (Secret Police) was Ceaușescu's chief instrument and it ruled with an iron hand, proliferating paranoia and fear, delivering torture and threatening to place people on its infamous 'blacklist'. Estimates suggest that as many as one person in 30 had been recruited as a Securitate by the 1980s – many Romanians couldn't trust their own families for fear of them being informers. Worse still, many of them were children. In March 1987 Ceaușescu embarked on 'Systematisation', a rural urbanisation program that would see the total destruction of 8000 villages (mainly in Transylvania) and the resettlement of their (mainly Hungarian) inhabitants into ugly apartment blocks.

The 1989 Revolution

In late 1989, as the world watched the collapse of one communist regime after another, it seemed only a matter of time before Romania's turn would come. The Romanian revolution was carried out with Latin passion and intensity – of all the Soviet bloc countries, only Romania experienced a government transfer that ended with a dead leader. The spark that ignited Romania occurred on 15 December 1989 when Father László Tőkés publicly condemned the dictator from his Hungarian church in Timișoara, prompting the Reformed Church of Romania to remove him from his post. Police attempts to arrest demonstrating parishioners failed and within days the unrest had spread across the city, leading to some 115 deaths. Ceaușescu proclaimed martial law in Timiș County and dispatched trainloads of troops to crush the rebellion. The turning point came on 19 December when the army in Timișoara went over to the side of the demonstrators.

On 21 December, anti-Ceaușescu demonstrators in Bucharest interrupted an address by Ceaușescu to a mass rally intended to shore up support for the dictator. They booed and shouted 'Timișoara!'. This moment is often seen as the decisive turning point in the country. The demonstrators retreated to the wide boulevard between Piața Universității and Piața Romană – only to be crushed a couple of hours later by police gunfire and armoured cars. Drenched by ice-cold water from fire hoses, they refused to submit, erecting barricades, under the eyes of Western journalists in the adjacent Hotel Inter-Continental. At 11pm the police began their assault using a tank to smash through the barricades, and by dawn the square had been cleared of debris and the corpses of insurgents. Estimates vary, but at least 1033 were killed.

The following morning thousands more demonstrators took to the streets, and a state of emergency was announced. Around noon Ceaușescu reappeared briefly on the balcony of the Central Committee building to try to speak again, only to be forced to flee by helicopter from the roof of the building. Ceaușescu and his wife Elena were arrested near

For an in-depth look at Romania since communism, check out Tom Gallagher's *Modern Romania: The End of Communism, the Failure of Democratic Reform, and the Theft of a Nation* (2008).

1976	1989	May 1990	June 1990
Fourteen-year-old Nadia Comăneci wins three gold medals and scores a perfect '10' at the Montreal Summer Olympics, the first '10' awarded in modern Olympic gymnastics history.	After 25 years in power, Nicolae Ceaușescu and his wife Elena are executed on Christmas Day in Târgoviște.	The National Salvation Front, led by Communist Party member Ion Iliescu, wins the first democratic elections held in Romania since 1946.	The Iliescu government brings in miners to quell protests in Bucharest. The mineriada, as it's later called, results in seven deaths and hundreds of injuries.

Târgovişte and taken to a military base there. On 25 December, they were condemned by an anonymous court and executed by a firing squad. Footage of the Ceauşescu family's luxury apartments broadcast on TV showed pure-gold food scales in the kitchen and rows of diamond-studded shoes in Elena's bedroom.

While these events had all the earmarks of a people's revolution, many scholars have advanced the notion that they were just as much the result of a coup d'état: the Communist Party, tired of having to bow down to Ceauşescu, had been planning an overthrow for months. Communist bystanders quickly came to power following Ceauşescu's fall, calling themselves the 'National Salvation Front' (FSN). Not until 2004 did Romania have a president who was not a former high-ranking communist.

The Securitate was finally abolished in late 1989, after Ceauşescu was ousted, leaving behind a damaging footprint of paranoia and mistrust that is still not entirely gone from the Romanian psyche today.

Attempts at Democracy

The years immediately following the revolution were rocky and the future was uncertain. The National Salvation Front took immediate control of the country. In May 1990 it won the first democratic elections since 1946, placing Ion Iliescu, a Communist Party member since the age of 14, at the helm as president. Protests ensued, but Iliescu sent in 20,000 coal miners to violently quash them. Iliescu was nonetheless re-elected in 1992 as the head of a coalition government under the banner of the Party of Social Democracy. New name, same policies. Market reforms remained nowhere in sight. In 1993 subsidies on food, transportation and energy were scrapped, prompting higher prices and widespread unemployment.

Iliescu was ousted in the 1996 presidential elections by an impoverished populace, who ushered in Emil Constantinescu, leader of the right-of-centre election alliance Democratic Convention of Romania (CDR), as president. Constantinescu's reform-minded government made entry into NATO and the European Union (EU) its stated priorities, together with fast-paced structural economic reform, the fight against corruption and improved relations with Romania's neighbours, especially Hungary.

Scandal and corruption surrounded the November 2000 electoral race. In May of that year the National Fund for Investment (NFI) collapsed. Thousands of investors – mainly pensioners who'd deposited their life savings into the government fund – took to the streets to demand their cash back (US$47.4 million, long squandered by the NFI).

After Constantinescu refused to run in the 2000 elections, Iliescu retook the helm as the country's president and his Social Democrat Party (PSD) formed a minority government, with Adrian Nastase as prime minister. The 2004 elections were marred by accusations of electoral fraud, and there were two rounds of voting before centre-right politician and former Bucharest mayor Traian Băsescu was announced the win-

1993	1994	1997	2004
The government removes subsidies on food, transport and energy, causing prices to skyrocket and employment figures to fall to an all-time low.	Eugène Ionesco (b 1909), the celebrated Romanian playwright, dies. Ionesco was half French and didn't write his first play until his late 30s.	The number of stray dogs in Bucharest reaches between 150,000 and 200,000 – twice as many as New York City, which is three times larger. Dogs bite 50 people per day.	Romania joins NATO, a major step in guaranteeing security, external stability and eventual EU membership.

ner, with 51% of the vote. The PNL (National Liberal Party) leader, Călin Popescu-Tăriceanu, became prime minister and swore in a new coalition that excluded the PSD.

The government's main goal, aside from addressing the many domestic issues, was integration with international bodies, most notably the EU. In 2002 Romania was invited to join NATO. Romania (and Bulgaria) finally joined the EU in 2007, their membership having been delayed by Romania's record of organised crime, corruption and food safety. Brussels would continue to be a big supporter of Romania's EU cause, granting billions of euros towards infrastructure, business development, environmental protection and social services.

Băsescu re-nominated the leader of the Democratic Liberal party, Emil Boc, as prime minister in December 2009, following which a coalition government of the Democrat Liberals and the Democratic Union of Hungarians in Romania (UDMR) was formed. Boc resigned in 2012 after street protests and increasing pressure from the opposition to call early elections. He was followed briefly by Mihai Răzvan Ungureanu, who was later trounced by Victor Ponta, leader of the Social Democratic Party, who formed a coalition with the National Liberal Party.

Trouble at the Top

The union of Băsescu as president and Ponta as prime minister was rocky from the start. Ponta went on to accuse Băsescu of breaching the constitution. Among his assertions, Ponta accused the president of pressuring prosecutors in legal cases and abusing his control of the secret service. Băsescu, in turn, accused Ponta of engineering a coup d'état. The conflict came to a head in the summer of 2012, when Ponta and his allies called for a national referendum to impeach Băsescu. The referendum failed because fewer than 50% of voters went to the polls.

Ponta was dogged by scandals of his own, including allegations he plagiarised his doctoral thesis at university. Băsescu went on to serve until the end of his term in 2014. Ponta eventually ran for president to succeed him, but was narrowly defeated at the polls in November of that year by the centre-right candidate, Klaus Iohannis. Ponta's career ended in disgrace after he was forced to resign in 2015 in the wake of the 'Colectiv' nightclub fire in October in which more than 60 people died.

Iohannis, an ethnic German and former mayor of Sibiu, ran on the familiar theme of anticorruption and won overwhelming support from the country's young people. At the time of writing the jury is still out on whether he will succeed where his predecessors have failed. His first major act in office was to launch a massive anticorruption campaign, which resulted in the jailing of mayors, judges and businessmen around the country.

Following spats between factions in the Romanian government in 2012, the EU postponed Romania's bid to join the group's visa-free Schengen Zone.

2007	2012	2014	2016
On 1 January Romania and Bulgaria become the 26th and 27th members of the EU.	Parliament, urged on by Prime Minister Victor Ponta, votes to impeach President Traian Băsescu, though he survives a national referendum.	Romanians elect ethnic-German Klaus Iohannis as president for a five-year term.	Reacting to the president's far-reaching corruption campaign, voters return the opposition, left-leaning Social Democrat Party (PSD) to power in parliamentary elections.

The Dracula Myth

Love it or loathe it, visit Romania and you can't ignore the omnipresence of Dracula; from mugs and T-shirts all the way to bat- and blood-themed menus and cape-bedecked waiters. But what's really chilling is that a blueprint for the pale, shape-shifting count we were all reared on in books and films actually existed – though not in a black cape and cloud of fog, but rather as a Wallachian warrior king with a predilection for extreme cruelty.

The Impaler

Author Leif Pettersen's *Backpacking with Dracula* (2016) is a highly amusing take on both the fictionalised and historical versions of 'Dracula' and the effect they've had on Romanian tourism.

Fifteenth-century prince Vlad Țepeș is often credited with being the inspiration for Dracula, the vampire-count originally featured in the classic Gothic horror story *Dracula* (1897). His princely father, Vlad II, was called Vlad Dracul. 'Dracula' actually means 'son of the house of Dracul', which itself translates as 'devil' or 'dragon'. Add to this diabolical moniker the fact that Vlad used to impale his victims – from which you get his surname: Țepeș (Impaler) – and it's easy to see why Dracula's creator, Irishman Bram Stoker, tapped into his bloodline. Even though Romanian shops are quick to bunch merchandise of the 19th-century vampire and 15th-century leader together, Vlad Țepeș is still a much-respected figure in Romania today; a symbol of independence and resistance for his stand against the Ottoman Empire.

Legend has it that Țepeș was born in 1431 opposite the clock tower in Sighișoara, and at the age of 17 he ascended to the throne of Wallachia. In 1459 his first act of murderous renown was against the Boyars (noblemen) of Târgoviște for the murder of his father and brother. The oldest Boyars were brutally impaled on spikes while the remainder were frogmarched 80km to Poienari where they were ordered to build an 850m-high fortress guarding the pass. You can still visit the ruins today.

The Vampire

Stoker undoubtedly read Emily de Laszowska Gerard's *Transylvanian Superstitions* (1885), which detailed how to kill vampires.

Bram Stoker's literary Dracula, by contrast, was a bloodsucking vampire – an undead corpse reliant on the blood of the living to sustain his own immortality. But who would have thought this oftentimes hyperbole-blown epistolary-style yarn about a lawyer visiting a megalomaniac aristocrat would almost single-handedly spawn a literary genre? Forget your *Vampire Chronicles* and *Twilight* series, because arguably neither would have been written without *Dracula*. And Victorian dramatics aside, this late-19th-century Gothic epic is a master-class in thriller writing, and so beautifully crafted in places it leaves an indelible impression on the reader's mind; none more so than the eerie passages following young Jonathan Harker's journey and imprisonment in Transylvania.

Countless films have loosely followed its storyline, and the novel has never been out of print.

Writer's Block

While he might have hit on the idea of writing a vampire story, initially Stoker couldn't think of where to locate it. He was also lost for a name for his bloodthirsty nobleman. But then he found a book on Vlad Dracula in Whitby Library whilst on holiday and met a Hungarian who told him at length about Transylvania (meaning 'the land beyond the forests'), and suddenly his story slotted together. It was only then that Stoker immersed himself in the Reading Room at the British Museum Library, swotting up on everything from geography to Romanian folklore and the mythology of vampires.

In the Footsteps of Dracula

For diehard *Dracula* fans, the good news is that the Transylvania chapters of the book are rooted in pure geographical fact, so you can actually see the places visited by its hero, Jonathan Harker. Despite visiting much of the world in his capacity as actor Henry Irving's manager, Irish-born Bram Stoker never actually set foot in Eastern Europe. Instead, he relied on exhaustive research from afar. Follow this itinerary to squeeze as many drops from both legends.

To catch the trail of the real Dracula, head to the remote **Poienari Citadel** (p69) on the Transylvania–Wallachia border, where the Impaler's wife committed suicide. Not far from Braşov – where he also had people impaled – is **Bran Castle** (p93), where Ţepeş was allegedly briefly imprisoned. The pretty Saxon citadel of Sighişoara may look to be straight out of a fairy tale, but it's also the birthplace of Vlad the Impaler. Visit the spooky **Casa Vlad Dracul restaurant** (www.casavladdracul. ro; Str Cositorarilor 5; 5 lei; ☉10am-10pm) for lunch.

Next, follow Jonathan Harker's footsteps to northern Transylvania's Bistriţa – known in the book as Bistritz – the medieval town he visited on the eve of St George's Day, when locals pleaded with him to turn back from his destination at Castle Dracula. From here it's a short drive up the lonely, forested Tihuţa Pass (which in the book is described as the Borgo Pass). Perched on top of the pass, in exactly the spot Harker described the castle as being, is the **Hotel Castel Dracula** (☏0266-264 010, 0266-264 020; www.hotelcasteldracula.ro; Piatra Fântânele; s/d/ste from 155/170/300 lei; [P][⊞]). This hotel is loosely Gothic with blood-red carpets and stuffed animals in the reception (not forgetting its occasional heart-attack-inducing crypt). The real reason to come, however, is the view. The rest is up to your imagination.

Best Dracula Films

Bram Stoker's Dracula (Francis Ford Coppola; 1992)

Nosferatu the Vampyre (Werner Herzog; 1979)

Horror of Dracula (Terence Fisher; 1958)

The Brides of Dracula (Terence Fisher; 1960)

THE DRACULA MYTH WRITER'S BLOCK

In the 1980s the original manuscript of *Dracula* was found in a barn in northwestern Pennsylvania. It now belongs to Microsoft co-founder Paul Allen.

Outdoor Activities & Wildlife

Romania is a great choice for nature-based activities. In addition to hiking and cycling, some highlights include birdwatching in the Danube Delta, wolf-tracking in the Carpathians, and crouching down in a hide watching for brown bears. There are also ample chances for horseback riding, caving, climbing and skiing.

Hiking

The proportion of agricultural land in Romania is around 60%. One third of Romania is constituted by mountains, another third hills and plateaus, while the remainder is plains.

Mountainous Transylvania and the more remote areas of Moldavia offer the best chances for leaving civilisation behind, though nearly all areas in Romania are covered by marked trails and hiking maps. You'll often find cabanas (huts or chalets) for overnighting in the upper elevations of the Carpathians. These normally have dorm-bed accommodation and a cafeteria or restaurant to get something to eat or drink.

Romania's hiking trails are well-marked, self-explanatory and accessible to anyone who is reasonably fit and in possession of a good map. Hotels and local tourist information offices can advise on the best walks in an area and transport options for getting a lift to the trailhead. Tourist offices also sometimes stock walking maps, but not always. Big bookshops are usually the best source for maps.

For more challenging treks, or if you simply want to understand more about an area's history or culture, a local guide or guided walk offered by a travel agency is recommended. There are some very solid tour options and guides working out of cities such as Braşov and Cluj-Napoca. Another credible source of guides can be found at www.alpineguide.ro. Tour companies worth looking into include:

Carpathian Travel Centre (p112) Sibiu-based travel agency offering Transylvanian hikes.

Discover Eco-Romania (www.eco-romania.ro) Hiking and walking tours in Transylvania and Maramureş, as well as a long list of more active pursuits, including wildlife-immersive treks.

DiscoveRomania (p89) Themed walking tours including Saxon Transylvania and rural Maramureş.

Roving România (p272) Walking and wildlife tracking tours as well as more culturally intensive offerings, including a Roma cultural experience tour.

Where to Hike

The Carpathians (aka Transylvanian Alps) offer endless opportunities for hikers, the most popular areas being the Bucegi and Făgăraş ranges, south and west of Braşov. The Bucegi has a flat-top plateau that can be reached by cable cars from Sinaia.

Well known for their karst formations and underground caves, the Apuseni Mountains, west of Cluj-Napoca, are also on the adventurer's radar. Other fruitful hiking areas include the Retezat National Park, which lies northwest of Târgu Jiu and south of Deva in Transylvania;

around Păltiniş, south of Sibiu; and, in Moldavia, the less visited Rarău and Ceahlău mountains near the Bicaz Gorges.

Staying Safe on the Trails

Here are a few common-sense tips to keep you safe while hiking:

➡ Stay on marked trails – especially in national parks.

➡ Have a decent map with you, and don't end up trekking in the dark (most good maps include details of walk durations on their reverse).

➡ Always wear sturdy shoes and make sure you're carrying enough water.

➡ Carry the telephone number of emergency rescue service Salvamont (☏0725 826 668), and check the weather forecast before setting out.

➡ Never attempt a difficult trail alone.

Cycling & Mountain Biking

Cycling and mountain biking are slowly developing in Romania, though the infrastructure of trails, maps and rental and repair shops is still rudimentary. Student-friendly cities like Timişoara, Cluj-Napoca and Iaşi, as well as Bucharest, have made the most progress in creating cycling lanes, although even here the network is spotty. Encountering careless drivers and the occasional pack of stray dogs are further concerns.

On the positive side, Romania is filled with long stretches of seldom-trafficked country roads, abandoned forest trails and some amazing vistas that certainly reward the effort of finding a bike and hitting the road. The best place to mountain bike is the plateau atop the Bucegi Mountains. From Sinaia (the town below) you can hire bikes; pay for an extra ticket on the gondola lift and go up for the day and work your way back down.

Cycling Romania (www.cyclingromania.ro) A great cycling resource; offers multi-day mountain-bike adventures to the Danube Delta or Transylvania.

Hooked On Cycling (www.hookedoncycling.co.uk) UK-based touring group offering extended self-guided tours through Transylvania.

Hiring a Bike

Ask at your hotel or local tourist information office about possible bike rentals in the area where you're staying. Rates vary but expect to pay from 5/30 lei per hour/day.

i'Velo (www.ivelo.ro), a nationwide cycling-promotion group, offers bikes for hire in big cities around the country, including Bucharest, Braşov, Timişoara and Iaşi.

Horse Riding

There are private riding clubs scattered around the country that can normally accommodate visitors. The local tourist information office should be your first port of call. Rates vary but expect to pay around 80 lei per hour for guided rides. Throughout the Carpathians, a network of horse riding-trails snakes through beautiful and remote areas.

Cross-Country Farm (p101) Horse-riding and agrotourism accommodation option located near Sighişoara.

Equus Silvania (www.equus-silvania.com) Offers guided horse rides, including winter rides, as well as overnight stays in Şinca Nouă, not far from Braşov.

Maggie's Ranch (www.maggiesranch.ro) Pretty guesthouse and a full array of horse rides and excursions at a ranch situated just east of Bran in Transylvania.

Merlelor (www.merlelor.com) Mountain rides through the Carpathians, as well as extended camping trips and more upscale affairs centred on fine wining and dining.

Caving & Rock Climbing

Romania has more than 12,000 caves *(peştera)*, many of which have been opened to the public. With the exception of a few large and well-visited caves, don't expect easy, visitor-friendly conditions. Instead, you may have to hike to the cave entrance and, once you've arrived, hoist and climb your way around. Pack a warm coat and wear sturdy shoes.

The **Apuseni Nature Park** (www.parcapuseni.ro), west of Cluj-Napoca, is undergirded by limestone and has the country's highest number of caves per square kilometre. Within the park's bounds are more than 1500 caves, plus Scărişoara, Romania's largest underground glacier. The two caves that are the best known and easiest to reach are the spectacular Ice Cave (p161), one of Romania's five glacier caves, and the Bears Cave (Peştera Urşilor; p161).

Apuseni Experience (p272) Oradea-based adventure outfit offering regional treks through the Apuseni Mountains, and can help tailor a caving trip.

Green Mountain Holidays (p139) Gets great reports for its caving trips in the Apuseni Mountains.

For rock climbing, the area around Braşov is particularly fruitful. The websites of **Climb Europe** (www.climb-europe.com) is a great reference guide, with links to maps and climbing points. Rock climbers take to the walls at the Piatra Craiului National Park, not far from Bran. The Bicaz Gorges in Moldavia offer spectacular challenges too, and there's some climbing near Băile Herculane.

Skiing & Snowboarding

Romania is finally on the winter adrenalin map, offering good-value accommodation, powder snow and uncluttered slopes. Recent investments have also seen many of the country's resorts getting state-of-the-art gondolas and new pistes added. Beginner, intermediate and

LEADING NATIONAL PARKS & RESERVES

NATIONAL PARK/ RESERVE	FEATURES	ACTIVITIES	BEST TIME TO VISIT
Apuseni Nature Park	cave system, boars, deer, bears	hiking, caving	Jun-Sep
Bucegi Nature Reserve	forests, abundant botanic species including edelweiss	hiking, biking, skiing	year round
Ceahlău Massif National Park	countless flower species, rare fauna	hiking	Jun-Sep
Danube Delta Biosphere Reserve	Europe's biggest wetlands, more than 5000 plant & animal species	boat tours, fishing, birdwatching	May-Sep
Iron Gates National Park (Porţile de Fier)	spectacular scenery, stunning gorges	hiking	May-Sep
Piatra Craiului National Park	wolves, deer, hazel-coloured bears	hiking, climbing	May-Oct
Retezat National Park	Unesco Biosphere Reserve, black mountain goats, bears, foxes, deer, monk eagles	hiking	May-Oct
Todirescu Flower Reservation	meadows of tulips, bluebells, chrysanthemums	hiking	Jun-Sep

expert slopes are marked as blue, red and black, respectively. The ski season generally runs from December to March, with some slopes operating by mid-November and staying open into April.

Tickets & Gear

It's usually not necessary to bring your own gear, as ski resorts should have decent skis and boards for hire. Ski-lift and day-pass prices vary according to the season and location. Check out www.ski-in-romania.com for images, webcams and information on resorts and snowfall forecasts.

Where to Ski

Transylvania is the centre of the action and the most popular places are reached as day trips from Braşov. Convenient Poiana Braşov – a 20-minute bus ride west of Braşov – has been upgraded in recent years, though it's still more of a beginner/intermediate option. For something more challenging, Sinaia in the Prahova Valley offers scope for the experienced skier, with wide bowls at its summit that funnel to gullies and half-pipes. Also nearby is the ski resort Predeal. South of Sibiu, you can find smaller lifts at pretty Păltiniş.

Outside of Transylvania, there are some fun smaller ski hills in Maramureş, at Izvoare and Borsa. The south side of the Apuseni Mountains has a couple of ski hills at Stâna de Vale and Gârda de Sus. In Moldavia, you can ski at Câmpulung Moldovenesc. The lifts there are due for renovation in 2017.

Health Spas

Check out the information provided by the **National Organisation of Spas** (www.romanian-spas.ro). **Contur Travel** (www.contur.ro) can arrange spa visits and maintains a useful website.

Some standout spas:

Băile Tuşnad (p120; www.bailetusnad.ro) A pensiune-filled valley in Transylvania with mineral baths and pools in the Harghita Mountains.
Covasna (p119) Known as 'the resort of 1000 springs' in Transylvania's Székely Land.
Mud Baths (p227) Lake Techirghiol, near Eforie Nord on the Black Sea, is famous for its dark sapropel mud, which, when slathered over your body is said to be restorative for skin and bones.
Sovata (p124) Between Târgu Mureş and Sighişoara in Transylvania; famed for its curative dip in a bear-shaped lake.

Birdwatching & Wildlife Spotting

The Danube Delta provides a major transit hub for birds migrating from as far off as the Russian Arctic to the Nile River. Here birdwatchers can hire boats or take tours or ferries on one of three channels through Romania's 3446-sq-km wetland. Almost the entire world's population of red-breasted geese (up to 70,000) winter here, as does 60% of the world's small pygmy cormorant population. In the summer white pelicans along with birds from up to 300 other species can be seen as well.

There are also birdwatching excursions in Transylvania's mountains and along the southern Black Sea coast. Migration season in spring runs from March to May, in autumn from August to October. It's particularly good in mid-April and October.

Ibis Tours (p215) Tulcea-based travel agency that organises specialised Danube Delta tours guided by ornithologists.
Roving România (p272) In Braşov; can help organise birding trips in and around Transylvania.

Romania is a great destination for spotting four-legged wildlife, with the most popular tours centred on tracking bears. Bears are an

THE BEAR & THE TRAVELLER

Thanks to its megalomaniac dictator (under Ceauşescu no one but he was allowed to hunt bears) 60% of Europe's brown bears are today found in Romania – a staggering 6000 bears. The chances of seeing one are high if you're trekking with a guide or going to a bear hide. A cousin of the grizzly bear, Romanian bears are smaller but have the same powerful hump of muscle on their back. They can also move at almost 50km/h.

Hikers have been killed by bears in recent years, usually because of accidentally surprising them, so there are a few tips to be mindful of. Try to pitch your tent in an open spot so bears can see you, and any used sanitary material or rubbish should be kept in a sealed bag. When walking through dense forest, talk loudly to announce your presence – the last thing a bear wants is to engage with you.

ever-present danger to hikers in Transylvania, and every year brings stories of an unsuspecting trekker mauled in the woods. However, for a much safer bear encounter (with a decent chance of seeing at least a few animals in their natural habitat), join a group excursion to a bear hide. Several companies offer such tours in ways that promote the security of both you and the animal. Most companies also offer wolf- and lynx-tracking excursions.

Transylvanian Wolf (p272) With award-winning Romanian guide Dan Marin at its helm, this company leads walks on the trail of animals such as wolves, bears and lynx.

Carpathian Nature Tours (p98) Conservation-minded operator based in Măgura village offering bear-tracking hikes and more.

Visual Arts & Folk Culture

The country's peasant roots have given rise to a thriving folk culture, and traditional arts and crafts, such as weaving, pottery and woodworking, are still important aspects of the country's identity. Roma music belongs to this legacy. Traditional Roma music is still played in the countryside, and more modern forms, such as manele, are popular among urban youth. Contributions to international arts include the early-20th-century sculptures of Constantin Brâncuși and, more recently, the films of the 'Romanian New Wave'.

Visual Arts

Painting

Medieval painting in Romania was marked by a strong Byzantine influence. Devised to educate illiterate peasants, paintings took the form of frescoes depicting scenes from the Bible on the outside walls of churches; they also appeared on iconostases inside churches and in miniature form as decorative frames for religious manuscripts.

The painted monasteries of Southern Bucovina (p204), dating from the 15th and 16th centuries, are home to Romania's loveliest and liveliest frescoes. The works are prized not only for their composition, but perhaps even more for their inventive application of colour and harmony.

Renaissance influences were muted in many areas by the cultural dominance of the Ottoman Empire, but can be seen here and there in western areas, and even in parts of Wallachia, which served initially as a vassal state of the Hungarian kingdom. The beautifully preserved frescoes on the wall of the 14th-century St Nicholas Church in Curtea de Argeş represent a rare synthesis of Byzantine themes, such as portraits of saints given a fleshier, three-dimensional cast, more characteristic of the Renaissance.

As art entered its modern phase in the 19th century, Romania trailed behind Western Europe. France, as the arbiter of painting styles, exerted a disproportionate influence. While many early Romanian attempts were knock-offs of French styles, by the mid- and late 19th century true Romanian masters were emerging.

The best of these masters, arguably, was Nicolae Grigorescu (1838–1907). Grigorescu absorbed French influences like realism and Impressionism, but brought them home with scenes celebrating Romanian landscapes, peasantry and soldiers. His portraits included unexpected subjects, such as Roma and Jewish women. He was a prolific painter, and art museums around the country carry his work.

Sculpture

Sculpture has been an active art form in the territory of modern Romania from the prehistoric days of the early Cucuteni people, whose nubile figurines must have titillated audiences way back in 6000 BC.

In 2009 one of Brâncuși's works, *A Portrait of Mme LR*, sold for US$37 million at a Christie's auction in Paris.

Fast-forward some 5000 years and the ancient Romans and Greeks brought the techniques of classical sculpture to settlements all along the Black Sea. The history and archaeology museums in Tulcea and Constanța are filled with these works of antiquity.

In the 19th century, at a time when realism was prized, sculpture often took the form of larger-than-life statues of national heroes. This rigid, didactic statue-making, however, was blown away in the early 20th century by the abstract works of Romanian master Constantin Brâncuși (1876–1957). Brâncuși turned the world of modern sculpture on its head with his dictum of using sculpture not to focus on an object's form, but rather its essence. His work is featured at Craiova's Art Museum, as well as in a series of open-air public works at Târgu Jiu, not far from where he was born.

Contemporary Romanian sculpture got a boost – or perhaps a setback – by a controversial work unveiled in 2012 at Bucharest's National History Museum. The bronze statue, by Vasile Gorduz (1931–2008), depicts a fully nude (and anatomically correct, but not particularly well-endowed) Roman Emperor Trajan holding a wolf to symbolise the synthesis of Roman and Dacian cultures. It provoked derision on all sides, but tellingly has emerged as the city's most photographed work of art.

Folk Culture

Romanian folk traditions have come under increasing threat from modern life, but remain surprisingly strong, particularly in Maramureș, parts of Transylvania and in the western region of Wallachia, called Oltenia. Folk crafts sit alongside the fine arts and have exerted strong influence over the centuries on Romanian painting, sculpture and music.

Arts & Crafts

Folk culture continues to thrive in traditional crafts such as pottery, weaving and woodworking. Romanian pottery is incredibly diverse. Materials and patterns vary according to the area where the pottery was made. The Ethnographic Museum (p71) in Craiova has an excellent display of regional pottery. Other important areas include Miercurea Ciuc and Baia Mare.

Similarly, textile weaving carries on into the modern age; many private homes in smaller towns and villages still have looms, and embroidery, patterns and materials can differ greatly from region to region. Weaving is used to produce bed clothing and towels as well as curtains and rugs. Romanian carpet tradition, not surprisingly, shares much in common with the Ottoman Turks. Even today, one of the most common carpets you'll see are the thin-weave, oblong rugs called *kilims*.

Maramureș is the centre of the country's woodworking expertise. Over the centuries, the inhabitants have used the abundant forests to create fabulous wooden churches. Traditionally, each family's woodworking skills are displayed on the enormous, elaborately carved wooden gates that front the family house. Wood was often used in making cooking utensils, and spoon-carving is still carried on throughout Maramureș and parts of Transylvania.

Folk & Roma Music

You won't travel far without hearing Romanian folk music, which is still common at family celebrations, holidays and weddings.

Traditional folk instruments include the *bucium* (alphorn), the *cimpoi* (bagpipes), the *cobză* (a pear-shaped lute) and the *nai* (a pan-pipe

---

Folk Albums

Band of Gypsies (Taraf de Haïdouks)

Art of the Bratsch (Anatol Ștefăneț)

Baro Biao (Fanfare Ciocarlia)

World Library of Folk & Primitive Music (edited by Alan Lomax)

Sacha Baron Cohen shot his 'Kazakhstan' scenes for the comic movie Borat: Cultural Learnings of America for Make Benefit Glorious Nation of Kazakhstan (2006) in the village of Glod, north of Târgoviște.

THE ROMANIAN 'NEW WAVE' IN FILM

Romanian film has traditionally not commanded worldwide attention, but that changed about 15 years ago with the emergence of a brilliant young generation of directors making films in a style that has come to be known as the 'Romanian New Wave'. While the films differ greatly in theme, they share a low-budget, low-key, hyper-realistic aesthetic that feels refreshing at a time when much of world cinema is dominated by big-budget blockbusters and comic-book movies.

One of the early big hits was director Cristi Puiu's *Death of Mr Lăzărescu* in 2005. This film tells the tragi-comic story of an old man and his futile efforts to get hospital care in Romania's dysfunctional medical system. It won the top prize at Cannes for young and upcoming directors.

That was followed up in 2007 by Cristian Mungiu's amazing *Four Months, Three Weeks and Two Days*. Set in Ceauşescu-era Romania, the film explores the frightening world of backstreet abortions, but more generally the limits of friendship and the inability of society to cope with basic problems. It won the Palme d'Or at Cannes for best film. Mungiu followed up that early success with the excellent *Beyond the Hills* (2012) and *Graduation* (2016).

Other well-known directors to have worked in this style include the late Cristian Nemescu, who was tragically killed in a car crash, Corneliu Porumboiu and Radu Muntean.

Andrei Ujică's 2010 *Autobiography of Nicolae Ceauşescu* tells a convincing story of the former dictator's descent into madness using nothing more than hours and hours of official footage, edited and spliced together. It's mesmerising.

of about 20 cane tubes). Many kinds of flute are used, including the *ocarina* (a ceramic flute) and the *tilinca* (a flute without finger holes).

Folk music can take many forms. A *doină* is a solo, improvised love song, a sort of Romanian blues with a social or romantic theme sung in a number of contexts (at home, at work or during wakes). The *doină* was added to the Unesco World Heritage list of intangible cultural elements in 2009. Another common form, the *baladă* (ballad), is a collective narrative song steeped with feeling.

Couples may dance in a circle, a semicircle or a line. In the *sârbă*, males and females dance quickly in a closed circle with their hands on each other's shoulders. The *hora* is another fast circle dance. In the *brâu* (belt dance), dancers form a chain by grasping their neighbour's belt.

Many modern bands have successfully incorporated folk elements into their acts. One of the most innovative has been the Timişoara-based metal group Negură Bunget, whose dark sounds draw on traditional instruments and folk rhythms. Taraf de Haïdouks was one of the few Roma bands to hit the big time in world music in the 1990s and 2000s, and became a favourite of actor Johnny Depp.

Manele, a modern form of hard-edged pop and dance music, emerged from the Roma, Balkan and ethnic music scene and took the country by storm in the 1990s and 2000s. The gritty lyrics, peppered with profanity and aimed at underclass youth, are frequently likened to a Romanian, home-grown hip-hop. Look for artists like Florin Salam and Nicolae Guţă, who is sometimes called the 'Father of Manele'.

New Wave Films

Four Months, Three Weeks and Two Days

Beyond the Hills

Death of Mr Lăzărescu

Boogie

Happiest Girl in the World

Child's Pose

The Romanian People

This Latin 'island' sitting in the far corner of southeastern Europe remains a fascinating enigma. It's a traditional culture in the throes of rapid modernisation, juiced in 2007 by EU membership, and still coping with a four-decade communist-totalitarian hangover. Sure, there are plenty of social problems to deal with and head-scratching moments when it comes to minority rights and social equality, but the signs are generally headed in the right direction. The energetic populace ensures that whatever happens, it's never dull.

An Island of Latins

Romania is often – correctly – described as 'an island of Latins surrounded by a sea of Slavs' (and Hungarians). Though the Romans occupied these parts for only a scant two centuries (2000 years ago), they bequeathed a language and temperament that places Romania firmly within the Latin family of nations, alongside Italy, Spain, Portugal and France. As with citizens of those other countries, Romanians tend to be warm, passionate, family-oriented, opinionated and highly impatient behind the wheel!

One thing you can usually rely on in face-to-face interactions is frankness and getting to the truth. Newcomers are often amazed by the candour of their host's enquiries as to their salary, views on homosexuality, the Roma, and anything else often deemed off-limits topics of conversation in other countries.

Romanian is spoken by around 90% of the population; nevertheless there are sizeable numbers of speakers of Hungarian, German, Romani, Ukrainian and Russian, and smaller numbers of Czech, Slovak, Bulgarian and Serbian speakers.

The Birth of Bling

As Westernisation accelerates, Romanians are lapping up the shiny brands foreign advertisers are hawking to them: mobile phones, prestige-brand cars, cosmetics and clothes. Indeed a whole new class has evolved, the *fitosi* (nouveau riche), obsessed with gadgetry and personal appearance. This propensity to want the best and newest slowed a bit during the global economic crisis of 2008–2010, though more recently it's kicked back into high gear again.

To an outsider all of this might seem shallow, but in truth many of those flashy cars return not to expensive houses but to modest flats – image these days seems to be everything. But try to put it into some perspective. After so many generations of suffering from limited choices, paranoia and oppression, it's no wonder many Romanians live by a *carpe diem* creed.

Hot Potatoes

The treatment of ethnic Hungarians (the nation's largest ethnic minority) remains a flashpoint and a thorn in the side of bilateral Hungarian–Romanian relations. Romania is bound by the European Charter for Regional or Minority Languages to recognise certain rights of Hungarian speakers, yet in practice those rights are sometimes vio-

WOMEN IN ROMANIAN SOCIETY

Romanian media portrayals of women can seem outdated, with TV shows peppered with dancing girls in barely a strip of clothing and anchor women on news channels dolled up like beauty queens. Juxtaposed to this is a worrying domestic-abuse record. While social mores are changing and evolving, this is still very much a man's country where women are expected to conform to being gentle and submissive, and males dominant and strong.

Surveys suggest as many as one in five women has been abused by her partner. In 2003 the country adopted its first law to prevent and combat domestic violence. That law was strengthened in 2012 by identifying various forms of abuse, including marital rape and economic mistreatment. Romania took another step forward in 2016 when it ratified the Council of Europe's convention on preventing and combating violence against women and domestic violence. The signs are hopeful. Romania's developing economy has seen a rapid increase in the number of female professionals taking their place in management positions in the workplace.

lated. One high-profile case concerned a decision by local authorities in Cluj-Napoca to refuse to post bilingual street signs in Hungarian.

Much of the friction is driven by right-wing fringe groups like Noua Dreaptă (New Right). This group routinely promotes anti-Hungarian feelings in Transylvania and indulges in garden-variety homphobia as well, such as organising anti-gay marches during the annual Bucharest Pride.

You're also likely to hear tirades from usually mild-mannered Romanians about the Roma minority. Rightly or wrongly, the average Romanian blames the country's besmirched image as a crime-ridden country on the practices of its Roma citizens.

Rapes are still difficult to convict in Romania because a witness and medical certificate are required, and most women are too scared to report the crime to police.

EU: Brain Drain & Gain

In the decade or so since Romania's accession to the EU in 2007, the country has witnessed profound changes in every sphere. Polls continue to show that about three quarters of Romanians support the EU and their country's membership, but scratch the surface in private conversation and you'll find it's been a mixed bag.

One of the biggest negatives, no doubt, has been the brain drain of talented young Romanians to countries around the EU, particularly to Italy, Spain and the UK. The IMF calls Romania the biggest exporter of human resources in the EU, with nearly one in five Romanians living outside the country. While EU membership can't be blamed entirely, the EU's open doors arguably made the lure of jobs abroad more powerful and accessible.

On the positive side of the ledger is a host of benefits and advantages that are hard to quantify, but equally difficult to ignore. Billions of euros in public EU funds have flowed into the country since accession. While the funds have swamped the country's ability to absorb them, Romanians have gained much cleaner air and water, better roads and a much more secure social benefit infrastructure. Romanians are free to travel, study and work where they want. The currency, the leu, has stabilised, and economic prospects are generally good.

In 2001 Romania finally repealed the criminalisation of homosexuality, though it has yet to recognise same-sex partnerships.

The Romanian Kitchen

Romanian dishes have a delightful, home-made character, incorporating fresh, organic produce into relatively uncomplicated but delicious meals. Many dishes use pork, paired with a staple like polenta, potatoes or cabbage. The recipes derive from peasant cooking, with liberal borrowings from neighbouring cultures such as Turkish, Hungarian, German and Slavic.

Comfort Food

Romanian food wasn't bred so much to dazzle as to satisfy. *Mămăligă*, a cornmeal mush (often translated as 'polenta' on English menus), was seemingly designed to warm and fill the stomach. You'll find it at restaurants, inns and family homes around the country – it can be disappointingly bland or stodgy in restaurants, but when home-made and served with fresh *smântână* (sour cream), it hits the spot.

Mămăligă pairs beautifully with *sarmale,* the country's de facto national dish (though it's actually an import from the days of Ottoman rule) and comfort-food extraordinaire. *Sarmale* are cabbage or vine leaves stuffed with spiced meat and rice; the *mămăligă* here provides an excellent backstop for soaking up the juices.

> If you want to make your own *mămăligă,* a couple of good books include Galia Sperber's *The Art of Romanian Cooking* and Nicolae Klepper's *Taste of Romania*.

Soups & Stews

Romanian meals always begin with soup, usually a 'sour' soup called *ciorbă*. The sour taste derives from lemon, vinegar, cabbage juice or fermented wheat bran added during preparation. Sour soups come in several varieties – the local favourite is *ciorbă de burtă*, a garlicky tripe soup. Others worth looking for include *ciorbă de perişoare* (spicy soup with meatballs and vegetables) and *ciorbă de legume* (vegetable soup cooked with meat stock).

The fish soup *(ciorbă de peste)* served in and around the Danube Delta is some of the best in the world. It's typically made from several types of fresh fish, including trout, pike-perch, sturgeon, carp and a giant Black Sea catfish known as *somn,* plus lots of fresh vegetables, garlic and other spices, all simmered in a cast-iron kettle.

Tochitură, another menu staple, is a hearty stew that could easily be filed away under the 'comfort food' category too. There are regional varieties, but it's usually comprised of pan-fried pork, sometimes mixed with other meats, in a spicy tomato or wine sauce, served with *mămăligă,* cheese and – this is the rub – topped with an egg cooked sunny-side up. How can it go wrong?

> Soups are often served with a small pepper on the side. Don't put the pepper in the soup; instead take a nibble of it along with a spoonful of soup. You might also be served clear or creamy garlic sauce *(mujdei).* The local habit is to take a spoonful of the garlic and mix it with the soup.

Street Eats

Romanians love to eat on the go. Look out for:

➡ covrigi – hot pretzels sprinkled with salt or sesame or poppy seeds

➡ gogoşi – doughnuts, dusted with sugar or stuffed with fruit

➡ *placinte* – warm sweet or savoury pastries, stuffed with fruit, curd cheese or meat

➡ *mici* – grilled rolls of spiced minced pork or beef, served with mustard

➡ *shoarma* – like a shawarma, though usually made from chicken or pork, with toppings like cabbage and tomato sauce

Going Meatless

Devout Orthodox Christians observe a vegan diet on Wednesdays and Fridays and for extended periods during religious holidays. On these days, some restaurants offer a *meniu de post* (menu without meat or dairy). This menu may include mains like *cartofi piure cu şniţele de soia* (mashed potatoes with soy schnitzels), *sarmale de post* (vegan cabbage rolls), *zacuscă de vinete cu ciuperci* (eggplant and mushroom dip) or *tocăniţă de legume de post* (vegan vegetable stew).

Aside from that, nearly every restaurant will have a list of vegetarian salads. *Salată de roşii* (tomato salad) is sliced tomatoes doused in olive oil and vinegar. Also popular is *salată de castraveţi* (cucumber salad) or tomatoes and cucumbers combined in a *salată asortată* (mixed salad).

For entrées, look for *murături* (pickled vegetables), *ciuperci umplute* (stuffed mushrooms), or potato dishes, including *cartofi ţărăneşti* (country-style potatoes), which is often served alongside meats.

Leave Room For Dessert

Romanian cooking excels in the sweets department, so be sure to leave plenty of room for a 'second' main course. More pedestrian – but still delicious – desserts include strudels, crêpes (*clătite*) and ice cream (*îngheţată*). The local favourite, though, has to be *papanaşi*. This is fried dough, stuffed with sweetened curd cheese and covered with jam and heavy cream.

Romanian Drinks

The Hard Stuff

Sure, Romanians enjoy a good beer or glass of wine, but when it comes to serious drinking, the only real contender is fruit brandy – schnapps, eau-de-vie – or as the Romanians say, *ţuică*. Typically, *ţuică* is made from plums (surveys say three-quarters of the nation's plums end up in a bottle), though apricots and pears can also be applied to this nefarious craft.

The best batches are from the backyard still, and nearly everyone has an uncle or grandpa who makes the 'best in Romania'. You'll often find *ţuică* sold in plastic bottles at roadside fruit stands, sitting there innocently next to the apples and watermelons.

THE ROMANIAN KITCHEN GOING MEATLESS

Dare to Try

răcituri – jelly made from pig's hooves

ciorbă de potroace – soup made from chicken entrails

brânză în coajă de brad – cheese wrapped in tree bark

Outside of the main wine-making regions, Drăgăşani in Wallachia is home to several of the country's most promising new wineries. These include Casa Isărescui, owned by the governor of the national bank, and Crama Bauer, Avincis and Prince Ştirbey. Look for these labels at good wine shops.

COOKING COURSES

A trip to Romania is a rare opportunity to learn the basics of Romanian cooking. While there are not many cooking schools or programs to choose from yet, the list is growing every year.

Mobile Cooking Romania (http://mobile-cooking-romania.com) A travel company offering package tours to major tourist destinations, combined with themed gourmet cooking classes and dining events with international chefs and sommeliers.

Société Gourmet (www.societegourmet.ro) This Bucharest-based outfit offers themed cooking classes. Most of the courses feature international cuisines, but there are also regional courses, such as regular weekend truffle hunts in Transylvania. It also has kids programs.

HOLIDAY TREATS

Romanian celebrations and rituals are intricately bound up with food.

Martyrs' Day (9 March) Little *mucenici* (martyrs) are baked on this day; in most of Romania they are pieces of unleavened dough in a figure eight. However, in Moldavia they're brushed with honey and sprinkled with walnuts, and in Wallachia they're boiled with sugar then covered with crushed walnuts and cinnamon.

Easter The high point of the Orthodox calendar. The main meal revolves around lamb; especially delicious is *stufat de miel,* a lamb stew made with green onions and garlic. Breads play an important side role, particularly *pască,* a traditional Easter sweet cake, and a sweet egg bread called *cozonac*.

Christmas Dinner centres on pork, starting with a soup of smoked pork, and ham or pork chops as the main course. *Sarmale* will also be served. Sweets include *cozonac,* walnut cake and even pumpkin pie. In Transylvania, you will find *singeretta,* sausages made with pig's blood, liver, kidneys and fat.

A shot of *ţuică* before a meal is a great way to break the ice, and Romanians say it does wonders for the appetite. Unless you're a seasoned drinker, though, hold the line at one or two shots. Home-made batches can run as high as 50% to 60% alcohol (100 to 120 proof).

Palincă (called *horincă* in Maramureş and *jinars* in the Cluj-Napoca region) is similar, only it's filtered twice and can be even stronger.

Wine & Beer

Though it definitely flies under the radar for wine production, Romania is a top-10 world winemaker by volume and produces many excellent wines.

The country's wineries turn out both reds (*negru* and *roşu*) and whites (*alb*). There are five traditional winemaking regions: Târnave plateau (outside Alba Iulia; whites), Cotnari (outside Iaşi in Moldavia; whites), Murfatlar (near the Black Sea coast, whites and reds), Dealu Mare (Prahova county; reds) and Odobeşti (in southern Moldavia; whites and reds). In recent years, the area around Drăgăşani, in Oltenia county northeast of Craiova, has emerged as one of the most exciting new wine regions, specialising in both red and white grapes.

For day-to-day tippling, though, Romanians are beer drinkers at heart, with quality ranging from passable to pretty good. Most breweries are owned by international brewers and it's sometimes easier to find a Tuborg or a Heineken in a pub than a Romanian label. That said, some of the better Romanian brands to look for include Ciuc, Ursus, Silva and Timişoara's local favourite, Timişoreana. All are broadly similar pilsner-style pale lagers, but each has its passionate defenders. Ursus and Silva both produce highly regarded darks.

In Bucharest, be sure to stop at the restaurent Caru' cu Bere (p50). Not only does it cook traditional Romanian food uncommonly well, it brews its own beer – and it's very good.

Wines to Watch

Cotnari's Fetească neagră (slightly sweet red)

Grasă de Cotnari (a sweet white)

Fetească Regală (sparkling wine)

Murfatlar (quality reds)

Tămâioasă Românească (sweet white)

Crâmposie Selecţionată (dry white)

Survival Guide

Directory A–Z

Accommodation

Romania has a wide choice of accommodation options to suit most budgets, including hotels, pensions, hostels and camping grounds. Book summer accommodation along the Black Sea coast well in advance. Elsewhere, advance booking is usually not necessary.

➡ **Hostels** Big cities like Bucharest and Cluj have modern-style hostels with internet access and laundry service and are open to all age groups.

➡ **Hotels** Hotels range from modest family-run affairs to boutiques and high-priced corporate chains – with a commensurate range of prices.

➡ **Pensions (pensiunes)** Small, locally owned inns that offer excellent value and are occasionally borderline luxurious.

Camping & Mountain Huts

Camping grounds (*popas turistic*) run the gamut from a handful of nicely maintained properties in scenic areas to grungy affairs, with wooden huts packed unattractively side-by-side like sardines. Bare mattresses are generally provided and sometimes you have to bring your own sleeping bag.

Often a better bet is camping rough. Wild camping is technically prohibited in parks and legally protected zones, but outside these areas you will rarely be disturbed, provided you exercise discretion, stay quiet and leave the area pristine when you leave. Camping can be great along the Black Sea coast, particularly in places like Sfântu Gheorghe or Vama Veche.

In most mountain areas there's a network of cabins or chalets (cabanas) with dormitories and occasionally restaurants. Prices are lower than those of hotels (about 40 to 60 lei for a bed) and no reservations are required, but arrive early if the cabana is in a popular location.

Hostels

Hostels in Romania are not as well developed as in other European countries. Large cities, such as Bucharest, Cluj-Napoca, Sibiu and Braşov, do have good-quality private hostels with group kitchens, laundry facilities, wi-fi and engaged, English-speaking staff.

Outside the big cities, though, the concept of a youth hostel means something quite different. These hostels are often only open from June to August and are located in university dormitories or other institutional spaces that have been repurposed as seasonal lodgings.

Hotels

Romanian hotels are rated according to a 'star' system, which provides a rough approximation of what you can expect – though stars are awarded according to a property's facilities and not on intangibles like appearance, location and value.

➡ The top end (four and five stars) is usually a guarantee of Western European levels of comfort and luxury. Expect in-room refrigerators, flat-screen TVs, climate control and key-card door locks. Five-stars will usually have a pool or sauna. A double in a four- or five-star hotel will run anywhere from 300 to 500 lei (higher in Bucharest).

BOOK YOUR STAY ONLINE

For more accommodation reviews by Lonely Planet authors, check out http://lonelyplanet.com/hotels/. You'll find independent reviews, as well as recommendations on the best places to stay. Best of all, you can book online.

➡ Three-star hotels hit the sweet spot between comfort and price. While three-star properties may not have pools or fancy fitness rooms, expect a well-managed property, with well-proportioned, clean rooms, air-conditioning, en suite baths and wi-fi. A three-star double typically costs around 200 to 250 lei per night outside of the capital and 300 to 400 lei in Bucharest.

➡ Two-star and lower properties are usually only acceptable if saving money is the main criterion. Furnishings and carpets are likely to appear frayed, beds will be uncomfortable and appear worn. A double room at a two-star property runs anywhere from 140 to 200 lei per night, depending on the location.

Pensions & Private Rooms

A pension (pensiune) is a small, privately run guesthouse where you'll normally get a clean, comfortable room and breakfast. Occasionally you'll have the option to take half or full board (one or both main meals). Singles and doubles typically run around 100 to 120 lei per room.

One rung down from a pension is a room (cazare) in a private home. Many Romanian families rent spare rooms in their homes as a way of supplementing income. You can spot these places by a 'cazare' sign in the window or by the homeowner holding a sign at the side of the road or at the train station.

Private rooms work best in a rural or farm setting, where the homes are decorated in traditional rural style and where the stays can include hearty meals and authentic extras like visits with shepherds, hikes or horseback rides.

SLEEPING PRICE RANGES

The following price ranges refer to a double room with a bathroom, including breakfast (Bucharest prices tend to be higher).

€ less than 150 lei

€€ 150–300 lei

€€€ more than 300 lei

Children

Travelling with children around Romania shouldn't create any specific problems – children often receive price breaks on local transport and for accommodation and entertainment; age limits for particular freebies or discounts vary from place to place, but are not often rigidly enforced; basic supplies needed for children are easily available in cities.

For general suggestions on how to make a trip with kids easier, pick up a copy of Lonely Planet's Travel with Children.

Customs Regulations

➡ You're allowed to import hard currency up to a maximum of €10,000 or the equivalent.

➡ Goods valued over €1000 should be declared upon arrival.

➡ For foreigners, duty-free allowances for items purchased outside of the EU are 4L of wine, 2L of spirits and 200 cigarettes. For more information, go to www.customs.ro.

Discount Cards

A **Hostelling International** (HI) card yields a token discount in some hostels (but note that an HI card is normally not necessary for staying in most private hostels). You can become a member by joining your own country's Youth Hostel Association (YHA) or IYHF (International Youth Hostel Federation); see www.hihostels.com for details.

Holders of an **International Student Identity Card** (ISIC) have the benefit of many discounts in Romania. A full list (in Romanian) of ISIC discounts as well as many helpful hints for student travellers in Romania can be found on the Romanian page of the ISIC website www.isic.ro.

USEFUL ACCOMMODATION WEBSITES

Hostelling International Romania (www.hihostels-romania.ro) Local Hostelling International site.

Lonely Planet (lonelyplanet.com/romania/hotels) Recommendations and bookings.

Tourist Info (www.turistinfo.ro) County-by-county listings of private rooms and pensions. In Romanian but easy to navigate.

Rural Tourism (www.ruralturism.ro) Scenic guesthouses and farmstays around the country.

Electricity

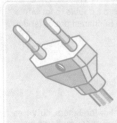

Type C
220V/50Hz

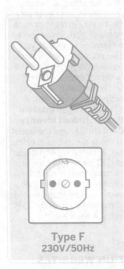

Type F
230V/50Hz

Embassies & Consulates

The website **Embassy Finder** (http://embassy-finder.com) maintains an up-to-date list of consulates and embassies around the world. Embassies are located in Bucharest, while several countries maintain consu-lates in other cities around the country. New Zealand does not maintain an embassy in Romania; official affairs are handled through the country's embassy in Belgium.

Australian Consulate (☎0374-060 845, 24h hotline 0061-1300-555-135; www.greece.embassy.gov.au; Str Praga 3; Ⓜ Calea Victoriei)

Canadian Embassy (☎021-307 5000; www.romania.gc.ca; Str Tuberozelor 1-3; ☺8.30am-5pm Mon-Thu, to 2pm Fri; Ⓜ Aviatorilor)

French Embassy (☎021-303 1000; www.ambafrance-ro.org; Str Biserica Amzei 13-15; ☺9am-noon Mon-Fri, 2.30-4.30pm Wed & Fri; Ⓜ Piaţa Română)

German Embassy (☎021-202 9830; www.bukarest.diplo.de; Str Gheorghe Demetriade 6-8; ☺8.30am-11.30am Mon, Tue, Thu & Fri, 2pm-4pm Wed; Ⓜ Aviatorilor)

Irish Embassy (☎021-310 2131; www.embassyofireland.ro; Str Buzeşti 50-52; ☺9.30am-12.30pm & 2-5pm Mon-Fri; 🚌24, 42, 45, 46)

Netherlands Embassy (☎021-208 6030; http://romania.nlembassy.org; B-dul Dimitrie Pompeiu 5-7; ☺9am-noon Mon, Tue & Thu; Ⓜ Pipera)

UK Embassy (☎021-201 7200; www.gov.uk; Str Jules Michelet 24; ☺8.30am-5pm Mon-Thu, to 4pm Fri; Ⓜ Piaţa Română)

US Embassy (☎consulate 021-270 6000, embassy 021-200 3300; https://romania.usembassy.gov/; B-dul Dr Liviu Librescu 4-6; ☺8am-5pm Mon-Fri; 🚌301)

Food & Drink

For an in-depth discussion of Romanian food and drink, see p254.

GLBTI Travellers

Public attitudes toward homosexuality remain generally negative. In spite of this, Romania has made significant legal progress in decriminalising homosexual acts and adopting antidiscrimination laws.

➡ There is no legal provision for same-sex partnerships.

➡ Bucharest remains the most tolerant city in the country, though here, too, open displays of affection between same-sex couples are rare.

➡ The Bucharest-based **Accept Association** (www.acceptromania.ro) is an NGO that defends and promotes the rights of gays and lesbians at a national level. Each year in June the group helps to organise the six-day festival **Bucharest Pride** (www.bucharestpride.ro; ☺Jun), with films, parties, conferences and a parade.

Health

Romania is a relatively safe country and visitors are not subject to any major health dangers that one wouldn't find in any other European country.

Before You Go

HEALTH INSURANCE

➡ EU citizens are entitled to free emergency medical care provided that they have a European Health Insurance Card (EHIC), available from health centres or via www.dh.gov.uk in the UK.

➡ Citizens from other countries will likely have to pay cash upfront for any medical treatment and then seek reimbursement later from their private or public health insurers.

➡ Be sure to save any and all paperwork provided by the hospital to present to your insurance company along with any reimbursement claim.

VACCINATIONS

There are no vaccinations required to enter Romania.

In Romania

AVAILABILITY & COST OF HEALTH CARE

Every Romanian city or large town will have a hospital or polyclinic that handles emergencies. In rural areas, the nearest hospital may be quite some distance away, though local people will be able to advise the best course of action.

➡ Romanian hospitals and medical centres may not look promising from the outside, but rest assured if something does go wrong, you will receive relatively prompt, professional care.

➡ If you need to go to the hospital, be sure to bring your passport, credit card and cash, as you may be required to prepay for services. EU citizens should bring their European Health Insurance Card (EHIC). You'll likely have to pay out of pocket for any medications, bandages or crutches, as the case may be.

➡ Romanian health care, particularly in public hospitals, is generally affordable by Western European (and certainly American) standards. Rates can be much higher in private clinics, though the quality of the care may be better as well.

Infectious Diseases

RABIES

Rabies cases are thankfully rare but still a concern given the number of stray dogs on the streets. If bitten by a homeless dog, seek medical attention within 72 hours (most main hospitals will have a rabies clinic).

TICKBORNE ENCEPHALITIS

Ticks are common in Romania's grasslands and open areas. Tick-borne encephalitis is a rare but debilitating virus that attacks parts of the brain. If you're planning on spending time hiking

---

EATING PRICE RANGES

The following price ranges refer to an average main course.

€ less than 20 lei

€€ 20–40 lei

€€€ more than 40 lei

---

and camping in the open air, consider a vaccination.

Tap Water

Tap water is generally considered safe to drink in Romania, though nearly everyone drinks bottled water: it's cheap and available everywhere.

Insurance

Travel insurance is not compulsory to enter Romania but a decent policy that covers medical expenses, theft or loss is always a good idea.

Worldwide travel insurance is available at www.lonelyplanet.com/travel-insurance. You can buy, extend and claim online anytime – even if you're already on the road.

Internet Access

Finding a Computer

Finding a computer to use for a few minutes of internet access has become harder as many hotels have dropped the former practice of making a computer terminal available for guests.

➡ Larger hotels will sometimes have a 'business centre', though this may incur an added fee.

➡ The situation with internet cafes is much the same. As more Romanians purchase their own computers, the number of internet cafes has dropped.

➡ Internet cafes normally charge 4 to 6 lei per hour.

➡ Other options include the tourist information offices,

---

which may have a terminal available for a few minutes of gratis surfing, or the local library.

➡ In this guide, we've used @ to indicate hotels that have computers available for guests.

Wi-fi

Romania is well-wired, and the majority of hotels, above a basic pension or guestroom, invariably offer some form of internet access, normally wi-fi, for you to use with your own laptop, smartphone or tablet device.

Many bars, cafes and restaurants offer free wi-fi for customers, though the strength and reliability of the signal can vary considerably. McDonald's and KFC outlets nationwide offer free wi-fi for customers.

➡ In this guide, we've used 🛜 to identify hotels, restaurants, cafes and bars that have wi-fi access for guests.

Legal Matters

Foreigners in Romania, as elsewhere, are subject to the laws of the host country. While your embassy or consulate is the best stop in any emergency, bear in mind there are some things it cannot do for you, like getting local laws or regulations waived because you're a foreigner, investigating a crime, providing legal advice or representation in civil or criminal cases, getting you out of jail, or lending you money.

A consul can usually issue emergency passports, contact relatives and friends,

TIPS FOR GETTING BETTER RESTAURANT SERVICE

Waiting tables can be a back-breaker and servers who do it night-in, night-out deserve respect. Still, it needs to be said that service at some Romanian restaurants can be absolutely exasperating: slow, inept, indifferent, even rude. Here are a few pointers to improve the dining-out experience.

➡ Greet the staff as you enter. A nicely timed 'bună ziua' (literally 'good day') can go a long way towards breaking the ice. A greeting lets the staff know you're there and gets things going on the right footing.

➡ Don't linger over the menu. If a menu is posted outside, give it a quick perusal to see what you might want before entering the restaurant. The server will usually take a drinks order first. When he or she brings the beverages, this is the time to order the food.

➡ Keep some small bills handy. These can be a lifesaver when it comes to paying and getting out fast. You'll need to signal the server that you want your bill, which will be brought in a folder or pouch. You're then free to stick the money in and go. Paying with a big bill inevitably means another delay as you wait for the change.

➡ Enjoy your meal and take your time. After all, you're on holiday. Unless you've got a train to catch, there's usually no need to rush.

advise on how to transfer funds, provide lists of reliable local doctors, lawyers and interpreters, and visit you if you've been arrested or jailed.

Romanian police take a dim view toward illegal drug use of any kind, including cannabis, as well as obvious displays of public drunkenness.

Money

ATMs

ATMs (cash points) are everywhere and give 24-hour withdrawals in lei with a variety of international bank cards, including Visa and MasterCard.

➡ Romanian ATMs require a four-digit PIN.

➡ Before leaving home, inform your bank where you're going, so the card security company does not (protectively) block your card once your Romanian transactions start coming through.

Credit & Debit Cards

International credit and debit cards, including Visa and MasterCard, are widely accepted at hotels, restaurants and shops in cities and large towns. In rural areas, you'll often need to pay with cash.

➡ American Express cards are typically accepted at larger hotels and restaurants, though they are not as widely recognised as other cards.

➡ Credit-card transactions require a PIN number, so it's best to work the details out with your bank prior to departure.

➡ You will need to have a valid credit card if you plan to hire a car.

➡ Credit cards can be used to get cash advances at most banks.

Currency

The Romanian currency is the leu (plural: lei), listed in some banks and currency exchange offices as RON. One leu is divided into 100 bani. Banknotes come in denominations of 1 leu, 5 lei, 10 lei, 50 lei, 100 lei, 200 lei and 500 lei. The coins come in 50 bani and relatively useless 10 bani pieces.

➡ The leu is a stable currency that has more or less held its own with respect to the euro and US dollar in recent years.

➡ Despite the fact that Romania is a member of the EU, the euro does not circulate. There is little point in converting your money into euro prior to arrival, since you will have to convert it to lei anyway.

➡ Some large hotels may quote rates in euro, but this is done for the convenience of international travellers. Hotel bills paid for with a debit or credit card will be charged in lei at the prevailing exchange rate.

➡ Try to keep small-denomination (1 leu and 5 lei) notes on hand for shops, transport tickets, cafes and tips for waiters. Using the 100 lei notes that ATMs often spit out can be difficult in practice.

Money Changers

The best place to exchange money is at a bank. You'll pay a small commission, but get a decent rate.

You can also change money at a private exchange booth (casa de schimb) but be wary of commission charges and always ask how many lei you will receive before handing over your bills.

You will usually need to show a passport to change

money, so always have it handy.

Never change money on the street with strangers; it's almost always a rip-off.

Tipping

Restaurants Tip 10% of the bill to reward good service.

Taxis Drivers won't expect a tip, but it's fine to round the fare up to reward special service.

Hotels Tip cleaning staff 3 to 5 lei per night or 20 lei per week to reward good service. In luxury hotels, tip doormen and concierges 5 to 10 lei for special assistance as warranted.

Personal services Tip hairdressers and other services around 10%.

Opening Hours

Shopping centres and malls generally have longer hours and are open from 9am to 8pm Saturday to Sunday. Museums are usually closed on Monday, and have shorter hours outside high season.

Banks 9am to 5pm Monday to Friday; 9am to 1pm Saturday (varies)

Museums 10am to 6pm Tuesday to Friday; 10am to 4pm Saturday and Sunday

Offices 8am to 5pm Monday to Friday; 9am to 1pm Saturday (varies)

Post Offices 8am to 7pm Monday to Friday; 8am to 1pm Saturday (cities)

Restaurants 9am to 11pm Monday to Friday; 10am to 11pm Saturday and Sunday

Shops 9am to 6pm Monday to Friday; 9am to 2pm Saturday

Post

The **Romanian Postal Service** (www.posta-romana.ro) is slow but reliable and fine for sending letters and nonessential parcels home. Buy stamps in post offices, as letters must normally be weighed to determine correct postage.

Delivery time within Europe is one week; overseas letters will take seven to 10 days.

Public Holidays

If you'll be travelling during public holidays it's wise to book ahead, as some hotels in popular destinations may be full.

New Year (1 and 2 January)

Orthodox Easter Monday (April/May)

Labour Day (1 May)

Pentecost (May/June, 50 days after Easter Sunday)

Assumption of Mary (15 August)

Feast of St Andrew (30 November)

Romanian National Day (1 December)

Christmas (25 and 26 December)

Telephone

Local & International Calls

Romania has a modern telephone network of landlines and mobile (cell) phones. It's possible to receive and make

WHO'S ON THE BILLS

One strike against the EU is the standardised currency, which makes cross-Europe travel a little less exciting than it once was. For now, the portraits on Romania's money still tell a tale of the country's history.

1 leu: Nicolae Iorga (1871–1940) The cofounder of the Democratic National Party was renowned as a rare voice against fascism as WWII loomed. He was eventually tortured and executed.

5 lei: George Enescu (1881–1955) Famous for composing 'Romanian Rhapsodies' (1903), he left Romania after communism took over.

10 lei: Nicolae Grigorescu (1838–1907) Romania's best-known painter progressed from Ruben copies to originals of traditional scenes around Romania.

50 lei: Aurel Vlaicu (1882–1913) The first Romanian to excel in flight (vampires included), he died in the crash of his Vlaicu II in 1913.

100 lei: Ion Luca Caragiale (1852–1912) This playwright was happy to mock everyone with his rather ironic stabs at the modernising of Romania at the end of the 19th century.

200 lei: Lucian Blaga (1895–1961) Poet, playwright, essayist, philosopher, professor and diplomat.

500 lei: Mihai Eminescu (1850–89) The mere mention of this national poet inspires Romanian pride. He suffered from manic-depressive psychosis and died at age 38.

PRACTICALITIES

➡ **Newspapers** Catch up on current affairs with the *Nine O'Clock* (www.nineoclock.ro), an online daily newspaper. Foreign papers can be found at some bookshops and gift stores of upmarket hotels.

➡ **Radio** State-run Romanian Radio is the main broadcaster, operating on AM and FM; programs are in Romanian.

➡ **Smoking** Smoking in prohibited in all public indoor spaces, including all hotels, bars, clubs and restaurants, though the rules may be spottily enforced.

➡ **TV** Televiziunea Română (TVR) is the state broadcaster, with several channels and regional studios in large cities. There are a few private channels, including Pro TV and Antena 1. Programs are in Romanian, though movies are often broadcast in their original language and subtitled.

➡ **Weights & Measures** Romania uses the metric system.

direct international calls from anywhere in the country. Romania's country code is ⌥40.

➡ All Romanian landline numbers have 10 digits, consisting of a zero, plus a city code and the number.

➡ The formula differs slightly depending on whether the number is in Bucharest or outside of Bucharest. Bucharest numbers take the form: 0 + two-digit city code (21 or 31) + seven-digit number. Outside of Bucharest, numbers take the form: 0 + three-digit city code + six-digit number.

➡ Mobile-phone numbers can be identified by a three-digit prefix starting with 7. All mobile numbers have 10 digits: 0 + three-digit prefix (7xx) + six-digit number.

Mobile Phones

Romanian mobile (cell) phones use the GSM 900/1800 network, which is the standard throughout much of Europe as well as in Australia and New Zealand and many other parts of the world. This band is not compatible with most mobile phones in North America or

Japan (though multiband phones do work across regions). Ask your provider if you're uncertain whether your phone will work.

➡ Using your own phone and SIM card in Romania could expose you to expensive roaming fees, particularly for long calls or data downloads. A cheaper option is to buy a prepaid Romanian SIM card, which gives you a temporary local number and charges local (cheaper) rates for calls, texts and data transfers. These cards only work with phones that are 'unlocked' (able to accept foreign SIM cards).

➡ Prepaid SIM plans start at about 20 lei per card and usually include some bonus minutes. They are offered by all three of Romania's main carriers: **Vodafone** (www. vodafone.ro), **Telekom Romania** (www.telekom.ro) and **Orange** (www.orange.ro).

➡ Buy prepaid SIM cards at any provider shop or independent phone seller. You can top up cards at phone shops, newspaper kiosks and even some ATMs. Shops around the country

also sell new or used phones that can be used in conjunction with local prepaid SIM cards.

➡ The situation is more complicated if you have a smartphone like an iPhone or Android device that may not be easily unlocked. With these phones, it's best to contact your home provider to consider short-term international calling and data plans appropriate to your needs.

➡ Even if you're not using your smartphone as a phone, it still makes a handy wi-fi device. Switch off the 'data roaming' setting to avoid unwanted roaming fees.

Pay Phones & Phonecards

➡ Public phones usually require a magnetic-stripe phonecard, which you can buy from post offices, newspaper kiosks, and some tourist offices and hotel reception desks.

➡ Phonecard rates start at about 10 lei and allow for a certain number of impulses (minutes).

➡ It's possible to dial abroad from a pay telephone.

Time

➡ All of Romania lies within the Eastern European time zone, GMT/UTC+2, one hour ahead of most of continental Europe. Romanian local time is two hours ahead of London and seven hours ahead of New York.

➡ Romania observes daylight saving time, and puts the clock forward one hour at 2am on the last Sunday in March and back again at 3am on the last Sunday in October.

➡ The 24-hour clock is used for official purposes, including transport schedules. In everyday conversation people commonly use the 12-hour clock.

Toilets

➡ Public toilets are few and far between and often not very clean. Use better facilities in restaurants or hotels when you have the chance.

➡ Toilets are labelled *toaletă* or simply 'WC'.

➡ Men should look for 'B' (*bărbaţi*). Women's toilets are marked with an 'F' (*femei*).

➡ The fee for a public toilet is usually 1 or 2 lei, collected by a toilet attendant sitting at the door. Have small bills ready.

➡ Some toilets have a plastic bin by their side – this is for used toilet paper.

Tourist Information

The **Romanian National Tourist Office** (www.romaniatourism.com) maintains a wonderful website with a trove of useful information. There's a large English-language section on festivals and events, accommodation and tips on what to see and do all around the country.

Romania's national network of tourist offices has made encouraging strides in recent years. Nearly all big cities (with the notable exception of urban centres in Wallachia like Craiova, Ploieşti and Piteşti) have decent tourist offices. Tourist information can still be tough to track down in rural areas.

If you turn up in a city that doesn't have a tourist office, you're pretty much on your own. Local bookshops or newsagents can sometimes sell a local map, but don't expect much help from local travel agencies. They are far more preoccupied with outbound travel by Romanians than with assisting visiting foreigners.

Travellers with Disabilities

Romania is not well equipped for people with disabilities, even though there has been some improvement over recent years.

➡ Wheelchair ramps are only available at some upmarket hotels and restaurants, and even in cities public transport is a challenge for anyone with mobility problems.

➡ **Romania Motivation Foundation** (www.motivation.ro) is a local organisation with offices around the country to assist people in wheelchairs and with mobility issues. It has a good website in English for people travelling in wheelchairs.

➡ Download Lonely Planet's free Accessible Travel guide from http://lptravel.to/ AccessibleTravel.

Visas

Citizens of EU countries do not need visas to visit Romania and can stay indefinitely. Citizens of the USA, Canada, Australia, New Zealand, Israel, Japan and many other countries can stay for up to 90 days without a visa. Other nationalities should check current requirements with the Romanian embassy or consulate in their home country. As visa requirements can change, check with the **Ministry of Foreign Affairs** (www.mae.ro) before departure.

Note that Romania, while a member of the EU, is not part of the EU's common border and customs area known as the Schengen area. In practice, this means that regardless of nationality you will have to show a passport or EU identity card when entering from EU member states Hungary and Bulgaria, as well as from non-EU states Ukraine, Moldova and Serbia.

Work

Working in Romania is possible only with a valid work permit issued by the **Ministry of Labor & Social Protection** (www.mmuncii.ro; Romanian only) and in conjunction with a Romanian employer. The procedure for obtaining a permit should be initiated before arriving. Working in Romania also normally requires a long-stay visa. The website of the Romanian **Ministry for Foreign Affairs** (www.mae.ro) has information in English on steps for obtaining such a visa.

Just Landed (www.justlanded.com) is a helpful resource for sorting out the bureaucracy and getting started.

Transport

GETTING THERE & AWAY

Travel to Romania does not pose any unusual problems. Bucharest has air connections with many European capitals and large cities, and train and long-haul bus services are frequent.

Flights, cars and tours can be booked online at lonelyplanet.com/bookings.

Entering the Country

All international visitors to Romania are required to have a valid passport (EU members must carry a valid EU ID card). The expiration date of the passport should exceed your travel dates by at least three months, though some airlines will not allow passengers to board unless the passport is valid for at least six months.

Air

Romania has good air connections to Europe and the Middle East. At the time of research there were no direct flights to Romania from North America or Southeast Asia.

Airports & Airlines

The majority of international flights to Romania arrive at Bucharest's **Henri Coandă International Airport** (OTP, Otopeni; ☑arrivals 021-204 1220, departures 021-204 1210; www.bucharestairports.ro; Şos Bucureşti-Ploieşti; ☑783). Several other cities have international airports that service mostly domestic flights, but normally also have flights to select European cities. The largest of these include:

Cluj Avram Iancu International Airport (CLJ; ☑0264-416 702, 0264-307 500; www.airportcluj.ro; Str Traian Vuia 149)

Iaşi Airport (Aeroportul Inter-naţional Iaşi, IAS; ☑0232-271 590; www.aeroport.ro; Str Moara de Vant 34)

Sibiu International Airport (SBZ; ☑0269-253 135; www.sibiuairport.ro; Şoseaua Alba Iulia 73)

Timişoara Traian Vuia International Airport (TSR; ☑0256-386 089; http://aerotim.ro/en; Str Aeroport 2, Ghiroda)

Romania's national carrier is Bucharest-based **Tarom** (☑call centre 021-204 6464, office 021-316 0220; www.tarom.ro; Spl Independenţei 17, City Centre; ☑9am-5pm Mon-Fri; ☑Piaţa Unirii). While the airline was previously the butt of jokes, in recent years it has transformed itself into a safe and reliable carrier. It operates an extensive network of domestic flights to cities around Romania. It also flies to major cities in Europe, including London and Paris, and the Middle East.

CLIMATE CHANGE & TRAVEL

Every form of transport that relies on carbon-based fuel generates CO_2, the main cause of human-induced climate change. Modern travel is dependent on aeroplanes, which might use less fuel per kilometre per person than most cars but travel much greater distances. The altitude at which aircraft emit gases (including CO_2) and particles also contributes to their climate change impact. Many websites offer 'carbon calculators' that allow people to estimate the carbon emissions generated by their journey and, for those who wish to do so, to offset the impact of the greenhouse gases emitted with contributions to portfolios of climate-friendly initiatives throughout the world. Lonely Planet offsets the carbon footprint of all staff and author travel.

Many other national carriers, particularly from Europe and the Middle East, operate regular flights to Romania, normally between their respective capitals and/or major cities and Bucharest.

Additionally, many budget carriers service the Romanian market, mainly to and from destinations in Italy, Spain, Germany and the UK. These include Bucharest-based **WizzAir** (www.wizzair.com) and **Blue Air** (www.blueairweb.com), as well as **EuroWings** (www.eurowings.com) and **Ryanair** (www.ryanair.com). Check the airline websites for the latest information on flights and routes.

Major carriers include the following:

Air France (www.airfrance.com)

Austrian Airlines (www.austrian.com)

British Airways (www.britishairways.com)

Lufthansa (www.lufthansa.com)

Swiss Airlines (www.swiss.com)

Turkish Airlines (www.turkishairlines.com)

Tickets

Fares vary depending on the route, the time of year, and the day of the week. Romania's high season is summer (June to August) and a short period around Christmas. The rest of the year is quieter and cheaper. Weekday flights tend to be more expensive than weekends, or trips that include a weekend stay.

For flights within Europe, travellers have the choice of several major, full-fare carriers as well as budget carriers. Budget options from Britain, Italy and Spain are particularly good.

For transatlantic and long-haul flights a travel agent or internet aggregator are probably still the best sources of cheap tickets. One feasible option is to find the best deal to a European hub, like London, and then try to find a budget flight from there. That might land you the cheapest deal, but bear in mind budget airlines rarely use main airports, and you're likely to have to change not just planes en route but airports too.

Land

Romania shares a border with five countries: Bulgaria, Hungary, Moldova, Serbia and Ukraine. Most crossings follow international highways or national roads. Romania has two bridge and three car-ferry crossings with Bulgaria over the Danube River. Highway border posts are normally open 24 hours, though some smaller crossings may only be open from 8am to 8pm. Ferries run during daylight and may have reduced operating hours in winter.

At the time of research, Romania was not a member of the EU's common customs and border area, the Schengen area, so even if you're entering from an EU member state (Bulgaria or Hungary), you'll still have to show a passport or valid EU identity card.

Border crossings can get crowded, particularly during weekends, so prepare for delays.

Bus

Long-haul bus services remain a popular way of travelling from Romania to Western Europe as well as to parts of southeastern Europe and Turkey. Bus travel is comparable in price to train travel, but can be faster and require fewer connections.

TO/FROM BULGARIA, TURKEY & GREECE

Bucharest is the hub for coach travel to Bulgaria, Greece and Turkey. Given Bucharest's position in the southeast of Romania, buses are often quicker and cheaper than trains.

Sofia-based **Etap Grup** (www.etapgroup.com) runs daily between Bucharest and Sofia (about 130 lei per person one way, seven to eight hours). Buses depart from Bucharest's **Autogara Filaret** (🚌 buses to Bulgaria 021-335 3290, buses to Greece 021-336 6780, domestic bus services 021-336 0692; www.acfilaret.ro; Piața Gării Filaret 1; 🚊 7, 47).

Bucharest-based **Murat Turism & Transport** (☑ 0735-515 081; www.muratturism.ro; Șos Viilor 33; 🚊 173) offers a daily bus service from the Romanian capital to İstanbul (160 lei, 11 to 12 hours) and to Athens (200 lei, 18 hours).

MAJOR INTERNATIONAL ROAD & FERRY CROSSINGS

Major international road and car-ferry crossings are located at or near the Romanian towns described here.

To/from Bulgaria Bridge crossings at Giurgiu and Calafat; ferry crossings at Bechet, Turnu Măgerele and Călărași; a highway crossing at Vama Veche.

Hungary Road crossings at Nădlac (Arad), Borș (Oradea), Cenad, Valea lui Mihai and Urziceni.

Moldova Road crossings at Rădăuți-Prut, Albița, Galați, Ștefănești and Sculeni.

Serbia Road crossings at Moravița, Comloșu Mare, Jimbolia and Porțile de Fier.

Ukraine Road crossings at Siret and Sighetu Marmației.

TO/FROM WESTERN EUROPE

Bus services to and from Western European destinations are dominated by two companies: **Eurolines** (www.eurolines.ro) and **Atlassib** (Map p46; ☎021-222 8971, call centre 080-10 100 100; www.atlassib.ro; Str Gheorghe Duca 4, Bucharest; Ⓜ Gara de Nord). Both maintain vast networks from cities throughout Europe to destinations all around Romania. Check the companies' websites for the latest schedules, prices and departure points.

For sample prices, a one-way ticket from Vienna to Bucharest costs roughly €70. From Paris, the trip is about €100.

Car & Motorcycle

Romania has decent road and car-ferry connections to neighbouring countries, and entering the country by car or motorcycle will present no unexpected difficulties.

At all border crossings, drivers should be prepared to show the vehicle's registration, proof of insurance (a 'green' card) and a valid driver's license. All visiting foreigners, including EU nationals, are required to show a valid passport (or EU identity card).

From Western Europe, the best road crossings are via Hungary at Nădlac (near Arad), along Hwy E68, and Borş (near Oradea), on Hwy E60. Both are major international transit corridors and are open 24 hours.

The main road connection to Bulgaria is south of Giurgiu on Hwy E85, across the Danube River. A second car bridge traverses the Danube at Calafat along Hwy E79, connecting to the Bulgarian city of Vidin.

Train

Romania is integrated into the European rail grid, and there are decent connections to Western Europe and neighbouring countries. Nearly all of these arrive at and depart from Bucharest's main station, **Gara de Nord** (☑ phone reservations 021-9522; www.cfrcalatori.ro; Piaţa Gara de Nord 1; Ⓜ Gara de Nord).

➡ Budapest is the main rail gateway in and out of Romania from Western Europe. There are two daily direct trains between Budapest and Bucharest, with regular onward direct connections from Budapest to Prague, Munich and Vienna.

➡ Buy international train tickets at major train stations or at CFR (Romanian State Railways) in-town ticket offices (identified by an 'Agenţia de Voiaj CFR' sign).

➡ For longer overnight journeys, book a couchette (*cuşetă*) or a berth in a sleeping car (*vagon de dormit*). The former are cheaper but less comfortable; they are in standard 2nd-class rail cars with seats that convert to makeshift beds at night. Sleeping cars have dedicated beds, though you're not actually likely to get much sleep since you'll still be awoken at border crossings to show tickets and passports. Book sleeping-car berths well in advance at train ticket windows or CFR offices.

RAIL PASSES

If you plan on doing a lot of rail travel or combining travel to Romania with neighbouring countries, you might consider an international rail pass. Romania is part of both the **InterRail** (www.interrail.eu) and **Eurail** (www.eurail.com) networks, and several passes offered by both include rail travel in Romania.

Passes typically allow for a number of train travel days within a period of 15 days or a month. Some passes allow for unlimited travel. InterRail passes are cheaper but can only be purchased by EU nationals or anyone living in Europe for at least six months prior to travel. Eurail passes are open to anyone. Check the websites for specific details and prices. Another rail-pass company worth checking out is **Rail Europe** (www.raileurope.com).

Romanian rail travel is included on InterRail's GlobalPass, which includes 30 European countries, and the Romanian country pass. Eurail passholders can choose from the Hungary–Romania Pass or the Eurail Balkan Flexipass. The latter

---

POPULAR INTERNATIONAL RAIL JOURNEYS

Most long-haul international rail trips arrive at and depart from Bucharest's main station, Gara de Nord. Travel times and the approximate cost of a second-class ticket to popular destinations are as follows (accurate at the time of research but subject to change):

Bucharest–Budapest (via Arad; 215 lei, 14 hours, two daily)

Bucharest–Belgrade (via Timişoara; 180 lei, 12 hours, one daily)

Bucharest–Sofia (via Ruse; 180 lei, nine hours, one daily)

Bucharest–Chişinău (via Iaşi; 140 lei, 13 hours, one daily)

Bucharest–Moscow (via Chişinău; 560 lei, 45 hours, one daily)

Bucharest–Istanbul (210 lei, 19 hours, one daily)

option allows for unlimited train travel in Romania as well as Bulgaria, Greece, Turkey, and much of former Yugoslavia.

Sea

Constanţa port has a passenger terminal on the Black Sea. Nevertheless, at the time of research, there were no scheduled sea arrivals in Romania.

Tours

It's generally cheaper to use a Romanian-based operator if you want a prebooked tour. Some recommended international tour agencies offering Romania tours:

➡ **Quest Tours** (www.rom tour.com) US-based operator offers several themed tours of Romania. Check the website or contact them for an up-to-date list of excursions and prices.

➡ **Romania Tour Store** (www.romaniatourstore. com) Local Romanian agency with guided multi-day tours to Transylvania, the painted monasteries of Bucovina and the Danube Delta, among others.

➡ **Transylvania Uncovered** (www.beyondtheforest. com) UK-based operator that books a variety of inclusive trips including themed travel to the painted monasteries, and travel to Transylvania and Maramureş. Check the website or contact them for the latest excursion and price info.

GETTING AROUND

Air

Given the distances and poor state of the roads, flying between cities is a feasible option if time is a primary concern.

The Romanian national carrier **Tarom** (www.tarom. ro) operates a comprehensive network of domestic routes and has a network of ticket offices around the country. The airline flies regularly between Bucharest and Cluj-Napoca, Iaşi, Oradea, Satu Mare, Suceava and Timişoara.

The budget carrier **Blue Air** (www.blueairweb.com) also has a comprehensive network of domestic destinations that overlap with Tarom, but also includes Sibiu, Bacău and Constanţa.

Flights between regional cities usually involve travel via Bucharest, and connections aren't always convenient.

Bicycle

Romania has great potential as a cycling destination, though cycling has not yet caught on to the extent it has in other European countries.

On the positive side, cycling offers an excellent way of seeing the country and meeting locals. Off the main highways, Romania is criss-crossed by thousands of kilometres of secondary roads that are relatively little trafficked and ideal for cycling.

On the negative side, there's not much cycling infrastructure in place, such as dedicated cycling trails and a network of bike-rental and repair shops. Many cities, including Bucharest, do have some cycling trails, but these are half-hearted efforts and frequently leave cyclists at the mercy of often ignorant and aggressive drivers.

It's possible to hire or buy bicycles in many major towns, though not all. The group **i'velo** (www.ivelo. ro) is trying to popularise cycling and has opened bike-hire outlets in several cities, including Bucharest, Timişoara, Braşov, Constanţa, Iaşi and Alba Iulia. Rates average about 5 lei per hour or 30 to 50 lei per day.

Several private companies and travel agencies offer extended bike tours, usually including transfers and overnights. One of the best is **Cycling Romania** (www. cyclingromania.ro).

Taking Your Bike on the Train

Bicycles can usually be transported on trains, though not every train will have room for bikes, including many newer IC trains. Check the timetable at www.cfrcalatori. ro. Trains that accommodate cyclists are marked with a bicycle sign.

If you are travelling with your bike, try to arrive at the train station early and inform the ticket seller you have a bike. You may have to buy a separate ticket for the bike, usually a flat fee of 10 lei, and be instructed to hand the bike over to the baggage window.

Even if the ticket seller says it's not possible, it's always worth taking your bike to the platform and trying to negotiate with the conductor. Frequently, if the train is not full he or she may allow you to board.

Boat

Passenger ferry or private boat is the only way of getting around much of the Danube Delta, where you can pick up ferries or hop on fishers' boats from Tulcea.

Bus

A mix of buses, minibuses and 'maxitaxis' – private vans holding anywhere from 10 to 20 passengers – form the backbone of the Romanian national transport system. If you understand how the system works – and that's a big if – you can move around regions and even across the country easily and cheaply.

Unfortunately, there appears to be little logic

behind how the system is organised and how it functions. Buses and maxitaxi routes change frequently; often these changes are communicated by word of mouth. Towns and cities will sometimes have a half-dozen different bus stations (autogara) and maxitaxi stops, depending on which company is operating a particular route and the destination in question.

In many cities and towns it's not possible to list firm bus stations and routes. In these cases, the helpful website **Autogari.ro** (www.autogari.ro) is a godsend. This is an up-to-date national timetable that is relatively easy to use and lists routes, times, fares and departure points. Another tried and true method is simply to ask around.

Once you've located the bus station and your bus, buy tickets directly from the driver. Have small bills handy, as drivers cannot usually provide change for big bills.

Fares vary according to the demand and number of competing bus companies, but are usually cheap. Figure on about 4 to 5 lei for every 20km travelled.

Car & Motorcycle

Driving around Romania has some compelling advantages. With your own wheels, you're free to explore off-the-beaten-track destinations, remote monasteries and tiny villages. Additionally, you're no longer at the whim of capricious local bus schedules and inconvenient, early morning train departures.

That said, driving in Romania is not ideal, and if you have the chance to use alternatives like the train and bus, this can be a much more relaxing option.

Roads are generally crowded and in poor condition. The country has only a few stretches of motorway (autostrada), meaning that most of your travel will be along two-lane national highways (DN, drum naţional) or secondary roads (DJ, drum judeţean). These pass through every village en route and are choked with cars and trucks, and even occasionally horse carts and tractors pulling hay racks. It's white-knuckle driving made worse by aggressive motorists in fast cars trying to overtake on every hill and blind curve. When calculating arrival times, figure on covering about 50km per hour.

Western-style petrol stations are plentiful, but be sure to fill up before heading on long trips through the mountains or in remote areas. A litre of unleaded 95 octane cost about 5 lei at the time of research. Petrol stations invariably accept credit cards, but you'll need to have a PIN to use them.

Hire

International companies like Avis, Budget, Hertz and Europcar have offices in large cities and at Henri Coandă International Airport in Bucharest. In addition, locally owned car-hire companies usually operate in large cities and can be cheaper. Book cars in advance over company websites to get the best rates. Drivers must normally be at least 21 years old, and the renter must hold a valid credit card.

Hitching

Hitching is a popular way of moving from town to town in Romania, where hitchers, usually students, line up on the main road just beyond the town or city limits and stick out their arms to hail a ride. That said, hitching occupies a grey area in Romanian law, is never entirely safe, and we don't recommend it. Travellers who hitch should understand that they are taking a small but potentially serious risk. If you decide to hitch anyway, note that it's common practice to pay the equivalent of the bus fare to the driver (about 1 to 2 lei per 10km).

Local Transport

Bus, Tram, Maxitaxi & Trolleybus

Romanian cities generally have good public-transport systems comprised of buses, trams, trolleybuses and, in some cases, maxitaxis. Bucharest is the only Romanian city with an underground

---

ROAD RULES

Motorists are required to buy and display a sticker, called a rovinieta (www.roviniete.ro), that can be purchased on the border, at petrol stations or online. A vignette valid for one week costs about 15 lei, for 30 days around 40 lei.

Other common traffic rules are as follows:

➡ Standard speed limits are 50km/h in town; 90km/h on national roads; 130km/h on four-lane expressways.

➡ The minimum driving age is 18.

➡ The blood-alcohol limit is zero.

➡ The use of seat belts is compulsory for front-seat passengers. Children under 12 are prohibited from sitting in the front seat.

➡ Headlights must be always on, even in bright daylight.

➡ Give way to traffic entering a roundabout.

ROMANIA ROAD DISTANCES (KM)

	Alba Iulia	Arad	Baia Mare	Bistriţa	Braşov	Bucharest	Cluj-Napoca	Constanţa	Deva	Iaşi	Miercurea Ciuc	Oradea	Piatra Neamţ	Piteşti	Ploieşti	Satu Mare	Sibiu	Suceava	Târgu Mureş	Timişoara
Arad	236																			
Baia Mare	236	319																		
Bistriţa	217	393	151																	
Braşov	229	429	392	267																
Bucharest	340	538	574	439	175															
Cluj-Napoca	94	270	142	281	123	432														
Constanţa	581	809	781	648	444	243	662													
Deva	84	150	290	301	279	388	178	631												
Iaşi	458	686	508	355	307	428	389	432	586											
Miercurea Ciuc	288	522	349	209	99	261	272	486	378	258										
Oradea	247	117	202	276	434	528	153	815	190	581	411									
Piatra Neamţ	358	620	383	244	236	310	342	425	422	118	140	463								
Piteşti	231	431	467	375	147	107	325	349	281	454	246	478	383							
Ploieşti	344	544	507	382	115	58	396	291	349	347	214	549	300	119						
Satu Mare	264	251	67	226	458	607	175	822	319	581	433	129	456	497	573					
Sibiu	73	274	322	271	156	265	167	538	126	413	255	320	295	188	271	343				
Suceava	408	588	318	191	328	434	300	562	492	140	247	467	107	475	392	403	406			
Târgu Mureş	137	378	227	93	174	347	106	554	221	321	151	260	201	282	289	282	124	284		
Timişoara	240	52	370	457	435	545	334	829	156	742	534	168	578	440	550	297	279	648	377	
Tulcea	600	813	777	591	384	304	665	147	666	335	406	817	345	401	262	846	540	437	558	825

metro. The method for accessing the systems is broadly similar. Purchase bus or tram tickets at newsagents or street kiosks marked *bilete* or *casă de bilete* before boarding, and validate the ticket once onboard. For maxitaxis, you usually buy a ticket directly from the driver. Tickets generally cost from 1 to 3 lei per ride.

Taxi

Taxis are cheap, reliable and a useful supplement to the public-transport systems. Drivers are required by law to post their rates on their doors or windscreens. The going rate varies from city to city but ranges from 1.39 to 1.79 lei per kilometre. Any driver posting a higher fare is likely looking to rip off unsuspecting passengers.

While it's usually OK to use a taxi parked at a taxi rank (provided the taxi is not one of those lined up at Bucharest's airport or main train station) or to hail one from the street, it's much safer to order taxis by phone from reputable companies or to ask a hotel or restaurant to call one for you. In Bucharest, try **Cobalcescu** (☑021-9451; www.autocobalcescu.ro), **Cris-Taxi** (☑021-9466; www.cristaxi.ro) or **Meridian** (☑English 021-9888, general 021-9444; www.meridiantaxi.ro).

Tours

Considering how remote much of Romania remains, it's not a bad idea to consider arranging a tour with local

agencies. Here are some of the standouts.

Apuseni Experience (☑0747-962 482, 0745-602 301; www.apuseniexperience.ro) Oradea-based outfit arranging multiday hiking and biking trips in the Apuseni Mountains.

Hello Bucovina (Map p201; ☑0744-292 588; www.hellobucovina.com; Aleea Nucului 1, bldg 1, apt 3; ⊙9am-5pm Mon-Fri) Suceava-based company offering day trips to the Bucovina painted monasteries and other regional sights, as well as more ambitious journeys to Ukraine and Moldova.

RoCultours/CTI (☑0723-160 925; www.rotravel.com/cti) Reliable agent with many cultural tours, and personalised itineraries listed on the website. It's best to contact them in advance.

Roving România (☑0724-348 272, 0744-212 065; www.roving-romania.co.uk; ⊙Apr-early Dec) Tailormade trips with Roving România allow small groups to access Transylvania's natural splendour and enjoy authentic village life.

Transylvanian Wolf (☑0744-319 708; www.transylvanian.ro; ⊙year-round) Family-run nature tour company leading walks on the trail of animals such as wolves, bears and lynx.

Train

Trains are a slow but reliable way of getting around Romania. The extensive network covers much of the country, including most of the

main tourist sights and key destinations.

The national rail system is run by **Căile Ferate Române** (CFR; www.cfrcalatori.ro); the website has a handy online timetable (*mersul trenurilor*).

Buy tickets at train-station windows, specialised Agenţia de Voiaj CFR ticket offices, private travel agencies, or online at www.cfrcalatori.ro.

Sosire means 'arrivals' and *plecare*, 'departures'. On posted timetables, the number of the platform from which the train departs is listed under *linia*.

Classes & Types

Romania has broadly three different types of passenger trains that travel at different speeds, offer varying levels of comfort, and charge different fares for the same destination.

➡ **InterCity**, listed in blue or green as 'IC' on timetables, are the most expensive and most comfortable but are not always much faster than 'IR' trains. IC trains often travel outside the country.

➡ **InterRegional**, listed in red as 'IR' on timetables, are the next rung down. These are cheaper and nearly as fast as 'IC' trains, but may not be as modern.

➡ **Regional**, listed in black as 'R' on timetables, are typically the oldest and slowest trains in the system, often sporting historic rolling stock.

Language

Romanian is a member of the Romance language family – as a descendant of Latin, it shares a common heritage with French, Italian, Spanish and Portuguese. Today, Romanian is the official language of Romania and Moldova (where it's called Moldovan), with about 24 million speakers.

Romanian pronunciation is pretty straightforward for English speakers, and if you read our coloured pronunciation guides as if they were English, you'll be understood. Note that ai is pronounced as in 'aisle', ew as the 'ee' in 'see' but with rounded lips, oh as in 'note', ow as in 'how', uh as the 'a' in 'ago', zh as the 's' in 'measure', and that the apostrophe (') indicates a very short, unstressed i sound. The stressed syllables are indicated with italics.

BASICS

Hello.	Bună ziua.	boo·nuh zee·wa
Goodbye.	La revedere.	la re·ve·de·re
Yes.	Da.	da
No.	Nu.	noo
Please.	Vă rog.	vuh rog
Thank you.	Mulţumesc.	mool·tsoo·mesk
You're welcome.	Cu plăcere.	koo pluh·che·re
Excuse me.	Scuzaţi-mă.	skoo·za·tsee·muh
Sorry.	Îmi pare rău.	ewm' pa·re ruh·oo

WANT MORE?

For in-depth language information and handy phrases, check out Lonely Planet's *Eastern Europe Phrasebook*. You'll find it at **shop.lonelyplanet.com**, or you can buy Lonely Planet's iPhone phrasebooks at the Apple App Store.

How are you?
Ce mai faceţi? — che mai fa·chets'

Fine. And you?
Bine. Dumneavoastră? — bee·ne doom·ne·a·vo·as·truh

What's your name?
Cum vă numiţi? — koom vuh noo·meets'

My name is ...
Numele meu este ... — noo·me·le me·oo yes·te ...

Do you speak English?
Vorbiţi engleza? — vor·beets' en·gle·za

I don't understand.
Eu nu înţeleg. — ye·oo noo ewn·tse·leg

ACCOMMODATION

Where's a ...? Unde se află ...? — oon·de se a·fluh ...

campsite	un teren de camping	oon te·ren de kem·peeng
guesthouse	o pensiune	o pen·syoo·ne
hotel	un hotel	oon ho·tel
youth hostel	un hostel	oon hos·tel

Can you recommend somewhere ...?	Puteţi recomanda ceva ...?	poo·te·tsi re·ko·man·da che·va ...?
cheap	ieftin	yef·teen
good	bun	boon
nearby	în apropiere	ewn a·pro·pye·re

I'd like to book a room, please.
Aş dori să rezerv o cameră, vă rog. — ash do·ree suh re·zerv o ka·me·ruh vuh rog

I have a reservation.
Am o rezervaţie. — am o re·zer·va·tsye

My name's ...
Numele meu este ... — noo·me·le me·oo yes·te ...

QUESTION WORDS

How?	Cum?	koom
What?	Ce?	che
When?	Când?	kewnd
Where?	Unde?	oon·de
Who?	Cine?	chee·ne
Why?	De ce?	de che

Do you have a ... room?	Aveţi o cameră ...?	a·vets' o ka·me·ruh ...
single	de o persoană	de o per·so·a·nuh
double	dublă	doo·bluh

How much is it per ...?	Cît costă ...?	kewt kos·tuh ...
night	pe noapte	pe no·ap·te
person	de persoană	de per·so·a·nuh

DIRECTIONS

Where's the ...?	Unde este ...?	oon·de yes·te ...
bank	banca	ban·ka
city centre	centrul oraşului	chen·trool o·ra·shoo·looy
hotel	hotelul	ho·te·lool
market	piaţa	pya·tsa
police station	secţia de poliţie	sek·tsya de po·lee·tsye
tourist office	biroul de informaţii turistice	bee·ro·ool de een·for·ma·tsee too·rees·tee·che

What's the address?
Care este adresa?   ka·re yes·te a·dre·sa

Can you show me (on the map)?
Puteţi să-mi arătaţi   poo·te·tsi suh·mi a·ruh·tats'
(pe hartă)?   (pe har·tuh)

How far is it?
Cît e de departe?   kewt ye de de·par·te

Is this the road to (Arad)?
Acesta e drumul   a·ches·ta ye droo·mool
spre (Arad)?   spre (a·rad)

How do I get there?
Cum ajung acolo?   koom a·zhoong a·ko·lo

EATING & DRINKING

Can you recommend a ...?	Îmi puteţi recomanda ...?	ew·mi poo·tets' re·ko·man·da ...
bar	un bar	oon bar

café	o cafenea	o ka·fe·ne·a
restaurant	un restaurant	oon res·tow·rant

I'd like (the) ..., please.	Vă rog, aş dori ...	vuh rog ash do·ree ...
bill	nota de plată	no·ta de pla·tuh
drink list	lista de băuturi	lees·ta de buh·oo·too·ri
menu	meniul	me·nee·ool
that dish	acel fel de mâncare	a·chel fel de mewn·ka·re

What would you recommend?
Ce recomandaţi?   che re·ko·man·dats'

What's the local speciality?
Care e   ka·re ye
specialitatea   spe·chya·lee·ta·te·a
locală?   lo·ka·luh

Do you have vegetarian food?
Aveţi mâncare   a·ve·tsi mewn·ka·re
vegetariană?   ve·je·ta·rya·nuh

I'll have ...	Aş dori ...	ash do·ree ...
Cheers!	Noroc!	no·rok

beer	bere	be·re
bottle	sticlă	stee·kluh
breakfast	micul dejun	mee·kool de·zhoon
cafe	cafenea	ka·fe·ne·a
coffee	cafea	ka·fe·a
cup	cană	ka·nuh
dinner	cină	chee·nuh
eggs	ouă	o·wuh
fish	peşte	pesh·te
fork	furculiţă	foor·koo·lee·tsuh
fruit	fructe	frook·te
glass	pahar	pa·har
juice	suc	sook
knife	cuţit	koo·tseet
lunch	dejun	de·zhoon
meat	carne	kar·ne
milk	lapte	lap·te
restaurant	restaurant	res·tow·rant
spoon	lingură	leen·goo·ruh
tea	ceai	che·ai
vegetable	legumă	le·goo·muh
water	apă	a·puh
wine	vin	veen

EMERGENCIES

| Help! | Ajutor! | a·zhoo·tor |
| Go away! | Pleacă! | ple·a·kuh |

Call ...!	Chemaţi ...!	ke·mats' ...
a doctor	un doctor	oon dok·tor
the police	poliţia	po·lee·tsya

I'm lost.
M-am rătăcit.   mam ruh·tuh·cheet

Could you help me, please?
Ajutaţi-mă, vă rog!   a·zhoo·ta·tsee·muh vuh rog

Where are the toilets?
Unde este o toaletă?   oon·de yes·te o to·a·le·tuh

I'm sick.
Mă simt rău.   muh seemt ruh·oo

I'm allergic to ...
Am alergie la ...   am a·ler·jee·ye la ...

I've lost my ...
Mi-am pierdut ...   myam pyer·doot ...

My ... was/were stolen.

Mi s-a/s-au furat ...	mee sa/sow foo·rat ...
bags	valizele	va·lee·ze·le
credit card	cartea de credit	kar·te·a de kre·deet
passport	paşaportul	pa·sha·por·tool
wallet	portofelul	por·to·fe·lool

I want to contact my consulate/embassy.
Aş dori să contactez   ash do·ree suh kon·tak·tez
consulatul/ambasada.   kon·soo·la·tool/am·ba·sa·da

SHOPPING & SERVICES

Where's the ...?	Unde este ...?	oon·yes·te ...
ATM	bancomat	ban·ko·mat
bank	bancă	ban·kuh
department store	magazin universal	ma·ga·zeen oo·nee·ver·sal
grocery store	magazin alimentar	ma·ga·zeen a·lee·men·tar
local internet cafe	un internet café în apropiere	oon een·ter·net ka·fe ewn a·pro·pye·re
newsagency	stand de ziare	stand de zee·a·re
post office	poşta	posh·ta

| tourist office | biroul de informaţii turistice | bee·ro·ool de een·for·ma·tsee too·rees·tee·che |

I'd like to buy (a phonecard).
Aş dori să cumpăr   ash do·ree suh koom·puhr
(o cartelă de telefon).   (o kar·te·luh de te·le·fon)

Can I look at it?
Pot să mă uit?   pot suh muh ooyt

Can I try it on?
Pot să probez?   pot suh pro·bez

My size is (40).
Port numărul   port noo·muh·rool
(patruzeci).   (pa·troo·ze·chi)

It doesn't fit.
Nu mi se potriveşte.   noo mee se po·tree·vesh·te

Do you have any others?
Mai aveţi şi altele?   mai a·vets' shee al·te·le

How much is it?
Cât costă?   kewt kos·tuh

That's too expensive.
E prea scump.   ye pre·a skoomp

There's a mistake in the bill.
Chitanţa conţine   kee·tan·tsa kon·tsee·ne
o greşeală.   o gre·she·a·luh

TIME & DATES

What time is it?
Cât e ceasul?   kewt ye che·a·sool

It's (two) o'clock.
E ora (două).   ye o·ra (do·wuh)

Half past (one).
(Unu) şi   (oo·noo) shee
jumătate.   zhoo·muh·ta·te

At what time ...?
La ce oră ...?   la che o·ruh ...

At ...
La ora ...   la o·ra ...

SIGNS

Intrare	Entrance
Ieşire	Exit
Deschis	Open
Închis	Closed
Informaţii	Information
Interzis	Prohibited
Toalete	Toilets
Bărbaţi	Men
Femei	Women

yesterday ...	ieri ...	ye·ri ...
tomorrow ...	mâine ...	mew·ee·ne ...
morning	dimineaţă	dee·mee·ne·a·tsuh
afternoon	după amiază	doo·puh a·mya·zuh
evening	seară	se·a·ruh

Monday	luni	loo·ni
Tuesday	marţi	muhr·tsi
Wednesday	miercuri	myer·koo·ri
Thursday	joi	zhoy
Friday	vineri	vee·ne·ri
Saturday	sâmbătă	sewm·buh·tuh
Sunday	duminică	doo·mee·nee·kuh

January	ianuarie	ya·nwa·rye
February	februarie	fe·brwa·rye
March	martie	mar·tye
April	aprilie	a·pree·lye
May	mai	mai
June	iunie	yoo·nye
July	iulie	yoo·lye
August	august	ow·goost
September	septembrie	sep·tem·brye
October	octombrie	ok·tom·brye
November	noiembrie	no·yem·brye
December	decembrie	de·chem·brye

NUMBERS

1	unu	oo·noo
2	doi	doy
3	trei	trey
4	patru	pa·troo
5	cinci	cheench'
6	şase	sha·se
7	şapte	shap·te
8	opt	opt
9	nouă	no·wuh
10	zece	ze·che
20	douăzeci	do·wuh·ze·chi
30	treizeci	trey·ze·chi
40	patruzeci	pa·troo·ze·chi
50	cincizeci	cheench·ze·chi
60	şaizeci	shai·ze·chi
70	şaptezeci	shap·te·ze·chi
80	optzeci	opt·ze·chi
90	nouăzeci	no·wuh·ze·chi
100	o sută	o soo·tuh

TRANSPORT

Public Transport

Is this the ... to (Cluj)?	Acesta e ... de (Cluj)?	a·ches·ta ye ... de (kloozh)
boat	vaporul	va·po·rool
bus	autobuzul	ow·to·boo·zool
plane	avionul	a·vyo·nool
train	trenul	tre·nool

What time's the ... bus?	Când este ... autobuz?	kewnd yes·te ... ow·to·booz
first	primul	pree·mool
last	ultimul	ool·tee·mool
next	următorul	oor·muh·to·rool

Where can I buy a ticket?

| Unde pot cumpăra un bilet? | oon·de pot koom·puh·ra oon bee·let |

One ... ticket (to Cluj), please.	Un bilet ... (până la Cluj), vă rog.	oon bee·let ... (pew·nuh la kloozh) vuh rog
one-way	dus	doos
return	dus-întors	doos ewn·tors

How long does the trip take?

| Cât durează călătoria? | kewt doo·re·a·zuh kuh·luh·to·ree·a |

Is it a direct route?

| E o rută directă? | ye o roo·tuh dee·rek·tuh |

At what time does it arrive/leave?

| La ce oră soseşte/ pleacă? | la che o·ruh so·sesh·te/ ple·a·kuh |

How long will it be delayed?

| Cât întârzie? | kewt ewn·tewr·zye |

Does it stop at (Galaţi)?

| Opreşte la (Galaţi)? | o·presh·te la (ga·la·tsi) |

How long do we stop here?

| Cât stăm aici? | kewt stuhm a·eech |

What station/stop is this?

| Ce gară/staţie e aceasta? | che ga·ruh/sta·tsye ye a·che·as·ta |

What's the next station/stop?

| Care este următoarea gară/staţie? | ca·re yes·te oor·muh·h·to·a·re·a ga·ruh/sta·tsye |

Please tell me when we get to (Iaşi).

| Vă rog, când ajungem la (Iaşi)? | vuh rog kewnd a·zhoon·jem la (ya·shi) |

I'd like a taxi ...	Aş dori un taxi ...	ash do·*ree* oon tak·*see* ...
at (9am)	la ora (nouă dimineaţa)	la o·ra (*no*·wuh dee·mee·*ne*·a·tsa)
now	acum	a·*koom*
tomorrow	mâine	mew·ee·ne

How much is it to ...?
Cât costă până la ...?   kewt kos·tuh pew·nuh la ...

Please take me to (this address).
Vă rog, duceţi-mă la   vuh rog doo·*chets*'·muh la
(această adresă).   (a·che·*as*·tuh a·*dre*·suh)

Please ...	Vă rog, ...	vuh rog ...
slow down	încetiniţi	ewn·che·tee·*neets*'
stop here	opriţi aici	o·*preets*' a·eech
wait here	aşteptaţi aici	ash·tep·*tats*' a·eech

Driving & Cycling

I'd like to hire a ...	Aş dori să închiriez o ...	ash do·*ree* suh ewn·kee·*ryez* o ...
bicycle	bicicletă	bee·chee·*kle*·tuh
car	maşină	ma·*shee*·nuh
motorbike	motocicletă	mo·to·chee·*kle*·tuh

How much for ... hire?	Cât costă chiria pe ...?	kewt kos·tuh kee·*ree*·a pe ...?
hourly	oră	o·ruh
daily	zi	zee
weekly	săptămână	suhp·tuh·*mew*·nuh

air	aer	a·er
oil	ulei	oo·*ley*
petrol	benzină	ben·*zee*·nuh
tyres	cauciucuri	kow·*choo*·koo·ri

I need a mechanic.
Am nevoie de un   am ne·*vo*·ye de oon
mecanic.   me·*ka*·neek

I've run out of petrol.
Am rămas fără   am ruh·*mas* fuh·ruh
benzină.   ben·*zee*·nuh

I have a flat tyre.
Am un cauciuc   am oon kow·*chook*
dezumflat.   de·*zoom*·flat

Is this the road to (Arad)?
Acesta e drumul   a·*ches*·ta ye *droo*·mool
spre (Arad)?   spre (a·*rad*)

GLOSSARY

The following are handy Romanian words. Hungarian (Hun) is included for key words.

Agenţia Teatrală – theatre ticket office (Hun: színház jegyiroda)

Agenţia de Voiaj CFR – train ticket office (Hun: vasúti jegyiroda)

Antrec – National Association of Rural, Ecological & Cultural Tourism

autogara – bus station (Hun: távolsági autóbusz pályaudvar)

bagaje de mână – left-luggage office (Hun: csomagmegőrző)

biserică – church (Hun: templom)

biserică de lemn – wooden church

cabana – mountain cabin or chalet

casă de bilete – ticket office (Hun: jegyiroda)

cascadă – waterfall

cazare – accommodation

CFR – Romanian State Railways

cheile – gorge

de jos – at the bottom

de sus – at the top

drum – road, trip

gara – train station (Hun: vasútállomás)

mănăstire – monastery (Hun: kolostor)

metropolitan – the head of a province of the church

pensiune – usually denotes a modern building or refurbished home, privately owned, that's been turned into accommodation for tourists

pensiunea – see *pensiune*

piaţa – square or market (Hun: főtér or piac)

plecare – departure (Hun: indulás)

sosire – arrival (Hun: érkezés)

ţară – land, country

Bulgaria

Cathedral of the Assumption of the Virgin (p417), Varna

Welcome to Bulgaria

Soul-stirring mountains rival golden beaches, while cities hum with nightlife and art. Within Bulgaria's beguiling blend of nature and history, unforgettable adventures are guaranteed.

Black Sea Beaches

Long, sandy beaches and fine weather reel Bulgarians into Black Sea resorts each summer. Foreign visitors, too, are wise to Bulgaria's coast, thanks to gorgeous seaside resorts such as Primorsko (and prices that compete well with Western Europe). Even the coast's two big cities, Varna and Burgas, have attractive beaches within minutes of their urban hearts. And while Sunny Beach, Sozopol and other favourites are thoroughly developed, there are still plenty of undiscovered coves.

Churches & Religious Art

No visitor to Bulgaria can fail to be impressed by its religious art, from vast gold-domed churches to miniature icon paintings. Sofia's Aleksander Nevski Church and 10th-century Rila Monastery draw visitors and pilgrims galore, while Tryavna's wood carvings and Bachkovo's apocalyptic murals are gathering fame. But Orthodox churches in even the tiniest villages have much to admire: emotive paintings of saints, often set in carved wooden screens (iconostases), appear magical when bathed in flickering candlelight. Almost as spectacular are the settings of many sacred buildings: granite cliffs, thrashing streams and lonely mountain passes.

Mountains & Forests

Bulgaria's untamed landscapes quicken the pulse of hikers, mountain bikers and skiers. Seven mountain ranges ripple across the country; glacial lakes sparkle, and tangles of forest conceal wolves, bears and lynx, a glimpse of Europe's primeval past. Networks of trails and *hizhas* (hiking huts) allow access to such raw beauty as mist-cloaked panoramas in the Stara Planina range and sunrise from Bulgaria's second-highest peak, Mt Vihren (2915m). Between trekking among Rodopi villages, thundering across ski fields in Bansko or birdwatching in Pirin National Park, Bulgaria has much to delight (and exhaust) lovers of the great outdoors.

Ancient History

Whispers of history emanate from Bulgaria's fortresses and ruins. Caves secreted in hold traces of Neolithic settlements. The Thracians left behind hauls of gold, and tombs that can still be explored. The Romans built breathtaking cities, the remains of which sit in the midst of modern cities such as Varna and Plovdiv. Tsars strutted along the ramparts of Tsarevets Fortress at former capital Veliko Târnovo. And these histories are no less relevant today, with Thracian art and Bulgaria's victory over the Ottomans continuing to inspire.

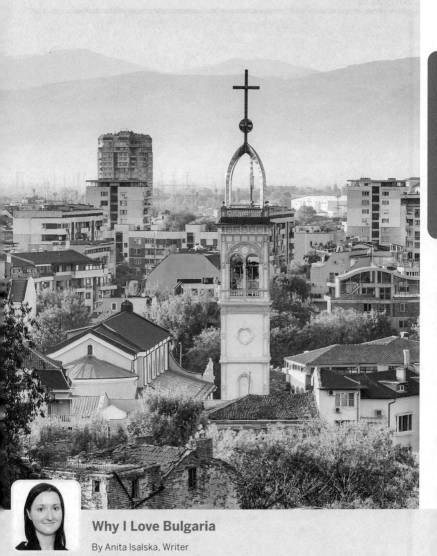

Why I Love Bulgaria

By Anita Isalska, Writer

Somewhere between panoramas of the Pirin Mountains and the cobbled nooks of old Plovdiv, Bulgaria grabbed my imagination – and it still hasn't let go. Bulgaria is a mysterious, multilayered country, with ski fields as fantastic as its beaches. But what keeps me in thrall is Bulgaria's mash-up of ancient and cutting-edge culture. What could be more alluring than heavy metal concerts in a Roman stadium, light shows over a medieval fortress, or crumbling mansions reborn as bars? Archaeological discoveries are made all the time, so there's something new and compelling each time I visit: the perfect excuse to keep coming back.

For more about our writers, see p512

Above: Plovdiv (p339)

Bulgaria

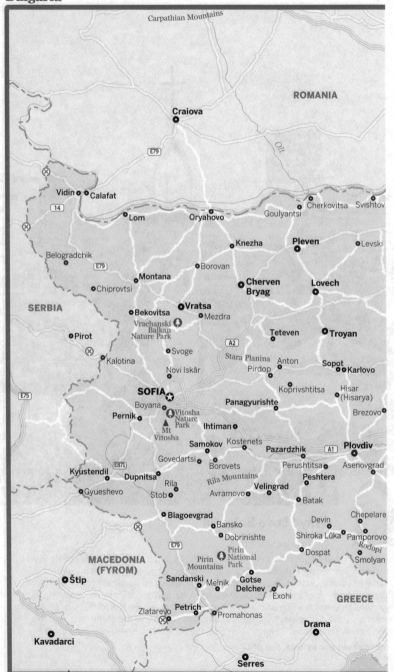

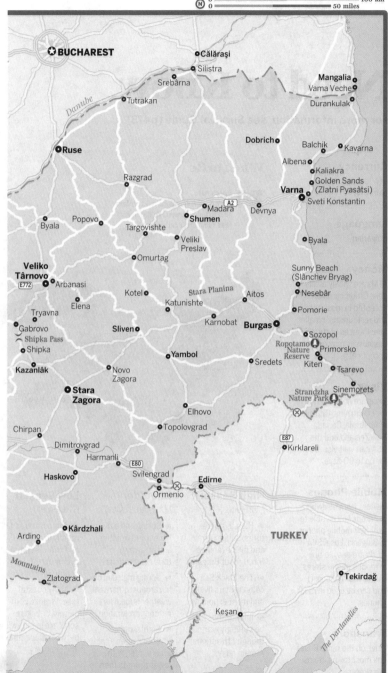

Need to Know

For more information, see Survival Guide (p473)

Currency
Lev/leva (singular/
plural; lv)

Language
Bulgarian

Money
ATMs are widely available. Credit cards are accepted in most hotels and restaurants; smaller guesthouses or rural businesses may only accept cash.

Visas
Visas are not required for EU citizens. Citizens of Australia, Canada, New Zealand and the USA can visit visa-free for up to 90 days.

Mobile Phones
Visitors from elsewhere in Europe will be able to use their mobile phones in Bulgaria. Local SIM cards are easy to buy in mobile phone stores (bring your passport) and can be used in most phones.

Transport
Drive on the right. Buses link most towns, trains are slower.

When to Go

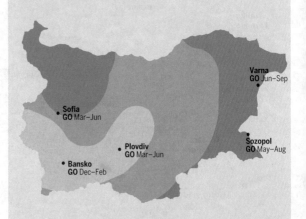

- Dry climate
- Warm to hot summers, mild winters
- Mild to hot summers, cold winters
- Mild summers, cold winters

Varna GO Jun–Sep

Sofia GO Mar–Jun

Plovdiv GO Mar–Jun

Sozopol GO May–Aug

Bansko GO Dec–Feb

High Season (Jun–Aug)
➜ High temperatures, sunny days and mild evenings throughout Bulgaria.

➜ The Black Sea coast is at its liveliest and most expensive.

➜ Inland cities can be stiflingly warm, though attractions remain busy.

Shoulder (Apr, May, Sep & Oct)
➜ Spring and autumn have warm weather and an array of cultural celebrations.

➜ Spring melt can be hazardous; otherwise, weather is ideal for outdoor exploration.

➜ Sights and attractions open again after winter, with fewer tourists than high summer.

Low Season (Nov–Mar)
➜ Temperatures fall rapidly in autumn, and snow is common over much of the country in winter.

➜ Many coastal resorts close completely, but ski resorts are in full swing between December and February.

Your Daily Budget

Budget: Less than 70 lv

➡ Dorm bed: 18–22 lv

➡ Room in a simple guest-house: 25–50 lv

➡ Meals from cafeterias: 5–10 lv

➡ Public transport tickets: around 1 lv

Midrange: 70–150 lv

➡ Double room in a midrange hotel: 60–80 lv

➡ Lunch and dinner in quality restaurants: 20–30 lv

➡ Taxi from airport to centre in Sofia or Plovdiv: 15 lv

Top End: More than 150 lv

➡ Double room in top-end hotel: 150–300 lv

➡ Three-course meals with wine in top-end restaurants: 30–55 lv

➡ Spa treatments: from 30 lv

Useful Websites

Anglo Info (www.angloinfo.com/bulgaria) Expat site with useful general information.

Beach Bulgaria (www.beachbulgaria.com) Seaside information and beach bookings.

Bulgarian Ministry of Foreign Affairs (www.mfa.government.bg) Visas, consulates and other practical basic information.

Bulgaria Travel (www.bulgariatravel.org) Official tourism portal.

Lonely Planet (www.lonelyplanet.com/bulgaria) Destination information, hotel bookings, traveller forum and more.

Vagabond (www.vagabond.bg) Features on culture and politics.

Exchange Rates

Australia	A$1	1.28 lv
Canada	C$1	1.34 lv
Europe	€1	1.95 lv
Japan	¥100	1.67 lv
New Zealand	NZ$1	1.22 lv
Romania	1 lei	0.43 lv
UK	UK£1	2.45 lv
USA	US$1	1.74 lv

For current exchange rates, see www.xe.com.

Important Numbers

The EU-wide emergency number ☑112 can be used in Bulgaria.

Bulgaria's country code	☑359
Ambulance	☑150
Fire	☑160
Police	☑166
24-hour pharmacy Information	☑178

Opening Hours

Standard opening hours are as follows.

Banks 9am to 4pm Monday to Friday

Bars 11am to midnight

Government offices 9am to 5pm Monday to Friday

Post offices 8.30am to 5pm Monday to Friday

Restaurants 11am to 11pm

Shops 9am to 6pm

Arriving in Bulgaria

Sofia Airport Sofia's metro runs between Terminal 2 and Serdika station (1 lv, 20 minutes); buy tickets in the station, located just outside the terminal exit. Bus 84 (1 lv, 40 to 50 minutes) also travels to central Sofia; buy tickets from the driver. Taxis (10 lv to 15 lv, 30 to 40 minutes) can be booked at the OK-Supertrans counter (staff will give you a slip of paper with the three-digit code of your cab).

Plovdiv Airport There's no airport shuttle bus; get a Violet Taxi to the centre (around 15 lv, 20 minutes).

Varna Airport Bus 409 (1 lv, 30 minutes) runs to central Varna and toward Golden Sands. A taxi from the airport costs 10 lv to 20 lv and takes 20 to 30 minutes.

Yes or No?

One cultural oddity that foreign visitors may find confusing at first is that Bulgarians shake their heads from side to side in a curved, almost wobbly motion to indicate 'yes', and gently jerk their heads up and backwards when they want to say 'no'. To add to the confusion, if Bulgarians know they are addressing a foreigner, they may reverse these gestures in an attempt to be helpful. If you are in any doubt about their real meaning, asking *'Da ili ne?'* (Yes or no?) will soon set you straight.

For much more on getting around, see p484

PLAN YOUR TRIP NEED TO KNOW

If You Like...

Churches & Religious Art

Rila Monastery This millennium-old monastery in Rila Mountains is decorated with frescoes by 19th-century master Zahari Zograf. (p324)

Boyana Church A Unesco-listed 13th-century sanctuary houses rare and movingly realistic murals of saints and royals. (p317)

Aleksander Nevski Church & Crypt Beneath the domes of Sofia's neo-Byzantine masterpiece lies Bulgaria's biggest collection of religious art. (p302)

Sveti Stefan Church Sixteenth- to 18th-century murals cover virtually the whole interior of this church in Nesebâr. (p413)

Nativity Church Arbanasi's five-chamber church, dating to the 17th century, has frescoes and remarkable hand-carved iconostases. (p375)

Church of Sveti Konstantin & Elena A copper-domed landmark for Plovdiv's old town, this whitewashed church has sumptuous 19th-century murals. (p342)

Beaches

Primorsko This laid-back resort town has the best beaches and its family-friendly shores are ideal for paddling. (p408)

Sunny Beach Bulgaria's most popular destination for foreign visitors, with soft sands and plenty of nightlife. (p412)

Sinemorets A far-southern town with white sandy beaches, clean water and a slow pace of life. (p410)

Varna Bulgaria's 'maritime capital' has a long sandy beach within easy walking distance of some big-city buzz. (p416)

Sozopol Distract yourself from Sozopol's ancient history at sun-kissed beaches or the excellent diving centre. (p403)

Albena Splash in the crystal waters lapping this resort's 4km-long beach, before unwinding at a spa. (p424)

Fortresses & Ruins

Tsarevets Fortress The seat of medieval tsars in Veliko Târnovo impresses with mighty walls and towers. (p365)

Roman Amphitheatre Plovdiv's theatre was built in the 2nd century AD, and still hosts drama and music performances. (p341)

Kaleto Fortress Almost blending into Belogradchik Rocks, this citadel was built over Roman-era foundations. (p432)

Baba Vida Fortress Originally a Roman fort, this fortress was built up by medieval Bulgarians and 17th-century Turks. (p433)

Hisar Vast Roman gateways and expansive ruined walls dominate this captivating little spa town. (p383)

Roman Thermae In the port of Odessos (modern-day Varna), see the remains of a huge public bathing complex. (p417)

Skiing & Snowboarding

Bansko Bulgaria's biggest and most popular resort also has by far the best après-ski fun. (p332)

Pamporovo A fast-developing modern resort with slopes for learners, though there's not much to the town. (p355)

Borovets Zoom down tree-lined runs to this sprawling resort, well-suited to intermediate skiers. (p327)

Chepelare This small ski area in a low-key Rodopi Mountain village has easy, family-friendly trails. (p352)

Mt Vitosha Not snow-sure, but Vitosha's well-connected slopes allow for an afternoon's skiing followed by Sofia nightlife. (p318)

Malîovitsa Get off the beaten piste at this rickety, pocket-sized ski area in the Rila Mountains. (p328)

Top: Mountaineer in Pirin National Park (p329)
Bottom: Sozopol (p403)

Myths & Legends

Belogradchik Rocks A geological wonderland infused with the tragic folk tale of a heartbroken nun. (p431)

Stob Pyramids Ecotrail Stories say these stone towers are the remains of a wedding procession frozen in shock. (p323)

Museum of Folk Craft & Applied Arts Some Bulgarian villagers don *kukeri* costumes, displayed in this Troyan museum, to chase spirits. (p382)

Halkata Rock This 8m rock formation near Sliven is thought to exert magical, gender-bending power. (p393)

Historical Museum Learn the mysteries of the Kibela (Cybele) Temple, unearthed in Balchik in 2007, at this local museum. (p425)

Hiking & Climbing

Rila Mountains This forested range has walking routes for all abilities, plus a school for climbers and mountaineers. (p323)

Pirin Mountains This landscape of glacial lakes and valleys has challenging climbs and remote hiking routes. (p329)

Rodopi Mountains Hikes in these mountains pass lush countryside, villages and wonders such as Trigrad Cave. (p354)

Stara Planina Bulgaria's 'Old Mountains' offer breathtaking scenery and a variety of peaks and valleys. (p381)

Blue Rocks Trek in the footsteps of Bulgaria's anti-Ottoman rebels in the craggy outskirts of Sliven. (p393)

Vrachanska Mountains Peaceful trails extend from quiet Vratsa, with more challenging routes toward Ledenika Cave. (p429)

Month by Month

January

New Year festivities in Bulgaria can be colourful affairs, especially in rural areas where old customs are still followed. Snow covers much of the country and it is a peak time for winter sports.

✹ St Vasil's Day

Traditionally, New Year's Day in the countryside is marked by young boys, known as *sourvakari,* tapping people with decorated twigs to wish them luck for the year ahead.

February

Cold and crisp, February is a quiet time of year in the cities, but the skiing and snowboarding season is often at its best. It's a good time for snowshoeing, too.

✹ Golden Grapes Festival

To celebrate the patron saint of wine in Melnik and other winemaking areas, vines are pruned, sprinkled with wine and blessed by a priest. The festival is celebrated on the first or 14th day of February, often both. (p338)

March

March straddles winter and spring, so the weather can be unpredictable. Snowfall is still possible in the mountains though ski season is winding down. Tourist sites start to gradually open up again after winter.

✦ Baba Marta

'Granny March' signifies the beginning of spring, and on 1 March Bulgarians give each other red and white woollen tassels, known as *martenitsi,* as good-luck tokens. You'll notice them tied to tree branches throughout the spring.

☆ March Days of Music Festival

One of Bulgaria's best classical music festivals, held in Ruse. Concerts take place over the last two weeks of the month (www.march musicdays.eu).

April

The weather begins to warm up, and what's left of the ski season officially ends. Depending on the year, Orthodox Easter celebrations usually take place during this month.

✦ Orthodox Easter

Easter is the most important festival of the Bulgarian Orthodox Church. Throngs of churchgoers attend 11pm masses where incense hangs thick in the air. Egg fighting competitions sometimes take place outside. Special bread loaves and dyed eggs are prepared.

May

May is often showery and warm, and is a good time to visit the coast before crowds descend and prices rise. Some of the biggest festivals begin this month.

✦ Re-enactment of the 1876 April Uprising

The momentous events surrounding the 1876 April Uprising are remembered by

Top: Rose Festival, Kazanlâk (p290)

Bottom: Traditional Orthodox Easter foods

GTS / SHUTTERSTOCK ©

patriotic locals in Kopriv-shtitsa (p385), who dress in period costume. It's held around 1 and 2 May.

 Goat Milk Festival

A blend of traditional Balkan village culture, cutting-edge art and thought-provoking debate unfurls in at the Goat Milk Festival (www.novakultura.org/goat-milk) in Gorna Bela Rechka village, 55km north of Sofia.

June

Summer is well under way, temperatures are rising and the tourist season on the coast begins. This is a great time for hiking, climbing and birdwatching.

Rose Festival

As the roses of surrounding valleys burst into flower, Kazanlâk and neighbouring villages bless visitors with rose water, sip rose liqueur and dance at street parades. The main event is held in Kazanlâk's main square on the first weekend in June. (p388)

Varna Summer International Festival

Ramping up in June and lasting throughout the summer in Varna, this is one of the oldest and biggest festivals in Bulgaria, comprising music, theatre and other cultural events. (p420)

July

High temperatures are recorded across the country in July. Both Bulgarian and foreign tourists flock to the coastal resorts, while the cities bake.

Sand Sculpture Festival

Admire the fantastic sand sculptures created by visiting artists in Burgas. There's a different theme each year and the sculptures remain all summer. (p399)

August

Temperatures are at their highest in August, with long, hot sunny days, warm evenings and little or no rain. Music festivals are in full swing.

Spirit of Burgas Festival

A popular Black Sea music event, Spirit of Burgas brings in rock, hip-hop and experimental acts and DJs for a beach party in early August.

International Jazz Festival

Top jazz musicians from across Europe and beyond flock to Bansko. Free concerts are held in the main square over a week. (p335)

September

Days are still hot in September, but begin to cool later in the month. A good time for birdwatching, as the Via Pontica migration begins.

Apollonia Arts Festival

Music, drama and dance in seaside Sozopol, attracting big names over the first week of the month. (p405)

Plovdiv Night of the Galleries

Plovdiv's galleries open their doors for free on one Friday evening late in September, alongside performances and open-air film screenings around town (www.night.bg).

October

Cooler days across Bulgaria come in October, but temperatures are still pleasant. Harvest and cultural festivals take place around the country.

November

Winter approaches and temperatures drop. Expect rain and cold, shorter days. The pace of life slows, but there's always something to see and do in the cities.

Young Wine Parade

Plovdiv celebrates the new wine vintage with parades, performances and opportunities to sample fresh local wines in the streets and houses of the old town (www.visitplovdiv.com).

December

Cold weather descends, with snowfall on higher ground. The ski season begins, though conditions aren't at their best until the end of the month. Christmas services in Orthodox churches are truly atmospheric.

Itineraries

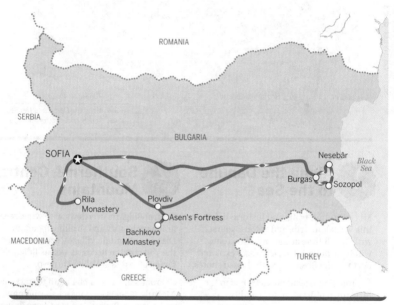

From Sofia to the Coast

10 DAYS

Explore Bulgaria's greatest hits, from the capital to the coast. Start in Sofia, stop off at its sassier sister Plovdiv, then wriggle your toes into sandy beaches along the Black Sea coast.

Begin in Bulgaria's lively capital city, **Sofia**. Over three days, take in the city's centrepiece, shimmering Aleksander Nevski Memorial Church, a couple of fascinating museums, and a day trip to the resplendent **Rila Monastery**.

Board a bus or train east to **Plovdiv**, Bulgaria's second city. Spend two days immersing yourself in the charming old town, Roman ruins, and bohemian nightlife, perhaps with a half-day out at spellbinding **Asen's Fortress** and **Bachkovo Monastery**.

Reach **Burgas** on the Black Sea coast by bus or train. Stay at least one night in this laid-back city, before hopping on a bus for the short trip south to the ancient town of **Sozopol**. Spend one or two days amid Sozopol's quaint cobbled lanes and attractive sandy beaches. If you're here in summer, catch the ferry up to **Nesebâr**, famed for its numerous medieval churches, and spend the day sightseeing. Return to Burgas to get the bus or train back to Sofia.

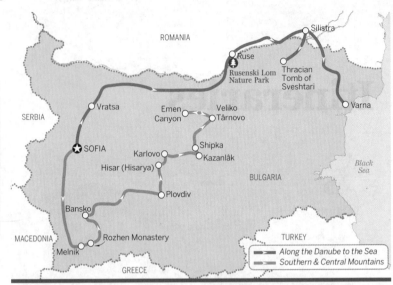

Along the Danube to the Sea
Southern & Central Mountains

1 WEEK — Along the Danube to the Sea

Mix mountain trails and historic sights on this week-long trip, and reward yourself with beach time at the end. This route winds through Bulgaria's lesser explored north to the Black Sea's sun-kissed shores.

From Sofia, head north by bus to the little town of **Vratsa**, to spend two days walking in the mountains or browsing museums. From here, travel by bus to Pleven where you can pick up another bus to elegant, appealing **Ruse**, for your first glimpse of the mighty Danube. Spend two nights in Ruse, taking in its grand Viennese-style architecture. On one of the days, head south of the city to **Rusenski Lom Nature Park** to see remarkable rock churches and caves, and maybe spot rare wildlife.

From Ruse head eastward to **Silistra**. Over a day or two, admire the Historical Museum's hoard of Roman gold and make an excursion to the **Thracian Tomb of Sveshtari**. Continue to the Black Sea coast at **Varna** for your final one or two days. Relax on the long, sandy city beach, enjoy a show or concert at one of the city's many cultural venues, or go clubbing along the vibrant seafront.

2 WEEKS — Southern & Central Mountains

Central Bulgaria overflows with wine, revolutionary history and thrilling mountains. Discover mountain villages, spa towns and the Valley of the Roses, as well as Bulgaria's famous fortress at Veliko Târnovo.

From Sofia, take a bus south to tranquil **Melnik**, famous for wine, chalky pyramids and National Revival–era mansions. Be sure to visit the serene **Rozhen Monastery** nearby. Continue by bus to **Bansko**, for two days of summer hikes or winter skiing.

From Bansko, meander by narrow-gauge rail through mountainous forests to Septemvri, then on to **Plovdiv**. Spend two or three days exploring Plovdiv's 19th-century house-museums and Kapana artistic quarter. Take a rest day simmering in the spa waters of **Hisar** just north, before continuing to atmospheric **Karlovo**, birth town of Bulgaria's most famous revolutionary hero.

Board a bus to **Kazanlâk**, gateway to the fragrant Rose Valley. Cross the mountains at Shipka Pass, stopping first in **Shipka** to see its dazzling church. Finally, unwind in the shadow of an impressive fortress in **Veliko Târnovo**, Bulgaria's medieval capital, allowing a day to hike nearby **Emen Canyon**.

Regions at a Glance

Sofia

Culture
Parks
Food & Drink

Cultural Riches

Bulgaria's capital is the country's cultural heart, with centuries-old religious art and cutting-edge installations. Seek Thracian treasures in the Archaeological Museum, peruse Bulgarian paintings at the National Art Gallery, or visit a battalion of Lenins at the Museum of Socialist Art.

Green Escapes

Experience a calmer side to Sofia amid the greenery of Borisova Gradina, spun with shady pathways and child-friendly play areas. Alternatively, City Garden and the university's Botanic Garden are pleasant escapes from the city bustle.

Diverse Dining

Sofia has some of Bulgaria's best and most varied restaurants. Go beyond high-quality traditional Bulgarian cuisine, and let your taste buds explore Turkish and Moroccan dishes, Italian gelato and coffee, and an increasing range of veggie options.

p296

Plovdiv & Southern Mountains

Art
Winter Sports
Culture

Unique Galleries

Plovdiv's old town is an impeccable host for some of the Balkans' most distinctive art galleries, housing vibrant contemporary sculpture, Mexican art and 200-year-old Bulgarian landscape paintings.

Ski Resorts

Rila, Pirin and Rodopi Mountains offer the country's best skiing. Bansko boasts the most reliable snow, plus guaranteed après-ski mayhem; Borovets draws big crowds to its 58km of pistes; while smaller resorts such as Chepelare are family friendly, with idyllic cross-country trails.

Cultural Energy

On one evening, watch opera in a Roman theatre. On the next, experience hard rock vibrating the walls of a box-sized alternative bar. Plovdiv has a breathtaking array of entertainment, with the revived Kapana quarter at the forefront.

p321

Veliko Târnovo & Central Mountains

History
Architecture
Hiking

Lavish Churches

Central Bulgaria's Orthodox churches, many dating to Byzantine times, are among the Balkans' most historically and aesthetically significant. Discover standout monasteries in Troyan and Dryanovo, and superb churches dotted around Veliko Târnovo.

Quaint Mansions

Bulgaria's heartland was crucial to the National Revival of the 18th and 19th centuries, and many richly decorated period mansions are now museums or B&Bs. Explore villages such as Koprivshtitsa and Etâr for a flavour of the past.

Windswept Walks

The Stara Planina mountain range stretches across Bulgaria's central spine for almost 550km. This rolling range is bisected with marked trails – perfect for both easy ambling and arduous long-haul trekking.

p359

Black Sea Coast

Beaches
History
Nightlife

Sun-Kissed Sand

Bulgaria's Black Sea coastline is the country's biggest tourist draw, boasting long and inviting sandy beaches. Top up your tan, try jet-skiing or parasailing at the big resorts, or find a hidden cove in the far north or south.

Ancient Towns

With histories stretching back millennia, the Black Sea's quaint towns are a joy to explore. Take a trip back in time through the cobbled lanes of Sozopol and explore the ruined medieval churches of Nesebâr.

Bold Nightclubs

The Black Sea coast has many of Bulgaria's best clubs. The big package resorts have the pick of the bunch, attracting international DJs and acts, while Varna is summertime party central for young Bulgarians.

p395

The Danube & Northern Plains

Outdoors
History
Cities

Untamed Landscapes

Northern Bulgaria encompasses a variety of landscapes, from the wild, mountainous northwest, ideal for hiking and rock climbing, to the diverse beauty of the Rusenski Lom Nature Park, famed for wildlife as diverse as wolves, eagle owls and dozens of bat species.

Forts & Ruins

The remains of ancient fortresses abound in region. The Roman fort of Sexaginta Prista in Ruse, Byzantine city walls in Silistra, and Ottoman fortifications in Vidin show how much this region was prized. Most spectacular is Kaleto Fortress, astride the looming Belogradchik Rocks.

Urban Charm

The Danubian city of Ruse boasts elegant architecture, excellent restaurants and the region's best museums. Beyond its leafy squares and belle époque buildings, it's also a great base for exploring the surrounding countryside.

p427

On the Road

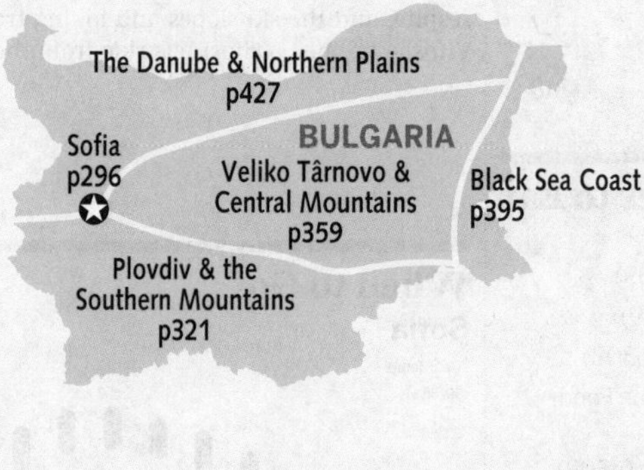

The Danube & Northern Plains
p427

BULGARIA

Sofia
p296

Veliko Târnovo &
Central Mountains
p359

Black Sea Coast
p395

Plovdiv & the
Southern Mountains
p321

Sofia

POP 1,200,000

Best Places to Eat

➡ Manastirska Magernitsa (p309)

➡ Ege Türk (p309)

➡ Sun & Moon (p308)

➡ MoMa Bulgarian Food & Wine (p309)

➡ Made In Home (p309)

Best Places to Sleep

➡ Hotel Niky (p307)

➡ Light Hotel (p307)

➡ Hotel Les Fleurs (p308)

➡ Art Hostel (p307)

➡ Canapé Connection (p306)

Why Go?

Bulgaria's pleasingly laid-back capital is often overlooked by visitors heading straight to the coast or the ski resorts, but they're missing something special. Sofia is no grand metropolis, but it's a largely modern, youthful city, with a scattering of onion-domed churches, Ottoman mosques and stubborn Red Army monuments that lend an eclectic, exotic feel. Recent excavation work carried out during construction of the city's metro unveiled a treasure trove of Roman ruins from nearly 2000 years ago, when the city was called 'Serdica'. Away from the buildings and boulevards, vast parks and manicured gardens offer a welcome respite, and the ski slopes and hiking trails of mighty Mt Vitosha are just a short bus ride from the centre.

When to Go
Sofia

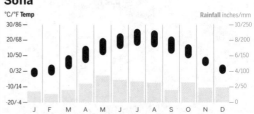

Mar–May Spring is warm and wet, and Easter is a colourful time to visit.

Jun–Aug Summer is very hot and dry, especially August, but there's plenty to see and do in the city.

Nov–Feb Winters in Sofia are often icy cold, with heavy snowfalls, but January is perfect for skiing.

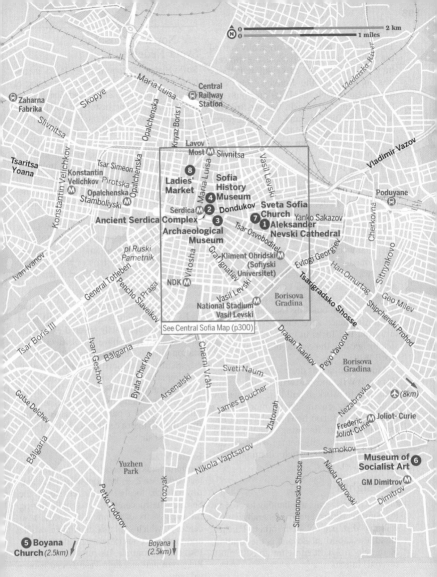

Sofia Highlights

1 **Aleksander Nevski Cathedral** (p302) Taking in the scope of this cathedral, with its gleaming gold domes.

2 **Ancient Serdica Complex** (p298) Bearing witness to a once-great Roman city.

3 **Archaeological Museum** (p299) Admiring Thracian craftsmanship going back 6000 years.

4 **Sofia History Museum** (p298) Travelling back in time to the 19th century, when Sofia was capital of Europe's newest country.

5 **Boyana Church** (p317) Admiring the 13th-century murals at this Unesco World Heritage site.

6 **Museum of Socialist Art** (p305) Revelling in the imagery of the country's not-so-distant communist past.

7 **Sveta Sofia Church** (p303) Venturing below the city's namesake church to see an ancient Roman necropolis.

8 **Ladies' Market** (p313) Walking through this exotic food market, the perfect spot to buy some Turkish treats.

History

The Thracian Serdi tribe originally settled the Sofia region as far back as the 8th century BC, but the city as we know it today was founded by the Romans, who conquered the region in AD 29 and built the town of Ulpia Serdica. In the late 3rd century AD 'Serdica' became a major regional capital, reaching a zenith in the early 4th century under Roman emperor Constantine the Great.

The city passed back and forth between the Bulgarians and the Byzantine Empire during the early Middle Ages, until the Ottomans, sweeping through the Balkans, captured it in 1382, and held it for nearly 500 years. The Ottomans built baths and mosques, such as the Banya Bashi Mosque, but many churches were destroyed or abandoned.

It was in Sofia that the celebrated anti-Turkish rebel Vasil Levski was hanged in 1873, after first being interrogated and tortured in the building that later became the Royal Palace. After the liberation of the city from the Turks in early 1878, Sofia officially became the capital of Bulgaria on 4 April 1879.

Much of Sofia was destroyed in bombing during WWII, and postwar socialist architects set to work rebuilding the heavily damaged city on the Soviet model, complete with high-rise housing blocks in the suburbs and the imposing socialist-realist buildings in the city centre, such as the old Party House, which dominates pl Nezavisimost.

◉ Sights

Most of Sofia's sights are handily located in the compact centre, and are generally within walking distance of each other. Further afield, the suburb of Boyana is the location of the city's biggest museum and its most revered church.

◉ Around Ploshtad Sveta Nedelya

Sveta Nedelya Cathedral CHURCH
(☑02-987 5748; pl Sveta Nedelya; ⊙8am-6pm; Ⓜ Serdika) Completed in 1863, this magnificent domed church is noted for its Byzantine-style murals. The church was targeted by communists on 16 April 1925 in a failed bomb attack aimed at assassinating Tsar Boris III.

◉ North of Ploshtad Sveta Nedelya

Sofia History Museum MUSEUM
(☑02-985 4455; www.sofiahistorymuseum.bg; pl Banski 1; adult/child 6/2 lv; ⊙10am-6pm Tue-Sun; Ⓜ Serdika, ☒20) The history of Sofia is presented on two floors of the magnificent former Turkish Mineral Baths, just behind the mosque. Exhibitions are divided thematically over eight chambers, with the most interesting rooms dedicated to the Bulgarian royal families of the late 19th and early 20th centuries, and the findings of recent archeological digs around town. There are plenty of signs in English.

The Mineral Baths – also known as the Turkish Baths – was completed in 1913. Its elegant striped facade and ceramic decorations recall the designs of the medieval churches in Nesebâr on Bulgaria's Black Sea coast.

Ancient Serdica Complex RUINS
(pl Nezavisimost; ⊙6am-11pm; Ⓜ Serdika) FREE This remarkable, partly covered excavation site, situated just above the Serdika metro station, displays the remains of the Roman city, Serdica, that once occupied this area. The remains were unearthed from 2010 to 2012 during construction of the metro. There are fragments of eight streets, an early Christian basilica, baths and houses dating from the 4th to 6th centuries. Plenty of signage in English.

Sveta Petka Samardzhiiska Church CHURCH
(bul Maria Luisa 2; ⊙9am-5pm; Ⓜ Serdika) This tiny church, located in the centre of the Serdika metro complex, was built during the early years of Ottoman rule (late 14th century), which explains its sunken profile and inconspicuous exterior. Inside are some 16th-century murals. It's rumoured that the Bulgarian national hero Vasil Levski is buried here.

Sofia Synagogue SYNAGOGUE
(☑02-983 1273; www.sofiasynagogue.com; ul Ekzarh Yosif 16; 2 lv; ⊙8.30am-12.30pm, 1-4.30pm; Ⓜ Serdika, ☒20) Sofia's Moorish-style synagogue was designed by Austrian architect Friedrich Gruenanger, and was consecrated in 1909. Built to accommodate up to 1170 worshippers, it is the second-largest Sephardic synagogue in Europe, and its 2250kg brass chandelier is the biggest in

Bulgaria. There's a small museum on the 2nd floor with an exhibition dedicated to the rescue of Bulgarian Jews during WWII.

Banya Bashi Mosque   MOSQUE

(bul Maria Luisa 2; ☉ dawn-dusk, prayer daily 1.30pm, 3.30pm & 8.45pm; Ⓜ Serdika, 🚌 20) Sofia's only working mosque was built in 1576. It's certainly an eye-catching edifice, and the red-brick minaret makes a convenient landmark. Visitors are welcome outside prayer times if modestly dressed.

Sofia Monument   MONUMENT

(bul Maria Luisa; Ⓜ Serdika) Erected in 2001 on the site where a gigantic statue of Lenin once stood, this 24m-high monument was created as a new civic symbol for the city. The bronze female figure at the top of the column, holding the wreath of victory in her right hand and balancing an owl on her left arm, represents Sofia, personification of wisdom and fate.

Drinking Fountains   FOUNTAIN

(ul Iskar; Ⓜ Serdika, 🚌 20) Bulgarians queue here throughout the day to fill plastic bottles from the taps of around a dozen fountains, situated in the open air just next to the former Mineral Baths and mosque.

⊙ Around Ploshtad Battenberg

Originally built as the headquarters of the Ottoman governor and his police force, it was at the **Royal Palace** (☏ 02-988 1974; pl Knyaz Al Batenberg 1; Ⓜ Serdika) that Bulgaria's national hero, Vasil Levski, was tried and tortured before his public execution in 1873. After the liberation the building was remodelled in Viennese style and in 1887, apparently undeterred by its grisly recent past,

Prince Alexander Battenberg moved in; it became the official residence of Bulgaria's royal family until the communist takeover. These days it provides a grand setting for the humble **Ethnographical Museum**.

Archaeological Museum   MUSEUM

(☏ 02-988 2406; www.naim.bg; ul Saborna 2; adult/child 10/2 lv; ☉ 10am-5pm Tue-Sun; Ⓜ Serdika) Housed in a former mosque built in 1496, this museum displays a wealth of Thracian, Roman and medieval artefacts. Highlights include a mosaic floor from the Church of Sveta Sofia, a 4th-century BC Thracian gold burial mask, and a magnificent bronze head, thought to represent a Thracian king.

Sveti Georgi Rotunda   CHURCH

(Church of St George; ☏ 02-980 9216; www.svgeorgi-rotonda.com; bul Dondukov 2; ☉ services daily 8am, 9am & 5pm; Ⓜ Serdika) Built in the 4th century AD, this tiny red-brick church is Sofia's oldest preserved building. The murals inside were painted between the 10th and 14th centuries. It's a busy, working church, but visitors are welcome.

Sveti Nikolai Russian Church   CHURCH

(☏ 02-986 2715; ul Tsar Osvoboditel 3; ☉ 7.45am-6.30pm; Ⓜ Serdika) This beautiful church with glittering mosaic exterior and golden domes was completed in 1914 for Sofia's Russian community, and named in honour of St Nikolai, the 'miracle worker'. The cramped interior features icons painted between the 11th and 14th centuries.

National Museum of Natural History   MUSEUM

(☏ 02-988 2894; www.nmnhs.com; bul Tsar Osvoboditel 1; adult/child 4/1 lv; ☉ 10am-6pm; Ⓜ Serdika, 🚌 9) You can almost sense the ghosts

---

SOFIA IN...

One Day

Start with the recent excavation works at the **Ancient Serdica Complex** and then pay a visit to nearby **Sofia History Museum**. Afterwards, walk over to Sofia's most impressive sight, the **Aleksander Nevski Cathedral**. Don't miss the **Sveta Sofia Church** next door with its subterranean necropolis. Enjoy a traditional Bulgarian dinner at kitschy (but in a good way) **Manastirska Magernitsa**.

Three Days

Follow the above itinerary, but on the second day admire the treasures on show at the **Archaeological Museum**, and take the opportunity to watch the changing of the guard at the neighbouring **President's Building** and to visit tiny **Sveti Georgi Rotunda**. Art-lovers will want to see the **National Gallery Quadrat 500**. On the final day, head out to **Boyana** to see the **National Museum of History** and lovely **Boyana Church**.

Central Sofia

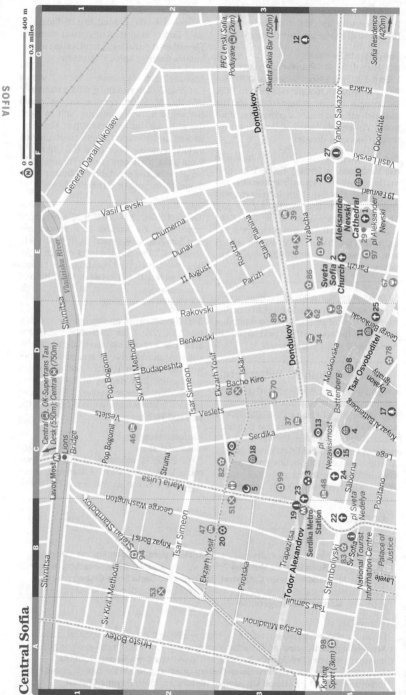

400 m
0.2 miles

Central (Ok-Supertrans Taxi Desk (550m); Central (750m)

Silvnitsa

Vladaiska River

General Danail Nikolaev

Vasil Levski

Chumerna

Dunav

II Avgust

Rositza

Stara Planina

Parizh

Dondukov

PFC Levski Sofia, Poduyane (2km)

Raketa Rakia Bar (150m)

12

Kraka

Yanko Sakazov

Oborishte

Sofia Residence (420m)

27

Vasil Levski

21

10

19 Fevruari

Aleksander Nevski Cathedral

1

29
97
pl Aleksander Nevski

Sveta Sofia Church
2
86

Parizh

67

Vrabcha

64
92

39

Rakovski

Benkovski

Dondukov

89

34

62

69

25

Georgi Benkovski

11

78

8

Tsar Osvoboditel

Moskovska

Dyakon Ignatiy

pl Battenberg

17

Knyaz Al Battenberg

Lege

Pozitano

Lavov Most

Lions Bridge

Pop Bogomil

Sv Kiril Methodii

Budapeshta

Tsar Simeon

Ekzarh Yosif

Iskăr

Bacho Kiro

61

70

Veslets

Serdika

46

37

Struma

13

99

pl Nezavisimost

3

48

15
24
pl Saborna

Maria Luiza

George Washington

82

7

18

5

51

23

19

Todor Aleksandrov

Serdika Metro Station

22

pl Sveta Nedelya

Stefan Stambolov

Knyaz Boris I

Tsar Simeon

94

47

20

Ekzarh Yosif

Pirotska

Trapezitsa

Stamboliyski

33
Sv Sofia

National Tourist Information Centre

Palace of Justice

Lavele

Sv Kiril Methodii

Hristo Botev

Bratya Miladinovi

Tsar Samuil

53

98

Karting Sport (3km)

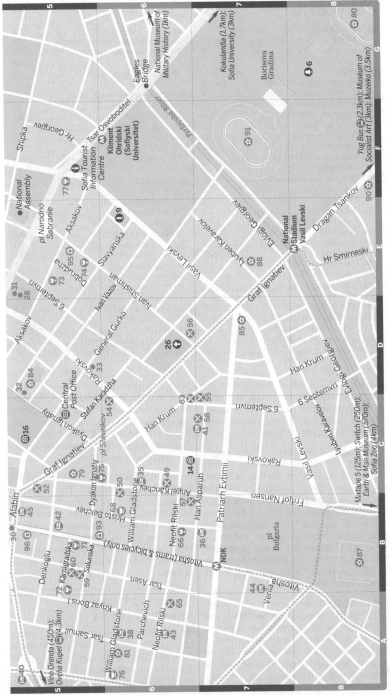

Central Sofia

of generations of school parties dutifully trooping through the musty halls of Bulgaria's oldest museum, founded in 1889. Rocks, minerals, stuffed birds and animals, and mounted insects are on display.

Ethnographical Museum MUSEUM
(☑02-988 1974; pl Knyaz Al Batenberg 1; adult/child 3/1 lv; ◷10am-6pm Tue-Sun; Ⓜ Serdika) Displays on regional costumes, crafts and folklore are spread over two floors of the former royal palace, and many of the rooms are worth pausing over themselves for their marble fireplaces, mirrors and ornate plasterwork. There are some interesting 19th-century Bulgarian paintings housed in an adjacent wing of the museum, and there's a crafts shop on the ground floor.

Sofia City Art Gallery GALLERY
(☑02-987 2181; www.sghg.bg; ul Gen Gurko 1; 2 lv; ◷10am-7pm Tue-Sat, 11am-6pm Sun; Ⓜ Serdika) The chunky building at the southern end of the City Garden park is an art gallery staging rotating exhibitions of mostly contemporary Bulgarian and international art over two floors. Enter from ul Knyaz Al Batenberg.

Sofia City Garden PARK
(Ⓜ Serdika) This small, central park, bounded on its northern end by ul Tsar Osvoboditel, is favoured by Sofia's chess-playing pensioners. It's home to the National Theatre (p313), and until 1999 held the mausoleum of Bulgaria's first communist ruler, Georgi Dimitrov.

President's Building NOTABLE BUILDING
(pl Nezavisimost; Ⓜ Serdika) The Bulgarian president's office isn't open to the public, but the changing of the guard ceremony (on the hour) is a spectacle not to be missed; for the full ceremony, replete with music, weapons and all manner of pomp, be there on the first Wednesday of the month at noon.

◎ Around Ploshtad Aleksander Nevski

★ **Aleksander Nevski Cathedral** CHURCH
(pl Aleksander Nevski; ◷7am-7pm; Ⓜ Sofiyski Universitet) One of *the* symbols not just of Sofia but of Bulgaria itself, this massive, awe-inspiring church was built between 1882

and 1912 in memory of the 200,000 Russian soldiers who died fighting for Bulgaria's independence during the Russo-Turkish War (1877–78). It is named in honour of a 13th-century Russian warrior-prince.

Designed by Russian architect Alexander Pomerantsev, the church was built in the neo-Byzantine style favoured in Russia at the time and is adorned with mosaics and gold-laden domes. The cavernous, incense-scented interior is decorated with naturalistic (though now rather faded) murals, pendulous chandeliers and elaborate onyx and alabaster thrones.

Visitors are welcome and there are daily services where you can hear evocative Orthodox chants and prayers.

Aleksander Nevski Crypt GALLERY
(Museum of Icons; pl Aleksander Nevski; adult/child 6/3 lv; ⊘10am-5.30pm Tue-Sun; Ⓜ Sofiyski Universitet) Originally built as a final resting place for Bulgarian kings, this crypt now houses Bulgaria's biggest and best collection of icons, stretching back to the 5th century.

Enter to the left of the eponymous church's main entrance.

★ **Sveta Sofia Church** CHURCH
(☑02-987 0971; ul Parizh 2; museum adult/child 6/2 lv; ⊘church 7am-7pm Apr-Oct, to 6pm Nov-Mar, museum 9am-5pm Tue-Sun; Ⓜ Sofiyski Universitet) Sveta Sofia is one of the capital's oldest churches, and gave the city its name. A subterranean museum houses an ancient necropolis, with 56 tombs and the remains of four other churches. Outside are the Tomb of the Unknown Soldier and an eternal flame, and the grave of Ivan Vazov, Bulgaria's most revered writer.

National Gallery Quadrat 500 GALLERY
(Kvadrat 500; ☑02-980 0093; www.nationalartgallerybg.org; ul 19 Fevruari 1; adult/child 10/5 lv; ⊘10am-6pm Tue-Sun; Ⓜ Sofiyski Universitet) This massive visual-arts gallery combines the holdings of the National Gallery and the former Museum of Foreign Art. The result is several hundred paintings spread out over 28 rooms. Works range from African tribal masks to countless

BULGARIA'S FIRST HEAD OF STATE

Emerging from five centuries of Ottoman rule, the leaders of the nascent state of Bulgaria decided they would rather like their country to be a monarchy. With no obvious native claimant to the throne, the Russian tsar suggested his 22-year-old nephew, a minor German prince named Alexander of Battenberg, to take up the position, and he was duly installed as Prince of Bulgaria in 1879, modern Bulgaria's first head of state.

The young ex-army officer was feted on his arrival in the country, but Alexander soon found that governing the fractious new state was anything but easy. In 1881, he suspended the constitution to rule as an absolute monarch, though in effect it was the prince's Russian backers who were really running the show.

Democracy was restored in 1883, and Alexander dismissed the Russian generals who had been controlling the country. In 1885, without the approval of the Russian tsar, the province of Eastern Rumelia was reunited with the rest of Bulgaria.

Alexander had made many enemies in his pro-Russian military, and in 1886, a group of army officers forced him to abdicate and handed him over to the Russian authorities. There was a swift counter-revolution, and the prince was soon recalled to Sofia. However, without Russian support, Alexander's position was untenable, and he formally abdicated in September 1886. A new prince, Ferdinand of Saxe-Coburg-Gotha, was elected in his place.

Alexander left Bulgaria for the last time and headed for Austria, where he took the title Count von Hartenau and married an actress, Johanna Loisinger. He died in 1893, aged just 36. Alexander retained a deep affection for the country he had briefly ruled and, according to his wishes, his remains were brought back to Sofia and interred in an elegant **mausoleum** (bul Vasil Levski 81; ⊙8am-6pm; Ⓜ Sofiyski Universitet) that is open to the public.

19th- and 20th-century paintings, mostly by lesser-known artists. Minor sketches by Renoir and Matisse and works by Gustave Courbet are on display.

Sofia University
Botanical Garden   GARDENS
(⌨02-988 1797; ul Moskovska 49; 2 lv; ⊙10am-6pm; Ⓜ Sofiyski Universitet) Sofia's small botanical garden includes a glasshouse filled with palms and cacti, a rose garden, and various trees and flowers (labelled in Bulgarian and Latin). The entrance is through what looks like a flower shop on bul Vasil Levski.

Vasil Levski Memorial   MONUMENT
(Ⓜ Sofiyski Universitet) A sombre monument, in the middle of a busy road, dates from 1895 and marks the spot where Bulgarian national hero Vasil Levski was hanged in 1873.

◉ South of Ploshtad
Aleksander Nevski

Sveti Sedmochislenitsi Church   CHURCH
(Church of the Seven Saints; ul Graf Ignatiev; ⊙7am-7pm; ⌨10) Set in a leafy garden, this church dedicated to Sts Cyril and Methodius and their five disciples was originally built as a mosque in 1528; it later became an

arms depot and a prison, before being consecrated as a church in 1903. Inside, there's a gilded iconostasis with icons painted by Anton Mitov.

Earth & Man Museum   MUSEUM
(⌨02-865 6639; www.earthandman.org; bul Cherni Vrâh 4; adult/child 4/2 lv; ⊙10am-6pm Tue-Sun; ⌨6) This rather old-fashioned museum is dedicated to geology, with two floors of minerals, crystals, ores and the like. There are some big and impressive geodes on show.

Peyo Yavorov
House-Museum   HISTORIC BUILDING
(⌨02-988 0887; ul Rakovski 136, 2nd fl; adult/child 3/2 lv; ⊙10am-5pm Mon-Wed & Fri, 1-5pm Thu; Ⓜ NDK) The Romantic poet and revolutionary Peyo Yavorov (1878–1914) briefly lived in a small apartment here; the three rooms have been restored to their original appearance, while ghoulish mementoes include Yavorov's death mask and the dress Yavorov's wife, Lora, was wearing when she killed herself in the study. Ring the doorbell for admittance.

Borisova Gradina   PARK
(⌨76, Ⓜ National Stadium Vasil Levski, Kliment Ohridski, ⌨5) Lying southeast of the city

centre, Sofia's most attractive park is filled with countless statues and flowerbeds and is a relaxing place for a stroll. It's a vast place, and is home to the Vasil Levski Stadium and CSKA Stadium, as well as several cafes and children's play areas.

The eastern end of the park is dominated by a gigantic communist monument built in 1956; it's known as the Mound of Brotherhood, and features a 42m-high obelisk and socialist-realist icons including a pair of partisan fighters, dramatically gesturing comrades clutching Kalashnikovs, and smiling, stoic workers. It has long been neglected by the authorities, and several of the socialist heroes are now missing limbs and have gained coats of graffiti, but small groups of pensioners come on occasion to lay flowers in remembrance of the red old days.

◉ East of Ploshtad Aleksander Nevski

Museum of Socialist Art   MUSEUM
(☏02-980 0093; ul Lachezar Stanchev 7, Iztok; 6 lv; ⊙10am-5.30pm Tue-Sun; Ⓜ GM Dimitrov) If you wondered where all those unwanted statues of Lenin ended up, you'll find some here, along with the red star from atop Sofia's Party House (pl Nezavisimost; Ⓜ Serdika). There's a gallery of paintings, where you'll rejoice in catchy titles such as *Youth Meeting at Kilifarevo Village to Send Worker-Peasant Delegation to the USSR*, and stirring old propaganda films are shown.

The museum isn't the easiest place to find. Catch the metro to the GM Dimitrov station, in the Iztok suburb; walk north up bul Tsankov and then turn right onto ul Lachezar Stanchev. The museum is housed in a gated Ministry of Culture building next to the Sopharma Business Towers. You can see the big red star in the garden.

National Museum of Military History   MUSEUM
(☏02-946 1805; www.militarymuseum.bg; ul Cherkovna 92; adult/child 8/2 lv; ⊙10am-6pm Wed-Sun; ☒9, 72, ☒20, 23) This out-of-the-way museum tells the story of warfare in Bulgaria, with most space given to the period from the 1876 April Uprising through to WWI. Weaponry, rebel flags, uniforms and decorations are on show, while outside is an impressive collection of Soviet-made military hardware including Scud missile launchers, tanks and MiG fighters.

🏃 Activities

There are several gyms, pools and sports centres dotted around Sofia. The Vitosha Nature Park (p318), outside of the city, has plenty of opportunities for hiking and skiing.

Sofia Run   RUNNING
(☏0885523630; www.sofiarun.com) Sofia Run offers easy one-hour, 3km jogging tours through the centre with an English-speaking runner guide. It also offers longer 10km tours for more-experienced runners. Prices vary according to the size of the group, but start from 10 lv, assuming a group of three runners. Book online or by email. Hotel pick-up available.

Courses

Study in BG   LANGUAGE
(☏0889624056; www.studyinbg.com; ul Rakovski 145; ☒9) Modern language centre offering Bulgarian-language lessons to foreigners. Private, one-to-one lessons cost 20 lv per hour on-site, or 30 lv elsewhere. Longer group courses are available. Enter from ul Gen Gurko.

Sofia University   LANGUAGE
(☏02-871 0069; www.deo.uni-sofia.bg; ul Kosta Lulchev 27; ☒9) Bulgarian-language courses for foreigners are offered by the university. Individual classes start at 23.50 lv per hour; group classes are considerably less. Accommodation is available.

🎫 Tours

There are a number of tours (both free and paid) you can join to explore Sofia and surrounds that are run by enthusiastic local volunteers; any donations, to keep these enterprises going, are much appreciated. Some youth hostels organise day trips for guests.

Organised tours are a convenient way to visit Rila Monastery (p324), which is awkward to visit in one day by public transport from Sofia.

Balkan Bites   FOOD & DRINK
(☏0877613992; www.balkanbites.bg; by donation; ⊙tours 2pm; Ⓜ Sofiyski Universitet, ☒9) This two-hour guided walking tour focuses on food and includes tastings and drinks at restaurants around town. The basic tour is free but a donation is expected. Walks depart at 2pm from the statue of Stefan Stambolov in Crystal Park.

New Sofia Pub Crawl TOURS

(☎0877613992; www.thenewsofiapubcrawl.com; tours 20 lv; ⏰9pm-1am; Ⓜ Sofiyski Universitet, 🚇9) Explore Sofia's secret haunts on this nightly knees-up. Expect lots of good chat and surprising insights into the social side of the city (plus the odd free drink). Meet by the statue of Stefan Stambolov in Crystal Park.

Sofia Green Tour ADVENTURE

(☎0885523630; www.sofiagreentour.com; ul Dyakon Ignatiy 5, Ivan Vazov National Theatre; tours by donation, winter hikes 10 lv, bicycle rental 10 lv; ⏰tours 11am; Ⓜ Serdika) This environmentally oriented tour company offers walking and biking tours of Sofia, as well as a winter hike (from December to April) in the Vitosha Nature Park, including a visit to Boyana Church. Tours normally meet at 11am in front of the Ivan Vazov National Theatre in the Sofia City Park. Book online or by email, or simply show up.

Free Sofia Tour WALKING

(☎0988920461; www.freesofiatour.com; cnr ul Alabin & bul Vitosha; ⏰11am & 6pm; Ⓜ Serdika) FREE Explore Sofia's sights in the company of friendly and enthusiastic English-speaking young locals on this two-hour guided walk. No reservation is needed; just show up outside the Palace of Justice on the corner of ul Alabin and bul Vitosha at 11am or 6pm.

City Sighteeing Bus Tour BUS

(☎0878575200; www.citysightseeing.bg; adult/child 20/10 lv; ⏰tours 10.30am & noon; Ⓜ Sofiyski Universitet) Get your bearings on this hop-on, hop-off bus tour that takes in more than 30 sights across Sofia. Tours are conducted in English and leave from the Aleksander Nevski Cathedral twice daily. Reservations are required from October to March; just show up the rest of the year.

★✦ Festivals & Events

Sofia International Film Festival FILM

(www.siff.bg; ⏰Mar) Movie buffs descend on the capital each March for a celebration of international independent films.

Sofia Underground ART

(SU; www.sofiaunderground.com; ⏰Apr) Contemporary-art festival featuring local and international artists; held in the basement of the NDK.

Sofia Dance Week DANCE

(⏰late Sep-early Oct) A varied program of modern dance, held over two weeks at the National Palace of Culture.

International Children's Folklore Festival DANCE

(⏰Jun) Five-day festival dedicated to childrens music, dance and costumes; it's usually in early June but the dates vary.

🛏 Sleeping

Accommodation in Sofia tends to be more expensive than elsewhere in Bulgaria, with hotel prices comparable to those in other large European cities.

There are several modern hostels scattered around town that offer dorm-bed accommodation (and often a couple of private singles and doubles), as well as free wi-fi, shared kitchens, and often a lounge or garden for relaxing.

★ Canapé Connection GUESTHOUSE $

(☎02-441 6373; www.canapeconnection.com; ul William Gladstone 12a; s/d from 50/64 lv; 📶; 🚇1, 6, 7) Formerly a hostel, Canapé reinvented itself as a guesthouse in 2016, retaining its same attention to cleanliness and a refreshingly simple, rustic design. The six rooms are divided into singles and doubles, with a

---

THE POET PEYO YAVOROV

One of Bulgaria's most admired lyric poets, Peyo Yavorov has a turbulent life story that sounds like it could have come from the pages of a lost Puccini opera. He was born in Chirpan in 1878, and by his early twenties his moody writing style had won many admirers. He was already a celebrated literary figure in Sofia when he joined the guerrillas fighting the Turks in Macedonia. His girlfriend Mina Todorova (whose parents had forbidden her relationship with the restless poet) died of consumption in Paris in 1910, and it was at her funeral that he met his next lover, Lora Karavelova, who lived with him at the house on ul Rakovski that now holds a museum dedicated to his memory. However, theirs was a stormy marriage and Lora, jealous of her husband's supposed affairs with other women, shot herself in 1913. Yavorov, by then a broken and penniless man, shot himself a year later.

larger room upstairs to accommodate families. There's a quiet garden outside to relax in. Note there's no breakfast, but you'll find several coffee places nearby.

Art Hostel
HOSTEL $

(☎02-987 0545; www.art-hostel.com; ul Angel Kânchev 21a; dm/s/d from 20/47/66 lv; @ ☎; ☐12) This bohemian hostel stands out from the crowd with its summertime art exhibitions, live music, dance performances and more. Dorms are appropriately arty and bright; private rooms are airy and very welcoming. There's a great basement bar and peaceful little garden at the back.

Hostel Mostel
HOSTEL $

(☎0889223296; www.hostelmostel.com; ul Makedoniya 2a; dm/s/d from 20/50/60 lv; P ☎; ☐1, 6, 7, 8, 10) Popular Mostel occupies a renovated 19th-century house, and has six- and eight-bed dorms, with either shared or private bathrooms, as well as a single and a couple of doubles; guests have use of a kitchen and a cosy lounge. Free beer, free pasta and all-you-can-eat breakfast round out the charms.

Hostel Gulliver
HOSTEL $

(☎0889656626; www.gulliver-hostel-sofia-bg.book. direct; bul Dondukov 48; dm/s/d 20/40/50 lv; @ ☎; Ⓜ Serdika, ☐20) Just a couple of blocks north of pl Aleksander Nevski, Gulliver is a clean and brightly furnished place with a couple of four- and five-bed dorms and some private doubles. All rooms have TVs and fridges. There's a communal kitchen and laundry.

Internet Hostel Sofia
HOSTEL $

(☎0889138298; www.internethostelsofia.hostel. com; ul Alabin 50a, 2nd fl; dm/s/d from 18/40/60 lv; @ ☎; ☐12) Centrally located hostel with a wide choice of large, clean rooms, with four- and six-bed dorms, singles, doubles, and private studios with separate entrances. Not immediately obvious from street level, the entrance is inside an arcade a couple of doors down from a McDonald's.

★ Hotel Niky
HOTEL $$

(☎02-952 3058; www.hotel-niky.com; ul Neofit Rilski 16; r/ste from 90/130 lv; P ⊖ ❀ ☎; Ⓜ NDK, ☐1) Offering excellent value and a good city-centre location, Niky has comfortable rooms and gleaming bathrooms; the smart little suites come with kitchenettes. It's a very popular place and frequently full; be sure to book ahead.

Light Hotel
HOTEL $$

(☎02-983 1243; www.hotellight.com; ul Veslets 37; s/d 60/90 lv; ❀ ☎; Ⓜ Lavov most) A beacon of light in a depressed (but safe) part of the city that offers excellent value. Rooms are sparsely furnished but spotlessly clean. Baths are gleaming and the mattresses firm. The breakfast buffet is monotonous (scrambled eggs and ham slices), but decent quality for the money. You'll find the staff is helpful, and the centre is just 10 minutes away on foot.

House
BOUTIQUE HOTEL $$

(☎02-952 0830; www.hotelthehouse.com; ul Verila 4; s/d from 45/55 lv; P ⊖ ❀ ☎; Ⓜ NDK) On a quiet side street off bul Vitosha, this attractively renovated townhouse has a wide choice of rooms, some quite small, but it's good value for central Sofia. Some guests may find the narrow wooden stairs awkward.

Red B&B
B&B $$

(☎0889226822; www.redbandb.com; ul Lyuben Karavelov 15; s/d from 40/60 lv; @ ; Ⓜ Vasil Levski National Stadium, ☐10) Attached to the Red House cultural centre in a wonderful 1920s building once home to Bulgaria's most famous sculptor, this six-room hotel offers digs with a difference. All rooms are individually decorated, and the general air is one of boho bonhomie. Shared bathrooms.

Arte Hotel
HOTEL $$

(☎02-402 7100; www.artehotelbg.com; bul Dondukov 5; r/ste from 100/200 lv; ❀ ☎; Ⓜ Serdika, ☐20) Welcoming city-centre hotel with bright, modern rooms and contemporary artworks adorning the walls. The central location, just next to the Serdika metro station, is a big advantage. Rooms come in standard and deluxe, with the biggest difference being room size. Prices drop slightly at weekends, and breakfast is an additional 20 lv.

Hotel Diter
HOTEL $$

(☎02-989 8998; www.diterhotel.com; ul Han Asparuh 65; s/d 70/100 lv; P ❀ @ ☎; Ⓜ NDK, ☐9) Occupying a restored, bright-blue 19th-century townhouse on a quiet street within easy walking distance of the trendiest parts of the city centre, the Diter is a cosy place with a variety of bright rooms. There's an on-site restaurant, bar and garden, but the breakfast buffet is meagre and costs an additional 8 lv with some room packages.

Scotty's Boutique Hotel BOUTIQUE HOTEL $$
(☎02-983 6777; www.scottyshotel.eu; ul Ekzarh Yosif 11; s/d from 70/90 lv; ❄🛜; Ⓜ Serdika, 🚊20) Opposite the synagogue, Scotty's is a small, stylish, gay-friendly hotel with just nine rooms, all individually designed and named after international cities, such as the Cape Town Room, which is kitted out with zebra-print details. The neighbourhood is central, though slightly depressed. Breakfast is bare bones: a breakfast roll and coffee.

Sofia Residence BOUTIQUE HOTEL $$$
(☎0885006810; www.residence-oborishte.com; ul Oborishte 63; r/ste from 200/300 lv; 🖨❄🛜🖂; 🚊9, 72, Ⓜ Sofiyski Universitet) A luxurious salmon-pink 1930s-era home with its own bistro, the Residence has nine rooms and sumptuous suites with cherry-wood flooring, antique-style furnishings and lots of space. The penthouse (260 lv) has a view over the Aleksander Nevski Church. Prices drop by 20% at weekends.

Arena di Serdica LUXURY HOTEL $$$
(☎02-819 9191; www.arenadiserdica.com; ul Budapeshta 2-4; r from 200 lv; 🅿🖨❄🛜🖂; Ⓜ Serdika) Rooms in this modern five-star hotel are plush but big and understated. The location is central, within easy walking distance of most sites, but on a quiet side street. The name comes from the remains of a 4th-century Roman amphitheatre that were uncovered during construction and are now preserved below the foyer. There's also a 'Roman-style' spa.

Visitors are welcome to gaze over the remains of the Roman amphitheatre inside the hotel (free, and open from 10am to 4pm).

Art Plaza Hotel BUSINESS HOTEL $$$
(☎02-980 0030; www.artplazahotel.bg; ul Hristo Belchev 46; s/d/ste 110/130/180 lv; 🅿❄@🛜; Ⓜ NDK, 🚊9) This swish, modern affiliate of the Best Western chain is one of the nicest hotels in the centre and a first choice among business travellers. The hotel offers 20 standard rooms, eight superior and six apartments, each with a unique design. Superior rooms are slightly larger, but similarly furnished to standards. The location is central yet quiet.

Sofia Hotel Balkan LUXURY HOTEL $$$
(☎02-981 6541; www.sofiabalkan.com; pl Sveta Nedelya 5; r/ste from 300/450 lv; 🅿❄@🛜; Ⓜ Serdika) The imposing building, part of the Presidential Palace, dates from the mid-

1950s and exudes a retro socialist-realist appeal. The interior has been retrofitted and boasts an elegant lobby, as well as bars, clubs, cafes and a casino. Marble floors, glittering chandeliers and large, plush rooms provide a level of comfort that should please the most demanding guests.

Hotel Les Fleurs BOUTIQUE HOTEL $$$
(☎02-810 0800; www.lesfleurshotel.com; bul Vitosha 21; r from 220 lv; 🅿🖨❄🛜; Ⓜ Serdika, 🚊10) You can hardly miss this very central hotel with gigantic blooms on its facade. The flowery motif is continued in the large, carefully styled rooms, and there's a very good restaurant on-site. The location, right at the start of the pedestrian-only stretch of bul Vitosha, is ideal.

🍴 Eating

Sofia has some of the country's best restaurants, including traditional and international cuisines. In summer, cafes occupy every piece of garden and footpath. Some are just basic spots for a coffee and a sandwich; others offer a more refined setting for cocktails and cakes.

Kiosks around town sell tasty local fast food such as *banitsa* (cheese pasties) and *palachinki* (pancakes), plus pizzas and burgers. The **Central Hali Shopping Centre** (Halite; bul Maria Luisa 25; ☺7am-9pm; Ⓜ Serdika, 🚊20, 22) is a good spot to pick up picnic supplies.

Vila Rosich BAKERY $
(☎02-954 3072; www.vilarosiche.com; ul Neofit Rilski 26; sandwiches & cakes 5-7 lv; ☺8am-9pm; 🛜🍴; Ⓜ NDK) Step into the back garden of this hidden bakery and enter what feels like a secret world of fresh-made breads and cakes. It's a perfect spot for an afternoon sweet, or a light cheese-stuffed croissant sandwich.

Sun & Moon VEGETARIAN $
(☎0899138411; www.sunmoon.bg; ul 6 Sepemvri 39; mains 8-12 lv; ☺10am-11pm; 🛜🍴; Ⓜ NDK) Very good vegetarian cooking, a warm, student-friendly atmosphere and a sunny, streetside terrace make this the ideal choice for a healthy, inexpensive lunch. Also has excellent homemade bread and baked goods, and great coffee.

Confetti ICE CREAM $
(☎02-988 4444; ul Graf Ignatiev 4; cones 2-4 lv; ☺9am-midnight; 🛜; Ⓜ Serdika, 🚊10, 12) Delicious, mouth-watering homemade ice

cream in countless variations that call out for sampling from the wide, oval-shaped front counter. The chocolate and vanilla tasted fresh from the ice-cream maker, and that was just the start of our exploration... Eat-in or takeaway.

Ege Türk   TURKISH $

(ul Tsar Simeon 108; mains 8-10 lv; ⊘9am-9pm Mon-Sat; Ⓜ Serdika, Lavov most) Hole-in-the-wall, diner-style restaurant deep within Sofia's Turkish quarter north of the Serdika metro station that serves arguably the city's best Turkish food. The modest menu features classic spicy Iskender and Adana kebabs, served here on a plate with rice and bulgur, as well as moussaka, and various stews, from beef to okra. Not much English spoken – simply point at your selection.

Skaptobara   BURGERS $

(☑0877333233; www.skaptobara.com; ul Iskâr 11a; burgers 10 lv; ⊘10am-midnight; 🕿🍴; Ⓜ Serdika, 🚊20, 22) Student-friendly burger joint opened by some former students of the American University in Bulgaria. The house burgers are served with spicy jalopenas on the side. Plenty of veggie and gluten-free options available. Crinkle-cut fries, imaginative cocktails and evening chill-out tunes on the terrace round out the charms.

Bistro Pesto   MEDITERRANEAN $

(☑0877174845; ul Angel Kânchev 18a; sandwiches 6 lv; ⊘10am-10pm; 🕿🍴; 🚊10, 12, 18 MB) Impossibly cute Italian-themed sandwich and coffee bar that makes for a great, inexpensive pit stop for lunch. The specialities here are panini (toasted sandwiches), but it also has very good salads, coffee and wine.

Krâchme Divaka   BULGARIAN $

(☑0886702996; www.divaka.bg; ul 6 Sepemvri 41a; mains 5-12 lv; ⊘10am-11pm; 🍴; Ⓜ NDK, 🚊10) In an appealing old house, this restaurant is a good choice for traditional Bulgarian food. Dishes include wine-soaked kebab with mashed potatoes, a filling potato-cream soup, and grilled trout, and there are plenty of vegetarian options.

Dream House   VEGETARIAN $

(☑02-980 8163; www.dreamhouse-bg.com; ul Alabin 50a, 1st fl; mains 5-8 lv; ⊘11am-10pm; 🍴; Ⓜ Serdika, 🚊10, 12) This informal vegetarian restaurant is up some grubby stairs, in an arcade just off the street. Options include stir-fries, curries, pancakes and homemade lemonade. There's an all-you-can-eat buffet on Sundays (10 lv) and daily, good-value lunch menus.

★Made In Home   INTERNATIONAL $$

(☑0876884014; ul Angel Kânchev 30a; mains 12-22 lv; ⊘11am-9pm Mon, to 10pm Tue-Sun; 🕿🍴; Ⓜ NDK) Sofia's very popular entrant into the worldwide, locally sourced, slow-food trend (the name refers to the fact that all items are made in-house). The cooking is eclectic, with dollops of Middle Eastern (eg hummus) and Turkish items, as well as ample vegetarian and vegan offerings. The playfully rustic interior feels straight out of a Winnie-the-Pooh book. Reservations essential.

★MoMa Bulgarian Food & Wine   BULGARIAN $$

(☑0885622020; www.moma-restaurant.com; ul Solunska 28; mains 8-22 lv; ⊘11am-10pm; 🕿🍴; Ⓜ Serdika) An update on the traditional *mehana* (taverna), serving typical Bulgarian foods such as grilled meats and meatballs, and wines, but in a more modern and understated interior. The result is one of the best nights out in town. Start off with a shot of *rakia* (Bulgarian brandy) and a salad, and move on to the ample main courses. Book ahead – this restaurant is popular.

Little Things   INTERNATIONAL $$

(☑0882490030; ul Tsar Ivan Shishman 37; mains 8-20 lv; ⊘noon-midnight; 🕿; 🚊10, 12) It's the little things – knick-knacks; toys, books, flowers – that give this charming spot its name, but it's the large portions of delightful, homestyle food that keep locals coming back for more. Mains include handmade meatballs, sinful pastas and creamy fish dishes; whatever you do, try the fig cheesecake.

Manastirska Magernitsa   BULGARIAN $$

(☑02-980 3883; www.magernitsa.com; ul Han Asparuh 67; mains 8-18 lv; ⊘11-2am; Ⓜ NDK) This traditional *mehana* is among the best places in Sofia to sample authentic Bulgarian cuisine. The enormous menu features recipes collected from monasteries across the country, with dishes such as 'drunken rabbit' stewed in wine, as well as salads, fish, pork and game options. Portions are generous and the service attentive. Dine in the garden in nice weather.

SkaraBar 2   BULGARIAN $$

(☑02-483 4431; www.skarabar.com; ul Benkovski 12; mains 6-12 lv; ⊘noon-midnight; Ⓜ Serdika, 🚊20, 22) The branch of a small local chain of popular grill restaurants features a bright, airy space with wooden floors, an open kitchen, exposed pipes and white tiles. The cooks here promise locally sourced beef, pork, lamb and even horsemeat, and a good choice of domestic wines. The speciality is grilled meatballs, but they also serve very good steaks and burgers.

Taj Mahal INDIAN $$
(📞0876600776; www.tajmahal.bg; ul 11 avgust 11; mains 16-22 lv; ⏱6-11.30pm Mon, noon-11.30pm Tue-Sun; 🔊📶; Ⓜ Sofiyski Universitet, 🚌20, 22) Sofia's longest-running Indian restaurant is also probably its best. Indian classics are served on three floors of what looks like an old mansion. Great appetisers and curries, with lots of vegetarian options. The 'salty' lassi, flavoured with cumin, is one of our favourites.

Annette MOROCCAN $$
(📞0885139676; www.annette.bg; ul Angel Kânchev 27; mains 10-20 lv; 🔊; Ⓜ NDK, 🚌10,12) With its cushion-filled couches, glowing candles and lanterns, and spicy aromas, this is a great place for authentic Moroccan cooking, including a big selection of tasty meze, and tagine meals such as lamb with figs and apricots, and chicken in wine sauce.

K.E.V.A BULGARIAN $$
(📞0877313233; School for Performing Arts, ul Rakovski 114; 6-15 lv; ⏱11am-midnight; 🚌10, 🚌9) All is not as it seems at K.E.V.A, a simple-looking place with a cheap menu: this restaurant offers five-star cuisine, lots of grilled meat dishes and meatballs, at cafeteria prices. A favourite hang-out of Sofia's arty elite and students from the attached School for Performing Arts, it also hosts regular mealtime theatrical performances.

Pastorant ITALIAN $$$
(📞02-981 4482; www.pastorant.eu; ul Tsar Asen 16; mains 12-29 lv; ⏱noon-10.30pm; 📶; Ⓜ NDK) This charming pea-green restaurant provides an intimate setting for high-quality Italian cuisine, including some inventive pasta and risotto dishes and traditional favourites such as saltimbocca and pesto chicken.

🍷 Drinking & Nightlife

There's a seemingly inexhaustible supply of watering holes all over Sofia. The cheapest places to grab a beer are the kiosks in the city's parks; if you're looking for a more so-

phisticated ambience, the city centre has plenty of swish new bars.

DaDa Cultural Bar BAR
(📞0877062455; http://blog.dadaculturalbar.eu; ul Georgi Benkovski 10; ⏱24hr; 🔊; Ⓜ Serdika, 🚌20, 22) A local institution, DaDa bar is far more than a place to drink. The mission here is culture, and expect to find live music, art installations, readings or happenings. The website usually has an up-to-date program. Friendly staff and a welcoming vibe.

Fabrika Daga CAFE
(📞02-444 0556; ul Veslets 10; ⏱8am-10pm Mon-Fri, 10am-10pm Sat, 10am-8pm Sun; 🔊; Ⓜ Serdika, 🚌20, 22) Classic third-gen coffee roaster with lots of exposed piping and a coffee menu scrawled on a chalkboard. Espressos, vacuum pots and French presses squeeze out java drinks from a wide variety of exotic beans. It also has a long list of salads and sandwiches, with vegan and vegetarian options. Handy spot for morning coffee and a breakfast roll or cake.

Raketa Rakia Bar BAR
(📞02-444 6111; ul Yanko Sakazov 15-17; ⏱11am-midnight; 🔊; 🚌11, Ⓜ Sofiyski Universitet) Unsurprisingly, this rakish communist-era retro bar has a huge selection of *rakia* on hand; before you start working your way down the list, line your stomach with meat-and-cream-heavy snacks and meals. Reservations essential.

One More Bar BAR
(📞0882539592; ul Shishman 12; ⏱8.30am-2.30am; 🔊; Ⓜ Sofiyski Universitet) Inside a gorgeous old house, this shabby-chic hot spot wouldn't be out of place in Melbourne or Manhattan: an extensive cocktail list, a delightful summer garden and jazzy background music add to its cosmopolitan appeal.

Memento CAFE
(📞0882422928; www.memento.cafe; pl Bulgaria 1, National Palace of Culture; ⏱8am-2am Mon-Fri, 9am-3am Sat, 10am-2am Sun; 🔊; Ⓜ NDK) A lively coffee bar perched on the northwestern end (right side if you're approaching from the centre) of the massive NDK. It also serves excellent local wines and small bites to eat, such as salads and sandwiches. A good choice to begin a night out.

Pavage COCKTAIL BAR
(The Cocktail Bar; 📞0877151152; ul Angel Kânchev 9a; ⏱9am-2am; 🔊; Ⓜ Serdika, 🚌10, 12) Enjoy

well-made cocktails in the open air at this secluded bar and club, just a couple of blocks east of bul Vitosha. Early evenings and through the week the vibe is relaxed, but weekend nights after 9pm can be more crowded as DJs bring out the clubbers.

Peroto   CAFE
(☑ 02-916 6411; www.ndk.bg; pl Bulgaria 1, National Palace of Culture; ⊙ 24hr; ☎; Ⓜ NDK) This non-stop library and coffeehouse, situated in the NDK, is an oasis of calm and good coffee. The perfect place, day or night, to relax with friends, surf the web or browse the books, though the latter are only in Bulgarian. To find it, enter the NDK and ask the guard to direct you to Peroto.

Motto   COCKTAIL BAR
(☑ 02-987 2723; www.motto-bg.com; ul Aksakov 18; ⊙ 10am-1pm; ☎; Ⓜ Sofiyski Universitet) By day, a pleasant place to stop for a coffee, beer and homemade lemonade in the tree-covered back garden. By night, a more raucous mood takes over, as stylish clubbers cram the bar for cocktails against a throbbing DJ beat.

Chucky's Coffee & Culture   CAFE
(☑ 0884068869; www.chuckys.bg; ul Hristo Belchev 29; ⊙ 9am-8pm Mon-Fri, 10am-7pm Sat & Sun; Ⓜ NDK) Locals claim this tiny stand-up in the trendiest part of the city centre does Sofia's best coffee, and that may certainly be true. Carefully chosen beans and blends, prepared using the latest filters, presses and vacuum packs.

JJ Murphy's   PUB
(☑ 02-980 2870; www.jjmurphys.bg; ul Kârni-gradska 6; ⊙ 10am-2am; ☎; Ⓜ Serdika) Popular city-centre Irish pub frequented by expats, with live music at weekends.

Ale House   BEER HALL
(☑ 0884320400; www.alehouse.bg; ul Hristo Belchev 42; ⊙ 11am-midnight; Ⓜ NDK, 🚌 9) No need to queue at the bar at this convivial beer hall – the tables have their own beer taps. Food is also served, and there's live music on Fridays and Saturdays.

Veda House   TEAHOUSE
(☑ 0882108108; www.vedahouse.bg; ul William Gladstone 2; teas from 3 lv; ⊙ 10.30am-11pm; 🚌 1, 6, 7) This sociable, vaguely Indian-themed teahouse has a lengthy (Bulgarian-only) menu of black and green teas, served in pretty little teapots. Light vegetarian and vegan meals are available, too.

Nightclubs

Switch   CLUB
(☑ 0877122890; bul Bulgaria 2; ⊙ 10am-2am Sun-Thu, to 4am Fri & Sat; ☎; Ⓜ NDK) High-dance club situated behind the NDK. Draws the best local and international DJs and live music. The club is sprawling, with lots of outdoor seating, though the dance floor is tiny and at 1am on a Saturday night is jammed to capacity.

ID Club   CLUB
(☑ 0898200000; www.idclub.bg; ul Kârnigradska 19b; ⊙ midnight-7am Tue & Thu-Sat; ☎; Ⓜ Serdika) Centrally located ID is a late-night dance club that draws a mix of gay and straight clientele for dancing, various theme nights and cabaret.

Yalta   CLUB
(☑ 0897870230; www.yaltaclub.com; bul Tsar Osvoboditel 20; ⊙ 9am-7pm Mon-Thu, 9am-7pm & 11pm-6am Fri, 11pm-6am Sat; ☎; Ⓜ Sofiyski Universitet) Shake it with Sofia's trendy types and local and international DJ stars at this hip, hyper spot that's been going strong since 1959 (it was Bulgaria's first modern nightclub).

Chervilo   CLUB
(☑ 0888111999; bul Tsar Osvoboditel 9; ⊙ 10.30pm-6am Tue-Sat; Ⓜ Sofiyski Universitet) This popular, upscale venue – the name translates as 'Lipstick' – is situated in Sofia's Military Club. The guest DJs, themed party nights and live acts draw Sofia's young and fashionable set at night. There's also a pleasant terrace for sitting out with a drink or two.

☆ Entertainment

If you read Bulgarian, or at least can decipher some of the Cyrillic, *Programata* is the most comprehensive source of entertainment listings; otherwise check out its excellent English-language website, www.programata.bg.

You can book tickets online at www.ticketpro.bg.

Cinemas

As well as a couple of modern multiplexes, Sofia has several smaller cinemas dotted around town. Most screen recent English-language films with Bulgarian subtitles, although cartoons and children's films are normally dubbed into Bulgarian.

Cultural Centre G8   CINEMA
(☑ 02-995 0080; www.g8cinema.com; ul William Gladstone 8; tickets 6-8 lv; ⊙ 9am-11pm; 🚌 1, 6, 7)

This trendy, art-house cinema does triple duty as a contemporary art gallery and secluded, garden drinking spot.

Euro Cinema
CINEMA

(☑02-980 4161; bul Stamboliyski 47; tickets 5-8 lv; ☺12.30-10pm Mon-Fri, noon-10pm Sat & Sun; Ⓜ Serdika) Cute retro cinema, close to the heart of the city, features the best in European and international art-house film.

Dom Na Kinoto
CINEMA

(☑02-980 7838; http://domnakinoto.com; ul Ekzarh Yosif 37; tickets 5-8 lv; 🚎20, 22) Shows a varied program of Bulgarian-language, independent and vintage foreign films.

Kino Odeon
CINEMA

(☑02-989 2469; bul Patriarh Evtimii 1; tickets 4-6 lv; Ⓜ NDK) Legendary cinema from communist days specialising in smaller European and art-house movies. Hosts several small film festivals throughout the year.

Cultural Centres

National Palace of Culture
CONCERT VENUE

(NDK; ☑02-916 6300; www.ndk.bg; pl Bulgaria; ☺ticket office 10am-8pm; 🕿; Ⓜ NDK) The NDK (as it's usually called) has 15 halls and is the country's largest cultural complex. It maintains a regular program of events throughout the year, including film screenings, trade shows and big-name international music acts.

Red House
ARTS CENTRE

(☑tickets 02-988 8188; www.redhouse-sofia.org; ul Lyuben Karavelov 15; ☺box office 3-9pm; 🕿; Ⓜ Vasil Levski National Stadium, 🚎10) Occupying a unique early 20th-century mansion, this avant-garde institution hosts everything from political and cultural debates (in various languages) to poetry readings and dance performances. Many events are free; check the website for the current program. There's also a B&B here.

Live Music

Sofia Live Club
LIVE MUSIC

(☑0886661045; www.sofialiveclub.com; pl Bulgaria 1; ☺8pm-7am; Ⓜ NDK) This slick venue, located in the National Palace of Culture (NDK), is the city's largest live-music club. All swished up in cabaret style, it hosts local and international jazz, alternative, world-music and rock acts.

Club Terminal 1
LIVE MUSIC

(☑0889219001; ul Angel Kânchev 1; tickets 6 lv; ☺9pm-6am Thu-Sat; 🕿; 🚎10, 12, 18) Live music on two floors, with several adjoining bars, marks this as the centre's best-known and most popular alternative music venue.

SOFIA FOR CHILDREN

Lions, tigers, elephants and bears are among the animals at Sofia Zoo (☑02-868 2043; www.zoosofia.eu; ul Srebarna 1; adult/child 4/2 lv; ☺8.30am-6pm; 🚎120), which also has play areas for children, and a couple of simple cafes. It's free for children under seven years old.

Muzeiko (☑02-902-0000; www.muzeiko.bg; ul Prof Boyan Kamenov 3; adult/child Sat & Sun 15/8 lv, Tue-Fri 10/6 lv; ☺10am-6pm Tue-Sun; 👪; Ⓜ GM Dimitrov) is a kid-friendly science and technology museum, with plenty of interactive exhibits and gadgetry to delight children from six to 16 years of age. There are playgrounds and climbing walls as well as more thoughtful exhibitions meant to teach younger minds about paleontology, astronomy, geology and more.

Young speed fans (over eight years old) can take the wheel of a motorised go-kart and zoom around the twisting, 1km-long track at Karting Sport (☑02-920 1447; www.karting-bg.com; bul Vardar 3a; per lap 2 lv; ☺9am-9pm May-Sep, 10am-6pm Oct-Apr; 🚎11, 77, 🚎4, 11, 22), a modern speedway circuit in the Krasna Polyana district. Kids and adults can enjoy active, outdoorsy fun at Kokolandia (☑0899966970; www.kokolandia.com; ul Nezabravka, Borisova Gradina; 3-5 lv; ☺9am-9pm May-Oct; 🚎84, 413), an adventure park inside Borisova Gradina. Divided into three increasingly challenging areas, it offers rope-climbing, treetop obstacle courses (harnesses provided) and rock-climbing walls.

Play areas can be found in Borisova Gradina, which has wide open green spaces that young children might enjoy. Sofia City Garden and Oborishte Park (Vladimir Zaimov Park; bul Yanko Sakazov; 🚎20) also have playgrounds and attractions like electric cars.

Sofia has several English-speaking nurseries and day-care centres, aimed more at expat families, but there are no reliable babysitting agencies working with foreign tourists. However, some top-end hotels may be able to provide such services.

Mixtape 5 — LIVE MUSIC
(☑ 0889838348; www.mixtape5.com; pl Bulgaria 1, NDK, Galleria Underpass; ☺ 9pm-3am; Ⓜ NDK) The best in Bulgarian and international live rock and alternative acts play here in two good-sized halls located behind the NDK.

RockIT — LIVE MUSIC
(☑ 0888666991; ul Georgi Benkovski 14; ☺ 9pm-4am Mon-Sat; Ⓜ Serdika, ☐ 20, 22) If you're into rock and metal, get your horns up here. This huge two-level building shakes beneath the weight of heavy live bands, DJs, and lots and lots of hair.

Swingin' Hall — LIVE MUSIC
(☑ 0896840161; www.swinginghall.bg; bul Dragan Tsankov 8; ☺ 9pm-4am; Ⓜ National Stadium Vasil Levski) Long-standing club offering an eclectic program of live music each night. The acts, ranging from jazz and blues to rock and folk pop, typically attract audiences of all ages.

Spectator Sports
Football (soccer) is Bulgaria's main sporting passion, and Sofia alone has several teams. The main clubs are CSKA (☑ tickets 02-866 8903; www.cska.bg; bul Dragan Tsankov 3; Ⓜ Vasil Levski National Stadium), which plays at the CSKA Stadium in Borisova Gradina, and PFC Levski (☑ 02-847 7958; www.levski.bg; ul Todorini kukli 47), based at the Georgi Asparoukhov Stadium.

Vasil Levski National Stadium — SPECTATOR SPORT
(www.nsb.bg; Borisova Gradina; Ⓜ National Stadium Vasil Levski) This 43,000-seat stadium is the home of the Bulgarian national football team, and is the main venue for international matches, athletics and other big sporting events. It also stages big concerts for visiting rock acts.

Theatre & Music
Ticket prices for theatre and live music vary enormously. For shows at the Opera House or the Ivan Vazov National Theatre, you might pay anything from 10 lv to 30 lv; shows at the NDK vary much more, with tickets costing from 30 lv to 80 lv for international acts and around 10 lv to 30 lv for local ones.

Bulgaria Hall — CLASSICAL MUSIC
(☑ tickets 02-987 7656; www.sofiaphilharmonie.bg; ul Aksakov 1; ☺ box office 9.30am-2.30pm, 3-7.30pm Mon-Fri, 9.30am-2.30pm Sat; Ⓜ Serdika) Home of the excellent Sofia Philharmonic Orchestra.

Ivan Vazov National Theatre — THEATRE
(☑ 02-811 9219; www.nationaltheatre.bg; ul Dyakon Ignatiy 5; ☺ ticket office 9.30am-7.30pm Mon-Fri, 11.30am-7.30pm Sat & Sun; Ⓜ Serdika) One of Sofia's most elegant buildings, the Viennese-style National Theatre opened in 1907, and is the city's main stage for Bulgarian drama.

National Opera House — OPERA
(☑ tickets 02-987 1366; www.operasofia.bg; bul Dondukov 30; ☺ box office 9am-2pm & 2.30-7pm Mon-Fri, 11am-7pm Sat, 11am-4pm Sun; ☐ 20, 22) Opened in 1953, this monumental edifice is the venue for classical opera and ballet performances, as well as special concerts for children. Enter from ul Vrabcha.

🛍 Shopping
Bul Vitosha is Sofia's main shopping street, mostly featuring international brand-name boutiques interspersed with restaurants. The Ladies' Market (Zhenski Pazar; ul Stefan Stambolov; ☺ dawn-dusk; Ⓜ Lavov most, ☐ 20, 22) feels like a little piece of the Middle East, with stalls selling all manner of fresh produce, meats, fish, cheeses and spices. Scattered around the city are also a few big modern shopping malls, housing international fashion chains, cinemas and supermarkets.

Vino Orenda — WINE
(☑ 0889623606; www.vinoorenda.com; bul Makedonia 50a; ☺ 10.30am-7.30pm Mon-Fri; ☐ 4, 5) Small, knowledgeable wine shop offering products from a variety of independent producers around the country. The engaging owner is more than happy to guide you through your options.

Rose of Bulgaria — COSMETICS
(☑ 0893356418; www.biofresh.bg; bul Vitosha 4; ☺ 10am-8pm; Ⓜ Serdika) This small boutique on bul Vitosha sells a range of locally made, rose-scented beauty products, including rosewater, perfume, colognes, soaps and shampoos.

Centre of Folk Arts & Crafts — GIFTS & SOUVENIRS
(☑ 02-989 6416; www.craftshop-bg.com; ul Parizh 4; ☺ 9.30am-6.30pm Mon-Sat, by appointment Sun; Ⓜ Serdika, ☐ 20, 22) Typical Bulgarian souvenirs such as hand-woven rugs, pottery, silver jewellery, woodcarvings and CDs of Bulgarian music are available in this crowded shop, though prices are rather high. There's another branch inside the

🛈 GIFTS & SOUVENIRS

Artists sell paintings, mainly of traditional rural scenes, near the Mineral Baths and around pl Aleksander Nevski, where you'll also find **stalls** (⊙dawn-dusk) selling reproduction religious icons, jewellery, souvenirs and embroidery. But be wary of the 'antiques': there are some genuine items here, but much of it's fake, and prices are very much aimed at tourists. The underpass below pl Nezavisimost has souvenir shops selling the usual array of postcards, paintings and books.

Royal Palace, at the exit from the Ethnographic Museum.

Tsum Retail Centre SHOPPING CENTRE
(☑02-926 0700; bul Maria Luisa 2; ⊙10am-8pm Mon-Sat, 11am-7pm Sun; ⓂSerdika) The monumental former state department store, built in 1956, is now a confusing warren of stalls selling clothing, jewellery, perfume and candles. It's eerily quiet, often seeming to have more staff than customers, but it does have free public toilets.

Mirella Bratova CLOTHING
(☑02-943 5420; http://mirellabratova.com; ul Ivan Shishman 4; ⊙10.30am-7pm Mon-Fri, to 6pm Sat; ⓂSofiyski Universitet) Stylish women's fashions designed by Sofia couturier Mirella Bratova are on display at this little shop, including knitwear, jewellery and accessories.

Greenwich Book Center BOOKS
(☑02-950 8337; www.greenwich.bg; bul Vitosha 37; ⊙9am-9pm Mon-Thu, to 10pm Fri, 10am-10pm Sat, to 9pm Sun; 🛜; ⓂSerdika, 🚌10) Offers a small selection of foreign-language souvenir books about Bulgaria, as well as guidebooks, maps and music CDs. There's a cafe in the basement.

Stenata SPORTS & OUTDOORS
(☑02-980 5491; www.stenata.com; ul Bratia Miladinovi 5; ⊙10am-8pm Mon-Fri, to 6pm Sat; ⓂSerdika) The best place in town to buy hiking, climbing and camping equipment, including backpacks, tents and sleeping bags.

🛈 Information

DANGERS & ANNOYANCES

Sofia is a relatively safe city and there are few specific dangers and annoyances. Watch for traffic when crossing the street, as drivers seem oblivious to pedestrian crossings; note that while bul Vitosha is pedestrian-only, the cross streets are not and cars still zip across.

As always, be careful with bags, wallets and purses on crowded public transport and particularly in busy areas such as the Ladies' Market and around pl Sveta Nedelya.

EMERGENCY

Ambulance (☑150)
Fire (☑160)
Mountain Rescue (☑0881470, 02-963 2000; www.redcross.bg)
Police (☑166)
Traffic Police (☑165)

INTERNET ACCESS

Most cafes, restaurants and bars offer free wi-fi for customers. Simply ask your waiter for the password. Nearly all hostels, guesthouses and hotels have free in-room wi-fi for guests. Larger hotels will also have a computer or 'business centre' for guest use.

Internet cafes have largely died out in central Sofia, though you may occasionally find a hanger-on, identified by the sign 'Internet'.

MEDIA

➡ **Programata** (www.programata.bg) A useful, widely available weekly listings magazine, with details of cinemas, restaurants and clubs. It's only in Bulgarian, but the website is in English.

➡ **Sofia City Info Guide** (www.sofia-guide.com) Published monthly, this includes basic practical information and reviews of hotels, restaurants and clubs and comes with a free city map. Available at hotel reception desks.

➡ **Sofia – The Insider's Guide** (www.inside sofia.com) A pleasingly opinionated quarterly publication featuring background information and advice for visitors, as well as restaurant and entertainment reviews. Available at some hotels and travel agencies.

MEDICAL SERVICES

Dr Ivan Dimitrov Dental Practice (☑02-952 2328; www.drivandimitrov.com; ul Dragshan 5; 🚌4) English-speaking dentist.

International Medical Centre (☑02-944 9326; www.imc-sofia.com; ul Gogol 28; ⊙8am-8pm Mon-Fri, 9am-3pm Sat; 🚌9, 306) The IMC has English- and French-speaking doctors who will make house calls at any time. It also deals with dental care.

Neomed Pharmacy (☑02-951 5539; bul General Totleben 2, entrance B; ⊙24hr; 🚌4, 5) Twenty-four-hour pharmacy.

Pirogov Hospital (☑emergency 02-915 4411; www.pirogov.bg; bul General Totleben 21; 🚌4, 5) Sofia's main public hospital for emergencies.

MONEY

Banks and ATMs are ubiquitous in the centre, and there are several foreign-exchange offices on bul Vitosha, bul Maria Luisa and bul Stamboliyski.

Unicredit Bulbank (www.unicreditbulbank.bg; cnr ul Lavele & ul Todor Alexandrov; ⊙9am-4pm Mon-Fri; Ⓜ Serdika)

United Bulgarian Bank (☑02-980 2235; www. ubb.bg; ul Sveta Sofia 5; ⊙9am-4pm Mon-Fri; Ⓜ Serdika)

POST

Central Post Office (ul General Gurko 6; ⊙7am-7pm Mon-Sat, 8am-1pm Sun) Centrally located bank branch and 24-hour ATM.

TOURIST INFORMATION

National Tourist Information Centre (☑02-933 5826; www.bulgariatravel.org; pl Sveta Nedelya 1; ⊙9am-5pm Mon-Fri; Ⓜ Serdika) Helpful, English-speaking staff and glossy brochures for destinations around Bulgaria. The office is a little hard to find, hidden near a small side street, a few steps southwest of pl Sveta Nedelya.

Sofia Tourist Information Centre (☑02-491 8344; www.info-sofia.bg; Sofiyski Universitet metro underpass; ⊙8am-8pm Mon-Fri, 10am-6pm Sat & Sun; Ⓜ Sofiyski Universitet) Lots of free leaflets and maps, and helpful English-speaking staff.

TRAVEL AGENCIES

Alexander Tour (☑02-983 5258; www. travelinbulgaria.eu; ul Pop Bogomil 40, 6th fl; ⊙9.30am-6pm Mon-Fri; Ⓜ Lavov most) Runs numerous tours around Bulgaria, including day trips from Sofia and longer, tailor-made tours.

Odysseia-In Travel Agency (☑02-989 0538; www.odysseia-in.com; bul Stamboliyski 20-V, 1st fl; Ⓜ Serdika) Organises hiking, skiing, climbing, birdwatching and other trips across the country. Oriented towards groups. Entrance is on ul Lavele.

Zig Zag Holidays (p478) Aimed at individuals, with a long list of hiking, climbing, caving,

wine-tasting and biking trips on the program. Day trips to Rila Monastery and Mt Vitosha. Entrance is on ul Lavele.

ⓘ Getting There & Away

AIR

The only domestic flights within Bulgaria are between Sofia and the Black Sea coast. **Bulgaria Air** (☑call centre 02-402 0400; www.air.bg; ul Ivan Vazov 2; ⊙9.30am-noon & 12.30-5.30pm Mon-Fri; Ⓜ Serdika) flies daily to Varna, with two or three daily flights running between July and September. Bulgaria Air also flies between the capital and Burgas.

BUS

Sofia's **Central Bus Station** (Tsentralna Avtogara; ☑info 0900 63 099; www.centralna avtogara.bg; bul Maria Luisa 100; ⊙24hr; 🕾; Ⓜ Central Railway Station) is located beside the train station and accessed via the same metro stop. It handles services to most big towns in Bulgaria as well as international destinations. There are dozens of counters for individual private companies, as well as an information desk and an **OK-Supertrans taxi desk** (☑02-973 2121; www.oktaxi.net; Centrail Bus Station; ⊙6am-10pm; Ⓜ Central Railway Station).

The smaller **Ovcha Kupel bus station** (☑02-955 5362, info 0875105097; http://avtogaraza pad.wix.com/avtogarazapad; bul Ovcha kupel 1, Zapad; ⊙6.30am-6pm; 🚌73, 103) – sometimes called Zapad (West) station – has a few bus services heading south, such as to Bansko, Blagoevgrad and Sandanski.

From tiny **Yug bus station** (☑02-872 2345; bul Dragan Tsankov 23; Ⓜ Joliot-Curie), buses and minibuses leave for Samokov (6 lv, one hour, every 30 minutes).

From the ramshackle **Poduyane bus station** (☑02-847 4262; ul Todorini Kukli, cnr ul Reka Veleka; 🚌79) – aka Iztok (East) station – buses leave infrequently for small towns in central Bulgaria.

DOMESTIC TRAIN SERVICES TO & FROM SOFIA

DESTINATION	1ST-/2ND-CLASS COST (LV)	DURATION (HR)	FREQUENCY (DAILY)
Burgas	26/20	7-8	4 fast & 2 express
Gorna Oryakhovitsa	23/18	4-4½	6 fast & 2 express
Plovdiv	10/8	2½-3	6 fast, 3 express & 4 slow
Ruse	30/24	6	3 fast
Sandanski	12/10	4	3 fast
Varna	39/31	7½-9	5 fast & 1 express
Vidin	17/14	5	3 fast

SUMMER BUS SCHEDULE - CENTRAL BUS STATION

DESTINATION	COST (LV)	DURATION (HR)	FREQUENCY
Albena	36	8	4-5 daily
Bansko	16	3	5-6 daily
Blagoevgrad	11	2	about hourly
Burgas	30	7-8	6-10 daily
Gabrovo	22	3-4	7 daily
Haskovo	22	6	12-14 daily
Kazanlâk	16	3½	4-5 daily
Lovech	14	3	2-3 daily
Nesebâr	37	7	5-10 daily
Pleven	15	2½	hourly
Plovdiv	14	2½	several hourly
Ruse	29	5	hourly
Sandanski	14	3½	10-12 daily
Shumen	31	6	7 daily
Sliven	24	5	8 daily
Smolyan	25	3½	6-7 daily
Sozopol	32	7	6-8 daily
Stara Zagora	22	4	8 daily
Varna	33	7-8	every 30-45min
Veliko Târnovo	22	4	hourly
Vidin	20	5	6-7 daily

TRAIN

Sofia's **Central Train Station** (☑ info 02-931 1111, international services 02-931 0972, tickets 02-932 2270; www.bdz.bg; bul Maria Luisa 102a; ☺ ticket office 7am-8.15pm; Ⓜ Central Railway Station) is the city's and country's main rail gateway. The station itself is a massive, cheerless modern structure that's been extensively renovated, but which feels empty and lacks many basic services. It's located in an isolated part of town about 1km north of the centre, though it's the terminus of a metro line and easy to reach. It's 100m (a five-minute walk) from the Central Bus Station.

Destinations for all domestic and international services are listed on timetables in Cyrillic, but departures (for the following two hours) and arrivals (for the previous two hours) are listed in English on a large computer screen on the ground floor.

Same-day tickets are sold at counters on the ground floor, while advance tickets are sold in the gloomy basement, accessed via an unsigned flight of stairs near some snack bars. Counters are open 24 hours, but normally only a few are staffed and queues are long, so don't turn up at the last moment to purchase your ticket, and allow some extra time to work out the confusing system of platforms (indicated with Roman numerals) and tracks.

❶ Getting Around

TO/FROM THE AIRPORT

Sofia Airport (☑ info 24hr 02-937 2211; www. sofia-airport.bg; off bul Brussels; ☎; ☐ 84, Ⓜ Sofia Airport), the city's and country's main air gateway, is located 10km east of the centre. The airport has two terminals (1 and 2). Most flights use the more modern Terminal 2, but a few budget carriers fly in and out of Terminal 1. Both terminals have basic services, ATMs and **OK-Supertrans Taxi** (☑ 02-973 2121; www.ok taxi.net; 0.79/0.90 lv day/night per km) desks.

Sofia's metro connects Terminal 2 to the centre (Serdika station) in around 20 minutes. Buy tickets in the station, which is located just outside the terminal exit. Bus 84 also shuttles between the centre and both terminals. Buy tickets (1 lv, plus an extra fare for large luggage) from the driver.

A taxi to the centre will cost from 10 lv to 15 lv. Prebook your taxi at the **OK-Supertrans Taxi** counter. They will give you a slip of paper with the three-digit code of your cab. The driver will be outside waiting.

CAR & MOTORCYCLE

Sofia's public transport is excellent and traffic can be heavy, so there's no need to drive a private or rented car in Sofia.

If you wish to explore further afield, however, a car might come in handy. The **Union of Bulgarian Motorists** (p485) provides emergency roadside service. Rental outlets include the following and all have desks at Sofia Airport:

Avis (☑ 02-945 9224; www.avis.bg; Sofia Airport, Terminal 2; ☉ 9am-10pm; Ⓜ Sofia Airport)

Hertz (☑ 02-945 9217; www.hertz.bg; Sofia Airport, Terminal 2; ☉ 9am-10pm; Ⓜ Sofia Airport)

Sixt (☑ 02-945 9276; www.sixt.com; Sofia Airport, Terminal 2; ☉ 8am-2.30am; Ⓜ Sofia Airport)

PUBLIC TRANSPORT

Sofia has a comprehensive public transport system based on trams, trolleybuses and underground metro. Public transport generally runs from 5.30am to around 11pm every day. The **Sofia Urban Mobility Centre** (☑ info 0700 13 233; www.sofiatraffic.bg) maintains a helpful website with fares and an updated transport map. Attractions in the centre are normally located within easy walking distance, and you're not likely to need the tram or trolley in most instances.

Metro

Sofia's shiny metro links the city centre to both Sofia Airport and the central train and bus stations. It's divided into two lines, with the lines crossing at central Serdika station. Other helpful stations include NDK, at the southern end of bul Vitosha, and Sofiyski Universitet, close to Sofia University. Tickets cost 1 lv, but cannot be used on other forms of public transport. Buy tickets at windows and ticket machines located in the stations.

Bus, Tram & Trolleybus

Tickets for trams, buses and trolleybuses cost 1 lv each (8 lv for 10 trips) and can be purchased at kiosks near stops or from on-board ticket machines. Consider buying a day pass (4 lv) to save the hassle of buying individual tickets.

Buses 64 and 107 run to Boyana for the Boyana Church. Bus 107 also runs to the National Museum of History.

TAXI

Taxis are an affordable alternative to public transport. By law, taxis must use meters, but those that wait around the airport, luxury hotels and within 100m of pl Sveta Nedelya may try to negotiate an unmetered fare – which, of course, will be considerably more than the metered fare.

All official taxis are yellow, have fares per kilometre displayed in the window, and have obvious taxi signs (in English or Bulgarian) on top. The standard legal fare is 0.79 lv per minute during the day, 0.90 lv per minute at night. Never accept a lift in a private, unlicensed vehicle.

OK-Supertrans (p316) Reliable, radio-taxi that operates around town and to and from the airport.

Yellow Taxi (☑ 02-91 119; www.yellow333.com) Order by phone or hail from the street.

AROUND SOFIA

The places mentioned here are accessible from Sofia by public transport, but beyond Boyana, it's worth staying at least one night to avoid excessive travel and to better appreciate the surroundings.

Boyana   БОЯНА

Boyana is a peaceful and prosperous suburb of Sofia, lying around 8km south of the city centre. Once a favourite retreat for communist leaders and apparatchiks, these days it's home to Sofia's wealthy elite and two of the capital's major attractions. However, there's little else to detain you here.

◉ Sights

Boyana Church   CHURCH

(☑ 02-959 0939; www.boyanachurch.org; ul Boyansko Ezero 3, Boyana; adult/child 10/1 lv, combined ticket with National Historical Museum 12 lv, guides 10 lv; ☉ 9.30am-5.30pm Apr-Oct, 9am-5pm Nov-Mar; ☐ 64, 107) Tiny 13th-century Boyana Church is included on Unesco's World Heritage list and its 90 murals are among the very finest examples of Bulgarian medieval artwork. A combined ticket includes entry to both the church and the National Museum of History, 2km away.

Highlights include the oldest known portrait of St John of Rila, along with representations of King Konstantin Asen and Queen Irina. There's little English signage and visitors are limited to 10 minutes inside.

National Museum of History   MUSEUM

(☑ 02-955 4280; www.historymuseum.org; ul Vitoshko Lale 16, Boyana; adult/child 10/1 lv, combined ticket with Boyana Church 12 lv, guided tours in English 30 lv; ☉ 9.30am-6pm Apr-Oct, 9am-5.30pm Nov-Mar; ☐ 63, 107, 111, ☐ 2) Housed in the former communist presidential palace, this museum occupies a stunning, if inconvenient, setting; unless a coach party turns up, you may have the place to yourself. The exhaustive collection includes Thracian gold treasures, Roman statuary, folk costumes, weaponry and icons, and outside you can see some Russian MiG fighters. There are regular temporary exhibitions, too.

Guided tours in English must be requested two weeks in advance by email. To get here, take public transport or a taxi (about 9 lv one way) from the city centre.

Vitosha Nature Park
ПРИРОДЕН ПАРК ВИТОША

The Mt Vitosha range, 23km long and 13km wide, lies just south of Sofia; it's sometimes referred to as the 'lungs of Sofia' for the refreshing breezes it deflects onto the capital. The mountain is part of the 22,726 hectare Vitosha Nature Park (www.park-vitosha.org), the oldest of its kind in Bulgaria (created in 1934). The highest point is Mt Cherni Vrâh (Black Peak; 2290m), the fourth-highest peak in Bulgaria, where temperatures in January can fall to -20ºC.

As well as being a popular ski resort in winter, the nature park is popular with hikers, picnickers and sightseers on summer weekends, and receives around 1.5 million visitors a year. There are dozens of clearly marked hiking trails, a few hotels, cafes and restaurants and numerous huts and chalets. Other draws include a centuries-old monastery in the hills above the suburb of Dragalevtsi and a fascinating 'stone river' at Zlatnite Mostove.

◉ Sights

Zlatnite Mostove   PICNIC AREA
(◔24hr) Zlatnite Mostove is a spray of large boulders – a 'stone river' – that runs down a slope from an altitude of about 1700m down to 1350m. The name, which translates to 'golden bridges', refers to the colour of lichen that grows on the stones. The boulders and green areas make for a popular sunbathing and picnicking spot. Hike up from near the Boyana Church. A taxi from the centre of Sofia will cost about 22 lv one way.

The boulder trail is a relatively rare geological phenomenon that dates from the Ice Age.

Dragalevtsi Monastery   MONASTERY
(✆02-967 3360; Dragalevtsi; ◔8.30am-noon, 1.30pm-6pm Tue-Sun; ▣66, 93) FREE This working monastery is probably the oldest

of its kind in Bulgaria. It was built around 1345, but abandoned only 40 years later. The monastery contains colourful murals and is revered as one of the hiding places of the ubiquitous anti-Turkish rebel leader Vasil Levski. The location is within the Vitosha National Park, about 1.5km south of the Dragalevtsi suburb of Sofia.

The monastery is reachable by public transport by buses 66 or 93; the former runs only on weekends and holidays. Wear comfortable shoes: the monastery lies on a hill and you'll have to hike to get up there.

🏃 Activities

The main activities are hiking in summer and skiing in winter (mid-December to April). All of the park's areas have good hiking; Aleko, the country's highest ski resort, is best for skiing.

Hiking

There are great hikes all through the Vitosha Nature Park. The most dramatic starting points are at Zlatnite Mostove and Aleko (accessible via the Simeonovo gondola). Bookshops stock hiking maps, including the very helpful *Vitosha Turisticheska Karta* (1:50,000). The best walks include the following:

Boyana Church–Zlatnite Mostove At the church, ask for directions to the path that hugs the Boyana River and leads to the 15m-high Boyana Waterfall. From there, obvious paths lead to Zlatnite Mostove; about three hours in total.

Zlatnite Mostove–Mt Cherni Vrâh A challenging hike, via Kumata Hut and Mt Sedloto (2018m); about three hours.

Aleko–Goli Vrâh A short trail (30 minutes) between the top of the gondola from Simeonovo and the chairlift from Dragalevtsi.

Aleko–Mt Cherni Vrâh A popular, but steep, 90 minutes on foot.

Aleko–Zlatnite Mostove Follow the trail to Goli Vrâh, around Mt Sredets (1969m) and pass Hotel Bor; about three hours.

Dragalevtsi chairlift–Goli Vrâh Follow the chairlift from the bottom; a three-hour steep climb.

Simeonovo Gondola   CABLE CAR
(✆0882111480; www.planinite.info; 8/10 lv one-way/return; ◔9am-5pm Sat & Sun, incl holidays; ▣122,123) At 6270m, this modern six-seater

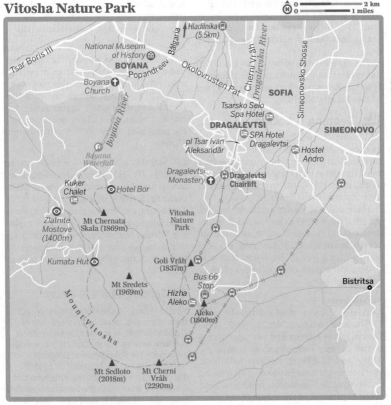

cabin is reputedly the longest lift of its kind in the country. The trip to the top lasts about 30 minutes. You can jump off at the junctions of Vtora or Chetvarta, from where hiking trails lead deep into the park, and then continue the trip later with the same ticket.

Dragalevtsi Chairlift
CABLE CAR

(☑02-967 1110; www.planinite.info; Dragalevski; 4/7 lv one-way/return; ☺9am-5pm Sat & Sun, incl holidays; 🚌66, 93) A two-person chairlift starts about 4km (by road) up from the centre of Dragalevtsi village; alternatively, it's about 3km on foot if you take the obvious short cut up the hill. One chairlift (2 lv, 20 minutes) goes as far as Bai Krâstyo, from where another (2 lv, 15 minutes) carries on to Goli Vrâh (1837m).

A pleasant option is to take the chairlift to Goli Vrâh, walk to Aleko (30 minutes) and catch the gondola down to Simeonovo (or vice versa).

Skiing

At 1800m above sea level, Aleko (www.ski vitosha.com; lift passes adult/child 35/21 lv) is Bulgaria's highest ski resort, and its six slopes are only 22km from the centre of Sofia. There is rarely enough snow here for skiing before mid-December, but the season can often last into April. Aleko was named in honour of the renowned writer Aleko Konstantinov, who kick-started the hiking craze back in 1895 when he led a party of 300 fellow outdoors enthusiasts to the top of Mt Cherni Vrâh.

The 29km of alpine ski runs (the longest of which is about 5km) range from easy to very difficult, and start as high as Mt Cherni Vrâh. Cross-country skiing is ideal along the 15km of trails, and snowboarding is also possible. As well as the Simeonovo gondola and Dragalevtsi chairlift there is a handful of other chairlifts and draglifts. A one-day lift pass costs about 35 lv.

The ski-rental shop at the start of the Simeonovo gondola and at Aleko both charge from 25 lv to 40 lv per day for a set of ski gear. A snowboard and boots costs 30 lv per day.

The ski school at Aleko caters mainly to Bulgarians, but instructors are multilingual. Five-day ski courses (four hours per day) are offered for around 140 lv.

🛏 Sleeping & Eating

In Vitosha Nature Park there are several modern hotels, which are usually much cheaper than those in the city centre. Ideally you'll have your own transport if you choose to stay here. Hikers can overnight at any of the numerous mountain huts.

There are restaurants scattered around, but it's a fun option to pack a lunch before heading out. Zlatnite Mostove, near the upper reaches of Vitosha Nature Park, is a popular spot for a picnic. Hotels and mountain chalets will almost always have a place to grab a meal.

Hostel Andro   PENSION $
(☑ 02-961 1506; www.hostel-andro.free.bg; ul Bor 10, Simeonovo; s/d from 30/50 lv; P @; ☐ 67) There's just one room and two apartments at this homely little place, each with TV, fridge and sparkling modern bathroom. The location is near the foot of Mt Vitosha in the upscale Simeonovo neighbourhood about 8km south of the centre of Sofia.

Hizha Aleko   HOSTEL $
(☑ 02-967 1113; www.motensport.com; Aleko; dm/apt from 12/50 lv; P ☎) This long-established *hizha* (hut), situated in the mountains at the base of Cherni Vrâh, offers a number of dorm rooms with two to 10 beds, and three apart-

ments, all with shared bathrooms. There's a restaurant (open 9am to midnight) and tearoom, and skiing gear is available to rent.

Kuker Chalet   CHALET $
(☑ 02-955 4955; www.kukerbg.com; Zlatnite Mostove; r 40-50 lv; P) One of the more comfortable 'huts', Kuker has 10 double rooms with TVs and bathrooms, and an on-site restaurant. Prices are slightly higher on Fridays and Saturdays. The chalet is located near the main road, about 100m north of Zlatnite Mostove.

SPA Hotel Dragalevtsi   LUXURY HOTEL $$$
(☑ 0879 471 135; http://spahotel-dragalevtsi.com; ul Karnobatski prohod 1, Dragalevtsi; s/d/ste from 100/130/170 lv; P ❄ @ ☎ ☎; ☐ 64, 66, 93) This bright, modern hotel in the Dragalevtsi neighbourhood is ideally located for exploring Vitosha Nature Park, and it has a spa centre, indoor pool and an excellent restaurant. Check the website for various package deals.

❶ Getting There & Away

Vitosha Nature Park has three main entry points: the western end, including the stone river at Zlatnite Mostove, is accessed by hiking trail or taxi from near the Boyana Church; the central area, below the Sofia suburb of Dragalevtsi, can be entered via the Dragalevtsi Chairlift; and the eastern end, below the Sofia suburb of Simeonovo, is served by the Simeonovo gondola (cabin lift) that leads to up to Aleko. The chairlift and gondola operate only on holidays and weekends.

To reach the Dragalevtsi lift and monastery from the centre of Sofia, use public bus 66 or 93; note bus 66 runs only on weekends and holidays. Buses 122 and 123 serve the base of the Simeonovo gondola.

Plovdiv & the Southern Mountains

Best Places to Eat

➡ Hemingway (p349)

➡ Mehana Chavkova Kâshta (p339)

➡ Hebros Restaurant (p348)

➡ Mehana Dedo Pene (p336)

➡ Restaurant Bulgare (p329)

Best Places to Sleep

➡ Todoroff Wine & Spa (p353)

➡ Kosovo Houses (p353)

➡ At Renaissance Square (p347)

➡ Villa Stresov (p328)

➡ Hostel Old Plovdiv (p347)

➡ Hotel Rojena (p338)

Why Go?

Spectacular mountains encircle spiritual sights in this swathe of inland Bulgaria. Europe's oldest continuously inhabited city, Plovdiv anchors the region. Roman ruins and a sparkling artistic quarter provide a thrilling backdrop to the city's calendar of festivals, which brims ahead of its reign as European Capital of Culture 2019.

Quiet winemaking villages snooze in Plovdiv's surrounds, while the Rodopi Mountains reach south, dotted with ski centres such as Pamporovo. To the west lie the Rila Mountains, home to a monastery that is a spiritual lighthouse for all of Bulgaria. Perhaps most spectacular is the Pirin Mountain range, which grumbles south of student-filled Blagoevgrad. High-octane Bansko is the region's leading ski and snowboard spot, but in spring and summer Pirin National Park comes to the fore: its hiking trails weave between gem-blue lakes, and up to arid peaks such as Mt Vihren.

When to Go
Plovdiv

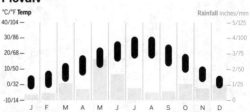

May & Jun Hiking among spring flowers in Rila and Pirin, or enjoying jazz or folk festivals in Plovdiv.

Sep & Oct Savouring wines in temperate Thrace, or autumnal spa bliss in the Rodopi Mountains.

Jan & Feb Ski by day and party by night on a winter break in Bansko or Pamporovo.

Plovdiv & the Southern Mountains Highlights

1 Rila Monastery (p324) Standing awestruck among beautiful frescoes in a millennium-old monastery.

2 Plovdiv (p339) Admiring Roman ruins by day, then sashaying into the Kapana quarter's arty nightlife.

3 Skiing in Bansko (p334) Thundering down pistes at Bulgaria's premier winter-sports town.

4 Melnik (p337) Peering at strange sandstone pillars while sipping famous wines.

5 Devin's Spas (p357) Sliding into silky spa waters in this fragrant town.

6 Historic Thrace (p339) Road tripping among wineries, ancient fortresses and enigmatic ruins.

7 Seven Rila Lakes (p328) Hiking wild mountain passes

to reach inky blue lakes and mysterious forests.

8 Rocky Rodopis (p352) Walking amid surreal rock formations or touring caves.

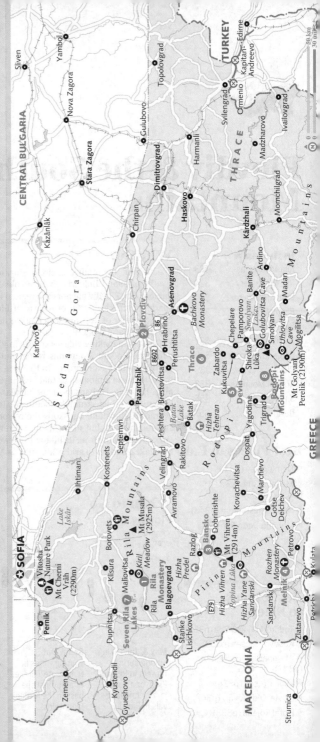

History

Archaeologists have uncovered tools, bones and other fragments of cave-dwelling peoples across Plovdiv and Bulgaria's southern mountains. But this land is most significantly marked by the Thracians, nomadic tribal peoples whose burial mounds still pepper the land. This warring group of tribes left no written records in their own language, but once dominated large parts of modern-day Bulgaria, northeastern Greece and today's European Turkey. Today's 'Bulgarian Thrace' – the section between the Sredna Gora Mountains, the Rodopi Mountains and the Black Sea coast – was the birthplace of legendary slave leader Spartacus, and Orpheus, the tragic, semi-mythical inventor of music.

Subsequent civilisations left more impressive ruins. Under Roman rule, which reached Philippopolis (Plovdiv) in 72 BC, spectacular structures such as theatres and stadia were built and the city became a strategic capital. After changing hands between the Bulgarians and the Byzantines, the region's most devastating period came when the Ottomans swept across Bulgaria, seizing Plovdiv in 1364. Meanwhile, villages in the strategic Rodopi mountain passes came under pressure to convert to Islam in return for special privileges; their descendants, Pomak communities, still thrive in the Rodopis today.

In the 18th century, Bansko-born Paisii Hilendarski began tramping from town to town, rousing the masses to reclaim their Bulgarian birthright. Uprisings followed, with initial stirrings in towns such as Perushtitsa quashed by the Ottomans. Plovdiv was freed in 1878, which sparked the National Revival period of architecture and art in earnest. This era's colourful remnants are easy to enjoy not only in Plovdiv but also Melnik and the tiny 'old towns' in Bansko and Blagoevgrad.

A burgeoning tourist scene allowed mountain towns such as Devin and Pamporovo to develop gradually from the 1930s. Communism descended to boost the region's manufacturing scene (though it did little for art and culture). Fortunately the 2000s brought a renaissance on that front, especially to Plovdiv; meanwhile, EU funding and private investment continues to slowly trickle into smaller southern mountain towns.

RILA MOUNTAINS
РИЛА ПЛАНИНА

The Rila Mountains, 70km south of Sofia, inspire awe for their spiritual history and stark beauty. The ancient Thracians called them 'mountains of water': around 200 glacial lakes gleam between these peaks, and ice-cold alpine streams thrash down from their heights.

Enormous and largely forested Rila National Park, a peaceful habitat for deer, wild goats and falcons, encompasses more than 800 sq km. At its heart is Mt Musala (2925m), the country's highest peak, and around 100 other mountains tower above 2000m. The steep ascent to Mt Musala is popular with hikers, as are trails around the glowing Seven Rila Lakes area.

Slightly north of the park lies Borovets, the region's main ski hub, while west of the park boundary stands Rila Monastery, Bulgaria's spiritual nucleus and a major tourist site.

Rila Village   РИЛА
POP 3600

This village 22km west of Rila Monastery is a sleepy place, kept awake by its transport links to the sacred Orthodox shrine. Most monastery-bound buses connect here, and there are a few cafes and hotels catering to pilgrims and tourists. Head to pl Vazhrajdane for restaurants and the Rila Tourist Information Center.

🏃 Activities

★ **Stob Pyramids Ecotrail**   WALKING

(2 lv; ⏱ 8.30am-6.30pm Mar-Oct, to 5pm Mon-Fri Nov-Feb) Gawp at an alien landscape of sandstone turrets along this magnificent ecotrail, which begins 5km south of Rila village. Stob's naturally formed chimneys and pyramids of ruddy sandstone, with rock clefts 40m deep, are a spectacular contrast to the village's surrounding meadows. Follow signs for the ecotrail from Stob village; there's a car park near the beginning of the trail.

🛏 Sleeping

Rila village's guesthouse and hotel offerings rather lack charm. Cosier accommodation offerings can be found along the road to Rila Monastery.

Rila Mountains

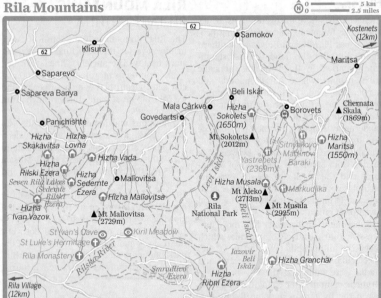

Valdis Hotel
GUESTHOUSE $

(☏0898920353; http://valdiscomplex.com; Rila; s/d/tr 40/50/60 lv) This simple guesthouse and inn, 5km east of Rila village and tucked away from the main road, has an idyllic riverside location and makes a convenient base for visiting Rila Monastery. The restaurant, with outdoor seating that overlooks thrashing water, serves breakfast (from 3 lv), and a selection of Bulgarian soups, omelettes and grilled meat dishes (mains 5 lv to 10 lv).

ⓘ Information

The **Rila Tourist Information Center** (pl Vazharajdane; ☼7am-1pm & 2-7pm) isn't always faithful to its opening hours, but it has bus timetables, monastery and hiking information, maps, and large placards with local information.

ⓘ Getting There & Away

Blagoevgrad–Rila buses operate hourly, the last returning to Blagoevgrad around 8pm (2 lv, 45 minutes). Two daily buses also serve Sofia (9 lv, two hours). If connecting from elsewhere, use Dupnitsa–Rila buses (three daily).

Three daily buses (2 lv) connect Rila village to Rila Monastery. If you're making a day trip from somewhere other than Rila village, start early to leave enough time for connections.

Rila Monastery

ELEV 1147M

Rising out of a forested valley in the Rila Mountains, Bulgaria's most famous monastery has been a spiritual centre for 1000 years. Rila Monastery's fortress-like complex engulfs 8800 sq m, and within its stone walls you'll find remarkably colourful architecture and religious art. Visitors can't fail to be struck by its elegant colonnades, archways striped in black, red and white, and the bright yellow domes of its main church, beneath which dance apocalyptic frescoes. All of this splendour, against a backdrop of mist-swirled mountains, has made Rila Monastery hugely popular among both pilgrims and curious visitors.

Most travellers visit Rila Monastery on a day trip, but you can stay at or near the monastery to experience its tranquillity after the tour buses leave, or explore the hiking trails that begin here.

History

The monastery was founded in AD 927, inspired by the powerful spiritual influence of hermit monk Ivan Rilski. By the end of the 14th century, it had become a powerful feudal fiefdom, attracting enormous donations from Bulgaria's tsars. Though it was plundered early in the 15th century, the monastery was restored in 1469, when Rilski's relics were returned from Veliko Tărnovo. Rila Monastery was vital to the preservation of Bulgarian culture and religion under Ottoman rule, despite being sacked by the Ottomans several times.

Rila's greatest modern catastrophe was a fire in 1833 that nearly engulfed all monastic buildings. An inundation of funds from Bulgarian and foreign donors allowed reconstruction to commence within a year. This rebuild during the Bulgarian Revival period gave the monastery new meaning, and it continues to represent indomitable Bulgarian identity. In 1961 the communist regime proclaimed Rila a national museum, and 22 years later it became a Unesco World Heritage site.

◎ Sights

The monastery compound is open from 6am to 10pm and includes a church, two museums, an icon gallery, guest rooms and even a post office.

The nearby 24m-high stone Hreliova Tower (1335), named after a significant benefactor, is the only 14th-century structure remaining here. The monastery's kitchen (1816) is in the northern wing's courtyard. Food was once prepared in giant cauldrons to cater for hundreds of pilgrims at a time – a single cauldron could fit an entire cow.

The upper balcony offers outstanding views over Rila Mountains.

Church of Rozhdestvo Bogorodichno   CHURCH
(Church of the Nativity; Rila Monastery) The highlight of Rila Monastery is this magnificent church, built from 1834 to 1837, with distinctive black-and-white archways and three yellow-painted domes. Its exterior frescoes are richly coloured scenes of Bible parables, including some blood-curdling illustrations of the punishments awaiting sinners; look out for demons gobbling the damned whole, or lassoing sinners into hell. Some are autographed by Zahari Zograf, the most eminent of Rila's painters. Taking photos inside the church is prohibited (though this is loosely enforced).

Within the church, you'll find an elaborate wooden iconostasis created by master artisans from Samokov and Bansko, plus an enormous low-hanging chandelier decorated with ostrich eggs. Note the need for proper attire: men and women should cover up from collarbone to knee. Holy water is on sale within the church, for the bargain price of 1 lv per bottle.

Ecclesiastical & Historical Museum   MUSEUM
(Rila Monastery; 8 lv; ◎8.30am-4.30pm) Rila Monastery's museum has a diverting collection of items and documents from across the centuries, including 14th-century wood carvings, Revival-era icons, and parchments revealing the financial history of this land-owning and profoundly influential monastery. Worthy of attention are the lavish silk and gold gifts sent from Russia to Rila. The museum's centrepiece, however, is Rafail's Cross, an early 19th-century double-sided crucifix.

Carved from a single piece of wood with 36 biblical scenes and around 600 human figures, Rafail's Cross is a feat of astonishing craftsmanship. Brother Rafail, the monk-artisan behind this masterpiece, went blind after its completion.

Icon Gallery   MUSEUM
(Rila Monastery; 3 lv; ◎8.30am-4.30pm) This single-room gallery features burnished 18th- and 19th-century icons of saints, with portraits of black-clad monks glowering above them.

Exposition Monastery Farm   MUSEUM
(Rila Monastery; 3 lv; ◎8.30am-4.30pm) Farming implements and traditional Bulgarian costumes are exhibited in this small stone-walled museum by the Samokov gate.

⊨ Sleeping

External accommodation is within 100m of Samokov gate. The monastery provides relatively spartan accommodation for those desiring the full Rila experience.

Gorski Kut   HOTEL $
(☑0888710348, 07054-2170; www.gorski-kut.eu; d/tr/ste 51/61/76 lv; P ❄) Between Rila village and the monastery, this pleasant family-run guesthouse has understated, airy rooms with balconies that gaze towards the mountains. It's signposted from the main road, 5km west of the monastery. Payment in cash only. Breakfast not included.

Hotel Tsarev Vrah   HOTEL $
(☑07054-2180; www.tzarevvrah.com; s/d/tr 45/50/66 lv) On land owned by Rila Monastery, the Tsarev Vrah has functional

WORTH A TRIP

AROUND THE RILA MONASTERY

Kiril Meadow (Rila) is a piece of tranquil nature compared to the tourist bustle at Rila Monastery, 7km southwest. This verdant, pine-backed area has picnic spots and a simple guesthouse-cafe. Kiril Meadow is also the starting point of well-marked hiking trails.

Closer to Rila Monastery, on the road to the meadow, a trail leads to another sight: **St Luke's Hermitage** (Rila). Built in 1798, the hermitage features a courtyard and the Church of Sveti Luka. Take the uphill walking trail for about 15 minutes to St Ivan's Cave, where Ivan Rilski lived and is buried; his picture by the roadside signals the start to the uphill trail.

Sveti Ivan (born 876) lived in caves for seven years, sleeping on bare stone and eating only foraged scraps, to attain greater closeness with God. These years of extreme asceticism, and his alleged miracles, brought him fame and followers across the Bulgarian Empire.

though unexciting rooms; most balconies offer forest views, but you can request a monastery-view room. The hotel cooks up tasty Bulgarian cuisine such as grilled river trout (mains 10 lv), best enjoyed at the leafy garden tables. It's signposted about 150m from the monastery's Samokov gate. Breakfast and other meals can be purchased at the restaurant.

Rila Monastery's Rooms MONASTERY $
(☑ 0896872010; www.rilamonastery.pmg-blg.com; r 30-60 lv) The monastery offers older, dorm-style western-wing rooms (the communal facilities have toilets but no showers) and some nicer en suite rooms. In summer, the latter can be booked by midday, so call ahead or arrive early. The reception office (in the southern wing) handles bookings. Breakfast not included.

✕ Eating

Most restaurants are near Samokov gate. Rila's local delicacy is *pasturva* (trout); prices are usually per 100g.

Restaurant Drushlyavitsa BULGARIAN $
(mains 6-13 lv; ⊘ 8am-10pm) On the left as you exit Rila Monastery's Samokov gate, this fine place has outdoor tables and a brook gushing practically beneath it. It's an atmospheric locale in which to dine on trout, tripe soup or grilled pork to a watery soundtrack.

Bakery BAKERY $
(snacks from 1.50 lv; ⊘ 8.30am-4.30pm) This popular little bakery, in a stone building opposite Rila Monastery's Samokov gate, attracts queues for its *banitsa* (cheese pastry) and sheep's-milk yoghurt.

Rila Restaurant BULGARIAN $
(mains 7-12 lv; ⊘ 8am-midnight) Part of the Tsarev Vrah hotel, Rila Restaurant specialises in Bulgarian grills and local fish and is set in a traditionally decorated 19th-century building.

🔒 Shopping

Souvenir shops within and outside the monastery sell books, postcards, candles and other religious souvenirs.

ℹ Getting There & Away

BUS

Tour buses such as **Rila Monastery Bus** (☑ 02-489 0883; www.rilamonasterybus.com; 50 lv) are a popular option for a day trip from Sofia.

By public transport, one daily morning bus (22 lv, 2½ hours) goes from Sofia's Ovcha Kupel bus station, returning in the afternoon.

There are more frequent connections via Dupnitsa (6 lv, 1½ hours) from Sofia's central bus station or Ovcha Kupel bus station. From here, irregular buses reach Rila Monastery (4 lv). Repeat the process back to Dupnitsa, which also has train connections to Sofia (6 lv, two hours, seven daily).

From Blagoevgrad, daily buses (9 lv, 45 minutes, 10 daily) reach Rila village. You then need to catch a bus from Rila village to the monastery (2 lv, three to five daily) so this route requires an early start.

TAXI

A taxi from Rila village to the monastery costs about 20 lv. At peak visiting times you can hail taxis outside the monastery for your return, but you may prefer to ask a driver to wait or return for you; allow one hour for a speedy visit, but ideally two.

Drivers usually park near the western Dupnitsa gate; the eastern entrance is called the Samokov gate.

Borovets БОРОВЕЦ

ELEV 1350M / POP 800

Though overshadowed by the more glamorous Bansko ski resort in the Pirin Mountains, Borovets claims 58km of pistes and a thumping après-ski culture that draws local and foreign visitors in droves between mid-December and early April. Just 72km southwest of Sofia, crouching beneath Mt Musala (2925m), this purpose-built ski resort is the oldest in Bulgaria. So perhaps it's no surprise that lifts are on the creaky side and infrastructure could do with a polish; but these are small quibbles against Borovets' crisp, pine-freshened air, tree-fringed ski runs and merry nightlife.

Borovets' reason for being is snow. It is eerily quiet outside ski season, though there are a few hiking trails worth plying in summer.

🏃 Activities

Skiing

Borovets has 58km of pistes among its main areas of Markudjika, Yastrebets and Sitnyakovo-Martinovi Baraki. Many are pleasant, tree-lined runs, and the majority are blue or red (beginner and intermediate level). There's more than 30km of cross-country runs around the resort, and night skiing between 5pm and 10pm each evening.

Snowsports fans might baulk at the number of drag lifts (10, alongside three chairlifts and a gondola), and the crowds. Still, Borovets compares exceedingly well with Western European ski resorts on price. Ski or snowboard instruction costs 49 lv per hour for individual learners, and six-day ski packages bundle together gear rental, daily ski instruction and lift passes for a bargain price (adult/child 500/320 lv). Guests at upmarket hotels can get good deals on training from in-house instructors.

Hiking

From Borovets marked hiking trails – some simply following established ski runs – provide access to the eastern Rila Mountains. Domino's hiking map of the Samokov area, on sale in some shops near the ski lifts, shows some of the routes. Seek local advice and tell your hotel your planned route and return time before setting out.

Some short and popular hikes:

Borovets–Chernata Skala Take the road towards Kostenets, and follow the signs pointing south to Hizha Maritsa; three hours (fairly easy).

Borovets–Hizha Maritsa From the Borovets to Chernata Skala road, continue along the southern road; 4½ hours (moderately difficult).

Borovets–Hizha Sokolets Follow the road south through Borovets; 2½ hours (moderately easy). Another trail (1½ hours) from Hizha Sokolets heads south to Mt Sokolets (2021m).

🛏 Sleeping

Independent travellers planning to ski (and overnight in) Borovets should book three to six months ahead for midrange or top-end hotels. Rates increase by around 25% in winter. Borovets' streets are unnamed and few, so addresses don't really exist.

For cheaper accommodation, it's wise to base yourself in Samokov, a pleasant though unexciting midsized town, 9km north. For something truly rural, villages such as Govedartsi have cheap guesthouses, though foreign visitors are few.

Hizha Musala HUT $

(☏ 0896661454; http://musalahut.com; dm 15 lv) Bulgaria's highest hiking hut, at 2389m, this simple mountain hostel is on the shores of the Musalenski Lakes, in the shadow of Mt Musala. Breakfast can be bought at its canteen.

Lodge HOTEL $$

(☏ 07503-3850; www.thelodgehotel.eu; d/ste from 110/140 lv; P 🛜 ≋) A pleasant alternative to Borovets' mega-resorts, this smaller-scale hotel has rooms that are immaculately clean, plus a little pool and sauna area.

TOP PICKS: BULGARIAN SKI RESORTS

· ·

Bansko (p332)

Borovets (p327)

Pamporovo (p354)

Chepelare (p352)

Malîovitsa (p328)

Management and staff are very warm. The hotel is inset from the main road, a few steps from Yastrebets lift.

Hotel Ela
HOTEL $$

(☑ 07503-2479; http://hotelela.com; d from 65 lv; P 🛜) With great-value rooms, free ski or bike storage, and a location mere paces from the gondola, this simple hotel is ideal for outdoorsy travellers with an eye for a bargain.

Hotel Rila
HOTEL $$

(☑ 07503-2658; www.rilaborovets.com; d from 92 lv; P ❄ 🛜 ⛐) Styled as a French alpine hotel (though it's more colossal than charming), Hotel Rila has a new gloss since being renovated. Located opposite the mountain near the main road's upper end, the hotel has rooms that are simply furnished – deluxe options are rather more chic than standards – and its impressive facilities include a heated pool and jacuzzis, a casino and a nightclub.

Flora Hotel
HOTEL $$

(☑ 07503-3100; www.flora-hotel.net; s/d/apt from 60/80/114 lv; P ❄ 🛜 ⛐) For friendly service and ski-rental spots on your doorstep, the four-star Flora is a reliable choice. Rooms are plain but clean, and there's a swimming pool with accompanying sauna and jacuzzi, and a restaurant and Irish-style pub to choose from. Kids under two sleep free. Children under 11 years stay for free when accompanied by two adults.

Alpin Hotel
HOTEL $$

(☑ 07503-2201; http://alpinborovets.com; d/ste from 88/129 lv; P ❄ 🛜) The spiky gothic roof of this small hotel sets it apart from the others at the mountain's base. Rooms are rather bare, but nicely equipped with big beds and flat-screen TVs.

Hotel Samokov
HOTEL $$

(☑ 07503-2309; www.samokov.com; s/d/apt from 58/88/134 lv; P 🛜 ⛐) The gargantuan Samokov has two restaurants, three bars, a nightclub, a shopping centre, a gym, a bowling alley and a ski school. Rooms are rather more bland than other resorts nearby, but prices are very competitive.

★ Villa Stresov
VILLA $$$

(☑ 02-980 4292, 0887924411; www.villastresov. com; d/villa from 167/607 lv; P 🛜) This dreamy villa is by far Borovets' most charming place

---

MALÎOVITSA & SEVEN RILA LAKES

Hikes in lake country and a low-key ski resort are the principal draws of remote Malîovitsa, 13km southwest of Govedartsi village at the foot of the Rila Mountains. Many hiking routes start here, the most popular leading to the spectacular Seven Rila Lakes (Sedemte Rilski Ezera). In midwinter, skiers and snowboarders (mostly locals) test 4km of pistes beneath monstrous Mt Malîovitsa (2729m), one of the tallest peaks in Rila National Park.

To get to the lakes from Malîovitsa village, first hike for about one hour to Hizha Malîovitsa (2050m). From Hizha Malîovitsa, it's a seven-hour hike to Hizha Sedemte Ezera, an older hut with simple dormitories. Alternatively, a little further north is Hizha Rilski Ezera (☑ 0886509409; www.rilskiezera.bg; dm/d/tr/q without bathroom from 25/70/100/125 lv, d/tr with bathroom 90/125 lv; ☉ Jun–mid-Sep), 2135m. The Rila Mountains' best hizha (mountain hut), it should be reserved ahead in peak summer.

From the Seven Lakes, it's an easy one-hour walk downhill to Hizha Skakavitsa (☑ 0886509409; dm from 25 lev); alternatively, head south for Rila Monastery (a six- to seven-hour hike).

With more than 200 summits above 1000m, it's no surprise the area attracts mountaineers and rock climbers. Climbing here is only for the experienced; contact the Central Mountain School (Hristo Prodanov Training Centre; ☑ 0882966319, 0885241403; Malîovitsa) to hire a guide for rock climbing or other mountain activities. The best season is between mid-June and mid-September.

For skiing, Malîovitsa's ski area has five drag lifts serving its 4km of pistes, of which the longest run is 1200m. Rent equipment from the Central Mountain School.

To get there, minibuses head from Sofia's Yug bus station to Samokov (4 lv to 6 lv, 1¼ hours); from there catch a minibus to Govedartsi or Malîovitsa (1.10 lv to 3.50 lv, 30 to 40 minutes, eight daily). Alternatively, book a direct, private transfer via Rila Shuttle (www.rilashuttle.com) for 38 lv for a minimum of five travellers.

to stay. The Swiss-style building is enclosed by a private garden, which bursts with rhododendrons in summer. The grand lounge and well-equipped kitchen are free for guest use, and all four double rooms have floral decorations and modern bathrooms. There's a pre-payment requirement and staff are hands-off, but this five-star retreat remains a stand-out.

Prices almost double between January and March. Staying at Villa Stresov is only advisable if you have your own vehicle.

✕ Eating & Drinking

Borovets' main streets feature cafes, bars and restaurants heavy on 'English breakfasts' and cocktails reminiscent of seaside summer holidays. A great many close outside ski season.

Restaurant Bulgare　　　BULGARIAN $$
(☑0888805544; mains 10-15 lv; ☺8am-midnight) Touristy but difficult to resist, this big restaurant ploughs its folksy furrow with no apology. Expect traditional woven tablecloths, and decor somewhere between ski chalet and Balkan *mehana* (tavern). Generously proportioned salads, whopping portions of grilled river trout and barbecued meats won't leave much room for dessert. It's open year-round.

Alpin Restaurant　　　INTERNATIONAL $$
(☑07503-2201; http://alpinborovets.com/restaurant; mains 9-12 lv; 🛜) Dark, polished wooden decor gives a cosy feel to the Alpin Hotel's restaurant. The menu spans nourishing soups and stews, barbecue, and classic skiing staples such as pizza and steaks.

Black Tiger　　　BAR
(☑0888144319; ☺9am-1am; 🛜) During ski season this bar-restaurant heaves with punters, whether they're chomping on pizza, chugging *rakia* (Bulgarian brandy) or settling in for karaoke. It's on the mountain's base amid the other restaurants and hotels.

ℹ Information

Central Borovets has exchange offices and ATMs, as do some of the larger hotels' lobbies.

A seasonal opening information and booking kiosk can be found near the Yastrebets chairlift.

Bulgaria Ski (www.bulgariaski.com) has information on snow conditions, accommodation and news on Bulgaria's ski resorts.

The **Bulgarian Extreme & Freestyle Skiing Association** (www.befsa.com) website has useful information about mountain safety and avalanche risks.

ℹ Getting There & Away

BUS

Samokov (9km north) is the main public transport hub to access Borovets. Buses head to Samokov from Sofia (6 lv, 1¾ hours, hourly) and Plovdiv (7 lv, two hours, four daily). From Samokov, board a minibus to Borovets (1.30 lv, 20 minutes, hourly) between 8am and 6pm. Minibuses stop opposite Borovets' Hotel Samokov.

TAXI

Taxis are good for out-of-town travel; note, however, that taxi rides within Borovets itself during peak ski season start at a considerable 10 lv. For airport transfers from Sofia or Plovdiv, consider using **Borovets Express** (www.borovetsexpress.com).

PIRIN MOUNTAINS
ПИРИН ПЛАНИНА

In the Pirin Mountains storms eclipse sunshine in a matter of moments – apt for a region named after ancient Slavic thunder god Perun. This land of giants, with more than 100 peaks surpassing 2000m in height, is greatly admired by hikers. But it's ski hub Bansko, Bulgaria's best developed winter-sports resort, that truly draws crowds.

From Bansko's southern edge spreads Pirin National Park (Unesco-listed in 1983), where 176 lakes glint among 400 sq km of fragrant pine forests and granite peaks. Fang-toothed predators make their home here – bears, wolves and jackals – but hikers are more likely to spot the park's abundant birdlife: wall-creepers, peregrine falcons and four types of woodpecker number among 170 species seen here.

West of the park, along the well-maintained route E79 running south from Sofia, lies pleasant student town Blagoevgrad; further south, encircled by dramatic sandstone towers, is wine-producing tourist favourite Melnik.

Blagoevgrad
БЛАГОЕВГРАД

POP 77,440

Blagoevgrad, 100km south of Sofia, graces few travel wishlists. But its leaf-lined squares, parks and dinky historic quarter are a nice surprise for travellers passing through. It also makes a convenient base to visit Rila Monastery, or a waystation en route to Melnik.

While many large Bulgarian towns have a harried vibe, Blagoevgrad locals are warm and approachable. An injection of foreign students into its student population of nearly 16,000, attending Neofit Rilski Southwest University and American University of Bulgaria, has shaped Blagoevgrad into a youthful and cosmopolitan place. Bisected by a small river and filled with grand squares, Blagoevgrad cannot brag about any A-list attractions but its minuscule Varosha district has charm and there are plenty of shady green spaces to dally in.

History

Blagoevgrad in Ottoman times was called Gorna Dzhumaya, but its large Turkish population was displaced after the Balkan Wars of 1912–13. It was renamed by the communists in 1950, after the 19th-century Bulgarian Marxist Dimitar Blagoev.

⊙ Sights

Between Park Loven Dom and bul Aleksandâr Stamboliyski, which runs parallel to the river on its eastern bank, is the old quarter, Varosha. Here you'll find renovated Bulgarian National Revival–period homes and art galleries.

A steep road (700m) from Varosha accesses **Park Loven Dom**, a shady and popular green space with great views over the city.

Church of Vavedenie
Presvetiya Bogoroditsi   CHURCH
(Church of the Annunciation of the Virgin; ul Komitrov; ⊙ 7am-8pm) In a small, serene garden, this church (1844) has a richly frescoed portico and a unique black-and-white chequered facade. Look for the extraordinary painting of the circle of life, including continents and astrological symbols. There are more murals and icons inside.

🏃 Activities

Escape summer's heat by tumbling down waterslides and splashing around at **Aqua Park** (☑ 073-881 880; http://aquapark-bg.com; ul Haydukovi 74; adult/child 5/2 lv; ⊙ 8am-8pm late May-Sep; 👧), 1km northeast of central Blagoevgrad.

🛏 Sleeping

★ **Hotel Varosha**   GUESTHOUSE $
(☑ 073-880 000; ul Bistrica 10; d/apt 35/70 lv; 🅿 ✳ 🛜) This four-room family guesthouse sits prettily at the northern end of Blagoev-

---

DON'T MISS

HIKING IN THE PIRIN MOUNTAINS

A network of marked hiking trails links huts and shelters throughout Pirin National Park, but the availability of paper maps is surprisingly patchy (even in information centres). Seek out Domino's Bansko, which has a small but detailed map in English of 12 hiking trails, and make use of the helpful http://pirinmap.com website, which has step-by-step routes and downloadable maps of the park.

The following hiking trails are especially photogenic:

Hizha Banderitsa (☑ 0898868999; dm/r from 10/15 lv) to **Baykushev's Pine** (one hour return) If you don't have much time in Pirin National Park, drive to the car park just shy of Hizha Banderitsa and take a short circuit to this 1380-year-old tree; find the viewing platform up a set of wooden stairs.

Hizha Bezbog to **Popovo Ezero** (1½ hours) Trek to this sapphire lake, the deepest in the national park. Local legends say that the tiny islet in the middle is the hat of an Orthodox priest who met an unfortunate end.

Hizha Yavorov to **Hizha Vihren** (☑ 0889834277, 07443-8279; dm from 12 lv; 9 hours) Best accessed from Razlog village. Experienced hikers can ply this route from northerly Hizha Yavorov south via the spectacular Premkata Saddle.

Hiking season runs from June to September. Spring snowmelt creates unexpected streams, while winter brings dangerous avalanches. Mountain guides are recommended in any season; these can be arranged at Bansko's **Pirin National Park Information Centre** (p336).

grad's Varosha neighbourhood. Rooms are crisply decorated with dark wood fittings, within a whitewashed traditional building whose upper floor juts out over its stone base. The owner's English-speaking daughter acts as a friendly interpreter for guests. Breakfast not included.

Hotel Korona HOTEL $

(☑ 073-831 350; www.hotelkorona.info; ul Nikola Vaptsarov 16; s/d/apt incl breakfast from 35/40/60 lv; ᴘ ✳ ☎) Located a five-minute walk from the centre, in a quieter residential area, the Korona is popular as much for its restaurant as for its lodgings. While rooms would benefit from a lick of paint, they are good value and have balconies. Larger rooms have bathtubs. Breakfast costs 5 lv.

Kristo Hotel HOTEL $$

(☑ 073-880 444; www.hotelkristo.com; ul Komitrov; s/d/apt 50/70/75 lv; ᴘ ✳ ☎) Chandeliers, four-poster beds and grand wooden furnishings combine to create Blagoevgrad's most atmospheric hotel, situated at the heart of charming Varosha district. Many rooms have invigorating views and a few have fireplaces. The hotel's excellent *mehana* is popular for weekend weddings – book ahead.

✕ Eating

Pizza Napoli PIZZA $

(☑ 073-882 388; http://pizza-napoli.bg; pl Hristo Botev 4; mains 8-12 lv; ◷ 8.30am-11pm; ☎) This swish Italian joint has a people-watching location by the main square. Its pizzas are the best choice on the menu, but Napoli also serves a range of ravioli, cannelloni and roasted meat dishes.

★ Kristo Restaurant BULGARIAN $$

(☑ 073-880 444; www.hotelkristo.com; ul Komitrov; mains 6-15 lv; ☎) The Kristo Hotel's superb restaurant presents a dilemma: the terrace overlooks lovely Vavedenie Presvetiya Bogoroditsi church, but its interior is a cosy yet classy blend of brass lamps, crimson rugs and other traditional touches. It serves Bulgarian *shashlik* (skewers), hotplates loaded with veggies and meat, and mountainous salads.

Starata Kashta BULGARIAN

(☑ 073-882 909; http://theold-house.com; ul Ivan Vazov 7; ◷ 9am-4pm Mon-Fri, from 10am Sat & Sun) In fine weather, sit in the shady courtyard; if it's chilly, dine beneath medieval

chandeliers inside. Either way, come with a hunger for plates heaving with tomatoes and *sirene* cheese, generous grilled meats, and listen out for occasional folk and other live-music acts.

☕ Drinking & Nightlife

Blagoevgrad has plenty of options when the sun goes down, from main-square cocktail bars to nightclubs secreted away along pedestrianised streets. Bars and club nights rise and fall as they compete to entice Blagoevgrad's young population. The action dies down in summer when students leave town.

★ PolCa CAFE

(☑ 0877553655; www.facebook.com/PolCa-5966 55820454566; ul Krali Marko 10; ◷ 7.30am-4pm Mon-Sat winter, to 3pm Mon-Fri summer) Blagoevgrad's friendliest cafe has a band of cheerful staff that stirs up soups, fresh salads and tasty sandwiches alongside an Italian-leaning menu of iced and classic coffees (from 1.50 lv). The family-run spot, popular with students, is managed by a small, multilingual team who happily offer local advice. It closes during high summer; check seasonal opening times on the Facebook page.

Moon CLUB

(www.facebook.com/clubxtreme; ul Vasil Koritarov 4; ◷ 11pm-6am Tue-Sat) Whether it's deep house, *chalga* (Bulgarian folk-pop) or live bands, things get raucous at this student-heavy nightclub (formerly known as Xtreme). Iron your shirt to get in, but prepare to get it hopelessly wrinkled on the dance floor, and probably drenched in cocktails. Check the Facebook page for upcoming events.

Underground BAR

(☑ 0897820513; www.facebook.com/underground. blagoevgrad; ul Dimitar Talev 5; ◷ 10.30pm-4am; ☎) Cheeky themed events – from retro '90s nights to shameless booze promotions – regularly lure students and 20-somethings to this popular brick-walled bar, just off the main square. Expect a mix of house, R&B, high-energy pop, and shots that pack a punch. Check the Facebook page for upcoming events.

Piano Bar BAR

(☑ 0898828828; ul Todor Alexandrov 23; ◷ 11pm-4am Thu-Sat; ☎) This stylish after-hours club features karaoke, occasional live rock or jazz bands, and a bubbly crowd of 20-somethings.

☆ Entertainment

For Hollywood blockbusters, visit the widescreen Cinemax (☑0876592700; www.cinemaxbg.com; pl Georgi Izmirliev Makedoncheto 9; tickets 6 lv). The well-respected Vaptsarov Theatre (☑073-885 250; www.blagoevgradtheater.eu; pl Georgi Izmirliev Makedoncheto) and Vaptsarov Chamber Opera (☑073-885 052; pl Makedonia) offer more edifying entertainment.

ℹ Information

Foreign-exchange offices can be found on ul Tsar Ivan Shishman, on the western riverbank. ATMs are near the main square and central pedestrian streets.

Internet Cafe (ul Petko Petkov 2; per hr 2 lv; ☉10.30am-11pm Mon-Sat) Look for the simple 'internet' sign, just off the main pedestrian street, to find this little place.

ℹ Getting There & Away

Blagoevgrad's adjoining **train station** (☑073-885 695; bul Sveti Dimitâr Solunski) and **bus stations** (☑073-884 009; bul Sveti Dimitâr Solunski) are about 2km from the centre; taxis from the centre cost around 4 lv.

BUS

See table for bus servicess from the main bus station. There is also one daily service to Thessaloniki, Greece (50 lv, nine hours).

TRAIN

Blagoevgrad is on the line between Sofia and Kulata (for Greece). To/from Sofia there are six daily trains (7.50 lv, 2½ to three hours), via Dupnitsa (3.60 lv, 45 minutes). Five daily services reach Sandanski (3.90 lv, one to 1½ hours) and continue to Kulata (4.60 lv, two hours) by the Greek border.

Bansko   БАНСКО

ELEV 925M / POP 9000

Buzzing Bansko is Bulgaria's premier ski resort and the most snow-sure in the country. Sunshine, thumping après-ski culture, and pistes at altitudes from 900m to 2600m draw locals, Brits and Russians each winter. As more and more hotels sprout up, overdevelopment in Bansko is a looming concern. This Pirin Mountains town gets mighty hectic during ski season; expect queuing bottlenecks on the main gondola lift from town.

Bansko isn't a faceless resort, though. The cobblestoned old town is speckled with 19th-century National Revival mansions and worthy museums. These stone-and-timber houses were buttressed by fortress-style walls, once holding hidden escape routes, protecting their inhabitants from the Turks.

Unlike many other ski towns, Bansko doesn't hibernate in summer and it makes a convenient base to explore pristine Pirin National Park, south of town. Visitors charmed by Bansko can only hope that development eases off, to preserve the character of this snow-and-sunshine town.

History

Built in the 10th century over an ancient Thracian settlement, Bansko grew to encompass several mountain villages by the 15th century. This town of craftspeople and livestock breeders bloomed as a centre of trade by the mid-18th century, thanks to its position on the caravan route between the Aegean coast and Danubian Europe. It spawned eminent traders, artisans, icon painters and woodcarvers, and Otets Paisii Hilendarski, the 18th-century monk who fuelled Bulgarian ethnic nationalism with his literary work and travels.

BUSES FROM BLAGOEVGRAD

DESTINATION	COST (LV)	DURATION	FREQUENCY
Bansko	6	1½-2hr	8 daily
Dupnitsa	4	1½hr	hourly
Melnik	7	2hr	2 daily
Plovdiv	13	4-4½hr	2 daily
Rila Village	2	45min	10 daily
Sofia	11	2-2¾hr	hourly

Bansko

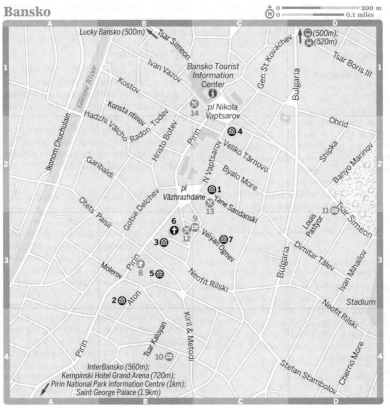

Bansko

◉ Sights

1 Bansko Permanent Icon
   Exhibition C2
2 Historical & Ethnographical
   Museum B3
3 House Museum of Neofit Rilski B3
4 House Museum of Nikola
   Vaptsarov C2
5 Museum of Otets Paisii
   Hilendarski B3
6 Sveta Troitsa Church B3
7 Velyan's House C3

◉ Activities, Courses & Tours

8 BTour B3

◉ Sleeping

9 Dvata Smarcha C3
10 Hotel Avalon B4
11 Park Hotel Gardenia D2

◉ Eating

12 Mehana Dedo Pene B3
13 Mehana Kasapinova Kâshta C2
14 Mehana Vodenitsata C1

◉ Sights

Sveta Troitsa Church   CHURCH
(Trinity Church; pl Vâzhrazhdane; ⊘7.30am-6pm)
Surrounded by 1m thick stone walls, this
19th-century church has the air of a fortress.
By contrast, the interior is a multicolour
marvel with flower-spangled ceilings and
columns painted rich shades of green and

crimson. In the churchyard, the 30m-high
clock tower (1850) is one of Bansko's most
recognisable landmarks.

Velyan's House   MUSEUM
(ul Velyan Ognev 5; 3 lv; ⊘9am-1pm & 2-5.30pm
Tue-Sat) This richly painted 18th-century
mansion stands out among Bulgaria's countless heritage properties. Admire elaborate

frescoes within the house-museum and around the courtyard, and peer at intricate wood carvings of the Debyrska School. Prettiest of all is the 'Blue Room', dedicated to the artist's wife.

House Museum of Nikola Vaptsarov
MUSEUM

(☎ 0749-88 303; pl Nikola Vaptsarov; 3 lv; ☉ 8.30am-1pm & 2-6pm) This house-museum was the birthplace of Nikola Vaptsarov (1909–42), a respected antifascist poet and activist. Influenced by communist ideology while a student, his populist writings caused his arrest and torture by the wartime fascist government; he wrote his most famous poem while awaiting execution. Period decor, photographs, documents and Vaptsarov's personal belongings are exhibited, alongside audiovisual displays about his life.

House Museum of Neofit Rilski
MUSEUM

(ul Pirin 17; 3 lv; ☉ 9am-noon & 1-5.30pm Wed-Mon) Occupying a Revival-era stone and wood building, this house-museum exhibits manuscripts by, and photos of, Rilski (1793–1881), the father of Bulgarian secular education, who created an early Bulgarian grammar textbook (1835) and a Bulgarian–Greek dictionary.

Bansko Permanent Icon Exhibition
MUSEUM

(☎ 0749-88 273; ul Yane Sandanski 3; 3 lv; ☉ 9am-noon & 1-5pm Tue-Sat) Housed within a former nunnery dating to 1749, this small museum exhibits a collection of 18th- and 19th-century icons painted by the Bansko School of art.

Museum of Otets Paisii Hilendarski
MUSEUM

(ul Otets Paisii 21; 3 lv; ☉ 9am-1pm & 2-5.30pm Tue-Sat) Commemorating the eponymous local monk, author and instigator of Bulgarian nationalism, this museum contains a chapel with a replica of the room at the Serbian Hilandarski Monastery on Greece's Mt Athos, where Paisii wrote his seminal and fulsome narrative of the history of the Slavs.

Historical & Ethnographical Museum
MUSEUM

(Radonova Kâshta; ul Aton 3; 3 lv; ☉ 9am-noon & 1-5.30pm Tue-Sat) This museum in a 19th-century mansion contains finds dating back to 6000 BC, plus antique, medieval and 19th-century National Revival–period items.

Activities

Skiing is the main activity, but there's a range of things to do, including hiking, visiting a nearby spa and riding a narrow gauge train. BTour can arrange guided day hikes to the top of Mt Vihren.

Dobrinishte, 6km south of Bansko, has mineral baths and spa retreats galore; see the **Bansko Tourist Information Center** (p336) for more information.

Skiing

Nestled at the base of Mt Vihren (2915m), Bansko enjoys long winters where snow cover sometimes last into May; snow cannons also keep pistes downy and white. The 75km of marked ski trails, at altitudes between 900m and 2600m, are best suited to intermediate skiers, though there are numerous blue (easy) pistes, a couple of kids runs too, and a fun park for skilled skiers and boarders to slalom and soar. You can zoom down 16km of uninterrupted piste from Todorka Peak to the base station.

Queuing is hard to avoid, due to reliance on Chalin Valog gondola to access the ski area. At the top of the gondola, Baderishka Polyana, another chairlift, accesses more trails at Shiligarnika. Bansko has 10 chairlifts and 16 drag lifts.

Lift passes in 2016 cost 46/32 lv per adult/child for one day or 272/132 lv for six; tariffs increase annually. There are often good deals bundling together lift passes, gear hire and winter-sports instruction.

Several outfits offer snowmobile safaris (from 90 lv for 30 minutes) and snowshoe walks (small groups from 240 lv); enquire at the **Tourist Information Center**.

InterBansko
OUTDOORS

(☎ 0899933343; www.interbansko.com; ul Pirin 92; ☉ 8am-8pm) This all-season outdoors store offers bike, ski and snowboard rental, winter-sports instruction, as well as guided summer excursions into the Bansko wilds. Gear hire starts at 30 lv per day for skis and boots (40 lv for snowboards). Guided day hikes start at 60 lv, while cultural excursions to Melnik, Plovdiv and beyond cost 80 lv to 100 lv. Opening hours can vary during summer.

✸✸ Festivals & Events

International Jazz Festival   MUSIC
(www.banskojazzfest.com; ☉early Aug) This enormously popular music festival, held from around 6 to 13 August, brings smouldering saxophonists and riotous jazz ensembles, both Bulgarian and international, to the heart of Bansko. Major events are held on an open-air stage at pl Nikola Vaptsarov, but check the website for the full program and venues.

Horizon Festival   MUSIC
(http://horizonfestival.net; ☉mid-May) A week-long festival of live music, DJ sets and hard partying (think hot tubs, flash mobs and daredevil skiing), in between late-season snowboarding or skiing in the mountains around Bansko.

Summer Theatre Festival   PERFORMING ARTS
(☉early Jul) During the first week of July, Bulgaria's biggest names in theatre come to Bansko for a celebration of the stage. Book accommodation early and check with the tourist office for a full calendar of events.

🛏 Sleeping

Bansko's abundant accommodation ranges from simple private rooms to five-star luxury hotels. Family-run guesthouses often close for periods outside the ski season, while most higher-end hotels remain open year-round. Book six months ahead for ski season, when rates can be up to 25% higher. Rates go up even higher over the Christmas–New Year holiday period.

Dvata Smarcha   PENSION $
(☎0749-82 632; ul Velyan Ognev 2; r from 35 lv) The lovely garden of this popular and reasonably priced pension encloses a well-run, friendly place with well-tended rooms and traditional home cooking. It's just south of the main square.

Saint George Palace   HOTEL $$
(☎0749-82424; www.saintgeorgepalace.com; ul Kosherinata 5; ste/apt from 66/82 lv; 🅿🛜) Roosting above Pirin National Park's northern fringe, 2.5km south of Bansko's old town, this slick hotel suits lovers of luxury and the outdoors. The buffed reception sets the tone for high-class service. There's a quality spa, ski hire on-site, and a free winter shuttle bus to the lifts. Suites and apartments are minimalist, but large and fashionably furnished.

NARROW-GAUGE RAILWAY

If you're in no hurry to press on from Bansko, consider trundling along Bulgaria's last narrow-gauge railway. This photogenic 114km route connects Bansko to Septemvri Station in five hours (6.10 lv, four daily), from where you can continue west to Sofia or east to Plovdiv and beyond.

At the two-hour mark after leaving Bansko is Avramovo Station, the highest Balkan train station at 1267m. The leisurely, visually stunning ride passes through narrow tunnels and dense forests and past bubbling rivers.

The train station ticket office only sells tickets 10 minutes before departure times, so plan ahead.

Prices rocket during winter. Breakfast not included.

Park Hotel Gardenia   HOTEL $$
(☎0749-86902; www.parkhotelgardenia.com; ul Tsar Simeon 72; s/d/apt 65/80/132 lv; ❄🛜🏊) Just 300m from Bansko's old town, the Gardenia has a superb location for travellers on a culture and hiking trip. The black, cream and beige decor of its ample-sized rooms is more business than traditional, but the expansive stone-and-wood *mehana* has a positively medieval feel. Sweetening the deal is an elliptical pool with subdued lighting, a menu of massage treatments (from 30 lv), and a swanky lobby bar.

Hotel Avalon   HOTEL $$
(☎0894488226, 0749-88 399; http://avalonhotel bansko.com; ul Eltepe 4; s/d/ste from 70/92/138 lv; 🅿@🛜) This friendly, British-run place, on a residential street just east of the old town, has airy rooms, some with jacuzzi, and ski storage. The restaurant serves a palate-pleasing variety of British pub classics, Indian dishes and mixed European fare. The owners can help organise airport transfers and local excursions. Check ahead as the hotel has an annual closure during June or July.

Lucky Bansko   HOTEL $$$
(☎879111222; http://luckybansko.com; ul Kir Blago Todev 4; ste/apt from 146/258 lv; 🅿❄@🛜🏊) Rain or shine, it's hard to go wrong with this amenity-rich aparthotel,

just off Rte 19 at the northern end of Bansko. Use of the spa and swimming pool is included in the price, while the neutrally decorated suites and apartments are equipped with fine kitchenettes and glossy modern bathrooms.

Kempinski Hotel Grand Arena
HOTEL $$$

(☎0749-88 888; www.kempinski.com; ul Pirin 96; d/ste from 200/300 lv; P✳@☎) Conveniently close to the ski lifts, this polished hotel has all the ingredients for luxury. Renovated rooms have alpine touches such as shaggy rugs; the large wellness centre has an indoor pool, steam baths and a menu of massage treatments; and there is plenty to entertain your party's younger skiers, including a kids pool and playground. Book far, far in advance: the Kempinski is deservedly popular.

Parking costs an extra 5 lv to 10 lv per day.

✗ Eating & Drinking

Bansko's traditional *mehanas* offer regional delicacies and excellent local wine, while grills and pizza places abound near the gondola in winter. Save room for *banska kapama*, a mouthwatering stew of cabbage, sausages and pork. Some *mehanas* close in summer, but there's still plenty of choice, especially around the old town.

★ Mehana Dedo Pene
BULGARIAN $$

(☎0749-88 348; www.dedopene.com; ul Aleksandar Buynov 1; mains 8-16 lv; ⊙8am-late) This homespun eatery in a 19th-century stone building is decked out with classic Balkan trimmings such as crimson tablecloths and nostalgic crockery. It serves a predictable but thoroughly satisfying range of soups, barbecued meats and claypot dishes. It's right near Sveta Troitsa church.

Mehana Kasapinova Kâshta
BULGARIAN $$

(☎0899948494; http://kasapinova-mehana.com; ul Yane Sandanski 4; mains 8-15 lv; ⊙10am-midnight) This 18th-century inn, just southeast of the main square, once entertained Bulgarian revolutionaries. These days it's hungry hikers and skiers who file in for excellent barbecue. Atmospheric touches include colourful rugs and animal skins draped on the stone walls, best admired with a glass of their locally produced wine.

Mehana Vodenitsata
BULGARIAN $$

(☎0888551110; cnr ul Hristo Botev & ul Ivan Vazov; mains 8-13 lv; ⊙11am-midnight) A traditional Bulgarian restaurant just west of pl Vaptsarov, the Vodenitsata offers hearty portions and live music. Barbecue is a speciality, and the place is popular with locals and visitors alike. It's open irregularly in summer.

Happy End
BAR

(off ul Pirin; ⊙11am-late; ☎) They forgot the '-ing', but never mind. This bar-disco, right near the ski lifts, has themed evenings and quality live acts, making it one of Bansko's favourite après-ski spots. The wood-floored outdoor bar has couches for ski-wearied travellers to slump into. Only open during ski season.

ℹ Information

Bansko Tourist Information Center (☎0749-88 580; infocenter@bansko.bg; pl Nikola Vaptsarov 1; ⊙9am-noon & 1-6pm Mon-Fri, 10am-noon & 1-6pm Sat, 10am-2pm Sun) The centrally located tourist information centre has friendly, informed, English-speaking staff who can advise on accommodation, bus and train times, cultural and outdoor activities, and upcoming events.

Pirin National Park Information Centre (☎0749-88 204; ul Pirin) This spiffy new information centre, at the southern end of ul Pirin on the border of Pirin National Park, has displays on local fauna and flora, and staff can provide tips on hiking trails. Most information is in Bulgarian, but some English and French is spoken by staff.

ℹ Getting There & Away

Bansko's adjacent **bus** (ul Patriarh Evtimii) and **train stations** (ul Patriarh Evtimii) are on the main road north of the centre, a 15-minute walk (or 4 lv taxi ride) to the old town.

BUS

Buses connect to Bansko from Sofia (15-18 lv, three hours, 15 daily), most heading via Blagoevgrad; from the latter to Bansko, it's 6 lv. Several more buses travelling to Gotse Delchev stop at Bansko.

From Bansko, six daily buses serve Blagoevgrad (6 lv, two hours). Two morning buses serve Plovdiv (14 lv, 2½ hours). Between mid-June and mid-September, three daily minibuses (4 lv) head to Hizha Banderitsa.

TRAIN

The most scenic route to Bansko is by **narrow-gauge railway**, which connects Bansko to Septemvri Station in five hours (6.10 lv, four daily), from where you continue west to Sofia or east to Plovdiv and beyond.

Melnik МЕЛНИК

POP 390

Steep sandstone pyramids form a magnificent backdrop in tiny Melnik, 20km north of the Bulgaria–Greece border. These natural rock formations, some 100m in height, resemble wizard hats and mushrooms, and they gave the village its name (the Old Slavonic word *mel* means 'sandy chalk').

But it's a 600-year-old wine culture that has made Melnik famous, and the village's wonderfully restored National Revival architecture looks all the better through a haze of cabernet sauvignon. Seeing the village only requires a day, even with an earnest ramble around its many ruins, though an overnight stop is best to soak up its peaceful charms after the tour buses leave.

History

Melnik has seen Thracian, Roman, Byzantine and early Bulgarian rule. Few traces remain, except some ancient pottery and the Roman bridge at the entrance to town. After an Ottoman doldrums, it had a resurgence during the National Revival period, helped along by a lively wine and tobacco trade. The once-notable Greek population among Melnik's 20,000 inhabitants was forcibly relocated by the Greek army in the 1912–13 Balkan Wars, when the village was largely burned.

◉ Sights & Activities

Melnik's main draws including rambling around town, admiring the historic architecture, and tasting the local wine. The grand old houses, many jutting out from cliffs, feature overhanging upper floors and handsome wooden balconies, most with cool stone basements for wine storage. Officially, all buildings must be built and/or renovated in the Bulgarian National Revival style.

Kordopulov House MUSEUM
(☑0887776917, 0877576120; www.kordopulova-house.com; 3 lv; ◎9.30am-6.30pm Apr-Sep, to 4pm Oct-Mar) Reportedly Bulgaria's largest Revival-era building, this whitewashed and wooden mansion beams down from a cliff face at the eastern end of Melnik's main road. Dating to 1754, the four-storey mansion was formerly the home of a prestigious wine merchant family. Its naturally cool rooms steep visitors in luxurious period flavour, from floral stained-glass windows to

Oriental-style fireplaces and a sauna. There are touches of intrigue, too, such as the secret cupboard that allowed the whole family to eavesdrop on wine-trading deals.

After visiting the house, descend into its enormous underground wine cellar (tastings available), with 180m of labyrinthine passageways.

Museum of Wine MUSEUM
(www.muzei-na-vinoto.com; ul Melnik 91; 5 lv; ◎10am-7pm) Learn the history and tools of Melnik's winemaking trade; ogle 400-plus bottles of wine; and work your way through a tasting menu at this fun museum attached to the Hotel Bulgari. Tour groups occasionally dominate the museum in summer, outside which time the opening hours can be erratic.

Wine Tasting

Melnik is awash in wines that have been celebrated for well over 600 years. Sip before you buy at excellent wine shops such as **Damianitza** (☑0746-30090; www.damianitza.bg; ◎11am-6pm), and enjoy high-quality local wine with a view at **Shestaka**.

Be warned: even in Melnik it's all too easy to end up with a glass of substandard stuff. Avoid plastic bottles on sale by roadsides and be wary of super-cheap house wines (some are frightful).

Shestaka Winery WINE
(Manolev Winery; ☑0887545795; www.shestaka.com; 2 lv; ◎9am-dusk) For atmospheric adventures in *degustatsia* (wine tasting), clamber up the cobblestones to 120-year-old Shestaka ('six-fingered') Winery; it's named after the founder, Iliya Manolev, who had an extra digit (as does his modern-day descendant Mitko). There is a wine cellar dug into the rocks, plus a shady hut with tables and chairs outside, which peer towards Melnik's sandstone pillars.

Mitko can help to organise longer winery tours around Melnik; enquire via the website. Shestaka Winery is along the hillside trail between the Bolyaskata Kâshta ruins and the Kordopulov House. Accommodation is also available (doubles 35 lv).

Churches & Ruins

Of Melnik's original 70 churches only 40, mostly ruined ones, survive. The still-standing 19th-century **Sveti Antoni Church** is dedicated to the patron saint of the sick; in the unenlightened past, the mentally ill would be brought here to be cured of demonic possession. A signposted path leads to the ruined Sveti Nikolai Church (1756), and to the Despot Slav's ruined Slavova Krepost. Both are visible from the Bolyaskata Kâshta, a 10th-century ruin of one of Bulgaria's oldest homes. The trail veers east along the ridge about 300m to the ruined Sveta Zona Chapel.

The Turkish Baths are difficult to recognise, standing just before the Mehana Mencheva Kâshta tavern. Just below the Kordopulov House, the 15th-century Sveta Varvara Church has retained its walls and floor.

🎎 Festivals & Events

Melnik owes so much to Sveti Trifon, patron saint of the vine, that Trifon Zarezan Festival (☉ 1 Feb) is celebrated twice: once on 1 February, and then again during the bigger event, Golden Grapes Festival (☉ 2nd weekend Feb).

🛏 Sleeping

Melnik's popularity among tourists has allowed a healthy, mostly midrange array of hotels and guesthouses to flourish; book ahead in summer. Private rooms are a budget, no-frills option (15 lv to 20 lv per person), usually with shared bathrooms; look for English-language 'Rooms' signs.

Sveti Nikola Hotel　　　　　　　HOTEL $
(☑ 07437-2211; http://melnik-svnikola.com; d 55; P ❋ ☎) At Melnik's eastern end, near the Historical Museum, Sveti Nikola's 10 crisply furnished rooms huddle above its stone-walled *mehana*.

★ Hotel Bolyarka　　　　　　　HOTEL $$
(☑ 07437-2383; www.melnikhotels.com; ul Melnik 34; s/d/apt 40/60/100 lv; P ❋ @ ☎) The right blend of old-world nostalgia and modern comfort has made this one of Melnik's favourite hotels. The Bolyarka has elegant rooms, a snug lobby bar, a Finnish-style sauna and one of Melnik's best restaurants. For a touch of added charm, reserve a deluxe apartment (130 lv) with fireplace.

Hotel Melnik　　　　　　　　　HOTEL $$
(☑ 0879131459, 07437-2272; www.hotelmelnik.com; ul Vardar 2; s/d/apt 40/60/120 lv; P ❋ ☎) This pleasant hotel is shaded by fig and cherry trees, and peeps down over Melnik's main road. White-walled rooms with simple furnishings don't quite match the old-world reception and the *mehana* with a bird's-eye view. But it's great value, smartly run, and the location – up a cobbled lane, on the right as you enter the village – is convenient whether you arrive by car or bus.

Lumparova Kâshta　　　　GUESTHOUSE $$
(☑ 07437-2218; www.lumparovamelnik.com; ul Melnik 102; s/d 50/100 lv; P) Experience Bulgarian Revival style with a modern twist at this atmospheric guesthouse, which features unique stained glass and wall frescoes created by local artists. It's up a steep path starting behind the village.

WORTH A TRIP

ROZHEN MONASTERY

Standing serenely in the hills 7km north of Melnik, Rozhen Monastery (Birth of the Virgin Mary Monastery; ☉ 7am-7pm) FREE has admirable 16th-century frescoes and a holy icon of the Virgin Mary. Its most significant building, the Nativity of the Virgin Church (1600), contains stained-glass windows, 200-year-old murals, woodcarvings and icon-ostases, with the icon of the Virgin its main focus for pilgrims. The monastery attracts fewer tourists than other monsteries in Bulgaria, so dress modestly and keep chatter at low volume.

First built in 1217, Rozhen Monastery was largely reconstructed in the late 16th century after a fire. Today's monastery was mostly built between 1732 and the late 18th century. Believers say the icon housed here was painted by St Luke, and that it miraculously survived being hurled into the sea, floating upright.

Treat yourself to a night at Hotel Rojena (☑ 0878832192, 0878424904; www.hotel rojena.net; Rozhen; d/tr/apt from 55/80/140 lv; P ❋ ☎ ❄) , tucked away on a quiet road 1.5km from Rozhen Monastery. Most rooms overlook an enticing outdoor pool, which is surrounded by lounge chairs, while the *mehana* (tavern) has shaded outdoor tables near a trickling fountain.

✕ Eating

Melnik's best eats are at hotel or pension restaurants, though other worthy spots abound. Try regional wine, *banitsa*, a local speciality, and mountain river trout.

Mehana Mencheva Kâshta　　BULGARIAN $
(📞 07437-2339; www.melnik-mehana.com; mains 6-11 lv; ⊙10am-11.30pm) This tavern has a lovely upper porch overlooking the main street down towards the end of the village. It's popular with locals and does the full run of Bulgarian dishes, with an emphasis on barbecued meats and yoghurt-slathered salads.

⭐**Mehana Chavkova Kâshta**　BULGARIAN $$
(📞 0893505090; www.themelnikhouse.com; 7-12 lv) Sit beneath 500-year-old trees and watch Melnik meander past at this superb spot. Like many places in town, grilled meats and Bulgarian dishes are specialities (try the *satch,* a sizzling flat pan of meat and vegetables); the atmosphere and friendly service give it an extra nudge above the rest. It's 200m from the bus stop, along the main road.

Chinarite Restaurant　　BULGARIAN $$
(📞 0878688328; http://chinarite.cbbbg.com; mains 7-12 lv; ⊙10am-10pm) Midway up the main road, by the bridge, Chinarite's folk-music soundtrack and sword-like *shish* kebab skewers will draw you in. Its summer garden is a relaxing spot to slurp a cool *tarator* soup (cucumber, garlic and yoghurt) or mull over a variety of Melnik wines.

ⓘ Information

There's an ATM by the Hotel Bulgari, past the central square, where the post office stands.

Melnik Tourist Information Centre (Obshtina Building; ⊙9am-5pm) Located behind the bus stop, on the *obshtina* (municipality) building's upper floor, this centre advises on accommodation and local activities, though opening times can be spotty (especially outside summer). Bus and train timetables are posted outside.

ⓘ Getting There & Away

Direct buses connect Melnik with Sofia (17 lv, 4½ hours, one daily) and Blagoevgrad (7 lv, two hours, two daily). Two daily minibuses go from Sandanski to Melnik, continuing to Rozhen, though there may be insufficient seats if local shoppers are out in force.

By train, the closest station is Damyanitsa, 12km west.

BULGARIAN THRACE

Named for the ancient Indo-Europeans who galloped across its valleys and plains, modern Thrace expands across central Bulgaria, northeastern Greece and northern Turkey. Bulgarian Thrace retains the fertile wine country that kept ancient Thracians well quenched, with remote villages and monasteries scattered in between.

Bulgaria's second city, Plovdiv, is reason enough to explore Thrace: its Roman ruins and revitalised arts scene combine to make it arguably the country's most interesting city. Frescoed Bachkovo Monastery, 30km south, comes a close second. In recent years enterprising locals have boosted attractions beyond these well-touristed spots; world-class wineries in Brestovitsa and beautifully preserved historic sites in Perushtitsa reward travellers veering off the beaten track.

Plovdiv　　ПЛОВДИВ

POP 341,560

With an easy grace, Plovdiv mingles invigorating nightlife among millennia-old ruins. Like Rome, Plovdiv straddles seven hills; but as Europe's oldest continuously inhabited city, it's far more ancient. It is best loved for its romantic old town, packed with colourful and creaky 19th-century mansions that are now house-museums, galleries and guesthouses.

But cobblestoned lanes and National Revival–era nostalgia are only part of the story. Bulgaria's cosmopolitan second city has always been hot on the heels of Sofia, and a stint as European Capital of Culture 2019 seems sure to give Plovdiv the edge. Music and art festivals draw increasing crowds, while renovations in the Kapana artistic quarter and Tsar Simeon Gardens have given the city new confidence. Once an amiable waystation between Bulgaria and Greece or Turkey, the city has flowered into a destination in its own right – and one that should be firmly stamped on any itinerary through central Bulgaria.

History

The remains of settlements dating to 7000 BC have been discovered around Plovdiv. Thracians settled here around 5000 BC, building a fortress at Nebet Tepe in the old town, calling it Eumolpias. Philip II of

Plovdiv

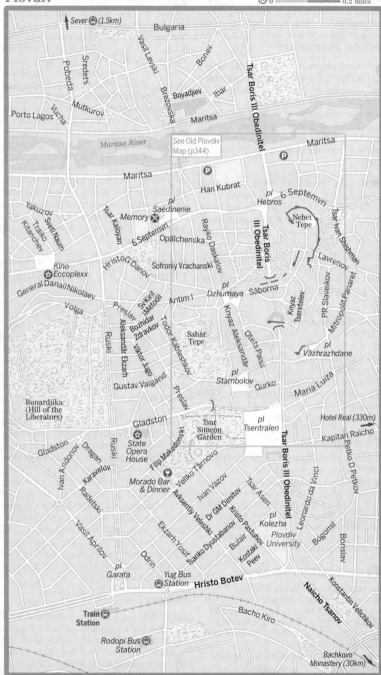

0 — 400 m
0 — 0.2 miles

↑ Sever (1.5km)

Bulgaria

Vasil Levski
Bonev
Boyadjiev
Ibar
Brezovska
Tsar Boris III Obedinitel
Maritsa

Porto Lagos
Pobeda
Vucha
Sredets
Mutkurov

Maritsa River

See Old Plovdiv
Map (p344)

Maritsa

Maritsa

Han Kubrat

pl
Hebros
6 Septemvri

Yakuzov
Sveti Naum
Traiko
Kitanchev
Tsar Kaloyan
Memory
pl
Saedinenie
6 Septemvri
Opălchenska
Rayko Daskalov

Nebet
Tepe

Tsar Boris
III Obedinitel

Tsar Ivan Shishman

Lavrenov

Kino
Eccoplexx
General Danail Nikolaev
HristoG Danov
Sofroniy Vrachanski
Antim I

Sv Kiril
i Metodii
Preslav
pl
Dzhumaya
Săborna

Knyaz
Tseretelev

PR Slaveikov

Mitropolit Panaret

Volga
Ruski
Aleksandăr Ekzarh
Bozhidar
Zdravkov
Viktor Jugo
Todor Kableshkov

Sahat
Tepe

Knyaz Aleksandăr
Otets Paisii

pl
Văzhrazhdane

Bunardjika
(Hill of the
Liberators)

Gustav Vaigand
Preslav

pl
Stambolov
Gurko

Maria Luiza

Gladston

Tsar
Simeon
Garden

pl
Tsentralen

Hotel Real (330m)

Kapitan Raicho

Gladston
Ivan A donov
Dragan
Karavelov
Ruski
State
Opera
House
Filip Makedonski

Morado Bar
& Dinner
Veliko Tărnovo
Ivan Vazov
Tsar Asen
Petko D Petkov
Leonardo da Vinci

Radetski
Vasil Aprilov
Ekzarh Yosif
Auksenty Veleshki
Dr GM Dimitov
Kristo Pastuhov
Tsanko Dyustabanov
Bulair
Kostaki
Peev
pl
Kolezha
Plovdiv
University
Bogomil
Borislav

Odrin
pl
Garata
Yug Bus
Station
Hristo Botev

Konstantin Velichkov

**Train
Station**
Bacho Kiro

Naicho Tsanov

Rodopi Bus
Station

Bachkovo
Monastery (30km)

Macedon (father of Alexander the Great) extended the settlement, humbly naming it Philippopolis in 342 BC. He strengthened the existing fortress, making Philippopolis an important military centre. However, the ruins that survive today largely come from the Roman annexation (AD 46) and thereafter. The Romans built streets, towers and aqueducts for the new city, named Trimontium ('three-hilled'). Unfortunately, Goths and Huns plundered and destroyed it in the mid-3rd century and in AD 447 respectively, and Trimontium languished. The Bulgar Khan Krum seized it in 812 and renamed it Pupulden, making it an important strategic outpost of the First Bulgarian Empire (681–1018).

Pupulden, or Philippopolis as the Byzantines called it, was controlled by Constantinople, Bulgars and even Latin Crusaders over the following centuries. After various skirmishes, the Ottomans conquered it in 1365, renaming the city Filibe. The city thrived and its merchants grew wealthy. Some of Bulgaria's finest and most lavish townhouses were built during the Bulgarian National Revival period. In the late 1850s, literary reformer Hristo Danov taught in the city and would later found the city's first publishing house.

While most of Bulgaria was freed following the Russo-Turkish War of 1877, the ensuing Congress of Berlin left Plovdiv and the south in Turkish hands. Only in 1885 did Plovdiv join the Bulgarian state. Industrial expansion came rapidly in the following century, with tobacco factories and fruit farms booming during WWII. More than 1500 of the city's Jewish citizens were rescued from wartime deportation.

◉ Sights

Plovdiv's appeal derives from its old town, largely restored to its mid-19th-century appearance and packed with house-museums and galleries. Unlike old towns in many other cities, Plovdiv's still has eminent artists living and working within its tranquil confines. The neighbourhood boasts Thracian, Roman, Byzantine and Bulgarian antiquities, the most impressive being the Roman amphitheatre. South of here, the modern centre features a shop-lined pedestrian mall, ul Knyaz Aleksandâr, which passes over the Roman Stadium to a square with fountains.

★**Roman Amphitheatre**   HISTORIC SITE
(Map p344; ul Hemus; adult/student 5/2 lv; ⊙ 9am-6pm Apr-Oct, to 5pm Nov-Mar) Plovdiv's magnificent 2nd-century AD amphitheatre, built during the reign of Emperor Trajan, was uncovered during a freak landslide in 1972. It once held about 6000 spectators. Now largely restored, it's one of Bulgaria's most magical venues, once again hosting large-scale special events and concerts. Visitors can admire the amphitheatre for free from several look-outs along ul Hemus, or pay admission for a scarper around.

Balabanov House   MUSEUM
(Map p344; ☑ 032-627 082; ul K Stoilov 57; 3 lv; ⊙ 9am-6pm Apr-Oct, to 5.30pm Nov-Mar) One of Plovdiv's most beautiful National Revival–era mansions, Balabanov House is an enjoyable way to experience old town nostalgia as well as contemporary art. The house was faithfully reconstructed in 19th-century style during the 1970s. The lower floor has an impressive collection of paintings by local artists, while upper rooms are decorated with antiques and elaborately carved ceilings.

Tsar Simeon Garden   PARK
(Map p344) Plovdiv's prettiest place to stroll, Tsar Simeon Garden was sculpted by Swiss architect Lucien Chevalas in 1892; he's now lovingly referred to as the 'minister of flowers'. In recent years the park's Goddess Demeter Fountain and central Viennese-style pavilion have been carefully restored. Tsar Simeon's Lake with the Singing Fountains combines light and water effects; arrive in the park's southwestern corner on a summer Thursday, Friday or Saturday evening around 9pm for the free show.

Atanas Krastev House   GALLERY
(Red Pony Art Gallery; Map p344; ☑ 032-625 792; http://redpony-bg.com; ul Dr Chomakov 5a; 2 lv; ⊙ 10am-6pm Mar-Nov) Close to Nebet Tepe hill, this late 18th-century house was the residence of local painter and conservationist Atanas Krastev until his death in 2003. Krastev's impact on preserving and showcasing Plovdiv's cultural riches has left him fondly remembered as 'mayor of the old town'. His self-portraits and personal collection of (mostly) abstract 20th-century Bulgarian paintings are displayed inside the beautifully furnished house, along with

PLOVDIV & THE SOUTHERN MOUNTAINS PLOVDIV

personal mementos. The garden is worth an amble for its red pony murals and scattered artefacts.

Ethnographical Museum
MUSEUM

(Map p344; ☑ 032-624 261; www.ethnograph. info; ul Dr Chomakov 2; adult/student 5/2 lv; ☺ 9am-6pm Tue-Sun May-Oct, to 5pm Nov-Apr) Even if you don't have time to step inside, it would be criminal to leave Plovdiv's old town without glancing into the courtyard of this stunning National Revival–era building. Well-manicured flower gardens surround a navy-blue mansion, ornamented with golden filigree and topped with a distinctive peaked roof. There is more to admire inside, especially the upper floor's sunshine-yellow walls and carved wooden ceiling, hovering above displays of regional costumes. The ground-floor displays of agrarian instruments are a shade less interesting.

Church of Sveti Konstantin & Elena
CHURCH

(Map p344; ul Sâborna 24; ☺ 8am-8pm Apr-Oct, to 5pm Nov-Mar) This is Plovdiv's oldest church and one of its most beloved. Dedicated to Emperor Constantine the Great and his mother, Helena, it was built on the spot where two Christian martyrs were beheaded in the year 304. Admire marvellous frescoes and a colourful carved ceiling in the exterior colonnade, and a baroque-style Viennese iconostasis and religious art spanning the 15th to 18th centuries inside. The separate bell tower, bright white with a coppery cap, stands 13m tall.

Archaeological Museum
MUSEUM

(Map p344; ☑ 032-633 106; www.archaeological museumplovdiv.org; pl Saedinenie 1; adult 5 lv, child under 7yr 5 free; ☺ 10am-6pm Tue-Sun) This 100,000-item museum is a tour de force of Thracian and Roman artefacts, as well as icons and ecclesiastical artefacts from recent centuries. Most dazzling is the weighty Thracian gold work, part of the Panagyurishte collection, Bulgaria's biggest-ever haul of ancient gold. The museum's most arresting space is a corridor flooded with natural light, which houses Roman-era statues and mosaics. Its enormous centrepiece is a 3rd-century mosaic of a river god encircled by geometric designs.

Ruins of Eumolpias
RUINS

(Map p344; ul Dr Chomakov; ☺ 24hr) [FREE] Some 203m high in the old town, a hill with spectacular views reveals sparse ruins of Eumolpias, a Thracian settlement in 5000 BC. The fortress and surrounding town enjoyed a strategic position, later bolstered by Macedonians, Romans, Byzantines, Bulgarians and Turks, who named it Nebet Tepe (Prayer Hill).

Church of Sveta Bogoroditsa
CHURCH

(Map p344; ☑ 032-623 265; ul Sâborna 40; ☺ 7am-7pm) Painted a fetching shade of butter-cream yellow, this three-nave church looks out proudly from a stone staircase at the base of the old town. Built in 1844 on the site of a 9th-century shrine, its 12th-century incarnations long ago sacked by the Ottomans, the church now contains icons and colourful murals, and bears an inscription of thanks to Bulgaria's liberators.

Sveta Marina Church
CHURCH

(Map p344; ul Dr Vulkovich 7; ☺ 8am-7pm) A little-visited 16th-century gem, Sveta Marina Church has suberb Old Testament murals on its outer walls, depicting scenes from Adam, Eve and a mischievous snake to a very cross Moses dashing stone tablets. The 17m-high wooden bell tower, dating to 1870, is unique in Plovdiv. The shadowy interior harbours an intricate 170-year-old iconostasis.

Hindlian House
MUSEUM

(Map p344; ☑ 032-628 998; ul Artin Gidikov 4; adult/student 5/1 lv; ☺ 9am-6pm Apr-Oct, to 5.30pm Nov-Mar) Once owned by merchant Stepan Hindlian, this opulent house was built between 1835 and 1840. It's full of exquisite period furniture and walls painted with real and imaginary landscapes of Venice, Alexandria and Constantinople. The magnificent panelled ceilings and 'Oriental-style' marble bathroom, with its domed ceiling and skylight, are high points.

Stadium of Philippopolis
HISTORIC SITE

(Map p344; ☑ 0876662881; www.ancient-stadium -plovdiv.eu; ☺ 9am-6pm) [FREE] While the once-huge 2nd-century Roman stadium is mostly hidden under a pedestrian mall, there are stairways from different sides allowing for exploration. A new on-site 3D movie (adult/student 6/3, child free; 10 screenings daily) offers an immersive experience of the stadium's glory days as a venue for gladiator matches.

GUIDED TOURS

If you're looking for a driver to help you explore Plovdiv and beyond, knowledgable **Hristo Petrov** (☑ 0879694681; hristo.petroff@yahoo.com) can take small groups on day trips by car. A typical rate for visiting Buzludzha in the central mountains from Plovdiv is around 150 lv.

For a tour with a personal touch, licensed guide **Svetlomir 'Patrick' Penov** (☑ 0887364711; www.guide-bg.com) crafts superb itineraries around Bulgaria for groups of up to four people. Tours can cover anything from Thracian treasures and wineries to horse riding, mountain biking and authentic village life. Longer trips can explore beyond Bulgaria's borders. Patrick has well over two decades of experience and can conduct tours in English or Spanish. Average daily rates are 200 lv to 250 lv.

Regional History Museum   MUSEUM
(Map p344; ☑ 032-623 378; ul Lavrenov 1; 2 lv; ⊙ 9.30am-6.30pm Wed-Mon, 12.30-6pm Tue Apr-Oct, to 5pm Nov-Mar) Plovdiv's Historical Museum concentrates on the 1876 April Uprising and the massacre of Bulgarians at Batak, which directly led to the Russian declaration of war on Turkey the following year. Built in 1848 by Dimitâr Georgiadi, the museum is also called the Georgiadi Kâshta.

City Gallery of Fine Arts   GALLERY
(Map p344; ☑ 032-635 322; www.galleryplovdiv. com; ul Sâborna 14a; 3lv; ⊙ 9.30am-6pm Apr-Oct, from 10am Sat & Sun Apr-Oct, 9.30am-5.30pm Mon-Fri, from 10am Sat & Sun Nov-Mar) Occupying an 1881 girls gymnasium, this gallery contains more than 7000 artistic works by 19th- and 20th-century masters, including Nikolai Pavlovich, Konstantin Velichkov and Georgi Danchov.

Permanent Exhibition
of Dimitar Kirov   GALLERY
(Map p344; ☑ 032-635 381; Kiril Nektariev 17; adult/student 5/1 lv; ⊙ 9am-6pm Mon-Fri Apr-Oct, to 5pm Nov-Mar) Housed in a grand old-town mansion where Plovdiv's budding artists worked in the 1960s, this special place celebrates the life and works of Dimitar Kirov, who died in 2008. Arguably Plovdiv's most original artist, Kirov produced work marked by bold and vivid uses of colour, from mosaics to abstracts.

Milyo Statue   STATUE
(Map p344) 'Milyo the idiot', as he's affectionately known, was a local prankster and mimic, fondly remembered in Plovdiv's shopping precinct in the form of a statue. Keep your voice low: Milyo cups his ear to eavesdrop on shoppers' conversations.

Icon Gallery   MUSEUM
(Map p344; ul Sâborna 22; adult/student 2/1 lv; ⊙ 9.30am-6pm Mon-Fri, 10am-6pm Sat & Sun) This small museum beside the Church of Sveti Konstantin & Elena has a sublime display of icons from the 15th century onwards.

Tsanko Lavrenov &
Mexican Art Exhibitions   GALLERY
(Map p344; ☑ 032-628 745; ul Artin Gidikov 11; adult/student 3/1 lv; ⊙ 9.30am-12.30pm & 1-5.30pm Mon-Fri, from 10am Sat) For something completely different, this time-warp 1846 house has displays of 1970s Mexican woodcuts, serigraphs and copies of pre-Columbian art downstairs (a gift to the communist state in 1981), and paintings by local artist Tsanko Lavrenov upstairs.

Zlatyu Boyadjiev Gallery   GALLERY
(Chomakov House; Map p344; ☑ 032-635 308; ul Sâborna 18; adult/student 5/2 lv; ⊙ 9am-6pm Apr-Oct, to 5.30pm Nov-Mar) Get two famous Bulgarians for the price of one at this tasteful National Revival–era mansion. Seventy-two paintings by Plovdiv native Zlatyu Boyadjiev (1903–76) are exhibited here, many idealising the Bulgarian peasantry. The figure after whom the house itself is named, Dr Stoyan Chomakov, fought against Ottoman domination and later bequeathed this house to the city of Plovdiv for posterity.

Dzhumaya Mosque   MOSQUE
(Map p344; pl Dzhumaya; ⊙ 6am-11pm) Bulgaria's first working mosque, this unmissable Ottoman building in the middle of Plovdiv's pedestrianised shopping zone was originally built in 1364. It was demolished and rebuilt in the mid-15th century. It is possible to enter (dress modestly), though the interior doesn't match up to the mosque's grand history and imposing 23m minaret.

Old Plovdiv

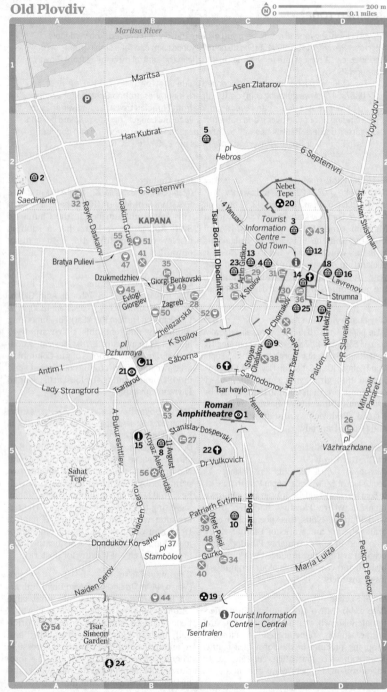

Maritsa River

N 0 ____ 200 m
0 ____ 0.1 miles

Maritsa

Asen Zlatarov

Han Kubrat

6 Septemvri

pl Hebros

6 Septemvri

5

2

pl Saedinenie

32

Rayko Daskalov

Ioakim Gruev

KAPANA

Tsar Boris III Obedinitel

4 Yanuari

Nebet Tepe

20

Tourist Information Centre – Old Town

3

43

Bratya Pulievi

55

51

41

47

35

Dzukmedzhiev

Giorgi Benkovski

49

45

Evlogi Giorgiev

Zagreb

50

28

52

Zhelezarska

K Stoilov

13

Artin Gidikov

23

4

K Stoilov

29

33

31

30

Dr Chomakov

42

Knyaz Tseretelev

12

14

7

48

16

Lavrenov

Strumna

36

25

17

Kiril Nektariev

PR Slaveikov

Palden

Tsar Ivan Shishman

Voyvodov

6 Septemvri

pl Dzhumaya

11

21

Sâborna

6

Stoyan Chalâkov

9

38

T Samodomov

Tsar Ivaylo

Hemus

Antim I

Lady Strangford

Tsaribrod

A Bukureshtliev

Roman Amphitheatre **1**

Stanislav Dospevski

53

27

15

Knyaz Aleksandâr

8

11 August

56

Dr Vulkovich

22

Sahat Tepe

Naiden Gerov

Patriarh Evtimii

Otets Paisii

39

48

Gurko

40

34

10

Tsar Boris

26

pl Vâzhrazhdane

Mitropolit Panaret

Petko D Petkov

46

Maria Luiza

Dondukov Korsakov

37

pl Stambolov

Naiden Gerov

44

19

54

Tsar Simeon Garden

24

pl Tsentralen

Tourist Information Centre – Central

Old Plovdiv

Cultural Center Thrakart   MUSEUM
(Map p344; ☑032-631 303; http://trakart.org/
museum; Podlez Arhaeologiski; 5 lv; ☺9am-7pm
Apr-Oct, to 6pm Nov-Mar) Visible through floor-
to-ceiling windows in the Tsar Obedinitel
underpass, Cultural Center Thrakart contains extensive Roman floor mosaics and
various artefacts from Roman (and earlier)
times. Concerts are performed on the centre's small stage.

Nedkovich House   MUSEUM
(Map p344; ☑032-626 216; ul Lavrenov 3; 3 lv;
☺9am-6pm Mon-Fri Apr-Oct, to 5.30pm Nov-Mar)
This butterscotch-coloured 1863 mansion
has a leafy courtyard and a marble fountain.
Its interior design showcases the European
classical and baroque styles favoured by its
former owner, a moneyed merchant from
Karlovo.

Roman Odeon   RUINS
(Map p344) Constructed at the end of the
1st century AD, the Odeon was once the seat
of the city council. It now hosts occasional
performances in its small, reconstructed
amphitheatre.

City Art Gallery   GALLERY
(Map p344; ☑032-635 322; www.galleryplovdiv.
com; ul Knyaz Aleksandâr 15; adult/student 4/2
lv; ☺9am-12.30pm & 1-5.30pm Mon-Fri, 10am-
5.30pm Sat) This branch of the City Gallery
of Fine Arts holds temporary exhibitions of
abstract art, housed within one of Plovdiv's
first Bulgarian Renaissance schools.

Center for Contemporary Art   GALLERY
(Chifte Banya; Map p344; www.arttoday.org/
site/news.php; pl Hebros; adult/student 2/1 lv;
☺10am-1pm & 1.30-6.30pm Tue-Sun) A stocky
16th-century Turkish bathhouse now

NATIONAL REVIVAL MANSIONS

Plovdiv's old town boasts some of the finest and best-restored 19th-century mansions in Bulgaria. These baroque-style houses were originally constructed during the National Revival period, a post-Ottoman era where Bulgarian art, literature and architecture flourished. They are instantly recognisable by their overhanging upper storeys, jutting eaves and bright exterior paintwork. Inside, they have finely carved woodwork (including gloriously intricate ceiling carvings) as well as painted wall decorations and ornamental niches. Many of these lovely buildings have been restored as house-museums with original 19th-century furniture and artwork, often with displays about local culture and history; they are well worth peeping inside, to get a flavour of the era. Still others have been renovated as restaurants and hotels, allowing you to bed down in grand Revival style.

features irregular, rotating displays of contemporary art. Free entry on Thursdays.

★ Festivals & Events

Kapana Fest CULTURAL
(www.facebook.com/kapanafest; ⊙ early Jun) Plovdiv's artiest neighbourhood hosts street parties, open-air musical performances and late-night carousing during this vibrant five-day festival of culture. Expect anything from conceptual art to folk costume fashion shows, and you can count on a lot of bunting. Check the Facebook page or ask at the tourist office about events.

Night of the Galleries ART
(http://night.bg; ⊙ last Fri in Sep) Plovdiv's heritage mansions and venerable galleries make an especially delightful stomping ground during the Europe-wide Night of the Galleries, where museums fling open their doors until the early hours of the morning and experimental art performances illuminate the Kapana district.

Unification Day CULTURAL
(⊙ 6 Sep) The nationwide anniversary of Bulgaria's 1885 unification with Ottoman province Eastern Roumelia is toasted with aplomb, and festivities are especially vigorous in Plovdiv, where the historic declaration was made. Events include a military roll-call in the main square, firework displays, and plenty of *rakia*.

International Folklore Festival CULTURAL
(cultura@plovdiv.bg; ⊙ 1st weekend Aug) Witness open-air Bulgarian folklore performances alongside traditional song and dance from a medley of other countries at this popular five-day festival.

Verdi Festival PERFORMING ARTS
(⊙ early Jun) Opera performances are held in Plovdiv's Roman amphitheatre during this two-week festival.

International Festival of Chamber Music MUSIC
(http://chamberfestivalplovdiv.com; ⊙ mid-Jun) Local and international chamber music acts perform during this long-running summer festival. Events unfold in atmospheric locations, including Plovdiv's Ethnographic Museum.

⊨ Sleeping

Plovdiv has abundant choice, from polished hostels to snug guesthouses and right up to chic high-end hotels. It's only quality campgrounds that seem to be lacking, with some out-of-town accommodation complexes phasing out their camping facilities. Prices increase during May and September when the international fairs are on. Book well in advance for events such as Plovdiv Jazz Festival and Kapana Fest.

Hikers Hostel HOSTEL $
(Map p344; ✆ 0896764854; www.hikers-hostel.org; ul Sâborna 53; 18-/12-bed dm 18/20 lv; @ ☎) In a mellow old-town location, Hikers has wood-floored dorms and standard hostel perks such as a laundry and a shared kitchen. Bonuses such as a garden lounge, hammocks and mega-friendly staff make it a worthy option. Staff can help organise excursions to Bachkovo Monastery (southern mountains), Buzludzha Monument (central mountains) and more. Off-site private rooms (from 43 lv) are available in the Kapana area.

Hotel Elite
HOTEL $

(Map p344; ☏032-624 537; ul Rayko Daskalov 53; s/d from 45/49 lv; ❄️ 📶) The name rather overstates its appeal, but Elite offers eight good-value rooms, scattered across four floors of a narrow building, just west of the Kapana bar district. Breakfast not included.

★ Hostel Old Plovdiv
HOSTEL $$

(Map p344; ☏032-260 925; www.hostelold plovdiv.com; ul Chetvarti Yanuari 3; dm/s/d/tr/q 26/60/90/110/130 lv; 🅿️📶) This marvellous old building (1868) is more akin to a boutique historical hotel than a run-of-the-mill hostel. Remarkably restored by charismatic owner Hristo Giulev and his wife, this genial place smack bang in the middle of the old town is all about warm welcomes and old-world charm.

Hotel Evmolpia
HOTEL $$

(Map p344; ☏0888636370; www.hotelevmolpia. com; ul Krikor Azaryan 4; d from 98 lv; ❄️📶) Newly opened in 2016, this perfectly positioned hotel is the brainchild of the team behind another charismatic spot in the old town, Hostel Old Plovdiv (p347). Hotel Evmopia's raison d'être is faithful representation of Plovdiv's Revival period: it brims with reverently chosen antiques and traditional handicrafts.

Old Plovdiv House
APARTMENT $$

(Map p344; ☏032-629 032; www.oldplovdiv bg.com; ul Georgi Benkovski 15; r/ste/apt from 50/90/110 lv; ❄️📶) These sleek suites and apartments have glossy modern bathrooms and supportive mattresses, right in the heart of lively Kapana district. One- and two-bedroom apartments have ample kitchens and plenty of sofa space to sink into, much needed after a day of navigating Plovdiv's shoe-wrecking ancient ruins and cobblestoned streets. Breakfast not included.

Dali Art Hotel
BOUTIQUE HOTEL $$

(Map p344; ☏032-621 530; www.hoteldali.hit. bg; ul Otets Paisii 11; d/ste from 60/74 lv; 🅿️❄️📶) This intimate boutique hotel, off the pedestrianised shopping street, has eight rooms furnished with the right mix of period style and modern amenities, plus reproductions of Salvador Dalí paintings. Though it's a little worn, furnishings with subtly surrealist flourishes make the hotel worthy of its name. Friendly service leaves the strongest impression. Ask ahead about the few available parking spots.

Hotel Real
HOTEL $$

(☏032-278 130; www.real-hotel.com; ul Georgi Voyteh 2; s/d/apt 78/89/117 lv; 🅿️❄️📶) If you're looking for a soft landing in Plovdiv, this is one of the most polished midrange hotels around. Rooms are somewhat beige, but comfortable. Service is very professional and Real has a transit-friendly location: just off the main road between Plovdiv and the airport, and less than 2km from Yug bus station. Breakfasts are made to order from a small menu.

Plovdiv Guest House
HOSTEL $$

(Map p344; ☏032-622 432; www.plovdivguest. com; ul Sâborna 20; dm/s/d/tr/q 20/50/68/76/88 lv; ❄️@📶) Though its interior has a boarding-school vibe and zero charm, there is no denying this backpacker option has thought of everything. Its seven-, eight- and 10-bed dorms are clean and feature en suite bathrooms, and there's a shared kitchen and common room with TV.

★ At Renaissance Square
BOUTIQUE HOTEL $$$

(Map p344; ☏032-266 966; www.renaissance -bg.com; pl Vâzhrazhdane 1; s/d from 115/145 lv; 🅿️❄️@📶) Re-creating National Revival–era grandeur is a labour of love at this charming little hotel, between the old town and Plovdiv's shopping streets. Its five rooms are individually decorated with handsome wood floors, billowy drapes, and floral wall and ceiling paintings. Friendly, English-speaking owner Dimitar Vassilev is a font of local knowledge who extends the warmest of welcomes.

Guesthouse Coco
BOUTIQUE HOTEL $$$

(Map p344; ☏0878801883; www.coco-plovdiv .com; ul Hristo Dyukmedzhiev 32; s/d/apt 139/169/269 lv; 🅿️❄️📶) This swish boutique guesthouse on the edge of the Kapana neighbourhood has a high-fashion-meets-vintage ambience unlike other places in Plovdiv. Its eight rooms and five suites have a mostly monochrome palette with flamboyant

---

ℹ️ PLOVDIV 2019

Events ranging from avant-garde fashion shows to spoken word and jazz will reach fever-pitch in the run-up to, and throughout, Plovdiv's tenure as European Capital of Culture 2019. Browse upcoming festivities on http://plovdiv 2019.eu.

touches such as chandeliers, and the service is upmarket but cheerful. Ask in advance if you need a parking space.

Hebros Hotel
BOUTIQUE HOTEL **$$$**

(Map p344; ☑ 032-260 180; www.hebros-hotel.com; ul K Stoilov 51a; s/apt from 140/200 lv; ❄ 🕿) Hebros Hotel is set in a lavish mansion that has housed wealthy furriers and communist party leaders over its fascinating 200-year history, so it's no surprise that demand to stay here is hot. One-of-a-kind bedrooms have antique furnishings and wood-carved bed frames, and there's a jacuzzi and sauna (an extra 25 lv), and an atmospheric restaurant.

Hotel Odeon
BOUTIQUE HOTEL **$$$**

(Map p344; ☑ 032-622 065; www.hotelodeon.net; ul Otets Paisii 40; s/d/apt 82/117/154 lv; ❄ 🕿) In keeping with its location across from the Roman Odeon, this hotel features Roman-style columns in some rooms and an elegant old-world feel throughout. Remarkably, for Bulgaria, the attached restaurant has a creative and extensive vegan menu, as well as sophisticated options for carnivores.

✕ Eating

When it comes to dining, Plovdiv is one of Bulgaria's stand-out cities. Bakeries and cafes abound (especially in Kapana and along ul Knyaz Aleksandâr), while the old town is lined with traditional Bulgarian eateries, ranging from casual *mehanas* to those with refined twists on classic Balkan dishes and Italian cuisine. It's rarely necessary to reserve, and most restaurants offer continuous service.

Klebarnitsa Kapana
BAKERY **$**

(Map p344; ☑ 0882330773; ul Ioakim Gruev 20; ⊙ 9am-7pm; ✐) This bakery has a sociable twist, with places to perch while you tuck into oven-warm bread, fresh pastries and other goodies.

Dreams
CAFE **$**

(Map p344; ☑ 032-627 143; http://dreams-plovdiv.com; pl Stambolov; sandwiches from 3 lv; ⊙ 8am-11pm; 🕿) This reliable cafe is anchored in prime people-watching territory, near the foaming fountains at pl Stambolov where shoppers, lovers and gelato-lickers linger. Sandwiches, pancakes and pastries dominate its menu of light meals, though the coffees and luminous cocktails might extend your stay. The outdoor tables are most popular, but there's also a spacious upstairs hall.

Grazhdanski Klub
BULGARIAN **$$**

(Citizens' Club; Map p344; ☑ 032-624 139; ul Stoyan Chalukov 1; mains 8-15 lv; ⊙ 8am-1am Mon-Fri, 10am-1am Sat & Sun; 🕿) A local favourite, this fabulous nook serves hefty portions of Bulgarian salads, grills and *satch* (meat and vegetables served on a hotplate), only a totter down the hill from the Roman Amphitheatre. Its cool, green courtyard is a haven in hotter months; inside is cosy.

Rahat Tepe
BULGARIAN **$$**

(Map p344; ☑ 0878450259; www.rahat-tepe.com; ul Dr Chomakov 20; mains 7-12 lv; ⊙ 10am-midnight; 🕿) Hands down the winner when it comes to shady beer-garden dining and lively atmosphere, Rahat Tepe's meals follow a simple formula: fresh, unfussy and filling. *Satch* (meat and vegetables on a hot plate) are enormous; salads and kebabs are similarly generous. Service gets chaotic at weekends, but it's ideal for a nosh after clambering around Nebet Tepe's ruins.

Gusto
ITALIAN **$$**

(Map p344; ☑ 032-623 711; www.gustobg.com; ul Otets Paisii 26; mains 6-14 lv; ⊙ 9am-1am) A few steps from pl Stambolov, Gusto strikes an agreeable note between sophisticated and friendly. There are diner-style booths upstairs; punters fight it out for several outdoor tables downstairs on the pedestrianised street. Choose from pizzas and great-value pasta dishes (from 6.50 lv), or slightly pricier, though beautifully executed, medleys such as duck with blueberries (14 lv) and sage-scented pork robed in prosciutto (10 lv).

Puldin Restaurant
BULGARIAN **$$**

(Map p344; ☑ 032-631 720; ul Knyaz Tseretelev 8; mains 15 lv; ⊙ 8am-midnight) Within the walls of an early 19th-century Dervish monastery, Puldin immediately impresses with its huge courtyard fresco of a wedding. Befitting the rustic setting, meals are traditionally Bulgarian, such as kebabs and platters of smoky local cheese.

★ Hebros Restaurant
BULGARIAN **$$$**

(Map p344; ☑ 032-625 929; ul K Stoilov 51; mains 15-27 lv; 🕿) Genteel service and a tranquil setting is exactly what you would expect from the restaurant of the boutique

Hebros Hotel. Classic Bulgarian flavours are gently muddled with Western European influences, creating mouthwatering morsels such as Smilyan beans with parmesan, rabbit with prunes, and grilled sea bream.

Memory
EUROPEAN **$$$**

(Map p340; ☑ 032-626 103; http://memorybg.net; pl Saedinenie 3; mains 15-25 lv; ⊙ 11am-1am) Candlelit tables in a secluded courtyard make Memory a venue to impress, with soul and jazz tunes completing the sultry mood. Its forte is creative interpretations of Western European flavours, such as lamb with mint risotto, and duck nestled in parsnip purée. Everything is lovingly presented, and whisked to tables by polite (if slightly stiff) waiting staff.

Hemingway
INTERNATIONAL **$$$**

(Map p344; ☑ 032-267 350; www.hemingway.bg; ul Gurko 10; mains 9-30 lv; ⊙ 9am-1am) Loosely channelling the cheek and chic of 1920s Paris with a modern twist, this classy spot near the Roman Odeon whips up some of Plovdiv's best dishes from a menu that borrows the best of Italian, French and American cuisines. Enjoy the dilemma of choosing from truffled parmesan fries, Pernod king prawns and mustard steak.

🍷 Drinking & Nightlife

Plovdiv's nightspots are widespread. Several vivacious spots occupy the Kapana district, which means 'the trap', referring to its tight streets in the areas north of pl Dzhumaya, between ul Rayko Daskalov to the west and bul Tsar Boris Obedinitel to the east.

Note that clubs undergo sporadic name changes, sometimes closing and reopening under new management – double-check locally with a free nightlife booklet such as *Programata*.

★ Basquiat Wine & Art
WINE BAR

(Map p344; ☑ 0895460493; https://basquiat.alle.bg; ul Bratya Pulievi 4; ⊙ 9am-midnight) A smooth funk soundtrack and great selection of local wines lure an arty crowd to this small Kapana bar. House wines start at 2 lv per glass; for something more memorable, the *malina* (raspberry-scented) wine packs a syrupy punch.

Kotka i Mishka
BAR

(Map p344; ☑ 0878407578; ul Hristo Dyukmedjiev 14; ⊙ 10am-midnight) The crowd at this hole-in-the-wall craft-beer hang-out spills onto the street – such is the bar's deserved popularity, even against stiff competition in buzzing Kapana, but it's too chilled to warrant its hipster label. Decorations – such as hamster cages hanging from the ceiling – of the industrial-feel brick bar are a nod to the name, meaning 'cat and mouse'.

Monkey House
CAFE

(Map p344; ☑ 0889678333; ul Zlatarska 3; ⊙ 10am-11pm) Coffee-lovers can rest easy in the stripped-bare decor of Monkey House, purveyors of Plovdiv's best flat white. The interior is ornamented with jaunty hallmarks such as bicycles and moustachioed pillows; seats range from tree stumps and wheelbarrows to comfy chairs; and light bulbs dangle on ropes from the beamed ceiling. It's terribly good fun, and the coffee's even better. Cocktails emerge after sundown.

Vino Culture
WINE BAR

(Map p344; ☑ 0892001926; ul Otets Paisii 5; ⊙ 5-11pm) Opening up from the blink-and-you'll-miss-it exterior is an airy brick-walled space where staff truly know their vintages. Delicious Bulgarian wines start at 2 lv per glass, while mixed Spanish and Italian tapas such as *pan tumaca* (tomato bread) and cured hams (from 3.30 lv) provide enough energy for you to sample another drop.

Sandak
BAR

(Map p344; ☑ 0888938075; www.facebook.com/whiskybarsandak; ul Abadzhiyska 10; ⊙ 5pm-midnight) Take a seat on the outdoor military storage boxes, or huddle up within this novel whisky bar in Kapana. The crowd is spirited, and there are occasional guitar-driven live-music acts to keep things fizzing until late.

Morado Bar & Dinner
BAR

(Map p340; ☑ 0896665213; ul Avksentiy Veleshki 19; ⊙ 10am-late) This glamorous venue marries cocktails, live music and pan-European dining on an open-air verandah. Events range from DJ sets and risqué dance shows to retro music nights or screenings of sports or music.

Dolce Fellini
CAFE

(Map p344; ☑ 0894540709; http://dolcefellini.com; ul General Gurko 15; ice cream 3 lv; ⊙ 7.30am-10pm Mon-Fri, from 8.30am Sat & Sun) Gelato flavours, from cookie to lemon, as well as dainty patisserie, custard puddings and smooth coffee seduce passers-by at this exceptional Italian-style cafe.

Bar Maria Luiza BAR

(Map p344; ☑ 0890356394; bul Maria Luiza 15; ☺ 8am-4am Mon-Sat, to midnight Sun; ☺) Too pretty to be merely a dive bar, the Maria Luiza has dedicated owners who keep adapting the decor to suit their whims. The colourful downstairs is particularly stylish, vaguely reminiscent of 1920s Paris. There's a dedicated local following.

Art Club Nylon BAR

(Map p344; www.facebook.com/clubnylon; ul Giorgi Benkovski 8; ☺ noon-4am Mon-Sat; ☺) A bastion of bohemia, this damp, bare-bones but always interesting spot hosts rock and indie bands, themed nights and plenty of drunken, late-night literary chatter.

Rock Bar Download BAR

(Map p344; www.facebook.com/rockbardownload; ul Ioakim Gruev 24; ☺ 10am-11pm) Hard rock and metal set this bar vibrating – when the football's not on, that is. It's only Download's pre-midnight closing time that doesn't feel rock 'n' roll. Check the Facebook page for live events; some solid heavy-metal acts pass through.

Apartment 101 BAR

(Map p344; ul William Gladston 8; ☺ 10am-1am Sun-Thu, to 2am Fri & Sat) A hip – but not painfully so – spot in a wonderfully ramshackle building with chill-out music and occasional live acts.

INTERNATIONAL DESTINATIONS

Union-Ivkoni (www.union-ivkoni.bg) serves Athens (127 lv, four hours, one daily) and Metro (www.metroturizm.com.tr) operates buses to İstanbul (40 lv, seven hours) several times day. Book online or buy tickets in Yug station.

Other private companies offer services to Thessaloniki (70 lv, eight hours, one daily), Paris (247 lv, two days, one daily), Vienna (130 lv, 18 hours, one daily) and other European destinations; buy tickets in Yug station.

Timetables are available on www.bgrazpisanie.com.

☆ Entertainment

Recent foreign films in original languages (with Bulgarian subtitles) screen at Lucky House of Cinema (Map p344; ☑ 0889200601; http://boxoffice.bg; ul Gladston 1; tickets 7 lv) and Kino Eccoplexx (Map p340; ☑ 032-644 004; http://kinoeccoplexx.com; bul 6 Septemvri 128; tickets from 6 lv).

Marmalad LIVE MUSIC

(Map p344; ul Bratya Pulievi 3; ☺ 9am-2am) This two-storey place is one of Kapana's best for live music. Split across a bar and a live-music venue, Marmalad hosts rock bands, karaoke, retro-themed nights and DJ sets.

Nikolai Masalitinov Dramatic Theatre THEATRE

(Map p344; ☑ 032-271 274; www.dtp.bg; ul Knyaz Aleksandâr 38; ☺ box office 10.30am-1.30pm & 4-7pm Mon-Fri) This historic theatre, dating to 1881, is one of the best in Bulgaria, and features Bulgarian-language performances ranging from Shakespeare and Greek tragedy to modern drama.

State Opera House OPERA

(Map p340; ☑ 032-625 553; http://operaplovdiv.bg; ul Gladston 15) Classic and modern European operas are performed in Bulgarian at this distinguished hall. Check the website for performances at other venues, including at Plovdiv's Roman Amphitheatre.

🛍 Shopping

The Kapana quarter, home to the city's artists and young creative community, is increasingly a great place to browse for jewellery and handmade souvenirs. Trendy clothes and shoe stores line the pedestrian mall ul Knyaz Aleksandâr. Continuing up ul Sâborna, you'll find several antique shops. Paintings by Bulgarian artists are sold in various cafes and galleries.

ℹ Information

Tourist Information offices are located in the centre (Map p344; ☑ 032-656 794; www.visitplovdiv.com; pl Tsentralen 1; ☺ 9am-6pm Mon-Fri, 10am-5pm Sat & Sun) and in the old town (Map p344; ☑ 032-620 453; ul Sâborna 22; ☺ 9am-1pm & 2-6pm Mon-Fri, 10am-1pm & 2-5pm Sat & Sun).

Mrezhata (☑ 032-628 501; ul Patriarh Evtimii 28; per hr 2 lv; ☺ 24hr) This internet cafe, a short walk from the pedestrian street, is almost always open.

BUSES FROM PLOVDIV

DESTINATION	STATION	COST (LV)	DURATION	FREQUENCY
Assenovgrad	Yug	1.20	30min	half-hourly
Bachkovo	Rodopi	4	1hr	hourly
Bansko	Yug	14	3½hr	2 daily
Blagoevgrad	Yug	13-15	3hr	3 daily
Burgas	Sever	20-26	4hr	5 daily
Chepelare	Rodopi	8.50	2hr	hourly
Devin	Rodopi	7	3hr	2 daily
Haskovo	Yug	4	1hr	5 daily
Hisar	Sever	4	45min-1hr	1 daily
Hisar	Yug	3.80	1hr	12 daily
Karlovo	Yug	3.90-5	1½hr	16 daily
Karlovo	Rodopi	5	1hr	13 daily
Karlovo	Sever	5	1hr	1 daily
Kazanlâk	Sever	9	2hr	3 daily
Nesebâr	Sever	22	4½-5hr	1 daily
Pamporovo	Rodopi	9	2-2½hr	hourly
Perushtitsa	Yug	3	40min	17 daily
Sliven	Yug	10	3hr	5 daily
Smolyan	Rodopi	10	2½-3hr	11 daily
Sofia	Yug	8-14	2½hr	half-hourly
Stara Zagora	Yug	5-7	1½hr	10 daily
Varna	Yug	22-26	7hr	2-5 daily
Veliko Târnovo	Sever	18	4½hr	3 daily

Plovdiv Hospital (☏ 032-959 221; www.mbal. net; bul Bulgaria 234) The general hospital, 3km northwest of Plovdiv's old town, has an emergency ward.

❶ Getting There & Away

At the heart of Bulgarian Thrace, Plovdiv is the region's main transport hub.

AIR

Plovdiv Airport (www.plovdivairport.com) is approximately 12km from town. At the time of research, Ryanair was offering flights between Plovdiv and London Stansted; other promised routes have been slow to materialise. There's no airport shuttle bus; get a Violet Taxi to the centre (around 15 lv).

BUS

Plovdiv has three bus stations, Yug, Rodopi and Sever; see table above for services and find more info on www.avtogara-plovdiv.info. Schedules can be found on www.bgrazpisanie. com.

Most destinations of interest to travellers are served from **Yug bus station** (Map p340;

☏ 032-626 937; bul Hristo Botev 47), diagonally opposite the train station and a 15-minute walk from the centre. A taxi from the centre costs about 5 lv; alternatively, local buses 7, 20 and 26 (0.80 lv) stop across the main street outside the station, on bul Hristo Botev. Both public and private buses operate from Yug bus station, and there's often no way of predicting whether you'll be getting a big, modern bus or a cramped minibus – though the latter is particularly likely for rural destinations.

Rodopi bus station (Map p340; ☏ 032-657 828) is accessed through the train station underpass. Services include the following.

Sever bus station (☏ 032-953 705; www. hebrosbus.com; ul Dimitar Stambolov 2), 3.5km from the old town in the northern suburbs, is accessible by local bus 99.

For Ruse, take a bus from Sever bus station to Veliko Târnovo and change there.

TRAIN

See table (p352) for direct services from Plovdiv's **train station** (bul Hristo Botev).

It's also possible to connect to more services to Burgas (up to five daily) via Karnobat (12 lv,

TRAINS FROM PLOVDIV

DESTINATION	COST (LV)	DURATION (HR)	FREQUENCY (DAILY)
Burgas	14.60	6	2
Karlovo	3.90	1½	6
Sofia	9	3	15
Stara Zagora	5.70	1½–2	13
Svilengrad	7.40-8.40	3½	2
Varna	18.10-21.60	6	4

3½ to four hours, daily) or Ajtos (13 lv, 3½ to four hours, three daily). Take a train to Dimitrovgrad (4 lv to 5 lv, one to 1½ hours, hourly) for more services to Stara Zagora and Svilengrad.

The train station is well organised, though the staff doesn't speak English. Computer screens at the station entrance and in the underpass leading to the platforms list recent arrivals and upcoming departures. At the time of writing, there was no luggage storage service in operation.

International bus and train tickets can be booked along with domestic tickets at Yug bus station and the train station.

ℹ Getting Around

Plovdiv is best experienced on foot. Much of the old town is off-limits to cars during daylight hours. Arriving by taxi during the day, your 'final destination' will be the Church of Sveta Bogoroditsa on ul Sâborna. At night the street is usually open. Although most taxi drivers conscientiously use meters, a few offenders charge rates as opprobrious as 4 lv per kilometre (especially from the airport); the daytime base rate should be around 0.9 lv per kilometre, slightly higher at night.

Major car-hire brands such as **Avis** (☑ 0885554445; Plovdiv Airport) have branches at Plovdiv Airport but they are usually only staffed to coincide with flight arrivals and departures. If booking pick-up from the airport outside of flight times, make your arrival time clear to the agency. **Motoroads** (www.moto roads.com) can arrange car hire (from 17 lv per day) with pick-up from central locations in Plovdiv.

RODOPI MOUNTAINS
РОДОПИ ПЛАНИНА

Vast stretches of serene pine forests, perilously steep gorges and hundreds of remarkable caves characterise the enthralling Rodopi Mountains. Covering nearly 15,000 sq km of territory, the mountains tumble across into Greece. Much of the border between the two countries is determined by the Rodopi range (85% of which is Bulgarian).

The ski resorts of Pamporovo and Chepelare, and spa town Devin receive a healthy supply of foreign visitors. But outside these areas, the region remains one of Bulgaria's wildest. In this expanse of majestic, thickly packed conifer forests, nearly 300 bird species have been spotted, as well as brown bears, wild goats and wolves. The Rodopi Mountains are exceptionally rich in wildflowers, including indigenous violets, tulips and the unique *silivriak* – a fragile flower said to have sprung up from the blood of Orpheus, the semidivine father of music, after he was torn to pieces by the frenzied bacchantes.

Chepelare   ЧЕПЕЛАРЕ
ELEV 1150M / POP 5800

Encircled by forested hills and scented with pine, low-key Chepelare is a calmer alternative to skiing hub Pamporovo, 11km south. The village spreads along the Chepelare River, with abundant guesthouses and a couple of museums to browse when you aren't on the slopes. The ski area is limited, but boasts one of Bulgaria's longest ski runs. A small trickle of cyclists and hikers pass through during summer, when the village is very quiet.

🏃 Activities

Skiing

Humble Chepelare lives and breathes skiing. There's a ski factory, ski museum (ul Vasil Dechev 25; 1.50 lv; ☺9am-12.30pm & 1.30-6pm Tue-Sat), and the village's most famous daughter is a superstar skier. Chepelare-born athlete Ekaterina Dafovska was the biathlon gold medallist of 1998's Nagano Winter Olympics. Dafovska's successors can be seen thundering down Mechi Chal I (3150m), Chepelare's competition-level slope, while mere mortals zoom down Mechi Chal II (5250m), itself a 720m vertical drop.The chairlift, 2km south on the Pamporovo road, is signposted. Hire gear at **Orion Ski** (☑ 03051-2142; www.orion-ski.com; Chepelare) and enquire at the tourist information centre about ski schools.

Chepelare Ski Resort   SKIING
(☑ 03051-3131; http://chepelaresport.com; day pass adult/child 40/24 lv; ☺ Dec-Mar) Schuss down 11.4km of pistes at Chepelare's small three-lift ski area, 2km south of the village. It's best suited to beginner and intermediate skiers. The area hasn't been very snow-sure in recent years, but there are snow cannons to top it up.

Hiking

From May to September, knot your hiking boots and strike out on a trail from Chepelare village.

Chepelare Panorama Walk the hour-long 'Path of Health' for views of the village; start by walking north 100m from Sveta Bogoroditsa Church before turning right up the hill.

Chepelare–Rozhen Circuit This five-hour trail leads from Chepelare to the Astronomical Observatory in Rozhen, before returning via Progled village.

Chepelare–Mechi Chal peak You'll need six or seven hours to trek to the top of Mechi Chal, take in the 'bear grave' site and wind back to the village.

🛏 Sleeping & Eating

The majority of accommodation in Chepelare consists of family-run guesthouses with dainty spa or sauna facilities. Outside ski season and the high summer months of June to August, things are quiet; booking well in advance is recommended.

The tourist offices in Chepelare and Smolyan can book private rooms (from 20 lv per person with shared bathroom). Hotel prices increase by around 20% in winter.

WORTH A TRIP

BACHKOVO MONASTERY & AROUND

The area around Plovdiv is filled with interesting things to see and do. About 30km south of Plovdiv stands the magnificent **Bachkovo Monastery** (www.bachkovskimanastir.com; Bachkovo; monastery free, refectory 6 lv, museum 2 lv, ossuary 6 lv; ☺ 6am-10pm) FREE, founded in 1083. Most of the complex dates from the 17th century onwards, with the Church of Sveta Bogoroditsa (1604) as its colourful centrepiece. The church is decorated with 1850s frescoes by renowned artist Zahari Zograf and houses a much-cherished icon of the Virgin Mary.

The rust-red ruin of the **Red Church** (Perushtitsa; 3 lv; ☺ 9am-6pm Apr-Sep, 8am-5pm Oct-Mar), a late Roman church, creates an enigmatic silhouette in the fragrant meadowlands outside Perushtitsa, 20km southwest of Plovdiv. The visitors centre tells the story of this rare brick construction, dating to the 5th century, while wooden walkways allow access to its skeletal remains, where you can glimpse faint frescoes. The ruin is 2km north of Perushtitsa town.

More than 3500 years ago, the Bessian tribe of ancient Thrace kept a sanctuary to the god of wine amid these verdant meadows. These days **Bessa Valley Winery** (☑ 0889499992; www.bessavalley.com; Ognyanovo village; ☺ 9am-noon & 2-5pm Mon-Fri), 30km west of Plovdiv, likes to think it's playing a part in preserving this heritage. Its quality merlot, syrah and cabernet sauvignon are sipped across Bulgaria and beyond. Book well in advance for tasting tours.

From sleeping to sipping to enjoying spa treatments, your every movement can be in reverence to juicy Thracian wines at the fabulous **Todoroff Wine & Spa** (☑ 0896689442, 03142-2166; www.todoroff-hotel.com; Brestovitsa; s/d/apt from 65/95/175 lv) in Brestovitsa, 15km southwest of Plovdiv. Use of the spa and traditional sauna comes included in the price.

Further afield, 50km south of Plovdiv, three **Kosovo houses** (☑ 03342-2333; www.selokosovo.com; Kosovo Village; d 70-80 lv, apt 80-120 lv; ☺ mid-Feb–early Jan) have been faithfully renovated in stone and wood to form a unique lodging concept. Each room overflows with traditional Rodopi touches, such as crimson rugs and polished antique furnishings.

PLOVDIV & THE SOUTHERN MOUNTAINS CHEPELARE

DON'T MISS

HIKING IN THE RODOPI MOUNTAINS

Exploring the idyllic forested region around Chepelare, Smolyan, Shiroka Lûka and Devin is the high point for nature lovers here.

Good maps are essential, such as Domino's *Western Rhodope Mountains* map (1:100,000). Tourist offices in Pamporovo, Chepelare and Smolyan irregularly stock the English-language *West Rhodopean Region* or *Western Rhodope Mountains* maps (1:100,000). Though several years old, Julian Perry's *Mountains of Bulgaria* remains a good guide for walkers. It describes a five- to seven-day trek from Hizha Studenents, near Pamporovo, to Hizha Rodoposki Partizanin, near Hrabrino, about 14km southwest of Plovdiv.

For shorter hikes, base yourself in Devin and choose from several marked trails. En route to Trigrad, via Nastan village (6km south), look out for the 'elephant rock'.

There are several good options for hikers looking for day walks, though trail markings are poorly maintained:

Batak–Hizha Teheran About four hours one way.

Chepelare–Hizha Igrev About three hours one way. From there, continue to Zabardo (4½ hours), Shiroka Lûka (six hours) or Pamporovo (eight hours).

Pamporovo–Progled An (easy) five-hour return trip.

Smolyan–Hizha Smolyanski Ezera About three hours one way.

If you're tackling multiday hikes, find details of *hizhas* (mountain huts) on www.bulgarian -mountains.com.

★**Hotel Shoky** GUESTHOUSE $
(📞 0887444004, 03051-3343; www.hotelshoky. com; ul 24 Mai 70; d/apt 40/65 lv; 🅿 🛜) This excellent-value guesthouse, on a quiet residential lane 750m west of the main road, is run by a family of champion skiers (their trophies are amassed in the reception area). Needless to say, advice about winter sports and hiking is insightful, and rooms are spotless, with classic Rodopi features such as wooden ceilings. There's a small spa and sauna area (5 lv). Breakfast extra 4 lv to 5 lv.

Hotel St George HOTEL $
(📞 0896797326; www.stgeorgehotel.bg; ul Belomorska 6; d/apt from 36/50 lv; 🅿 🛜) Simple, cosy rooms and well-equipped modern apartments fill this traditional stone building at the northern end of Chepelare, on the main Plovdiv–Smolyan road. Service is friendly and thorough, and there's a ski storage room. Breakfast is an extra 5 lv.

Hotel Savov HOTEL $$
(📞 0888687957; http://hotel-savov.eu; ul Vasil Dechev 7; d/tr/ste from 51/61/82 lv; 🅿 🛜) Just north of the main square, this homely place offers large, airy doubles, and cosy suites with sitting areas. Staff can help with bicycle, car or ski rental. You can buy breakfast from the restaurant downstairs.

Vienski Salon BULGARIAN $
(📞 03051-4486; ul Vasil Dechev 14; mains 5-8 lv; ⏱ 8am-11pm) Not quite a 'Viennese salon', as the name suggests, but this unfussy spot serves everything from breakfast *banitsa* to Rodopi specialities such as grilled fish, through to pizza and syrupy baklava. It's 200m north of the main square.

❶ Information

The **Tourist Information Centre** (📞 03051-2110; ticchepelare@gmail.com; ul Dicho Petrov 1a; ⏱ 8.30am-12.30pm & 1.30-5.30pm) can provide info on buses, hiking, skiing and local attractions.

❶ Getting There & Away

The bus station is across a footbridge, 200m northeast of the square. Buses leave hourly for Smolyan (4 lv, one hour), via Pamporovo. Between 6am and 6.30pm, regular services reach Plovdiv (9 lv, 90 minutes).

Pamporovo ПАМПОРОВО
ELEV 1650M

One of Bulgaria's four major ski resorts, southerly Pamporovo enjoys plenty of blue skies above its spruce-lined pistes. As is the case with Bansko, the country's premier spot in the Pirin Mountains, the ruthless quest for expansion has left Pamporovo's forests scarred, and has littered its skyline with cranes and an ever-increasing number of apartment blocks. But unlike Bansko, there's no historic nucleus, just a resort that sprawls along kilometres of pedestrian-unfriendly roads.

Outside busy winter season, Pamporovo is quiet (except for its many building sites); and its lack of a meaningful centre and non-skiing attractions means it can be quietly skipped during the summer.

🏃 Activities

Pamporovo claims the title of Bulgaria's winter-sports sunshine capital, with around 250 days of sun each year. Significant snowfall between mid-December and mid-April usually brings great conditions for snowboarders and skiers, though recent winters have been unreliable regarding snowfall.

Pamporovo's smallish ski area is served by nine drag lifts and five chairlifts. There are 25km of pisted runs (the longest more than 4km), most of them suited to beginner and intermediate skiers and boarders, with a highest point of 1937m. Additionally, it has more than 30km of cross-country trails. A two-day lift pass costs 108 lv per person, though prices increase each year.

Ski instruction is easiest to organise as a multiday package. Joining a ski school for four-hour lessons over three days costs about 90 lv, and private instruction is considerably higher. Many instructors speak English or German.

More than a dozen places offer gear rental; many of them are attached to hotels. Prices vary, but for three days, renting a set of skis, boots and poles costs from 60 lv. Rent via the **Sport Shop** (☑ 0887636000; www.perelikpamporovo.com; ☺ Dec-Mar) in Hotel Perelik, or book on http://pamporovo. me for the best prices (you can pick up your gear by the ski lifts or at Malina Village). The best deals often involve bundling together accommodation, lift passes and gear hire.

🛏 Sleeping & Eating

Pamporovo's hotel scene mostly involves all-inclusive resorts geared towards winter-sports tourists, and the vast majority snooze outside the frosty months. Reserve several months ahead for winter; for summer, book ahead to ensure your desired hotel is operating.

★ **Aparthotel Kamelia** HOTEL **$$**
(☑ 0309-50 500; www.kamelia-hotel-pamporovo. com; 1-/3-bedroom apt 60/100 lv; P🛜) Airy apartments in this welcoming all-season hotel have oodles of space, and many overlook evergreen forests. The restaurant oozes Rodopi atmosphere with its big fire, wooden beams and woollen rugs; the luxurious pool is decorated with Grecian statues; and the spa centre (15 lv) has a tiled steam room and a jacuzzi. It's at the southern end of Pamporovo's sprawl, south of the main road.

There is a children's room and ski kindergarten, plus winter-sports gear storage. Prices double during ski season.

Malina Village CHALET **$$**
(☑ 0309-58 388; http://malina-pamporovo.com; 2-/4-person chalets from 82/125 lv; P🛜) If Pamporovo's towering resort hotels don't appeal, bunk down in a cosy triangular chalet instead. The wooden huts in Malina Village, in western Pamporovo, are sprinkled among spruce forests, and each one has a small kitchen, living room and bathroom. It's a five-minute walk to the ski lifts.

ℹ Information

Browse www.bulgariaski.com for snow reports, advice and accommodation information for all Bulgarian ski resorts, and check out http:// pamporovo.me for specifics on Pamporovo events and lift-pass prices.

ℹ Getting There & Away

Hourly Smolyan–Chepelare buses pass Pamporovo, as do Smolyan–Plovdiv and Smolyan–Sofia buses. Five daily buses from Sofia go directly to Pamporovo (22 lv, four hours), and regular buses leave from Plovdiv (12 lv, 2½ hours). The bus stop is at the 'Ski Lift No 1' chairlift at the central T-junction.

Smolyan СМОЛЯН

ELEV 1000M / POP 30,640

Sprawling Smolyan is the southern Rodopi Mountains' administrative centre, and a convenient base for hikers. Steep and forested mountains rise abruptly on its southern flank, lending a lovely backdrop to a town that's otherwise time-worn and gritty.

The town is an alternative place to stay if you're skiing Pamporovo or Chepelare, though it's certainly not the most beautiful. It's the transport hub for villages such as Shiroka Lûka and Devin, and a base for exploring the seven (somewhat swampy) Smolyan Lakes and the caves of Golubovitsa and Uhlovitsa.

◎ Sights

Historical Museum   MUSEUM
(✆ 0301-62 727; www.museumsmolyan.eu; Dicho Petrov 3; 5 lv; ✆ 9am-6pm Tue-Sat May-Sep, 9am-noon & 1-5pm Tue-Sat Oct-Apr) Larger and much better presented than many of Bulgaria's regional museums, this multifloor exhibition space preens from a steep hill behind Smolyan's civic centre. The ground floor displays Palaeolithic artefacts and Thracian weaponry, with a Thracian helmet and doe-headed bronze lamp among its standout artefacts. The upper floors feature whimsically arranged folk costumes, Rodopi weaving and woodcarving, and fantastically hairy *kukeri* outfits (worn at New Year celebrations). No photography allowed.

Smolyan Art Gallery   GALLERY
(✆ 0301-62 328; Dicho Petrov 7; 3 lv; ✆ 9am-noon & 1-5pm) This excellent gallery features 1800 paintings, sketches and sculptures by local, national and foreign artists. Especially interesting are the upper floor Rodopi realism works.

Cathedral of Saint Vissarion   CATHEDRAL
(✆ 8am-6pm) This Orthodox cathedral is the third-largest in Bulgaria, and impossible to miss on Smolyan's main street. It's topped by a UFO-like dome, which measures 17m in diameter. Aptly, this space-age spiritual site is right opposite the planetarium.

🛏 Sleeping

★ Three Fir Trees House   PENSION $
(✆ 088855988, 0301-81 028; www.trieli.hit.bg; ul Srednogorets 1; s/d/apt with shared bathroom 30/40/80 lv; @ 🛜) Welcomes rarely come warmer than at this relaxing, family-run guesthouse, 400m east of the main bus station. Rooms have a pleasant, cosy style and there's an excellent breakfast (5 lv) featuring produce fresh from the garden. The helpful English- and German-speaking owner can arrange walking tours and rental cars, plus there's a good-value laundry service (6 lv).

Hotel Spartak   GUESTHOUSE $
(✆ 0301-64 632; www.hotelspartak.bg; ul Spartak 21; s/d/apt from 30/40/100 lv; P 🛜) This hospitable 14-room guesthouse has a quiet location on a residential street south of the main road, 800m west of the cathedral. Rooms are simple, with occasional Rodopi trimmings such as carved wooden bed frames, and there's a smart *mehana* below. Breakfast can be bought from the attached restaurant.

✗ Eating & Drinking

Starata Kâshta   BULGARIAN $
(ul Studenska 2; mains 6-9 lv; ✆ 4.30pm-midnight) The attractive National Revival–style house has a few rough-hewn outdoor tables and benches, and a menu of Bulgarian classics such as grills and cheese-strewn salads. It's up the steps from bul Bulgaria.

Riben Dar   SEAFOOD $$
(✆ 0301-63 220; ul Snezhanka 16; mains 6-12 lv) In the western neighbourhood of Nevyasta, this hospitable restaurant and guesthouse specialises in seafood, such as mountain trout. Riben Dar is at the top of the town, and has ravishing Rodopi views; drive or take a taxi (3 lv to 5 lv).

WORTH A TRIP

SMOLYAN'S MYSTERIOUS CAVES

Two caves south of Smolyan are worth a detour. Visitors can explore the 330m of passageways in Uhlovitsa Cave (✆ 0889121014; adult/child 4/2 lv; ✆ 10am-4pm daily summer, Wed-Sun winter), 25km south of Smolyan and 3km northeast of Mogilitsa village, which fires the imagination with its rock formations and waterfalls (most spectacular in winter). Entry is by hourly guided tour. Located 3km south of Uhlovitsa Cave, off the road between Smolyan and Mogilitsa, the Golubovitsa Cave is only accessible by boat, as the first 25m or so is completely underwater. After that, you walk by lantern-light. Special equipment and a guide is essential; ask at Smolyan's tourist office.

ℹ Information

Tourist Office (☑ 0301-62 530; www.smolyan.
com; bul Bulgaria 5; ⊙ 9am-5.30pm Mon-
Sat) An excellent source of info for Smolyan
and nearby towns and for outdoor activities;
can help book tours, and provides transport
information.

ℹ Getting There & Away

Most buses to/from Smolyan use the **main bus
station** (☑ 0301-63 104; bul Bulgaria 85) at
Smolyan's western end. Six daily buses serve
Sofia (25 lv, 3½ hours). Hourly buses reach Plovdiv (10 lv, 2½ to three hours), via Chepelare (6 lv,
one hour) and Pamporovo (4 lv, 30 minutes)
between 6am and 7pm. Buses also depart from
here to Shiroka Lûka and Devin (8 lv, 90 minutes,
six daily on weekdays, one to three at weekends).

Devin   ДЕВИН
POP 7200

Thirsty travellers gulp Devin's waters long
before they set foot in town. The name of
this placid mountain town is emblazoned on
one of Bulgaria's bottled water brands, and
its famed mineral springs entice bathers
and curists for a long soak. Spa hotels ably
meet the demand, but otherwise the town
is tranquil to a fault: there are few standout
attractions and restaurants.

Still, this sleepy town, clasped by spruce
forests, is a good base for exploring two of
the Rodopi Mountains' major caves: Trigrad
and Yagodina. Luxuriant spa treatments and
a fragrant ecotrail provide further excuses to
dawdle in Devin.

⊙ Sights & Activities

The lovely **Struilitsa Ecotrail** follows the
Devinska River from the mineral baths up
to the remnants of a medieval settlement.
From here, you can climb further to **Kavur-
skoto Kale**, the remains of a stronghold
where locals once made a desperate last
stand against the Turkish onslaught. This
triangular route, returning to the baths,
takes about three hours.

🛏 Sleeping

The bliss of snoozing in a plush hotel, after sweaty stints in a sauna, is an excellent
reason to stay the night in Devin. Midrange
to top-end spa hotels dominate the scene,
but check credentials carefully: some guesthouses claim to be 'spa hotels' but have little
more than a tepid jacuzzi.

Spa Hotel Evridika   HOTEL **$$**
(☑ 03041-3727,0888137222;www.spahotelevridika.
com; ul Osvobozhdenie 25; s/d/apt 69/89/102 lv;
❄ 🕏 ☰) This warm, intimate place has a
handful of doubles and roomy apartments
with kitchenettes, all with balconies peering
over spruce trees. Service is personalised
and friendly, and there's a restaurant with
Bulgarian and international fare, a summer
garden, and the (literal) topper: a sky bar
with mineral pool and jacuzzi, with sweep-
ing views of the Rodopi forests. All in all,
this is hard to beat for the price.

Hotel Elite   HOTEL **$$**
(☑ 03041-2240; www.elite-devin.com; ul Undola 2;
s/d/apt 50/65/80 lv; 🅿 ❄ 🕏) On the central
pedestrian street, the Elite has large rooms
with gleaming modern bathrooms; doubles
have bathtubs. The basement mini-spa includes a sauna, a jacuzzi and massage treatments (from 25 lv). Note that there is an
extra 15 lv charge for children aged between
two and 14.

★ **Complex Ismena**   HOTEL, VILLA **$$$**
(☑ 03041-2757, 0884707970; www.ismena.bg; ul
Osvobozhdenie; d/ste/4-bed chalets 140/166/266
lv; ⊙ Mar-Dec; 🅿 🕏 ☰) Mock-Tudor villas sit
serenely beneath the Rodopi Mountains at
this luxurious spa complex. Villas have bal-
conies, polished wooden floors and plenty of
space, with trimmings such as flowers and
fuzzy blankets adding a hint of alpine flair.
The wellness centre has the full monty of in-
door and outdoor (seasonal) pools, a steam
bath, a sauna and massage treatments. Its
location away from Devin's centre enhances
the leisurely feel.

The hotel website often features promo-
tional pricing, so book ahead.

Orpheus Spa & Resort   HOTEL **$$$**
(☑ 03041-2041; www.orpheus-spa.com; Tzvetan
Zangov 14; d/ste 132/182 lv; 🅿 🕏 ☰) Devin's
poshest address is this giant gingerbread
mansion, overlooking a pool crowned with
an enormous faux crystal. Rooms are ornate
but have traditional features in the wood-
framed windows and decor. The spa centre
feels decadent, with an Egyptian-style tiled
hammam, and treatments involving gold
dust, diamonds and caviar.

🍴 Eating

In a town where glamorous hotels contrast
a rather humdrum town centre, the best

WORTH A TRIP

THE CAVES OF TRIGRAD & YAGODINA

The most accessible and developed Rodopi caves are south of Devin, near Trigrad and Yagodina. Admission to both caves includes a guided tour.

Trigrad Cave (Dyavolskoto Gurlo Peshtera; ☑0889903642; Trigrad; adult/student 3/2 lv; ⊙9am-4pm May-Sep, shorter hours rest of year), also called 'Devil's Throat Cave', was burrowed out by the Trigrad River over millennia. A 20-minute guided tour, requiring three or four tourists, leads you into grottoes with dangling stalactites. As you descend into the cave, you can hear a 42m-high waterfall. Exiting involves a daunting set of steep steps. You'll need private transport to reach the cave, 2km north of Trigrad village via a narrow mountain road.

Yagodina (☑0889903642; www.yagodinska-peshtera.com; 5 lv; ⊙9am-4.15pm May-Sep, shorter hours rest of year) is the Rodopi Mountains' longest cave at 8.5km, and its many abysses and labyrinthine tunnels also make it one of Bulgaria's deepest grottoes. The 45-minute tours leave on the hour and highlight curtain-like rock formations and knotty stalagmites, resembling towers of profiteroles. The cave is a winding 20km drive south of Devin.

---

restaurants are often within spa complexes and guesthouses.

Starata Varba   BULGARIAN $$
(☑0886842844; ul Rodopi; mains 9-16; ⊙10am-11pm) The 'Old Willow Tree' is a local favourite for its juicy salads, frisbee-sized omelettes and meat dishes, grilled simply with a squeeze of lemon or drowned in forest-mushroom sauce. The outdoor seating on a wooden deck adds to the appeal. It's south of the stream at the eastern end of ul Rodopi.

Oriental Restaurant   TURKISH $$
(☑03041-2041; www.orpheus-spa.com; Tzvetan Zangov 14; mains 8-16 lv; 🔊) Within the Orpheus Spa & Resort, the Oriental serves Turkish kebabs and is decorated with the requisite couches, pillows and gauze.

ℹ Information

Find ATMs along the main street and at Orpheus Spa & Resort (p357).

There is no municipal tourist office but the regional tourist office (p357) in Smolyan can help with maps, public transport timetables and information across the region. **Devin Museum** (ul Orfei; 1 lv; ⊙10am-noon & 3-5pm Mon-Sat) and hotel staff are best placed to give local advice.

ℹ Getting There & Away

From **Devin bus station** (☑03041-2077; ul Osvobozhdenie 24), services reach Smolyan (5 lv, 1½ hours, six daily) via Shiroka Lûka and Plovdiv (7 lv, three hours, two daily). For Sofia, minibuses depart every other day; alternatively, catch a bus to Plovdiv, which has numerous bus and train connections to the capital.

Veliko Târnovo & Central Mountains

Best Places to Eat

➔ Han Hadji Nikoli (p372)

➔ Sevastokrator (p375)

➔ Magnolia (p389)

➔ Pri Hadjiyata (p394)

➔ Starata Loza (p378)

Best Places to Sleep

➔ Hotel-Mehana Gurko (p371)

➔ Hotel IT Shipka (p390)

➔ Camping Veliko Tarnovo (p370)

➔ Dream of Happiness (p377)

➔ Hotel Merien Palace (p391)

Why Go?

Forbidding mountains and floral valleys compose the varied landscape at Bulgaria's heart. What unites its perilous hills and colourful villages is revolutionary history, etched into the landscape.

In the Central Mountains, monasteries at Troyan and Dryanovo triumphed over repeated attempts to destroy them – even sheltering revolutionary fighters between their frescoed walls. Just south in Koprivshtitsa, a town famed for its charming 19th-century mansions, the 1876 April Uprising brewed. Ensuing battles for Bulgaria's independence from Ottoman control unfolded in the thickly forested Shipka Pass.

The fortress at Veliko Târnovo, once the capital of the Bulgarian tsars, remains the region's crowning attraction. Just as captivating is Kazanlâk's Valley of the Roses, aflame with blooms each May and June, and the Thracian tombs in its surrounds. Little-explored intrigues lie east: Shumen's colossal monuments, Madara's archaeological reserve and the boulder-strewn hiking terrain around Sliven.

When to Go
Veliko Târnovo

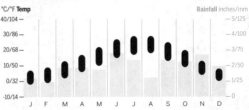

| **May–Jun** Rose festivals in and around Kazanlâk, and Koprivshtitsa's uprising re-enactment. | **Aug–Sep** Escape the heat while hiking in cooler climes in the Stara Planina. | **Oct** Enjoy Veliko Târnovo's Sound and Light Show under clear skies, along with its student nightlife. |

Veliko Tǎrnovo & Central Mountains Highlights

① **Veliko Tǎrnovo** (p365) Striding along medieval ramparts and cobbled lanes.

② **Valley of the Roses** (p386) Breathing the scent of fresh rose oil.

③ **Shipka Pass** (p389) Driving between hilltop monuments, golden church domes and a Soviet UFO.

④ **Koprivshtitsa** (p385) Delighting in lovingly painted mansions.

⑤ **Founders of the Bulgarian State Monument** (p361) Craning your neck at futurist sculptures in Shumen.

⑥ **Stara Planina** (p381) Hiking the windswept wilds of Bulgaria's grand 'old mountain'.

⑦ **Troyan Monastery** (p383) Gasping at 19th-century frescoes in this sandstone monastery.

⑧ **Emen Canyon** (p375) Looking over steep views from this cliffside ecotrail towards a waterfall.

⑨ **Tryavna** (p377) Marvelling at hand-carved wood iconostases'.

⑩ **Etǎr** (p379) Strolling among quaint buildings and craft shops at touristy (but irresistible) Etǎr.

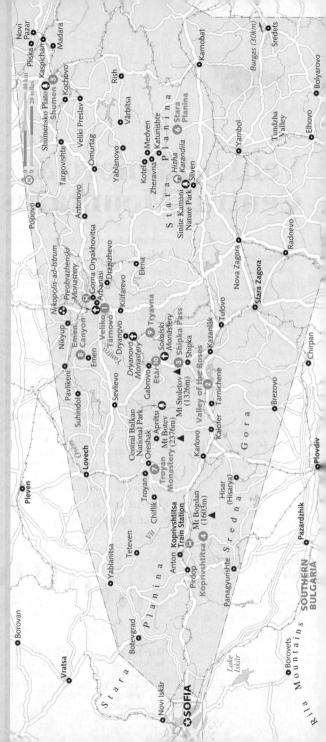

History

Settlers have been drawn to this hilly swath of inland Bulgaria for millennia. Historians have unearthed traces of Palaeolithic cave dwellers in grottoes such as Bacho Kiro, as well as remnants of Neolithic settlements in the hills around modern Veliko Tårnovo. Thracian tribes dominated the land until Romans marched in, establishing impressive cities such as Nikopolis-ad-Istrum, laying the first walls of Veliko Tårnovo's citadel and the mighty gates in Hisar, and fortifying existing Iron Age fortresses in Shumen.

From the 7th century, skirmishes between Byzantium and the emerging First Bulgarian Empire seemed never-ending, until defeats in central Bulgarian Pliska and Preslav signalled the end. The Byzantines enjoyed a decisive victory in the 11th century.

The region's fortunes turned in 1185, when brothers Asen and Petår energised an uprising that would finally cast off Byzantine rule for the Second Bulgarian Empire, with Veliko Tårnovo (then Tårnovgrad) as its capital. Good times rolled until 1393 when the Ottomans besieged Tårnovgrad. Under 500 years of Ottoman control, treasured monasteries such as Dryanovo and Preobrazhenski were wrecked and the region's significance dwindled. But rebellion was quietly being plotted in those same sacked monasteries, as well as revolutionary centres such as Koprivshtitsa.

The 1876 April Uprising finally loosened the chains: Tårnovgrad was freed in the ensuing Russo-Turkish War, with its most decisive battles fought at Shipka Pass. The ensuing 18th- and 19th-century Bulgarian National Revival period bestowed wondrous architecture on towns such as Koprivshtitsa, Karlovo and Tryavna. From 1946 the communist regime suppressed some artistic life while bringing its own distinctive architecture to the fore, with notable remnants in Shumen and Shipka. But in the 21st century, preserving the legacy of Revival-era towns has taken priority.

Shumen ШУМЕН

POP 87,000

Fans of Soviet-era design, rejoice. While Shumen's numerous concrete blocks don't inspire, an extraordinary brutalist monument peers down over the city. Sprinkling variety among this Soviet severity are Shumen's National Revival–era mansions, green parks interlaced with walking trails, and a 3000-year-old fortress. Furthermore, the city's name is emblazoned on beer cans across Bulgaria, as the home of popular Shumensko pivo.

History

Settlements in Shumen date back to the 5th millennium BC. Thracians and then Romans settled and fortified today's Shumen. After the Turkic Bulgar migrations in the 6th century AD, nearby Veliki Preslav and Pliska became the centres of the medieval Bulgarian kingdom. In 1388 the Ottomans captured Shumen, and it became an important market town. In the final days of Ottoman domination, it was part of the Turks' strategic quadrangle (with Ruse, Silistra and Varna) of towns fortified against Russian advances in 1877. Reminders of Ottoman multi-ethnicity remain with Shumen's minority Jewish, Armenian and Muslim communities.

◎ Sights

★ Founders of the Bulgarian State Monument   MONUMENT
(Shumensko Plato Nature Park; adult/child 3/1 lv; ☺ 8am-8pm May-Sep, 8.30am-5pm Oct-Apr) Visible within a 30km radius, this tremendous Soviet-era monument was opened in 1981 to commemorate the First Bulgarian Empire's 1300th anniversary. Enormous futurist sculptures depict Bulgaria's medieval rulers, and the complex includes the Balkans' largest outdoor mosaic triptych.

Statues of Bulgarian khans tower 18m high around this angular complex, constructed with 50,000 cu metres of concrete and 2500 tonnes of steel. The inscription beneath Khan Omurtag's mighty statue translates roughly as 'Even if a man lives well, he dies and another comes into existence; let the one who comes later, when he sees this inscription, remember the one who made it'. A granite lion atop the monument weighs an estimated 1000 tonnes.

From central Shumen, a circuitous 5km road leads to the hilltop monument; it's uphill all the way from ul Saedinenie, south of Hotel Rai. A taxi from the city centre costs around 5 lv, and then you can walk back down the steps.

An information centre, about 300m from the monument, has details about the

VELIKO TÅRNOVO & CENTRAL MOUNTAINS SHUMEN

Shumen

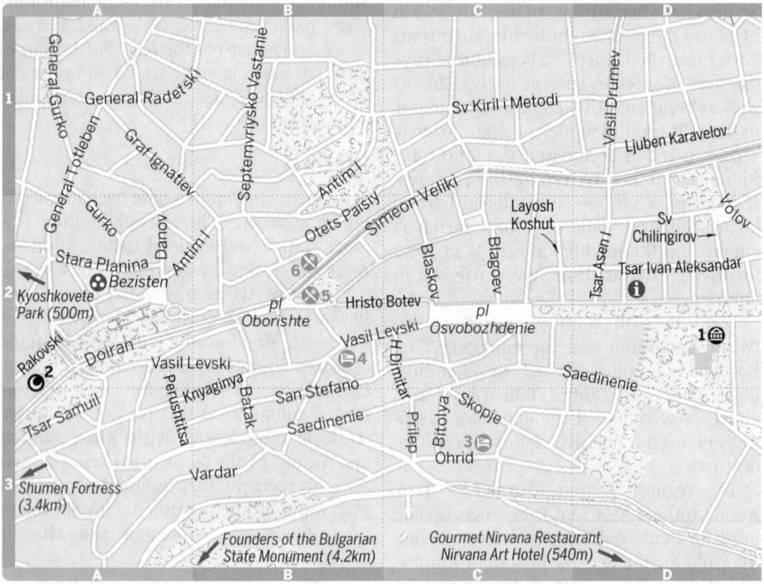

structure and surrounding flora. A 3km path passes the information centre and car park, finishing at Shumen Fortress.

Regional Museum of History MUSEUM
(☎054-875 487; http://museum-shumen.eu; bul Slavyanski 17; 3 lv; ⊙10am-6pm daily Apr-Oct, 9am-5pm Mon-Fri Nov-Mar) This brick museum on the main road exhibits Thracian and Roman artefacts from Madara, Veliki Preslav and Pliska, along with ancient claypot burials and a re-creation of the Tomb of Smyadovo, a significant 4th-century-BC grave. The upper floor exhibits jewellery, 19th-century lanterns and fine work by Shumen's National Revival–era goldsmiths.

Shumen Fortress FORTRESS
(adult/student 3/1 lv; ⊙9am-7pm daily summer, to 5pm Mon-Fri winter) Standing proudly over Shumen at a height of 455m, this 3000-year-old fortress dates back to the Iron Age. Thracian, Roman and Byzantine fortifications followed, and its strategic significance heightened during the Second Bulgarian Empire (1185–1396) when Shumen rose to prominence as one of northeast Bulgaria's most significant settlements. Ottoman ruler Ali Pasha invaded in 1388, looting and burning the fortress.

Tombul Mosque MOSQUE
(Sherif Halil Pasha Mosque; ☎054-802 875; ul Rakovski 21; adult/child 4/2 lv; ⊙9am-6pm) Shumen's Tombul Mosque was built in 1744 in a fusion of oriental and French baroque styles. At 1730 sq metres, it's the largest mosque still in use in Bulgaria. The 40m-high minaret has 99 stone steps and local belief states that the courtyard fountain gushes sacred water.

Sleeping

Hotels in Shumen are geared towards business travellers, so some drop their prices at weekends. The friendliest digs are in family-run guesthouses, while high-end amenities abound in Shumen's rather-impersonal business hotels.

Hotel Rai HOTEL $
(☎054-802 670; http://shumen-hotel-rai.alle.bg; ul Ohrid 26a; s/d/tr/apt 33/46/54/59 lv; ❄@📶) Within a butter-yellow building that fringes Shumensko Plato Nature Park, this family-run hotel is furnished in a cosy, grandmotherly style with bonus internet terminals in the rooms. Staff are friendly and eager to please, and breakfast costs a mere 2 lv.

in all), plus there's a traditional restaurant attached. Staff are warm and speak English.

🍴 Eating & Drinking

Shumen's best restaurants stand along ul Tsar Osvoboditel, near the main square, or within high-end lodgings such as Nirvana Art Hotel and Grand Hotel Shumen. Look out for *Gorna Oryakhovski sudzuk*, a spicy regional flat sausage.

Minaliat Vek Restaurant　　　BULGARIAN $$
(☑054-801 615; www.minaliatvek.com; bul Simeon Veliki 81; mains 9-17 lv; 🖥) This local favourite, which is part of the Minaliat Vek Hotel, seeks to re-create the 'old time' tastes its name suggests. The long list of Bulgarian specialities ranges from triple pork fillet baked in chewy *kashkaval* (cheese), to grilled fish, tripe soup and refreshing salads. There is also an extensive menu of *rakia* (Bulgarian brandy).

Mehana Popsheitanova Kashta　BULGARIAN $$
(☑054-802 222; ul Tsar Osvoboditel 158; mains 5-12 lv; ⊙noon-11pm; 🖥) This wood-framed traditional restaurant has big outdoor benches and also big portions. Try the skewered chicken with cooked red peppers, onions, tomatoes and mushroom.

Gourmet Nirvana Restaurant　　INTERNATIONAL $$$
(☑054-800 127; www.hotelnirvana.bg; ul Nezavisinost 25; mains 12-25 lv; 🖥🍴) Refined dining within this neoclassical hotel is worth the 10-minute drive south from central Shumen. Sophisticated fish dishes, Mediterranean grills and vegetarian-friendly Italian fare

★**Nirvana Art Hotel**　　BOUTIQUE HOTEL $$
(☑054-800 127; www.hotelnirvana.bg; ul Nezavisimost 25; s/d/apt from 79/89/140 lv; 🅿🖥🖥🖥) Marvellously at odds with Shumen's Soviet feel, this unique hotel resembles a Middle Eastern palace with its elegant white archways and elaborate trellises. Individually decorated rooms are painted in calming shades of sky blue and apricot. There's a seasonal outdoor pool, a wellness centre with spa and hammam, and massage treatments begin at a reasonable 25 lv.

Hotel-Restaurant Minaliat Vek　HOTEL $$
(☑054-801 615; www.minaliatvek.com; bul Simeon Veliki 81; s/d/ste 58/70/95 lv; 🅿🖥🖥) This great-value hotel in the western part of Shumen inhabits a restored 18th-century building and is managed by chirpy staff who speak a smattering of foreign languages. Rooms are basic but nicely maintained, the wi-fi signal is strong and a small choice of breakfasts costs an extra 5 lv per person.

Hotel Zamaka　　　HOTEL $$
(☑054-800 409; www.zamakbg.eu; ul Vasil Levski 17; s/d/ste 50/70/85 lv; 🖥🖥) This lovely hotel snoozes away in a quiet residential neighbourhood west of the main square. Airy, light-filled rooms are arranged around a garden courtyard (nine rooms and three suites

> **ⓘ WALKING TRAILS**
>
> Walking and cycling trails interlace Shumensko Plato, the protected area fanning out from the Founders of the Bulgarian State Monument. Find routes and a map on www.shumenskoplato. net.

such as cannelloni are laid gracefully on tables overlooking a peaceful garden.

Nightclub Colosseum CLUB
(☑ 054-830 444; www.facebook.com/Colosseum Oficial; ul Simeon Veliki; ☺ 11pm-4am Wed-Mon; ☏) Shumen's most popular club nights unfold inside this cavernous disco, which has more than a decade's worth of late nights under its belt. Check its Facebook page for events, from student nights to DJ parties and retro.

ⓘ Information

The **tourist information centre** (☑ 054-857 773; www.shumen.bg/en/tourism; bul Slavyanski 17; ☺ 9am-5pm Mon-Fri) has maps, tips and local information. The **souvenir booth** (☺ 9am-1pm, 2-6pm) adjoining the Museum Complex of Pancho Vladigerov sells maps of local attractions (2.50 lv).

ⓘ Getting There & Away

The bus and train stations are adjacent each other at Shumen's eastern end. From the **bus station** (☑ 054-830 890; ul Rilski Pohod), buses serve Burgas (14 lv, three hours, two to four daily), Ruse (6 lv to 10 lv, 2½ hours, one daily), Dobrich (13 lv, two to 2½ hours, two daily), Silistra (13 lv, three hours, three daily), Veliko Târnovo (13 lv, two to 2½ hours, three daily), Sofia (31 lv, six hours, seven daily) and Varna (7 lv, 1½ hours, nine daily). Private buses, such as those operated by **Etap Adress** (☑ 054-830 670; www.etapgroup.com; bul Madara 33), also stop (at the same station) in Shumen on the Sofia–Varna route. Twice-daily buses reach Istanbul, Turkey (60 lv, nine hours).

From the **train station** (☑ 054-860 155; ul Stantsionna) direct daily services reach Varna (6 lv to 7 lv, two hours, 10 daily) and Sofia (20 lv to 26 lv, six to 6½ hours, three to four daily). Services reach Ruse (12 lv, 3½ to 4½ hours, one daily) via Gorna Oryakhovitsa. Aside from one direct train, reaching Plovdiv (18 lv to 20 lv, seven to nine hours, 10 daily) also requires changing trains at various stations. Seven daily trains reach Madara (1.50 lv to 3 lv, 15 minutes).

Madara МАДАРА

POP 1300

A striking rock carving, the Madara Horseman, has secured this quiet village's place in history. Madara, 15km east of Shumen, was an important town for the horse-riding, nomadic Thracians around 7000 years ago, and was later settled by the Romans. Madara was also a key location during the 7th-century foundation of the Bulgarian state. Though the village is languid today, it remains famous for its archaeological reserve: caves, chapels and the horseman, which was carved dramatically into the cliff face during the 8th-century Bulgar khanate.

The reserve is also an excellent place for walkers, with trails up to a ruined fortress offering sweeping views over white cliffs that jut from tangles of forest, and a tapestry of green fields.

⊙ Sights

**Madara
Archaeological Reserve** HISTORIC SITE
(adult/child 5/2 lv; ☺ 8.30am-8pm Apr-Oct, to 5pm Nov-Mar) The carved figure of a horseback warrior, spearing a lion while his dog trots behind, is this archaeological reserve's highlight. The Madara Horseman (Madarski Konnik), 1.5km east of Madara village, was sculpted 23m high into the cliff face during the 8th century, to commemorate the victorious Khan Tervel and the creation of the First Bulgarian Empire (681–1018). Bulgaria's only known medieval rock carving, it's a Unesco World Heritage site. Caves, chapels and an ecotrail are signposted within the reserve.

Follow the stone stairs to view the horseman. About 200m right of the stairs, find the 12th- to 14th-century **St Panteleimon Chapel**, an icon-filled cave-sanctuary. A steep uphill trail left of the stairs leads to the ruin of the 4th- to 5th-century **Madara Fortress** (about 20 minutes), with its uplifting views over the surrounding plains.

🛏 Sleeping

A mountain hut lies just northwest of the Madara rider, plus there is a campground 500m walk from the archaeological complex. A couple of more comfortable guesthouses can be found in Madara village, 1.5km west of the archaeological complex, but most people stay in busy, amenity-packed Shumen, 15km west.

Guesthouse Valentina
GUESTHOUSE $

(☑ 0895990260; ul Madarski konnik 44; d 40 lv; P ☎) This four-room family guesthouse in Madara village is off the main road, 1km west of the archaeological complex. You can enjoy cliff views from the cheerful yard, which is full of flowers, birds and garden gnomes, and the rooms are simple and tidy.

Hizha Madarski Konnik
HUT $

(☑ 0896688536; dm 20 lv) This bare-bones mountain hut, 200m northwest of the Madara rider on the main road, offers dorm beds geared towards hikers passing through.

ⓘ Getting There & Away

Public transport to Madara is limited, and the horseman is 2km up a steep road from the village. A taxi from Shumen costs 30 lv return, including waiting time. Madara itself has no taxis.

Seven daily Shumen–Varna trains stop at Madara (3 lv, 15 minutes). Shumen–Madara buses are unreliable, though there is one daily bus to Kaspichan, from where you can catch a minibus to Madara.

Veliko Târnovo
ВЕЛИКО ТЪРНОВО

POP 68,783

Medieval history emanates from Veliko Târnovo's fortified walls and cobbled lanes. One of Bulgaria's oldest towns, Veliko Târnovo has as its centrepiece the magnificent restored Tsarevets Fortress, citadel of the Second Bulgarian Empire.

Historic Târnovo is tucked into the dramatic bends of the Yantra River, clasped by an amphitheatre of forested hills. Bulgaria's 19th-century National Revival splendour is easy to relive along historic lanes such as ul Gurko; similarly evocative is handicraft market Samovodska Charshiya, which retains much the same atmosphere it had two centuries ago.

The modern town has burst these tidy seams, splaying west from busy bul Bulgaria. Today's Târnovo has Bulgaria's second-largest university and is home to a multicultural expat scene. Its location between Bucharest and Istanbul has made it a backpacker favourite, though it's worth more than a stopover if you're to see it from the heights of its fortress down to its tangle of ramshackle lanes.

History

The strategic geography of Târnovo's hills attracted settlers from early times. Neolithic people in 5500 BC, and Thracian tribes three millennia later, inhabited Tsarevets Hill (on which the fortress stands today) and Trapezitsa Hill opposite. The Romans built the fortress' first walls and, in the 6th century, Byzantine Emperor Justinian created a citadel. Slavic tribes captured it in the 7th century, but it was soon fought over in the interminable wars between Byzantium and the First Bulgarian Empire.

In 1185, under brothers Asen and Petâr, Târnovgrad became a hotspot for rebellion against weakening Byzantine rule. With their foundation of the Second Bulgarian Empire, it replaced the destroyed Pliska and Veliki Preslav as the new capital, becoming second only to Constantinople in importance. Trade and culture flourished for the next 200 years.

On 17 July 1393 the Ottomans captured Târnovgrad, destroying the citadel. No longer very strategic in the middle of a vast empire, the town stagnated through Ottoman times until Bulgarian nationalism asserted itself during the mid-19th century. In 1877, during the Russo-Turkish War, Russian General Gurko liberated Târnovgrad.

Because of its importance during the Second Bulgarian Empire, Veliko Târnovo (as it was renamed) was the location for the writing of Bulgaria's Constitution in 1879, and was where the independence of the Bulgarian state was officially proclaimed in 1908. An earthquake in 1913 had drastic effects, destroying around one-third of the town, though gradual rebuilding restored some of the period architecture to its former glory.

◎ Sights

★ Tsarevets Fortress
FORTRESS

(adult/student 6/2 lv, scenic elevator 2 lv; ⊙ 8am-7pm Apr-Oct, 9am-5pm Nov-Mar) The inescapable symbol of Veliko Târnovo, this reconstructed fortress dominates the skyline and is one of Bulgaria's most beloved monuments. The former seat of the medieval tsars, it boasts the remains of more than 400 houses, 18 churches, the royal palace, an execution rock and more. Watch your

Tsarevets Fortress

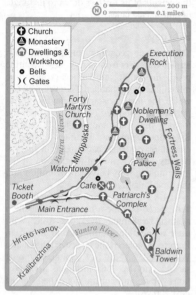

0 ─────── 200 m
0 ─────── 0.1 miles

- **Church**
- **Monastery**
- **Dwellings & Workshop**
- **Bells**
- **)(Gates**

Execution Rock

Forty Martyrs Church

Nobleman's Dwelling

Mitropolska

Yantra River

Royal Palace

Fortress Walls

Watchtower

Ticket Booth

Cafe

Patriarch's Complex

Main Entrance

Hristo Ivanov

Yantra River

Kraibrezhna

Baldwin Tower

step: there are lots of potholes, broken steps and unfenced drops. The fortress morphs into a psychedelic spectacle with a magnificent night-time Sound & Light Show (p371).

Tsarevets Museum-Reserve is located on Tsarevets Hill, which has been settled since time immemorial due to its strategic location. Thracians and Romans used it as a defensive position, but the Byzantines built the first significant fortress here between the 5th and 7th centuries AD. The fortress was rebuilt and fortified by the Slavs and Bulgars between the 8th and 10th centuries, and again by the Byzantines in the early 12th century. When Tărnovgrad became the Second Bulgarian Empire's capital, the fortress was truly magnificent, but with the Turkish invasion in 1393, it was sacked and destroyed. Tourists can thank the communists for returning it to a semblance of its former glory (although some archaeologists grumble about the faithfulness of the restoration).

Not much English-language information is provided, but guided English-language tours (10 lv) can be arranged by enquiring at the tourist-information centre.

Entering the structure, pass through two gates and veer left (northeast) for the fortress walls – some were once 12m high and 10m thick. Further along the walls are the unrecognisable remains of a 12th-century monastery, various dwellings and workshops and two churches. To the north lie remains of a 13th-century monastery, and Execution Rock, from which traitors were pushed into the Yantra River. Alleged traitor Patriarch Joachim III was the most famous figure to take the plunge, in 1300.

The complex's eastern path is less remarkable; return to the middle, using the hilltop Patriarch's Complex as a landmark. Past one of several modern bells (used in the Sound and Light show) are a ruined nobleman's dwelling and two churches to the left (east).

Below the Patriarch's Complex are the foundations of the Royal Palace, from where 22 successive kings ruled Bulgaria. Once covering 4500 sq metres, the palace included an appropriately enormous throne (measuring about 30m by 10m) and Roman columns, probably transferred from nearby Nikopolis-ad-Istrum.

From the palace, head west to the main path and up the steps to the Patriarch's Complex, also called the Church of the Blessed Saviour. Once about 3000 sq metres in size, it was probably built around 1235 and has been extensively restored. The city views from the front steps are more impressive than the modern murals inside, depicting 14th- and 15th-century Bulgarian history.

Returning towards the main entrance, veer left along the path hugging the southern wall. At its end is the restored Baldwin Tower, where Baldwin I of Flanders – the perfidious Crusader who led the sacking of Christian Byzantium in 1204 – got his just deserts, imprisoned and executed after his defeat by the Bulgarians a year later. There are great views from the top.

Sarafkina Kâshta   MUSEUM
(ul General Gurko 88; adult/student 6/2 lv; ☉9am-6pm Tue & Thu-Sat, noon-6pm Wed) Built for a wealthy banker in 1861, this National Revival–style house-museum spans five storeys (when viewed from the river). Within, 19th-century earrings, bracelets and other delicate silverware are on display, alongside antique ceramics, woodcarvings and traditional costumes and jewellery.

Sarafkina Kâshta offers insights into the wigged world of Veliko Tărnovo's society women, a ball-frequenting, fashioned-focused crowd devoted to following the latest point-lace techniques from Western Europe. It's a tantalising glimpse of moneyed Veliko Tărnovo society during its 19th-century golden age.

Asenevtsi Monument   MONUMENT

In the shape of a sky-piercing sword and dominating Veliko Tărnovo's river views, this 1985 monument celebrates medieval Bulgarian might. The horsemen flanking its central column are Asenevtsi brothers Asen, Petar and Kaloyan and Asen's son Ivan, under whom Bulgaria flourished in the 12th and 13th centuries. The surrounding greenery is a popular place for summer live-music events.

Samovodska Charshiya   AREA

During its 19th-century heyday, this lane hosted dozens of vendors from local villages, carefully laying fruit and vegetables, butter and cheeses onto small carpets laid on the cobbled ground. Inns, blacksmiths and craft shops helped Samovodska Charshiya grow into Veliko Tărnovo's biggest market square in the 1880s. Today it retains the nostalgic feel, with handicrafts, traditional sweets and leatherware on offer from numerous boutiques.

Ulitsa Gurko   HISTORIC SITE

The oldest street in Veliko Tărnovo, ul Gurko is a must-stroll with arresting views towards the Yantra River and Asen Monument. Its charmingly crumbling period houses – which appear to be haphazardly piled on one another – provide a million photo ops and conversations that start with 'Imagine living here...' Sturdy shoes a must.

Forty Martyrs Church   CHURCH

(www.st40martyrs.org; ul Mitropolska; adult/student 5/1 lv; ☺9am-6pm Apr-Oct, 9.30am-5.30pm Nov-Mar) The Forty Martyrs Church, in the old Asenova quarter, was built in 1230 to celebrate Tsar Asen II's victory over the Byzantines. It was used as a royal mausoleum and then as a mosque by the Turks, before its reuse as a church after Bulgaria's liberation in 1878.

Multimedia Visitors Centre   MUSEUM

(Tsarevgrad Tarnov Wax Museum; ul Nikola Pikolo 6; adult/child 10/5 lv; ☺9am-7pm Tue-Sun, noon-7pm Mon) Eerily lifelike wax figures of medieval characters are the main attraction of this museum en route to Tsarevets Fortress. Between waxy visages of peasants and kings, multimedia panels give multilingual rundowns of Veliko Tărnovo's history. Kids will get a kick out of eyeballing citizens of yore, especially the throne room featuring an intensely concentrating Tsar Asen, or playing dress-up in period costumes. Less-youthful travellers might find the entrance fee a little steep.

Church of Sveti Petar & Pavel   CHURCH

(Church of St Peter & St Paul; ul Mitropolska; adult/student 4/2 lv; ☺9am-6pm) North of Tsarevets Fortress and the Forty Martyrs Church, this sturdy little church mingles elements of Byzantine and classic Bulgarian styles and houses fragments of murals from the 13th to 17th centuries.

Church of Sveti Dimitâr   CHURCH

(ul Patriarh Evtimii) Across the river, enclosed by a high wall, is Tărnovo's oldest church, the beautifully proportioned Church of Sveti Dimitâr. Built in the so-called Tărnovo style, it was named after St Dimitrios, patron saint of Thessaloniki (Greece). During its 1185 consecration, Tsars Asen and Petâr proclaimed an uprising against Byzantine rule, which would create the Second Bulgarian Empire (1185–1396).

State Art Museum   GALLERY

(Boris Denev Gallery; Asenovtsi Park; adult/student 4/2 lv; ☺10am-6pm Tue-Sun) Named for an early 20th-century Veliko Tărnovo artist, this gallery is housed in a grand neoclassical building near the Asen Monument, in a tight bend of the Yantra River. Spread across two floors, displays comprise 19th- and 20th-century art, mostly religious icons and local landscape paintings. Entry is free on Thursdays.

Museum of National Revival & Constituent Assembly   MUSEUM

(ul Ivanka Botev; adult/student 6/2 lv; ☺9am-6pm Wed-Mon, noon-6pm Tue) Within a former Turkish town hall built in 1872, this is where Bulgaria's first National Assembly was held to write the country's first constitution in 1879. The ground floor charts administrative and daily life in Veliko Tărnovo from the 15th to 19th centuries, using costumes, books and photos, building up to the Bulgarian National Revival. The former assembly hall, upstairs, displays portraits of local personalities, while the basement has old photos and some valuable icons.

Veliko Târnovo

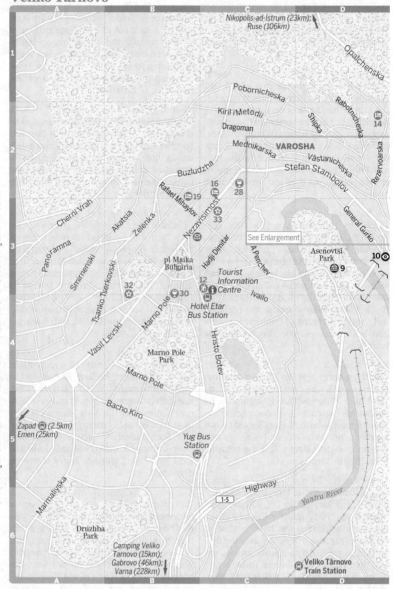

Veliko Târnovo

Archaeological Museum MUSEUM
(☏062-638 841; http://museumvt.com; ul Ivanka
Boteva 2; adult/student 6/2 lv; ⊗noon-6pm Mon
& 9am-6pm Tue-Sun Apr-Oct, to 5.30pm Nov-
Mar) Housed in a grand old building with a courtyard full of Roman sculptures, the archaeological museum contains Roman artefacts and medieval Bulgarian exhibits, including a huge mural of the tsars, plus some ancient gold from nearby Neolithic settlements.

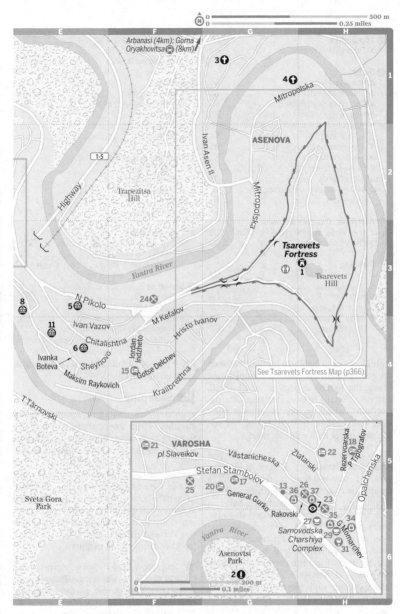

🏃 Activities

Hiking and mountain biking are the most popular ways to work up a sweat in Veliko Tãrnovo's surrounds; the best months are May to October.

Free Veliko Turnovo Walking Tours WALKING

(☑ 0887199921; www.facebook.com/freevtwalk; tourist information centre; ☉ 11am daily Apr–mid-Nov) FREE Engaging walking tours lead visitors around Veliko Tãrnovo's highlights,

Veliko Târnovo

with plenty of history and humour between the statue photo ops and restaurant plugs. Check the Facebook page or email ahead, and consider the less-regular 6pm 'alternative tours', which explore the city's seamier side. Tours last up to three hours, but you can skip out early if short on time.

The VT Foodies   CULTURAL TOUR
(thevtfoodies@mail.com; ⊙ tours at 11.30am weekdays May–mid-Nov by request) FREE Guided by charming food enthusiast Mila, nibble your way from traditional bakeries to markets and dizzyingly sugary desserts. Tours are free, though tips are welcome; food providers hope you'll return for another taste (often with 10% off). Tours usually begin from the corner of ul Stambolov and ul Rakovski. Email at least 24 hours ahead, and mention any dietary requirements.

✷ Festivals & Events

International Folklore Festival   CULTURAL
(☑ 062-630 223; www.cioff.org; ⊙ late Jun–mid-Jul) The city's most popular festival brings acts from Bulgaria, the Balkans and beyond for a program of folk music, dancing and

street parties. Details and exact dates available from mid-April.

⌂ Sleeping

High utility costs put the squeeze on smaller guesthouse and hotel owners, who struggle to make ends meet. But while hotels come and go, Veliko Târnovo's accommodation scene suits all budgets. Higher-end hotels are comfortable, though impersonal, while hostels have plenty of personality but tend to be bare-bones. The best balance is found at family-run guesthouses and apartments, especially near Samovodska Charshiya in the Varosha district, and along the lower (southeastern) end of ul Gurko.

★ **Camping Veliko Tarnovo**   CAMPGROUND $
(☑ 0619-42 777; www.campingvelikotarnovo.com; ul Vasil Levski 70, Dragizhevo; per tent/campervan/adult/child 6/16/7/6 lv; ⊙ Apr-Oct; P 🐾 🎾 🐕) This friendly campground snoozes among green meadows in Dragizhevo village, a 15km drive east of Veliko Târnovo. Efficiently run by cheerful British couple Nick and Nicky, the camping area draws a mix of families and adventure travellers. There's laundry service (12 lv), bike hire (15 lv) and a pool for kids to splash in.

Hotel Anhea
HOTEL **$**

(☑ 062-577 713; www.anheabg.com; ul Nezavisimost 32; s/d/tr from 30/45/55 lv; ✳ ⌘) This superb budget hotel in an early 1900s building has a restful air, despite its central location. Crisp beige and cream rooms are arranged across two buildings, between which lies a peaceful courtyard and breakfast area – this secret garden is decorated with pretty iron railings, fountains and overseen by resident rabbit Emma.

Slavianska Dusha
GUESTHOUSE **$**

(☑ 062-625 182; www.slavianska-dusha.com; ul Nikola Zlatarski 21; s/d/tr/apt from 30/40/50/70 lv; P ✳ ⌘) This jolly guesthouse is a real family affair, with the father as builder, son as chef and mother managing daily operations. Rooms are simple, spacious and ultra-clean, with some enjoying heavenly views over Veliko Tărnovo's terracotta rooftops.

Kâshata Private Flats
APARTMENT **$**

(The House; ☑ 0887253693, 062-604 129; www. thehouse-bg.com; pl Slaveikov 4; 2/4-person apt from 50/90 lv; ✳ ⌘) Live like a local at these city-centre apartments. All are plain, though well maintained with comforts such as TVs and little sofas. Most have balconies and they are occasionally enlivened by original features (such as the 100-year-old wooden beams in the attic flat). The English- and Russian-speaking host is a garrulous soul and very flexible to accommodating travellers' needs.

Hostel Mostel
HOSTEL **$**

(☑ 0897859359; www.hostelmostel.com; ul Iordan Indjeto 10; campsites/dm/s/d incl breakfast 18/20/46/60 lv; @ ⌘) The famous Sofia-based Hostel Mostel has a welcoming branch in Tărnovo, with clean, modern dorm rooms and doubles with sparkling bathrooms. It's just 150m from Tsarevets Fortress – good for exploring there, but a long walk from the city centre. Service is cheerful and multilingual, and there's barbecue equipment out back.

Hikers Hostel
HOSTEL **$**

(☑ 0889691661; www.hikers-hostel.org; ul Rezervoarska 91; dm/d from 14/52 lv; @ ⌘) Tărnovo's most laid-back hostel, Hikers has an unassuming location high in Varosha's old quarter (a 10-minute walk from the city centre) with lovely, lofty views. Dorms are spartan but clean, as are the two private rooms (one is without windows). Laundry facilities cost 4 lv.

★ Hotel-Mehana Gurko
HISTORIC HOTEL **$$**

(☑ 0887858965; www.hotel-gurko.com; ul General Gurko 33; s/d/apt incl breakfast from 70/90/130 lv; P ✳ @ ⌘) Sitting pretty on Veliko Tărnovo's oldest street, with blooms spilling over its wooden balconies and agricultural curios littering the exterior, the Gurko is one of the best places to sleep (and eat) in town. Its 21 rooms are spacious and soothing, each individually decorated and offering great views.

Hotel Comfort
HOTEL **$$**

(☑ 0887777265; www.hotelcomfortbg.com; ul P Tipografov 5; d 40-140 lv, apt 100 lv; P ✳ ⌘) With jaw-dropping views of the fortress and surrounding hills from most rooms, plus a stellar location just around the corner from the Samovodska Charshia market square, this family-owned hotel is a winner. Room prices vary enormously, depending on their view and floor. English is spoken by the amiable staff.

Hotel Premier
HOTEL **$$**

(☑ 062-615 556; www.hotelpremier-bg.com; ul Sava Penev 1; s/d 76/96 lv, ste from 210 lv; P ✳ ⌘ ☀) Hotel Premier is a smart and central option, located on a side street near the post office. Amenities are geared at business travellers, though there is plenty of scope for pampering with its rooftop pool, sauna (14 lv) and

DON'T MISS

THE SOUND & LIGHT SHOW

Marvel as Veliko Tărnovo's medieval skyline is bathed in multiple sounds and colours at the Sound & Light Show (☑ 0885080865; www.soundandlight.bg; ul N Pikolo 6; 20-25 lv). This 40-minute audiovisual display uses choral music and flashes of light in a homage to the rise and fall of the Second Bulgarian Empire.

Historical insights are few, but it's an undeniably impressive spectacle: Tsarevets Hill is awash in crimson and green, while strings, cymbal clashes and traditional song swell to a crescendo.

The starting time is anywhere from 8pm to 9.30pm, depending on the time of year, so check the website or ask at the tourist information centre. Otherwise, simply listen for the bells and look for the laser beams.

comprehensive menu of spa treatments (19 lv to 117 lv).

Hotel Bolyarski
HOTEL **$$$**

(☑ 062-613 200; www.bolyarski.com; ul Stefan Stambolov 53a; s/d/ste incl breakfast from 70/130/180 lv; P❋🔊🛋) The schmick Bolyarski roosts on the bluff on ul Stambolov, with magical views of the town and river. Its modern, well-kept rooms are pitched at business travellers. The fitness centre, pool and sauna will suit anyone seeking a follow-up workout to marching around Tsarevets Hill.

✖ Eating

Bulgarian and Italian restaurants dominate Veliko Tǎrnovo's dining scene, with good options for all budgets. Ul Stefan Stambolov has abundant choice (the best restaurants have terraces overlooking the river) but folksy, family places on ul Gurko and around Samovodska Charshiya are most atmospheric.

Stratilat
INTERNATIONAL **$**

(☑ 062-635 313; ul Rakovski 11; mains 5-9 lv; 🕘9am-11pm; 🛜) It's certainly touristy, but a large outdoor terrace perched above hectic ul Stambolov makes this cafe-restaurant enormously popular among visitors to the historic Samovodska Charshiya quarter. It's best for coffees and cakes, but Stratilat also churns out grills and salads day and night.

★ Shtastliveca
BULGARIAN **$$**

(☑ 062-606 656; www.shtastliveca.com; ul Stefan Stambolov 79; mains 10-20 lv; 🕚11am-1am; 🛜) 🍴 Inventive dishes and amiable service have solidified the 'Lucky Man' as a favourite among locals and expats. Sauces pairing chocolate and cheese are drizzled over chicken, while strawberry and balsamic vinegar lend piquancy to meaty dishes, and there is a pleasing range for vegetarians.

The nod to vintage style in its floral decor gives it a calming feel, and downstairs tables enjoy the best views.

Ivan Asen
BULGARIAN **$$**

(☑ 0882650065; www.ivan-asen.com; pl Tsar Asen 1; mains 8-15 lv; 🕘10am-11pm) Don't be deterred by its touristy location near Tsarevets Fortress. Stone walls and pillars infuse it with a commanding air, while dishes are as robust as you'd expect from a restaurant named after the Bulgarian Empire's bolshiest ruler. Fill up on *satch* (a stew served on a hotplate), roasted pork, or trout with prosciutto. Risottos and pizza also served.

Hotel-Mehana Gurko
BULGARIAN **$$**

(☑ 062-627 838; ul General Gurko 33; mains 7-15 lv; 🛜) This traditional-style *mehana* (tavern) at the Hotel Gurko is a cosy place with great views and tasty Bulgarian specialities. Portions are hearty and service is prompt and friendly.

★ Han Hadji Nikoli
INTERNATIONAL **$$$**

(☑ 062-651 291; www.hanhadjinikoli.com; ul Rakovski 19; mains 17-30 lv; 🕘10am-11pm; 🛜) Countless Veliko Tǎrnovo inns were ransacked under Ottoman rule, as they were popular meeting places for revolution-minded locals. Fortunately Han Hadji Nikoli survived, and today the town's finest restaurant occupies this beautifully restored 1858 building with an upstairs gallery. Well-executed dishes include Trakia chicken marinated in herbs and yoghurt, mussels sautéed in white wine and exquisitely prepared pork neck.

Popular with tour groups.

🍷 Drinking & Nightlife

★ Tam
BAR

(☑ 0889879693; ul Marno Pole 2A; 🕓4pm-3am Mon-Sat) Open the nondescript door, and up the stairs you'll find the city's friendliest, most-open-minded hang-out. Tam is the place to feel the pulse of VT's arty crowd. You might stumble on art installations, movie screenings, or language nights in English, French or Spanish. Punters and staff extend a genuine welcome and drinks flow late.

Sammy's Bar
BAR

(☑ 0885233387; ul Nezavisimost; 🕚11am-3am) The lofty views from this bar and beer garden are as refreshing as the selection of herb-garnished lemonades (2.80 lv). So it's no wonder that Sammy's, just off busy ul Nezavisimost, has become a trusted local haunt.

Shekerdzinitsa
CAFE

(ul Giorgi Momarchev 13; 🕘9am-6pm Tue-Sun) Centuries of Veliko Tǎrnovo history can be tasted in the Turkish 'sand coffee' at this characterful little cafe near the old-market neighbourhood. Most tempting of all are takeaway treats such as sticks of *lokum* (rose-scented sweets with pistachios), hen-shaped lollipops and *halva* (blocks of honey-flavoured semolina).

Cafe Provence
CAFE

(☎ 0876223882; ul Stefan Stambolov 36; ⊙ 10am-10pm) Retreat from the bustle of the city's main drag into this calming cafe, where satiny chairs and distressed furnishings evoke a salon feel. Hot drinks and gateaus fit the loose French theme, with occasional Bulgarian twists such as the 'Rose de Provence', a coffee swirled with local rose oil (2.80 lv).

Tequila Bar
BAR

(ul Stefan Stambolov 30; ⊙ 3pm-late) Overlooking the main street, and around the corner from Samovodska Charshiya, Tequila Bar is a festively painted, as-fun-as-you'd-expect student bar with good cocktails and cheap beer.

☆ Entertainment

Melon Live Music Club
LIVE MUSIC

(☎ 062-603 439; bul Nezavisimost 21; ⊙ 6pm-2am) Popular spot for live music, from rock and R&B to Latin jazz. Admission to live events is around 4 lv or 5 lv.

Club Jack
CLUB

(www.jack-club.com; ul Magistraka 5; ⊙ 10pm-4am) This house and dance-music club draws a young, well-dressed crowd at weekends with its popular formula of themed nights, cocktail promotions and local DJs. The student-dominated crowd means it usually hibernates outside university term time.

🛍 Shopping

★ Samovodska Charshiya
ARTS & CRAFTS

(ul Rakovski) Veliko Târnovo's historic quarter is a true centre of craftsmanship, with genuine blacksmiths, potters and cutlers, among other artisans, still practising their trades here. Wander the cobblestone streets to discover bookshops and purveyors of antiques, jewellery and art, housed in appealing National Revival houses.

Galeria Manya
ARTS & CRAFTS

(☎ 0886432861; ul Rakovski 12; ⊙ 10am-6pm) Hirsute costumes and scowling wooden masks startle passers-by from the window of this folk store in the thick of Samovodska Charshiya. The shop specialises in ornaments and costumes relating to *kukeri* processions, an end-of-winter tradition in which evil spirits are banished by shaggy-costumed dancers.

Book Cave
BOOKS

(☎ 0898229910; www.bulgarianbuddies.com; ul Opalchenska 9; ⊙ 10am-1pm & 1.30-5pm Mon-Sat) A sturdy favourite among locals, expats and tourists, this bookstore at the bottom of the Varosha district is run by an enormously helpful owner and is the city's best place to buy, exchange or donate secondhand books. In winter it's closed on Monday and Tuesday.

Icons Krasimir Ivanov
ARTS & CRAFTS

(☎ 0885060544; cnr ul Rakovski & ul Kapitan Diado Nikola; ⊙ 10am-7pm) Lovely hand-painted icons (60 lv to 400 lv) by elder artist Krasimir Ivanov, and detailed ink sketches of old Târnovo (20 lv), are sold at this store-workshop.

ℹ Information

Foreign-exchange offices and ATMs are plentiful on the main drag and in the shopping mall.

Hospital Stefan Cherkezov (☎ 062-626 841; ul Nish 1) Modern hospital with an emergency room and English-speaking doctors.

Tourist Information Centre (☎ 062-622 148; www.velikoturnovo.info; ul Hristo Botev 5; ⊙ 9am-6pm Mon-Sat Apr-Oct, Mon-Fri Nov-Mar) Helpful English-speaking staff offering local info and advice.

ℹ Getting There & Away

BUS

The most central bus terminal is **Hotel Etar Bus Station** (www.etapgroup.com; ul Ivailo 2), served by hourly buses to Sofia (20 lv, three to 3½ hours) and Varna (20 lv, 3½ hours). There are also two daily buses to Dobrich (20 lv, four hours), two to Kavarna (21 lv, 4½ hours) via Albena, and services to Shumen (13 lv, two hours, seven daily). The station is just south of the tourist information centre.

Two non-central bus stations also serve Veliko Târnovo, with a broader range of destinations and services. **Zapad Bus Station** (☎ 062-620 014, 062-640 908; ul Nikola Gabrovski 74), about 3km southwest of the tourist information centre, is the main intercity one. Local buses 10, 12, 14, 70 and 110 go there, along ul Vasil Levski. There's also a left-luggage office. Closer to the centre is **Yug Bus Station** (☎ 062-620 014; ul Hristo Botev 74), 700m south of the tourist information centre.

For online information and to book advance bus tickets (with discounts), search http://bus-ticket.bg and http://online.union-ivkoni.com.

To reach Romania by bus, go first to Ruse: from its main bus station, five daily minibuses make the three-hour trip to Bucharest.

BUSES FROM VELIKO TÂRNOVO

DESTINATION	COST (LV)	DURATION (HR)	FREQUENCY (DAILY)
Burgas (from Zapad)	18-25	4	4
Karlovo (from Zapad)	19	4	1
Kazanlâk (from Zapad)	9	2½	5
Pleven (from Zapad)	14	2	1
Plovdiv (from Zapad)	19	4	4
Ruse (from Yug or Zapad)	8-12	2	6
Shumen (from Yug)	13	3	6
Sliven (from Zapad)	8	2	7
Sofia (from Yug)	22	4	regularly
Troyan (from Zapad)	10	2	1
Varna (from Yug)	21	4	regularly

TRAIN

Check train schedules with the tourist information centre, or on www.bdz.bg, as Veliko Târnovo's two main train stations are located 10km apart. Irregular trains link the two stations (1.50 lv, 20 minutes, nine daily).

The slightly more walkable of the two is **Veliko Târnovo Train Station** (☑ 062-620 065), 1.5km west of town (though staff can be unhelpful).

From Veliko Târnovo Train Station, there is one daily direct train to Plovdiv (12 lv, 4½ hours); alternatively, travel via Stara Zagora (6.50 lv, three hours, five daily), which adds an hour to the total journey time. You can reach Sliven (9 lv, 3½ to four hours, four daily) via Tulovo or Dabovo. For the coast, there is one direct service to Varna (14 lv, four hours). For Burgas you'll need to travel via Dabovo, or via Stara Zagora and Karnobat. Day-trip destinations such as Tryavna (3 lv, one hour, eight daily) and Dryanovo (2.10 lv, 30 minutes, nine daily) are also reachable from this station. Buses 10, 12, 14, 70 and 110 connect the train station to the centre of town. Alternatively, take a taxi (3 lv to 6 lv).

Gorna Oryakhovitsa train station (☑ 062-826 118), 8.5km northeast of town, is along the main line between Sofia and Varna. There are daily services to/from Sofia (14.60 lv, four to five hours, eight daily), some via Tulovo or Mezdra. Direct trains also reach Varna (13 lv, 3½ to four hours, five daily) and Ruse (7 lv, two to 2½ hours, seven daily). There are also daily connections to Stara Zagora (7.40 lv, three hours, four daily) and Shumen (8.40 lv, two to 2½ hours, eight daily).

From Veliko Târnovo, minibuses wait opposite the market along ul Vasil Levski to get to this train station. Taxis cost about 12 lv to 15 lv.

ⓘ Getting Around

Walking is ideal for seeing Târnovo. Taxis are good for zipping around the central areas (charging day/night 0.70/0.80 lv per kilometre), but sometimes refuse to drive in the old quarters, especially Varosha, due to the narrow streets. Take advantage of any free pick-up services offered by your accommodation.

If driving, be warned that traffic along the town's central road is always sluggish and parking can be painful. Paid parking is available on pl Slaveikov and at a couple of sites near the fortress. A more distant car park, and some unpaid street parking, can be found near the industrial zone, north of Varosha.

For car rental (from 45 lv per day), ask at the tourist information centre for the best offers, or enquire with Motoroads (www.motoroads.com).

Around Veliko Târnovo

Preobrazhenski Monastery

Outstanding clifftop views compete with murals by renowned painter Zahari Zograf at this serene monastery (Transfiguration Monastery; church admission 2 lv; ☺7am-7pm), 7km north of Veliko Târnovo. It was officially founded in 1360, though its origins extend 200 years earlier. Like many Bulgarian monasteries, it was destroyed under Ottoman rule. Rebuilt in 1825, its Zograf murals (painted 1849–51) include a wheel of life and menacing scenes between demons and sinners. It was spared annihilation by a 1991 landslide (note the boulders either side of the church).

Bus 10 from Veliko Tărnovo passes the monastery; disembark at a turn-off on the road headed to Ruse. From here it's a shady, uphill 3km walk. A taxi from Veliko Tărnovo costs about 6 lv one way.

If there's no one around, pop your 2 lv donation into the tin in the church.

Emen   Емен

Thrashing beneath lofty limestone cliffs, the Negovanka River has sculpted deep creeks and pretty waterfalls in captivating nature reserve Emen Canyon (Emenski Kanion), 22km west of Veliko Tărnovo. For soaring views across the canyon, hike the Negovanka Ecotrail along 90m-high bluffs. The trail begins with a steep clamber up rocky steps from Emen Cave (it's safer not to enter) to a spectacular vantage point over the gorge. The path then weaves among tree-shaded clifftops before a muddy descent to a 10m-high waterfall.

It takes about two hours to the waterfall and back. Don't attempt the slippery trail after rainfall or in winter, and don't step out on to the disastrously unmaintained wooden walkways and bridges; stick to the path.

There is a narrow, cobblestone car park by the cave, but it may be better to leave your vehicle in Emen village's central car park. From here, set out through Emen's northeastern streets uphill towards the river. The

---

WORTH A TRIP

ARBANASI

This hilltop getaway, 8km by road from Veliko Tărnovo, has an agreeable mix of historical and outdoor activities. Nearly 90 of Arbanasi's churches, monasteries and mansions are state-protected cultural monuments. Wealthy nobles who resided here during the Bulgarian Revival period have left behind heritage houses, now converted into museums or guesthouses.

Walking trails and horse-riding excursions are popular ways to experience its leafy surrounds. Busloads of visitors arrive at weekends; stick around after sunset to enjoy excellent *mehanas* and valley views without the crowds.

The Nativity Church (Regional Museum of History; ul Rozhdestvo Hristovo; adult/student 6/2 lv; ☉9am-6pm Wed-Mon, noon-6pm Tue) is considered the main sight. The five chambers in Arbanasi's oldest surviving church are covered in kaleidoscopic frescoes (dating to between 1632 and 1649), featuring a pantheon of saints and moving depictions of Mary and Christ. Don't miss the wooden iconostasis, intricately carved by Tryavna-school artisans.

Dark-eyed saints with gold haloes glower down from every painted arch inside the 16th-century Church of Sveti Arhangeli Mikhail & Gavril (ul Sofronii Vrachanski; adult/student 6/2 lv; ☉9am-6pm Tue-Sun, noon-6pm Mon), built over a ruined medieval building. The wooden iconostases were carved by Tryavna artisans.

Be sure to stop by the 17th century Konstantsalieva House (cnr ul Kapitan Pavel Gramadov & ul George Kandilarov; adult/student 6/2 lv; ☉9am-6pm Tue-Sun, noon-6pm Mon) to learn how Arbanasi's well-heeled residents prospered during Bulgaria's National Revival period, sipping coffee from silver cups and donning fox-skin coats and silks to show up their neighbours at church.

For activities, the Arbanasi Horse Base (☑0886999449, 0898459880; ☉8am-noon & 1-6pm) offers guided horse-riding excursions in the lush hills around Arbanasi. Prices for short rides start at 25 lv.

Stop for a meal at highly rated Sevastokrator (☑062-655 553; www.sevastokrator.com; ul Sveti Nikola 13; mains 10-15 lv; ☉8am-10pm), whose terrace peers over some of the finest forest views in Arbanasi. The highlights here are beautifully executed 'stone kebabs', where juicy mushrooms, cabbage and pork are muddled together on a hot plate.

Complex Bulgarka (☑0889207020; www.hotelbulgarka.com; ul Konstantin Rusevich 4; apt incl breakfast 120-170 lv; P❄🏠) is a heritage hotel that's hosted rebels, refugee monks and even a Romanian prince over the centuries. Its three apartments are elegantly furnished with plump leather sofas and shiny bathrooms. The hosts happily help to organise fishing and horse-riding trips.

trail is signposted from the Vishovgrad–Emen road, at the northern fringe of Emen, although the signs can be hard to spot and read.

Dryanovo Monastery

A history of destruction and revolution, as dramatic as its cliff-backed location, entices visitors to Dryanovo Monastery (www.dryanovo.bg; ⊙8am-8pm) FREE. Originally founded in the early 13th century, when relics of St Michael were transported from Batak, the complex was plundered by the Ottomans. It was rebuilt in the late 17th century at its present location, astride the gorge about 6km from Dryanovo village, sheltered by limestone bluffs. The highlight is its frescoed church, sporting a huge gold and red chandelier.

History

Revolutionary sentiment simmered within the monastery walls over the decades that followed its 17th-century rebuild. Key events of the 1876 April Uprising were plotted here and monks gave shelter to revolutionary fighters such as Vasil Levski. During the Russo-Turkish War (1877–8), more than 100 locals made a valiant last stand against the Turks for nine days. The Turks eventually won, burning the place down yet again. The villagers' bravery is commemorated with a mausoleum in the monastery grounds.

🏃 Activities

After taking in the monastery, hikers can explore the Dryanovo Ecotrail, a well-marked, circular path that starts and finishes near the monastery. The hike takes about four hours, and passes through lush, hilly forests.

The Bacho Kiro Cave (adult/child 3/1 lv; ⊙9am-6pm Apr-Oct, 10am-4pm Nov-Mar) became Bulgaria's first tourist cave way back in 1937, and today it's often twinned with a visit to the monastery. Entry is by semi-guided tour, which involves a little historic preamble (usually in Bulgarian only), after which you can take a short or long (25 minutes or one hour) walking route around the cave.

🛏 Sleeping & Eating

Komplex Drianovski Manastir   HOTEL $
(☎0676-75 253; http://drianovski-manastir.com; r/apt 50/60 lv; ❄) Virtually attached to the Dryanovo Monastery, this small hotel complex has a wing of 11 clean rooms and three apartments above a simple *mehana*.

Mehana Andyka   BULGARIAN $$
(☎0676-72 230; www.andyka.com; mains 8-12 lv; ⊙9am-midnight) This relaxing restaurant has a wooded setting between cliffs and next to the rushing river, about 300m before the Bacho Kiro Cave entrance. It serves soups from tripe to white bean, an extensive range of sausage and other meat hotpots, and salads galore.

ℹ Getting There & Away

Buses from Veliko Târnovo to Gabrovo can leave you at the turn-off to the monastery (4km south of Dryanovo), from where you'll have to walk the last 1.5km. Car parking costs 1 lv per hour.

WORTH A TRIP

NIKOPOLIS-AD-ISTRUM

The broken remains of a Roman 'victory city', built in AD 110, cover this isolated site, 20km north of Veliko Târnovo. The foundations of Nikopolis-ad-Istrum (adult/child 6/2 lv; ⊙9am-6pm Apr-Oct, 10am-4pm Nov-Mar) were laid by Emperor Trajan after a successful battle against the Dacians. Destroyed by Slavs in the late 6th century, the city experienced a brief period of resettlement in the 9th century, after which it slumbered for centuries. Its ruins, including streets, towers, gates, a city square and town hall, were discovered in 1871.

If driving from Veliko Târnovo, head north towards Ruse and take the signposted turn-off to the left (west) after about 20km. This access road is rough in parts.

By bus, take the same northerly route and dismount at the turn-off to Nikyup; from there, it's a 4km signposted walk. By taxi from Veliko Târnovo, the journey costs roughly 15 lv each way.

Tryavna   ТРЯВНА

POP 10,000

Famous for its dexterous woodcarvers, whose work has graced churches and mansions across Bulgaria, Tryavna is a relaxing day trip from Veliko Tårnovo or Kazanlâk (respectively, a 60- and 90-minute drive). Bulgaria's 19th-century glory days come alive along Tryavna's romantic bridges and cobbled streets, lined with National Revival–period homes. Amid tourists clinking glasses in numerous *mehanas*, Tryavna's centuries-old woodcarving tradition lives on in the artisans who still train here.

⊙ Sights

Restored period houses and churches, decorated with Tryavna's distinctive woodcarvings, are the main attractions in town. Tryavna's historic heart is pl Kapitan Dyado Nikola, dominated by a 21m-high clock tower (1814), with Roman-style stone Arch Bridge (1844) nearby. The bridge leads to ul PR Slaveikov, one of Bulgaria's most pleasing cobblestone lanes, chockfull of house-museums and traditional *mehanas*.

★ Daskalov House   MUSEUM

(Museum of Woodcarving & Icon Painting; www.tryavna-museum.com; ul PR Slaveikov 27; adult/student 2/1 lv; ⊙9am-6pm) As well as faithfully representing 19th-century design styles within its walls, Daskalov House contains the fascinating **Museum of Woodcarving and Icon Painting**. There are magnificent examples of the Tryavna school of woodcarving, including a re-created workshop. The superb carvings within the 1808 mansion are the result of a fierce competition between two craftsmen, Ivan Bochukovetsa and Dimitar Oshanetsa. Note the 'July sun', a starburst carved in the wooden ceiling, that won the contest.

Church of Sveti Arhangeli Mihail   CHURCH

(cnr ul Pencho Raikov & ul Chuchura; 1 lv) Overlooking the square near the clock tower is slate-roofed St Archangel Michael, Tryavna's oldest church. Local lore dates it to the 12th century. It was burnt down by the Turks, but rebuilt in 1819, and holds remarkably intricate Tryavna-school woodcarvings.

Museum of Icons   MUSEUM

(☑0896755938; ul Breza 1; 2 lv; ⊙10am-6pm Wed-Sun summer, 9am-4.30pm Wed-Sun winter) Housed in a former chapel, Tryavna's Museum of Icons contains more than 160 religious icons from the erstwhile collections of famous local families. The museum is beyond the train line, and signposted from ul PR Slaveikov.

Angel Kânchev House-Museum   MUSEUM

(ul Angel Kânchev 39; 2 lv; ⊙9.30am-1.30pm & 2-6pm Wed-Sun summer, 10am-4pm Wed-Sun winter) It's impossible to miss the dark wooden building with a steeply overhanging upper floor along ul Angel Kânchev. Now housing the Angel Kânchev House-Museum, the 1805 building contains exhibits about revolutionary hero Kânchev and the liberation of Tryavna during the Russo-Turkish War.

Tryavna Museum
School of Painting   MUSEUM

(adult/student 2/1 lv; ⊙9am-6pm summer, to 5pm winter) Housed in the restored Staroto Shkolo (the town's old school, built in 1836), the Tryavna Museum School of Painting has exemplary works by local artists.

⊨ Sleeping

Though many are within modern constructions, Tryavna's numerous guesthouses and hotels often live up to the charisma of the town's historic buildings. There are lodgings to suit most budgets, with the majority aimed at travellers in the midrange bracket. The tourist office can help arrange private rooms for about 25 lv per person.

★ Dream of Happiness   GUESTHOUSE $

(☑0892281441; http://dreamofhappiness.tryavna.biz; ul Angel Kânchev 63; d 50 lv; P ❄ 🛜) This whimsically named guesthouse offers comfortable rooms in a spotlessly clean house on Tryavna's main drag. Rooms are immaculate, there's a tranquil private garden, and a shared kitchen if you're tired of dining out on *kebabcheta* (spicy grilled sausage). Ebullient staff can share tips on local dining and wine. Ask ahead for directions to its car park, accessible via a back street.

You can request an extra bed for 10 lv.

Hotel Tigara   HOTEL $

(☑0889393154; www.tigara.tryavna.biz; ul D Gorov 7a; d/apt 35/60 lv) This friendly, family-run place in the centre, near the History Museum, has trim, balconied rooms.

Art-M Gallery Hotel   HOTEL $$

(☑0887097373; www.artmgallery.com; ul Angel Kânchev 20; d 78-98 lv; P 🛜) Attached to a little

TRYAVNA WOODCARVING

Local legends say Tryavna's association with intricate woodcarvings began with a gifted young boy, Vitan, who learned the art from a monk. Generations of woodcarvers, passing their skills from father to son, helped Tryavna bloom into a hub for this painstaking craft during the Bulgarian National Revival period. Designs chiselled from local walnut, birch, poplar and oak trees were used to decorate monasteries in Gabrovo, Veliko Târnovo, Arbanasi and Rila. Tryavna carvers were sought after by builders and house owners as far away as Serbia, Turkey and modern-day Iran.

By the early 19th century more than 40 Tryavna workshops were producing wooden cradles, frames, icons, friezes, doors and crosses, each individually designed. Ornate and detailed flower and starburst motifs became particularly associated with the Tryavna school. Some beautiful exhibits include the 'July sun ceiling' inside Tryavna's Daskalov House (p377), home to the Museum of Woodcarving and Icon Painting.

Carving courses for tourists are available, starting at around 60 lv per hour; see the local tourist information centre (p378) for details.

gallery, this boutique place is winning hearts for warm service and its atmospheric period building. Rooms within the slate-roofed hotel are comfortable, wooden-floored and have accents such as regional artwork and sloping ceilings in attic rooms. The location, opposite the clock tower and paces from the bridge leading to cobblestone ul PR Slveiykov, couldn't be finer.

Zograf Inn   GUESTHOUSE $$
(☑ 0677-64 970; http://zograf.tryavna.biz; ul PR Slaveikov 1; d/apt from 59/78 lv; 🖻) In the heart of Tryavna, near the clock tower, the Zograf occupies a renovated historic house. Rooms are good value, though (unlike the National Revival–style building) they are simple and modern. Hearty breakfasts cost an extra 4 lv. Ask ahead for car space in its tiny garage.

✖ Eating & Drinking

In keeping with the town's nostalgic feel, Tryavna's plentiful restaurants and cafes almost invariably serve traditional Bulgarian food. Find several options along ul PR Slaveikov.

★ Starata Loza   BULGARIAN $$
(☑ 0677-64 501; http://starata-loza.tryavna.biz; ul PR Slaveikov 44; mains 6-15 lv; ⊙10am-10pm; 🖻) The traditional Bulgarian *mehana* experience is given a whimsical twist with decorative touches such as wine casks bulging out of the walls. Meals are nicely cooked, from barbecued river fish to salty *shopska* (tomato, cucumber and cheese salad), while the service is genial and very efficient. It's opposite the entrance to Daskalov House.

Restaurant Trevnenski Kat   BULGARIAN $$
(☑0677-62 066; http://trevnenski-kat.tryavna. biz; ul Angel Kânchev 55; mains 8-12 lv; ⊙8am-midnight) This atmospheric restaurant in an imposing National Revival–style house has worn wooden floors and carved ceilings, and a good range of homemade Bulgarian cooking.

Biraria Tryavna   BREWERY
(☑0667-63 727; http://lucs.tryavna.biz; ul Pencho Raikov 5; ⊙noon-late) Sup local brews by the river at this cheerful tavern, enormously popular with visitors and with a refreshing beer garden. It's close to the Starata Skola, less than 100m north of the Arch Bridge.

Kafe Paraliite   CAFE
(☑0898545407; ul Osmimart 8; ⊙9am-8pm) Perch on a crescent-moon-shaped stool, gulp coffee from colourful Troyan pottery and nibble a meringue stuffed with hazelnuts at this friendly cafe near the clock tower.

ℹ Information

An ATM and some restaurants are around the square.

Tourist Information Centre (☑ 0677-62 247; www.tryavna.bg; ul Bacho Kiro 1; ⊙ 9am-12.30pm & 2-5pm Mon-Fri) In the town-hall building; can help with bus and train schedules, and arrange private rooms.

ℹ Getting There & Away

The bus and train stations are 100m apart, west of ul Angel Kânchev, the main road through the old town.

Most public transport to Tryavna goes via Gabrovo (4 lv, 30 minutes); half-hourly to hourly minibuses connect the two. Occasional direct buses reach Sofia (23 lv, four hours, one to two daily).

By train, Tryavna is accessible from Veliko Târnovo (3 lv, one hour, eight daily). For Sofia, change trains at Gorna Oryakhovitsa.

Etâr   ЕТЪР

Step into Bulgaria's rustic past at Etâr's open-air historic village, 8km southeast of Gabrovo. This family-friendly complex has superb places to shop, and you can watch artisans shaping pottery and metalwork. Beyond the museum, travellers can unwind along walking trails and visit sublime Sokolski Monastery.

⊙ Sights

★ **Sokolski Monastery**   MONASTERY
(☑ 0886308017; Vodnitsi; ⊙ 7am-5pm) A sky-blue church, posing against forested valleys, is the centrepiece of this 1833 monastery. What began as a humble wooden church outside Sokola Cave (Falcon Cave) expanded into the outbuildings and well-preened garden here today. Like many cloisters in Bulgaria, Sokolski Monastery sheltered revolutionary fighter Vasil Levski. The monastery is a 2.5km drive southwest of Etâr's Open-Air Museum, near Vodnitsi village.

The stone fountain at the centre of the garden was crafted in 1868 by Kolyu Ficheto, Bulgaria's pre-eminent National Revival–era architect. Its eight spouts are a nod to eight Gabrovo rebels who were captured and hanged.

There are souvenir and snack stands inside and outside the complex, as well as an excellent sweet shop selling rooster-shaped bonbons and *lokum*.

★ **Etâr Ethnographic
Open-Air Museum**   MUSEUM
(☑ guides 066-810 571; www.etar.org; Etâr; adult/child 5/2 lv; ⊙ 8.30am-6pm) If ambling down cobbled lanes with a stick of halva in hand sounds like an agreeable foray into Bulgaria's past, a day in Etâr will delight. Nearly 50 shops and workshops cluster along the lanes of this historic complex, set between trees along a tributary of the Yantra River. Officially an open-air museum, Etâr feels like a movie set with its costumed performers

and traditional handicrafts. The museum is on the Gabrovo–Shipka road, a 17km drive north from Shipka.

Etâr's 19th-century National Revival–style buildings, gaily painted in peach and periwinkle blue, house the workshops of bakers, cartwrights, cobblers, furriers, glass workers, hatters, jewellers, leather workers, millers, potters, weavers and more. Yes, it's rather twee, but if you're looking to take home a memento of bygone days in the Balkans, there are quality goods from silverware to pottery on sale. Some of the workshops are powered by water from a stream running through the complex; the Karadzheika Watermill dates to 1780.

Aside from shopping, it's possible to peer inside traditional cottages, watch an old sawmill and pause inside the Holy Epiphany Church, a replica of an 1868 temple in Radovtsi village.

Enter the complex either on the northern side (near the Hotel Stranopriemnitsa), at the central administration building, or on the far southern side, near the large car park. A multi-entry, one-day ticket is usually required, and guided tours (in English, French or German) are available for another 7 lv per person (minimum of five people).

🏃 Activities

There is excellent hiking in the forested hills around Etâr. A large map standing opposite the entrance to the ethnographic village details 15 different trails through the nearby Bulgarka Natural Park, plus the time required to hike them. Some trails can be done as loop day hikes, starting and finishing at Etâr.

🛏 Sleeping & Eating

Because of its guaranteed influx of tourists, Etâr's accommodation offerings don't need to work hard to bring in guests. There are a few acceptable guesthouses and hotels in walking distance of the historic complex, but Etâr also makes an easy day trip from Shipka (10km), Tryavna (12km) or Kazanlâk (25km).

Hotel Stranopriemnitsa   HOTEL $
(☑ 066-810 580; stranopriemnica@etar.org; s/d/tr incl breakfast 36/60/84 lv) At the northern (Gabrovo) end of the historic complex, this hotel is decent value, though rooms don't live up to the promise of the olde-worlde hotel exterior.

VELIKO TÂRNOVO & CENTRAL MOUNTAINS ETÂR

Todorovi Guesthouse
GUESTHOUSE $

(☑0879080862; bul Derozhinski 102, Etâr village; s/d 30/45 lv; ☎) Five hundred metres north of the historic complex lies this bare-bones guesthouse, which is a clean and convenient budget stop. Breakfast costs an additional 4 lv.

Mehana Etâr
BULGARIAN $

(☑0879851462; mains 7 lv; ☉10am-7pm) A bit quieter than most of the eateries upriver within the ethnographic museum, Mehana Etâr has affectionate service and shaded outdoor tables. There is an ample menu of Bulgarian fare, such as shish kebabs smoked on a barbecue and gleaming salads of peppers and tomato. It's a few paces south of the complex, on the opposite side of the river.

Renaissance Tavern
BULGARIAN $

(mains 8-10 lv; ☉8.30am-6pm) Sure, its location within Etâr's historic complex may be touristy, but if you want your sausages smoked in the open air or your heaving platefuls of *shopska* salad served on wooden tables outside, then the canteen-style Renaissance is a good choice, especially for families.

❶ Getting There & Away

Etâr is best served from the city of Gabrovo, which has local buses (1 lv) for the 20-minute trip. Alternatively, take a Gabrovo–Kazanlâk bus and disembark at the turn-off near Lyubovo, from where it's a 2km walk. A taxi from Gabrovo costs about 10 lv. From Etâr, a taxi to Tryavna (25 lv to 30 lv) saves the trouble of bussing via Gabrovo.

Driving is more convenient, and Etâr makes a good day trip from Veliko Târnovo, Shipka or Tryavna.

Lovech
ЛОВЕЧ

POP 38,000

Bulgaria's 'town of lilacs' has a fortress, old town and unique covered bridge among its intriguing attractions. Spring is an especially lovely time to visit, when abundant lilac bushes add fragrance to the town. Foreign tourists are few, but Bulgarian weekend visitors arrive in groups to traipse through cobbled lanes in the historic Varosha quarter, and shop for handicrafts within the covered bridge. Lovech is a convenient detour if you're travelling between Sofia and Veliko Târnovo.

◉ Sights

The most colourful photo opportunity in Lovech is from ul Osamska, near the entrance to the Covered Bridge on the western bank of the Osâm River. From here you can see riverside mansions, painted canary yellow and coral pink, hanging over the water's edge.

The **Varosha quarter**, flowing from the eastern end of the Covered Bridge, is Lovech's cobblestone old town with around 150 restored National Revival-period structures. From here, ul Marin Poplukanov leads to Lovech's museums and eventually **Stratesh Hill**, where an imposing **Vasil Levski statue** stands before the entrance to the fortress.

Covered Bridge
BRIDGE

(Pokritiyat Most) A touch of Florence in the heart of Bulgaria, this covered bridge is the only such structure in the Balkans. Renowned Bulgarian architect Kolyu Ficheto masterminded the bridge, with stone foundations and wooden buildings, between 1874 and 1876. A fire in 1925 destroyed the wooden parts, but faithful reconstruction in the spirit of Ficheto's original began two years later. Today this dark wooden bridge is packed with craft and art shops, as well as cheap souvenirs and snacks.

Hisar Fortress
RUINS

(adult/student 4/2 lv; ☉9am-noon & 2-7pm Apr-Oct, 8am-noon & 1-5pm Nov-Mar) One of Bulgaria's few remaining Ottoman citadels overlooks Lovech from a steep hill, enveloped by a bend in the Osâm River. Extensive ruins of mortar and crushed limestone walls, dating to between the 8th and 10th centuries, spread across the 1200-sq-metre site. Its major points of interest are an 8m-high **main gate** and the remains of an early Byzantine domed **basilica**. Paved pathways lead around the site and give inspiring views across the hills.

From Varosha, it's a 10- to 15-minute uphill walk.

Vasil Levski Museum
MUSEUM

(ul Marin Poplukanov 14; 3 lv; ☉9am-1pm & 2.30-6pm summer, 9am-noon & 1-5pm winter) This museum examines the life and trials of one of Bulgaria's best-known revolutionaries, Vasil Levski, through items from his life (including weapons) and artwork inspired by the dashing freedom fighter. Explanations are almost all in Bulgarian, but you'll be handed a manual to explain the various exhibits, plus there's an enormous mural to admire.

🛏 Sleeping & Eating

Lovech has a reasonable range of accommodation, mostly aimed at tourists on mid-range budgets and business travellers. Its several riverside and Varosha-quarter guesthouses represent the best mix of value and charm.

Hotel Varosha　　　　HOTEL **$**
(☑068-603 377; www.hotelvarosha.com; pl Todor Kirov 36; s/d/tr/f from 40/50/70/80 lv; ☐🐕) Rooms are a little plain at this hotel near the eastern-bank entrance to the Covered Bridge, but there is accommodating, English-speaking staff and the location can't be beaten. It's worth an extra 5 lv to 10 lv to stay in a 'superior room' with warm, satiny decor and a balcony.

Hotel Varosha 2003　　GUESTHOUSE **$$**
(☑068-622-277; www.varosha2003.com; ul Ivan Drasov 23; d/ste/apt incl breakfast 60/80/120 lv; ☐✳🐕) Bed down in a Bulgarian Revival at-mosphere at family-run Varosha 2003, with its flower-filled balconies overlooking the river. Rooms with smooth wood floors are among the most comfortable in town, while breakfast and evening meals are served in a pretty garden terrace.

Hotel Lovech　　　　HOTEL **$$**
(☑068-604 717; www.hotellovech.com; ul Târgovska 12; s 30-70 lv, d 46-110 lv incl breakfast; ☐✳🐕✖) On the western bank of the Osâm River, rooms in this rather austere structure are divided between the cheaper, older part of the hotel and the more comfortable, renovated wing. It's chock-full of amenities geared towards business travellers, including a casino, cocktail bar and reasonable restaurant. The spa centre, with Turkish bath and sauna, plus an open-air pool (summer only) is included in the price.

Mehana Gallereya　　BULGARIAN **$$**
(ul Vasil Levski; mains 7-12 lv) Located beside the art gallery, this *mehana* features a large courtyard, good service and standard Bulgarian dishes such as hotplates of meat and veg, soups and grills.

HIKING IN THE STARA PLANINA

The Stara Planina (Old Mountain) range, also known as the Balkan Mountains, stretches across the length of Bulgaria, from its border with Serbia to the Black Sea. Nearly 30 peaks are taller than 2000m, with Mt Botev (2376m), north of Karlovo, as its highest point. Bulgaria's Rila and Pirin ranges dwarf the Stara Planina peaks (which average 700m in height), but still their verdant nature reserves and rippling hills are very inviting for hikers.

Good maps are essential. For short treks, Domino has a series of *Stara Planina* (1:50,000) maps covering different sections of the range. Dedicated hikers can consult Julian Perry's *Walking in Bulgaria's National Parks*, which includes four excellent central mountain walks, and his *Mountains of Bulgaria*. Hardened hikers ply the strenuous 25-day Kom–Emine 'Friendship Route', which stretches almost 700km across the entire Bulgarian part of the range (part of the trans-European E3 trek).

Guided hikes are a superb way to explore the Stara Planina, and local insight can be essential when it comes to local culture and the condition of different trails. **Bulgaria Walking** (http://bulgariawalking.com) offers tough trekking tours up to Mt Botev.

Some of the more interesting hikes include the following. Trail markings are of variable quality.

Cherni Osêm to Hizha Ambaritsa Four hours.

Dryanovo Ecotrail Four hours.

Etâr to Sokolski Monastery One hour.

Gabrovo to Hizha Uzana Seven hours.

Karlovo to Hizha Hubavets Three hours, or continue to Hizha Vasil Levski (another two to three hours) and Mt Botev (further two to three hours).

Shipka Monastery to Shipka Pass Three hours.

Sliven to Hizha Karandila Three hours.

ⓘ Information

The main square, pl Dimitrov, has banks, exchange offices and a post office.

Tourist Information Centre (Covered Bridge; ⊙ 9am-1pm & 2-5pm Mon-Fri) This tourist information booth within the Covered Bridge can give directions and has pamphlets about the local area. Some English is spoken.

ⓘ Getting There & Away

From the adjacent bus and train stations, take a taxi (preferable) or walk along ul Tsacho Shishkov, veer right and follow the signs to the centre.

From the **bus station** (☑ 068-603 620; pl Garata), hourly buses on weekdays reach Troyan (7 lv, 45 minutes). Regular buses serve Sofia (10 lv to 14 lv, 3½ hours, nine daily) and Pleven (9 lv, one hour, eight daily). Less regularly, direct buses reach Burgas (28 lv, six hours, one daily), Veliko Târnovo (8 lv, 1½ to two hours, four daily), Kazanlâk (15 lv, 3½ hours, four daily) and Plovdiv (20 lv, five hours, one daily).

From the **train station**, daily trains serve both Troyan (3 lv, one hour, four daily) and Levski (3 lv, one hour, four daily). From the latter, change for Sofia (in total 15 lv) and the important railway hub of Gorna Oryakhovitsa for Veliko Târnovo (in total 7 lv) and beyond.

Troyan ТРОЯН

POP 22,000

Colourful pottery, plum brandy and a serene monastery are Troyan's calling cards. Along with woodcarving, tanning and metalwork, pottery helped the town rise to acclaim during the Bulgarian National Revival period. *Troyanska kapka* pottery, decorated with an unmistakable swirling-droplet design, is a popular souvenir that's sold around Bulgaria.

Modern Troyan has a grand communist-era square, and wood-beamed houses leaning over the Beli Osâm River. Though major attractions are few, it's an agreeable place in which to pause on the way to Troyan Monastery (which actually stands south of Oreshak village, 5km east of Troyan), or as a way station between prettier Karlovo and Lovech.

◉ Sights

Museum of Folk Craft & Applied Arts MUSEUM
(☑ 0670-62063; pl Vûzhrazhdane; adult/student 4/2 lv; ⊙ 9am-5pm daily Apr-Oct, Mon-Sat Nov-Mar) One of Bulgaria's most engaging folk-art attractions, this museum displays a colourful range of traditional pottery, along with *kukeri* costumes, woolly masks and sequined garb designed to scare away evil spirits during end-of-winter village rituals. Spread across two floors (the upper level featuring a stunning carved ceiling), the exhibitions feature plenty of English-language detail about Troyan's pottery school, founded in 1911, and other village traditions.

🛏 Sleeping & Eating

Troyan's hotel scene is a little lacklustre, but it has some decent midrange options serving business travellers and monastery visitors.

Cafes and pizza places can be found around the corner of ul Vasil Levski and pl Vûzhrazhdane.

Troyan Plaza Hotel HOTEL $$
(☑ 0670-64 399; www.troyanplaza.com; ul PR Slaveykov 54; s/d/ste incl breakfast 65/80/120 lv; 🅿@🛜) Old-fashioned but perfectly serviceable, this cordial place has 51 rooms and six suites, plus a restaurant serving local produce and a pub. Helpful staff can steer you towards local activities such as horse riding and archery.

Prices are 15% higher at weekends.

Hotel Park HOTEL $$
(☑ 0878303939; www.phtroyan.net; Park Kâpincho; s/d/apt 50/70/100 lv; 🅿🛜) Formerly known as the Panorama, this hillside hotel in the park above town has the most scenic location in Troyan, though its rooms could do with a serious revamp. Reach it by taxi for around 3 lv from the centre.

Café Antik CAFE
(☑ 087052233; Ploshtad Vûzhrazhdane; mains 8-15 lv; ⊙ 8am-midnight) Sip a drink beneath wooden awnings to the rushing sounds of the river at this nicely located cafe-restaurant, behind the folk museum and overlooking the water. It's a good bet for coffee on the terrace when it's warm, or a shot of strong Troyan brandy when it's cold. There's a menu of rotating daily specials, such as soups and salads.

ⓘ Information

Pick up maps and advice on local attractions at the sporadically open **Cultural Information Centre** (pl Vûzhrazhdane; ⊙ 9.30am-1pm & 2-6.30pm Mon-Sat).

TROYAN MONASTERY

Bulgaria's third-largest monastery, Troyan Monastery (☑0876156500; Oreshak; photos 5 lv, video 15 lv; ☺6am-10pm) FREE showcases vivid, apocalyptic murals within its serene walls. Beaten in size only by Rila and Bachkovo, this monastery, 10km southeast of Troyan, has a pale sandstone Church of the Holy Virgin as its centrepiece. Inside glow frescoes painted by Zahari Zograf, the leading mural artist of the Bulgarian National Revival period, depicting saints and searing scenes of the Last Judgement. The monastery has a few cafes, restaurants, souvenir shops and art galleries around it.

Parts of the 16th-century monastery survived attacks by the Turks between the 16th and 18th centuries, but most of today's monastery dates to 1835. Zograf's finest frescoes (painted in the 1840s) are outside on the back wall, depicting Judgement Day with fire-breathing monsters, pitchfork-wielding demons corralling the damned, and angels summoning the dead out of their coffins. The monastery is also renowned for its hand-carved wood altar and iconostasis, crafted in the mid-19th century by Tryavna's famed school of woodcarvers.

The 19th-century revolutionary leader Vasil Levski formed and trained insurgents here, and urged the monks themselves to fight the Turks in 1876. This history is highlighted in the small 3rd-floor museum (open by request).

Guesthouse Oreshaka (☑0889704232; www.oreshaka.bg; Oreshak; r 40 lv; P ⓢ) offers simple rooms just outside the monastery walls.

The National Exhibition of Crafts & Arts (☑0888008411, 06952-2816; www.fairoreshakbg.com; ul Stara Planina 256, Oreshak; adult/student 2/1 lv; ☺9am-5.30pm), 500m north of Troyan Monastery along the main road, is something between an open-air museum and a shoppers' paradise. This handicrafts complex exhibits marvellous examples of traditional Bulgarian woodcarving, carpet weaving and jewellery across nine halls.

From Troyan, some buses bound for Gabrovo, Apriltsi or Cherni Osâm (3 lv, 20 minutes, seven daily) reach the monastery.

❶ Getting There & Away

Troyan's **bus station** (☑0670-62172; ul Dimityr Ikonomov-Dimitrykata 23) is a 350m walk south from pl Vûzhrazhdane; its ticket office for **Neshev** (http://neshevbg.com) closes at 6pm. From the bus station, two daily buses serve Sofia (14 lv to 15 lv, three hours). Buses passing through Lovech (4 lv to 5 lv, 45 minutes, seven daily) have immediate connections to Pleven. For Troyan Monastery (3 lv, 20 minutes, seven daily), take buses bound for Gabrovo, Apriltsi or Cherni Osâm.

Train travel is much slower and less advisable; the station is near the bus station. Services to Sofia (16 lv, six to seven hours, four daily) go via Pleven or Levski.

Hisar ХИСАР

POP 9300

There's something in the water in Hisar: a near-miraculous cocktail of minerals, if this spa town's healing reputation is to be believed. Hisar (also known as Hissar or Hisarya) has been famed for its mineral waters since Roman times, when it was named Diokletianopolis (after the Emperor Diocletian). Most visitors are here either to fill bottles directly from its 16 springs, or to ease into the silky waters at hotel spas. Just as invigorating is the sight of Hisar's Roman ruins, including more than 2.3km of walls and towering fortress gates, among the best preserved in Bulgaria.

◉ Sights

More than 2.3km of Roman walls, refortified by the Byzantines, thread their way through Hisar. Among Bulgaria's best preserved and most arresting Roman ruins, the walls are 3m thick in places, with gates as high as 13m. Built to protect a 30-hectare span of the town and its mineral baths from invaders, the walls were too formidable even for 6th-century Slavic raiders. One of the best photo ops is the stocky southern fortress gate; reach it by walking south along bul Ivan Vazov, past soothing Momina Salza Park.

More ruins lie along unnamed roads heading towards the centre from the main road. These unfenced, unsupervised ruins include remains of an amphitheatre, baths and some dwellings.

Momina Salza Spring
FOUNTAIN

Join the locals filling water bottles at this elegant colonnade. Sipping these lukewarm and mineral-rich waters is reputed to boost everything from liver function to metabolism; whether or not you're convinced of its healing powers, you may see people filing to the spring armed with gallon-sized bottles to fill. Find it on the walk between bul Hristo Botev and the southern fortress gate (near Izvora restaurant).

Archaeological Museum
MUSEUM

(2 0337-62 796; http://museum.hisar.bg; ul Stamboliyiski 8; 2 lv; ⊙ 9am-12.30pm & 1.30-5.30pm summer, 8am-noon & 1-4.30pm winter) This small museum, arranged across a pretty courtyard, is divided between archaeological displays from Neolithic tools to late-Thracian jewellery, and a small exhibition of folk costumes and looms. Exhibits rather lack description, but it's a pleasant way to complement a walk along Hisar's Roman walls.

🛌 Sleeping

Accommodation is plentiful in Hisar, with the majority of hotels offering spa facilities, ranging from small spas and saunas to outdoor pools and a daunting range of therapies. Midrange spa hotels can feel clinical; characterful ones carry a bigger price tag. Shoestring travellers can look out for 'rooms' signs along bul General Gurko.

Hotel Hissar
HOTEL $$

(2 0337-62 781; www.hotelhissar.com; ul General Gurko; s/d/apt from 105/115/162 lv; P ❄ @ ☲) Standard, beige-paletted rooms at the Hissar are pleasant enough, but things get more luxurious within the deluxe rooms (doubles from 150 lv), which have plum-coloured trimmings and velveteen sofas. Most rooms have balconies overlooking the outdoor pool, rimmed by thick greenery.

Augusta Spa Hotel
SPA HOTEL $$

(2 0337-62 244; www.augustaspa.com; ul General Gurko 3; s/d from 69/88 lv; P ❄ ⊛ ☲) Some rooms at this spa hotel, within a Lego-block of a building, are a little clinical – apt perhaps, given its popularity among visitors with respiratory and skin ailments – though refurbished ones are more plush. Spa facilities include mineral-rich indoor and outdoor pools, plus a slide and kiddies' pool, and a gym and salt cave (from 12 lv per visit).

You can dip into Augusta's spa waters (9am to 9pm) without being a guest (from 8 lv).

Hotel Chinar
SPA HOTEL $$$

(2 0337-62 288; www.hotelchinar.bg; ul Vasil Petrovich 5; s/d/apt incl breakfast from 90/130/195 lv; P ❄ ⊛) Stately rooms at the Chinar are a little worn in places, but they have distinguished touches such as carved wooden bedheads and pristine bathrooms, while apartments are ample. Use of the spa comes with the room rate, and there is a menu of spa treatments.

🍴 Eating

National
BULGARIAN $$

(bul General Gurko; mains 12-15 lv; ⊙ 9am-midnight) Adjoining Hotel Chinar, this classy *mehana* spills into a tranquil garden where roses creeps up the wooden trellis. The menu ranges from Bulgarian stews to osso buco (15.50 lv).

Provence
EUROPEAN $$

(2 0876414144; bul General Gurko 5; mains 8-20 lv; ⊙ 11am-midnight) No lavender fields here, but beyond the mustard-coloured walls lies a peaceful courtyard where geraniums bloom from pots, lulled by a soothing pop soundtrack. Pan-European dishes are as diverse as Tuscan-style rabbit (16 lv), Bulgarian pork neck and wild mushroom risotto (9 lv).

Izvora
BULGARIAN $$

(2 0896864987; bul Ivan Vazov; mains 7-15 lv; ⊙ 10am-10pm) This hearty, home-style *mehana* with adjoining bathhouses, serving Bulgarian dishes such as milk salad (yoghurt and cucumber) and juicy barbecued meats, is just 100m from the fortress walls.

ℹ Information

The small **tourist information centre** (2 0337-62 141; bul General Gurko; ⊙ 9am-noon & 1-6pm Mon-Sat), opposite the National restaurant, sells maps (2 lv). Hours are limited outside summer.

ℹ Getting There & Away

The **train station** (ul Geo Milev) and **bus station** (2 0337-62 069; ul Geo Milev) are adjacent to each other. Buses reach Pleven (20 lv, five hours,

KOPRIVSHTITSA

Behind colourful house fronts and babbling streams broods Koprivshtitsa's revolutionary spirit. This museum-village immediately pleases the eye with its numerous restored National Revival–period mansions. It's a peaceful, touristy place, but Koprivshtitsa was once the heart of Bulgaria's revolution against the Ottomans. Todor Kableshkov declared an uprising against the Turks on 20 April 1876 from Kalachev Bridge (also called 'First Shot' Bridge).

Today, Koprivshtitsa's few streets are dotted with historic homes interspersed with rambling, overgrown lanes, making it a romantic getaway and a safe and fun place for children.

Koprivshtitsa boasts six house-museums. To buy a combined ticket for all (adult/student 6/3 lv), visit the souvenir shop Kupchinitsa (near the tourist information centre) or Kableshkov House (ul Todor Kableshkov 8; adult/student 4/2 lv; ⏱9.30am-5.30pm Tue-Sun Apr-Oct, to 5pm Nov-Mar).

With its triple-arched entrance and interior restored in shades from scarlet to sapphire blue, Oslekov House (ul Gereniloto 4; 3 lv; ⏱9.30am-5.30pm Apr-Oct, 9am-5pm Nov-Mar, closed Mon) is arguably the most beautifully restored example of Bulgarian National Revival–period architecture in Koprivshtitsa. It was built between 1853 and 1856 by a rich merchant executed after his arrest during the 1876 April Uprising. Now a house-museum, it features informative, multilingual displays (Bulgarian, English and French) about 19th-century Bulgaria.

Accommodation is plentiful in this attractive historic village, though booking is recommended for summer weekends. Traditional fare is served at Dyado Liben (⏱0887532096; bul Hadzhi Nencho Palaveev 47; mains 8-15 lv; ⏱11am-midnight; ⏱), an atmospheric 1852 mansion with tables set in a warren of halls, graced with ornately painted walls and heavily worn wood floors.

The Tourist Information Centre (⏱07184-2191; www.koprivshtitza.com; pl 20 April 6; ⏱9.30am-5.30pm Tue, Wed & Fri-Sun Apr-Oct, to 5pm Nov-Mar) on the main square can advise on rooms and places to eat.

Without private transport, getting to Koprivshtitsa can be inconvenient: the train station is 9km north of the village, requiring a taxi or shuttle bus (2 lv, 15 minutes), which isn't always dependably timed to meet incoming and outgoing trains.

one daily) via Lovech (18 lv, four hours), and Plovdiv's northern bus station (3.50 lv, 50 minutes, one daily). Most trains for Plovdiv require a connection in Dolna Mahala (3 lv, one to 1½ hours, six daily). To reach Sofia by train, travel via Plovdiv.

Karlovo КАРЛОВО

POP 30,340

Revolutionary history and a picturesque old town make Karlovo, nestled in the foothills of the Stara Planina, an edifying stop. Roughly equidistant from Koprivshtitsa and Kazanlâk, Karlovo's National Revival-era architecture and churches are sumptuous and well preserved. Significantly for the many Bulgarian visitors filing through, the town is venerated as the birthplace of Vasil Levski, leader of the revolution against the Turks in the early 1870s.

◉ Sights

Karlovo's main sights are along ul Vasil Levski. Walking north from the train or bus station, find pl Vasil Levski, where the revolutionary's statue depicts him with a lion (his nickname among rebel peers). Close by is pale-pink Sveti Nikola Church (ul Vasil Levski 10; ⏱7am-7pm) and the History Museum (ul Vûzrozhdenska 4; 3 lv; ⏱8am-noon & 1-5pm), full of agrarian tools and bright woven costumes. Continuing north, admire the fantastic exterior frescoes of power-blue Sveta Bogoroditsa Church (cnr ul Vasil Levski & ul 27 Decembri; ⏱7am-7pm), before stopping for a traditional 'sand coffee' at cultural centre Buhalov Han (Owl Inn; cnr ul Evlogi Georgi & ul Vasil Levski; 2 lv; ⏱8.30am-5pm).

Further up ul Vasil Levski, the closed Kursum Mosque (ul Vasil Levski), built in 1485, occupies the park. Continue up the mall to pl 20 Yuli, then head left (west) for about 300m, past the clock tower, to Vasil Levski Museum (☑0335-93 489; www.vlevskimuseum -bg.org; ul Gen Kartzov 57; 3 lv; ⊙8.30am-1pm & 2-5pm Mon-Fri).

🛏 Sleeping & Eating

White Guesthouse
GUESTHOUSE $

(☑0878152726; ul Tsar Simeon 6; s/d/tr 27/37/45 lv; ❄🤖) With white walls and wooden floors, rooms here feel a little bare. Still, the place is spotless, rooms are kitted out with TVs, fridges and nice bathrooms, and it's managed by a friendly owner who speaks some English. It's tucked within a quiet residential building on a side street off main-drag ul General Kartsov, 150m east of Vasil Levski Museum.

Shterev Hotel
HOTEL $

(☑0335-93 380; www.shterevhotels.com; pl 20 Yuli; s 33-40 lv, d 40-50 lv, ste 68-85 lv; P❄🤖) Overlooking Karlovo's monumental square and its popular cafes and restaurants, the Shterev enjoys a fine location, though its rooms are somewhat bland.

Restaurant Dionisi
BULGARIAN $$

(☑0335-93 412, 0885244346; ul Evlogi Georgiev; mains 9-12 lv; ⊙11am-11pm Mon-Sat) Over near pl Sveti Nikolai, Restaurant Dionisi does hearty, home-cooked fare, including a range of meat and veg soups.

❶ Getting There & Away

The **train station** (☑0335-94 641; Rte E871) is served by trains on the Sofia–Burgas line, via Kazanlâk and Sliven. Direct trains reach Sofia (7.40 lv, 2½ to three hours, four daily), Burgas (14 lv, 4½ hours, one daily), Koprivshtitsa (3 lv, one hour, one daily) and Plovdiv (4 lv, 1½ hours, six daily).

The **bus station** (☑0885218139; ul Vasil Levski), 200m north of the train station, has services to Sofia (18 lv, three hours, two daily); Plovdiv (5 lv, one to 1½ hours, five daily, sometimes via Hisar), Pleven (16 lv, 1½ hours, one daily) and Lovech (14.50 lv, 1½ hours, one daily).

Kazanlâk   КАЗАНЛЪК

POP 47,300

Bulgaria's Valley of the Roses, nestled at the foot of the Stara Planina mountains, is thought to produce almost two-thirds of the world's rose oil. When flowers bloom in the valleys each May and June, visitors flock to Kazanlâk, the dusty town at the core of this fragrant industry. Roses are Kazanlâk's main lure, but Thracian history has also left a powerful mark. A major 4th-century-BC tomb is here, while the so-called 'Valley of Thracian Kings', a chain of ancient burial mounds, extends north towards Shipka.

Modern Kazanlâk has a working mosque and sizeable Turkish and Pomak Muslim populations, making it one of Bulgaria's more multicultural cities. The town itself doesn't compete with the loveliness of its surrounding valleys, with a jumble of Soviet-style buildings and shabby marketplaces flowing from the well-groomed main square. But it has pockets of great beauty, especially in the 19th-century buildings along its riverbank.

◉ Sights

Thracian Tomb of Kazanlâk
TOMB

(Tyulbe Park) In hilly Tyulbe Park, a 15-minute walk northeast of Kazanlâk's centre, is one of the archaeological finds of the century: a brilliantly frescoed, 4th-century-BC tomb of a Thracian ruler. Discovered in 1944 during construction of a bomb shelter, it's now a Unesco World Heritage site. Tragically for would-be tomb raiders, visitors aren't currently allowed inside, but you can explore the replica (p386) next door.

Along the *dromos* (vaulted entry corridor), a double frieze depicts battle scenes. The burial chamber is 12m in diameter and covered by a beehive dome typical of Thracian 3rd-to-5th-century-BC design. The dome's murals depict events such as a funeral feast and chariot race.

Replica Thracian Tomb of Kazanlâk
MUSEUM

(Tyulbe Park; adult/child 3/1 lv; ⊙9am-5.30pm) This museum has a full-scale replica of the 4th-century-BC tomb next door. Photography inside the museum costs an extra 5 lv.

Museum of Roses
MUSEUM

(☑0431-64 057; bul Osvobozhdenie 10; adult/ student 3/1 lv; ⊙9am-6.30pm) Kazanlâk's shiny Museum of Roses opened in June 2016 in Park Rozarium, 500m north of pl Sevtopolis. The museum guides visitors through the history of rose-oil production and the 300-year-old production methods that continue to be used today. Its light-flooded atriums are packed with antique perfume-making equipment and photographs of rose pickers past.

Kazanlâk

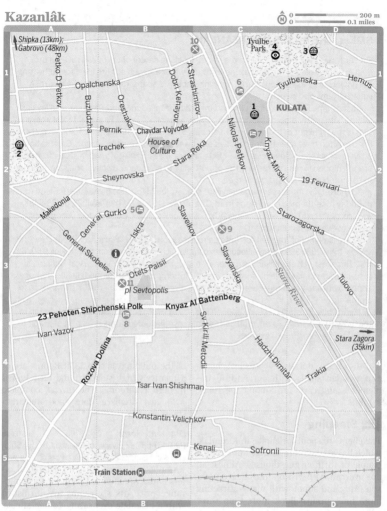

Kazanlâk

◉ Sights

1 Kulata Ethnological Complex	C1
2 Museum of Roses	A2
3 Replica Thracian Tomb of Kazanlâk	D1
4 Thracian Tomb of Kazanlâk	C1

⊜ Sleeping

5 Diamond Hotel	B2

6 Hotel Teres	C1
7 Hotel-Restaurant Chiflika	C2
8 Roza Hotel	B4

⊗ Eating

9 Banicharnitsa Violeta Asenova	C3
10 Magnolia	C1
11 New York Pub & Grill	B3

Kulata Ethnological Complex   MUSEUM
(☎ 0431-63 762; bul Nikola Petkov 18; 3 lv; ⊙ 8am-noon & 1-6pm) Just down from Tyulbe Park and the Thracian tomb, you'll find the appealing Kulata (Tower) district, site of the Kulata Ethnological Complex. A replica of

DON'T MISS

SMELL THE ROSES IN KAZANLÂK

For centuries, Kazanlâk has been the sweet-smelling centre of European rose-oil production. The Valley of the Roses' underground water and rich soil are ideal for cultivating the flowers, and the region churns out pink-packeted soaps, moisturising balms, rose liqueurs, jams and sweets.

Roses come into flower from around mid-May to mid-June, and Kazanlâk's valleys are aflame with pretty blooms at this time of year. Kazanlâk's Rose Festival (☺1st weekend Jun) is the highlight of the season, but smaller villages such as Razhena, Kanchevo and Rozovo often have rose-themed festivities at weekends during the season. Celebrations often involve rose picking, costume-clad dancers, blessing visitors with a shake from a branch dipped in rose water, and the opportunity to buy scented souvenirs. An entrance fee of around 10 lv is usually charged.

To thoroughly immerse yourself in rose season, join a tour. Guide Nikolay Tsutsov runs multiday rose-themed excursions from Cucovata House (☑0887804223, 03133-5483; www.cucovata.com) in Kalofer village, 40km west of Kazanlâk. Book up to a year in advance to avoid disappointment.

There is plenty of fragrant fun outside rose season. At Enio Bonchev Rose Distillery (☑02-986 3995; www.eniobonchev.com; Tarnichene; with/without rose picking 9.60/6 lv), 27km west of Kazanlâk in Tarnichene village, you can learn the history of Bulgaria's rose-oil trade (and inhale its soothing smell). Touring the 1909-founded distillery's huge copper vats and small museum is possible year-round, but call or email in advance to fix a time.

Meanwhile, Kazanlâk's newly opened Museum of Roses is a worthy introduction to the industry's history. Finally, you can sample rose-flavoured goodies as part of a visit to Kulata Ethnological Complex.

---

a 19th-century one-storey peasant's home and wooden sheds with agricultural implements and carts are among the rustic exhibits.

🛏 Sleeping

Travellers are spoilt for choice in Kazanlâk, which has abundant midrange hotels and a couple of thriftier guesthouses. Almost all are overrun with visitors during rose season (May and June), with many attracting large tour groups. Book more than three months ahead if visiting in summer.

Hotel Teres   HOTEL $
(☑0431-64 272; www.hotelteres.com; ul Nikola Petkov; d 50 lv; P❋🛜) For a quieter locale than the centre of town, this friendly hotel in a pretty whitewashed wooden building is a gratifying spot. It has clean, modern rooms, a lobby bar and an adjacent restaurant. Find it directly below the hill of the Thracian tomb.

Hotel-Restaurant Chiflika   HOTEL $
(☑0431-21 411; www.hotelchiflikakazanlak.bg; ul Knyaz Mirski 38; d 35-46 lv; P❋@🛜) Just south of the Thracian tomb, the Chiflika has a faux-traditional look, though the bones

of the building date to 1851. Rooms are of a relatively high standard and have buffed modern bathrooms. The tavern, complete with cosy fireplace, does good Bulgarian standbys.

Diamond Hotel   HOTEL $$
(☑0431-63 192; www.hoteldiamant.bg; ul Shipchenska Epopeya 2; d 65-76 lv; P❋🛜) Facing Kazanlâk's History Museum, Diamond offers a hint of old-world glamour for a midrange price. Its six rooms are furnished with a nostalgic eye: satiny golden sheets, textured floral wallpaper and twinkly chandelier-style lamps. A choice of breakfasts is on offer (7 lv).

Ask for directions to the tiny underground garage if there is no street parking available.

Roza Hotel   HOTEL $$
(☑0431-50 005; www.hotelrozabg.com; ul Rozova Dolina 2; r 50-110 lv; P❋@🛜) Despite its setting in an office complex, Roza Hotel is a homely hideaway, thoughtfully managed by friendly staff. Its private terrace, bedecked with flowers, overlooks the main square. Rooms on the hall's right-hand side are smaller, with beds jammed in lengthways,

whereas the slightly larger ones on the left have more elbow room (and are slightly more costly).

Free tea, coffee and fruit are available throughout the day in the breakfast nook. Parking costs an extra 4 lv per 24 hours.

🍴 Eating

New York Pub & Grill INTERNATIONAL $
(☑ 0431-62 464; www.newyorkpub-bg.com; pl Sevtopolis; mains 5-10 lv; ⊙ 9am-10pm; 🛜) There's no risk of imagining you're in the Big Apple, but this enormously popular spot is beloved for its wide menu of pizzas and grills, and everything is fresh and high quality.

Banicharnitsa Violeta Asenova BAKERY $
(Otets Paisii 33; banitsa from 0.80 lv; ⊙ 7.30am-9pm) Kazanlâk's best breakfast nook is this tiny hole-in-the-wall place opposite the open market, serving a variety of flaky cheese (and other) pies from the *banitsa* and *byurek* family of Balkan pastry. Go early, as service stops when the fresh-baked goodies run out.

★ Magnolia BULGARIAN $$
(☑ 0431-89 546; www.magnolia-kazanlak.com; bul Nikola Petkov 1; mains 5-14 lv; ⊙ 10am-10pm) Inside this peach-coloured building, just across the river from the Thracian tomb, lies an unmissable *mehana* with a menu of well-executed Bulgarian classics such as meaty claypot medleys (from 5 lv) and mixed grills (12 lv). Choose between the Bulgarian Renaissance–style dining room or, better yet, the white-tiled courtyard with its walls draped in vines.

ℹ️ Information

ATMs are on the square and especially on the section of ul 23 Pehoten Shipchenski Polk that runs between the square and ul Petko Stajnov.
Tourist Information Centre (☑ 0431-99 553; ul Iskra 4; ⊙ 9am-1pm & 2-6pm Mon-Fri, 10am-4pm Sat & Sun) Assists with hotels, excursions and general information about the town.

ℹ️ Getting There & Away

From the bus and train stations, it's a 10-minute walk (or 2 lv taxi ride) northwards to the square. Kazanlâk's **bus station** (☑ 0431-63 200; ul Sofronii Vrachanski) has connections to Sofia (17 lv, three hours, five daily), Plovdiv (9 lv, two hours, three daily) and Gabrovo (6 lv, one to 1½ hours, eight daily) via Shipka. Daily buses also reach Ruse (16 lv, 3½ hours) via Veliko Târnovo, and Svilengrad (12 lv, 2½ hours).

Minibuses for Stara Zagora (4 lv, 45 minutes) run half-hourly from just outside the main station. Along the road by the roundabout, town bus 6 runs to Shipka (1.80 lv, 25 minutes, half-hourly); the central stop for this bus is at the corner of Knyaz Al Battenberg and ul Kiril i Metodii.

Kazanlâk **train station** (☑ 0431-62 012; ul Sofronii Vrachanski) serves Sofia (10 lv, 3½ hours, three daily) and Burgas (12 lv, three hours, three daily), via Karlovo (5 lv, 1½ hours, six daily) or Stara Zagora. Daily services reach Sliven (6 lv, two hours, four to six daily). Trains to or from Plovdiv involve changing at Karlovo or Stara Zagora station.

Shipka   ШИПКА

Humble mountainside Shipka has stirring monuments that span the breadth of Bulgarian history. Forbidding Shipka Pass, the one good route through the Stara Planina, was where the Russian army and Bulgarian volunteers decisively thwarted an Ottoman counter-attack in the 1877 Russo-Turkish War. In their memory, a stone monument now crowns the pass, while an exquisite Russian-style church shines out of quiet Shipka village, 13km south.

Shipka also boasts a seam of tombs, dating back to the 4th century BC. The countryside between Kazanlâk and Shipka has been dubbed 'Valley of the Thracian Kings', thanks to hundreds of grass-topped burial mounds and archaeological sites. Shipka makes an excellent day trip from Kazanlâk, though staying a night or two allows you to tomb-hop and visit the offbeat Buzludzha Monument ruin.

◎ Sights

Buzludzha Monument RUINS
(Shipka) The concrete UFO looming over Shipka Pass is central Bulgaria's most peculiar sight. This former assembly hall slid into disrepair after the fall of communism, but its space-age silhouette has turned it into an irresistible stop for travellers. At the time of writing, authorities had reopened its front doors after months of barring them shut and forbidding visitors. We strongly recommend admiring it from outside: there's a high risk of injury from broken glass or falling masonry inside the unmaintained building.

Buzludzha Monument stands on a 1441m peak overlooking the pass. On the drive up, look for the steely monument of clenched fists. Next to the UFO, the concrete shard pointing skywards is crowned with a red star. Rumours that the star was made of rubies led to locals looting and chipping the site (it's really glass). While local people have mixed feelings about Buzludzha, news that the monument will eventually be transformed into a history museum have been largely well received.

The monument is accessible along a pitted, zigzagging road branching from the E85 between Shipka and Kazanlâk. It's a 30-minute drive from Kazanlâk.

Nativity Memorial Church   CHURCH
(Church of St Nikolai; ⊙8.30am-5.30pm May-Oct, to 5pm Nov-Apr) A magenta-and-white ice-cream cone of a church glows above tumbledown Shipka village, its golden onion domes glittering from thick woodlands. Part of Shipka Monastery, the magnificent structure was built in 1902 as a dedication to soldiers who died at Shipka Pass during the Russo-Turkish War (1877–8). To get there, follow the *Hram Pametnik* sign for 1.2km through the village, or walk 300m up from the restaurant along the Kazanlâk–Gabrovo road.

The church's design is heavily influenced by Russian architecture and features five golden domes and 17 church bells, within a 53m-high bell tower that can be heard for several kilometres when rung. Thirty-four marble plaques on the outside walls list the names of soldiers who perished in the Russo-Turkish War. Inside the crypt Russian soldiers are interred, and there are some wonderful frescoes depicting scenes from Russian history.

Souvenir and food stands can be found in the car park of this enormously popular sight. Indoor photography permits cost 5 lv.

Ostrusha Tomb   TOMB
(adult/student 3/1 lv; ⊙9am-5pm May-Nov) Discovered in 1993, the sarcophagus within this whopping Thracian burial mound was carved from a single 60-tonne stone during the 4th century BC. The site continues to puzzle archaeologists – a horse's skeleton has been found, but no human remains – with the biggest mystery being how the granite (not native to the region) was hauled to Shipka. The mound is 3km south of Shipka village.

Byzantines damaged many Thracian burial mounds, and Ostrusha Tomb is no exception. Most frescoes have, tragically, been chipped off, but the serene face of a woman on one of the ceiling panels hints at the tomb's past splendour.

Freedom Monument   MONUMENT
(Shipka Memorial; ⊙9am-7pm Apr-Oct, to 4.30pm Nov-Mar) **FREE** About 13km along a winding road north of Shipka village is the Shipka Pass. Almost 1000 steps lead to the top of Mt Stoletov (1326m), dominated by the impressive, 32m-high Freedom Monument. It was built in 1934 as a memorial to more than 7000 Russian troops and Bulgarian volunteers who died in the Battle of Shipka Pass, which culminated in August 1877. The fighters successfully repelled numerous attacks by around 27,000 Turkish soldiers.

To reach the pass from Kazanlâk or Shipka, take a bus to Haskovo, Gabrovo or Veliko Târnovo and ask the driver to let you off at the Shipka Pass (Shipchensky prokhod).

🛏 Sleeping & Eating

The popularity of the Shipka Pass Freedom Monument has allowed cafes to bloom at the base of the monument, near the Hotel-Restaurant Shipka. Shipka village has a very quiet restaurant scene, aside from a cafe at the northern end of town; enjoy more choice in Kazanlâk.

★ Hotel IT Shipka   GUESTHOUSE $
(☏0896755090; www.shipkaithotel.com; ul Kolyo Adjara 12; s/d/apt 37/49/86 lv; ✳ 🛜 🌊) In a quiet residential area 500m east of Shipka village square, this friendly, family-run guesthouse has attractive, modern rooms with great views of either the Valley of Roses, or the mountain and the shimmering domes of the Nativity Memorial Church. The hotel's restaurant serves home-cooked Bulgarian fare, and there's a small outdoor swimming pool, an infrared sauna and a steam room.

Ring ahead and English-speaking owner Ivan will collect you from the bus stop on the main square. He can also arrange local hiking and other outdoor activities. All rooms have either air-conditioning or ceiling fans. Breakfast costs 6 lv for for a home-cooked spread of pancakes, pastries and more.

Hotel-Restaurant Shipka
HOTEL $

(☑ 0888356479; shipkahotel@abv.bg; Shipka Pass; d 40-60 lv; P ⓐ) If vertiginous views from the top of the pass appeal more than snoozing down in Shipka village, this hotel features 13 simple rooms, each with fridge and TV. The restaurant downstairs (8am to midnight) dishes up Bulgarian food. Little English is spoken, but staff are sympathetic. It's 50m up from the car park at the top of the pass.

❶ Getting There & Away

Bus 6 runs half-hourly on weekdays (and hourly at weekends) between the local bus stop near Kazanlâk bus station and Shipka village (1.80 lv, 25 minutes). Alternatively, the hourly bus between Kazanlâk and Gabrovo stops at the village and Shipka Pass, as do buses to Veliko Târnovo.

Stara Zagora
СТАРА ЗАГОРА

POP 137,850

As a business city and major road and rail connection, Stara Zagora (meaning 'old beyond the mountains') doesn't loom large on tourist itineraries. Nonetheless, this bubbly city is a fine place to stop for a night or two: the dining scene is superb, pedestrianised streets lined with trendy cafes lead right to Roman ruins, and there are numerous parks in which to idle. It's best known for Zagorka, a leading Bulgarian beer that has been brewed here since 1902.

◎ Sights

Eski Mosque
MOSQUE

(Museum of Religions; ☑ 042-919 214; ul Pazarska 1; adult/child 3/1 lv; ⊙ 10am-6pm Tue-Sat) One of Bulgaria's oldest Muslim shrines, the cavernous interior of 15th-century Eski Mosque has splendid rococo and floral designs. Now presented as a 'Museum of Religions', a few Bulgarian-only display cases feature religious miscellany, but the real reason to visit is the mosque's beautiful interior. It lies just east of central October 5 Park.

Roman Theatre
RUINS

(bul Mitropolit Metodii Kusev) **FREE** The 3rd-century-AD Forum Augusta Trayana is well preserved and hosts summertime concerts. Just north of the park, it can be freely explored on foot.

World of Zagorka
BREWERY

(http://zagorkatours.bg; ul Han Asparuh 41; adult/child 6/4 lv; ⊙ noon-6pm Fri-Sun, by appointment) Guzzle down some beer history at this brewery museum. You can peruse barley-processing equipment and a 1902 bottle, and admire photos of the good old days of brewing. Best of all, there's beer tasting at the end. It's 2km north of central Stara Zagora, by the eastern edge of Zagorka Park.

Neolithic Dwellings Museum
MUSEUM

(☑ 042-600 299; adult/child 5/2 lv; ⊙ 9am-12.30pm & 1-5.30pm Tue-Sat) This two-room museum displays the remains of an 8000-year-old Stone Age house, once 7m in height, along with interesting details on how Bulgarians from the 6th millennium BC lived. Jewellery, tools and household items are exhibited, some of which – such as enamelled animal-headed vessels – are astonishingly detailed for their age. To find the museum, enter the hospital gates and walk straight through the complex to an outdoor staircase, which leads to the museum.

🛏 Sleeping

Hotel La Roka
HOTEL $

(☑ 042-919 427; www.hotel-laroka.com; ul Tsar Ivan Shishman 38; s/d/ste 55/59/69 lv; P ✳ ⓐ) This classy little hotel represents marvellous value thanks to its comfortably furnished rooms, red-and-gold decor and relaxing common room area with TV and buttery leather sofas. Breakfast costs an additional 5 lv.

★ Hotel Merian Palace
HOTEL $$

(☑ 042-611 100; www.merianpalace.com; bul Ruski 8; s/d/apt incl breakfast 95/115/150 lv; P ✳ ⓐ ▧) Sparkling bathrooms and well-furnished rooms with flat-screen TVs are the norm at this tastefully modern hotel near the train and bus stations. Most luxurious are the 'VIP apartments' (320 lv) with creamy leather sofas and maroon carpets. There's a wellness centre with a sauna (8 lv), and genteel service is the cherry on the cake.

Hotel Vereya
HOTEL $$

(☑ 042-919 373; www.hotel-vereya.com; ul Tsar Simeon Veliki 100; d/apt from 70/120 lv; P ✳ ⓐ) Plump mattresses and welcoming cream rooms lift the Vereya above other business hotels in town. 'VIP apartments' (150 lv) are enormous and artily decorated. The hotel is well situated on the town's liveliest square, the so-called 'Complex', full of cafes and restaurants.

Parking is an extra 10 lv per day. Breakfast costs 5 lv.

✗ Eating

Most restaurants and cafes are on the pedestrian sections of bul Metropolit Metodii Kusev and bul Tsar Simeon Veliki, which cross one block west of the October 5 Park. Stara Zagora has a taste for Western European dining, so you can expect to find Italian and French flavours muddled among filling Bulgarian grills.

Restaurant Uniqato   ITALIAN $$
(☑ 042-661 155; www.uniqato.com; ul Sava Silov 36; mains 10-20 lv; ⊙11am-midnight; ☑) Stara Zagora's best dining can be enjoyed at this sophisticated Italian place, with its stone-baked pizzas, prosciutto-draped salads and juicy meatballs spoken of reverently by locals. Vegetarians are well catered for, with dishes such as eggplant lasagna and goat's cheese ratatouille. The range of desserts, from cheesecakes to panna cotta, is refreshingly broad compared to most Bulgarian restaurants – leave room.

Mehana Chevermeto   BULGARIAN, EUROPEAN $$
(☑042-630 331; http://chevermetosz.com; ul Bratya Zhekovi 60; mains 10-15 lv; ⊙8am-midnight; ☎) With its traditional decor and soothing setting by a pond, the restaurant of the Hotel Ezeroto has family ambience and high-quality traditional fare. A vast wine list and range of cured meat platters precede Bulgarian mainstays such as baked claypot dishes, though there's also plenty of Mediterranean influence sprinkled among the grilled fish and mozzarella salads.

❶ Information

The friendly **Tourist Information Centre** (☑042-627 098; www.tour.starazagora.bg; bul Ruski 27; ⊙9am-6pm Mon-Fri, 9am-12.30pm & 1.30-4pm Sat) has free maps and local info.

❶ Getting There & Away

From the **bus station** (☑042-605 349; ul Slavyanski) three are services to Sofia (17 lv to 22 lv, four hours, hourly), Burgas (16 lv, three hours, hourly), Sliven (7 lv, 1¼ hours, hourly), Varna (23 lv to 33 lv, five hours, six daily), Veliko Târnovo (13 lv to 23 lv, three hours, six daily), Plovdiv (5 lv to 8 lv, three hours, hourly) Kazanlâk (4 lv, 45 minutes, eight daily) and Ruse (25 lv, five hours, one daily).

Private companies offer different prices for international destinations such as Athens, Frankfurt and more.

Stara Zagora's **train station** (☑042-626 752; ul Papazchev) is a five-minute walk south from the bus station, at the southern edge of Stantsionna Gradina park. See table for direct routes.

Indirect alternative routes include Sofia via Plovdiv, and Burgas via Karnobat or Zimnica. To reach Ruse (11 lv, six hours), change at Gorna Oryakhovitsa.

Sliven   СЛИВЕН

POP 96,400

Encircled by rocky crags, Sliven is famed for its role in the 19th-century revolution. The hilltop caves and boulders that now form Blue Rocks Nature Park, north of town, once concealed *haidouks*, the rebels who helped secured Bulgaria's freedom from the Ottomans. Against the backdrop of this proud history, this welcoming town offers glimmers of inspiration in its well-preserved house-museums, and cultural draws along its pretty pedestrianised mall.

Outside these areas, Sliven is a rather dusty place where post-Soviet gloom hangs heavy. Nonetheless, local desires to plant Sliven more firmly on the tourist map are seeing it improve by the day.

DIRECT TRAIN SERVICES FROM STARA ZAGORA

DESTINATION	COST (LV)	DURATION (HR)	FREQUENCY
Burgas	10	2½–3	2 daily
Kazanlâk	3-4	1–1½	2 daily
Plovdiv	6-7	2	hourly
Sofia	14	4	5 daily
Varna	15-19	4½	4 daily
Veliko Târnovo	7-8	3	4 daily

Sliven

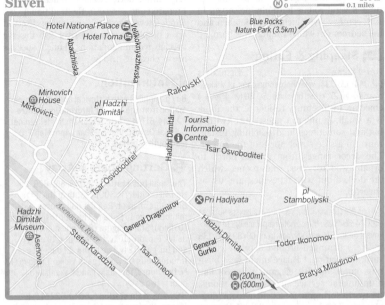

◉ Sights

Blue Rocks Nature Park NATURE RESERVE
(Sinite Kamani; chairlift one way/return 3/6 lv;
⊙ chairlift 8.30am-5pm Tue-Sun, noon-5pm Mon)
Despite its enigmatic name, there's little
more than a bluish haze hanging over this
rubbly nature park. But these hills have
revolutionary history: within their folds
once hid the *haidouks,* the freedom fighters who plotted against the Turks during
Bulgaria's centuries of Ottoman rule. Most
visitors take the chairlift to the top and picnic overlooking views of the valley, or follow trails to the caves in which *haidouks*
planned acts of sabotage against the Ottomans. The best time to visit is between May
and September.

As an alternative to the chairlift, you can
walk uphill following a winding trail (1½
hours). From the top of the chairlift, a path
leads about 300m to the main road; cross it
and proceed 500m through the woods. Follow the road downhill to bypass information centres (pick up a map). Ragged, often
steep trails to the *haidouk* caves are sporadically signposted from the main wood
into the wilds.

The park is also home to rock formations
with legends as strange as their shapes.
Halkata, 'the ring', is thought to weave love

spells from its 8m stone bulk; stories say
that passing through the circle ensures a
couple long life and happiness. Even more
eyebrow-raising is the claim that passing
through the circle with a willingness to
change sex can transform a visitor from
male to female, or vice versa. Other rocks
are thought to resemble camels and frogs;
get more information from the tourist information centre (p394).

Irregular minibus 25 from central Sliven
reaches the main road, a short walk from
the lifts, but it's far easier to get a taxi (4 lv).
Keep a taxi number for the way back, as they
don't reliably ply the lifts.

Mirkovich House MUSEUM
(☑ 044-622 796; ul Mirkovich 10; adult/child 2/1 lv;
⊙ 10am-6pm Tue-Fri, to 5pm Sat & Sun) The temporary art exhibitions are a fine excuse to
explore this creaky period house, where the
crimson rugs and elaborate carved wooden
ceilings give an agreeable flavour of the
1930s and '40s.

Hadzhi Dimitâr Museum MUSEUM
(☑ 044-622 496; ul Asenova 2; adult/student 2/1
lv; ⊙ 9am-noon & 2-5pm daily Apr-Oct, closed
Sun Nov-Mar) This house-museum dedicated
to the rebel-movement leader is set in a
lovely wooden building arranged around

a cobblestone courtyard. The building features several rooms faithfully preserved in 19th-century style, including a kitchen and the bedroom in which Dimitâr was born.

🛏 Sleeping & Eating

Hotel Toma
GUESTHOUSE $

(☑ 044-623 333; www.hoteltoma.com; ul Velikoknyazhevska 27; d incl breakfast 50-60 lv; ❀ @ 🛜) Once an 18th-century residence, the Toma is a small, family-run guesthouse (with a big and sometimes loud adjoining restaurant) up a side street north of the square. The decor ranges from animal horns to ornate woodcarvings, and rooms, which are decked out with tapestries, are just as cheerful.

Hotel National Palace
BUSINESS HOTEL $$

(☑ 044-662 929; http://nationalpalace.bg; ul Velikoknyazhevska 31; s/d/ste/apt from 69/89/108/138 lv; P 🛜) Arranged around a pretty courtyard, the National Palace might be a business hotel, but it's elegant, with cordial, multilingual service and spotless rooms. It's worth springing for a deluxe room (doubles from 97 lv) with headboard lighting and flat-screen TV, but lodgings throughout are crisp and well maintained. Parking is 5 lv per 24 hours.

★ Pri Hadjiyata
BULGARIAN $

(☑ 0878553222; ul Yordan Kyuvliev 11; mains 5-12 lv; 🛜) This festive local favourite set around a shaded courtyard, with indoor seating for winter, does excellent Bulgarian food prepared and served in the traditional way. *Satch* (stew baked in a clay pot and served on a hotplate), ribs and river fish deserve special recommendations. Lunch specials are as cheap as 3.50 lv.

ℹ Information

Buy pamphlets with historical and hiking information from the **Tourist Information Centre** (☑ 044-611 148; http://tourism.hostsliven.net; bul Tsar Osvoboditel 1; ⊘ 9am-4pm Mon-Fri), just south of pl Hadzhi Dimitâr.

ℹ Getting There & Away

The small **bus station** (☑ 044-662 629; bul Hadzhi Dimitâr) is 300m south of the large Billa supermarket. Regular daily buses and minibuses go to Sofia (22 lv, four to five hours, 10 daily), Stara Zagora (8 lv, one hour, 18 daily), Plovdiv (10 lv, three hours, 12 daily) and Burgas (12 lv, two hours, 12 daily). Less frequent bus services reach Veliko Târnovo (13 lv, two hours, four daily) and Kazanlâk (8 lv, 1½ hours, two daily).

Sliven's **train station** (☑ 044-622 614) is 1km south of the bus station. Direct trains serve Sofia (23 lv, 5½ hours, one daily), Varna (11 lv, 3½ hours, one daily) and Burgas (7 lv, 1½ hours, two daily); travel via Karnobat for more services. Daily trains reach Kazanlâk (6 lv, two hours, five daily). For Stara Zagora (6 lv, two to three hours, five daily), change trains at Tulovo. For Plovdiv (12 lv, five hours, 10 daily), travel via Karlovo or Zimnica. To get to Ruse, one or two changes are required.

Black Sea Coast

Best Places to Eat

➡ Ethno (p401)

➡ Ribarska Sreshta (p409)

➡ Mehane Neptun (p407)

➡ Bay (p424)

➡ Gloria Mar (p415)

Best Places to Sleep

➡ Art Hotel (p406)

➡ Graffit Gallery Hotel (p420)

➡ Boutique Hotel St Stefan (p415)

➡ Hotel Regina Maria Spa (p426)

➡ Yo Ho Hostel (p420)

Why Go?

Bulgaria's long Black Sea coastline is the country's summertime playground, attracting not just Bulgarians but tourists from across Europe and beyond. The big, purpose-built resorts here have become serious rivals to those of Spain and Greece, while independent travellers will find plenty to explore away from the parasols and jet skis.

Sparsely populated sandy beaches to the far south and north, the bird-filled lakes around Burgas, and picturesque ancient towns such as Nesebâr and Sozopol are rewarding destinations. The 'maritime capital' of Varna and its seaside rival, Burgas, are two of Bulgaria's most vibrant cities. Both are famous for summer festivals and nightlife as well as many museums and galleries.

Those with their own transport will have even greater choice, with the wild Strandzha Nature Park in the south and the picturesque Kaliakra Cape and Dobrudzha region in the north theirs to discover.

When to Go
Burgas

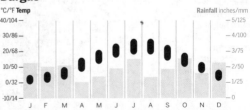

Apr–May Spring on the coast is pleasantly warm and relaxed, with fewer tourists.

Jun–Aug Reliably hot, dry, sunny days in summer bring the crowds to the beaches.

Nov–Mar Winters are chilly, resort hotels close for the season, but you'll have the place to yourself.

Black Sea Coast Highlights

1 Sozopol
(p403) Exploring the cobblestoned lanes of this lovely old former Greek harbour.

2 Archaeological Museum (p417) Learning of the Black Sea coast's rich Thracian, Greek and Roman origins in Varna.

3 Summer Palace of Queen Marie (p425) Strolling through Romanian Queen Marie's picturesque seaside cottage in Balchik.

4 Nesebâr (p412) Marvelling at how this tiny, cobblestoned peninsula was once home to some 80 medieval churches.

5 Strandzha Nature Park (p410) Hiking and cycling through this remarkably diverse natural landscape.

6 Sinemorets (p410) Soaking up the sun near the Turkish border, where the river meets the sea.

7 Burgas (p397) Enjoying the spoils of one of Bulgaria's most attractive cities, with some great restaurants and a pristine seaside park.

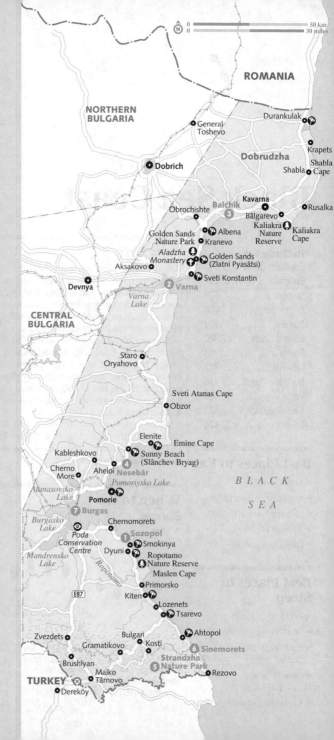

History

The towns along the Black Sea coast share a common historical origin. Archaeological and historical museums are filled with artefacts from the Copper and early Bronze Age (about 4000–1500 BC). A superb collection from this era – including possibly the world's earliest worked gold jewellery – can be admired in the Varna Archaeological Museum.

From the 7th century BC, Greek merchants founded Black Sea ports such as Apollonia Pontica (modern-day Sozopol), Odessos (Varna), Mesembria (Nesebâr), Krounoi/Dionysopolis (Balchik) and Pirgos (Burgas).

The Romans were the next great people to dominate the region, appearing on the scene in the 1st century AD. They conquered Mesembria and Odessos, and eventually built the exquisite Thermae complex (Roman baths) in Varna. The Roman presence lasted only a few short centuries before the empire began to fragment.

The rise and fall of the Bulgarian empires, the first (681–1018) and second (1185–1396), found the coastal cities along the Black Sea caught between the Bulgarians to the north and the remnants of the Eastern Roman Empire – Byzantium – to the south. The entire coastal region fell to the Ottoman Empire in the 14th century, though cities such as Varna and Sozopol thrived as important commercial ports.

In the 19th century, the coastal region joined with the rest of the country to form independent Bulgaria, though fierce fighting with the retreating Ottoman Empire lasted into the 20th century.

SOUTHERN COAST

Burgas БУРГАС
POP 200,000

For most visitors, the port city of Burgas (sometimes written as 'Bourgas') is no more than a transit point for the more obviously appealing resorts and historic towns further up and down the coast. If you do decide to stop over, you'll find a lively, well-kept city with a neat, pedestrianised centre, a long, uncrowded beach, a gorgeous seafront park, and some interesting museums. A clutch of reasonably priced hotels, as well as some of the best restaurants in this part of the

---

> **TOP BULGARIAN BEACHES FOR...**
>
> **Urban swimming:** Burgas
>
> **Safe, shallow water:** Primorsko
>
> **24-hour fun:** Sunny Beach (Slânchev Bryag)
>
> **A low-key hideaway:** Sinemorets
>
> **Romantic setting:** Sozopol

country, makes it a practical base for exploring the southern coast, too.

Nature lovers also come to Burgas for the four lakes just outside the city, which are havens for abundant bird life. You can birdwatch, kayak or take an impromptu plunge into a salt pool.

History

Greek colonists from Apollonia (modern-day Sozopol) expanded their territory into the Burgas region as far back as the 6th century BC. Later, the Romans came along and Emperor Vespasian founded a city here, named Deultum, in the 1st century AD. The name Burgas first appeared on maps in the 17th century, when fisher folk from the wider region settled here. The city grew quickly after the completion of the railway from Plovdiv (1890) and the development of the port (1903). Today it's a major industrial and commercial centre, home to the largest oil refinery in the Balkans.

◉ Sights

Maritime Park PARK
Stretching lazily along the Black Sea coast and filled with manicured flower beds, fountains, busts of Bulgarian worthies, abstract sculptures and cafes, this park is the pride of Burgas. There are spectacular views over the sea from the terraces, and steps lead down from here toward the beach.

Archaeological Museum MUSEUM
(☑ 056-843 541; www.burgasmuseums.bg; bul Aleko Bogoridi 21; adult/student 5/2 lv; ◷ 10am-6pm Mon-Sat) This small museum houses a diverting collection of local finds including Neolithic flint tools, a wooden canoe from the 5th century BC, Greek statuary and the remarkably well-preserved wooden coffin of a Thracian chieftain. It's all well laid out and signposted in English.

BLACK SEA COAST BURGAS

Burgas

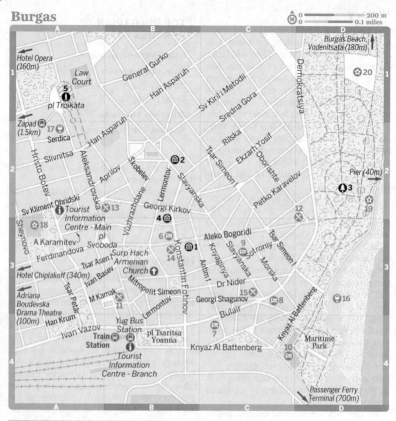

Burgas

◉ Sights

1 Archaeological Museum	B3
2 Ethnographic Museum	B2
3 Maritime Park	D2
4 Natural History Museum	B3
5 Soviet Army Monument	A1

🛏 Sleeping

6 Fotinov Guest House	B3
7 Hotel Bulair	C4
8 Hotel Luxor	C3
9 Old House Hostel	C3
10 Primoretz Grand Hotel & Spa	C4

✕ Eating

11 BMS	B3
12 Boulevard	D2
13 Ethno	B2
14 Rosé	B3
15 Satsanga	C3

◉ Drinking & Nightlife

16 Bar Neptun	D3
17 Mezetto	A2

✦ Entertainment

18 Burgas Opera House	A3
19 Sea Casino Cultural Centre	D2
20 Summer Theatre	D1

Natural History Museum   MUSEUM

(☎ 056-843 239; www.burgasmuseums.bg; ul Konstantin Fotinov 30; adult/student 5/2 lv; ⊙ 10am-6pm Mon-Sat) Old-fashioned but informative displays on local flora, fauna and geology. Exhibits of rocks, seashells, butterflies and bee-

tles occupy the ground floor; upstairs there's a collection of stuffed birds and animals.

Ethnographic Museum   MUSEUM

(☎ 056-842 587; www.burgasmuseums.bg; ul Slavyanska 69; adult/student 5/2 lv; ⊙ 10am-6pm

Mon-Sat) Regional folk costumes, jewellery and furniture are on show at this museum, as well as displays covering the local weaving and fishing industries. Everything is labelled in Bulgarian.

Soviet Army Monument   MONUMENT
(pl Troikata) Standing sentinel over pl Troikata is this towering Red Army memorial. Comprising a column surmounted by a saluting Russian soldier and figurative panels, it remains a major city focal point.

🏃 Activities

Burgas' 3km-long strip of beach (🕒 9am-6pm Jun-Sep) is surprisingly pretty for an urban beach. The water and sand tend to get nicer the further north along the coast you wander, but it's all clean and safe and patrolled by lifeguards in summer. The beach is lined with bars and fish restaurants, and umbrellas and loungers can be hired.

Mud and Salt Baths   HEALTH & FITNESS
(Solnitsite Beach; 🕒 dawn-dusk) **FREE** North of Burgas, hyper-saline Atanasovsko Lake affords visitors the chance to bathe in health-giving saltwater and mud. Head to Solnitsite Beach, 3km north of the northern end of Maritime Park (following the shore); bring a swimsuit that can get muddy, flip flops and a towel. Choose from several salt or mud lagoons, including some eerie red-salt pools, then wash yourself off in the sea afterward.

Kayak Safaris BG   KAYAKING
(📞 0877500031; www.kayaksafarisbg.webs.com; tours 65 lv) Run by a couple of long-time expats, Kayak Safaris BG operates slow-moving kayaking tours along the Fakiska river, one of the tributaries that feeds Lake Mandrensko, south of Burgas. The two- to three-hour excursions operate on weekdays from May to September. The company offers hotel pick-up and drop-off for an additional charge. Call or email to reserve and arrange details.

⭐ Festivals & Events

Burgas Sand Sculptures Festival   ART
(📞 0889360430; www.sandfestburgas.com; adult/child 3.50/1 lv; 🕒 early Jul-Sep) Artists create fantastic sand sculptures each summer in July. The works are put on display through the end of summer at Ezero Park, near the northern end of Maritime Park.

ST ANASTASIA ISLAND

St Anastasia Island (📞 0882004124; www.anastasia-island.com; return boat trip adult/child 12/7 lv; 🕒 departures 10am, 11.30am, 1pm, 3pm Jun-Aug) is a small volcanic island that makes for a fun day of exploring. The island, which has served as a religious retreat, a prison and pirate bait (according to legend, a golden treasure is buried in its sands), is today dominated by a lighthouse and a monastery, where visitors can sample various healing herb potions. Three or four ships leave daily in summer from the passenger ferry terminal south of the bus and train stations.

Emil Tchakarov Music Festival   MUSIC
(🕒 Jul-Sep) Series of classical music concerts, opera and ballet to remember the late Bulgarian composer Emil Tchakarov, who was born in Burgas in 1948.

International Folklore Festival   CULTURAL
(🕒 late Aug) Burgas's main festival, with shows during the evening at the Summer Theatre in Maritime Park and various locations around the city.

Burgas Sea Song Festival   MUSIC
(🕒 Jul & Aug) Showcases up-and-coming popular music acts from around the country and offers new talents a chance to perform. Held in Maritime Park.

🛏 Sleeping

Few foreign tourists hang around in Burgas for longer than it takes to get the next bus or

LIFE'S A BEACH

Every day during summer, lifeguards work between 9am and 6pm at the resorts and popular beaches; they usually rescue a few tourists who ignore the warnings and don't swim between the flags. It is extremely important to pay attention to these warnings on the Black Sea – there are often very strong currents at play and there are fatalities every year. Topless bathing is acceptable at the major resorts, but less so elsewhere.

BLACK SEA COAST BURGAS

train out again, but there's a good choice of mostly midrange hotels.

Old House Hostel
HOSTEL $

(☑ 056-841 558; www.burgashostel.com; ul Sofroniy 3; dm/d 17/33 lv; ❋ 🛜) This charming hostel makes itself right at home in a lovely 1895 house. Dorms are airy and bright (and bunk-free!), while doubles have access to a sweet little courtyard. The location is central and about 400m from the beach.

Hotel Bulair
HOTEL $

(☑ 056-844 389; www.hotelbulair.com; ul Bulair 7; r 60 lv; P ❋ 🛜) In a converted 19th-century townhouse on a busy road, the 14-room Bulair is very handy for the bus and train stations. Guests have access to the spa and wellness centre at the nearby Primoretz Grand Hotel & Spa.

Hotel Opera
BOUTIQUE HOTEL $$

(☑ 0885578000; www.burgashotel.com; ul Lyuben Karavelov 36; s/d/ste incl breakfast 60/70/120 lv; P ↩ ❋ 🛜) This appealing boutique hotel has large, colourful rooms and especially soft mattresses. Guests get a 20% reduction in the excellent restaurant. It's on a quiet side street about five minutes' walk west of the city centre.

Hotel Luxor
HOTEL $$

(☑ 056-847 670; www.luxor-bs.com; ul Bulair 27; s/d 70/80 lv; P ❋ @) This vaguely Egyptian-inspired place is centrally located and has comfortable, three-star rooms and an Italian restaurant with a pretty terrace.

Fotinov Guest House
HOTEL $$

(☑ 0878974703; www.hotelfotinov.com; ul Konstantin Fotinov 22; s/d 70/80 lv; ❋ 🛜) Conveniently located right in the city centre, with a selection of brightly coloured rooms

---

HOTEL PRICES

All accommodation prices listed in this chapter (unless stated otherwise) are what you should expect to pay during the high season (July and August). During the shoulder season (May, June, September and early October), room prices drop by up to 50%, so along with the continually good weather and greatly reduced crowds, this may be the best time to visit. Note that many hotels and restaurants in the resort towns only open for the summer season.

---

featuring fridges, kettles and cable TV. The multilingual staff are friendly and helpful, and there's even a small sauna.

Hotel Chiplakoff
BOUTIQUE HOTEL $$

(☑ 056-829 325; www.chiplakoff.com; ul Ferdinandova 88; s/d 70/80 lv; P ❋ @) A 10-minute walk west of the centre, this hotel occupies an attractively restored art nouveau mansion, designed by the same architect who built the city's grand train station. Rooms are large and contemporary in style, and the original spiral staircases have been retained; there's no lift, however.

Primoretz Grand Hotel & Spa
LUXURY HOTEL $$$

(☑ 056-812 345; www.hotelprimoretz.bg; ul Knyaz Al Battenberg 2; r from 220 lv; P ❋ 🛜 ⛱) This huge, five-star complex at the southern end of the city beach looks out of scale in Burgas, but its excellent facilities include a spa and indoor and outdoor pools. Sea views cost a little extra, as does the wi-fi and parking, which seems a bit cheeky at these prices.

🍴 Eating

It's no exaggeration to say that Burgas boasts some of the best restaurants along the coast. For more budget-conscious travellers, outlets along ul Aleksandrovska and bul Aleko Bogoridi sell pizza, kebabs and ice cream. There are several summertime bars along the beach, most of which also serve food.

Satsanga
VEGETARIAN $

(☑ 0885070443; ul Slavyanska 14; mains 6-10 lv; ⏱ 10am-10pm; 🛜 🍴) One of the few vegetarian-only restaurants in town, clean and upbeat Satsanga does a full range of international veg hits, drawing inspiration from Asian, Middle Eastern and Mexican cooking. The friendly owner is a good source of local information.

Vodenitsata
BULGARIAN $

(Water Mill; ☑ 0899174715; Kraybrezhna aleya; mains 5-10 lv; ⏱ 10am-2am) Standing on the seafront overlooking the beach, this traditional wood-cabin affair is consistently packed out with locals. Good value specialities include grilled fish, barbecues, steaks and salads.

BMS
CAFETERIA $

(ul Aleksandrovska 20; mains 4-7 lv; ⏱ 8am-10pm) Cheap, self-service, cafeteria-style

BIRDING IN THE BURGAS LAKES

Four lakes surrounding Burgas (Pomoriysko, Atanasovsko, Mandrensko and Burgasko) comprise 9500 hectares and represent the largest wetland system in Bulgaria. The area is home to some 260 bird species, nearly 70% of the country's total.

The **Poda Conservation Centre** (☏056-500 560; www.bspb-poda.de; adult/child 5/2 lv; ☺9am-7pm Apr-Sep, to 5pm Oct-Mar; 🚌17), about 8km south of Burgas, was established in 1998 to protect the habitat and offers visitors an excellent chance to spot numerous scarce and endangered birds.

Also boasting a signposted 2.5km ecotrail, the conservation centre lies at the westernmost point of the Black Sea and along a key bird migration route. Late August and September sees the highest numbers of migrating birds, but each part of the year brings something different; key species include Dalmatian pelicans, herons, avocets and terns.

The Poda centre is easiest to reach by car, following the main road south to Sozopol (look for signs for the 'Poda' turn-off). Burgas public bus 17 runs here from the Zapad bus station. See the Poda website for bus departure times.

chain offering simple but filling fare such as sausages, salads and stews. There are some outdoor tables and it also serves beer.

★**Rosé** INTERNATIONAL $$
(☏0885855099; bul Aleko Bogoridi 19; mains 8-20 lv; ☺8am-11pm; 🛜) Choose from a wide menu of grilled meats and fish, including a superlative lamb-shank offering, or fresh pasta, at this superb restaurant in the city centre. Finish off with a cake or home-made ice cream. Rosé also does a very good breakfast, including a rarity for Bulgaria: gluten-free muesli.

★**Ethno** SEAFOOD $$
(☏0887877966; ul Aleksandrovska 49; mains 7-20 lv; ☺11am-11.30pm; 🛜) This downtown restaurant does splendid things with seafood: the Black Sea mussels alone are worth a trip to Burgas. With inviting blue-and-white surrounds that recall the city's Greek heritage, superb (English-speaking) service and a summery vibe, Ethno is classy without being uptight.

Boulevard ITALIAN $$
(☏056-825 555; bul Aleko Bogoridi 60; mains 6-20 lv; ☺10am-midnight; ❄🛜) Conveniently located at the entrance to Maritime Park, this casual, vaguely Italian restaurant is not as fancy as it looks at first glance. The pizzas are considered among the best in town, but it also offers seafood and risotto dishes higher up the food chain. The up-stairs area is air-conditioned, though the prettiest table is below a big tree outside.

 Drinking & Nightlife

In summer, nightclubs and bars materialise among the trees of Maritime Park.

Bar Neptun CLUB
(☏0878101789; www.neptunburgas.com; Maritime Park; ☺9pm-4am) Among the more reliable summertime clubs, with a varied program including 'retro nights', dance and Bulgarian music. Located on the central beach, near the southern end of Maritime Park.

Mezetto PUB
(☏0898405555; pl Troikata 4; ☺9am-1am; 🛜) Pleasant wine and beer bar, located on the side of one the city's main squares. Wide selection of draught beers, including reputedly the only place in town for Guinness. They also have a nice bar food menu, with burgers and light bites (mains 5 lv to 8 lv). No credit cards.

☆ **Entertainment**

Sea Casino Cultural Centre ARTS CENTRE
(☏056-911 868; Maritime Park; ☺10.30am-7.30pm Mon-Fri) The city's renovated 1930s casino is now a cultural centre, hosting a varied program of concerts, exhibitions, film screenings and readings. Ask at the tourist information centre if something is on during your visit.

Burgas Opera House OPERA
(☏056-840 762; www.operaburgas.com; ul Sv Kliment Ohridski 2; tickets 10-30 lv; ☺box office 11am-2pm & 3-7pm) A regular program of opera, ballet and concerts is held at the city's

opera house. Buy tickets at the venue box office or online over the website.

Summer Theatre THEATRE
(☎ 056-844 274; www.letenteatar.com; Maritime Park) Live music, dance and drama performances often take place here.

Adriana Boudevska Drama Theatre THEATRE
(☎ 056-841 494; www.burgteatre.com; ul Tsar Asen I 36a) This stylish venue hosts classic and contemporary drama, though will only be of limited interest to most visitors as performances are normally staged in Bulgarian.

❶ Information

There are two branches of the tourist information centre; both offices have English-speaking staff and plenty of brochures. **Tourist Information Centre - Main** (☎ 056-841 542; www.goto burgas.com; ul Hristo Botev; ☺ 8.30am-5.30pm Mon-Fri) is at the entrance to the underpass below ul Hristo Botev. Another **branch** (☎ 056-825 772; pl Tsaritsa Yoanna, Yug Bus Station; ☺ 8.30am-5.30pm Mon-Fri) is within the terminal of the Yug bus station.

Numerous banks with ATMs can be found along ul Aleksandrovska and ul Aleko Bogorid. **Raffeisen Bank** (☎ 056-851 422; www.rbb. bg; ul Ferdinandova 5; ☺ 8.30am-5pm Mon-Fri) Changes cash and travellers cheques and has ATMs.

Unicredit Bulbank (☎ 02-933 7212; www. unicreditbulbank.bg; ul Aleksandrovska 22; ☺ 8.30am-5pm Mon-Fri) Handy 24-hour ATM.

❶ Getting There & Away

AIR

Bulgaria Air (www.air.bg) links **Burgas Airport** (BOJ; ☎ information 056-870 248; www. bourgas-airport.com; Sarafovo; ☎; 🚌15), 10km northeast of town, with Sofia daily (April to October). In summer, **Wizz Air** (www.wizzair. com) connects Burgas with London Luton, Budapest, Prague and Warsaw. Other carriers fly to destinations in Germany and Russia.

BUS

Outside the train station at the southern end of ul Aleksandrovska, **Yug bus station** (☎ 0884981220; www.bgrazpisanie.com; pl Tsaritsa Yoanna) is where most travellers will arrive or leave. There are regular buses to coastal destinations. Departures are less frequent outside summer. A **left-luggage office** (☺ 6am-10pm) is located inside the station.

A number of agencies around Yug bus station, including **Viva Travel** (☎ 056-841 245; www.viva -travel.net; ul Bulair; ☺ 9am-6pm Mon-Fri), run coaches to Istanbul each day (50 lv, seven hours).

From the less convenient **Zapad bus station** (☎ 056-831 427, 0884981270; www.bgraz pisanie.com; ul Maritsa 2), 2km northwest of pl Troikata, buses leave for Malko Târnovo (9 lv, 1½ hours, two daily) in the Strandzha Nature Park and Veliko Târnovo (25 lv, four hours, one daily).

The Burgas Bus website (www.burgasbus.info) is in Bulgarian only but has a handy timetable for both major bus stations (on the upper left side of the opening page).

TRAIN

The historic **train station** (☎ information 056-845 022; www.bdz.bg; ul Ivan Vazov;

BUSES FROM BURGAS

DESTINATION	COST (LV)	DURATION	FREQUENCY
Kiten	8	1hr	every 1-1½hr
Nesebâr	6	40min	every 30-40min
Plovdiv	20	4hr	several daily
Pomorie	4	30min	every 1-1½hr
Primorsko	7	1hr	several daily
Sinemorets	15	1½hr	1 daily
Sofia	30	7-8hr	several daily
Sozopol	5	40min	every 45min
Sunny Beach (Slânchev Bryag)	6	45min	every 30-40min
Tsarevo	10	2hr	several daily
Varna	14	2hr	every 30-40min

TRAINS FROM BURGAS

DESTINATION	COST (LV)	DURATION (HR)	FREQUENCY (DAILY)
Kazanlâk	12	3	2
Plovdiv	16	5-6	5
Sliven	8	1¾	4
Sofia	21	7-8	5
Stara Zagora	11	3	4

⊙ information office 6am-10pm), sporting a fresh coat of paint, was built in 1902. There are clearly marked ticket windows for buying both domestic and international tickets. There's also an ATM and a cafe.

Sozopol   СОЗОПОЛ

POP 5700

Ancient Sozopol, with its charming old town of meandering cobbled streets and pretty wooden houses, huddled together on a narrow peninsula, is one of the coast's real highlights. With two superb beaches, a genial atmosphere, plentiful accommodation and good transport links, it has long been a popular seaside resort and makes an excellent base for exploring the area. Although not quite as crowded as Nesebâr, it is becoming ever more popular with international visitors. There's a lively cultural scene, too, with plenty of free concerts and other events in summer.

The new town, known as 'Harmanite', lies south of the tiny bus station. The best beach is in this part of town, but otherwise, it's mainly modern hotels and residential areas.

History

Sozopol is the oldest settlement on the Bulgarian Black Sea coast, founded in an area belonging to an ancient Thracian tribe in 611 BC by Greek colonists from Miletus, who called their home Apollonia Pontica in honour of the god Apollo. One of these early settlers was the philosopher and astronomer Anaximander.

Apollonia, ruled by an elected Council of Archons, flourished as a major trading hub, but in 72 BC the town was sacked and mostly destroyed. Its famous bronze statue of Apollo was taken to Rome as booty.

Under the Byzantine Empire, and renamed Sozopolis (City of Salvation), the town was an important religious centre. It fell to Khan Tervel in 705, was recaptured by the Byzantines in 759 and finally reverted to the First Bulgarian Empire (681–1018) in 969. Under Turkish rule, centuries later, ship-building and fishing were mainstays of the economy.

During the communist era, the town was promoted as a holiday resort, although not until the 1990s did it really take off, with Russians and Germans being among the more numerous foreign visitors.

◉ Sights

Sozopol's sights are clustered in the old town, with the main attraction simply being the criss-crossing cobblestoned lanes that trace paths between 19th-century and stone-and-timber houses built on ruins that have been here more than 1000 years.

Archaeological Museum   MUSEUM
(⏷0550-22 226; ul Han Krum 2; adult/child 7/3 lv; ⊙8.30am-6pm Jun-Sep, 8.30am-6pm Mon-Fri Oct-May) Housed in a drab concrete box near the port, this museum has a small but fascinating collection of local finds from its Apollonian glory days and beyond. In addition to a wealth of Hellenic treasures, the museum occasionally exhibits the skeleton of a local 'vampire', found with a stake driven through its chest. Enter from the building's northern side.

Church of Sveta Bogoroditsa   CHURCH
(Holy Virgin; ul Anaksimandâr 13; donation 1 lv; ⊙10am-6pm) This 15th-century church was built below street level, as required at the time by the Ottoman rulers. Set in a courtyard with a giant fig tree, it is one of the most picturesque in town, with an exquisite wooden iconostasis and a pulpit carved with bunches of grapes.

Fishing Harbour   HARBOUR
Boats line up picturesquely along the fishing harbour, along the western edge of the peninsula. Many of the boats can be chartered for short-term excursion or evening rides. Simply ask along the dock.

Sozopol

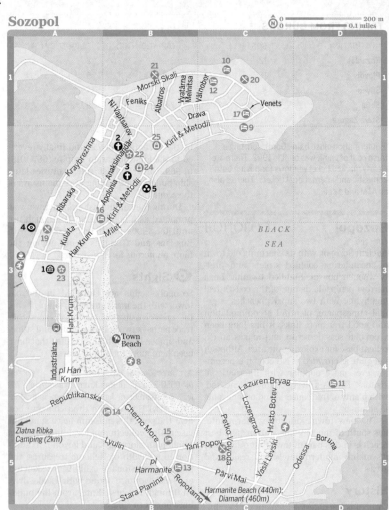

**Southern Fortress Wall
& Tower Museum** RUIN, MUSEUM
(☏ 0550-22 267; www.sozopol-foundation.com;
ul Milet 50; adult/child 7/5 lv; ⊙ 9am-6pm) This
museum occupies a former granary and
part of the fortification walls of the medieval town, dating from the 5th century
AD. At this time, Sozopol was considered
an important defensive post of the Byzantine Empire, with its capital at Constantinople (Istanbul). Visitors pass by some
interior defensive walls and a well going
back to the 3rd century BC. That said, it's
a bit underwhelming. Even if you skip the

museum, walk under the arch to see the
sea views.

Church of Sveti Georgi CHURCH
(ul Apolonia; donation 1 lv; ⊙ 9am-2pm & 3-8pm)
This attractive church boasts a fine painting of St George and the Dragon over the
entrance and an impressive 19th-century
iconostasis. The custodians here are rather
keen to enforce the dress code (no shorts).

🏃 Activities

The town's two beaches, Harmanite Beach
(ul Ropotamo; ⊙ 9am-6pm Jun-Sep) and Town

Sozopol

Beach (⊙9am-6pm Jun-Sep), are attractive, though waves can be quite high.

There's also a beautiful sand beach, **Smokinya**, located 4km south of Sozopol. Find it along the highway heading south or, hugging the coast, along ul Via Pontika. Look for signs to 'Smokinya' or 'Camping Smokinya'.

Sozopol Diving Center   DIVING
(☏0885245526; www.dive-sozopol.com; ul Yani Popov 27) This outfit offers supervised beginner dives from around 80 lv, as well as a range of specialist dives such as wreck dives (140 lv) and PADI courses. Two-day excursions, including accommodation, start from around 180 lv per person.

Sailing Boats   BOATING
(Sozopol Harbour; adult/child 10/6 lv) Several large sailboats moored in the Old Town port on the western side of the peninsula offer evening sightseeing cruises in summer. Boats normally depart at around 6pm and 7.30pm and the cruise lasts for about an hour.

✵ Festivals & Events

Apollonia Arts Festival   ART, MUSIC
(www.apollonia.bg; ⊙end Aug–mid-Sep) This is the highlight of Sozopol's cultural calendar, with concerts, theatrical performances, art exhibitions, film screenings and more held across town.

⊖ Sleeping

Sozopol has numerous private homes offering rooms. Look for signs along Republikanska in the new town and pretty much anywhere in the old town. Choose the new town if you're looking for a traditional beach holiday or if you're coming by car. The old town is smaller, quainter and closed off to most vehicle traffic.

★ **Justa Hostel**   HOSTEL $
(☏0550-22175; ul Apolonia 20; dm 20 lv; ☜) This clean, cosy, centrally located hostel sits in the centre of the Old Town, a few minutes' walk from the beach. Dorm-bed accommodation with shared bath and shower. The price includes traditional breakfast (pancakes) and coffee.

DON'T MISS

SVETI IVAN

Sveti Ivan is the largest Bulgarian island in the Black Sea (0.7 sq km). It lies 3km north of Sozopol's old town, and can be visited by private boat (for around 50 lv) from the town's **Fishing Harbour**.

The island's history stretches back to Thracian and Roman times, and includes a monastery from the 4th century AD. Sveti Ivan made international headlines in 2010 with the purported discovery of the remains of St John the Baptist.

Sv Ivan is also an important bird sanctuary, with some 70 species of birds reported here. Visits are restricted during the spring nesting season.

Sasha Khristov's Private Rooms
PENSION **$**

(☑ 0550-23 434; ul Venets 17; s/d from 20/30 lv; ☎) This lovely family home in the Old Town faces the art gallery at the end of the Sozopol peninsula. It comprises good-sized rooms and a large apartment. Book ahead in summer.

Hotel Orka
HOTEL **$**

(☑ 0888752200; www.sozopol-orka.com; ul Pârvi Mai 2; d/tr/apt 50/65/80 lv; ✴ @) In the centre of the new town, this is a neat, family-run hotel not far from the beach. Rooms are plain but clean, with balconies, TVs and fridges.

Zlatna Ribka Camping
CAMPGROUND **$**

(☑ 0550-22 534; www.zlatna-ribka.com; Tsarski Beach; tent/caravan sites from 30/45 lv; ☺ Jun-Sep; P ☎ ⛱) Around 2km west of Sozopol's old town, Zlatna Ribka is a well-ordered campsite on its own private beach, with guarded spaces for 150 caravans and tents. On-site facilities include a restaurant, shops, a bakery, a surf school and other water sports, and lifeguards patrol the beach. Buses between Sozopol and Burgas stop outside the gates.

★ Art Hotel
HOTEL **$$**

(☑ 0878650160, 0550-24 081; www.arthotel-sbh. com; ul Kiril & Metodii 72; d/studios 80/100 lv; ✴ ☎) This peaceful old house, belonging to the Union of Bulgarian Artists, is within a walled courtyard toward the tip of the peninsula, away from the crowds. It has a small selection of bright, comfortable rooms with balconies, most with sea views; breakfast is served on the terraces overlooking the sea.

Hotel Radik
HOTEL **$$**

(☑ 0550-23 706; ul Republikanska 4; d/studios/apt from 68/75/95 lv; P ✴ ☎ ⛱) Run by a lovely English expat-Bulgarian couple, the Radik is cheap, cheerful and perfectly located 100m from the Old Town and a quick stagger to the beach. Rooms have sea views and balconies; studios and apartments have good kitchenettes.

Hotel Anaxemander
HOTEL **$$**

(☑ 0882683361; www.hotel-anaxemander.eu; ul Odessa 38; d/tr/apt 70/80/100 lv; P ✴ ☎) On a rocky promontory in a quiet corner of the new town, the Anaxemander has light and airy rooms, all with sea views and terraces, while the larger, two-bedroom apartments come with small kitchens and bathtubs.

The hotel runs various excursions, including yacht trips.

Doctor's House
HOTEL **$$**

(☑ 0550-22 731; www.doctorshousesozopol.com; ul Morski Skali 35; r 60-80 lv, apt 100-140 lv; P ✴ ☎) Perched over the sea at the northern tip of the peninsula, the Doctor's House has basic twin-bedded rooms, and larger apartments sleeping up to four people. All rooms have balconies and sea views. It has a restaurant and even its own chapel.

Hotel Diamanti
HOTEL **$$**

(☑ 0550-22 640; www.hoteldiamanti.com; ul Morski Skali 8; d/apt from 80/120 lv; ✴ ☎) Old town Diamanti has a variety of rooms, some with sea views, including apartments with kitchenettes; larger apartments are available in a second building nearby. There's also a terrace restaurant, with live music in summer.

Hotel Villa List
HOTEL **$$**

(☑ 0550-22 235; www.hotellist-bg.com; ul Yani Popov 5; s/d from 80/120 lv; ✴ @ ⛱) With a superb setting just off the town beach, big rooms with balconies and an outdoor pool with a view over the sea, Villa List is understandably very popular, and frequently fully booked in summer.

✖ Eating

Fish, naturally enough, is the local speciality, and several reasonably priced restaurants are strung out along the port area. The best restaurants in town are on ul Morksi Skali, on the far northeastern end of the peninsula. These are mainly traditional affairs with some spectacular views.

Diamant
BULGARIAN **$**

(ul Ropotamo; mains 5-8 lv; ☺ 9am-11pm Jun-Sep) Nothing special, but one of the better Harmanite beachfront restaurants, serving traditional grills, soups, fish and cheap three-course lunch deals from around 5 lv. It's one of a string of several similar restaurants on ul Ropotamo, located toward the southern end of Harmanite Beach.

Biju
SEAFOOD **$**

(☑ 0878726928; ul Kraybrezhna 51; mains 5-10 lv; ☺ 11am-11pm) This simple harbour-side restaurant is good value, specialising in a variety of fresh fish dishes. Bulgarian staples such as *kebabcheta* (spicy grilled sausages) and salads are also available.

BOATING IN THE ROPOTAMO NATURE RESERVE

The **Ropotamo Nature Reserve** (☑0887767706; www.ropotamo-reserve.com; boat rides adult/child 10/5 lv; ☉Jun-Sep) is located 10km south of Sozopol, along the main road to Primorsko. Visitors can hike or picnic, but most come for a 30- to 40-minute slow boat ride along the Ropotamo River. To get to the parkland entrance by public transport, take any bus south of Sozopol, and get off at the prominent, well-signposted bridge where the highway crosses the river. Boats leave at regular intervals throughout the day.

The reserve was established in 1940 to protect fragile landscapes of extensive marshes and the largest sand dunes in Bulgaria, as well as rare flora such as the endemic sand lily. It also protects some 257 species of birds, reptiles and mammals, including white-tailed eagles, wild boars, jackals and 10 species of bat. The reserve also encompasses Thracian megaliths and tiny Sveti Toma Island, which hosts Bulgaria's only wild cacti.

Albatros
BULGARIAN $$

(☑0897909089; www.hoteli-albatros.com; ul Yani Popov 10; mains 7-14 lv; ☉9am-11.30pm; ☏) No sea views, but no touts either, this handy new town restaurant, below a hotel of the same name, serves great grills, fish and some of the best homemade chips (French fries) we've tasted. There are a few street-side tables or a handsome dining room.

Panorama
SEAFOOD $$

(ul Morski Skali 21; mains 8-20 lv; ☉11am-11pm) This lively place has an open terrace with a fantastic view toward Sveti Ivan island. Fresh, locally caught fish is the mainstay of the menu. It's one of the best of many seafood spots on this street.

★ Mehane Neptun
BULGARIAN $$$

(☑0550-22 735; ul Morski Skali 45; mains 15-30 lv; ☉10am-11pm) Occupying a promontory overlooking the sea and Sveti Ivan Island, the awesome views here and delicious fish combinations, such as mouth-watering stuffed squid, are only partly marred by the sometimes indifferent service. Try to book a sea-view table outdoors for around dusk and settle in for a memorable evening.

☆ Entertainment

Live music, dancing and other shows are often staged through the summer at the modern **open-air theatre** (ul Han Krum) near the Archaeological Museum.

Art Club Michel
LIVE MUSIC

(☑0889801120; ul Apolonia 39; tickets 3-5 lv; ☉6pm-2am) With its walled garden just off one of the old town's main streets, this mellow place is good for live music, especially jazz.

🛍 Shopping

In summer, the streets in the old town are lined with stalls selling the usual array of tourist tat, but there are some better-quality souvenirs to be found.

Gallery Bissera
GIFTS & SOUVENIRS

(☑0550-24 092; ul Apolonia 52; ☉9am-10pm) Set up in an old wooden barn, Gallery Bissera offers a range of local paintings and ceramics, as well as some antique oddments.

Art Gallery Laskaridi
GIFTS & SOUVENIRS

(☑0550-23 906; ul Kiril & Metodii 19; ☉9am-8pm) Sells contemporary art, jewellery and pottery, as well as souvenir books about Sozopol. The gallery is located in a historic house that sits behind ruins of ancient churches.

ℹ Information

There's no tourist information office.

Many banks with ATMs can be found along the old town's main streets, and around the new town's main square.

ℹ Getting There & Away

The small public **bus station** (☑0550-23 460; www.bgrazpisanie.com; ul Han Krum) is just south of the old town walls. Buses leave for Burgas (5 lv, 40 minutes) about every 30 minutes between 6am and 9pm in summer, and about once an hour in the low season.

In summer, hourly buses go to Primorsko (6 lv, 30 minutes) and Kiten (6 lv, 40 minutes). Public buses leave two to three times a day for Sofia (32 lv, seven hours).

Fast Ferry (☑0988908629, booking 0885808001; www.fastferry.bg; Sozopol Harbour) operates from a kiosk at the harbour and runs three daily high-speed catamarans or hydrofoils to both Nesebâr (one way/return from 27/54 lv, 40 minutes) and Pomorie (one way/return from 22/44 lv, 30 minutes), June to September.

ⓘ Getting Around

Sozopol is easy to get around on foot. If you need a car, there are several agencies around pl Harmanite and ul Ropotamo in the new town which can arrange car rental from about 70 lv per day.

Primorsko ПРИМОРСКО

POP 3680

Primorsko (meaning 'by the sea'), 52km southeast of Burgas, is in many ways the ideal seaside resort. It's pretty and clean, and laid-back enough to feel like a holiday, yet it still has plenty of places to eat and drink. The town's two beaches are among the nicest on the coast.

🏃 Activities

The main activities in Primorsko revolve around the town's two main beaches. **North Beach** curls around the northern end of town and is accessible from ul Briz. **South Beach** stretches on for a few kilometres and is accessible from ul Cherno More. Both have life guards on duty from 9am to 6pm from June to September.

🛏 Sleeping

Primorsko has loads of hotels and guest-houses, though the best tend to book up quickly in summer. Even if you don't have a reservation, residents offering rooms line the road into town.

Zora Guest House GUESTHOUSE $
(☑ 0878510406; ul Zora 2; d/apt 50/100 lv; P✳🛜) This largish guesthouse is located in the centre of town, about equidistant (300m) for both the northern and southern beaches. The rooms are plainly furnished, but clean and well-maintained. Rooms come with a fridge and some have balconies or efficiency kitchens.

Hotel Plovdiv HOTEL $$
(☑ 0550-32 372; www.hotel-primorsko.com; ul Briz 9; d/ste 80/120 lv; ✳🛜🏊) On a quiet street overlooking North Beach, the Plovdiv is ex-cellent value. Rooms are basic but bright and perfectly comfortable. There's a res-taurant and a children's pool. The hotel is open throughout the year, and prices drop considerably out of season.

Spektar Palace HOTEL $$
(☑ 0550-31 043; www.spektar-palace.com; ul Treti Mart 82; d/tr 60/80 lv; ⊘ May-Oct; P✳🛜🏊) This modern hotel is situated away from the beaches and closer to the town's entrance on the western end. Because of the location (300m to South Beach) it represents very good value and easy access to the bus sta-tion. Spektar has large rooms and excellent facilities, including a small pool and gym.

🍴 Eating

Kebabs, pizzas and burgers from stalls around town seem to be standard fare for most visitors. Some of the better restaurants are on ul Cherno More.

Birariya Dionisii BULGARIAN $
(☑ 0878656220; ul Cherno More 28, cnr ul Hristo Botev; mains 4-6 lv; ⊘ 11am-11pm May-Oct) This small, traditional tavern in the southeastern part of town, not far from the top of South Beach, serves up the usual range of Bulgar-ian specialities as well as pizzas, salads and locally caught fish.

Restaurant Ahtamar BULGARIAN $$
(☑ 0885888969; ul Ropotamo 26; mains 7-15 lv; ⊘ 11am-11pm May-Oct) One of the few places in town that tries to go beyond the usual range of grills and salads. The speciality here is local fish, prepared in inventive ways. The owner is friendly and can help you sort through the list of Bulgarian wines. The restaurant is located near the exact centre of Primorsko, one block north of the main street, ul Treti Mart.

Chaika BULGARIAN $$
(☑ 0550-32 990; ul Cherno More; mains 5-20 lv; ⊘ 11am-midnight May-Oct) Grilled octopus, mackerel and other fishy dishes feature here; other options include stuffed peppers and goulash. There's outdoor seating in the shady little park behind the restaurant. The restaurant is situated in a red stucco build-ing near where ul Kiril & Metodii meets ul Cherno More, just at the top of South Beach.

ⓘ Getting There & Away

Primorsko's bus station, 1km from the town centre, is where all public transport arrives and departs. From here there are buses to Kiten (1 lv, 10 minutes, roughly every hour), Tsarevo (4 lv, 30 minutes, six daily) and Sozopol (6 lv, 35 minutes, several daily). In addition, a few buses travel daily to Burgas (7 lv, one hour) and Sofia (35 lv, eight hours).

Tsarevo ЦАРЕВО

POP 5800

Spread lazily over two small peninsulas jutting out into the Black Sea, Tsarevo is a quiet, elegant little town, once a popular holiday spot for the Bulgarian royal family. Called Vasiliko until 1934, it was renamed Tsarevo ('royal place') in honour of Tsar Boris III; the communists then renamed it Michurin (after a Soviet botanist) in 1950, and it reverted once again in 1991. The centre, on the larger, northern peninsula, has a calm, affluent atmosphere and feels more like a real town than some of Tsarevo's seaside-resort neighbours.

⊙ Sights & Activities

With two main beaches, swimming is the main activity, though quiet Tsarevo does not feel like a full-on beach resort in the same way that nearby Primorsko does.

Sea Gardens PARK

Offering dramatic panoramic views across the Black Sea, these peaceful gardens overlook the northern peninsula's rocky headland at the end of the main road, ul Han Asparuh.

North Beach BEACH

(⊙9am-6pm Jun-Sep) The smaller of Tsarevo's two main beaches, North Beach lies on the northern side of the northern peninsula and is accessible via a stairway that begins on ul Hristo Botev at the intersection with ul Samuil.

South Beach BEACH

(⊙9am-6pm Jun-Sep) Bigger and prettier than its northern neighbour, South Beach (or Nestinarka Beach), across the wide bay, occupies a cove along the southern peninsula. Sadly, this is no hideaway beach, as it's also shared by several modern hotels. The beach is about 2km from the town centre.

Angel Divers DIVING

(☑0590-99 379; www.angel-divers.com; Lozenets; beginner dives from 100 lv) At the heart of the Hotel Lalov Egrek complex in Lozenets, 4km north of Tsarevo, is this top-class diving centre, where there's a dedicated training pool on-site and a wide variety of diving courses on offer. PADI-certified courses are aimed at everyone from beginners to advanced divers.

🛏 Sleeping

There are several hotels in town to suit a range of budgets. If swimming and spending time at the beach are at the top of your 'to do' list, nearby Lozenets is an attractive option.

Hotel Lalov Egrek RESORT $$

(☑0590-99 379; www.hotel.lalov.net; Lozenets; s/d/apt 80/120/140 lv; P ⊜ ✳ ᐢ ☲) Around 4km north of Tsarevo, on the outskirts of Lozenets, this beachfront complex enjoys stunning sea views and has an excellent restaurant. There's access to two popular beaches and an in-house diving centre.

Hotel Ribarska Sreshta HOTEL $$

(☑0590-52 455; www.hotelribarska.com; ul Kraymorska, Tsarevo Harbour; d/tr/ste 60/85/100 lv; ✳ ᐢ) Looking like a small, stranded cruise liner sitting on the northern side of the fishing harbour, this place has compact, attractive rooms with sea-facing balconies. There's an excellent fish restaurant downstairs, and full board is available for 40 lv per person.

Hotel Zebra HOTEL $$

(☑0590-55 111; www.hotel-zebra.com; ul Han Asparuh 10; s/d 60/76 lv; P ✳ @ ᐢ ☲) Near the scenic Sea Gardens, on the northern peninsula, this modern complex offers superb value. The large, comfortable rooms all have balconies and sparkling bathrooms, and there's an outdoor pool and a restaurant.

Family Hotel Diana HOTEL $$

(☑0590-54 855; ul Hristo Botev 2; r from 60 lv; P ✳ ᐢ) The Diana is a modern affair with a good location, about 50m up from North Beach, a block north of the centre. Many rooms offer Black Sea views and terraces. There's an on-site restaurant and free parking (rare in tiny Tsarevo), though there's no lift to the third floor.

✗ Eating

Tsarevo has several good restaurants, including one of the country's best places for fish and seafood.

★ Ribarska Sreshta SEAFOOD $$

(☑0590-52 451; www.hotelribarska.com; ul Kraymorska, Tsarevo Harbour; mains 8-14 lv; ⊙11am-midnight; ᐢ) Even if you're not staying at the hotel, consider lunch or dinner at this authentic fish restaurant. There's an extensive menu of fresh fish, including a local favourite: small bluefish (grilled or fried). Choose from a long list of appetisers and

STRANDZHA NATURE PARK

The remote **Strandzha Nature Park** (☑ 05952-3635; www.strandja.bg; ⊙ 9am-noon, 1-6pm Wed-Sun), established in 1995, occupies a good chunk of the country's southeast, stretching from low-lying central mountains to the southernmost strip of the Black Sea coast. At 1161 sq km, the park is Bulgaria's largest protected area. It shelters a diverse range of flora and fauna, as well as various ancient ruins.

The park is ideal for hiking, as it's sparsely populated and relatively flat. Several short hikes (1km to 8km long), and longer treks (about 20km) between the coast and the centre of the park, are detailed in the colourful *Nature Park Strandzha* map (1:70,000). Strandzha is also ideal for swimming as the country's most remote stretches of sandy beach lie within the park's borders.

Malko Târnovo, a small, provincial town 80km south of Burgas, is the administrative centre of the park, and a logical base for exploring the area. Alongside the park's visitor centre and an interesting **History Museum** (☑ 05952-3664; ul Konstantin Petkanov 1a, Malko Târnovo; adult/child 5/3 lv; ⊙ 8am-5pm Mon-Fri, 9.30am-noon & 2-5pm Sat & Sun May-Oct, 8am-noon & 1-4pm Mon-Fri Nov-Apr), the town is also the beginning or end for many of the park's hiking and cycling paths.

salads, and wash it down with *rakia* (Bulgarian brandy) as you gaze out over the harbour.

ℹ Getting There & Away

Tsarevo's bus station is at the top of ul Mikhail Gerdzhikov, toward the highway, about 2km west of the centre. Buses to Burgas (10 lv, 75 minutes) run roughly every 30 minutes to one hour between 6am and 8pm via Kiten (2 lv, 20 minutes) and Primorsko (4 lv, 30 minutes). There are two daily buses to Sofia (37 lv, eight hours).

Sinemorets СИНЕМОРЕЦ
POP 300

If you have your own transport, tiny Sinemorets, with its two lovely white beaches, is a relaxing place to leave the crowds behind. The natural attractions haven't escaped the attention of the developers, sadly, but despite the presence of several modern hotels near the main beach, the atmosphere of remote, slow-paced village life remains. Sinemorets lies within the boundaries of the Strandzha Nature Park and hiking trails lead from just outside the town into the park.

🏃 Activities

There are two public **beaches**: the main beach (sometimes called Butamya Beach) is located to the southeast of town (follow ul Butamya, the main drag, east and then down a steep hill); a smaller and more attractive beach lies to the north of the centre, where the Veleka River empties into the Black Sea.

🛌 Sleeping

Hotels normally open up in May and run through September. Most places offer some kind of board option for meals. Given the shortage of good restaurants, this may make sense.

Casa Domingo HOTEL **$$**
(☑ 0590-66 093; www.casadomingo.info; ul Ribarska; s/d/apt from 50/65/130 lv; 🕸🏊) This attractive modern complex has a range of rooms, studios and apartments, set in a pretty garden with an open-air pool and restaurant. Breakfast is 6 lv extra and there are reductions for children under 12 years old. To get here, head east along the main street, ul Butamya, about halfway through the town and turn right (south).

Asti Arthotel HOTEL **$$**
(☑ 0590-65 504; www.asti.bg; ul Silistar 8; d/apt 80/140 lv; ⊙ May-Sep; 🅿❄🕸🏊) All of the Asti's 26 apartments have terraces and tiny kitchenettes, and there are also three smaller double rooms. There is a tennis court, pool, playground and restaurant, and bikes are available for rent. To find it, head east along the main street, ul Butamya, about 1km, almost to the main beach, and turn right along an unmarked street. The hotel is signposted.

Dayana Beach Hotel HOTEL **$$**
(☑ 0590-65 502; www.dayanabeach.com; ul Silistar; s/d 60/80 lv; ⊙ May-Sep; 🅿❄🕸🏊) Close to the main beach, this modern family hotel has bright rooms with verandahs, TVs

and fridges. The hotel sits behind the Asti Arthotel.

Eating

The greatest concentration of places to eat is along ul Butamya, which runs west to east through the centre of town.

Zafo   SEAFOOD $$

(📞 0888401916; www.zafosinemorec.com; ul Buta-mya 6; mains 8-16 lv; ⊙ 11am-11pm May-Sep; 🕙)
This pretty garden restaurant located along the main street near the centre of town offers grilled meats and fresh fish. It's popular in the evenings and gets quite festive as the *rakia* flows.

❶ Getting There & Away

Public transport to/from Sinemorets is poor. There's one daily bus leaving Burgas in summer (14 lv, two hours), otherwise you'll need to make your way to Ahtopol and change there for one of the four daily minibuses to Sinemorets (2 lv, 15 minutes).

CENTRAL COAST

Pomorie ПОМОРИЕ

POP 13,500

Like neighbouring Nesebâr, Pomorie sits on a narrow peninsula, and until it was ravaged by fire in 1906 it was almost as picturesque. There, however, the similarities end. The old town centre, situated on the far eastern end of the peninsula, has a lazy charm, and there's a pleasant and usually not very crowded beach. Pomorie is very much a Bulgarian resort and is almost entirely by-passed by foreign tourists.

Pomorie Lake, to the north, is a saline coastal lagoon where sea salt is produced and medicinal mud is extracted. The lake is also an important sanctuary for birds, including terns, avocets and stilts. The NGO Green Balkans (www.greenbalkans.org) is active in species conservation here and operates a visitor centre to educate the public on the lake's flora and fauna.

❂ Sights & Activities

The main sight for most visitors is the beach, though there are a couple of important religious buildings to see. Nature enthusiasts and birders will want to visit the Pomorie Lake Visitor Centre to see first hand the conservation efforts taking place in the region.

Pomorie Lake
Visitor Centre   NATURE RESERVE

(📞 0885108712; www.greenbalkans.org; adult/child 4/2 lv; ⊙ 9.30am-noon & 1.30-6.30pm Tue-Sun)
This interactive visitor centre provides information on bird- and species-conservation efforts on Pomorie Lake undertaken by the NGO Green Balkans. From the terrace, visitors can see the main breeding colonies (with fieldscopes and binoculars provided). There's also an ecotrail that passes along the dyke on the side of the lake. The centre is situated along the southern edge of the lake, about 1km west of the beachfront promenade.

Salt Museum   MUSEUM

(📞 0596-25 344; www.saltmuseum.bg; adult/child 4/2 lv; ⊙ 8am-6pm Mon-Fri, 10am-4pm Sat & Sun Jun-Sep, 8am-4pm Mon-Fri Oct-May) Pomorie Lake has been an important source of salt, via salt panning, through the ages. Visitors learn the techniques of panning as well as the history of salt extraction. The museum is located next to the Pomorie Lake Visitor Centre, along the southern edge of the lake.

Preobrazhenie
Gospodne Church   CHURCH

This most atmospheric of the town's churches is located in the oldest part of the settlement, on the far eastern end of the outcropping. The church dates from 1765.

☐ Sleeping

Hotel Pri Amerikaneca   HOTEL $$

(📞 0596-22 824; www.attheamericans.com; ul Knyaz Boris I 9, cnr ul Vitosha; r 100 lv; 🅿 🌐 @ 🕙)
The curiously named 'At the Americans' is a modern seafront hotel in the old town, with its own private beach. The 12 spacious studios all have balconies and panoramic sea views, and there's a restaurant and cocktail bar on-site. It's located south of the main beachfront promenade, on the extreme southeastern end of the peninsula.

Zeus Hotel   HOTEL $$

(📞 0888866174; www.zeus-hotel.com; ul Rak-ovska 9, cnr ul Aheloi; s/d 65/85 lv; 🌐 🕙) The town-centre Zeus has a variety of cosy rooms, all with balconies, fridges and TVs. Prices drop by up to 50% outside the summer season. To find it, follow ul Aheloj toward the centre about 200m from the main beachfront promenade (ul Kraybrezhna).

✖ Eating

The beachfront promenade, ul Kraybrezhna, is lined with restaurants, while better options (with multilingual menus) are found near the Preobrazhenie Gospodne Church.

Restaurant Tsarevets　　　BULGARIAN $$
(☑0875148517; ul Knyaz Boris I 5; mains 7-20 lv; ⊙11am-11pm) One of the better options in town, near the Preobrazhenie Gospodne Church on the extreme southeastern end of the peninsula, offering grilled pork, chicken and fish dishes. The back terrace looks out onto the beach of the nearby Hotel Pri Amerikaneca.

❶ Getting There & Away

There are two bus stations in Pomorie. The main station is 3km west of the town centre; regular buses and minibuses between Burgas and Nesebâr and/or Sunny Beach usually stop only at the main station. The smaller central station is situated to the southeast, closer to the beach resorts. Roughly hourly minibuses marked 'Pomorie Central' (Поморие Център) leave from Burgas (4 lv, 30 minutes) and Sunny Beach (3 lv, 30 minutes).

Nesebâr　　　НЕСЕБЪР

POP 11,600

On a rocky outcrop 37km northeast of Burgas, connected to the mainland by aN artificial isthmus, pretty-as-a-postcard Nesebâr is famous for its surprisingly numerous, albeit mostly ruined, medieval churches. It has, inevitably, become heavily commercialised, and transforms into one huge, open-air souvenir market during the high season; outside summer, it's a ghost town. Designated by Unesco as a World Heritage site, Nesebâr has its charms, but in summer these can be overpowered by the crowds and the relentless parade of tacky shops.

History

Greek colonists founded what became the thriving trading port of Mesembria in 512 BC, although most of their temples and towers were submerged after the level of the Black Sea rose around 2000 years ago.

Under Byzantine rule, during the 5th and 6th centuries AD, several grand churches were erected and the fortifications extended. After the Bulgar invasion in 812, the town was renamed Nesebâr; over the following centuries, it passed back and forth between Byzantium and the First Bulgarian Empire (681–1018), but remained largely unscathed, finally falling to the Turks in 1453.

During the Bulgarian National Revival of the 18th and 19th centuries, Nesebâr prospered, and wealthy merchants built grand villas here, some of which remain today. Nesebâr ceased to be an active trading town from the early 20th century, and these days it survives almost entirely on tourism.

◉ Sights

Nesebâr was once home to about 80 churches, but many have been lost to time. Of the survivors, most are now in ruins. Characteristic of the Nesebâr style are the strips of white stone and red brick, and facades decorated with green ceramic discs.

Sveta Sofia Church　　　RUINS
(Old Metropolitan Church; ☑0554-46 019; www.ancient-nessebar.com; ul Mitropolitska; ⊙dawn-dusk) **FREE** The impressive ruins of this 5th-century church form the centrepiece of

---

WORTH A TRIP

SUNNY BEACH (SLÂNCHEV BRYAG)

Bulgaria's biggest purpose-built seaside resort, Sunny Beach (Slânchev Bryag) is the Black Sea coast's hyperactive answer to the Spanish costas, and probably the most expensive place in the country.

The appeal is clear, though, with several kilometres of sandy beach that attracts more international sun worshippers than any other resort in the country. If you're just looking to top up your tan by day and go clubbing all night, this is the place to come. You won't even notice that you're in a country called Bulgaria.

Sunny Beach is a package-holiday resort, so almost everyone staying here will be on a pre-booked, often all-inclusive, deal arranged in their home countries. Of all the coastal resorts, this is the least user-friendly for independent travellers, so if you really want to stay here, it's best to book through an agent at home (or lay your hat in nearby Nesebâr instead).

a busy plaza surrounded by cafes and artists' street stalls.

Sveti Stefan Church   CHURCH
(☑0554-46 019; www.ancient-nessebar.com; ul Ribarska; adult/child 6/3 lv; ⊘9am-7pm Mon-Fri, 10.30am-2pm & 2.30-7pm Sat & Sun May-Sep, 9am-5pm Mon-Fri, 10am-5pm Sat & Sun Oct-Apr) Built in the 11th century and reconstructed 500 years later, this is the best-preserved church in town. If you only visit one, this is the church to choose. Its beautiful 16th- to 18th-century murals cover virtually the entire interior. Come early, as it's popular with tour groups.

Archaeological Museum   MUSEUM
(☑0554-46 019; www.ancient-nessebar.com; ul Mesembria 2; adult/child 6/3 lv; ⊘9am-7pm Mon-Fri, 9.30am-2pm & 2.30-7pm Sat & Sun Jun-Sep, reduced hours Oct-May) Explore the rich history of Nesebâr – formerly Mesembria – at this fine museum. Greek and Roman pottery, statues and tombstones, as well as Thracian gold jewellery and ancient anchors, are displayed here. There's also a collection of icons recovered from Nesebâr's numerous churches.

Ethnographic Museum   MUSEUM
(☑0554-46 019; www.ancient-nessebar.com; ul Mesembria 32; adult/child 3/2 lv; ⊘10.30am-2pm & 2.30-6pm Tue-Sun Jun-Sep, on request Oct-May) Inside a typical wooden National Revival building, constructed in 1840 for a wealthy merchant, this museum features exhibitions of folk costumes and traditional weaving.

Christ Pantokrator Church   CHURCH
(☑0554-46 019; www.ancient-nessebar.com; ul Mesembria; adult/child 3/2 lv; ⊘9am-7pm Mon-Fri, 9.30am-2pm & 2.30-7pm Sat & Sun Jun-Sep, reduced hours Oct-May) Typical of the characteristic Nesebâr construction is this well-preserved church, built in the mid-14th century. An unusual feature at the eastern end of the exterior of the church is the frieze of swastikas, an ancient solar symbol. The church now houses a small gallery dedicated to old maps.

Sveta Paraskeva Church   CHURCH
(☑0554-46 019; www.ancient-nessebar.com; ul Hemus; adult/child 3/2 lv; ⊘10.30am-2pm & 2.30-7pm Jun-Sep, to 6pm May & Oct, on request Nov-Apr) With only one nave and one apse, the Sveta Paraskeva Church is a fine example of 13th-century architecture. The church now houses a small exhibition of murals that have survived through the ages, including

> ### ⓘ SEEING THE CHURCHES
> The ruins, including the main church, Sveta Sofia, are free to enter or to observe. Five churches – Sveti Stefan, Sveti Spas, Christ Pantokrator, Sveta Paraskeva and the Church of St John the Baptist – contain modest exhibitions and require a separate admission fee. Various combined admission tickets are available, and include access to the Archaeological Museum, with the Ethnographic Museum and one or more of the churches.

some from the lost St George the Elder church, which was destroyed in 1958.

Church of St John the Baptist   CHURCH
(☑0554-46 019; www.ancient-nessebar.com; ul Mitropolitska; adult/child 3/2 lv; ⊘10.30am-2pm & 2.30-7pm Jun-Sep, to 6pm May & Oct, on request Nov-Apr) This church was built in the 10th century and features some of the best-preserved murals from the 14th and 17th centuries. The church is built on the foundations of an earlier church from the Byzantine period dating from the 6th century.

Sveti Spas Church   CHURCH
(Church of the Blessed Saviour; ☑0554-46 019; www.ancient-nessebar.com; ul Aheloi; adult/child 3/2 lv; ⊘10.30am-2pm & 2.30-7pm Jun-Sep, to 6pm May & Oct, on request Nov-Apr) This modest, single-nave church was built in 1609, below ground level, as dictated by the Ottoman authorities of the time. It features some well-preserved murals depicting the life of Christ and the Virgin Mary.

Town Gate   GATE
The town gate leads to the old town. The well-preserved fortification walls here date from the 5th century AD.

🏃 Activities

Around 1.5km southwest of the peninsula, in the 'new town', is **South Beach**. There are also beaches on the extreme eastern end of the outcropping.

Aqua Paradise   WATER PARK
(☑0885208055; www.aquaparadise-bg.com; adult/child 40/20 lv, after 3pm 30/15 lv; ⊘10am-6.30pm; 🚸) Organised watery fun is on hand at Aqua Paradise, a huge water park on the southern outskirts of Sunny Beach just as you enter Nesebâr, with a variety of pools, slides and chutes. A free minibus, running

Nesebâr

200 m
0.1 miles

BLACK SEA

Emona
Neptun
Kraybrezhna
Neptun
Han Asparun
Rusalka
17
15
Sadala
Slavyanska
11
12
Vrachanski
4
Hemus
Venera
Mitropolitska
6
Ivan Asen II
Hemus
5
Aheloi
Hemus
Tervel
Mesembria
Ivan Alexander
13 7
16
3
Kraybrezhina
Mitropolitska
Ribarska
2
Tsar Simeon
10
8
14
Mesembria
Mena
Water Taxis
to Sunny Beach
Chaika
1
9
Harbour
Fast
Ferry
Bus
Station

Trolleybus to
Sunny Beach
(summer only)

Nesebâr New
Town (400m);
South Beach (1km)

Nesebâr

◉ Sights

⊜ Sleeping

◉ Eating

every 15 minutes, makes pick-ups at signed stops around Nesebâr and Sunny Beach.

⊨ Sleeping

In summer you'll need to book accommodation in advance. Private rooms are the best option for budget travellers – locals offering rooms meet tourists off the bus.

Hotel Tony GUESTHOUSE **$**
(☑ 0554-42 928; ul Kraybrezhna 20; r 40-50 lv; ⊙ Jun-Sep; ❋) Thanks to its low prices and excellent location overlooking the sea, the Hotel Tony books out quickly: be sure to reserve well in advance. Rooms are simple but clean, and the chatty host is very helpful.

★ Boutique Hotel
St Stefan BOUTIQUE HOTEL **$$**
(☑ 0554-43 603; www.hotelsaintstefan.com; ul Ribarska 11; r/ste 80/160 lv; ℗❋ᗆ) One of the nicest hotels in Nesebâr, the St Stefan offers rooms with views out over the harbour and Black Sea. There's a small sauna on the premises as well as a terrace for drinks and light meals. Rooms feature original artwork by Bulgarian artists. Breakfast costs 8 lv. Book well in advance for summer dates.

Prince Cyril Hotel HOTEL **$$**
(☑ 0887897971; hotelprincecyril@gmail.com; ul Slavyanska 9; d 60-80 lv; ❋ᗆ) Located on a quiet, cobbled, souvenir-stall-free lane, this is a friendly place with a variety of rooms, all with TV and fridge, but not all with air-

con; check out a few first and try to avoid the cramped, top-floor, fan-only rooms.

Royal Palace Hotel HOTEL **$$**
(☑ 0554-46 490; www.nessebarpalace.com; ul Mitropolitska 19; s/d 80/110 lv; ℗⊜❋ᗆ) In the old town centre, the Royal Palace offers stylish and comfortable rooms with fridges and TVs (though there's only one single). There's a good restaurant and summer garden, and various package deals are often available.

✗ Eating & Drinking

All restaurants in Nesebâr are geared toward the tourist trade, and prices are roughly twice what you'll pay away from the coastal resorts. Try to avoid those that employ touts.

Zlatnoto Runo BULGARIAN **$$**
(☑ 0554-45 602; ul Rusalka 6; mains 8-20 lv; ⊙ 10am-midnight) Overlooking the sea on the southeastern end of the peninsula, 'Golden Fleece' serves a varied menu, including roast lamb and rabbit, plus some inventive seafood dishes, like octopus with blueberry sauce.

Plakamoto SEAFOOD **$$**
(☑ 0888807239; ul Ivan Alexander 9; mains 8-20 lv; ⊙ noon-11pm) With tiers of seating offering gorgeous sea views, and a menu crammed with splendid seafood dishes, this is the go-to place for a dinner (or lunch) to remember.

Mehana Pri Shopite BULGARIAN **$$**
(☑ 0897910754; ul Neptun 12; mains 10-20 lv; ⊙ 9am-11pm; ☑) Set in a traditional, tavern-style courtyard around a twisted, 300-year-old fig tree, this is a welcoming place with great food, including fresh fish, grills, steaks and vegetarian options.

★ Gloria Mar BULGARIAN **$$$**
(☑ 0893550055; www.gloriamar-bg.com; ul Krajbrezhna 9; mains 12-30 lv; ⊙ 11am-11pm) For our money, the best dining option in touristy Nesebâr. Fresh seafood, wood-fired pizzas and grilled meats, as well as harder-to-find risottos and paellas. There's an extensive wine list and dining on three levels, including a rooftop terrace. It's on the southern side of old Nesebâr, facing the marina and passenger ferry terminal.

❶ Getting There & Away

Nesebâr is well connected to coastal destinations by public transport, and the town's **bus station** (☑ 0554-42 721; www.bgrazpisanie. com) is on the small square just outside the city walls. The stop before this on the mainland is for the new town. Buses run in season every few minutes to Sunny Beach (1 lv, 10 minutes). Longer-haul destinations include Burgas (6 lv, one hour, hourly), Varna (14 lv, two hours, four daily) and Sofia (37 lv, seven hours, three daily).

In season, a slower, tourist-friendly **trolleybus** (adult/child 3/1 lv; ☺ Jun-Sep) runs from just outside the town gate of Nesebâr to the southern end of Sunny Beach, near Hotel Kotva. The trolley goes every 10 to 15 minutes. A **water taxi** (adult/child 10/5 lv) runs every 15 minutes from the port on the northern side of Nesebâr, facing Sunny Beach, to the central part of the Sunny Beach resort.

In season, high-speed **Fast Ferry** (☑ 0885808001; www.fastferry.bg; Passenger Ferry Port; ☺ 8.30am-8.30pm Jun-Sep) hydrofoils and catamarans run daily from Nesebâr's passenger ferry port (on the southern side of Nesebâr) to Pomorie and Sozopol. Buy tickets from a small stand along the water in front of the terminal building, online or on board. See the website for the current schedule and prices.

NORTHERN COAST

Varna   BAPHA

POP 334,700

Bulgaria's third city and maritime capital, Varna is the most interesting and cosmopolitan town on the Black Sea coast. A combination of port city, naval base and seaside resort, it's an appealing place to while away

a few days, packed with history yet thoroughly modern, with an enormous park to amble round and a lengthy beach to lounge on. In the city centre you'll find Bulgaria's largest Roman baths complex and its finest archaeological museum, as well as a lively cultural and restaurant scene.

History

In 585 BC, Greeks from Miletus settled in the area of modern Varna, founding the city of Odessos, which thrived as a major commercial centre, taken over by the Romans in the 2nd century AD.

The city became a key port under the Byzantines, and gained its modern name of Varna (possibly derived from the word for 'water') during the period of the First Bulgarian Empire (681–1018). Varna was used by British troops as a port during the Crimean War (1853–56), after which Turkey allowed its allies Britain and France to sell their products throughout the Ottoman Empire, making Varna a great trading centre once more.

In 1866 a railway between Ruse and Varna was built, providing a direct route from the Danube to the Black Sea coast, and Varna became a major shipbuilding centre and port. In 1921 Varna was established as Bulgaria's first seaside holiday resort, and its status as the country's summertime playground was enhanced by the founding of the International Festival in 1926, which has been going strong ever since.

PRIMORSKI PARK

Established in 1878, this large and attractive green space, overlooking the sea, stretches for about 8km and is said to be the largest of its kind in Europe. It's full of promenading families and old ladies knitting lace in summer, and there's always something going on. In addition to greenery and views, the park is home to some of the city's leading attractions.

Aquarium (☑ 052-632 066; bul Primorski 4, Primorski Park; adult/child 4/2 lv; ☺ 9am-5pm Tue-Sun; ☒ 8, 9, 109, 409) Worth a look to see the tanks filled with seahorses, piranhas and conger eels.

Copernicus Planetarium (☑ 052-684 444; www.astro-varna.com; Primorski Park 4; adult/child 4/2 lv) Varna's retro planetarium is a beautiful building in its own right, though the nightly presentations are in Bulgarian only.

Natural History Museum (☑ 052-610 243; www.nature.museumvarna.com; Primorski Park; adult/child 5/2 lv; ☺ 10am-5pm Tue-Sun Apr-Oct, 10am-5pm Mon-Fri Nov-Mar; ☒ 8, 9, 109, 409) Flora and fauna of the Black Sea region.

Zoo Park (☑ 052-820 612; www.varna-zoo.com; Primorski Park; adult/child 1.50/1 lv; ☺ 8am-8pm Jun-Aug, 8.30am-6.30pm Sep-May; ☒ 8, 9, 109, 409) Around 70 different types of animals, including some llamas and big cats.

ROMAN BATHING

Like all self-respecting Roman cities, Odessos (modern-day Varna) was graced with the very best public bathing facilities, and the vast thermae here were a visible, powerful symbol of the fruits – and engineering skill – of Roman civilisation. Far from being simply a place in which to wash up, the baths were an integral part of civic life. They were a place to socialise, make business deals, eavesdrop on the latest gossip, snooze, read and eat. All classes were allowed, though men and women were admitted at different times.

Larger baths, such as the one in Odessos, had a palaestra, or exercise hall, where wrestling and other athletic activities took place, often accompanied by music. Bathers would then rub themselves down with oil and sweat for a while in the sudatorium (a kind of sauna) before scraping it off with a strigil, examples of which are on show in the Archaeological Museum. A plunge in the hot water of the caldarium would follow. They would then move on to the more bearable temperature of the tepidarium, finishing off with a dip in the icy frigidarium. The remains of these shallow pools can still be seen in Varna's Thermae, as well as the furnace and hypocaust system that provided under-floor heating and hot water.

⊙ Sights

★ **Archaeological Museum**   MUSEUM
(☑ 052-681 030; www.archaeo.museumvarna. com; ul Maria Luisa 41; adult/child 10/2 lv; ⊙ 10am-5pm Tue-Sun Apr-Sep, Tue-Sat Oct-Mar; ☐ 8, 9, 109, 409) Exhibits at this vast museum, the best of its kind in Bulgaria, include 6000-year-old bangles, necklaces and earrings said to be the oldest worked gold found in the world. You'll also find Roman surgical implements, Hellenistic tombstones and touching oddments including a marble plaque listing, in Greek, the names of the city's school graduates for AD 221. All of the exhibits are helpfully signposted in English, with excellent explanatory text. There's a large collection of icons on the second floor.

**Cathedral of the Assumption
of the Virgin**   CHURCH
(☑ 052-613 005; www.mitropolia-varna.org; pl Kiril & Metodii 2; ⊙ 8am-6pm; ☐ 8, 9, 109, 409) Varna's cathedral (1886) is topped with golden onion domes. Note the murals (painted in 1950) and colourful stained-glass windows, though you'll have to pay 5 lv if you want to take photos inside.

Roman Thermae   RUINS
(☑ 052-600 059; www.archaeo.museumvarna. com; cnr ul Han Krum & ul San Stefano; adult/child 5/2 lv; ⊙ 10am-5pm Tue-Sun May-Oct, 10am-5pm Tue-Sat Nov-Apr) The well-preserved ruins of Varna's 2nd-century-AD Roman Thermae are the largest in Bulgaria and the fourth-largest of its kind in Europe. Visitors are allowed to clamber around the various chambers of the bath complex and admire

surviving pieces of the advanced floor- and water-heating systems. The baths survived in their original form for only a century or two before the complex was abandoned. It was too costly to maintain as the empire began to decline.

St Michael the Archangel Church   CHURCH
(ul 27 Yuli; ⊙ 8am-6pm; ☐ 8, 9, 109, 409) St Michael the Archangel Church was founded in 1865 and is historically significant as the first place where religious services were given in Bulgarian. The building also contained Varna's first school. The church is small and badly lit, but there are some fine wooden icons.

Sveti Atanas Orthodox Church   CHURCH
(☑ 052-633 925; www.sv-atanasii-varna.org; ul Graf Ignatiev 19; ⊙ 8am-6pm) The beautiful Sveti Atanas Church overlooks the Roman Thermae. Dating from 1838, it features numerous icons and an intricately carved bishop's throne.

Sveti Nikolai Church   CHURCH
(☑ 052-622 727; ul Knyaz Boris I 35; ⊙ 8am-6pm) The pretty Sveti Nikolai Church, right in the city centre, is worth a visit for its saintly murals. It's always busy, and is a popular venue for weddings.

🏃 Activities

Varna has a long stretch of public beach (⊙ 9am-6pm), starting in the south, near the port, and stretching north some 4km. Generally, the quality of the sand and water improve and the crowds thin as you stroll north. The easiest way to access the beach is

Varna

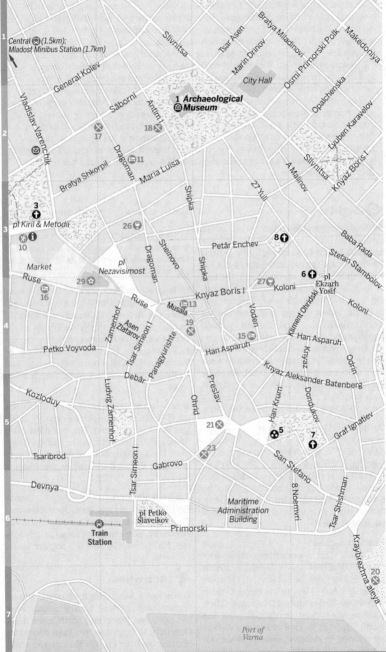

Central (1.5km);
Mladost Minibus Station (1.7km)

Slivnitsa

Tsar Asen

Bratya Miladinovi

Makedoniya

Osmi Primorski Polk

General Kolev

Marin Drinov

City Hall

Opalchenska

Vladislav Varenchik

Sáborni

Antim I

1 Archaeological Museum

Lyuben Karavelov

17

Bratya Shkorpil

Dragoman

18

Maria Luisa

A.Malinov

Slivnitsa

Knyaz Boris I

11

Shipka

27 Yuli

3

pl Kiril & Metodii

26

Sheinovo

Petâr Enchev

8

Baba Rada

10

Dragoman

Shipka

Stefan Stambolov

Market

Ruse

pl Nezavisimost

6

pl Ekzarh Yosif

27

Koloni

Koloni

29

Ruse

Knyaz Boris I

16

Musala

13

Voden

Kliment Ohridski

Han Asparuh

Zamenhof

Asen Zlatarov

19

15

Tsar Simeon I

Panagyurishte

Han Asparuh

Knyaz

Odrin

Petko Voyvoda

Debâr

Knyaz Aleksander Batenberg

Kozloduy

Ludvig Zamenhof

Ohrid

Preslav

Han Krum

Dondukov

Graf Ignatiev

Tsaribrod

21

5

7

23

San Stefan

Devnya

Gabrovo

8 Noemvri

Tsar Simeon I

Tsar Shishman

pl Petko Slaveikov

Maritime Administration Building

Kraybrezhna aleya

Train Station

Primorski

20

Port of Varna

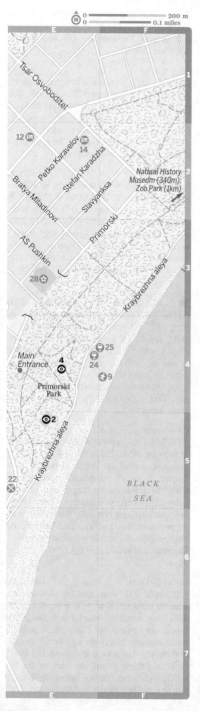

BLACK SEA COAST VARNA

to walk south on bul Slivnitsa to Primorski Park and follow the stairs to the beach.

Running alongside the beach is the long coastal lane, Kraybrezhna. You'll find a stretch of clubs here that have beach access and offer daybeds and umbrellas for rent (5 lv to 10 lv).

Plateau Cycling　　　　　　CYCLING
(☎ 0897478989; www.plateaucycling.com; tours from 90 lv) Offers whole- or half-day guided cycling trips around Varna and the Black Sea coast, as well as longer bespoke tours around eastern Bulgaria and southern Romania. Tours include hybrid bikes and gear, as well as pick-ups, drop-offs, luggage

transfers and cold drinks. See the website and the calendar for what's on offer; book by phone or email.

Baracuda Dive Center   DIVING

(☑052-610 841; www.baracudadive.com; half-day beginning instruction from 110 lv) Offers diving instruction for beginners and advanced divers, as well as guided diving excursions along the Black Sea coast. Rates include equipment.

Free Varna Tour   WALKING

(☑052-820 690; www.visit.varna.bg; pl Kiril & Metodii; ⊙Jun-Sep; 🚌8, 9, 109, 409) FREE The Varna Tourist Information Centre offers a free three-hour walking tour of Varna on select days from June to September. Tours leave at 10.30am in front of the centre offices. Tours leave almost daily in July and August, and less frequently in June and September. Consult the office for the dates and to book a place.

🎪 Festivals & Events

Varna has a lively cultural calendar year round, culminating with the annual Varna Summer International Music Festival. The Varna city's Department of Culture maintains an excellent website (www.varna culture.bg) of the year's festivals and major events.

Varna Summer International Music Festival   MUSIC

(www.varnasummerfest.org) One of the country's leading festivals of orchestral and chamber music, as well as ballet, is held every year in June and July. Events are held at the Open-Air Theatre, the City Art Gallery and the Festival Hall.

🛏 Sleeping

Varna has no shortage of accommodation, although the better (or at least more central) places get very busy during summer.

Private rooms are plentiful, and pensioners with spare rooms occasionally turn up at the train station to greet new arrivals. Prices tend to be from 15 lv to 20 lv per person, but make sure you don't end up in some out-of-the-way suburb.

★ Yo Ho Hostel   HOSTEL $

(☑0884729144; www.yohohostel.com; ul Ruse 23; dm/s/d from 14/30/40 lv; @🛜; 🚌8, 9, 109) Shiver your timbers at this cheerful, pirate-themed place, with four- and 11-bed dorm rooms and private options. Staff offer free pick-ups and can organise camping and rafting trips. The location is an easy walk to the main sights.

Flag Hostel   HOSTEL $

(☑0897408115; www.varnahostel.com; ul Bratya Shkorpil 13a, 4th fl; dm from 22 lv; P🐕🛜; 🚌8, 9, 109, 409) The Flag is a long-established, sociable spot with a party atmosphere. The three dorms are basic with comfortable single beds (no stacked bunks). Free pick-ups from the bus and train stations.

Hotel Hi   HOTEL $$

(☑052-657 777; www.hotel-hi.com; ul Han Asparuh 11; s/d/ste 80/120/200 lv; P❄@🛜) In a quiet neighbourhood south of the main thoroughfare, Hi is a friendly place featuring stylish, cosy rooms – some very small – with TVs and minibars. Doubles come in 'standard' and 'lux' varieties, with the latter being slightly bigger and with a sofa seating area.

★ Graffit Gallery Hotel   BOUTIQUE HOTEL $$$

(☑052-989 900; www.graffithotel.com; bul Knyaz Boris I 65; s/d from 160/190 lv; P🐕❄🛜🍴; 🚌8, 9, 109, 409) With its own art gallery and themed rooms, this modern designer hotel is one of Varna's more colourful options. Super-efficient staff, a chic spa and gym, and a superb on-site restaurant (7.30am to midnight) make this a top option. Enter from ul Makedonia.

Grand Hotel London   HOTEL $$$

(☑052-664 100; www.londonhotel.bg; ul Musala 3; r/ste from 200/230 lv; P🐕❄🛜) Varna's grandest and oldest hotel opened in 1912. Rooms come in 'standard' and 'deluxe', with the latter being larger and offering early-20th-century furniture. Both types are spacious and elegantly furnished, with carpets and print curtains and bedspreads. Bathrooms are clean and fully modernised. Discounts offered for stays of at least five days.

Hotel Capitol   HOTEL $$$

(☑052-688 000; www.capitol.bg; ul Petko Karavelov 40; s/d 100/130 lv; P❄@🛜; 🚌8, 9, 109, 409) This smallish, smart hotel, just a few blocks off central bul Slivnitsa, is popular with business travellers and is a nice top-end choice. The rooms are clean and quiet, especially those facing the back of the hotel. There's a tiny garage below the hotel if you're travelling by car.

Eating

Varna has some of the best eating on the Black Sea coast, with everything from beachside shacks to fine dining.

Dom na Arkitekta
BULGARIAN $

(ul Musala 10; mains 4-10 lv; ⊗8am-9pm) The Architect's House is a fine old wooden National Revival–style building with a leafy courtyard that makes for a good-value lunch spot. Grills, steaks and salads are on the menu, along with more traditional Bulgarian 'delicacies' such as chicken gizzards with onions.

★ Stariya Chinar
BULGARIAN $$

(☑0876520500; www.stariachinar.com; ul Preslav 11; mains 10-20 lv; ⊗8am-midnight) This is upmarket Balkan soul food at its best. Try the baked lamb, made to an old Bulgarian recipe, or the divine barbecue pork ribs; it also boasts some rather ornate salads. Outdoor seating is lovely in summer; park yourself in the traditional interior when the cooler weather strikes.

Orient
TURKISH $$

(☑052-602 380; www.orientbg.com; ul Tzaribrod; mains 9-16 lv; ⊗9am-midnight) The best place in Varna for Turkish food, including spicy kebabs, grilled meats, stews and salads. There's a nice range of appetisers, including favourites such as tabouli and hummus. Eat inside or outside under the umbrellas.

Bistro Dragoman
SEAFOOD $$

(☑052-621 688; www.bistro-dragoman.net; ul Dragoman 43; mains 6-16 lv; ⊗10am-11pm; 🚌8, 9, 109, 409) This welcoming little place specialises in delicious takes on seafood and locally caught fish. This being the Balkans, grilled meats are also on the menu.

Pri Monahinite
BULGARIAN $$

(☑052-611 830; www.monahini.com; bul Primorski 47; mains 12-24 lv; ⊗11am-10pm; 🕾; 🚌20) Set in the courtyard of a little church, 'At the Nuns' is a good choice for roast lamb, grilled pork and other meaty offerings. It also has an extensive wine list.

★ Di Wine Restaurant & Wine Cellar
MODERN EUROPEAN $$$

(☑052-606 050; www.diwine.bg; ul Bratya Shkorpil 2; mains 12-30 lv; ⊗11am-11pm; 🚌8, 9, 109, 409) This formal but friendly restaurant is, in the eyes of many, Varna's best fine-dining spot, with a big menu of tempting dishes including rack of lamb, T-bone steaks, guinea fowl, salmon and trout, as well as cheaper barbecue dishes. There are plenty of very good wines to try, too.

Mr Baba
SEAFOOD $$$

(☑0896505050; www.mrbaba.net; bul Primorski; mains 15-30 lv; ⊗8am-midnight; 🕾; 🚌20) The coast-long trend for novelty ship restaurants has come to Varna, with this handsome, wooden-hulled venture stranded at the far southern end of the beach off bul Primorski, near the port. It features a pricey but tasty menu of steak and fish dishes, including sea

---

WORTH A TRIP

KALIAKRA CAPE

Kaliakra (Beautiful) Cape is a 2km-long headland (the longest along the Bulgarian coastline), about 13km southeast of the town of Kavarna.

Most of the cape is part of the 687-hectare **Kaliakra Nature Reserve** (☑0896798912; www.bbf.biodiversity.bg; Kaliakra Cape; 3 lv; ⊗9am-7pm Apr-Oct), the only reserve in Bulgaria that partly protects the Black Sea (up to 500m offshore). The reserve also protects fragile wetlands at Bolata and Taukliman (Bay of Birds), about 100 remote caves and over 300 species of bird.

Between August and October you can spot migrating birds passing by, including storks and pelicans. Most of the year, the official lookouts along the cape and near Rusalka are ideal spots to watch groups of increasingly rare dolphins.

The history of the area is explained in some detail at the **Archaeological Museum**, wonderfully located inside a cave.

Further north, the tiny seaside town of Krapets, makes an excellent base for exploring the region. Try **Villa Kibela** (☑02-870 3495; www.villakibela.com; Krapets; r 80-100 lv; P ❄ ☎) 🐾, a welcoming place that also arranges walking tours and fishing trips.

bass, trout and bluefish. Indoor and outdoor seating. Reserve in advance.

Drinking & Nightlife

Varna's trendiest bars are found along the beach on Kraybrezhna aleya, in Primorski Park, although many of these exist in the summer months only. To find the epicentre of this beach nightlife, enter the park at the southern end of bul Slivnitsa and walk down the stairs. Many places operate during the day as beach resorts and morph into clubs after sunset.

Makalali Beach Bar   CLUB
(📞 0882828220; Kraybrezhna aleya; ⊙ 8am-4am Jun-Sep) Yet another bar along Kraybrezhna aleya in Primorski Park where you can lounge on the beach all day, and then drink and dance all night.

Palm Beach   CLUB
(📞 0889422553; www.facebook.com/PalmBeach Varna; Kraybrezhna aleya; ⊙ 24hr) By day, a great place to relax by the beach and enjoy coffee and drinks at the bar. By night, a beachside nightclub, with music and dancing that can go all the way till morning.

Sundogs   PUB
(📞 0988936630; www.sundogspub.com; ul Koloni 1; ⊙ 9am-midnight; 🛜) Big with expats and locals, this very welcoming watering hole is a great place to make new friends, chase down excellent pub grub with a good selection of beers, or show off your smarts at regular pub quiz nights.

Pench's   COCKTAIL BAR
(📞 052-616 696; www.penchis.com; ul Dragoman 25; ⊙ 2pm-2am; 🚌 8, 9, 109, 409) Want cocktails? Oh, they've got cocktails: Pench's is a two-time world-record holder for having the largest number of cocktails available at a single bar. Choosing one may be the hardest decision you'll ever make.

☆ Entertainment

Festival Hall & Congress Centre   PERFORMING ARTS
(📞 052-685 214; www.fccvarna.bg; bul Slivnitsa 2; ⊙ box office 10am-9pm) This big, boxy concert hall at the entrance to Primorski Park hosts the film and music festivals as well as music and dance performances throughout the year. Consult the website for the program. Buy tickets at the venue box office.

Varna Opera Theatre   OPERA
(📞 box office 052-665 022; www.tmpcvarna.com; pl Nezavisimost 1; ⊙ ticket office 10am-1pm & 2-7pm; 🚌 8, 9, 109, 409) Varna's grand opera house hosts performances by the Varna Opera and Philharmonic Orchestra all year, except July and August, when some performances are staged at the Open-Air Theatre in Primorski Park.

❶ Information

There are numerous banks with ATMs around the city centre.

Internet Doom 7 (📞 052-612 043; bul Tsar Osvoboditel 20; per hr 2 lv; ⊙ 24hr) The most central of several branches around town.

Tourist Information Centre (📞 052-820 690; www.visit.varna.bg; pl Kiril & Metodii; ⊙ 9am-7pm; 🚌 8, 9, 109, 409) Plenty of free brochures and maps, and helpful multilingual staff. The Tourist Information Centre also operates free three-hour walking tours of the city on select days from June to September.

BUSES FROM VARNA CENTRAL BUS STATION

DESTINATION	COST (LV)	DURATION (HR)	FREQUENCY (DAILY)
Burgas	14	2½	several daily
Kavarna	7	1½	7
Plovdiv	26	7	5
Ruse	15	4	5
Shumen	7	1	6
Silistra	10	2	2
Sofia	33	7	10
Veliko Târnovo	21	4	8
İstanbul	60	10	1

GOLDEN SANDS & ALADZHA MONASTERY

Golden Sands (Zlatni Pyasâtsi), 18km up the coast from Varna, was Bulgaria's original purpose-built resort, with the first hotel opening here in 1957. Today it's Bulgaria's second-largest coastal resort, with a 4km stretch of sandy beach, and some of the best nightlife on the coast.

The usual water sports are available on the beach. Diving is also popular, and there are several outlets along the beach, including the PADI-certified **Harry's Diving Center** (☑ 052-356 701; www.divewithharry.com; ☺ May-Oct).

Virtually all visitors staying in Golden Sands will be on a pre-booked package tour, and many of the hotels tend to be booked solid through the summer. However, there are so many hotels you should be able to find a room somewhere.

A major local attraction accessible by trail from Golden Sands is the **Aladzha Monastery** (☑ 052-355 460; www.archaeo.museumvarna.com; adult/child 5/2 lv; ☺ 10am-5pm May-Oct, 10am-5pm Tue-Sat Nov-Mar). Little is known about this bizarre rock monastery; the caves were first inhabited by 11th-century hermits, but what remains today was created during the 13th and 14th centuries, including some remarkable frescoes.

❶ Getting There & Away

AIR

Varna's international **airport** (VAR; ☑ 052-573 323; www.varna-airport.bg; Aksakovo; 🚌 409) has scheduled and charter flights from all over Europe, as well as regular flights to and from Sofia. From the centre, bus 409 goes to the airport.

BUS

Varna has two bus stations; the scruffy **central bus station** (Avtoexpress; ☑ information 052-757 044, tickets 052-748 349; www.bgrazpisanie.com; bul Vladislav Varenchik 158; ☺ 24hr; 🚌 148, 409) is about 2km northwest of the city centre. There are basic cafes and a **left luggage office** (per hr 1 lv; ☺ 7am-7pm).

The **Mladost minibus station** (☑ 052-500 039; www.bgrazpisanie.com; ul Dobrovoltsi 7; 🚌 148, 409) is 200m southwest of the central bus station and serves minibuses operating along the Black Sea coast, including to Balchik (5 lv, 50 minutes, hourly), Kavarna (7 lv, 1½ hours, hourly), Burgas (14 lv, 2½ hours, every 40 minutes to one hour) and Nesebâr (12 lv, 1½ hours, six daily) via Sunny Beach (11 lv, 1¼ hours).

TRAIN

Facilities at Varna's **train station** (☑ 052-662 3343; www.bdz.bg; pl Slaveikov; 🚌 8, 9, 109) include a left-luggage office (p423) and cafe. Rail destinations from Varna include Ruse (14 lv, four hours, two daily), Sofia (24 lv, seven to eight hours, seven daily), Plovdiv (24 lv, seven hours, three daily) and Shumen (7 lv, 1½ hours, 10 daily).

❶ Getting Around

The most useful bus for visitors is 409, which connects the airport to the heart of Varna, stopping near the Tourist Information Centre, before heading onward to the resort at Golden Sands (Zlatni Pyasâtsi). This bus also passes the central bus station in Varna and stops outside Sveti Konstantin. It runs about every 15 minutes between 6am and 11pm. Bus 109 runs between the train station and Golden Sands. Buy tickets from the driver.

If you need a rental car, **Hertz** (☑ 052-510 250; www.hertz.bg; Varna Airport; ☺ 9am-6pm) and **Sixt** (☑ 052-599 490; www.sixt.com; Varna Airport; ☺ 9am-9pm) have offices at the airport.

Sveti Konstantin
СВЕТИ КОНСТАНТИН

Sveti Konstantin is sedate beach resort about 9km northeast of Varna, with hotels attractively spaced out among parkland. Established in 1946 under the name of Druzhba (Friendship), it was later renamed Sveti Konstantin i Elena, but is now more commonly known simply as Sveti Konstantin. It's less commercial than the other resorts and has long been popular with older holidaymakers; it still has a number of 'rest homes' for retired civil servants and trade-union members, and the resort is famous for its therapeutic mineral waters and health treatments.

◉ Sights & Activities

Much of the beach (☺ 9am-6pm Jun-Sep) is carved up into private stretches of sand appropriated by the various hotels, but there are plenty of areas accessible to nonguests, too.

Sveti Konstantin & Elena Monastery

MONASTERY

(www.varnamonastery.bg; ☉ dawn-dusk, closed Sun morning) **FREE** This tiny church and monastery was built in the early 18th century on the site of a holy healing spring, though it has been rebuilt and remodelled since then. The spring remains, under the communion table. The church houses relics of St Valentine, as well as its patron saints.

Chateau Euxinograde

CHATEAU

(☏ 052-393 165; euxinograde@government.bg; adult/child 12/3 lv, wine tastings per person from 10 lv; ☉ tours 9am, noon & 3pm Tue-Sun) Located about 2km south of Sveti Konstantin, along the main road to Varna, the 90-hectare Euxinograde complex boasts a 19th-century palace featuring elaborate period furnishings, botanical gardens with rare plants, and the wine collections of Prince Ferdinand and Tsar Boris III, which include a Chateau Margaux from 1904. Guided tours (in Bulgarian) are conducted three times daily. The complex also includes a winery with tastings (though the minimum number of participants is seven). Book tours and tastings in advance by email.

🛏 Sleeping & Eating

Most of the major hotels have good restaurants, and prices are reasonable compared with the bigger resorts elsewhere on the coast.

International House of Scientists Frederic Joliot-Curie

HOTEL $$

(☏ 052-361 161; www.ihsvarna.com; s/d 60/90 lv, renovated 90/100 lv; P ☕ ❄ @ ☎) Although it looks like a remnant of another era, this '60s tower block west of the bus stop offers good value, and it's definitely worth the extra leva for the neater modernised rooms. It has a mineral-water pool, a pharmacy and a cactus garden. Various balneological treatments are available. To find it, look for the high-rise hotel near the bus stop.

Sirius Beach Hotel

HOTEL $$$

(☏ 052-361 224; www.siriusbeach.com; s/d 100/150 lv; P ❄ @ ☎) With its flashy glass tower and mock-up ship restaurant, the four-star Sirius is an unmistakable landmark. Set on a narrow curve of beach, it's a typical resort-style hotel, and there are indoor and outdoor pools, a kids' play area and a spa. To find it from the bus stop, walk toward the beach and veer to the left (north).

★ Bay

MIDDLE EASTERN $$$

(☏ 0887003003; www.thebay.bg; mains 15-25 lv; ☉ 11am-11pm) Discover the best food in Sveti Konstantin, and arguably in all of greater Varna, at this beachside Lebanese restaurant and cocktail bar. The specialities are fish and barbecue, though the chef has added creative Middle Eastern touches, such as a mashed chick-pea salad flavoured with yoghurt and eggplant. The grills are outstanding, as are the views onto a small beach.

ℹ Getting There & Away

Bus 409 leaves regularly from the bus stop outside Varna's tourist information centre to near Sveti Konstantin (2 lv, one hour).

Balchik БАЛЧИК

POP 12,000

After the vast, artificial resorts further down the coast, Balchik is a breath of fresh sea air. A small, pretty town and fishing port huddled below white-chalk cliffs, it's a low-key

ALBENA

With its lovely 4km-long beach and shallow water, the big purpose-built resort of Albena is a great place for water sports. On the downside, it's relatively expensive and not particularly user-friendly for independent travellers, but that doesn't mean you can't drop by as a day visitor and take advantage of its facilities. Jet-skiing, parasailing, waterskiing and surfing are all available. If that sounds a little too active, several hotels in the resort have excellent spa centres.

The bus station is around 800m from the beach and there are regular minibuses to/from Balchik (4 lv, 30 minutes) and Varna (6 lv, 45 minutes). If you decide to drive your own vehicle note that entry to the resort costs 6 lv per car (10 lv Saturday and Sunday).

Balchik

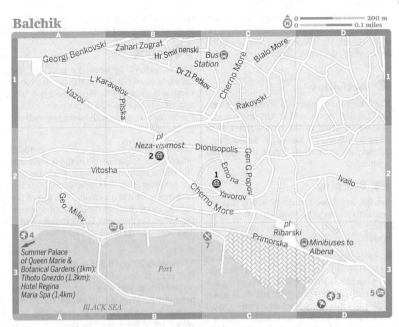

Balchik

⊙ Sights
1 Art Gallery C2
2 Historical Museum B2

⊕ Activities, Courses & Tours
3 Balchik Beach D3
4 New Beach A3

⊟ Sleeping
5 Hotel Helios D3
6 Hotel Mistral B3

⊗ Eating
Francis Drake .... (see 6)
7 Old Boat C3

holiday spot that feels a world away from the likes of Albena, the lights of which can be seen winking across the bay at night. The main attraction here is the palace, with its lovely botanical gardens, a couple of kilometres west along the seafront promenade.

⊙ Sights

★Summer Palace of Queen Marie & Botanical Gardens
PALACE

(Dvorets; ☏ 0579-74 552; www.dvoreca.com; adult/child 10/2 lv; ☺ 8am-8pm May-Oct, 8.30am-5pm Nov-Apr) At the far western end of the seafront, this palace was completed in 1926 by King Ferdinand of Romania for his English wife, Queen Marie, when Balchik was part of Romania. Size-wise, it's a relatively modest villa, though the architecture – a blend of local, Gothic and Islamic styles topped with a minaret – is unique. Behind the palace are the extensive botanical gardens. The complex also includes a water mill, a winery and the tiny Chapel of Sveta Bogoroditsa.

Historical Museum
MUSEUM

(☏ 0579-72 177; www.dobrudzha.com; ul Vitosha 3; adult/child 5/2 lv; ☺ 9am-1pm & 2-6pm) The diverse collection here includes valuable remnants from excavations carried out at the nearby Kibela (Cybele) Temple (referred to at the museum as the 'Temple of the Pontic Mother of Gods'), which dates back to the 3rd century BC and was buried in an earthquake 1500 years ago. It was discovered only in 2007 during construction of a hotel. There is also Roman statuary and medieval pottery, with lots of helpful signage in English.

Art Gallery
GALLERY

(www.dobrudzha.com; ul Otec Paisii 4; adult/child 5/1 lv; ☺ 9.30am-1pm & 2-5.30pm Tue-Sat) The permanent collection of this gallery holds about 1500 works of art from Bulgarian and foreign artists, though the main draws tend to be the highly interesting rotating exhibitions, such as a recent exhibit on Scythian coins.

Activities

Balchik's main beach (ul Primorska; ⊙9am-6pm Jun-Sep) is situated at the eastern end of town, in front of the Helios Hotel. New Beach (⊙9am-6pm Jun-Sep) is smaller and quieter, about midway along the seafront promenade.

🛏 Sleeping

Balchik has a good range of hotels that are suited to all budgets, from small family-run affairs to resort complexes. There are no hostels.

Hotel Helios HOTEL $$
(📞0579-76 970; www.heliosbg.com; ul Primorska 32; d/apt 100/140 lv; P🌸@☀) Occupying the only real patch of sandy beach in Balchik, Helios is a modern, resort-style hotel and all rooms have balconies, many with superb sea views. Prices drop by up to 50% out of high season.

Hotel Mistral HOTEL $$
(📞0579-71 130; www.hotelmistralbg.com; ul Primorska 8b; s/d 100/126 lv; ⊜🌸🛜) One of the best waterfront hotels, the four-star Mistral is an upmarket place with large rooms, all with sea-facing balconies. In addition to the usual amenities, the hotel rents bikes for guests and the open-air restaurant features pretty views out over the marina. Prices drop by up to half outside the summer season.

★Hotel Regina Maria Spa HOTEL $$$
(📞052-953 466; www.reginamariaspa.com; r/ste 150/230 lv; P🌸🛜☀) On the far western end of the seafront, 1.5km from the centre, the four-star Regina Maria offers smart rooms in a variety of styles, all with sea views. Golfing packages and fishing trips can be arranged. There's both an indoor and outdoor

pool, a rocky beach out front, and a spa with loads of fitness and wellness offerings.

Eating

The waterfront between the port and the palace is lined with open-air restaurants, of varying quality, most offering fresh fish. The restaurants tend to rise in price and quality the further west you walk along the seafront promenade.

Tihoto Gnezdo SEAFOOD $
(mains 5-12 lv; ⊙9am-11pm) On the far western end of the seafront promenade, just beyond the Summer Palace of Queen Marie, this unfussy restaurant is a welcome relief from the bigger, more touristy dining options along the water. Don't expect haute cuisine, but it does salads and grilled fish very well.

Old Boat SEAFOOD $$
(ul Primorska 20; mains 6-15 lv; ⊙8am-1am) The Old Boat is one of the very first seafront restaurants as you walk westward along the promenade. With an attractive waterfront setting overlooking the harbour, this is a casual place for fresh fish, such as grilled mackerel, shark fillet and bluefish.

Francis Drake SEAFOOD $$$
(📞0579-71 130; www.hotelmistralbg.com; ul Primorska 8b; mains 15-30 lv; ⊙9am-11pm; 🛜) The restaurant of the Hotel Mistral is the place for some classier cuisine. Fried turbot, smoked salmon and locally caught fish are among the offerings.

ℹ Getting There & Away

Balchik's **bus station** (📞0579-74 069; www.bgrazpisanie.com) is at the top of ul Cherno More, a steep 1.5km walk from the port. Several buses travel daily to Varna (5 lv, 50 minutes, hourly), Kavarna (5 lv, 45 minutes) and Golden Sands (4 lv, 30 minutes). A couple of buses make the long-haul daily to Sofia (36 lv, seven hours). Hourly minibuses to Albena (3 lv, 20 minutes) use a handy **bus stop** (ul Primorska) just along the main road, ul Primorska, near the main beach.

The Danube & Northern Plains

Best Places to Eat

➡ Garden Restaurant (p435)

➡ New House (p435)

➡ Riverside (p442)

➡ Classic Pizzeria (p433)

➡ Sladost (p442)

Best Places to Sleep

➡ Hotel Drustar (p441)

➡ City Art Hotel (p435)

➡ Hotel Kiprovets (p431)

➡ Pelican Lake Guesthouse (p440)

➡ Old Town Hotel (p433)

Why Go?

Though it's one of the poorest parts of Europe, northern Bulgaria is a rewarding region to explore. Unspoilt mountain landscapes, wild nature reserves and peaceful monasteries await discovery. The mighty Danube River shimmers along most of the country's border with Romania, and the riverside city of Ruse, famed for its Viennese-style architecture, is the gateway to Bucharest.

The enigmatic rock churches and rich wildlife of the Rusenski Lom Nature Park and, further east, serene Lake Srebârna, home to numerous rare bird species, are well worth visiting. Away from the Danube, the bizarre rock formations at Belogradchik and the Sveshtari Thracian burial tomb are top national sights.

When to Go
Vidin

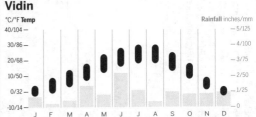

Mar–May Spring days are warm and festival season begins. Late spring is ideal for birdwatching.

Jun–Aug Summers are hot and dry, and it's a great time for hiking and sunbathing.

Nov–Jan Winters can be harsh, but the countryside looks picturesque in the snow.

The Danube & Northern Plains Highlights

1 Belogradchik Rocks
(p431) Clambering over massive sandstone and limestone formations.

2 Thracian Tomb of Sveshtari (p434) Peering into a perfectly preserved Thracian burial tomb.

3 Ruse (p433) Strolling through the parks and gardens of this most elegant of Bulgarian cities on the Danube.

4 Ivanovo Rock Monastery (p439) Marvelling at the lives of monks who retreated to caves here in the Rusenski Lom Nature Park.

5 Srebârna Nature Reserve (p440) Spotting rare fowl along this Unesco-protected birdwatching biosphere.

6 Vratsa's Historical Museum (p429) Gawking at the Rogozen Treasure, a collection of more than a hundred Thracian silver jugs and plates.

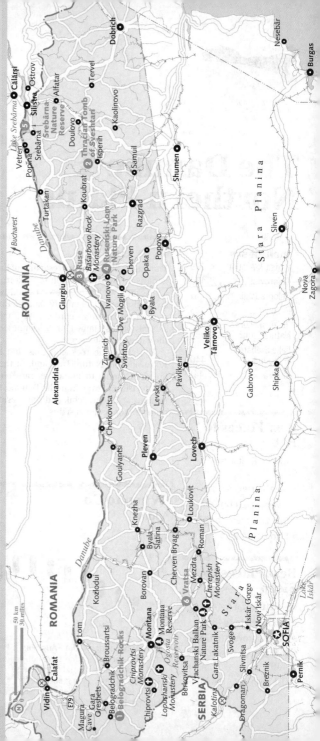

History

There's been human habitation along the Danube for at least 40,000 years. History museums in Vratsa and Silistra hold remnants of tools and artefacts used by ancient peoples in these parts.

Northern Bulgaria was home to powerful Thracian tribes, including the Getae, one of the most advanced. One of the highlights of a trip through the region is to pop into local historical museums, such as at Vratsa, and see the gold and silver bounty of Thracian civilization. The excavated Thracian burial tomb of Sveshtari is a must-visit.

The Romans ushered in another accelerated period of development in the first centuries AD. They established the province of Moesia along the Danube, and Roman fortifications arose at major towns, such as Ruse, Bononia (Vidin) and Durostorum (Silistra).

After 1362, Ottoman Turks swarmed into the northern Balkans; within 30 years, they possessed Bulgaria, holding it for five centuries. Vidin is famous for its Ottoman fortress, Baba Vida, on the Danube.

The remote monasteries here played a key role in the Bulgarian National Revival of the 19th century. They often offered sanctuary to rebel fighters in their battles with the Turks and still proudly display their nationalist sentiments.

Vratsa & Around ВРАЦА

POP 74,700

With its striking location just below a steep, narrow gorge in the Vrachanska Mountains, Vratsa makes a handy base for exploring the Vrachanski Balkan Nature Park, as well as Lopushanski and Cherepish Monasteries. It's a quiet, well-kept little town with plenty of laid-back pavement cafes, and there are a couple of worthwhile museums to visit, too.

The centre of Vratsa is pl Hristo Botev, named in honour of the 19th-century revolutionary whose giant statue stands here. Cafes and civic buildings congregate around this square, though most of the action is further east along the pedestrian street of bul Nikola Voyvodov, which finishes at the market near the train station.

◉ Sights

Historical Museum   MUSEUM
(☑ 092-620 220; www.vratsamuseum.com; bul Hristo Botev 2; adult/child 4/1 lv; ☺ 9am-12.30pm & 1-6pm) This regional historical museum traces the history of the town and surrounding area from Thracian and Roman times through to the 19th century. The pride of the collection is the Rogozen Treasure, a collection of more than 100 Thracian silver jugs and plates that were discovered accidentally by a local farmer in 1985. Also here are neolithic clay idols, Roman pottery and displays relating to local hero Hristo Botev. The 17th-century tower outside doubles as the museum's souvenir shop.

Vrachanski Balkan
Nature Park   NATIONAL PARK
Numerous species of birds, 700 types of trees and about 500 caves distinguish this nature park of 288 sq km, southwest of Vratsa. Although some of the rocky outcroppings are fragile, they're still open to rock climbers and hang-gliders.

Ledenika Cave   CAVE
(☑ 0888245509; www.vratza.bg; guided tours per person 6 lv; ☺ 9am-5pm Apr-Oct, 10am-4pm Nov-Mar) The 'ice' cave, as its Bulgarian name translates to, is 16km west of Vratsa, within the Vrachanski Balkan Nature Park. It's

---

WORTH A TRIP

CHEREPISH MONASTERY

Founded in the 14th-century, Cherepish Monastery was torched, toppled and rebuilt repeatedly during the Ottoman period. Like many other monasteries, it was used by rebels as a hiding place before and during the Russo-Turkish War (1877–78). The museum displays icons and has Bulgarian-language books about the monastery and local history. There's basic guesthouse accommodation (20 lv per person) if you want to stay.

The monastery is 30km southeast of Vratsa on the Mezdra–Zverino route. Buses from Sofia heading toward Mezdra, Vratsa, Montana or Vidin pass the monastery; disembark at the Zverino turn-off and walk west 6km. If driving from Sofia, the most aesthetically appealing approach is the slower but scenic road through the stunning Iskâr Gorge, via Novi Iskâr.

sheathed in ice for much of the winter, but thaws in summer, when visitors on guided tours arrive to explore it. There's no public transport, so you'll have to hike (three hours from Vratsa) or take a taxi (15 lv).

Sveti Sofronii Vrachanski Ethnographical & Revival Complex   MUSEUM

(☑092-624 573; www.vratsamuseum.com; ul Targovska; adult/child 3/1 lv; ☺9am-5.30pm Mon-Fri) This interesting museum complex consists of four National Revival–era buildings displaying traditional costumes, instruments, toys, domestic interiors and silk-weaving apparatus. There's also a collection of vintage vehicles, including a sleigh and 19th-century carriages. The gardens are free to wander around in; buy a ticket at the Vaznesenie School building and ask them to open the other buildings for you.

🏃 Activities

Within **Vrachanski Balkan Nature Park** there are relaxed hiking trails in the forested hills southwest of the main square and tougher treks along the river road towards **Ledenika Cave**, where several marked hiking trails exist. Rock climbing – for the truly fearless – is performed on the sheer mountain cliffs that straddle the road.

🛏 Sleeping

Hotel Hemus   HOTEL $$

(☑092-624 150; www.hotelhemus.com; pl Hristo Botev 1; s/d 55/70 lv; ⓟⓢⓢⓢ) This high-rise hotel on the main square remains the best accommodation option in town, though the rooms and corridors have a mustiness about them that cries out for renovation. Room prices are reasonable for the central location, and there's a small pool and a pleasant terrace restaurant on the premises.

Hotel Chaika   HOTEL $$

(☑092-621 369; www.chaika.net; d 45-65 lv, ste 70-160 lv; ⓟⓢ) This inn with a very good garden restaurant is located 1km south of town, along the road to Ledenika Cave. The gorge setting is spectacular, though the plain rooms are just okay. Room prices reflect size and views, and several have terraces. Walk 20 minutes from the centre, or take a taxi (4 lv from the train or bus station).

🍴 Eating & Drinking

Trakiiska Printsesa   INTERNATIONAL $

(☑0888099966; bul Nikola Voyvodov 12; mains 4-9 lv; ☺8am-midnight; ⓢⓢ) On Vratsa's main pedestrian street, this is a pleasant place for a coffee or a variety of light meals. Salads, risottos, fish and pasta dishes are served. The chicken fettuccine is very good.

Pintata   BULGARIAN $$

(☑092-621 873; ul Sofroniy Vrachanski 17; mains 8-15 lv; ☺11am-midnight Mon-Fri, 6pm-midnight Sat; ⓢ) A good choice for dinner, this is arguably the best restaurant in the centre. The little garden lies behind an unpromising street and feels like an oasis. There's a nice list of *rakia* (Bulgaria brandy) and wine, and some very good salads and meat dishes. It's located in the northern end of the centre, about 300m north of pl Hristo Botev.

ℹ Information

Some 200m south of Vratsa town centre heading to the gorge, the **Natura Information Centre** (☑092-660 318; www.vr-balkan.net; ul Pop Sava Katralfilov 27-29; ☺9am-noon & 1-5pm Apr-Oct, closed Sat & Sun Nov-Mar) is the first port of call for information on hiking and sights in the Vrachanski Balkan Nature Park. You'll recognise the unusual building on sight: a former mosque from Ottoman times.

ℹ Getting There & Away

BUS

The **bus station** (☑092-622 558; bul Vasil Kanchev 98) is 200m east of the train station. Buses travel hourly to/from Sofia (10 lv, two hours) and even more frequently between 6am and 9am. One or two buses daily serve Pleven (10 lv, 2½ hours) and three or four to Vidin (13 lv, 2½ hours).

TRAIN

Services from the oversized **train station** (☑092-624 415; bul Vasil Kanchev) include Sofia (8 lv, two hours, five daily), Montana (3.60 lv, one hour, six daily) and Vidin (10 lv, three hours, four daily); the latter passes through Gara Oreshets, from where you can get a taxi to Belogradchik.

For more distant destinations, connect to nearby Mezdra train station, 20 minutes to the south, and change there. From Mezra four daily trains serve northern Bulgarian destinations such as Pleven (6.50 lv, one to two hours), Ruse (15.30 lv, four hours) and Varna 20 lv, six to nine hours).

Chiprovtsi   ЧИПРОВЦИ

POP 1500

Famous for its traditional carpets and quaint monastery, Chiprovtsi is little more than a rather quiet village tucked into the foothills of the Stara Planina (Balkan Range) mountains. It has a fascinating history as a mining town and a bastion of Catholicism in Orthodox Bulgaria. In more recent years, it's become a popular weekend destination for Sofia city dwellers but, truth be told, there's not much to see or do (and that may be part of the appeal).

Sights

Chiprovtsi Monastery MONASTERY
(☑ 0878970388; ☺ 8am-8pm) FREE Founded in the 10th century, this working monastery, dedicated to Sveti Ivan Rilski (St John of Rila), was destroyed and rebuilt several times over the years – what you see today dates largely from the early 19th century. It's roughly 7km northeast of Chiprovtsi village; take any bus between Montana and Chiprovtsi.

Historical Museum MUSEUM
(☑ 095-542 168; ul Vitosha 2; 2 lv; ☺ 8am-noon & 1-5pm Mon-Fri, 9am-5pm Sat-Sun) This small museum, situated in the centre of Chiprovtsi above a small stream, tells the story of the village, focusing on its gold- and silver-mining traditions and its unusual (for Bulgaria) history as a Catholic and Saxon enclave. Also on display are period weapons, traditional costumes and colourful examples of the local Chiprovtsi carpets.

Sleeping & Eating

Chiprovtsi has one very nice hotel and a handful of acceptable guesthouses. Reserve in advance.

Pavlova Kâshta GUESTHOUSE $
(☑ 095-542 242; ul Pavleto 17; r 35 lv) The Pavlova Kâshta is a dusty white-stone building offering basic, though airy and clean, rooms. The adjacent *mehana* (tavern) does good Bulgarian meals.

★**Hotel Kiprovets** HOTEL $$
(☑ 0886853311; ul Ivan Stanislavov 4; r/apt 45/65 lv; ᴘ ᴡ) Far and away the nicest accommodation option in town. The room decor blends modern elements such as tiled floors and flat-screen TVs with old-fashioned touches like wood-beamed ceilings. The family owners couldn't be nicer, and there's an excellent restaurant and barbecue onsite. Worth keeping in mind for lunch or dinner even if you're not sleeping here.

WORTH A TRIP

LOPUSHANSKI MONASTERY

Some 21km west of Montana, near the village of Georgi Damyanovo, the **Lopushanski Monastery** (☑ 0887-397 301; www.lopushanski-monastery.domino. bg; Georgi Damyanovo; ☺ 8am-6pm) FREE, completed in 1853, enjoys a serene setting and holds icons painted by brothers Stanislav and Nikolai Dospevski. During the periodic rebellions against Ottoman rule, Lopushanski (also known as St John the Precursor) provided a safe haven for revolutionaries.

The **Lopushanski Monastery Guesthouse** (Balova Shouma Inn; ☑ 0887-397 301; www.lopushanski-monastery. domino.bg; Georgi Damyanovo; r from 25 lv; ❄) is situated within the grounds of the monastery. The attached cafe has indoor and outdoor seating in a peaceful location and serves decent food.

Information

Chiprovtsi Tourist Information Centre
(☑ 0885258405; bul Petar Parchevich; ☺ 9am-5pm Mon-Fri) Located in the municipal administration building in the centre of town. Don't expect much in the way of maps or information, though the staff may be able to answer basic questions.

Getting There & Away

Several daily buses and minibuses connect Montana and Chiprovtsi (5 lv, one hour). By car, Chiprovtsi is about 50km from Belogradchik (one hour).

Belogradchik
БЕЛОГРАДЧИК

POP 5150

The crisp mountain air and the weird and wonderful rock formations that rise from a lonely horizon of hills are what draw visitors to little Belogradchik, on the eastern edge of the Stara Planina mountain range. Although rather remote, Belogradchik's charms are starting to attract more visitors.

Sights

Belogradchik Rocks ROCK FORMATIONS
The massive Belogradchik sandstone and limestone rock formations cover an area of

around 90 sq km and tower over the town. The rocks, standing up to 200m high, were sculpted over millions of years by natural compression. Several hiking trails of varying difficulty lace through the rocks. The tourist information centre has a map of the routes.

The 'Monks', the 'Bear', the 'Shepherd Boy' and 'Adam and Eve' are just some of the named formations.

Kaleto Fortress
FORTRESS

(☑ 093-653 001; www.muzeibelogradchik.com; ul Tsolo Todorov; 6 lv; ☉ 9am-6pm Jun-Sep, to 5pm Oct-May) Almost blending in with the surrounding rocks, the Kaleto Fortress was originally built by the Romans and later expanded by the Byzantines, Bulgarians and Turks. Most of what you see today was completed in the 1830s. You can wander round three courtyards and explore the defensive bunkers; accessing the highest rocks involves a precarious climb up steep ladders.

The fortress lies about 1km west of the centre. The location is signposted. To find it, follow ul Tsolo Todorov uphill to the end of the street.

Museum of Nature and Science
MUSEUM

(☑ 093-653 231; www.muzeibelogradchik.com; adult/child 3/2 lv; ☉ 9am-noon, 2-5pm Apr-Oct) Affiliated with Belogradchik's history museum, the nature department displays unusual local flora and fauna. To get here, proceed from the large, modern Hotel Skalite in the centre up ul Vasil Levski, turn right, and follow the path for 600m. From here there are great views over the Belogradchik rocks.

Activities

Not far from Belogradchik, visitors have the chance to combine two usually unrelated but enjoyable activities: caving and wine-tasting. The Magura Cave (☑ 089-448 1955; Rabisha; adult/child 5/3 lv; ☉ 10am-5pm Apr-Oct, to 4pm Nov-Mar) is one of the largest in Bulgaria, with a total length of about 3km. It's known for the size of its stalagmites and stalactites, as well as surviving cave art going back several thousand years.

After tramping around, indulge in something a tad more refined: a tasting at the nearby Magura Winery (☉ 093-296 230, 02-857 0015; www.magurawinery.bg; Rabisha; tasting packages per person from 25 lv). Check the winery website for several different tasting options. Both the cave and winery are about 20km north of Belogradchik.

🛏 Sleeping

Drakite Guesthouse
GUESTHOUSE $

(☑ 093-653 930; www.drakite.com; ul Treti Mart 37; r from 30 lv; P 🛜) This modest guesthouse is located in the western part of the town, about 400m down from the entrance to the Kaleto Fortress. There are five rooms, some with balconies and en suite bathrooms. The property is run by a helpful English-speaking local who also organises fishing trips and transport. The whole house can be rented for 175 lv per day.

Guesthouse Geto
GUESTHOUSE $

(☑ 093-653 388; http://getobelogradchik.alle.bg; ul Treti Mart 47; r from 30 lv; P ✳ 🛜 🐾) This cosy guesthouse is located in the western part of the town, about 400m down from the entrance to the Kaleto Fortress. Modest rooms come with balconies and private baths, and some have separate kitchens. There's a communal kitchen and a hot tub as well. Guests can hire bikes for around 10 lv per day.

⭐ Hotel Skalite
HOTEL $$

(☑ 094-691 210, 0884514154; www.skalite.bg; pl Vazrazhdane 2; s/d from 80/100 lv; P ✳ @ 🐾) This modern four-star place in the town

---

LEGENDS OF THE ROCKS

For centuries the Belogradchik rock formations have fired the imaginations of local people. These twisting, contorted pillars of stone seem to take on the most curious shapes, both human and animal.

One legend tells the tragic tale of Valentina, a young nun renowned for her beauty. One day, during a holy festival, a young nobleman came along and was immediately smitten. The two began an illicit affair, which was only discovered when Valentina gave birth to a child in the convent. The Mother Superior and a council of monks decided to expel her. As she left, in tears, her lover came riding towards her on his white horse. At this moment, the sky turned black and terrifying thunder rent the air. The ground opened up and consumed the convent and everyone was turned to stone where they stood – including Valentina, who was transformed into the rock known today as the 'Madonna'.

VIDIN

Resting on a bend in the Danube in the far northwest of Bulgaria, the town of Vidin feels a long way from anywhere, and unless you're crossing into Romania, there seems little obvious reason for you to wend your way here. But don't dismiss it so easily. Vidin does enjoy some fine riverside views and its one major attraction, the majestic **Baba Vida Fortress** (☑ 094-601 705; www.museum-vidin.domino.bg; Kraidunavski Park; adult/child 4/2 lv, combined ticket with Archaeological Museum 5 lv; ⊙ 9am-5pm Mon-Fri, 10am-5pm Sat & Sun), is one of the best preserved Ottoman fortresses in the country.

Baba Vida is a marvellously intact 17th-century Turkish upgrade of 10th-century Bulgarian fortifications. These in turn were built on the ruins of a 3rd-century Roman fort called Bononia. You'll find it at the northern end of Vidin's pretty riverside park.

Vidin makes a convenient overnight if you're coming over the bridge from Romania. The **Old Town** (Hotel Staryat Grad; ☑ 094-600 023; www.oldtownhotel.dir.bg; ul Knyaz Boris I 2; s/d/tr 60/80/100 lv; ❄ 🛜) is a charming boutique hotel situated in a renovated townhouse. For a meal, try the central **Classic Pizzeria** (☑ 0878656402; www.vidinrestaurants. com; ul Knyaz Al Battenberg 23; mains 8-15 lv; ⊙ 11am-11pm; 🛜). Its big menu includes grilled meats and fish.

centre has the best rooms and facilities in Belogradchik, including a spa, a gym, a restaurant and an appealing terrace bar. Prices rise slightly at weekends.

✖ Eating

Mislen Kamak　　　　　　　BULGARIAN $
(☑ 0879830207; mains 6-10 lv; ⊙ 10am-2am) Magnificent views over the Belogradchik rocks make up for mediocre food at this terrace restaurant located just south of the centre. The menu features salads and grilled meats, and a long list of *rakia* drinks. On summer weekends, arrive before traditional meal times to snag an outdoor table. To find it, follow the uphill path that starts behind the Hotel Skalite.

Restaurant Pri Ivan　　　　　BULGARIAN $$
(☑ 0879207712; www.priivan.com; ul Yuri Gagarin 3; mains 10-15 lv; ⊙ 8am-midnight) Pri Ivan is arguably the best of a tiny number of restaurants in town and offers a variety of traditional Bulgarian and Balkan dishes, including lots of salads and grilled-meat specialities. To find the restaurant, proceed past the large, modern Hotel Skalite up ul Vasil Levski about 200m and then turn left.

❶ Information

The tourist information centre
(☑ 0877881283; ul Poruchik Dvoryanov 1a; ⊙ 9am-5pm Mon-Fri) can help with information on local accommodation, and supplies free maps and leaflets.

❶ Getting There & Away

Belogradchik's **bus station** (bul Saedinenie 1) has a couple of daily departures to Vidin (5 lv, one hour) and a 6am service to Sofia (16 lv, four hours) via Montana.

The nearest train station is 9km away at Gara Oreshets, but there are no public buses that make the trip there. The only option is to take a taxi (about 8 lv). Several daily trains from Gara Oreshets serve Vidin (5 lv, 30 minutes), Vratsa (7 lv, 20 minutes) and Sofia (10 lv, 3½ hours).

Ruse　　　　　　　　РУСЕ
POP 150,00

One of Bulgaria's most elegant cities, Ruse, sometimes written 'Rousse', has more than a touch of Mitteleuropa (Central Europe) grandness not seen elsewhere in the country. It's a city of imposing belle époque architecture and neatly trimmed leafy squares, as if a little chunk of Vienna had broken off and floated down the Danube. Its past is abundantly displayed in several museums and in its ruined Roman fortress, standing guard high over the Danube.

Ruse is also a base for visiting the nearby rock monasteries and other attractions at Rusenski Lom Nature Park.

History

Named Sexaginta Prista or the 'Port of Sixty Ships' by the Romans, the fortress at Ruse once stood guard over the Danube. The town declined under the Byzantines and Bulgarians, but its fortunes revived under the Turks, who called it Roustchouk. It developed great economic and cultural importance and, in 1866, became the first station on the first railway line in the entire Ottoman Empire, which linked the Danube with the Black Sea at Varna.

Ruse also became a centre for anti-Turkish agitation during the 19th-century uprisings when Bucharest, just a few hours to the north, was the headquarters of the Bulgarian Central Revolutionary Committee. By the end of the Russo-Turkish War (1877–78), Ruse was the largest, most prosperous city in Bulgaria; the legacy of those days lingers in the city's lovely turn-of-the-century architecture.

◎ Sights

Roman Fortress
of Sexaginta Prista   ARCHAEOLOGICAL SITE
(☑ 082-825 002; www.museumruse.com; ul Tsar Kaloyan 2; adult/child 4/1 lv; ☺ 9am-noon & 12.30-5.30pm Tue-Sat) Archaeological work is ongoing at this former Roman fortress at a high point along the Danube. Research attests to some 2000 years of continued military use, from an ancient Thracian settlement through the Roman period in the first centuries AD to the Slavs, Bulgarians and Turks. There are Roman fragments on display as well as older Thracian artefacts.

National Transport Museum   MUSEUM
(☑ 082-803 516; ul Bratya Obretenovi 5; adult/child 4/2 lv; ☺ 9am-noon & 2-5.30pm Mon-Sat)

The country's only National Transport Museum is housed in the building of Bulgaria's first railway station. It exhibits vintage locomotives from the late 19th and early 20th centuries, as well as carriages that once belonged to Tsar Boris III, Tsar Ferdinand and Turkish sultan Abdul Aziz.

Ruse Regional
Museum of History   MUSEUM
(☑ 082-825 002; www.museumruse.com; pl Aleksandar Battenberg 3; adult/child 4/1 lv; ☺ 9am-6pm) The 5th-century BC Borovo Treasure, consisting of silver cups and jugs adorned with Greek gods, is one of the highlights of Ruse's main history museum. Other artefacts on display include Thracian helmets, Roman statues and 19th-century costumes.

Sveta Troitsa Church   CHURCH
(Holy Trinity; pl Sveta Troitsa 9; ☺ 7am-6pm) Built in 1632 below ground level – according to the Turkish stipulation that churches should be as unobtrusive as possible – Sveta Troitsa has a fine gilt wood iconostasis and wooden pillars painted to look like marble, as well as some well-preserved icons.

Pantheon of the National Revival   MONUMENT
(☑ 082-820 998; www.museumruse.com; Park na Vazrozhdentsite; adult/child 2/1 lv; ☺ 9am-noon & 12.30-5.30pm) The gold-domed Pantheon of the National Revival was built in 1978 to commemorate the 100th anniversary of the deaths of 453 local heroes who fought the Ottomans in the Russo-Turkish War.

THE DANUBE & NORTHERN PLAINS RUSE

WORTH A TRIP

THE THRACIAN TOMB OF SVESHTARI

About 90km to the east of Ruse stands one of the country's most impressive archaeological sites: a former Thracian settlement with a nearly perfectly preserved three-chamber burial tomb. The Unesco-protected Sveshtari tomb (☑ 084-735 279; http://whc.unesco.org/en/list/359; Sveshtari, near Isperih; adult/student 10/5 lv; ☺ 9.30am-4.30pm Wed-Sun) dates from about 300 BC and brilliantly shows off the advanced state of Thracian civilisation through its high-quality construction, fine artwork, and exquisite burial gifts. The highly detailed reliefs include carvings of 10 female figures on the walls of the central chamber, which are said to be unique among tombs so far discovered in the Thracian territories.

Access to the tomb is by guided-tour only in groups of 10 or fewer. Register at the visitor centre on arrival and then wait until a tour spot opens up. Visitors are free to walk throughout the sprawling compound and visit an adjoining Muslim shrine from the 16th century.

The Sveshtari compound is located about 8km from the town of Isperih, and can be difficult to reach without private transport. Infrequent trains run to Isperih, but from there it's a long hike or taxi (about 10 lv). Taxi services also make the run from Ruse and back. Ask at the Ruse Tourist Information Centre (p438).

Inside, you can see the marble tombs of revolutionary leaders and a small collection of swords and rifles, but little is explained in English.

Museum of the
Urban Lifestyle in Ruse   MUSEUM
(Kaliopa House; ☑ 082-820 997; www.museum ruse.com; ul Tsar Ferdinand 39; adult/child 4/1 lv; ⊙ 9am-noon & 12.30-5.30pm) Built in 1866 this elegant townhouse features some re-created period rooms, with 19th-century furniture, paintings and chandeliers upstairs. Downstairs there are changing exhibitions on social themes such as education, childhood and domestic life. During the mid-1800s the house served as the consulate of Prussia.

🛏 Sleeping

Ruse has several excellent hotels, though most are aimed at business travellers and are priced accordingly. Budget travellers have the options of a guesthouse and a few older hotels.

English Guest House   B&B $
(☑ 082-875 577; vysachko@abv.bg; ul Rayko Daskalov 34; s/d/tr from 40/60/70 lv; P ❄ @) This centrally located guesthouse in a renovated townhouse has a selection of simple rooms, including pricier options with en suites. There's a common kitchen and living room with a TV and fireplace. Guests have use of the garden. The owners can advise on transport and offer sightseeing day trips.

★ City Art Hotel   BOUTIQUE HOTEL $$
(☑ 0885158403; www.cityarthotel.com; ul Veliko Târnovo 5; s/d 70/90 lv; ❄ 🛜) City Art offers 19 artfully styled rooms with trendy colour schemes, giant headboards and upbeat philosophical quotations stencilled on the walls. The building is a renovated 19th-century hat-maker's shop on a quiet street near the centre. There's a Chinese restaurant, Bamboo, in the back courtyard.

Hotel Riga   HOTEL $$
(☑ 082-822 042; www.en.hotel-riga.com; bul Pridunavski 22; s 60-80 lv, d 90-110 lv; P ❄ @ 🛜) This communist-era high-rise is trying hard to modernise and is worth serious consideration. The updated, slightly more expensive 'Executive' rooms sport cutting-edge design, superclean baths and comfortable beds. The garden restaurant overlooks the Danube, and the top-floor Panorama restaurant is one of the better restaurants in town.

> **ℹ DANUBE BRIDGE**
>
> Some 6km downstream from Ruse, a double-decker highway and railway bridge links the city with **Giurgiu** on the Romanian side of the Danube. Built in 1954, the Danube Bridge was originally called the Friendship Bridge, and at 2.3km in length and towering 30m above the water, it's the longest steel bridge in Europe.

The garden merits a visit even if you're not staying here.

Charlino Plaza   HOTEL $$
(☑ 082-825 707; www.charlino-plaza.com; ul Kaloyan 24, pl Dunav; s/d 50/70 lv; P ❄ 🛜) Twenty-two rooms, including a presidential suite, spread out over four floors at this grand Viennese-style mansion located on a central square. The rooms recall the late 19th and early 20th centuries, with richly textured carpets and curtains. There's also a restaurant, a bar and a garden.

Anna Palace   HOTEL $$
(☑ 082-825 005; www.annapalace.com; ul Knyazheska 4; s/d/ste from 75/90/140 lv; P ❄ @) In a bright-yellow neoclassical mansion just up from the river, the luxurious Anna Palace has large rooms done out in a fin de siècle style (think brocade curtains and richly printed wallpapers). Some of the front rooms have river views. There are smaller discounted attic singles.

🍴 Eating

The centre of the city, around pl Svoboda, is filled with restaurants and pavement terraces.

★ Garden Restaurant   BULGARIAN $
(☑ 0886005658; www.hotel-riga.com; bul Pridunavski 22; mains 6-12 lv; ⊙ 11am-1am Apr-Sep; 🛜) This outdoor restaurant is part of the Riga Hotel complex, and features a beautiful view out over the Danube, water fountains and lots of green. Choose from a long list of grilled meats and fish. The atmosphere borders on magical in the evening as the *rakia* starts to flow and the last rays of sun glint over the river.

New House   BULGARIAN $
(☑ 0892000627; ul Hristo Danov 5; mains 5-10 lv; ⊙ 11am-midnight) The simple, no-frills interior hints at the owners' intention: to

Ruse

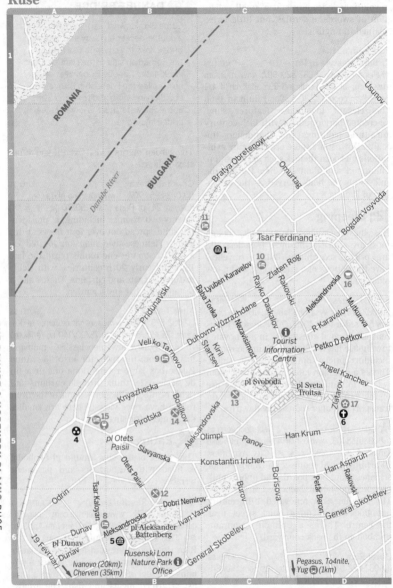

THE DANUBE & NORTHERN PLAINS RUSE

create a foodie destination in the centre of Ruse. The menu emphasises healthy choices, mixing the best of Bulgarian dishes such as *tarator* (cold cucumber and yoghurt soup) and moussaka, with a modern take on fresh ingredients and authentic prepara-

tion. Good-value lunch specials make this a winning choice at midday.

Happy Bar & Grill　　　INTERNATIONAL $$
(☏ 0888154222; www.happy.bg; pl Svoboda 4; mains 7-14 lv; ☺ 11am-11pm; ☜🖉👪) Don't

er times, choose a table in the handsome, contemporary interior.

Chiflika   BULGARIAN $$

(☑ 082-828 222; ul Otets Paisii 2; mains 9-20 lv; ⊙ 11am-2am Mon-Sat, noon-1am Sun) Set in several rooms following an old-world *mehana* theme, with a good dollop of kitsch, Chiflika features wooden benches, rugs, fleeces on the walls, and waiters in pantaloons. This is one of the few places in Ruse where you can sample hearty traditional food. On the big menu are clay-pot meals, including an excellent chicken *gyuvetch* (overn-baked stew), soups, grills and more adventurous options.

🍷 Drinking & Nightlife

Club Admiral   PUB

(☑ 0888002023; www.admiralruse.com; ul Slavyanska 5; ⊙ 10am-midnight Mon-Fri, noon-midnight Sat; 🛜) Describing itself as a 'Scottish pub', Admiral is a big, lively place with a traditional pub, smarter piano bar and a summer garden where food is also served.

Sofa Coffee Time   CAFE

(ul Tsar Osvoboditel, cnr ul Aleksandrovska; ⊙ 8am-2am; 🛜) This trendy little coffee bar with

be put off by the fast-food appearance of the exterior. This is actually a very good and well-run restaurant, with a menu that includes pizza and pasta, seafood, sushi, steaks and salads. The terrace is a festive option for a warm summer evening. At oth-

comfy sofas inside and seating outside is always busy. It also serves cocktails and light meals.

☆ Entertainment

The Ruse Opera House (☑ 082-825 037; www.ruseopera.com; pl Sveta Troitsa 7) is known for hosting top productions. Buy tickets at the box office or online, or ask at the tourist information centre.

❶ Information

There are numerous banks with ATMs and foreign-exchange offices along ul Aleksandrovska and pl Svoboda.

Rusenski Lom Nature Park Office (☑ 082-872 397; www.lomea.org; ul General Skobelev 7; ☺ 9am-5.30pm Mon-Fri) Provides camping and hiking information and maps; can arrange trips to the Ivanovo Rock Monastery.

Tourist Information Centre (☑ 082-824 704; www.rusetourism.org; ul Aleksandrovska 61; ☺ 9am-6pm Mon-Fri, 9.30am-6pm Sat & Sun; ☎) The helpful tourist information office hands out free city maps and leaflets. Can advise on day trips and transport options.

❶ Getting There & Away

BUS

Yug bus station (☑ 082-828 151; www.bgraz pisanie.com; ul Tsar Osvoboditel 156) The city's main bus station, located 2.5km south of the city centre. Most buses, including international services to Bucharest, depart from here. It's well laid out, with kiosks representing the various private bus companies. Look for destinations posted on company timetables, and buy tickets from windows or directly from the drivers.

Sample services:

Burgas (18 lv, 4½ hours)

Pleven (11 lv, 2½ hours)

Silistra (12 lv, about two hours) Bus and minibus departures every hour or so.

Sofia (30 lv, five hours)

Varna (15 lv, four hours)

Veliko Târnovo (12 lv, two hours)

Pegasus (☑ 0877344747; www.pegasusbg. com; ul Tsar Osvoboditel 156, Yug Bus Station) runs four daily minibuses to central Bucharest (22/35 lv one way/return) and the city's international airport (29 lv) from Yug bus station, dropping off at Piaţa Unirii in the centre of the Bucharest, just outside the Hotel Horoscop (rather than the bus station).

Iztok bus station (☑ 082-845 064; ul Ivan Vedar 10) is situated 4km east of the centre; it has infrequent buses to nearby destinations

such as Ivanovo and Cherven in the Rusenski Lom Nature Park.

TRAIN

The grand but decaying **train station** (☑ 082-820 222; www.bdz.bg; pl Stamboliyski 1) is adjacent to the Yug bus station, about 2.5km south of the town centre. It has several daily trains to both Sofia (19 lv, six hours) and Veliko Târnovo (7.50 lv, two to three hours), and two more to Varna (12 lv, four hours).

For Romania, one daily train serves Bucharest (20 lv, 3½ hours). Show up at least 30 minutes before the train departure time for customs and passport checks.

In the station, the **Rila Bureau** (☑ 082-828 016; Train Station; ☺ 9am-5.30pm) sells international train tickets. It's best to buy a Bucharest ticket on the day of travel as there are sometimes delays.

❶ Getting Around

Reliable local taxi company **To4nite** (☑ 082-212 222; www.to4nite.com; bul Tsar Osvoboditel 156, Yug Bus Station) offers regional taxi service to attractions located in the nearby Rusenski Lom Nature Park, including to the Basarbovo Rock Monastery (26 lv return), Ivanovo Rock Monastery (37 lv) and Cherven Fortress (48 lv return). Offers package trips as well.

Rusenski Lom Nature Park
ПРИРОДЕН ПАРК РУСЕНСКИ ЛОМ

This 32.6 sq km nature park, sprawling south of Ruse around the Rusenski Lom, Beli Lom and Malki Lom Rivers, is a superb spot for birdwatching; 172 species are recorded here, including Egyptian vultures, lesser kestrels and eagle owls. It's also home to 67 species of mammals and 24 types of bats.

Most visitors, however, are drawn first to the park's cliff churches. Around 40 medieval rock churches exist in and around some 300 local caves. A handful are accessible, the most famous of which are Basarbovo and Ivanovo. The park also contains the second-longest cave in Bulgaria, the Orlova Chuka Cave, between Tabachka and Pepelina villages. Thracian and Roman ruins are also found here.

◉ Sights

Basarbovo Rock Monastery   MONASTERY
(Sv Dimitar Bassarbovski; ☑ 082-800 765; Basarbovo; ☺ 9am-6pm) **FREE** This towering monastery, about 12km south of Ruse near the

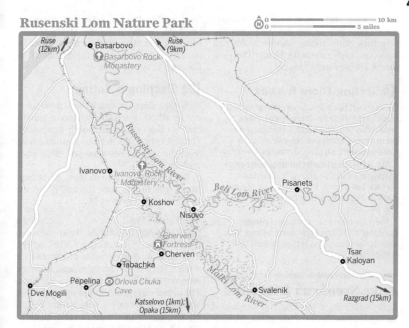

village of Basarbovo, is the country's only working rock monastery. Established some time before the 15th century, the complex has been much restored and extended over time. Visitors can explore a rock-carved church with colourful icons and a little museum.

Cherven Fortress FORTRESS

(Citadel; Cherven; adult/child 4/1 lv; ⊙9am-noon & 1-6pm Mar-Nov) Just outside the village of Cherven, about 30km south of Ruse, are the remains of a remarkably intact 6th-century hilltop citadel. Several streets, towers and churches have also been discovered, and there are great views of the river valleys and peaks from the top. Wear comfortable walking shoes because it's a long climb up from the car park to the citadel.

Ivanovo Rock Monastery MONASTERY

(Sv Archangel Michael; ☑0889370006; Ivanovo; adult/child 4/1 lv; ⊙9am-6pm Apr-Nov) This nonworking monastery, a Unesco World Heritage site, is situated in a cave about 40m above ground at an isolated spot 4km from the village of Ivanovo. Built during the 13th century, it houses 14th-century murals, including a Last Supper scene, which are regarded as some of the finest in Bulgaria.

It's accessible by car, or on foot (30 minutes), from the village.

Orlova Chuka Cave CAVE

(Eagle Peak Cave; ☑0885500294; www.orlova chuka.eu; Pepelina; adult/child 6/2 lv; ⊙10am-5pm Apr-Oct) Lying 2km from Peplina village, the country's second-longest cave is accessible for around 3km of its length. Visitors pass through several chambers, the first called the 'Concert Hall' for its good acoustics. Entry is by guided tour only, taking place at even-numbered hours throughout the day. Guides rarely speak English, but anyway the real attraction here is the natural beauty of the cave.

🍴 Sleeping & Eating

The tourist information office in Ruse and the **information centre** (☑081-162 285; ul Olimpiiska 75, Ivanovo; ⊙9am-5pm Mon-Fri) in Ivanovo can provide information on accommodation. Restaurants are few and far between in the Rusenski Lom Nature Park; consider packing a lunch for your visit.

Art Villa Orlova Chuka GUESTHOUSE $

(☑0899504756; www.artvillaorlovachuka.com; ul Orlova Chuka, Pepelina; r from 40 lv) This comfortable guesthouse is located in the village of Pepelina, about 2km from the Orlova

Chuka cave and 20km from the Ivanovo Rock Monastery in the Rusenski Lom Nature Park. Some rooms have en suites and balconies with mountain views. There's a shared kitchen and a garden.

ℹ️ Getting There & Away

Buses depart twice daily on weekdays from Iztok bus station in Ruse for Cherven, via Ivanovo and Koshov (4 lv, 45 minutes). The best way to get to Ivanovo from Ruse, however, is by the more-frequent train (3 lv, 30 minutes, seven daily).

Ask at the Ruse **tourist information centre** (p438) for details on getting to Basarbovo via local bus directly from the city centre. In summer buses depart hourly; in winter they are less frequent.

The Ruse-based taxi company **To4nite** (p438) offers return sightseeing outings from Ruse to the attractions in the Rusenski Lom Nature Park.

Lake Srebârna & Around

Lake Srebârna, a shallow lake connected to the Danube by a narrow canal, features unique types of vegetation and unusual floating islands made of reeds. It also hosts more than 160 species of waterbirds, including colonies of endangered small cormorants and Dalmatian pelicans. There are elevated lookout posts set around the lake for birdwatching. The 80-sq-km area around the lake, known simply as Srebârna Nature Reserve, is a Unesco World Heritage site.

Srebârna village is the most convenient place to access the lake and has the best facilities. The nearby village of Vetren (4km to the west) is a good spot for fishing, and there are plenty of hikes and other outdoor activities to be enjoyed.

◉ Sights & Activities

The **Museum of Natural History** (☑086-772 469; Srebârna; adult/student 5/1 lv; ⊙9am-6pm Mon-Fri) in Srebârna village presents a good overview in English of birdlife and other fauna around Lake Srebârna. The main activities are birdwatching, hiking and fishing. Walkers can take the rocky, relatively flat 4km ecotrail that starts from Srebârna village and runs along the lake.

Pelican Travel   BIRDWATCHING
(☑0885671058; www.pelican-travel.org; ul Petko Simov 16, Srebârna) Guided birdwatching tours and nature walks (from 40 lv per group) are conducted by Englishman Mike

Black of the Pelican Lake Guesthouse in Srebârna. Pelican Travel also arranges birdwatching and other outdoor tours throughout Bulgaria and further afield, such as to Romania's Danube delta.

🛏️ Sleeping & Eating

Srebârna village and nearby Vetren have several guesthouses, though they can be hard to find as village streets are poorly signposted. The best bet is to get detailed location advice from the guesthouse when you make your booking.

Restaurants are rare in these parts. Srebârna village has one centrally located restaurant, the Complex Diva.

Guesthouse Luba   GUESTHOUSE $
(☑086-772 462, 0889441116; www.srebarna-bg. com; ul Lebed 35, Srebârna; s/d 30/50 lv; 🅿️) This handsome guesthouse is situated on a quiet street in Srebârna village, a couple of minutes' walk away from Lake Srebârna. The owner can speak a little English, but the website is in Bulgarian only. Rooms are attractive and clean. Guests can take meals in a small, traditional tavern on the premises.

Complex Diva   GUESTHOUSE $
(☑0898751478; www.complexdiva.com; ul Dunav 19, Srebârna; s/d 25/35 lv) This Srebârna village guesthouse, restaurant and general store lacks architectural appeal, but does offer excellent value, clean rooms and a great location at the centre of the village. Each of the 12 rooms is simply furnished but has smart hardwood floors and comfortable beds. The restaurant is the only place in town to grab a bite. No credit cards.

Kalimaritsa   GUESTHOUSE $
(☑086-762 554; www.housekalimaritsa.bg; ul Dunav 12, Vetren; d/apt 40/65 lv) A Vetren restaurant that doubles as a guesthouse, the Kalimaritsa's grapevine-bedecked courtyard garden is lovely. Rooms are a bit musty and old-fashioned with their big floral carpets and garish fabrics, but they're passable for an overnight stay. Dining features grilled meats and fish (mains 5 lv to 8 lv).

★ Pelican Lake Guesthouse   B&B $$
(☑0885671058, 086-772 322; www.srebarna birding.com; ul Petko Simov 16, Srebârna; s/d/ste 40/60/100 lv; 🅿️❄️🛜) The cosy English-owned Pelican Lake Guesthouse has two adjoining rooms with a shared bathroom. The hosts provide a wealth of local knowledge and activities, and bird-

watching tours are free for guests. There's a small shared kitchen and a relaxing garden. Breakfast is 8 lv extra and evening meals are available on request. No credit cards.

ⓘ Information

There's no formal tourist information office in the area. Neither Srebârna village nor Vetren have ATMs.

ⓘ Getting There & Away

There is no bus station in either Srebârna village or Vetren. Buses traversing the main Silistra–Ruse route drop passengers on the roadside 1.5km from the centre of Srebârna village.

To reach Vetren, enter Srebârna village and keep following the main street, ul Dunavska. After 4km, you'll reach Vetren, which stops at the river.

Silistra   СИЛИСТРА

POP 35,000

Sitting on the Danube, with picturesque views across the water to the Romanian shore, sedate Silistra feels a little out on a limb and visitors are thin on the ground. There's more than meets the eye here, though. Silistra was an important city, known as Durostorum, during Roman times and served as a fortress for the Roman province of Moesia. This rich historical heritage can be seen at the Archaeologicial Museum and in a preserved Roman tomb from the 4th century.

◉ Sights

Scattered ruins, including a hulking section of the 6th-century fortress wall and a number of early churches, can be seen between the main square and the riverfront.

Silistra has one of Bulgaria's prettiest riverside parks, and one of the treats of a visit here is simply to stroll the banks and look out over the Danube.

★ **Archaeological Museum**   MUSEUM
(☏086-820 386; ul Simeon Veliki 72; adult/child 2/1 lv; ⊙9.30am-noon & 12.30-5pm Tue-Sat) The Archaeological Museum houses an impressive array of locally excavated Roman and Slavic artefacts, housed on two floors and helpfully signposted in English. Highlights include a rebuilt-to-scale Roman chariot (the original fittings are in a glass case) on the ground floor, and a stunning collection

ⓘ FERRY CROSSING TO ROMANIA

The frontier crossing with Romania stands 1km east of Silistra centre (follow ul Drastar). From there it is possible to catch a car-passenger ferry to the Romanian city of Călăraşi. The ferry runs every 30 minutes or so, though boats usually wait until they are full. At the time of research the fare per car was about 25 lei, payable only in Romanian currency; there are exchange booths nearby.

of gold and silver coins that go back to the time of Alexander the Great.

The museum also organises group tours (minimum of five people) to the nearby Roman tomb of Durostorum (Silistra's Roman name). The tomb dates from the turbulent 4th century and is noteworthy for its remarkable frescoes, depicting the master and his wife, who were buried here, as well as their servants. Tours are infrequent and must be booked in advance at the museum.

Art Gallery   GALLERY
(ul Simeon Veliki 49, cnr pl Svoboda; 1 lv; ⊙9-11.30am & 2-5.30pm Mon-Fri) The Art Gallery is in a grand yellow-and-white Viennese-style building on the central square. Inside you can view hundreds of 19th-century and contemporary Bulgarian artworks. Some of the modern works, especially, are breathtaking, though sadly there's not much English signage.

🛏 Sleeping

Sleeping options in Silistra are limited to a few relatively expensive hotels.

Hotel Silistra   HOTEL $$
(☏086-833 033; hotel_silistra@abv.bg; ul Dobruzhda 41; s/d/apt 45/60/90 lv; ☏) In the centre of town on the 5th floor of a shiny business centre, this place has nine big, fresh-looking rooms with laminated-wood floors. There's a restaurant and nightclub on the ground floor.

★ **Hotel Drustar**   LUXURY HOTEL $$$
(☏086-812 200; www.hoteldrustar.com; ul Kapitan Mamarchev 10; s/d 130/160 lv; ⓟ🖪✳@☒) This modern five-star hotel, set in parkland overlooking the Danube, offers attractive, spacious rooms with balconies; ask for a

river view, and watch the aerial display put on by the numerous resident swallows. Facilities include a big outdoor pool and an excellent restaurant. Half-board packages are especially good value.

🍴 Eating

Silistra isn't exactly overflowing with excellent restaurants, but there are a couple worth seeking out.

★ Riverside
BULGARIAN $$

(☑ 0888002691; ul Geno Cholakov 1; mains 6-12 lv; ⊙ 11am-midnight; 🛜) This casual, modern restaurant, just off the park lining the Danube River and near to the Drustar Hotel, serves excellent Bulgarian food, including perfectly spiced veal meatballs and fresh salads. Sit inside or outdoors at a small group of tables within the park. It's situated on one end of the Central Park shopping centre.

Sladost
BULGARIAN $$

(☑ 086-822 177; ul Hristo Smirnenski; mains 7-14 lv; ⊙ 11am-10pm) Sladost is best known around town for its cakes and baked goods, but it also runs an excellent restaurant serving some of the city's best grilled fish and fish soup. It's located 700m east of the Hotel Drustar on an unnamed street that lines the Danube. From the centre, walk north on ul Hristo Smirnenski to the river.

ℹ️ Information

There's no tourist information office. Silistra is a large town, with plenty of banks, ATMs, shops and pharmacies in the centre.

ℹ️ Getting There & Away

Hourly buses and minibuses leave Silistra **bus station** (☑ 086-820 280; www.bgrazpisanie. com; ul Moskova 1) for the Yug bus station in Ruse (12 lv, two hours). Buses also head to Varna (10 lv, two hours, one or two daily), Sofia (36 lv, six hours, three or four daily) and Shumen (12 lv, two to three hours, two or three daily).

From the **train station** (☑ 086-821 813; www. bdz.bg; ul Haralampi Dzhamdzhiev 1; ⊙ 9am-8.30pm), one daily train goes to Ruse (four hours, 12 lv).

Understand
Bulgaria

Bulgaria Today

With a proliferation of new cultural projects and vacillating feelings about its EU membership, Bulgaria's social and political landscape is rapidly evolving. Sceptics feel Bulgaria's new dawn as part of the EU is losing its lustre; meanwhile accusations of political corruption grumble on. But among young people, there's plenty of reason to feel optimistic about modern Bulgaria.

Best on Film

The World is Big & Salvation Lurks around the Corner (2008) A man takes his amnesiac grandson on a journey to rediscover the past.
The Goat Horn (1972) Harrowing tale of revenge in Ottoman-occupied Bulgaria.
Peach Thief (1964) An evocative romance between a Bulgarian Army officer and a prisoner, set during WWI.

Best in Print

Street Without a Name: Childhood & Other Misadventures in Bulgaria (Kapka Kassabova; 2008) Thought-provoking memoir of a young woman's experiences in communism's last years.
Circus Bulgaria (Deyan Enev; 2010) Surrealist collection of stories based on Bulgarian legends and oddities.
The Porcupine (Julian Barnes; 1992) The former ruler of a fictional post-communist country goes on trial.

Best in Music

Le Mystère des Voix Bulgares (1990) A now-legendary set of folk recordings from the national female choir.
Gadna Poroda by Azis (2011) The best *chalga* (Bulgarian pop-folk) album by the country's biggest star.
Song of the Crooked Dance (1927–42) A collection of vintage folk songs and traditional dances.

Growing Pains

Accession to the EU in 2007 was a crowning achievement for post-communist Bulgaria. But years later, Bulgarians regard their progress with a thoughtful eye. In 2015 Bulgaria had the lowest GDP in the EU, and an International Day of Happiness survey found Bulgarians with Europe's lowest levels of contentment. High fuel prices – which formed part of the bitter groundswell of protests that toppled Boyko Borisov's first term as prime minister in 2013 – continue to hinder small businesses.

Along with Romania, Bulgaria's first few years of EU membership were subject to migration controls. These were lifted in 2014, allowing Bulgarians to work permit-free across the EU. But after years of being held at arm's length by longer-term EU members, the country now finds itself wrestling with the thorny topic of migration into Bulgaria. An 80km wire fence was built along the Bulgaria–Turkey border in 2016, a crude attempt to curb illegal migration; at the time of writing, there were plans for a fence along the Greek border, too.

Freedom of movement has turned out to be a double-edged sword. Young Bulgarians thrive on their new-found mobility, many choosing to work abroad in Spain, Germany, Italy and beyond. The older generation are increasingly unnerved by the trend, some claiming they are unable to find young Bulgarians to work in small businesses at home. Others blame Bulgarian gloom on the fragmentation of families, a by-product of ambitious Bulgarians roving elsewhere to earn money.

Positive effects in recent years mustn't be overlooked. An injection of EU funding for cultural treasures, Sofia's expanded metro system, Plovdiv being crowned European Capital of Culture 2019, the smoking ban in restaurants and bars – the victories are considerable. Accusations of corruption still bubble beneath the surface though, and EU membership has not proved the silver bullet Bulgarians were hoping for. More change is coming now that Bulgaria has met requirements to join the Schengen Zone. Meanwhile economic instability has prompted a deceleration of the process to adopt the euro as currency. Bulgaria's 21st-century rebirth was never going to be easy.

Heritage Renaissance

Bulgaria's cultural treasures have experienced a rough ride, and the fight for their preservation isn't over. Under Ottoman rule, churches were sacked and Bulgarian language quashed. After being wrested from Ottoman oppression, art and architecture flourished under the National Revival period, but the rise and fall of communism made the country's cultural life stagnate.

Many National Revival–era buildings languished in paperwork limbo after the fall of communism. Archaeological discoveries around this time, such as a string of tombs discovered in the 1990s in Kazanlâk's Valley of Thracian Kings, suffered from a lack of funding and publicity. Limited investment in safeguarding cultural heritage, combined with a hunger from private collectors, resulted in thieves seizing priceless treasures, with Roman coins and Thracian masks especially prone to disappearing from museums.

But over the last few years, green shoots have sprouted for Bulgaria's cultural treasures. A rare Thracian-Roman silver mask-helmet, stolen in 1995, was recovered in 2015 and redisplayed in Plovdiv's Museum of Archaeology. Roman ruins uncovered during the construction of Sofia's metro system, the Ancient Serdica Complex, opened to great excitement in 2016. Historic neighbourhoods have been spruced up, such as Plovdiv's Kapana area, where young artists were incentivised to move into faded properties and transform them into galleries and cafes. Archaeological finds in recent years have reignited excitement in Bulgarian history, too: excavation of the country's largest Thracian burial mound, Maltepe, and further digs at Ruse's Roman city Sexaginta Prista were among 2016's highlights.

An uphill battle remains for Bulgaria's historic riches. For every site restored with a little help from the EU piggy bank, others lie waiting their turn. Meanwhile, historians despair that tourist revenue never seems to convert back into investment for further archaeological endeavours. Still, though progress is slow and frustrations abound, the road ahead for Bulgaria's heritage is brighter than it has ever been.

POPULATION: **7.19 MILLION**

AREA: **110,879 SQ KM**

GDP GROWTH (2016): **3.5%**

INFLATION RATE (2015): **-0.2%**

AVERAGE MONTHLY SALARY (2016): **748 LV (€383)**

if Bulgaria were 100 people

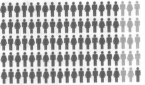

85 would be Bulgarian
9 would be Turkish
5 would be Roma
1 would be Other

belief systems
(% of population)

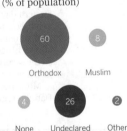

60 Orthodox
8 Muslim
4 None
26 Undeclared
2 Other

population per sq km

BULGARIA   UK   USA

≈ 30 people

History

Bulgaria's history is awash in blood, gold and wine. Its most famous ancient inhabitants, the Thracians, were a civilisation of masterful horsemen, wine-drinkers and lovers of song, who left behind hauls of gold. Across Bulgaria loom grand churches and fortresses, commissioned by medieval Bulgarian tsars whose battles spanned centuries, while the most colourful way in which Bulgaria's history lives on is through National Revival architecture. Countless towns glow with pastel-coloured mansions from the 1800s, contrasting against brutalist blocks that came during post-WWII communism.

Beginnings

A Concise History of Bulgaria by RJ Crampton is a scholarly and comprehensive overview of the country's history from prehistoric times to the present day.

Cave excavations near Pleven and in the Stara Planina (Balkan Range) confirm human habitation since the Upper Palaeolithic Period (40,000 BC). However, archaeologists believe cave-dwelling neolithic peoples (6000 BC) were Bulgaria's earliest permanent settlers. Excavations in Mursalevo, western Bulgaria, reveal an impressive degree of town planning among dwellings that date back eight thousand years. In Stara Zagora, burial mounds have been excavated, and burnt wheat and barley provide evidence of early farming. Bulgaria's chalcolithic (copper-using) cultures developed during the fourth millennium BC; a superb collection of chalcolithic artefacts – including possibly the world's earliest worked gold jewellery – can be admired in the Varna Archaeological Museum.

The Thracians

Several diverse Indo-European tribes, the Thracians, settled in modern-day Bulgaria and attracted a reputation for ferocious warfare and bacchanalian pursuits. Their earliest settlements were based around cave systems and 'sacred' springs. Later, they built more permanent villages with elevated, rudimentary fortresses. Herodotus described them as the second-most numerous people (after Indians) in the world, with global domination only out of grasp because of their lack of unity.

Most powerful were the Sofia-area Serdi; the Getae, from the Danube region; and the Odrysai, from the Rodopi region. The tribes

TIMELINE	6000–5000 BC	4000–1000 BC	611 BC
	Bulgaria's earliest neolithic settlers occupy caves, abandoning them around 5000 BC for mud huts. Farming develops.	Thracian tribes dominate modern-day Bulgaria; around 3000 BC, settlements include coastal Mesembria; around 2000 BC they expand into Greece and Anatolia.	Greek settlers from the Anatolian city-state of Miletus establish Apollonia Pontica (Sozopol) on the Black Sea coast – the first classical democracy on Bulgarian territory.

quarrelled, but had a shared culture and language and common religious rites. They were feared warriors and horsemen – as weaponry pieces in museums reveal. The 2nd-century BC Greek historian Polybius described the chronic wars of attrition between the Thracians and the Greek colonists at Byzantium (later, Constantinople, and then İstanbul).

But it wasn't all nocturnal ambushes, high-speed javelin attacks, and impaling heads on spears (just a few of the Thracians' wartime tactics). Semi-mythical musician and underworld explorer, Orpheus, was born here: his talent for getting the party started worked seamlessly with that of wine god Dionysus, who was worshipped in orgiastic rituals. The Thracian elite practised polygamy, while unmarried girls were encouraged to be promiscuous. Breathless ancient Greek historians also mentioned Thracians' tattoos – men and women proudly wore geometric and animal designs – and recreational drug use.

The Thracians were accomplished artists and traded jewellery, copper and gold. Excavations near Kazanlâk have unearthed the astonishing gold funerary mask of a Thracian king. The Thracians also influenced Greek and Roman religion, while some Bulgarian names, such as 'rila' (for Rila Monastery) and 'yantra' (the river through Veliko Târnovo) probably originate from Thracian. However, lacking their own written record, the Thracians' history and culture remain opaque; since Thracian history is known largely from Greek sources, Greek scholars have long been tempted to Hellenise Thracian achievements.

Today's famous Thracian remains include tombs dating from about 4000 BC (in Varna's Archaeological Museum) and several burial mounds in the area around Kazanlâk and Shipka, referred to as the Valley of Thracian Kings. Other Thracian artefacts lie in museums in Haskovo, Smolyan, Sofia and Sliven. Other settlement remains are at Burgas and Nesebâr on the Black Sea, and Plovdiv's Nebet Tepe fortress site.

Greeks, Macedonians & Romans

From the 7th century BC, Greek merchants seeking safe harbours and trade opportunities founded Black Sea ports such as Apollonia Pontica (modern-day Sozopol), Odessos (Varna), Mesembria (Nesebâr), Krounoi/Dionysopolis (Balchik) and Pirgos (Burgas). These ports exported wheat, fish and salt, while Greek pottery was traded for Thracian metalwork and jewellery.

The Greeks avoided Bulgaria's interior, being heavily outnumbered by Thracians there, so few inland towns attest to Greek settlement. Still, the Greeks did influence Balkan religion, arts and culture, and the Bulgarian language retains many Greek words and place names.

The Thracian Getae tribe would send 'messengers' to their god, Zalmoxis, by hurling them onto a row of upturned spears.

Georgi Kitov (1943–2008) unearthed some of Bulgaria's most astonishing archaeological treasures in the Valley of Thracian Kings, though his bulldozer methods appalled his contemporaries. Fellow archaeologists haven't been kind about the quality of Kitov's scholarship, so he is remembered variably as Bulgarian hero and tomb-raiding self-promoter.

---

335 BC	AD 46	293	443–47
Macedonian king Alexander the Great extends the Thracian holdings of his father Philip II by marching to the Danube, the northernmost border of his massive empire.	Rome annexes the eastern Balkans, and modern-day Bulgaria is divided into provinces: Thrace (south), Moesia (north) and Ulpia Serdica (today's Sofia) as the capital of Inner Dacia.	Roman emperor Diocletian establishes the 'Tetrarchy' (rule of four), reorganising imperial administration. Regional 'capitals' are established, including Serdica (Sofia), which becomes important.	Forces of Attila the Hun cross the Danube, sweeping into Roman territory and sacking Serdica and Philipopolis (Plovdiv), forcing Rome to pay tribute in gold.

A more dangerous adversary for the Thracians arose in the 4th century BC, when Macedonian King Philip II (and later his son, Alexander the Great) conquered Thrace. Philip's new capital, Philippopolis (Plovdiv) became an important military outpost. Odessos (Varna) and Serdica (Sofia) were also occupied.

Macedonian rule ended when Rome defeated them in 168 BC. By the middle of the 1st century AD, Romans occupied Mesembria (Nesebâr) and Odessos (Varna), site of Bulgaria's largest Roman ruins, the Thermae complex.

After AD 46, Bulgaria was divided into the provinces of Thrace, in the south, and Moesia, in the north. Roman fortifications arose at major Thracian and Greek towns along the Danube, such as Ruse and Bononia (Vidin), and at Deultum (Burgas) along the Black Sea coast.

Ulpia Serdica (Sofia) subsequently became the Roman capital of Inner Dacia province (today's northwestern Bulgaria); the impressive Sveti Georgi Rotunda, or Church of St George, attests to this period. By the late 3rd century AD, Ulpia Serdica had become a major regional imperial capital, where Diocletian and subsequent emperors held court.

Bulgaria's other Roman towns include Sevtopolis (Kazanlâk), Ulpia Augusta Traiana (Stara Zagora), Nikopolis-ad-Istrum (north of Veliko Târnovo) and Trimontium (Plovdiv), site of a magnificent (and still working) amphitheatre. From the 3rd century AD onwards Goths, Huns and other warring tribes wreaked havoc, though raids were sporadic and short-lived.

Byzantium & the Bulgars: War & Peace

In AD 330 Roman emperor Constantine the Great founded Constantinople (modern İstanbul) at ancient Byzantium. Constantinople became the Eastern Roman Empire's capital, with a co-emperor ruling in Rome. Bulgaria (and most Balkan territory) fell under the eastern half. All through the 6th-century rule of Emperor Justinian the Great, Bulgaria was relatively stable, and great structures such as Sofia's original Church of Sveta Sofia were built. However, Slavs, Avars and Bulgars would increasingly threaten the Byzantine Balkans.

From 632, Turkic Bulgars migrated southwest. These warlike Central Asian tribes were archetypical steppe nomads – skilled horsemen, archers and superstitious pagans. The Bulgars roamed from the Caspian Sea to the Black Sea steppes and, when united under Khan Kubrat, soon were roaming Bulgaria, too. The Byzantines could not repel or assimilate this horde; the Turkic tribes gradually settled down, subjugating the Slavs, Greeks and Thracian remnants.

Khan Asparuh (r 681–701) created the First Bulgarian Empire (681–1018), based at Pliska near modern-day Shumen. The empire expanded

---

The ancient Thracians favoured quick-fire war tactics: they rushed their foes down hillsides, rained down spears and made repeated attacks to tire their enemies.

The Shortest History of Bulgaria by Nikolay Ovcharov runs quickly through the high points of Bulgaria's past, cramming a lot of interesting facts into just 70 brightly illustrated pages.

681	814	855	863
After Turkic Bulgar tribes sweep down from the Black Sea steppes, Khan Asparuh establishes the First Bulgarian Empire at Pliska. Centuries of chronic fighting with Byzantium ensue.	Khan Krum dies unexpectedly while preparing to besiege Constantinople; the Bulgars make peace two years later.	Byzantine monks Kiril and Metodii undertake a mission to the Moravian Slavs; their monk-disciples later spread the Cyrillic alphabet in Ohrid, in Bulgarian-controlled Macedonia.	Byzantine Orthodox prelates baptise Knyaz Boris and his court; Constantinople's dramatic competition with the Pope only ends in 870, when Bulgaria wins national-church status.

south and west under Khan Tervel (r 701–721), who helped the Byzantine army repel an Arab advance on Constantinople.

Periods of bloody conflict and wary peace followed between Byzantium and the Bulgars. Khan Krum 'The Dreadful' (r 803-814) ruthlessly expanded the empire and besieged Constantinople after the Byzantines destroyed Pliska, and used the skull of vanquished adversary Emperor Nikephoros as a drinking vessel thereafter.

Golden Times

After Krum's sudden and unexpected death, several 9th-century khans annexed further territory: Khan Omurtag (r 814–831) pressed into modern-day Hungary in 829, and Khan Presian's reign (r 837–852) ended with Bulgarian control over southeastern Europe, including modern-day Romania, Moldova, Macedonia and parts of Greece. Presian's territorial gains brought many Macedonian and other Slavs into his empire; along with Christianity's imminent arrival, this would dramatically change the Bulgars' ethnicity and culture.

Presian's son, Knyaz (Prince) Boris I (r 852–889) cleverly exploited the Constantinople–Rome rivalry; both sought spiritual control over Bulgaria, and Boris played both sides. In 863 he, his family and his court were baptised by Byzantine prelates, but only in 870 did Bulgaria officially go Orthodox, not Roman Catholic. Bulgaria's ruling class was soon immersed in Byzantine court practices, spirituality and culture. (Today, the Church considers Boris a saint).

Boris displayed further political acumen in sheltering the persecuted disciples of two Byzantine missionary monks, Kiril and Metodii (Cyril and Methodius), who had in 855 gone to convert Moravia's Slavs (in today's Slovakia) to Orthodoxy, devising an understandable liturgical language (Old Church Slavonic). Under Boris' and later tsars' sponsorship, theological schools in Macedonia and Bulgaria would develop the Cyrillic alphabet. Bulgarian churchmen thus won freedom from both Rome and Constantinople, with the liturgy in their own emerging Slavic language, not Greek or Latin.

Following Byzantine imperial practice, Boris retired to a monastery in 889 for his final years. However, when his son Vladimir tried to restore paganism, Boris deposed and blinded him. Younger brother Simeon (r 893–927) stretched Bulgaria's borders from the Adriatic to the Aegean, and the Dnieper River in the north. Ruling from a new capital, Preslav, Tsar Petâr (r 927-968) oversaw a cultural golden age of church building, fine arts and manuscript production. However, Preslav was badly damaged during 960s wars with the Kievan Rus and Byzantium and never recovered.

HISTORY GOLDEN TIMES

The 9th-century Bulgar ruler Khan Krum 'the Dreadful' earned his sobriquet from his ferocity in battle and his penchant for sipping wine out of enemy skulls. He is thought to have especially enjoyed forcing visiting diplomats to drink from the skulls of his former foes.

Thracian Historical Sights

Thracian Tomb of Sveshtari (Razgrad Province)

Valley of Thracian Kings (Shipka)

Thracian Tomb of Kazanlâk (Kazanlâk)

Archaeological Museum (Sofia)

917	972	1014	1185–1396
Boris' third son, Tsar Simeon (r 893–927) expands borders from Romania and Bosnia to the Peloponnese, becoming Europe's strongest power.	Byzantines capture and burn the Bulgarian capital, Preslav; the leadership relocates to Ohrid, their capital until the Byzantine reconquest in 1018.	Byzantine forces win decisively at the Battle of Kleidion/Belasitsa in southwestern Bulgaria, auguring the Bulgarian Empire's demise four years later.	Aristocrat brothers Asen and Petâr rebel against a weakening Byzantium, establishing the Second Bulgarian Empire, with Veliko Târnovo the capital. Tsar Ivan Asen II (1218–41) expands Bulgaria's borders.

Decline & Fall

After Preslav's destruction, Tsar Samuel (r 997–1014) moved the capital to Ohrid (in modern-day Macedonia; his castle still towers above Ohrid's massive lake). However, he lost the 1014 Battle of Kleidion/Belasitsa to the Byzantines; according to a legend, Emperor Basil II (r 976–1025) had 15,000 captured Bulgarian soldiers blinded and returned to Samuel, who died of shock. While Samuel actually died months later, the defeat was impressive – Basil was nicknamed Voulgaroktonos ('Bulgar-Slayer' in Greek). In 1018, Ohrid fell, and Bulgaria was annexed.

Byzantium's later decline led aristocratic brothers Asen and Petâr to rebel; their Second Bulgarian Empire (1185–1396) had Veliko Târnovo as capital. Bulgaria now cast a wary eye westward: in the perfidious Fourth Crusade of 1204, Western knights invaded Constantinople, destroying the Byzantine state. In 1205, self-declared 'emperor' Baldwin of Flanders foolishly invaded Bulgaria: he was captured and terminally imprisoned in the tower at Tsarevets Fortress in Veliko Târnovo.

Asen's diplomatically savvy son, Tsar Ivan Asen II (r 1218–41), became southeastern Europe's most powerful ruler, and Veliko Târnovo became an important cultural centre. In 1230 he defeated Byzantine successor armies at the Battle of Klokotnitsa. After his death, however, Bulgaria disintegrated between Tatar and Arab invasions and internal fighting.

Bogomilism was a secretive medieval Bulgarian sect based on dualism – the existence of two deities, one evil, the other good. In 1118, sect leader Basil the Physician was burned at the stake in Constantinople (an extremely rare punishment meant to intimidate his followers).

The Turkish Yoke

After 1362 Ottoman Turks swarmed into the northern Balkans; within 30 years, they possessed Bulgaria, holding it for five centuries.

Despite some rosy depictions of life under the Turks, they regarded non-Muslims as second-class citizens, so many Bulgarians were deprived of major rights and suffered harsh punishments for the most insignificant of offences. Like most of the Balkans, Bulgaria was isolated from Christian Western Europe, and missed out on its cultural and intellectual advances. In all, up to half of Bulgaria's population was either killed or enslaved (young boys were seized and converted into the sultan's Janissary guard, while girls were kidnapped into Turkish harems). Churches and monasteries were destroyed, closed or turned into mosques. Sporadic uprisings were quashed ferociously, and many Bulgarians fled.

Ottoman aristocrats inhabited the cities, consigning Bulgarians to the mountains and villages. Haidouks (armed rebels) fought the occupiers from the hills. As elsewhere in Ottoman lands, the Turks courted mountain-dwelling populations in strategic regions such as the Rodopi Mountains – here, Bulgarian converts to Islam (today's Pomaks) won

The Legend of Basil the Bulgar-Slayer by Paul Stephenson offers a scholarly reinterpretation of the illustrious Byzantine emperor and his campaigns in Bulgaria.

1396	1444	1598	1686
Bulgaria's last native king, Tsar Ivan Shishman (1371–96), is defeated and Bulgaria is annexed by the Ottoman Empire, beginning 500 years of harsh Islamic rule.	A Hungarian-led Crusade against the Turks ends disastrously at the Battle of Varna.	The First Târnovo Uprising against Turkish rule briefly liberates Veliko Târnovo. A new tsar is crowned, but the revolt is brutally crushed. Thousands of Bulgarians flee to Wallachia.	Austrian victories against the Turks inspire revolts in northern Bulgaria, but the so-called Second Târnovo Uprising is squashed.

exemption from taxes and enjoyed legal rights denied to their Christian neighbours.

Bulgaria's national, cultural and Christian identity survived largely because of monks in monasteries (such as Rila) that the Turks tolerated or couldn't control. They carefully preserved rituals, traditions and important manuscripts, keeping Bulgarian culture alive until it could re-emerge safely.

National Revival

The Bulgarian monasteries that had preserved Bulgarian culture and history sparked the 18th- and 19th-century National Revival. This reawakening coincided with similar nation-state sentimentality in Western Europe, and was influenced by monk Paisii Hilendarski – his name was taken from his time at the Serbian-sponsored Hilandar Monastery at Mount Athos, Greece.

Hilendarski collected information to compile the first history of the Slav-Bulgarian peoples in 1762. He roamed the land, reciting his history to illiterate people (the Turks forbade Bulgarian-language publications). It was an instant hit, stirring long-suppressed nationalist feelings. Hilandarski's emphasis on the great deeds of Bulgaria's medieval tsars fuelled populist pride.

By the early 19th century the Bulgarian economy had grown, with merchants from Plovdiv and Koprivshtitsa supplying wool, wine, metals and woodcarvings to Turkey and Western Europe. An educated and prosperous urban middle class emerged, especially after the Crimean War, when the victorious allies persuaded Turkey to open up to foreign trade.

Travels in European Turkey in 1850 by Edmund Spencer is a firsthand travelogue providing rare insight into the later years of Ottoman rule in the Balkans.

HISTORY NATIONAL REVIVAL

LADISLAS' CRUSADE & THE BATTLE OF VARNA

By the early 15th century, the Ottomans possessed Bulgaria, Serbia and Transylvania, with Hungary in their sights and Constantinople under siege.

Trying to save Europe, Pope Eugenius IV ordered a crusade. In 1443, King Ladislas (Władysław III) of Hungary and Poland transported his 25,000-man army via Venetian ships. Victories in Serbia, and Sofia's capture, forced Ottoman Sultan Murad II to concede Serbia and agree to a 10-year truce in 1444.

However, the Pope and other crusade sponsors wanted all of Europe liberated, forcing Ladislas to break his agreement. With a smaller force, he marched to Varna; while the promised reinforcement fleet never arrived, one furious sultan accompanied by 80,000 soldiers did. Ladislas was beheaded and his army destroyed (though folktales would describe a resurrected Ladislas taking a pilgrimage to Jerusalem). Nine years later, Constantinople fell, and Ottoman expansion continued.

1762–1878	1853–56	1876	1877–78
The National Revival era; monk Paisii Hilendarski's groundbreaking Slav-Bulgarian History captivates Bulgarians. Bulgarian-language education is allowed and the Bulgarian Orthodox Church is established.	The Crimean War brings British and French troops to Bulgaria, with Varna an important garrison; Turkey is compelled to open up Bulgaria to international trade.	Koprivshtitsa's April Uprising is suppressed; civilian massacres cause international outrage. The Ottomans reject Bulgarian autonomy at the November Constantinople Conference.	Russo-Turkish War; Tsar Alexander II's army invades Bulgaria and destroys the Ottoman forces. The resulting Treaty of San Stefano envisages the Turks ceding 60% of the Balkan Peninsula to Bulgaria.

Bulgarian merchants built grand private homes and public buildings in the distinct National Revival style. Woodcarvers from Tryavna and painters from Samokov developed a unique Bulgarian style in designing them. Bulgarian art, music and literature also flourished, and Bulgarian-language schools were opened. Towns and villages built *chitalishta* (reading rooms), providing a communal forum for cultural and social activities and political chatter. Turkish recognition of an autonomous Bulgarian Orthodox Church followed in 1870.

Revolution & Freedom

The 1876 April Uprising in Koprivshtitsa came after long planning by revolutionaries such as Georgi Rakovski, Hristo Botev and Bulgaria's iconic hero Vasil Levski. The Turks indiscriminately massacred 30,000 Bulgarian civilians, destroyed scores of villages and plundered hundreds more.

Western Europe was outraged; Russia cited the massacre in declaring war on Turkey in 1877. Some 200,000 Russian soldiers died for Bulgarian freedom, as the Russian army (and its Bulgarian volunteers) crushed the Turks. With Russian forces only 50km from İstanbul, the Ottomans capitulated. As part of the Treaty of San Stefano, signed on 3 March 1878, Turkey finally recognised Bulgarian autonomy and ceded Bulgaria 60% of the Balkans.

However, Russophobic Western European powers reversed this with the Treaty of Berlin, signed on 13 July 1878. It awarded the area between the Stara Planina ranges and the Danube, plus Sofia, to an independent Bulgarian principality. The Thracian Plain and Rodopi Mountains became Ottoman 'Eastern Rumelia'. Macedonia, renamed 'Western Rumelia', also remained Ottoman, as did Aegean Thrace. This ill-conceived treaty infuriated every Balkan nation, sparking decades of war: between 1878 and WWII, Balkan countries (including Bulgaria) fought six wars over border issues.

Revolutionary Sights

Shipka Pass (Stara Planina)

Koprivshtitsa

Blue Rocks (Sliven)

Sveti Arhangeli Mihael Church (Perushtitsa)

National Museum of Military History (Sofia)

The Nascent State

On 16 April 1879, Bulgaria's new national assembly adopted its first constitution in Veliko Tãrnovo. On 26 June, Germany's Prince Alexander Battenberg was elected head of state. On 6 September 1885 the Bulgarian Principality and Eastern Rumelia were reunified after a bloodless coup. Central European powers were angered by this contravention of the Berlin Treaty, and Turkish troops massed for war.

The Austro-Hungarian Empire incited Serbia to fight Bulgaria, but Serbian troops were quickly repelled; the Bulgarian army advanced deep into Serbia, prompting Austria to call for a ceasefire. The Great Powers finally recognised the reunified Bulgaria.

1885	1908	1912–13	1915–19
A bloodless coup sees Bulgaria reunited with the Ottoman-controlled southlands. Turkish armies mobilise, while a Serbian invasion is defeated. Bulgaria's new borders are internationally recognised.	Amid internal Turkish political chaos, Prince Ferdinand declares full independence from Turkey and becomes tsar of the new Bulgarian kingdom.	Bulgaria and neighbouring states fight the Ottomans in the First Balkan War (1912), reclaiming territory. Dissatisfied with its share, Bulgaria attacks allies Greece and Serbia in the Second Balkan War (1913).	Bulgaria joins the Germans in WWI; defeated, the Treaty of Neuilly-sur-Seine punishes Bulgaria by awarding land to its neighbours, while the government faces crippling reparations.

War and its Discontents

Alexander's forced abdication in 1886 brought Prince (later King) Ferdinand Saxe-Coburg-Gotha to power. Prime minister Stefan Stambolov helped accelerate economic development, while two important political parties were founded: the Social Democrats (the communist forerunners) and the pro-peasant Agrarian Union. In 1908, King Ferdinand I took advantage of the Young Turks revolt to declare complete independence from Turkey.

After a decade of guerrilla warfare against the Turks in Macedonia and Greece, Montenegro, Bulgaria, Greece and Serbia united in 1912. In this, the First Balkan War, Serbian troops easily swept down through Macedonia, and Greek naval power denied Turkey reinforcements. However, Bulgaria's invaluable infantry bore the brunt of the Turkish counter-attack; this, and the Bulgarian obsession with Macedonia, caused a disgruntled Bulgaria to attack its allies (the Second Balkan War) in 1913. Quickly defeated, Bulgaria lost hard-won territory; Turkey grabbed back Adrianople (today's Edirne), too.

Unsurprisingly, a bad-tempered Bulgaria joined the Central Powers (ironically, allying it with Turkey) in 1915. Bulgarian soldiers spent the next years staring down Allied troops at the 'Salonika Front' (today's Macedonia–Greece border). However, by 1918 Ferdinand's pro-German policies forced his abdication. His son, Boris III, took over.

The 1919 Treaty of Neuilly-sur-Seine awarded Aegean Thrace to Greece and southern Dobrudzha to Romania. Bulgaria was also humiliated by war reparations, inciting political and social unrest. The 'radical' ruling Agrarian Party renounced claims to Macedonia (now divided between Greece and the newly established Kingdom of Serbs, Croats and Slovenes). A right-wing military coup followed in 1923. Two years later, at Sofia's Sveta Nedelya Cathedral, communist terrorists failed to assassinate Boris III, killing around 150 bystanders instead. In 1934 the right-wing Zveno group's military coup gave Tsar Boris dictatorial powers.

Commmunist politician Georgi Dimitrov became famous worldwide when he was accused, along with three others, of starting the infamous Reichstag fire in Berlin in 1933. Dimitrov used his trial as a platform to expound communist ideas.

World War II

Bulgaria declared neutrality when WWII began. However, German troops advancing toward Greece menacingly massed along the Danube, and Hitler offered up Macedonia to entice Bulgaria, which, once again, joined the (losing) Germanic side.

Allowing the Nazis free passage, Bulgaria declared war on Britain and France, but not Russia. Bulgarian soldiers occupied Macedonia and northern Greece and deported 13,000 Greek and Macedonian Jews to Nazi death camps, in order to delay doing the same with their own Jews, due to public opposition.

1940	1941	1945–46	1949
Southern Dobrudzha, occupied by Romania since 1913, is returned to Bulgaria for a nominal fee; a population exchange follows.	After first declaring neutrality, Bulgaria joins the Axis powers after German troops are stationed along the Danube, and declares war on Britain and France, but not on the Soviet Union.	After winning 1945 elections, the communists under Georgi Dimitrov declare the People's Republic of Bulgaria, with Soviet backing.	After a show trial, the Bulgarian Supreme Court sentences deputy prime minister Traicho Kostov to death on grounds of encouraging anti-Soviet feeling. Similar staged trials of prominent communists.

On 28 August 1943, one week after meeting Hitler, Tsar Boris III died. Boris' infant son, Tsar Simeon II, succeeded him. Allied air raids in winter 1943–44 damaged Sofia and other towns. A coalition government sought peace, but failed, leading Russia to invade. On 9 September 1944 the part-communist resistance coalition, the 'Fatherland Front', took power. Even before war's end, 'people's courts' saw thousands of 'monarch-fascist' supporters imprisoned or executed.

Elderly Bulgarian mystic, Baba Vanga, rose to fame for allegedly foreseeing the date of Stalin's death, the break-up of the USSR and the 9/11 attacks. Former dictator Todor Zhivkov is thought to have consulted her more than once.

Red Bulgaria

The Fatherland Front won November 1945 elections, with communists controlling the new national assembly. Leader Georgi Dimitrov's Soviet-styled constitution declared the People's Republic of Bulgaria on 15 September 1946. The royal family were exiled. The Stalinist regime held show trials for 'traitors', collectivised agriculture and undertook industrialisation and modernisation programs. Dimitrov's successor, Vâlko Chervenkov, was dubbed 'Little Stalin' for his unquestioning loyalty.

Dictator Todor Zhivkov's long rule as head of state (1954–89) saw prosperity under Soviet protection. Bulgaria received cheap oil and electricity, plus exporting and contracts with Eastern Bloc and Non-Aligned Movement states. However, the secret police became an instrument of Zhivkov's totalitarianism, dealing ruthlessly with dissidents and diaspora critics. The service was rumoured to have masterminded the 1981 assassination attempt on Pope John Paul II by a Turkish gunman. (However, Bulgaria has always denied this and conflicting theories exist). As the Soviet bloc weakened in the 1980s, and Bulgaria's economy, too, nationalism surged, targeting Turks, Pomaks and Roma, who were pressured to adopt Bulgarian names. A Turkish exodus ensued, though many returned and prospered later.

The Transition to the West

Voices from the Gulag: Life and Death in Communist Bulgaria, edited by Tzvetan Todorov, is a collection of firsthand accounts from inmates, guards and bureaucrats of the communist system's horrors.

By 1989 *perestroika* had reached Bulgaria. On 10 November, an internal Communist Party coup dismissed Zhivkov, and the party allowed elections, renaming itself the Bulgarian Socialist Party (BSP). A broad opposition coalition, the Union of Democratic Forces (UDF), failed to unseat the BSP in the June 1990 parliamentary elections – making Bulgaria the first ex-Soviet state to resurrect communists.

While the incompetence of both blocs caused frequent changes in government, elections were generally irrelevant in transition-era Bulgaria, as power and wealth consolidated around overnight millionaires, bodyguards, former spies and other adventurers in the new 'capitalism'. Throughout the 1990s, an impoverished public held protests over government failures. In 1997, prime minister Ivan Kostov pledged to fight

1978	1984	1989–90	1991–2000
In one of the most infamous Cold War espionage events, Bulgarian dissident writer Georgi Markov is assassinated in London with a poisoned umbrella tip by a Bulgarian secret agent.	A nationalistic campaign to assimilate the ethnic Turkish population causes a mass exodus of Turks, though many return after communism ends.	Democratic revolutions see Todor Zhivkov's communist regime collapse; Zhelyu Zhelev becomes Bulgaria's first non-communist head of state.	Transition times; massive inflation, corruption and plummeting wages make Bulgaria Europe's poorest country. Successive governments fail, while organised crime flourishes.

crime and corruption while attracting investment. However, doing this while making painful NATO- and EU-mandated reforms was difficult.

In 2001 Bulgarians elected their once-exiled king as prime minister. Simeon Saxe-Coburg-Gotha had formed the National Movement Simeon II (NMSII) only two months earlier. His coalition included the Movement for Rights and Freedoms (MRF), the ethnic Turkish party of wealthy businessman Ahmed Dogan, and promised economic prosperity, plus NATO and EU membership. Although Simeon's popularity did not endure, those goals were reached – Bulgaria joined NATO in 2004 and the EU in 2007.

Subsequent years brought further political turmoil with a banking crisis and vehement political protest. Loss of trust in prime minister Plamen Oresharski brought down his government in July 2014, after nearly a year of fierce protests. This made way for boomerang politician Boyko Borisov, who had resigned his government in February 2013, only to return for a second time as part of a coalition government in November 2014. Meanwhile, a trickle of EU funding allowed for the rejuvenation of some of Bulgaria's historic sights, and in 2015 Plovdiv was formally approved by the EU Council as the European Capital of Culture for 2019, giving some reason for young Bulgarians to be optimistic about their country's future and its place on the European stage.

Bulgaria's former tsar and later prime minister, Simeon Saxe-Coburg-Gotha, is distantly related to Britain's Queen Elizabeth II.

2001	**2004**	**2007**	**2014**
Bulgaria's formerly exiled child-king, Simeon Saxe-Coburg, becomes prime minister.	Bulgaria, along with other former Warsaw Pact nations, joins NATO.	Despite European misgivings over stalled reforms, Bulgaria joins the EU, becoming its first 'Cyrillic' country. Brussels pressures the government to tackle organised crime and environmental problems.	Year-long protests against the Plamen Oresharski government, and loss of faith in its ability to tackle Bulgaria's banking crisis, causes it to topple on 23 July. Boyko Borisov's coalition steps in on 7 November.

Outdoor Activities & Wildlife

Bulgaria is a true adventure playground. Hiking, biking and rock climbing are popular, with numerous trails in the spellbinding Stara Planina and in national parks such as Pirin. The Black Sea coast draws snorkellers and windsurfers, while skiers and snowboarders flock to Borovets and Bansko each winter.

Activities

Hiking

The Balkani Wildlife Society (www.balkani.org) is active in environmental conservation programs around the country and in raising public awareness of wildlife issues.

Hiking has long been enormously popular in Bulgaria; it was even encouraged as a patriotic activity during communist times. Today it's the sheer joy of Bulgaria's 37,000km of marked trails that brings walkers.

The trans-European hiking trails E3, E4 and E8 all cross through the country, while the E3 trail, which begins in Spain, follows the crest of the Stara Planina range from Belogradchik eastward to the coast at Cape Ermine, and is signposted along the way. The Bulgarian stretch is roughly 720km in length; if you want to go the whole way, count on taking at least 25 days. The E4 and E8 trails both pass through Rila National Park and offer varied scenery and difficulty.

Walkers are well supported, with numerous *hizhas* (mountain huts) along the more popular tracks, as well as in real wilderness areas. While some are very basic affairs, intended only as no-frills overnight shelter, others are more comfortable, sometimes with attached cafes. It's one of the more positive legacies of the old communist regime, which believed that hiking was a healthy and productive proletarian pastime.

The Rila Mountains are a rugged, rocky, heavily forested range with plunging glacial valleys and rich plant life. One of the most attractive and accessible walking routes heads into the Malîovitsa range, south of the small town of the same name and based around soaring Mt Malîovitsa (2729m).

Another relatively easy and very pleasant walk runs along the Rilska River toward Rila Monastery, before reaching Kiril Meadow.

The Pirins offer some of the very finest walking country in Bulgaria. It's an alpine landscape of glacial valleys and lakes, and the climate is blessed with a moderating Mediterranean influence.

The Sredna Gora is the highest, most visited section of the Stara Planina, with hundreds of marked tracks and the largest number of *hizhas*. The Stara Planina is noted for its sudden weather changes, and some of Bulgaria's highest rainfalls and strongest winds have been recorded here, so be prepared.

Guides are invaluable when hiking in Bulgaria, both because of remote and tricky terrain and for the insights they can give into the landscape's geology and myths; find a guide via Hiking Guide Bulgaria (www.bulguides.com) from around 120 lv per day. For organised hiking tours, contact Odysseia-In (p315) in Sofia.

Rock Climbing & Mountaineering

The Rila, Pirin and Stara Planina mountain ranges each have numerous locations where you can rock climb and mountaineer. In these perilous peaks, and with snow and low temperatures persisting at higher levels into summer, a qualified guide is essential. Find local guides with mountaineering or rock and ice climbing expertise through www.bulguides.com (from 230 lv per day).

The Bulgarian Climbing & Mountaineering Federation (www.bfka.org) has information, advice and links to regional clubs. The website www.climbingguidebg.com is also a good resource.

Rila Mountains

There are well over 200 peaks higher than 1000m in the alpine, lake-dappled Rila range. Malîovitsa village is home to the Central Mountain School (p328), which offers rock-climbing activities and guides. Climbing here is only for the experienced. Mid-June to mid-September has the best conditions.

Pirin Mountains

This range features more than a hundred peaks above 2000m. The northern face of Mt Vihren (2915m) is the most popular climb in this region and can be accessed from Bansko, though it is extremely challenging; indeed most climbing routes in the Pirin Mountains are only suitable for experienced climbers. **BTour** (Map p333; ☑0887243793, 0886205953; www.btour.org; ul Pirin 27; ⊙10am-7pm) can arrange family-friendly and beginner-level rock climbing from Bansko (from 70 lv per person, minimum group of three). May to September has the best conditions, but ask about conditions locally.

Stara Planina

The 550km-long Stara Planina (Balkan Range) has more than 350 climbing routes from Vratsa. The most frequented section is the Vratsa Rocks in the far west, the largest limestone climbing area in Bulgaria. Mt Botev (2376m), inside the Central Balkan National Park, is a popular climb, with easy access from Karlovo. Learn more at the Natura Information Centre (p430). Spring or autumn are the best times to climb.

Skiing & Snowboarding

Bansko is the number one skiing and snowboarding resort in the country, and it continues to expand rapidly, particularly with hotel developments encroaching on its mountainous horizon. It has the most modern facilities, the longest snow season and the biggest international profile. It boasts 75km of marked ski trails (from 900m to 2600m in elevation), and all abilities are catered for, plus there's a stunt park for experienced snowheads to leap and slalom. The ski season runs between mid-December and April, helped in part by the use of artificial snow cannons. It's at its best from January to March.

Pamporovo, sited at 1650m in the Rodopi Mountains, and with 25km of trails, is a family-friendly place and great for beginners. The more experienced will be drawn to the giant slalom run and, most difficult of all, the infamous 1100m-long Wall.

Nearby Chepelare is quieter and further from hotel developers' radars, but it has 30km of cross-country tracks and some of the longest runs in Bulgaria. Mechi Chal I (3150m long) is a black-level run used for

See www.bulgariaski.com for comprehensive information about the country's skiing resorts and snow reports.

OUTDOOR ACTIVITIES & WILDLIFE ACTIVITIES

MINERAL BATHS

After all that cycling, skiing and hiking, soothe your muscles in nerve-ticklingly warm water at these spa hotspots and natural pools.

Hisar (p383) Dating back to Roman times, the mineral-rich waters in Hisar are renowned whether you soak in or sip the stuff.

Mud and Salt Baths (p399) Just north of Burgas, squelch around Atanasovsko Lake's mud pools and red-tinged waters.

Devin (p357) Sink into healing waters at this Rodopi Mountains spa town, which has hotels for all budgets.

Pomorie (p411) This coastal spot is well known for mud-bath treatments, offered by numerous hotels.

Dobrinishte (p334) Only 6km from Bansko, the cheap and cheerful mineral baths here are an enjoyable way to relax after skiing.

international competitions, while Mechi Chal II (5250m) is a combined red/green slope with a 720m vertical drop.

Borovets, in the Rila Mountains, has three main ski areas comprising 58km of pistes, many of them scenic and fringed with trees, plus well over 30km of cross-country runs.

Just 10km from central Sofia, Vitosha is a convenient destination for weekending city folk and has slopes to suit all levels of skiers and snowboarders. Other, smaller (and cheaper) ski resorts such as Malîovitsa are mainly patronised by Bulgarian holidaymakers and there's little to detain visiting skiers beyond a day.

Water Sports

During the summer, big Black Sea package resorts such as Sunny Beach (Slânchev Bryag) and Golden Sands (Zlatni Pyasâtsi), as well as some smaller seaside towns, offer organised water sports, including jet-skiing, waterskiing, parasailing and windsurfing. Often these are quite casual affairs set up at various points along the beaches.

Scuba diving has become popular in recent years, and there are several places along the coast where you can try it. Popular tourist towns such as Varna, Sozopol and Nesebâr are the places to go, and there's a diving resort just north of Tsarevo. As well as standard training courses and boat dives, there's also the opportunity to explore wrecks.

Birdwatching & Wildlife Watching

Bulgaria is a haven for all kinds of wildlife, including such elusive creatures as brown bears and wolves, plus more than 400 species of birds (around 60% of the European total).

The Bulgarian Society for the Protection of Birds (www.bspb.org) is a good source of bird news and the latest conservation projects.

Birdwatching is a popular hobby and several companies run birdwatching tours. The nesting period (May to June) and migration period (September to October) are the best times to come. The Via Pontica, which passes over Bulgaria, is one of Europe's major migratory routes for birds. Top picks for birdwatchers include Lake Srebârna, home to Dalmatian pelicans and rare cormorants; Pomorie Lake, with more than 200 bird species; and Kaliakra Nature Reserve, frequented by migratory birds.

Cycling & Motorbiking

Though not always advisable as a means of getting around cities, cycling is an excellent way of exploring some of the more off-the-beaten-track areas of Bulgaria's wild and wonderful countryside.

Malko Tărnovo in southeastern Bulgaria has some enjoyable cycling trails, as does the coastal area around Varna. Inland, Veliko Tărnovo's surrounds have good options for cyclists.

There are surprisingly few businesses that rent out bikes. It's a good idea to either bring your own or book a package or tour. Alternatively, seek out accommodation at a guesthouse or campground that offers bike rental, such as Camping Veliko Tarnovo (p370) or **Guesthouse Djambazki** (☑0888573133; www.house-djambazki.com; bul Iskar 53, Govedartsi; s/d/tr from 70/100/150 lv; P✱🞀🞕).

Motoroads (www.motoroads.com) has a good choice of mountain bikes (minimum five-day rental from 240 lv) and motorcycles (minimum five-day rental from 485 lv). Motoroads also organises a series of self-guided trips, including five-day motorcycle tours of the Black Sea coast and Bulgarian monasteries (each from 1270 lv).

Odysseia-In (p315) runs mountain-biking trips through the Rodopis and along the coast. Its self-guided five-day cycling trip along the Black Sea coast costs around 1020 lv.

Cycling Bulgaria (www.cyclingbulgaria.com) is another big outfit offering interesting excursions, from a one-day Mt Vitosha ride from Sofia (66 lv) to eight-day tours of the Western Balkan mountain range (from around 960 lv).

The reputable Plateau Cycling (p419) runs whole- or half-day guided cycling trips around Varna and the Black Sea coast, including bikes and pick-ups.

Horse Riding

Seeing the open countryside from atop a horse can be a magical experience, and there are several companies around the country offering horse-riding tours in some of the most spectacular areas such as Stara Planina, the Pirin Mountains and the Black Sea coast. Arbanasi is an especially good destination for equine enthusiasts, with a family-friendly riding school (p375) on the eastern edge of the sleepily scenic hilltop village; short rides cost from 25 lv.

Nature & Wildlife

Though small, Bulgaria packs in a huge and diverse array of flora and fauna, helped by the varied climate and topography, relatively sparse human population, and the fact that almost a third of the country is forested.

WILDLIFE-WATCHING TOURS

There are several companies that run interesting wildlife tours, led by English-speaking professionals.

Neophron (www.neophron.com) Birdwatching, botany and other wildlife-spotting tours, with interesting focuses such as wolves, vultures and dragonflies.

Via Pontica Tours (www.viapontica.com) Specialist birdwatching, butterfly, insect and botanical tours.

Wild Echo (www.wildechotours.com) Birdwatching and bat-, butterfly-, wolf- and bear-viewing tours. Formerly known as Spatia Tours.

Pelican Travel (www.pelican-travel.org) Wildlife and cultural tours of Bulgaria; also operates a guesthouse in twitcher's haven Lake Srebârna.

Wildlife Photography (www.cometobg.com) Wildlife photography tours and workshops.

Zig-Zag Holidays (www.zigzagbg.com) Birdwatching and botany tours.

Animals

Bulgaria is home to some 56,000 kinds of animal, including over 400 species of birds, 38 types of reptile, over 200 species of freshwater and saltwater fish (of which about half are found along the Black Sea coast), and 27,000 types of insect.

Many larger animals are elusive and live in the hills and mountains, away from urban centres, but if you are keen to see some natural fauna, join an organised tour. Alternatively, hike in the Strandzha Nature Park, the Rusenski Lom Nature Park (home to 66 species of mammal), the Rila National Park, or the Pirin National Park (where 45 species of mammal, such as European brown bears, deer and wild goats, thrive).

Bird lovers can admire plenty of feathered friends at Burgas Lakes, the largest wetland complex in the country, and home to about 60% of all bird species in Bulgaria; the Ropotamo Nature Reserve, with more than 200 species of birds; Lake Srebârna, also with over 200 bird species; the Strandzha Nature Park, with almost 70% of all bird species found in Bulgaria; and the Rusenski Lom Nature Park, home to 170 species of water birds. White storks, black storks, Dalmatian pelicans, sandpipers, corncrakes and pygmy cormorants are some of the species that can be seen in these areas. Inland, Blue Rocks Nature Park near Sliven is home to the insect-spearing red-backed shrike, as well as golden eagles and vultures.

NATIONAL PARKS

The Bulgarian government has officially established three national parks – Rila, Pirin and Central Balkan – where the flora, fauna and environment are (in theory) protected. Bulgaria also has 11 'nature parks' (unlike the national parks, they include permanent settlements) and nature reserves, which are unique managed ecosystems. The latter category receives the strictest protection, and access is often regulated or even prohibited.

NATIONAL PARK OR RESERVE	FEATURES	ACTIVITIES	BEST TIME TO VISIT
Central Balkan National Park	mountains, forests, waterfalls & canyons; wolves, otters, wildcats, rare birds & bats	hiking, caving & horse riding	May-Sep
Pirin National Park	mountains & lakes; bears & birds	hiking, snowshoeing & skiing	Jan, Feb & Jun-Sep
Rila National Park	alpine forests & pastures; deer, wild goats & eagles	hiking	May-Sep
Ropotamo Nature Reserve	marshes & sand dunes; rare birds	boat trips & hiking	Apr-Jul
Rusenski Lom Nature Park	rivers & valleys; rare birds; rock churches	birdwatching & caving	Jun-Sep
Sinite Kamani (Blue Rocks) Nature Park	hills & rock formations; *haidouk* caves	hiking & birdwatching	May-Sep
Strandzha Nature Park	varied forest & beaches; birds & mammals; archaeological ruins	hiking & birdwatching	Jun-Aug
Vitosha Nature Park	mountain trails	hiking, skiing & snowboarding	Jan, Apr-Aug & Dec
Vrachanski Balkan Nature Park	forest, varied tree life & caves	hiking & caving	Jun-Sep

ENDANGERED SPECIES

Bulgaria has one of the largest brown bear populations in Europe. Rough estimates put the figure at anything from 400 to 700 individuals. There are thought to be around 300 to 500 bears in the southeastern Rodopis, and up to 200 in the Central Balkan National Park. However, unless you're on a wildlife-spotting tour, you're extremely unlikely to see a bear.

Bulgaria is thought to have up to 1200 wolves, though sadly they are considered a threat to livestock and can be shot by farmers. Numbers of the critically endangered Eurasian lynx are uncertain. Again, you'll be very lucky to see these animals in the wild.

Rare insects include the Bulgarian emerald dragonfly, only discovered in 1999. It is thought only to inhabit a small area of the Eastern Rodopi Mountains and neighbouring areas of Greece and Turkey.

Various species of rare birds, including Egyptian vultures, lesser kestrels and great eagle owls, are protected in the Rusenski Lom Nature Park, while small cormorants, ferruginous ducks and Dalmatian pelicans thrive in the Srebârna Nature Reserve. The imperial eagle is one of Bulgaria's most threatened birds – only around 24 pairs are believed to exist in the wild today. Saker falcons have been brought close to extinction in Bulgaria due to the illegal falconry trade and egg collectors; after a 90% population reduction over a decade, conservation projects have been attempting to reverse the decline.

Common and bottlenose dolphins and harbour porpoises live in the Black Sea – though, sadly, in decreasing numbers.

Plants

About 250 of Bulgaria's 10,000 or so plant species are endemic and many have indigenous names, such as Bulgarian blackberry and Rodopi tulip. The *silivriak,* with its pale pink flowers, grew all over Europe before the last Ice Age, but is now found only in southern Bulgaria, particularly in the Rodopi Mountains, where it's reasonably abundant. The wonderfully named Splendid Tulip, with its large red flowers, is extremely rare, and was only discovered in 1976, near Yambol.

The Unesco-protected Pirin National Park boasts more than 1300 species of flora, and the Central Balkan National Park encompasses ancient fir, spruce and hornbeam forests and mountain meadows, and supports some 2340 plant species, several of which are found nowhere else.

The rare *silivriak* is also known as the Orpheus flower; legend says that its flowers were stained pink with the blood of the divine musician after he was hacked to pieces by the frenzied Bacchantes.

Visual Arts, Craft & Music

Bulgaria has an ancient tradition of icon painting and these religious images are still the most memorable examples of Bulgarian artistry. Five centuries of Turkish rule suppressed much of native Bulgarian culture, but the National Revival of the late 18th to 19th centuries saw a creative blossoming as writers and artists strove to reignite the national consciousness. During the communist era, however, the arts were tightly controlled and heavily influenced by Russia and socialist ideology. Today, artistic activity in Bulgaria is at an all-time high.

Icons & Religious Art

Get up to date on the artistic revival in Plovdiv, European Capital of Culture 2019, at www. plovdiv2019.eu.

Most of Bulgaria's earliest artists painted on the walls of homes, churches and monasteries. The works of these anonymous masters are considered national treasures, and rare surviving examples can be seen in churches and museums across the country, including the lovely Boyana Church, near Sofia.

Throughout the Ottoman occupation, the tradition of icon painting endured, as a symbol of national culture and identity. The highpoint for Bulgarian icon painting came during the National Revival period, and the most famous artist of the time was Zahari Zograf (1810–53), who painted magnificent murals in the monasteries at Rila, Troyan and Bachkovo.

Icon painting continues to be a highly regarded branch of the arts in Bulgaria, with artists such as Silvia Dimitrova creating luminous works for display not only in Sofia, but as far afield as London and Oxford. Hand-painted icons by contemporary artists are sold at galleries, churches and markets; Sofia, Veliko Tárnovo and Oreshak are good places to shop.

Painting & Sculpture

Bulgarian painting has had little exposure overseas, but well-regarded Bulgarian artists of the last 150 years include Georgi Mashev, who created probing portraits and historic scenes; modernist Tsanko Lavrenov; and painter of pastoral landscapes Zlatyu Boyadzhiev. Head and shoulders above them all is Vladimir Dimitrov (1882–1960), often referred to as the 'Master'. Dimitrov, who during his life was as famous for his asceticism as his art, is known for his colourful, sometimes psychedelic, images of 19th-century peasants, and you will see his work in galleries across Bulgaria.

Bulgarian sculpture developed in the 19th and 20th centuries, and one of the leading lights of the period was Andrey Nikolov (1878–1959), who was influenced by contemporary French styles. His home in Sofia is now a cultural centre and hotel. He designed the stone lion outside Sofia's Tomb of the Unknown Soldier and more examples of his naturalistic sculptures are on show in the city's National Art Gallery.

CHRISTO & JEANNE-CLAUDE

Among the 20th century's most internationally famous Bulgarian artists were Christo and Jeanne-Claude. Born in Gabrovo, Christo Javacheff (b 1935) studied at Sofia's Fine Arts Academy in the 1950s and met his French-born wife, Jeanne-Claude (1935–2009), in Paris in 1958. They worked in collaboration, creating their first outdoor temporary installation, *Stacked Oil Barrels*, at Cologne Harbour in 1961. Thereafter, the couple, who moved to New York in 1964, crafted (usually) temporary, large-scale architectural artworks, often involving wrapping famous buildings in fabric or polypropylene sheeting to highlight their basic forms. In 1985 they created *The Pont Neuf Wrapped*, covering the Parisian landmark in golden fabric for 14 days, while in 1995 the Reichstag in Berlin was covered entirely with silver fabric. In 2005, *The Gates*, an impressive installation consisting of 7503 vinyl gates spread over 32km of walkways, was unveiled in New York's Central Park. Learn more about their artistic legacy at www.christojeanneclaude.net.

Contemporary Bulgarian artists include the sculptor Todor Todorov, abstract painter Kolyo Karamfilov, and Daria Vassilyanska, who paints luminous scenes of dances and villagers. However, the most widely recognised Bulgarian of recent times is Christo, of husband-and-wife duo Christo and Jeanne-Claude.

Pottery

One of Bulgaria's oldest crafts is pottery, and the most distinctive style is known as *Troyanska kapka,* literally translated as 'Troyan droplet', after its town of origin and the runny patterns made by the paint on the glazed earthenware body. Developed in the 19th century, it's still produced both for everyday domestic consumption and as souvenirs. Everything from cooking pots, plates and jugs to vases, ashtrays and more decorative items can be bought at market stalls, and from souvenir shops and independent workshops. Easily identifiable, the pottery comes in a few basic colours, including a lovely cobalt blue, green, brown and yellow, and pieces are decorated with concentric circles, wavy lines and teardrops.

Carpets

Fabrics have been woven in Bulgaria as long ago as the neolithic era, as evidenced by fragments of weighted spindles found in archaeological digs. Carpets and rugs were spun in earnest during the 9th century, but were most popular and creative during the Bulgarian National Revival period. Today, weaving is a dying art, practised only by a dwindling band of elderly village ladies. Troyan and Oreshak remain excellent places to understand this fading art, as well as to buy authentic samples.

Carpets and rugs made in the southern Rodopi Mountains are thick, woollen and practical, while in western Bulgaria they're often delicate, colourful and more decorative. The carpet-making industry began in Chiprovtsi around the late 17th century, with patterns based mainly on geometric abstract shapes. The more popular designs featuring birds and flowers, commonly seen in tourist shops today, were developed in the 19th century.

Music

From serene choral harmonies to sexy, sweaty folk-pop, Bulgaria's music scene couldn't be more diverse. Bulgaria's millennium of

The remarkable late-9th-century ceramic icon of Sveti Teodor, found in Veliki Preslav, is regarded as one of the masterpieces of early Bulgarian art.

ecclesiastical music continues to leave a strong impact, while traditional folk isn't confined to twee tourist restaurants: it enlivens village festivals and can be heard across the country. Meanwhile, folk's spin-off genre, *chalga,* is an energetic, Turkish-influenced pop style that dominates the airwaves.

Choral Music

Music from *Le Mystère des Voix Bulgares* was included in the capsule aboard the *Voyager 2* space probe in the hope of reaching alien ears.

Bulgarian ecclesiastic music dates back to the 9th century and conveys the mysticism of chronicles, fables and legends. To hear Orthodox chants sung by a choir of up to 100 people is a moving experience. Dobri Hristov (1875–1941) was one of Bulgaria's most celebrated composers of church and choral music, and wrote his major choral work, *Liturgy No 1,* for the Seven Saints ensemble, Bulgaria's best-known sacred-music vocal group, based in Sofia's Sveti Sedmochislenitsi Church.

The Sofia Boys' Choir, formed in 1968, brings together boys from various schools in the capital, aged 8 to 15, and has performed around the world to great acclaim. As well as their traditional Easter and Christmas concerts, they are known for their Orthodox choral music and folk songs.

Folk Music

Bulgarian folk music gives an instant aural impression of the country. Some is jauntily melodic, featuring traditional instruments such as the *gaida* (bagpipes), *gadulka* (a bowed stringed instrument) and *kaval* (flute). Other folk songs feature arresting polyphonic harmonies, or vocals that float in a haunting minor key. As in many peasant cultures, Bulgarian women were not given access to musical instruments, so they usually performed the vocal parts. Women from villages in the Pirin Mountains are renowned for their unique singing style, best enjoyed at festivals such as Pirin Sings. Preserved historic villages, such as in Etâr, have a rich calendar of folk music concerts.

Jazz

For news about the angelic-voiced Sofia Boys' Choir, see www. sofiaboyschoir. altpro.net.

Bulgaria's jazz scene began in earnest after World War I, when the USA's Great Depression nudged Bulgaria-born immigrants back home with an acquired taste for jazz. Like many forms of entertainment, Bulgaria's flourishing jazz scene was squashed under communism because it represented everything disliked by the regime: Western European influences, free artistic expression, and experimentation. After communism fell, jazz's popularity exploded back into the open and the country now hosts an impressive array of festivals, including A to JazZ (www.atojazz.bg) in Sofia, the Plovdiv Jazz Festival (www.plovdiv jazzfest.com), and the International Jazz Festival (www.banskojazzfest. com) in Bansko.

RECOMMENDED LISTENING

Gadna Poroda (2011) Pop-folk performed by Bulgaria's biggest *chalga* star, Azis.

Gladiator (1988) Frenetic hair-metal and heavy guitars by Impulse, a band who once toured with The Scorpions.

Vkusut Na Vremeto (1982) Psychedelic rock anthems by Shturcite, the 'Bulgarian Beatles'.

Folk Impressions (2012) Traditional folk songs from the renowned Sofia Boys' Choir.

Bulgarian Rhapsody Vardar By Pancho Vladigerov; arguably the composer's most popular work.

Chalga

Turn on a radio or TV in Bulgaria and it won't be long until *chalga* struts, vibrates and hip-thrusts your way. This unavoidable, love-it-or-hate-it genre fuses Balkan, Turkish, Arabic and flamenco rhythms to produce fast-paced pop music. Concerts and music videos almost unerringly feature shining bare torsos, minuscule bikinis and intense seductive stares. Big names include the silver-haired, always sparkling Azis, who has used his fame to fight for gay rights, and legendary Ruse-born diva Gloria.

Despite being loosely translated as 'Bulgarian pop-folk', most modern *chalga* gives only the vaguest nod toward folk music, preferring instead to focus on rippling synthesisers, warbling vocals and the all-important bikini girls. While many Bulgarians distance themselves from this brash musical genre, plenty of clubs around Bulgaria play little else. We guarantee you'll tap your toes to *chalga* at least once on your travels in Bulgaria.

Beyond the suggestive rhythms of *chalga*, Bulgarian pop artists include sweet-voiced Mariana Popova, rock band FSB, and Poli Genova, whose song *If Love Was a Crime* won Bulgaria their highest-yet Eurovision Song Contest position (number four) in 2016.

VISUAL ARTS, CRAFT & MUSIC MUSIC

The Bulgarian People

Philosophical, sceptical and with a brooding sense of humour, Bulgarians can initially appear reserved – but this soon gives way to warmth and wit. Having seen their national identity crushed over centuries of brutal foreign occupation, most Bulgarians are fiercely proud of their history and weave it into modern daily life. Look out for young people wearing T-shirts emblazoned with 19th-century heroes such as Vasil Levski, or attaching martenitsi, ancient pagan good luck charms, to their iPhones.

The National Psyche

In *Street Without a Name*, Bulgarian-born travel writer Kapka Kassabova recalls her childhood under communism and offers a thought-provoking perspective on Bulgaria today.

After five gruelling centuries of occupation under the Ottoman Empire came the National Revival, under which Bulgaria's culture and language freely flourished. More recently, four decades of totalitarian communist rule fell away, necessitating another phoenix-like renaissance. The hardships endured by generations of Bulgarians have sharpened national pride and tinged the country's psyche with a worldly-wise, cynical outlook on life, while high levels of corruption and uneven economic fortunes have taught them not to expect too much of politicians and bureaucrats.

On the whole, Bulgarians are welcoming and hospitable. Most are eager that you leave their country with good impressions, though in many places, a hint of Soviet inflexibility colours the service industry. Still, most Bulgarians are informal and easy-going, and delight in social get-togethers fuelled by plenty of alcohol. Bulgarians have rather freer attitudes toward personal space than most Western Europeans; don't be surprised if strangers ask to join you at tables in restaurants if no other seats are available.

Young people are especially curious about visitors to their country; they are usually highly engaged with European and worldwide politics.

Daily Life

Like many other Eastern European nations, Bulgaria remains a largely conservative and traditional society. Macho culture prevails. Attitudes toward women can be old-fashioned, especially in rural areas – despite women in these communities carrying clout in agricultural and domestic decision-making. Cities are more progressive, though excessive chivalry is occasionally used as a form of chauvinism.

Hostility toward the LGBT community is not uncommon. Many Bulgarians believe gay, lesbian and bisexual individuals should remain closeted; there is even less understanding of transgender people. Fortunately, younger, urban Bulgarians are bucking the trend, though change is slow.

Most Bulgarians celebrate the feast day of the saint after whom they are named as well as their birthday.

Rural life goes on much as it has done for the last century or so. You'll still see headscarfed old women toiling in the fields and donkeys pulling carts along the dirt tracks running through tumbledown villages. Meanwhile, in cities Western boutiques, casinos and strip clubs have proliferated. Pouting, scantily clad women are popular motifs used for advertising everything from alcohol to shopping centres, while a profusion of strip clubs and escort agencies has appeared in the big cities, colourfully touted in tourist magazines alongside reviews of restaurants and museums.

Multiculturalism

Despite invasions and occupations throughout its history, Bulgaria remains a fairly homogenous nation, with around 80% of the population declaring themselves Bulgarian.

In the mid-1980s the government mounted a program to assimilate the country's Turkish inhabitants (then 10% of the country) by forcing them to accept Bulgarian names. Mosques were also closed down and even wearing Turkish dress and speaking Turkish in public were banned. Mass protests erupted, and in early 1989 about 300,000 Turkish Bulgarians and Pomaks left for Turkey (though many subsequently returned to Bulgaria when the repressive policies were overturned).

Relations between Bulgarians and the ethnic Turkish minority have improved since, but racial tensions remain. Far-right political parties have received increasing support over recent years and new ones established, like the 2013-founded Nationalist Party of Bulgaria, which has drawn comparisons to Greece's extremist Golden Dawn. Their aggressively nationalistic rhetoric has been directed against both Turkish Muslims and Roma. There have also been violent attacks on Roma neighbourhoods, while Syrian refugees have also suffered xenophobic attacks.

Bulgaria's Roma, who form roughly 4% of the population, suffer disproportionate rates of unemployment, social deprivation, illiteracy, poverty and prejudice. They tend to live in ghettos and can be seen begging on the streets all over the country. Along with other East and Central European nations, Bulgaria signed up to the Decade of Roma Inclusion program from 2005–15. In terms of employment opportunities and raising awareness of Roma exclusion, some inroads were made, but effects are slow to trickle down (particularly for remote communities) and prejudice remains widespread.

Bulgaria is home to about 200,000 Pomaks, the descendants of Slavs who converted to Islam during the Ottoman occupation in the 15th century. In the past, they have been subjected to the same assimilatory pressures as the Turks. Some villages in the Rodopi Mountains are almost entirely Pomak, and there are small communities around Ruse and Lovech.

Religion

Orthodox Christianity has been the official religion since 865, though modern Bulgaria is a secular state that allows freedom of religion. The majority of the population – around 60% – still professes adherence to the Bulgarian Orthodox Church, although only a fraction of this number regularly attends church services.

In the 2011 census, about one-quarter of Bulgarians did not declare a religion, most of them young people from cities such as Sofia, Plovdiv and Varna. Protestant and Catholics together formed less than 2% of the Bulgarian population.

Roughly 10% of the population is Muslim – ethnic Turks, Pomaks and many Roma. Over the centuries the Islam practised in Bulgaria has incorporated various Bulgarian traditions and Christian beliefs and has become known as Balkan Islam.

There's also a tiny Jewish population, mainly living in Sofia.

Bulgarians wear red and white threads to celebrate Baba Marta Day on 1 March, tying them to tree branches when they first see a stork or blossom. The custom is thought to welcome spring and bring good luck.

THE BULGARIAN PEOPLE MULTICULTURALISM

The Orient Within by Mary Neuburger investigates the story of Bulgaria's Muslim minority population, their relationship with the modern state and ideas of national identity.

Bulgarian Wine

Bulgaria's excellent wines are a product of its varied climate zones, rich soil and proud tradition. Foreign interest and investment in recent years have made Bulgarian wines increasingly known and appreciated abroad. Wine-loving travellers can sample them at rustic wineries, in gourmet urban restaurants and bars, and even at roadside stands. The tourist offerings of local wineries vary enormously; if you are keen to sample wine, check ahead, join an organised wine-tasting tour, or head for well-trodden wine towns like Melnik.

History of Winemaking in Bulgaria

Degustatsija na vino is Bulgarian for 'wine tasting'.

Bulgaria's winemaking tradition goes back to the Thracians, who worshipped wine god Dionysus and planted grape varietals still cultivated today. Roman, Byzantine and medieval Bulgarian civilisations continued the tradition. While the Muslim Ottomans discouraged vintners, the 18th- and 19th-century National Revival period saw aristocratic mansions (some still in use) doubling as wine salons. After a damaging late-19th-century phylloxera outbreak, French experts recommended which endemic varietals to continue (such as Mavrud, Pamid and Gamza). Today, modern techniques and know-how have helped make Bulgarian wines increasingly visible in foreign supermarkets.

Winemaking Regions

Bulgaria has five wine-producing regions, each with unique microclimates and grape varietals.

Thracian Lowlands (South Bulgaria)

Beginning south of the Stara Planina range and extending to the Sakar Mountain and Maritsa River, this region enjoys hot, dry summers, while the mountains protect it from cold northern winds. This region produces one of Bulgaria's most famous wines, the red Mavrud, plus merlot, cabernet sauvignon, muscatel and Pamid.

Wineries

➡ Todoroff Wine & Spa (p353) Sleep, sip and spa at this fabulous winery-hotel in Brestovitsa, 15km southwest of Plovdiv. Surrounded by rolling meadows and vineyards, even the hotel's banisters are decorated with wrought-iron grapes. Book well ahead for the excellent wine tastings in Todoroff's atmospheric underground wine cellar (14 to 30 lv, or 44 to 50 lv with a meal).

No time to join a winery tour? Stock up on bottles of Bulgaria's best at Vino Orenda (p313) in Sofia.

➡ Bessa Valley Winery (p353) More than 3500 years ago, the Bessian tribe of ancient Thrace kept a sanctuary to the god of wine amid these verdant meadows. These days Bessa Valley Winery, 30km west of Plovdiv, likes to think it's playing a part in preserving this heritage. Its quality merlot, syrah and cabernet sauvignon are sipped across Bulgaria and beyond. Book well in advance for tasting tours of the impressive facilities.

Struma River Valley (Pirin Mountains)

In Bulgaria's southwest, bounded by the River Struma and the Pirin Mountains, this region is marked by an arid, Mediterranean climate and soil. Signature wines include Shiroka Melnishka Loza from Melnik, and Keratzuda from Kresna, a village between Blagoevgrad and Sandanski.

Wineries

➡ Damianitza (p337) Leading Melnik wine producer Damianitza has a shop poised on the main road, shortly after you enter Melnik village. Tastings are free, and no hard sell is required once you've tasted its dry red Uniqato or oaky No Man's Land Cabernet Sauvignon. At the time of writing, Damianitza's wine tours were on hiatus for a renovation, but check its website.

➡ Shestaka Winery (p337) Shestaka ('six-fingered') Winery in Melnik is named after its founder, Iliya Manolev, who had an extra finger (as does his descendant Mitko). You can visit the wine cellar dug into the rocks (admission 2 lv), or drink a glass outside, with views toward Melnik. Mitko can help to organise longer winery tours; enquire via the website.

Damianitza's 'No Man's Land' wine is made from grapes grown in the once off-limits border-zone fields between Bulgaria and Greece.

Eastern (Black Sea Coastal)

Running down the Black Sea coast from Romania to Turkey, this region's long summers and mild autumns create ideal conditions for grape growing. Almost one-third of Bulgaria's vineyards are here, with varietals ranging from Dimyat, Traminer, Gewürztraminer, riesling, Muscat Ottonel and sauvignon blanc.

Wineries

➡ Chateau Euxinograde (p424) Book well ahead for group tastings at this 19th-century palace featuring elaborate period furnishings and verdant gardens. The winery is known for good whites and a French-style brandy, Euxignac.

➡ Di Wine (p421) Browse an extensive wine list at this inventive restaurant in Varna.

Northern (Danube Plain)

Between the Danube and the Stara Planina range, and hemmed in by the Serbian border and the eastern Dobrudzha Valley, these sun-kissed plains produce a signature Gamza, a fruity and fresh red dinner wine. Cabernet sauvignon and merlot are also crafted here, as are whites such as chardonnay, riesling and sauvignon blanc. Other common northern wines include Muscat Ottonel, Aligoté and Pamid.

Wineries

➡ Magura Winery (p432) Flood your taste buds with local wine on a tasting tour in Magura Cave in Belogradchik. Book wine tastings a few days in advance.

➡ Han Hadji Nikoli (p372) This historic Veliko Târnovo tavern is a superb place to sample regional wines, either from the broad wine list in the restaurant or at the classy wine bar. Han Hadji Nikoli also boasts six of its own wines.

The Valley of Roses (Sub-Balkan)

South of the Stara Planina mountain range and north of Plovdiv, this narrow region produces dry whites, such as distinctive pinkish Misket – better here than anywhere else in Bulgaria.

Wineries

➡ Vini Sliven (www.vini.bg) Look out for Chardonnay, Misket and Rkatsiteli wines grown in the sandy soil of these 1920-founded vineyards around Shivachevo village, 30km west of Sliven.

Winston Churchill used to order Melnik red wine by the barrel.

BULGARIAN WINE WINEMAKING REGIONS

Bulgarian Cuisine

Fresh fruit, vegetables, dairy and grilled meat form the basis of Bulgarian cuisine, which has been heavily influenced by Greek and Turkish cookery, as well as home-grown Balkan traditions. Pork and chicken are the most popular meats, while tripe also often features. You will also find recipes including duck, rabbit and venison, and fish is plentiful along the Black Sea coast and in the Rodopi Mountains. Yoghurt and two types of cheese are also key ingredients.

Grilled Meats & Stews

The Food & Cooking of Romania & Bulgaria by Silvena Johan Lauta features 65 easy-to-follow traditional regional recipes.

Grilled meats *(skara),* especially pork, are among the most popular dishes served in Bulgarian restaurants, *mehana* (taverns) and snack bars. You can't escape the omnipresent *kebabche* (grilled spicy pork sausages) and *kyufte* (a round and flat pork burger), which are tasty, filling and cheap staples of Bulgarian menus, usually served with chips, fried potatoes or salad. The *kyufte tatarsko,* a seasoned pork burger filled with melted cheese, is another variant. The Greek-influenced *musaka* (moussaka), made with minced pork or veal and topped with potatoes, is a quick lunchtime staple of cafeterias.

Shish kebabs *(shishcheta),* consisting of chunks of chicken or pork on wooden skewers with mushrooms and peppers, as well as various steaks, fillets and chops, are widely available.

Meat stews and 'claypot meals' (hot, sizzling stews served in clay bowls) are traditional favourites. *Kavarma,* normally made with either chicken or pork, is one of the most popular dishes. Exact recipes vary from one region to the next, but the meat is cooked in a pot with vegetables, cheese and sometimes egg, and is brought sizzling and bubbling to your table.

Pig, cow and lamb offal, in various forms, is a distressingly common feature of many a restaurant menu. If you're in the mood for something different, though, you could try such delights as stomach soup *(shkembe chorba)* or perhaps brain *(mozâk)* or tongue *(ezik),* which come in various forms, including in omelettes. Spleens and intestines also turn up in soups and grills.

Salads & Starters

Salads are an essential part of most Bulgarian meals, and are often eaten as a starter, but some are so large that they could be a full meal in themselves. There's a bewildering array of salads available at most restaurants.

Shopska salad, which is made with chopped tomatoes, cucumbers, green peppers and onions and covered with feta cheese, is so popular it's regarded as a national dish. *Snezhanka* ('Snow White'), or milk salad, is made with cucumbers and scoops of plain yoghurt, with garlic, dill and crushed walnuts; it's essentially a more solid version of *tarator* (chilled cucumber and yoghurt soup), and is especially tempting in summer.

Ruska (Russian) salad features boiled potatoes, pickles, eggs and chopped ham, while the hearty *ovcharska* salad includes ham, mushrooms, chopped tomatoes, cucumbers, peppers, cheese and olives. Rather lighter, and more common, green and Greek salads are served everywhere, and restaurants often have their own inventive concoctions worth trying.

Appetisers, or starters, are eaten before a meal, sometimes with a glass of *rakia* (fruit brandy). Plates of sliced, dried sausage *(lukanka)*, stuffed vine leaves *(losovi sarmi)*, roast peppers stuffed with cheese and egg *(chuska byurek)* and fried, breaded cheese *(sirene pane* or *kashkaval pane)* are all very popular.

Street Food

If you just fancy a quick bite, there's a wide choice of cheap and tasty street food available all over Bulgaria. By far the most popular takeaway snack is the *banitsa,* a flaky cheese pastry, freshly baked and served hot from simple counters and kiosks. They are often eaten for breakfast. Fancier bakeries will offer variations of the basic *banitsa,* adding spinach, egg, ham or other ingredients. Sweet versions *(mlechna banitsa)* are made with milk.

Sweet and savoury pancakes *(palachinki),* croissant-shaped buns *(kiflichki),* filled with marmalade, chocolate or cheese, and deep-fried yoghurt doughnuts *(mekitsi)* are all worth sampling.

Bulgarians are great snackers and in big towns you will see vendors in parks selling toasted sunflower seeds wrapped in paper cones. Steamed corn on the cob is served on street corners and around parks, and bagel-like, ring-shaped bread rolls dusted in poppy or sesame seeds *(gevrek)* are commonly sold by street vendors.

Cheese & Yoghurt

It's amazing how much Bulgarians make of their two types of cheese, *sirene* ('white'; brine cheese, similar to feta) and *kashkaval* ('yellow'; hard cheese, often melted in omelettes). Those who are lactose-intolerant or non-cheese-lovers should read menus carefully.

Bulgarians claim to have invented yoghurt *(kiselo mlyako;* literally 'sour milk'), and, indeed, the bacteria used to make yoghurt is called *lactobacillus bulgaricus,* named in honour of its Bulgarian origins. Yoghurt is used in many sweet and savoury dishes, including salads and desserts, and drinking yoghurts are very popular; *ayran* is a refreshing, chilled, slightly salty, thin yoghurt drink that makes an ideal accompaniment to light meals.

Drinks

Coffee is the beverage of choice for most Bulgarians, though tea is also popular. Most common are the herbal *(bilkov)* and fruit *(plodov)* varieties; if you want real, black tea, ask for *cheren chai,* and if you'd like milk, ask for *chai s'mlyako* (though some bewildered waiters may bring tea and milk in separate cups).

If you're looking for a quick and easy Bulgarian recipe, www.findbgfood.com gives instructions for several popular dishes.

SHOPSKA SALAD

Although it might seem one of the most 'traditional' of Bulgarian dishes, the origins of *shopska* salad are unclear, and it may have been created as recently as the 1950s. Usually a medley of tomato, cucumber and crumbly *sirene* cheese, every restaurant will have a different twist, from a sprinkle of oregano to handfuls of roasted red peppers. They are usually crowned with a solitary olive, whose plumpness and freshness foretells the quality of the salad overall.

Beer *(bira)* is sold everywhere, either in bottles or in draught *(nalivna)* form, which is generally cheaper. Leading nationwide brands include Zagorka, Kamenitza, Ariana and Shumensko, while there are several regional brews, which are rarely available far beyond their home areas. Lower-alcohol fruit beers have become popular in recent years.

The national spirit is *rakia,* a clear and potent kind of brandy. Distilled from plums, grapes or apricots and ideally served ice cold, there are numerous brands available (as well as some powerful homemade versions made from quince, cherries and apples). It's drunk as an aperitif, and served with ice in restaurants and bars, which often devote a whole page on their menus to a list of the regional *rakias* on offer. *Shopska* salad is considered a superbly salty accompaniment to *rakia.*

Bulgaria produces huge quantities of both white and red *vino* (wine), which varies greatly in quality.

Where to Eat & Drink

Cafes & Markets

Traditional Bulgarian Cooking by Atanas Slavov gives more than 140 recipes you might like to try out, including all the favourites such as *kavarma, banitsa* and *shopska* salad.

Cafes are cheaper affairs and include basic self-service cafeterias offering pre-cooked meals, soups and salads. In the cities, small basic cafes or snack bars offer drinks and snacks, sometimes with a few chairs outside, or just a table to lean on. Some bake their own produce, especially *banitsa.* Look out for signs reading закуска *(zakuska;* breakfast).

Self-caterers will find plenty of choice at Bulgaria's many street markets; this is where most locals do their shopping, and much of the produce will be fresh (though in many villages, locals whisper that produce touted as organic and locally grown is quietly imported).

Mehana

A *mehana* (tavern) is a traditional restaurant, often decorated in a rustic style, adorned with rugs and farming implements, and offering only authentic Bulgarian cuisine. Some of these, of course, are tourist traps, luring foreign tourists with noisy 'folk shows' and waiters in fancy dress, though the genuine places provide a pleasant atmosphere in which to sample the very best of local food. Look out for those frequented by locals. Rounding up a bill is common; some waiting staff simply don't bring back change.

Restaurants

Most outlets providing seating describe themselves as restaurants, and this covers a pretty broad range of dining spots and every imaginable type of cuisine.

In the big cities and coastal resorts, most restaurants will offer menus in English and, occasionally, other languages. Reservations are rarely necessary, unless you are in a large group or the restaurant is especially popular. Bills will usually be 'rounded up', and a service charge of 10% is sometimes added. If it isn't, a small tip is expected.

Survival Guide

Directory A–Z

Accommodation

Accommodation is most expensive in Sofia and other big cities, notably Plovdiv and Varna. Elsewhere, prices are relatively cheap by Western European standards. Demand and prices are highest in coastal resorts between July and August, and in the skiing resorts between December and February. Outside the holiday seasons, these hotels often close down, or operate on a reduced basis.

➡ **Guesthouses** Usually small, family-run places and great value, with cosy rooms and home-cooked breakfasts.

➡ **Hizhas** The mountain huts in Bulgaria's hiking terrain are convenient, though basic, places to sleep.

➡ **Hotels** Bulgaria has a good range of hotels from budget to top-end.

Camping

Most campgrounds are open only between May and September. They are mainly popular with Bulgarian families, and are rarely convenient for anyone relying on public transport. Camping in the wild (ie outside a camping ground) is usually prohibited, and stiff fines can apply if you're caught doing so in a national park.

Hostels

Sofia has more hostels than anywhere else. You will also find hostels in Veliko Târnovo, Varna, Plovdiv, Bansko and Burgas. Most are clean, modern and friendly places in central locations.

Hotels

Usually, the most attractive, and often best value, places are the smaller, family-run hotels. Towns famous for their spas, skiing or beaches usually have a wide range of high-quality hotels, often with spa centres or saunas on-site.

Monasteries

About a dozen of the 160 monasteries around Bulgaria offer accommodation to anyone, of either sex, from pilgrims to foreign tourists. Some rooms are actually inside the monastery, such as at the Rila and Cherepish monasteries, or at guesthouses within metres of the monastery gates, for example at the Troyan, Lopushanski and Dryanovo monasteries. Some only offer rooms on a sporadic basis and availability may be unreliable; contact the monasteries directly to see if they have room. Be prepared to dress modestly and adhere to evening lock-out times throughout your stay.

Mountain Huts

Anyone, especially those enjoying long-distance treks or shorter hikes, can stay at any *hizha* (mountain hut). Normally a *hizha* only offers basic, but clean and comfortable, dormitory beds with a shared bathroom, and cost from 15 lv to 35 lv per person per night. Most are open only from May to September, but those situated at or near major ski slopes are often also open in winter. They are privately run, frequently change hands, and often only Bulgarian is spoken. It's sometimes advisable to ask a Bulgarian speaker to call them in advance.

Private Rooms

Stays in private rooms can often be arranged through an accommodation agency in a town centre, or at a bus or train station. Rooms cost anywhere between 10 lv and 45 lv per person. You may see signs outside private homes advertising rooms

BOOK YOUR STAY ONLINE

For more accommodation reviews by Lonely Planet authors, check out http://lonelyplanet.com/hotels/. You'll find independent reviews, as well as recommendations on the best places to stay. Best of all, you can book online.

available, either in Bulgarian (Свободни Стаи) or, quite often, in English or German. The pensioners who hang around outside bus and train stations offering rooms in their homes are invariably living on very low incomes, so by paying them directly, without the commissions taken off by agencies, you will have the satisfaction of knowing that you're helping them get by. These days, due to the increasing number of hostels and social accommodation websites such as Airbnb, this kind of private room arrangement is much less common.

Children

Children play a big part in the social and cultural scenes of family-friendly Bulgaria. Aside from bars, children are welcomed with open arms at restaurants, hotels and attractions.

The Black Sea coast, and winter sports areas such as Bansko, are the most family-friendly regions. Bigger hotels here often have playgroups and kids' clubs. More rural areas may appeal to older children, as activities such as horse riding, cycling and wildlife-watching are available. All big towns have public parks with playgrounds, as well as attractions that children might enjoy, like zoos, which you can find in both Sofia and Varna.

For inspiration and tips on family travel, pick up a copy of Lonely Planet's *Travel with Children* guide.

Practicalities for Parents

➡ **Baby care** Most of the necessities for travelling with toddlers, such as disposable nappies (diapers), baby food and fresh or powdered milk are readily available in shops and supermarkets across the country. Public nappy-changing facilities are not common in public toilets

> ## BOOKING SERVICES
>
> **Bulgaria Monasteries** (www.bulgariamonasteries.com) For contact details to book monastery stays.
>
> **Hostelling International** (www.hihostels.com) Has hostels in Sofia and Plovdiv.
>
> **Lonely Planet** (www.lonelyplanet.com/bulgaria/hotels) Recommendations and bookings.
>
> **Zig Zag Holidays** (www.zigzagbg.com) Based in Sofia, this outfit can arrange accommodation in the mountains and villages.

but they can be found in toilets at higher-end restaurants and hotels.

➡ **Babysitting** Agencies are only common among the expatriate community in Sofia. Some top-end hotels offer this service, however, and ski creche facilities are increasingly common in luxurious hotels at winter sports hubs such as Bansko.

➡ **Breastfeeding** Public breastfeeding is not very common in Bulgaria, though awareness-raising groups are working to change attitudes.

➡ **Cots and car seats** Top-end, international chain hotels in cities, and hotels in coastal resorts, usually have cots available. International car rental firms can provide children's safety seats for a nominal extra cost, but it's essential to book these in advance.

➡ **Restaurants** Most restaurants in Bulgaria welcome families with children, although few offer specific children's menus, and fewer still have high chairs. You're more likely to find these kinds of facilities in and around the Black Sea resorts and in some places in Sofia. There are plenty of Western-style restaurants and international fast-food chains if your little ones are fussy eaters.

Customs Regulations

➡ Whether you're inspected by customs officers depends

on how you enter the country, but bona fide tourists are generally left alone.

➡ If you're travelling between Bulgaria and another EU country, then normal EU rules on what you can import or export apply.

➡ If you enter or leave the country with more than €10,000 on you (in any currency), you must declare it.

➡ Check with the customs service in your home country for advice on what you can import duty-free from Bulgaria.

➡ For information about exporting unusual items (such as valuable archaeological artefacts) by air, contact the National Customs Agency (www.customs.bg).

Discount Cards

International Student (ISIC), Youth (IYTC) and Teacher (ITIC) discount cards can be used in Bulgaria, and offer a range of discounts on transport, accommodation, restaurants, shopping, entertainment venues and tourist attractions. Many places that accept these cards don't advertise the fact, so it's always worth asking. Cards may be bought in Bulgaria at branches of the Usit Colours (www.usitcolours.bg) travel agency. Check online at www.isic.org for current details and for participating companies.

Electricity

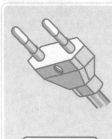

Type C
220V/50Hz

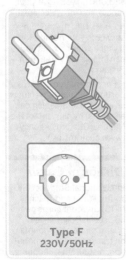

Type F
230V/50Hz

Embassies & Consulates

The following embassies are all in Sofia.

Australian Embassy (☑02-946 1334; http://greece.embassy. gov.au; ul Trakia 37; ⓡ78, 79)

Canadian Embassy (☑02-969 9710; www.canadainternational. gc.ca; ul Pozitano 7; ⊙8.30am-1pm Mon-Fri; Ⓜ Serdika, ⓡ1, 6, 7)

French Embassy (☑02-965 1100; www.ambafrance-bg.org; ul Oborishte 27-29; ⊙9am-noon Mon-Fri; ⓡ9, Ⓜ Sofiyski Universitet)

German Embassy (☑02-918 380; www.sofia.diplo.de; ul Frederic Joliot-Curie 25; ⊙8.15-11.30am Mon-Thu, 8.15-10.30am Fri; Ⓜ Joliot-Curie)

Irish Embassy (☑02-985 3425; www.embassyofireland.bg; ul Bacho Kiro 26-30; ⊙9.15am-4.45pm Mon-Fri; Ⓜ Serdika, ⓡ20, 22)

UK Embassy (☑02-933 9222; www.ukinbulgaria.fco.gov.uk; ul Moskovksa 9; ⊙9am-5pm Mon-Fri; Ⓜ Serdika, ⓡ20, 22)

US Embassy (☑02-933 9222; www.ukinbulgaria.fco.gov.uk; ul Moskovksa 9; ⊙9am-5pm Mon-Fri; Ⓜ Serdika, ⓡ20, 22)

Food & Drink

Eating out in Bulgaria is remarkably cheap, at least for Western travellers, and even if you're on a tight budget you'll have no problem eating well. For more information see p470.

GLBTI Travellers

Homosexuality is legal in Bulgaria but gay culture is very discreet as a result of prevailing macho attitudes and widespread homophobia. Same-sex relationships have no legal recognition and gay couples cannot adopt children or seek IVF treatment.

In common with other Eastern European countries, Bulgaria is a very conservative society. Discrimination is illegal, but many Bulgarians react negatively to open displays of affection between same-sex couples, and a depressingly high number consider homosexuality a mental illness. Attitudes, among younger people at least, are changing, and there are several gay clubs and bars in Sofia and small scenes in Varna and Plovdiv. There is an annual Gay Pride march in Sofia (www.sofiapride.org), although this has been the focus of protests and even violence in past years.

One of Bulgaria's biggest music stars, Azis, is an openly gay, cross-dressing Roma, who has spoken about the double discrimination he faces towards his sexuality and ethnicity.

For more information see www.gay.bg and www.gay-bulgaria.info.

Health
Before You Go
HEALTH INSURANCE

Citizens of other European Economic Area countries (EU plus Norway, Iceland and Liechtenstein) should pick up a European Health Insurance Card (EHIC) before travel, which entitles you to the same immediate medical treatment that's available to Bulgarian nationals. However, you should also consider buying an insurance policy that covers you for the worst possible scenario, such as an accident requiring an emergency flight home.

VACCINATIONS

No vaccinations are required for travel to Bulgaria, but vaccination against typhoid and hepatitis A may be recommended.

In Bulgaria
AVAILABILITY & COST OF HEALTH CARE

Every major town and city has government hospitals of an acceptable, though not always high, standard. Private clinics are preferable.

INFECTIOUS DISEASES

Rabies This disease is fatal if untreated, and is a potential concern considering the number of stray dogs in Bulgaria. Do not approach feral dogs; if you are bitten by a dog, bat or any other mammal, seek medical attention immediately.

Tick-borne Encephalitis Spread by tick bites, this is a serious infection of the brain and is present in some rural areas of Bulgaria. Contraction risks are low, but if you are camping in rural areas, protect against bites by using sprays and wearing long-sleeved shirts and long trousers. Check for ticks if camping; remove any invaders head-first using tweezers and seek medical advice.

TAP WATER

Bulgarian tap water is generally safe and drinkable, but may have an odd taste. There have been reports of contamination in some rural areas. It's best to use bottled mineral water, which is widely available and cheap.

Insurance

A travel insurance policy to cover theft, loss and medical problems is a sensible idea. There are a wide variety of policies available, with some policies offering lower and higher medical-expense options, so check the small print.

Some policies specifically exclude 'dangerous activities', which can include scuba diving, motorcycling and even trekking. A locally acquired motorcycle licence is not valid under some policies.

You may prefer a policy that pays doctors or hospitals directly rather than you having to pay on the spot and claim later. If you have to claim later, make sure you keep all documentation. Some policies ask you to call back (via reverse charges) to a centre in your home country where an immediate assessment of your problem can be made.

Check that the policy covers ambulances as well as an emergency flight home.

EATING PRICE RANGES

The following price ranges refer to a standard main course. Unless otherwise stated, service charge is included in the price.

€ less than 10 lv

€€ 10–20 lv

€€€ more than 20 lv

Worldwide travel insurance is available at www.lonelyplanet.com/travel-insurance. You can buy, extend and claim online anytime – even if you're already on the road.

Internet Access

Most hotels and hostels offer free internet access to guests, and wi-fi hotspots can be found in many restaurants, cafes and other businesses. Some hotels offer laptops for guest use.

With the increasing availability of wi-fi, internet cafes have become something of a rarity in Bulgaria. Where internet cafes do exist, access is usually cheap, between 2 lv and 3 lv per hour, although these are often cramped, smoky bunkers where teenage boys play deafening computer games, and connections can be painfully slow.

In reviews the @ symbol is used to show premises that provide computers for internet access, or plug-in facilities for laptops, while the wi-fi symbol 🛜 denotes places that offer wireless internet access.

Legal Matters

Bulgaria is a member state of the EU and more or less follows the same legal system as most of the rest of Europe, and anyone arrested has the right to information, a lawyer, and a translator or translated document of any charges. The days of ripping off foreign travellers are long gone: traffic police have to abide by a certain code of ethics. But residents do complain bitterly about corruption within some government departments, especially customs. If you do get into serious trouble with the police, it's best to contact your embassy.

Maps

Even for dedicated satnav users, road maps are a good idea if you're driving around Bulgaria (though recent ones can be frustratingly tricky to track down). Domino's *Bulgaria Road Atlas* (1:330,000) and Freytag & Berndt's *Bulgaria Road Map* (1:400,000) are high quality, though Marco Polo's *Bulgaria* (1:800,00) is the most freshly updated.

For hikers, maps are even more crucial. It's

SLEEPING PRICE RANGES

The following price ranges refer to a double room with bathroom in high season. Unless otherwise stated, breakfast is included in the price.

€ less than 60 lv

€€ 60–120 lv (to 200 lv in Sofia)

€€€ more than 120 lv (more than 200 lv in Sofia)

recommended to buy hiking maps online before you reach Bulgaria, or get them at bookshops in Sofia (before you reach remote hiking terrain; map availability in villages is very variable, even at tourist offices). A good place to find maps in the capital is **Zig Zag Holidays** (☏02-980 5102; www.zigzagbg.com; bul Stamboliyski 20-V; ☺9.30am-6.30pm Mon-Fri; ⓂSerdika), which sells maps covering the various national parks and mountain ranges. Elsewhere, local travel agencies or tourist information centres are your best bet.

Money

ATMs

ATMs that accept major credit cards (ie Visa, Master-Card and American Express) are common, found in all sizeable towns and cities. The total amount you can withdraw depends on your bank's own restrictions.

Credit & Debit Cards

You cannot rely on using a credit card exclusively in Bulgaria; use it to get cash from banks and for major purchases only. Credit cards are commonly accepted in hotels, restaurants and shops in the big cities, towns and tourist resorts, but acceptance is less widespread in more rural areas. Some places, particularly the more expensive hotels, will add a 5% surcharge to your bill if you use a credit card.

Currency

The local currency is the lev (plural: leva), comprised of 100 stotinki. It is almost always abbreviated to lv (лв). The lev is a stable currency. For major purchases such as organised tours, airfares, car rental and midrange and top-end hotels, prices are often quoted by staff in euros, although payment is possible in leva, too. Bulgaria has no immediate plans to adopt the euro as its national currency.

Bulgarian banknotes come in denominations of 2, 5, 10, 20, 50 and 100 leva. Coins come in 1, 2, 5, 10, 20 and 50 stotinki and 1 lev. Prices for smaller items are always quoted in leva or a fraction of a lev, eg on a bus ticket the fare will be listed as '0.50 lv' rather than '50 stotinki'. Some shops will not bother to give change less than 1 lv in value. It's wise to bring exact change or small bills for minor attractions, which seldom seem to have change.

Exchange Rates

Australia	A$1	1.28 lv
Canada	C$1	1.34 lv
Europe	€1	1.95 lv
Japan	¥100	1.67 lv
New Zealand	NZ$1	1.22 lv
Romania	1 lei	0.43 lv
UK	UK£1	2.45 lv
USA	US$1	1.74 lv

For current exchange rates, see www.xe.com.

Money Changers

Foreign exchange offices can be found in all large towns, and current rates are always displayed prominently. They are no longer allowed to charge commission, but that doesn't always stop them trying; always check the final amount that you will be offered before handing over your cash. Avoid exchange offices at train stations, airports or in tourist resorts as rates are often poor.

When changing money, make sure that the foreign banknotes you have are not torn, marked or grubby, otherwise they may be refused. Similarly, make sure that any leva given to you are not torn or marked. The best currencies to take to Bulgaria are euros, pounds sterling and US dollars. You may have trouble changing less familiar currencies, such as Australian or Canadian dollars, but you should be able to find somewhere in a city such as Sofia, Plovdiv or Varna that will accept most major international currencies.

It's also easy to change cash at most of the larger banks found in cities and major towns; the exchange rates listed on the electronic boards in bank windows may offer slightly higher rates than foreign exchange offices, but they may charge a commission.

Scams

Foreigners may be approached on the street (especially in Sofia or Varna) and asked to change money, but this is illegal and there's a high chance you'll be given counterfeit leva, short-changed or robbed, so don't do it!

Taxes & Refunds

The value-added tax (VAT) of 20% is included in all prices quoted in Bulgaria, and is

TIPPING

Bars Serving staff don't expect tips per round, though leaving a small tip when you leave is appreciated.

Hotels Expectation of a tip for hotel staff is rare except in very high-end places.

Restaurants In some restaurants a 10% service charge is already added, although waiters may still round up the bill or not return with your change.

Taxis Metered-taxi drivers usually expect to keep the change from a fare.

included in all prices listed in our reviews. Some restaurants add a service charge of 10%, and some top-end hotels and tour-guide services list pre-VAT prices.

Opening Hours

Standard opening hours are as follows.

Banks 9am to 4pm Monday to Friday

Bars 11am to midnight

Government offices 9am to 5pm Monday to Friday

Post offices 8.30am to 5pm Monday to Friday

Restaurants 11am to 11pm

Shops 9am to 6pm

Post

The standard cost of sending a postcard is 0.40 lv within Bulgaria, while a letter up to 50g costs 0.65 lv. Postcards and letters weighing up to 20g cost 1 lv to elsewhere in Europe and 1.40 lv to the rest of the world. Get the most up-to-date rates at www.bgpost.bg.

To send a parcel from Bulgaria, it will save you hassle to bring it unwrapped to the post office. Anything heavier than 2kg must often be taken to a special customs post office (ask at the post office for information).

Public Holidays

During official public holidays all government offices, banks, post offices and major businesses will be closed. Hotels, restaurants, bars, national parks/reserves and museums usually stay open (unless the holiday coincides with a normal day off), as do most shops and petrol stations; border crossings and public transport continue to operate normally.

New Year's Day 1 January

Liberation Day 3 March

PRACTICALITIES

→ **Newspapers** Seek out *Vagabond* (www.vagabond.bg), a glossy, English-language lifestyle magazine, published monthly and available at bookshops and newsstands in Sofia, and some coffeeshops in Varna, Plovdiv and Stara Zagora. *Novinite* (www.novinite.com) is an online English-language source of Bulgaria-wide news.

→ **Smoking** Around 45% of Bulgarians smoke – one of the highest proportions in Europe. Since 2012, smoking has officially been banned in all public spaces, including restaurants, bars, hotels, cinemas and workplaces, but is still permitted at outside restaurant tables.

→ **Radio** Key radio stations include Radio Bulgaria (BNR; www.bnr.bg), which has a daily one-hour English-language broadcast, and BG Radio (91.9FM; www.bgradio.bg).

→ **Weights & Measures** Bulgaria uses the metric system.

Orthodox Easter March/April/May

May Day 1 May

St George's Day/Bulgarian Army Day 6 May

Cyrillic Alphabet/Culture and Literacy Day 24 May

Unification Day 6 September

Bulgarian Independence Day 22 September

Christmas 25 & 26 December

Telephone
Domestic & International Calls

→ To call Bulgaria from abroad, dial the international access code (which varies from country to country), add ☑359 (the country code for Bulgaria), the area code (minus the first zero) and then the number.

→ To make an international call from Bulgaria, dial ☑00 followed by the code of the country you are calling, then the local area code, minus the initial 0.

→ To make domestic calls within Bulgaria, dial the area code, which will be between 2 and 5 digits long, followed by the number you wish to call. If you are making

a domestic call from your mobile phone, you will also have to insert the country code (☑+359) first, unless you are using a Bulgarian SIM card.

→ To call a Bulgarian mobile phone from within Bulgaria, dial the full number, including the initial 0.

→ Find phone numbers of local businesses via www.goldenpages.bg.

Mobile Phones

→ Mobile (cell) phones are as commonplace in Bulgaria as anywhere else, and many hotels, restaurants and other businesses give mobile numbers as their prime contact number.

→ Mobile telephone numbers have different codes to land lines (eg 087, 088 or 089) and are indicated by the abbreviations 'GSM' or 'mob'.

→ Bulgaria has three main mobile service providers which cover most of the country: M-Tel (www.mtel.bg), Telenor (www.telenor.bg) and Vivacom (www.vivacom.bg).

→ Visitors from other European countries should be able to use their own mobile phones as usual, but check your provider's roaming rates. Travellers from outside Europe may have to purchase a Bulgarian SIM card in order to use their handsets on the Bulgarian mobile network.

Phonecards

Prepaid phonecards, for use in public telephones, are available from newspaper kiosks and some shops in denominations ranging from 5 lv to 25 lv. Cards for domestic or international calls can be used in public phone booths and some also accept credit cards.

Time

Bulgaria is on Eastern European Time (GMT/UTC plus two hours), except during daylight saving time, when clocks are put forward by one hour between the last Sunday in March and the last Sunday in October. There are no time-zone changes within the country.

If it's noon in Sofia, it's 2am in Los Angeles, 5am in New York, 10am in London, 11am in Paris and 7pm in Sydney, not taking into account daylight saving (where applicable) in these countries. The 24-hour clock is commonly used throughout Bulgaria, and always used for bus and train timetables.

Toilets

Most toilets are of the sit-down European variety, though squat toilets exist at some tourist attractions (especially monasteries) and near the Turkish border. All hotels provide toilet paper and soap, but these are rarely offered anywhere else.

Public toilets are usually found at bus and train stations, underpasses and parks, and standards of cleanliness are generally poor. You will be charged between 0.30 lv and 0.50 lv per visit, sometimes more for toilet paper. Much better (and free) facilities are available within modern shopping malls and Western fast-food franchises.

Tourist Information

Bigger cities, and smaller towns popular with tourists, have dedicated tourist information centres, which provide free maps, leaflets and brochures, although a good many, strangely enough, are staffed by speakers of only Bulgarian. National parks often have information centres offering advice.

Burgas (www.gotoburgas.com)

Ministry of Tourism (www.tourism.government.bg)

National tourism portal (www.bulgariatravel.org)

Plovdiv (www.visitplovdiv.com)

Ruse (www.tic.rousse.bg)

Sofia (www.visitsofia.bg)

Varna (www.visit.varna.bg)

Veliko Târnovo (www.velikoturnovo.info)

Travellers with Disabilities

Unfortunately Bulgaria is not an easy destination for travellers with disabilities. Uneven and broken footpaths pose challenges, and ramps and toilets designed for disabled people are few and far between, other than in a handful of top-end hotels in Sofia and other big cities. Public transport is not generally geared toward the needs of travellers with disabilities.

One organisation worth contacting is the Center for Independent Living (www.cil.bg) in Sofia.

Download Lonely Planet's free Accessible Travel guide from http://lptravel.to/AccessibleTravel.

Visas

Citizens of other EU member states and Australia, Canada, Israel, Japan, New Zealand, the USA and several other

---

ETIQUETTE

Greetings Bulgarians are polite and a little reserved on first meetings, so a handshake is most appropriate.

Personal space Bulgarian attitudes to personal space are more relaxed than some other cultures. People may approach closely when speaking to you, or join your table at crowded restaurants.

Queues The Bulgarian attitude toward queuing can be somewhat fluid; idle or distracted travellers can expect queue-jumpers to pounce.

Gifts Flowers and bottles of spirits are well received by Bulgarian hosts, if you're lucky enough to be invited to dinner.

Tipping Rounding up a bill, or leaving 10% of the total, is standard tipping practice.

Public transport In Bulgaria it is considered very poor form not to relinquish your seat for a pregnant or elderly person.

countries can stay in Bulgaria visa-free for up to 90 days. Other nationals should check the current requirements with their nearest Bulgarian embassy or consulate before their departure. Visas cannot be obtained at border crossings. At the time of writing, Bulgaria was not a member of the Schengen zone, and its application to join had long been pending.

Visitors wishing to extend their visit to Bulgaria beyond the 90-day limit have to apply for a residence permit at the National Migration Directorate (http://migration. mvr.bg); application forms can be downloaded from the website. This is likely to be a time-consuming, bureaucratic nightmare, and nobody here will speak anything but Bulgarian. It's probably far better to contact the Bulgarian Embassy in your own country for advice before you travel if you envisage being in the country for more than three months. The Bulgarian Ministry of Foreign Affairs (www.mfa.bg) has useful information, in English, on visas and other immigration matters.

Volunteering

There are a number of opportunities for volunteering in Bulgaria. Various international organisations have ongoing projects in the country, and there are also many local groups that welcome foreign volunteers.

British Society for the Protection of Birds (www.rspb.org. uk) Occasional opportunities to assist with fieldwork relating to endangered species.

Bulgarian Archaeological Association (www.archaeology. archbg.net) Find out about volunteering opportunities on archaeological digs in Bulgaria.

Green Balkans (www.green balkans-wrbc.org) Rescue centre for the rehabilitation of injured animals, with a network of volunteers who transport creatures back to their habitats.

Habitat for Humanity (www. habitatbulgaria.org) Organises house-building and community-based projects in poorer neighbourhoods.

World Wide Opportunities on Organic Farms (www.wwoof bulgaria.org) Can direct you to current projects and openings for volunteers on farms around the country.

Women Travellers

In general, travelling around Bulgaria poses no particular difficulties for women. For the most part, sober men are polite and respectful. However, Bulgarian women won't normally go to a bar or nightclub unaccompanied, and single foreign women may attract attention. If you do attract unwanted advances, saying *Az sâm omâzhena* ('I am married') gives a pretty firm message.

For overnight train journeys, choose a sleeper compartment rather than a couchette. Women in big cities and coastal resorts dress as they please; in more rural areas, modest clothing is the norm. At some monasteries and religious sites, you may be asked to wear a shawl or headscarf (they are usually available to borrow), though this is increasingly uncommon if the visitor is otherwise covered from collarbone to knee.

Feminine hygiene products, such as tampons, are widely available in supermarkets and pharmacies across the country.

Work

Since Bulgaria joined the EU in 2007, there are no longer any labour restrictions on citizens of other EU countries, but with high levels of domestic unemployment and some of the lowest wages in Europe, Bulgaria isn't an obvious destination for foreign job seekers. In fact, local people lament the 'brain drain' as Bulgarian youth seek work in other European countries.

The government is keen for foreigners to establish businesses as long as most of the staff are Bulgarian, but paperwork can still be labyrinthine. Most foreigners working in Bulgaria are employed by multinational companies in jobs arranged before arriving in the country.

If you intend to seek employment in Bulgaria and are not an EU, EEA or Swiss citizen, you will need a work visa; contact your local Bulgarian embassy for details. If you do find a temporary job, the pay is likely to be very low. Do it for the experience, rather than the money, and you won't be disappointed. Teaching English is one way to make some extra cash, but the market is often saturated.

If you arrange a job before you arrive, your employer should plough through the frightening mass of paperwork from relevant government departments and pay the various fees. If you land a job *after* you arrive, or you're considering setting up a business in Bulgaria, contact expats for current advice about the plethora of required forms and fees.

Work Your Way Around the World by Susan Griffith provides practical advice on a wide range of issues.

Transport

GETTING THERE & AWAY

Most international visitors enter and leave Bulgaria via Sofia Airport, and there are frequent flights to the capital from other European cities. Bulgaria is also easily accessible by road and rail from neighbouring countries, and Bulgaria's railway is part of the InterRail system and so can be included in a longer European rail journey. Long-distance coaches reach Bulgarian cities from Turkey, Greece, Serbia and Macedonia. There are regular ferry crossings that carry both vehicles and foot passengers across the Danube from Romania.

If you prefer something more structured, an increasing number of companies offer organised tours and package holidays to Bulgaria.

Flights, cars and tours can be booked online at lonely planet.com/bookings.

Entering the Country

As Bulgaria is a member of the EU, citizens of other EU nations will face minimal border formalities.

Delays are common at border crossings, and customs officials are generally an unfriendly and suspicious lot; expect to be questioned on what business you have in coming to Bulgaria and where you intend on staying.

See p480 for more visa information.

Air

Bulgaria has good air links with numerous European cities, as well as some cities in the Middle East. There are currently no direct flights to Bulgaria from further afield, so visitors from, for example, North America or Australia will need to pick up a connecting flight elsewhere in Europe.

Airports & Airlines

Sofia Airport (www.sofia -airport.bg) is the main point of entry to the country. Varna Airport (www.varna-airport. bg) and Burgas Airport (www.bourgas-airport.com) serve the coast, and are particularly busy during the summer when they are used by charter flights. For central Bulgaria, direct flights from a couple of European cities, including London, reach Plovdiv Airport (www.plovdiv airport.com).

The national carrier is Bulgaria Air (www.air.bg). It has an unblemished safety record, and operates flights to destinations across Europe (including London, Paris, Frankfurt and Madrid) and the Middle East, as well as domestic routes to the Black Sea coast.

Tickets

Air tickets to Bulgaria vary greatly in price, and it pays to shop around, starting with global flight comparison site

---

CLIMATE CHANGE & TRAVEL

Every form of transport that relies on carbon-based fuel generates CO_2, the main cause of human-induced climate change. Modern travel is dependent on aeroplanes, which might use less fuel per kilometre per person than most cars but travel much greater distances. The altitude at which aircraft emit gases (including CO_2) and particles also contributes to their climate change impact. Many websites offer 'carbon calculators' that allow people to estimate the carbon emissions generated by their journey and, for those who wish to do so, to offset the impact of the greenhouse gases emitted with contributions to portfolios of climate-friendly initiatives throughout the world. Lonely Planet offsets the carbon footprint of all staff and author travel.

www.skyscanner.net. You're likely to find the best deals online, and there are a few websites dedicated to Bulgarian flights:

➡ www.balkanholidays.co.uk
➡ www.bulgariaflights.com
➡ www.flybulgaria.bg

Land

Bus

TO/FROM GREECE

The main departure/arrival points for buses to/from Greece are Sofia, Plovdiv, Burgas and Varna; several bus companies ply these routes. For information, see www.bgrazpisanie.com and www.eurolines.bg.

TO/FROM MACEDONIA

Buses between Macedonia and Bulgaria arrive at and depart from Sofia and Blagoevgrad. See www.matpu.com for more details (in Bulgarian) on buses to destinations in Macedonia, or see www.bgrazpisanie.com for English-language schedules.

TO/FROM ROMANIA

Regular buses to/from Romania depart from and arrive at Sofia, Ruse and Varna.

TO/FROM SERBIA

Buses travel between Sofia and Serbia. To reach Belgrade, change buses in Niš.

TO/FROM TURKEY

Several companies operate bus services to/from Turkey, and this is the quickest, most comfortable and safest way to travel between the two countries. Find schedules on www.bgrazpisanie.com.

Car & Motorcycle

In order to drive on Bulgarian roads, you will need to display a **vignette** (15/30 lv for one week/month) sold at all border crossings into Bulgaria, petrol stations and

BORDER CROSSINGS

You can expect delays at each of Bulgaria's border crossings, especially if you are using public transport. Delays at the Turkish border tend to be longest. The following list is not exhaustive:

Greece to Bulgaria

➡ Promahonas (Serres)–Kulata
➡ Ormenio (Alexandroupoli)–Svilengrad
➡ Thermes (Xanthi)–Zlatograd

Macedonia to Bulgaria

➡ Deve Bair–Gyushevo
➡ Delčevo–Stanke Lisichkovo (Blagoevgrad)
➡ Novo Selo–Petrich

Romania to Bulgaria

➡ Giurgiu–Ruse; toll-bridge (€6 per car)
➡ Calafat–Vidin; toll-bridge (€6 per car)
➡ Calarasi–Silistra; ferry
➡ Negru Vodă–Kardam
➡ Vama Veche (Varna)–Durankulak

Serbia to Bulgaria

➡ Dimitrovgrad–Kalotina
➡ Zaječar–Vrâshka Chuka (Vidin)
➡ Strezimirovtsi (Serbia)–Strezimirovtsi (near Pernik)

Turkey to Bulgaria

➡ Dereköy–Malko Târnovo
➡ Edirne–Kapitan Andreevo

post offices. Rental cars hired within Bulgaria should already be equipped with a vignette.

Petrol stations and car-repair shops are common around border crossing areas and along main roads.

Train

Bulgarian International train services are operated by Bulgarian State Railways (BDZ; www.bdz.bg).

Macedonia

At present, no trains travel directly between Bulgaria and Macedonia. The only way to Skopje by train from Sofia is to get a connection in Niš (Serbia).

Romania

Most visitors travel to/from Romania by train and either depart from or travel through Ruse. For more information, see www.cfr.ro. Trips include Ruse to Bucharest (20 lv, 3½ hours) and Sofia to Bucharest (50 lv, 10 hours).

Serbia

Parts of the Balkan Express between Belgrade and İstanbul, via Sofia, were undergoing repairs at the time of writing, necessitating some rail-replacement buses near İstanbul. Night and day trains travel between Belgrade and Sofia (40 lv to 80 lv, 11 hours); for more details, see www.serbianrailways.com.

Turkey

The daily Bosfor (Bosphorous Express) travels through Bulgaria, between Bucharest and İstanbul (14 hours), stopping at Ruse along the way. From Ruse to İstanbul, the journey costs roughly 50 lv, more for a couchette.

The Balkan Express travels daily between İstanbul and Belgrade (Serbia), via Bulgaria, passing through Plovdiv and Sofia. The journey from Sofia to İstanbul takes around 12 hours and costs roughly 60 lv to 70 lv.

River

Oryahovo Ferries travel from this northern Bulgarian town across the Danube to Bechet in Romania.

Silistra From Silistra, travellers can cross a land border into the Romanian town of Ostrov, before taking the onwards Ostrov–Călăraşi ferry.

Sea

Very few visitors enter or leave Bulgaria by sea. The only scheduled sea route into and out of Bulgaria is provided by a weekly cargo ferry between Ukraine and the port of Varna, which also accepts passengers and vehicles. UKR Ferry (www.ukrferry.com) travels between Ilyichevsk in the Ukraine and Varna (from around US$100, about 30 hours).

Tours

Most tourists visit Bulgaria on package tours, the vast majority either based on the Black Sea coast or in the skiing resorts, while others come on tours specialising in birdwatching or hiking.

One of the few foreign companies that offers organised sightseeing holidays to and around Bulgaria is the London-based Exodus (www.exodus.co.uk). It has eight-day tours of the Pirin and Rodopi Mountains starting from around £930 per person, including flights from London. Check the website for exact prices, which vary through the year, and for other tours.

Balkan Holidays (www.balkanholidays.co.uk) is a leading specialist company offering package skiing and beach holidays in Bulgaria. A week in Golden Sands in summer costs from around £300 per person, while a week in Bansko with skiing pass costs from £330, including flights from London.

GETTING AROUND

Air

The only scheduled domestic flights within Bulgaria are between Sofia and Varna and Sofia and Burgas. Both routes are operated by Bulgaria Air (www.air.bg).

Bicycle

Generally, cycling isn't the most practical (or safest) way of getting about in urban or built-up areas, and accidents involving cyclists are common on the busy roads of Sofia. Many roads are in poor condition, major roads are often choked with traffic, and bikes aren't allowed on highways. On the other hand, traffic is light along routes between villages and long-distance buses and trains will carry your bike for an extra 2 lv (buy a permit at the ticketing desk).

Cycling is a more attractive option in the Black Sea resorts, where there are plenty of places renting out bikes. Spare parts are available in cities and major towns, but it's better to bring your own. Mountain bikes are a more attractive option in the countryside, and are sporadically available for rent, especially at campsites. For a dedicated two-wheeled tour of Bulgaria, week-long cycling holidays (starting at 900 lv) can be found at www.cyclingbulgaria.com.

Tap in to the country's cycling community on the Bulgarian Cycling Association website (www.bulgaria-cycling.org).

Boat

The only domestic sea transport in Bulgaria consists of a seasonal service between tourist towns on the Black Sea Coast. During the summer months the high-speed **Fast Ferry** (☑0885808001; www.fastferry.bg) operates from Nesebâr's passenger ferry port to Sozopol (from 27 lv one way) and Pomorie (from 11 lv one way).

Bus

Buses link all cities and major towns and connect villages with the nearest transport

---

BRIDGES TO ROMANIA

➡ Crossing the Danube Bridge (formerly the 'Friendship Bridge') from Giurgiu in Romania into Ruse will incur a toll of €6 (12 lv) per vehicle. You are not permitted to cross at Giurgiu without transport.

➡ The New Europe Bridge (also known as 'Danube Bridge 2') between Vidin and Calafat in Romania also incurs a toll of €6 (12 lv) per vehicle.

OVERVIEW OF TRANSPORT OPTIONS

Bus The most reliable transport links between cities are by bus. Local buses reach most villages, though these services are usually infrequent, or seasonal in ski or beach destinations.

Car The most convenient way to get around, especially if your itinerary includes small Bulgarian villages. Drive on the right; the steering wheel is on the left side of the car.

Taxi As well as short journeys within cities, engaging a local driver is a good way to reach day-trip destinations without the inconvenience of infrequent buses; make sure to agree on a fare before setting out.

Train Slower than buses and frequently delayed, trains are a scenic (if not speedy) way to cover ground in Bulgaria.

hub. Several private companies operate frequent modern, comfortable buses between larger towns, while older, often cramped minibuses run on routes between smaller towns. Buses provide the most comfortable and quickest mode of public transport in Bulgaria, though the type of bus you get can be a lottery.

Though it isn't exhaustive, many bus and train schedules can be accessed at www.bgrazpisanie.com.

Biomet (☑02-813 3332; www.biomet.bg) Runs between Sofia and Veliko Târnovo, Varna and Burgas, with less frequent routes to Ruse and Silistra.

Etap-Grup (☑02-945 3939; www.etapgroup.com) Another extensive intercity network, with buses between Sofia, Burgas, Varna, Ruse and Veliko Târnovo, as well as routes between Sofia and Sozopol, Primorsko, Tsarevo and Pomorie.

Union-Ivkoni (☑02-989 0000; www.union-ivkoni.com) Links most major towns and many smaller ones, including Sofia, Burgas, Varna, Plovdiv, Pleven, Ruse, Sliven and Shumen.

Car & Motorcycle

The best way to travel around Bulgaria – especially when visiting remote villages, monasteries and national parks – is to hire a car or motorbike. **Union of Bulgarian Motorists** (☑02-935 7935, road assistance

02-91 146; www.uab.org) is the main national organisation for motorists, though little information is available in English.

Before you can drive on motorways, you will need to purchase and display a 'vignette' in your vehicle. For a car, this costs 15/30 lv for one week/month. Vignettes can be bought at border crossings when first entering the country or at post offices and some petrol stations once inside Bulgaria. Rental cars hired within Bulgaria should already have a vignette.

Driving Licences

Check with your car rental agency whether your driving licence from home meets their requirements; some operators may ask for an international driving licence.

Note that drivers of private and rented cars (and motorcycles) must carry registration papers.

Hire

To rent a car in Bulgaria you must be at least 21 years of age and have had a licence for at least one year. Rental outlets can be found all over Bulgaria, but are most common in the bigger cities, at airports, and at Black Sea resorts. Prices start at around 60 lv to 80 lv per day.

Insurance

Third-party liability insurance is compulsory, and it is important to hold proof

of insurance. Buying comprehensive insurance in your home country is the best idea, but make sure it's valid in Bulgaria. The Green Card – a routine extension of domestic motor insurance for EU citizens, covering most European countries – is valid in Bulgaria.

The National Bureau of Bulgarian Motor Insurers (www.nbbaz.bg) has some useful advice.

Road Conditions & Hazards

Bulgaria's roads are among the most dangerous in Europe, and the number of road deaths each year is high. Speeding and aggressive driving habits are common; during summer (July to September), an increase in drink-driving and holiday traffic can contribute further to accidents.

Sofia and roads along the Black Sea coast can be particularly traffic-clogged and nerve-jangling.

Aside from the well-maintained main highways, road conditions in Bulgaria can be poor. Drivers must cope with potholes, roads under reconstruction, slow-moving vehicles, horses and carts, and often erratic driving by other motorists.

Mountain roads can be narrow and suffer from rockfall, while pitted roads and lack of markings are the biggest issues in Bulgaria's rural interior.

BULGARIA ROAD DISTANCES (KM)

	Burgas	Dobrich	Gabrovo	Haskovo	Kulata	Kyustendil	Lovech	Pleven	Plovdiv	Ruse	Shumen	Silistra	Sliven	Smolyan	Sofia	Stara Zagora	Varna	Veliko Tărnovo	Vidin	Vratsa
Vidin																				126
Veliko Tărnovo																			328	193
Varna																		228	515	421
Stara Zagora																	316	126	388	251
Sofia																231	469	241	199	116
Smolyan															258	161	477	287	457	329
Silistra													135	474	443	355	248	228	478	376
Sliven														232	279	161	477	287	457	329
Shumen												113	248	356	381	218	90	140	429	329
Ruse											115	122	216	135	393	232	203	106	356	254
Plovdiv										298	283	396	159	102	156	88	398	192	355	237
Pleven									194	146	219	268	228	296	174	180	304	120	208	108
Lovech								35	159	150	225	272	193	261	167	145	313	85	243	119
Kyustendil							257	264	200	410	471	525	359	302	90	288	559	331	289	206
Kulata						154	350	357	260	503	564	619	419	207	183	348	652	424	382	299
Haskovo					346	278	206	241	78	293	302	374	132	141	234	61	371	187	433	316
Gabrovo				141	403	310	65	100	146	152	186	274	130	241	220	80	274	46	308	172
Dobrich			317	388	695	602	356	347	455	212	133	92	299	541	512	367	51	271	558	451
Burgas		185	234	213	388	520	462	299	334	270	148	262	114	357	385	182	134	224	538	406
Blagoevgrad	464	613	321	272	82	72	268	275	194	421	482	543	353	244	101	282	571	342	300	217

➡ Never rely completely on road signs. Outside cities and major tourist destinations, many are written in Cyrillic only. One useful map to take on your travels is the *Bulgaria Road Atlas* (1:330,000) published by Domino in Cyrillic and English, and widely available at bookshops in Bulgaria.

Road Rules

Road signs are rare, but official speed limits (50km/h in built-up areas, 90km/h on main roads and 130km/h on motorways) are enforced by traffic police, and speed cameras have been installed on main routes.

There are a number of road rules you are required, by law, to follow.

➡ Drivers and passengers in the front must wear seat belts, and motorcyclists must wear helmets.

➡ All vehicles must have a warning triangle, reflective jacket and first-aid kit on board.

➡ The blood-alcohol limit is 0.05%.

➡ Children under 12 years are not allowed to sit in the front seat.

➡ Headlights must be on low beam at all times, year-round. Hire cars may already be configured to do this, so check at the rental office.

➡ Mobile phones may only be used with a hands-free system.

➡ If you have an accident, you must wait with your vehicle and have someone call the local police and ☐112 for assistance.

➡ There are still some cases of corrupt traffic police targeting motorists, especially those in expensive foreign cars, and demanding on-the-spot 'fines' (or bribes) for alleged offences. There has been a crackdown on such racketeering, but if you are unlucky enough to be approached in this way (and it looks like a scam)

either ask to pay at a police station or insist on a receipt, with the officer's full details. The 'charge' may well be dropped. There are also occasional reports of impostors masquerading as traffic police attempting to extort fines. Again, be sure to ask for ID before handing over any cash.

Hitching

Hitching is officially illegal in Bulgaria, but people still do it. For some travellers, hitching in rural Bulgaria is seen as preferable to being restricted by infrequent public transport.

Hitching is never entirely safe, and we don't recommend it. Travellers who hitch should understand that they are taking a small but potentially serious risk.

The upsurge in crime over the last few years has dissuaded some Bulgarians from offering lifts to hitchhikers.

Bulgaria's borders are not particularly 'user-friendly', and you may face extra questioning and delays if you are travelling in a stranger's vehicle, so hitching across borders is not recommended.

Local Transport

Buses & Minibuses

➡ Private and public buses and minibuses ply routes between smaller villages, eg along the Black Sea coast and between urban centres and ski resorts in winter. Tickets for minibuses cost roughly the same as for public buses but are usually bought from the driver. Destinations (in Cyrillic) and, often, departure times are indicated on the front window. Most minibuses leave from inside, or very close to, the major public bus station.

➡ In Sofia, minibuses called *marshroutki* run between the

city centre and the suburbs, acting like shared taxis.

➡ Most Bulgarian towns have cheap and efficient public bus services that tend to be quite crowded, as this is how most locals get around.

➡ Trolleybuses also operate in several city centres, drawing their power from overhead cables. They tend to be priced similarly to standard city buses.

Taxi

Taxis, which must be painted yellow and equipped with working meters, can be flagged down on most streets in every city and town throughout Bulgaria. They can be very cheap, but rates do vary. Taxis can be chartered for longer trips at negotiable rates, which you can approximate by working out the distance and taxi rate per kilometre, plus waiting time.

All drivers must clearly display their rates on the taxi's windows. These rates are divided into three or four lines:

➡ The first line lists the rate per kilometre from 6am to 10pm (about 0.60 lv to 0.80 lv per kilometre is average), and the night-time rate (sometimes the same, but often about 10% more).

➡ The second lists, if applicable, the call-out fee (of about 0.50 lv) if you preorder a taxi (rarely necessary).

➡ The third line lists the starting fee (0.30 lv to 0.50 lv).

➡ The final line lists the cost for waiting per minute (0.15 lv to 0.30 lv).
Some drivers try to overcharge unwary foreigners by claiming the meter 'doesn't work' (it must work by law) or offering a flat fare (which will always be at least double the proper metered fare). Dishonest drivers congregate outside airports, train and bus stations and big city centres and in the resorts along the Black Sea coast. Negotiating a flat fare only

TRAIN TICKETS

All tickets are printed in Cyrillic. Other than the place of departure and destination, tickets also contain other important details:

➡ Клас – *klas* – '1' (1st class) or '2' (2nd class)

➡ Категория – *kategoriya* – type of train, ie T (express), 255 (fast) or G (slow passenger)

➡ Влак – *vlak* – train number

➡ Час – *chas* – departure time

➡ Дата – *data* – date of departure

➡ Вагон – *vagon* – carriage number

➡ Място – *myasto* – seat number

makes sense if you are asking for a multistop journey, or if waiting time needs to be factored into a day trip by taxi.

Train

The Bulgarian State Railways (БДЖ; www.bdz.bg) boasts more than 4070km of tracks across the country, linking most sizeable towns and cities, although some are on a spur track and only connected to a major railway line by infrequent services.

Most trains tend to be antiquated, shabby and not especially comfortable, and journey times are usually slower than buses. On the plus side, the scenery is likely to be more rewarding.

Trains are classified as *ekspresen* (express), *bârz* (fast) or *pâtnicheski* (slow passenger). Unless you absolutely thrive on train travel or you want to visit a more remote town, use a fast or express train.

Two of the most spectacular train trips are along Iskâr Gorge, from Sofia to Mezdra, and on the narrow-gauge track between Septemvri and Bansko. Railway buffs often go on these trips for no other reason than the journey itself.

Train travel in Bulgaria is a normally safe and enjoyable experience, but there have been reports of robberies, pickpocketing and minor annoyances (such as drunkenness) on some cross-border routes, such as to/from Turkey or Serbia. If you are travelling late at night, sit with other passengers rather than in an empty compartment, and if you are making a long overnight trip across the border, try booking a bed in a couchette.

Classes

First-class compartments seat six people, eight are crammed into 2nd class, and the intercity express has individual seats in an open carriage.

Sleepers and couchettes are available between Sofia and Burgas and Varna but must be booked in advance.

Fares for 1st class are around 25% higher than for 2nd class. The carriages won't be any cleaner, but it's always worth paying the extra just to have a bit more space.

Costs

Train travel within Bulgaria is cheap by Western European standards, with a 1st/2nd class express cross-country trip between Sofia and Varna coming in at approximately 25/30 lv. If you're travelling in a group (three to six people) you may get a small discount.

Reservations

For frequent train services between the main cities there is rarely a problem if you simply turn up at the station and purchase a ticket for the next train (but be careful to allow at least 30 minutes to queue up).

Advance tickets are sometimes advisable on train services such as the intercity express to the Black Sea during a summer weekend. Advance tickets can be bought at specific counters within larger train stations.

It is not usually possible to buy tickets for travel that does not start from your current location (for example, buying a Plovdiv–Veliko Târnovo ticket isn't possible from Sofia).

Language

Bulgarian is a member of the South Slavic language family, with Macedonian and Serbian as close relatives. It's the official language of Bulgaria, with 9 million speakers.

Bulgarian is written in the Cyrillic alphabet. The pronunciation is pretty straightforward for English speakers – just read our coloured pronunciation guides as if they were English, and you'll be understood. Note that ai is pronounced as in 'aisle', uh as the 'a' in 'ago' and zh as the 's' in 'measure'. Vowels in unstressed syllables are generally pronounced shorter and weaker than they are in stressed syllables. The stressed syllables are indicated with italics. Polite and informal options are provided where relevant, indicated by the abbreviations 'pol' and 'inf'.

BASICS

Hello.	Здравейте.	zdra·*vey*·te
Goodbye.	Довиждане.	do·*veezh*·da·ne
Yes.	Да.	da
No.	Не.	ne
Please.	Моля.	*mol*·ya
Thank you.	Благодаря	bla·go·*dar*·ya
You're welcome.	Няма защо.	*nya*·ma zash·*to*
Excuse me.	Извинете.	iz·vee·*ne*·te
Sorry.	Съжалявам.	suh·zhal·*ya*·vam

How are you?
Как сте/си? (pol/inf) kak ste/si

Fine, thanks. And you?
Добре, благодаря. do·*bre* bla·go·*da*·rya
А вие/ти? (pol/inf) a vee·e/te

What's your name?
Как се казвате/ kak se *kaz*·va·te/
казваш? (pol/inf) *kaz*·vash

My name is ...
Казвам се ... *kaz*·vam se ...

Do you speak English?
Говорите ли go·vo·*ree*·te lee
английски? ang·*lees*·kee

I don't understand.
Не разбирам. ne raz·*bee*·ram

ACCOMMODATION

Where's a ...?	Къде има ...?	kuh·*de* ee·ma ...
campsite	къмпинг	*kuhm*·peeng
guesthouse	пансион	pan·see·*on*
hotel	хотел	ho·*tel*
youth hostel	общежитие	ob·shte·*zhee*·tee·ye

Do you have a ... room?	Имате ли стая с ...?	ee·ma·te lee *sta*·ya s ...
single	едно легло	ed·*no* leg·*lo*
double	едно голямо легло	ed·*no* go·*lya*·mo leg·*lo*

How much is it per night/person?
Колко е на вечер/ *kol*·ko e na ve·cher/
човек? cho·*vek*

DIRECTIONS

Where's the (market)?
Къде се намира kuh·*de* se na·*mee*·ra
(пазарът)? (pa·*za*·ruht)

What's the address?
Какъв е адресът? ka·*kuhv* e ad·*re*·suht

QUESTION WORDS

How?	Как?	kak
What?	Какво?	kak·vo
When?	Кога?	ko·ga
Where?	Къде?	kuh·de
Who?	Кой? (m sg)	koy
	Коя? (f sg)	ko·ya
	Кое? (n sg)	ko·e
	Кои? (pl)	ko·ee
Why?	Защо?	zash·to

Can you show me (on the map)?
Можете ли да ми покажете (на картата)? — mo·zhe·te lee da mee po·ka·zhe·te (na kar·ta·ta)

How far is it?
На какво растояние е? — na kak·vo ras·to·ya·nee·e e

EATING & DRINKING

I'd like (the) ..., please.	Дайте ми ..., моля.	dai·te mee ... mol·ya
bill	сметката	smet·ka·ta
drink list	листата с напитките	lees·ta·ta s na·peet·kee·te
menu	менюто	men·yoo·to
that dish	онова блюдо	o·no·va blyoo·do

What would you recommend?
Какво ще препоръчате? — kak·vo shte pre·po·ruh·cha·te

Do you have vegetarian food?
Имате ли вегетерианска храна? — ee·ma·te lee ve·ge·te·ree·an·ska hra·na

I'll have ...	Ще взема ...	shte vze·ma ...
Cheers!	Наздраве!	na·zdra·ve
beer	бира	bee·ra
bottle	шише	shee·she
breakfast	закуска	za·koos·ka
cafe	кафене	ka·fe·ne
coffee	кафе	ka·fe
cup	чаша	chas·ha
dinner	вечеря	ve·cher·ya
eggs	яйца	yai·tsa
fish	риба	ree·ba
fork	вилица	vee·lee·tsa
fruit	плод	plod
glass	чаша	chas·ha
juice	сок	sok
knife	нож	nozh
lunch	обед	o·bed
meat	месо	me·so
milk	мляко	mlya·ko
restaurant	ресторант	res·to·rant
spoon	лъжица	luh·zhee·tsa
tea	чай	chai
vegetable	зеленчук	ze·len·chook
water	вода	vo·da
wine	вино	vee·no

EMERGENCIES

Help!	Помощ!	po·mosht
Go away!	Махайте се!	ma·hai·te se
Call ...!	Повикайте ...!	po·vee·kai·te ...
a doctor	лекар	le·kar
the police	полицията	po·lee·tsee·ya·ta

I'm lost.
Загубих се. — za·goo·beeh se

Where are the toilets?
Къде има тоалетни? — kuh·de ee·ma to·a·let·nee

I'm sick.
Болен/Болна съм. (m/f) — bo·len/bol·na suhm

I'm allergic to ...
Алергичен/Алергична съм на ... (m/f) — a·ler·gee·chen/ a·ler·geech·na suhm na ...

SHOPPING & SERVICES

Where's the ...?	Къде се намира ...?	kuh·de se na·mee·ra ...
ATM	банкомат	ban·ko·mat
bank	банката	ban·ka·ta
department store	универсален магазин	oo·nee·ver·sa·len ma·ga·zeen
grocery store	гастроном	gas·tro·nom
local internet cafe	най-близкият интернет	nai·blees·kee·yat een·ter·net
newsagency	киоск	kee·osk
post office	пощата	po·shta·ta
tourist office	бюрото за туристическа информация	byoo·ro·to za too·ree·stee·ches·ka een·for·ma·tsee·ya

I'd like to buy (a phonecard).
Искам да си купя (една телефонна карта). — ees·kam da see koop·ya (ed·na te·le·fon·na kar·ta)

Can I look at it?

Мога ли да го
разгледам?
*mo·ga lee da go
raz·gle·dam*

Do you have any others?

Имате ли още?
ee·ma·te lee osh·te

How much is it?

Колко струва?
kol·ko stroo·va

That's too expensive.

Скъпо е.
skuh·po e

There's a mistake in the bill.

Има грешка в
сметката.
*ee·ma gresh·ka v
smet·ka·ta*

TIME & DATES

What time is it?

Колко е часът?
kol·ko e cha·suht

It's (two) o'clock.

Часът е (два).
cha·suht e (dva)

Half past (one).

(Един) и половина.
(e·deen) ee po·lo·vee·na

At what time ...?

В колко часа ...?
v kol·ko cha·suh ...

At ...

В ...
v ...

yesterday ...	вчера ...	*vche·ra ...*
tomorrow ...	утре ...	*oot·re ...*
morning	сутринта	*soot·reen·ta*
afternoon	следобед	*sle·do·bed*
evening	вечерта	*ve·cher·ta*

Monday	понеделник	*po·ne·del·neek*
Tuesday	вторник	*vtor·neek*
Wednesday	сряда	*srya·da*
Thursday	четвъртък	*chet·vuhr·tuhk*
Friday	петък	*pe·tuhk*
Saturday	събота	*suh·bo·ta*
Sunday	неделя	*ne·del·ya*

January	януари	*ya·noo·a·ree*
February	февруари	*fev·roo·a·ree*
March	март	*mart*
April	април	*ap·reel*
May	май	*mai*
June	юни	*yoo·nee*
July	юли	*yoo·lee*
August	август	*av·goost*
September	септември	*sep·tem·vree*
October	октомври	*ok·tom·vree*
November	ноември	*no·em·vree*
December	декември	*de·kem·vree*

TRANSPORT

Public Transport

| **Is this the ...
to (Burgas)?** | Това ли е ...
за (Бургас)? | *to·va lee e ...
za (boor·gas)* |
|---|---|---|
| **boat** | корабът | *ko·ra·buht* |
| **bus** | автобусът | *av·to·boo·suht* |
| **plane** | самолетът | *sa·mo·le·tuht* |
| **train** | влакът | *vla·kuht* |

| **What time's
the ... bus?** | В колко часа
е ... автобус? | *v kol·ko cha·suh
e ... av·to·boos* |
|---|---|---|
| **first** | първият | *puhr·vee·yat* |
| **last** | последният | *po·sled·nee·yat* |
| **next** | следващият | *sled·vash·tee·yat* |

Where can I buy a ticket?

Къде мога да си
купя билет?
*kuh·de mo·ga da see
koop·ya bee·let*

| **One ... ticket
(to Varna),
please.** | Един билет
... (за Варна),
моля. | *e·deen bee·let
... (za var·na),
mol·ya* |
|---|---|---|
| **one-way** | в едната
посока | *v ed·na·ta
po·so·ka* |
| **return** | за отиване
и връщане | *za o·tee·va·ne
ee vruhsh·ta·ne* |

How long does the trip take?

Колко трае
пътуването?
*kol·ko tra·ye
puh·too·va·ne·to*

Is it a direct route?

Има ли прекачване?
ee·ma lee pre·kach·va·ne

At what time does it arrive/leave?

В колко часа
пристига/тръгва?
*v kol·ko cha·suh
prees·tee·ga/truhg·va*

How long will it be delayed?

Колко закъснение
има?
*kol·ko za·kuhs·ne·nee·ye
ee·ma*

SIGNS	
Вход	Entrance
Изход	Exit
Отворено	Open
Затворено	Closed
Информация	Information
Забранено	Prohibited
Тоалетни	Toilets
Мъже (М)	Men
Жени (Ж)	Women

NUMBERS

1	един (m)	e·deen
	една (f)	ed·na
	едно (n)	ed·no
2	два (m)	dva
	две (f&n)	dve
3	три	tree
4	четири	che·tee·ree
5	пет	pet
6	шест	shest
7	седем	se·dem
8	осем	o·sem
9	девет	de·vet
10	десет	de·set
20	двайсет	dvai·set
30	трийсет	tree·set
40	четирийсет	che·tee·ree·set
50	петдесет	pet·de·set
60	шестдесет	shest·de·set
70	седемдесет	se·dem·de·set
80	осемдесет	o·sem·de·set
90	деветдесет	de·vet·de·set
100	сто	sto

Does it stop at (Plovdiv)?
Спира ли в (Пловдив)? spee·ra lee v (plov·deev)

How long do we stop here?
След колко време sled kol·ko vre·me
тръгваме оттук? truhg·va·me ot·took

What station/stop is this?
Коя е тази гара/ ko·ya e ta·zee ga·ra/
спирка? speer·ka

What's the next station/stop?
Коя е следващата ko·ya e sled·va·shta·ta
гара/спирка? ga·ra/speer·ka

Please tell me when we get to (Smoljan).
Кажете ми моля ka·zhe·te mee mol·ya
когато пристигнем ko·ga·to prees·teeg·nem
в (Смолян). v (smol·yan)

How much is it to ...?
Колко струва до ...? kol·ko stroo·va do ...

Please take me to (this address).
Моля да ме докарате mol·ya da me do·ka·ra·te
до (този адрес). do (to·zi ad·res)

I'd like a taxi ... Искам да ees·kam da
поръчам po·ruh·cham
такси ... tak·see ...

at (9am) в (девет часа v (de·vet cha·sa
сутринта) soo·treen·ta)

now сега se·ga

tomorrow за утре za oot·re

Please ... Моля ... mol·ya ...

slow down намалете na·ma·le·te

stop here спрете тук spre·te took

wait here чакайте тук cha·kai·te took

Driving & Cycling

I'd like to hire Искам да ees·kam da
a ... взема под vze·ma pod
наем ... na·em ...

bicycle един e·deen
велосипед ve·lo·see·ped

car една кола e·dna ko·la

motorbike един e·deen
мотопед mo·to·ped

How much for Колко струва kol·ko stroo·va
... hire? на ...да се na ...da se
наеме? na·e·me

hourly час chas

daily ден den

weekly седмица sed·mee·tsa

air въздух vuhz·dooh

oil масло mas·lo

petrol бензин ben·zeen

tyres гуми goo·mee

I need a mechanic.
Трябва ми монтьор. tryab·va mee mon·tyor

I've run out of petrol.
Нямам бензин. nya·mam ben·zeen

I have a flat tyre.
Пукнала ми се е pook·na·la mee se e
гумата. goo·ma·ta

Is this the road to (Rila)?
Това ли е пътят за to·va lee e puh·tyat za
(Рила)? (ree·la)

GLOSSARY

aleya – alley, lane
avtogara – bus station

banya – bath; often signifies mineral baths in general
BDZh – abbreviation for the Bulgarian State Railways
bul – abbreviation of boulevard; main street or boulevard

chalga – upbeat Bulgarian folk-pop music, based on traditional melodies but played on modern instruments
charshiya – a street or area of traditional craft workshops

dvorets – palace
dzhumaya – mosque

ezero (m), ezera (f) – lake

gara – train station
gradina – garden; often referring to a public park

haidouks – Bulgarian rebels who fought against the Turks in the 18th and 19th centuries
hali – indoor market
hizha – hut; often refers to a mountain hut

house-museum – a home built in a style typical of the Bulgarian National Revival period and turned into a museum

iconostasis (s), iconostases (pl) – a screen, partition or door in an Eastern Orthodox church that separates the sanctuary from the nave; often richly decorated
iztok – east

kâshta – house
khan – king within a Bulgar tribe, or the subsequent Bulgarian empires; also known as a *tsar*
kilim – hand-woven woollen carpet, normally with colourful geometric patterns
kino – cinema
knyaz – prince
krepost – fortress

mehana – tavern

obshtina – municipality; also another word for town hall

peshtera – cave
pl – abbreviation of ploshtad; town or city square

planina – mountain
Pomaks – literally 'helpers'; Slavs who converted to Islam during the era of Turkish rule

rakia – Bulgarian brandy, normally made from grapes, occasionally from plums or other fruit
reka – river
sveti (m), sveta (f) – saint

svobodni stai – 'free rooms': advertised rooms for rent in private homes

Troyanska kapka – 'Troyan droplet'; traditional glazed pottery with a distinctive 'drip' design
tsar – see *khan*

ul – abbreviation of ulitsa; street

varosha – centre of an old town
veliko – great, large
vrâh – mountain peak

zakuska – breakfast

Behind the Scenes

SEND US YOUR FEEDBACK

We love to hear from travellers – your comments keep us on our toes and help make our books better. Our well-travelled team reads every word on what you loved or loathed about this book. Although we cannot reply individually to your submissions, we always guarantee that your feedback goes straight to the appropriate authors, in time for the next edition. Each person who sends us information is thanked in the next edition – the most useful submissions are rewarded with a selection of digital PDF chapters.

Visit **lonelyplanet.com/contact** to submit your updates and suggestions or to ask for help. Our award-winning website also features inspirational travel stories, news and discussions.

Note: We may edit, reproduce and incorporate your comments in Lonely Planet products such as guidebooks, websites and digital products, so let us know if you don't want your comments reproduced or your name acknowledged. For a copy of our privacy policy visit lonelyplanet.com/privacy.

OUR READERS

Many thanks to the travellers who used the last edition and wrote to us with helpful hints, useful advice and interesting anecdotes:

Adrian Ineichen, Alex Harford, Andrew Coker, Ben Fugill, Charley Harris, Chiara Motta, Dimitar Vlaevsky, Felice Oxborrow, Flavius Streianu, Graham Meale, Jaap van Beelen, Jim Blackstone, Jim Van Leemput, Joaquín Tabales, John McKellar, John Roxburgh, Katarzyna Piriankov, Kay Martin, Marco Nawijn, Marinela Stere, Mayte Penelas, Melanie Luangsay, Mihai Bursesc, Mike Black, Olav van der Stoep, Peter Phillips, Richard Mortel, Raquel Buades, Richard Snarsky, Sarah Foxwell, Scott Allsop, Sonya Jetcheva, Thomas & Sona Hoisington, Tom Flannaghan

WRITER THANKS

Mark Baker

First, thanks to my co-writers and editors at Lonely Planet for their help in this project. A big thanks, too, to Lonely Planet readers and website users who sent in suggestions, complaints and compliments on previous editions. On the ground in Romania, I'd like to thank friends Florina Presadă, Ioana Lupea, Ana Raluca, Ruxandra Predescu, Dalia Tabacaru, Ştefania Oprina, Crina Becheanu, Elena Loghin, Diana Podasca, Narcisa Suruianu, Mirela Petra, Lori Alexe, Paula Gusetu Nimigean, and her husband Costi. In Bulgaria, my gratitude goes out to Tatyana Spasova, Martina Ivanova Staneva-Antonova and Dani Nencheva, among many others.

Steve Fallon

Mulţumesc foarte mult to those who provided assistance, ideas and/or hospitality along the way in Maramureş, Crişana and the Banat, including: Dan Carpov and Rada Pavel in Baia Mare; Ion Hotea, who pulled me out of a ditch (literally) in Mănăsteria; and Duncan and Penny Ridgley in Breb. Thanks, too, to co-authors Mark Baker and Anita Isalska for help and ideas along the way. As always, my efforts here are dedicated to my partner, Michael Rothschild.

Anita Isalska

Big thanks to the following for fantastic Bulgaria tips: Denitsa Leshteva and Plovdiv's helpful tourism team; Hristo Giulev; Sophia Bozhkova and the VT tourism crew; Mila Todorova; Samokov TIC; Ivan Dzhamulov; and especially my insightful co-author Mark Baker. Thanks to my intrepid parents, who met me at Rila Monastery and gave me fresh eyes on this extraordinary place. To those who offered their time during my research in Transylvania, including Andrea Rost, Sana Nicolau, Cristina Cofaru, Cristiana Fica, Mark Tudose, Crina Prida, Colin Shaw, Karla Zimmerman and my fellow writer Steve Fallon. Love to Normal Matt, who enhanced my time in Sibiu and cheered me through the write-up.

ACKNOWLEDGEMENTS

Climate map data adapted from Peel MC, Finlayson BL & McMahon TA (2007) 'Updated World Map of the Köppen-Geiger Climate Classification', Hydrology and Earth System Sciences, 11, 163344.

Cover photograph: Aerial view of Old Town, Brasov, Transylvania, Romania, Dziewul/Shutterstock ©

THIS BOOK

This 7th edition of Lonely Planet's *Romania & Bulgaria* guidebook was researched and written by Mark Baker, Steve Fallon and Anita Isalska. The previous edition was written by Mark Baker, Chris Deliso, Richard Waters and Richard Watkins. This guidebook was produced by the following:

Destination Editor Brana Vladisavljevic

Product Editor Vicky Smith

Senior Cartographer David Kemp

Book Designer Katherine Marsh

Assisting Editors Andrew Bain, Imogen Bannister, Nigel Chin, Bruce Evans, Victoria Harrison, Rosie Nicholson, Susan Paterson, Saralinda Turner

Assisting Cartographer Alison Lyall

Cover Researcher Naomi Parker

Thanks to Jenna Myers, Claire Naylor, Karyn Noble, Tony Wheeler, Tracy Whitmey, Amanda Williamson

Index

NOTES

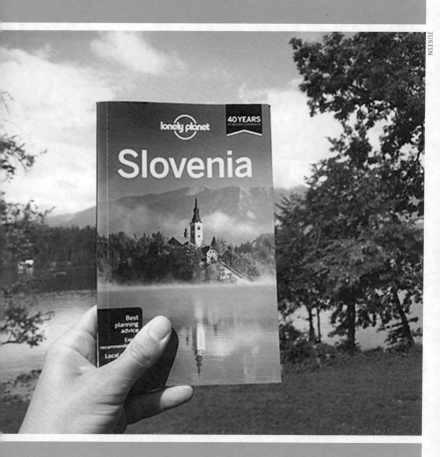

Map Legend

Sights

- Beach
- Bird Sanctuary
- Buddhist
- Castle/Palace
- Christian
- Confucian
- Hindu
- Islamic
- Jain
- Jewish
- Monument
- Museum/Gallery/Historic Building
- Ruin
- Shinto
- Sikh
- Taoist
- Winery/Vineyard
- Zoo/Wildlife Sanctuary
- Other Sight

Activities, Courses & Tours

- Bodysurfing
- Diving
- Canoeing/Kayaking
- Course/Tour
- Sento Hot Baths/Onsen
- Skiing
- Snorkelling
- Surfing
- Swimming/Pool
- Walking
- Windsurfing
- Other Activity

Sleeping

- Sleeping
- Camping

Eating

- Eating

Drinking & Nightlife

- Drinking & Nightlife
- Cafe

Entertainment

- Entertainment

Shopping

- Shopping

Information

- Bank
- Embassy/Consulate
- Hospital/Medical
- Internet
- Police
- Post Office
- Telephone
- Toilet
- Tourist Information
- Other Information

Geographic

- Beach
- Gate
- Hut/Shelter
- Lighthouse
- Lookout
- Mountain/Volcano
- Oasis
- Park
- Pass
- Picnic Area
- Waterfall

Population

- Capital (National)
- Capital (State/Province)
- City/Large Town
- Town/Village

Transport

- Airport
- Border crossing
- Bus
- Cable car/Funicular
- Cycling
- Ferry
- Metro station
- Monorail
- Parking
- Petrol station
- S-Bahn/Subway station
- Taxi
- T-bane/Tunnelbana station
- Train station/Railway
- Tram
- Tube station
- U-Bahn/Underground station
- Other Transport

Note: Not all symbols displayed above appear on the maps in this book

Routes

- Tollway
- Freeway
- Primary
- Secondary
- Tertiary
- Lane
- Unsealed road
- Road under construction
- Plaza/Mall
- Steps
- Tunnel
- Pedestrian overpass
- Walking Tour
- Walking Tour detour
- Path/Walking Trail

Boundaries

- International
- State/Province
- Disputed
- Regional/Suburb
- Marine Park
- Cliff
- Wall

Hydrography

- River, Creek
- Intermittent River
- Canal
- Water
- Dry/Salt/Intermittent Lake
- Reef

Areas

- Airport/Runway
- Beach/Desert
- Cemetery (Christian)
- Cemetery (Other)
- Glacier
- Mudflat
- Park/Forest
- Sight (Building)
- Sportsground
- Swamp/Mangrove

DA   07/17 ✓

OUR STORY

A beat-up old car, a few dollars in the pocket and a sense of adventure. In 1972 that's all Tony and Maureen Wheeler needed for the trip of a lifetime – across Europe and Asia overland to Australia. It took several months, and at the end – broke but inspired – they sat at their kitchen table writing and stapling together their first travel guide, *Across Asia on the Cheap*. Within a week they'd sold 1500 copies. Lonely Planet was born.

Today, Lonely Planet has offices in Franklin, London, Melbourne, Oakland, Dublin, Beijing and Delhi, with more than 600 staff and writers. We share Tony's belief that 'a great guidebook should do three things: inform, educate and amuse'.

OUR WRITERS

Mark Baker

Mark is a freelance travel writer with a penchant for offbeat stories and forgotten places. He's originally from the United States, but now makes his home in the Czech capital, Prague. He mainly writes travel guides on Eastern and Central Europe for Lonely Planet as well as several other leading travel publishers, but finds real satisfaction in digging up stories in places that are too remote or too quirky for the guides. He also contributes to publications such as the *Wall Street Journal* and *National Geographic Traveler*. Prior to becoming an author, he worked as a journalist for the *Economist*, Bloomberg News and Radio Free Europe, among other organisations. When he's not travelling, these days he's teaching Central European history and journalism at Anglo-American University in Prague or out riding his bike. He has a master's degree in International Affairs from Columbia University in New York.

Steve Fallon

A native of Boston, Massachusetts, Steve graduated from Georgetown University with a Bachelor of Science in modern languages. After working for several years for an American daily newspaper and earning a master's degree in journalism, his fascination with the 'new' Asia led him to Hong Kong, where he lived for over a dozen years, working for a variety of media and running his own travel bookshop. Steve lived in Budapest for three years before moving to London in 1994. He has written or contributed to more than 100 Lonely Planet titles. Steve is a qualified London Blue Badge Tourist Guide.

Anita Isalska

Anita is a travel journalist, editor and copywriter whose work for Lonely Planet has taken her from Greek beach towns to Malaysian jungles, and plenty of places in between. After several merry years as an in-house editor and writer – with a few of them in Lonely Planet's London office – Anita now works freelance between the UK, Australia and any Balkan guesthouse with a good wi-fi connection. Anita writes about travel, food and culture for a host of websites and magazines. Read her stuff on www.anitaisalska.com.

Published by Lonely Planet Global Limited
CRN 554153
7th edition – Jul 2017
ISBN 978 1 78657 543 2
© Lonely Planet 2017   Photographs © as indicated 2017
10 9 8 7 6 5 4 3 2 1
Printed in China